A COMMENTARY TO *Pushkin's Lyric Poetry,* 1826–1836

Publications of the Wisconsin Center for Pushkin Studies

David M. Bethea and Alexander Dolinin
Series Editors

A COMMENTARY TO *Pushkin's Lyric Poetry,* 1826–1836

Michael Wachtel

THE UNIVERSITY OF WISCONSIN PRESS

Publication of this book has been made possible, in part, through support from the Department of Slavic Languages and Literature at the University of Wisconsin–Madison and from Princeton University.

The University of Wisconsin Press
1930 Monroe Street, 3rd Floor
Madison, Wisconsin 53711-2059
uwpress.wisc.edu

3 Henrietta Street
London WC2E 8LU, England
eurospanbookstore.com

Printed in the United States of America

Library of Congress Cataloging-in-Publication Data

Wachtel, Michael.
A commentary to Pushkin's lyric poetry, 1826–1836 / Michael Wachtel.
p. cm. — (Publications of the Wisconsin Center for Pushkin Studies)
Includes bibliographical references and index.
ISBN 978-0-299-28544-9 (pbk. : alk. paper) — ISBN 978-0-299-28543-2 (e-book)
1. Pushkin, Aleksandr Sergeevich, 1799–1837—Poetic works. I. Title. II. Series: Publications of the Wisconsin Center for Pushkin Studies.
G3356.W33 2011
891.71'3—dc22

2011011570

In loving memory of my mother
Miriam Rados Wachtel
23 November 1928–13 July 2009

Contents

1827

1828

1829

1830

1831

1832

1833

1834

1835

1836

Preface

The purpose of this book is less to fill a lacuna than to bridge a gaping chasm in the existing scholarly literature. Given the centrality of Pushkin's work to the Russian literary tradition and the virtually hagiographical reverence that attends any object or location associated with him, one can only marvel that to this day no adequate commentary to his lyric poetry exists in any language. This regrettable situation cannot be attributed to a lack of qualified scholars or to their insufficient devotion to the task. Rather, it is the result of a very peculiar set of historical circumstances. The team that oversaw the first Academy edition of Pushkin's works (the Jubilee Edition of 1937) was probably the most formidable group of Pushkinists ever assembled. However, Stalinist watchdogs overseeing the project forced them to limit themselves to textological questions, to determine for each poem a "definitive" text (with variants) and to trace its publication history. No other form of explanation or gloss was allowed to intrude on Pushkin's words. After Stalin's death, some of these same scholars (notably Boris Tomashevskii and Tatiana Zenger-Tsiavlovskaia) were allowed to produce their own Pushkin editions; yet they were again severely constrained in their commentaries, with no single poem ever warranting more than a few lines of explanation. The detailed source study and contextual work (historical, biographical, etc.) that informed numerous articles and books were reduced to a bare minimum or simply passed over in silence.

Russians love to say – usually with eyes heavenward – that Pushkin's verse is remarkable for its simplicity and transparency. Insofar as this platitude has any validity whatsoever, it concerns syntax and lexicon (and there are striking exceptions even then). Such claims of simplicity are not only superficial, but also fundamentally misleading, for few poets so consistently and so consciously embedded their verse in the literary culture of their time and, for that matter, of previous times. Pushkin's lyric poetry is teeming with references to other poets and poems; his mind was constantly alert to their accomplishments and to possibilities that they had left unexplored. To an extraordinary extent, Pushkin's own achievement is in rewriting rather than writing. To appreciate his verse, it is essential to reconstruct his poetic context.

A commentary is not an interpretation, but rather a framework that makes informed interpretation possible. It is not merely literary, but concerns anything in the text that may require elucidation for readers of a later era – whether historical, biographical, or cultural (in the broadest sense of the word). For this reason, any serious commentary runs the risk of becoming so ambitious as to be unfinishable. To avoid this fate, I concentrate on some elements at the expense of others. My emphases largely reflect my own interests and the needs of my anticipated readership, but they also were chosen to complement the Russian commentary that does not yet exist, but – with luck – will be produced in the not-too-distant future.

The present commentary is written primarily for an audience of students and scholars who can read Pushkin in the original, but whose native language is not Russian. Such readers require a different type of help than Russian native speakers, who, for example, require no assistance in deciphering "simple" syntax or in determining where an accent falls. Other aspects of my work, while traditionally omitted from Russian commentaries, may well be of value to Russian scholars. First, I consider the metrical and stanzaic form of each poem and, where possible, conceptualize it historically in terms of genre and theme. As Tomashevskii has shown in one of the greatest Pushkin studies ever written ("Strofika Pushkina"), formal questions were for Pushkin always also semantic questions. Second, I pay especially close attention to Pushkin's Western sources, citing wherever possible (in the original French, English, and – when relevant – Italian, Polish, Serbian, and Latin) the specific edition that Pushkin was using. As far as Russian sources are concerned, I have been far less scrupulous about searching out the exact version Pushkin knew. Pushkin was acquainted with his contemporaries' verse through published versions, hand-written copies, and recitations. Given the propensity of Soviet editors to modernize spelling and unify punctuation, it would require immense bibliographical and archival efforts to find editions of these poems in the precise form that Pushkin knew them. Moreover, it is not clear that the rewards of such labors would be significant. Following the standard practice of Russian commentaries, I cite other Russian poets in accessible modern (and modernized) editions. There may be cases where nuances are lost as a result, but I leave such questions to the scrutiny of future scholars.

Certain elements of my commentary necessarily fall short of what a full-scale Russian edition would entail. I base my work on the Academy edition, volume 3, part 1 (which I follow page by page) and do not generally revisit their editorial decisions. To the extent I do, I base my work on subsequent scholars' discoveries, not on my own study of manuscripts or facsimiles. With very few exceptions (and those are explicitly noted), I focus on the "canonical" text established by the editors of the Academy edition. I make no systematic study of the variants, though I mention them when they seem to me particularly revealing. (Unless otherwise noted, references to the drafts come from the same Academy edition, volume 3, part 1 [final section] and part 2.) Nor do I make any claim to trace the history of scholarship – or even the principal lines of critical inquiry – on any given poem. When I refer to secondary literature, I do so only to satisfy the curiosity of an inquisitive reader who may wish to know how I came to a particular conclusion. Abbreviated references (linked to the bibliography) to specific points are included immediately after the point in question; if I have referred repeatedly to an article in glossing a poem, I list it under the rubric "literature" at the end of the entry on that poem. Scholars who are aggrieved to discover that their works are not listed in my bibliography are urged to remember the specialized nature of my project. The absence of a book or article should not be construed as a statement about its value.

To avoid weighing down the book with constant references, I do not cite the most obvious sources: the commentaries of Lerner (in the prerevolutionary Vengerov edition); of Tomashevskii and of Tsiavlovskaia; Chereiskii's *Pushkin i ego okruzhenie* (my main source for biographical data and birth and death dates). I generally do not cite works of a compilatory nature such as Veresaev's *Sputniki Pushkina*, the *Putevoditel' po Pushkinu*, the *Khronika zhizni i tvorchestva A. S. Pushkina*. Though I rely throughout on the *Slovar' iazyka Pushkina*, I cite it only rarely, either because (in a few instances) I question it or because the definition seems unusual enough to warrant attribution. The first volume of the excellent *Pushkinskaia entsiklopediia: Proizvedeniia* (Saint Petersburg, 2009), which covers all works (including lyric poems) beginning with the letters A through D, reached me just as I was submitting my final version of the manuscript. I had time only to make a few brief references to it.

Acknowledgments

Most of this book was written in 2007 and 2008, during a year-long sabbatical from teaching at Princeton University. My research was generously supported by Princeton as well as by the National Endowment for the Humanities and the Guggenheim Foundation. I cannot sufficiently thank these three institutions for allowing me the extraordinary pleasure of spending a year in the company of Russia's greatest poet and generations of his most ingenious readers.

In the final stages of manuscript preparation, a two-week grant from the Likhachev Foundation permitted me to travel to Saint Petersburg and consult the books in Pushkin's personal library. I am particularly grateful to Elena Vladimirovna Vitenberg of the Likhachev Foundation and to Tatiana Ivanovna Krasnoborod'ko, the curator of Pushkin's library (housed in Pushkinskii Dom), for making this work possible.

In the course of writing this book, I have been assisted by more people than I can enumerate here. I am truly grateful to all of them. I take this opportunity to thank explicitly the four people who had the most profound influence on my work, particularly since it would be impractical to recognize each of their myriad contributions in the text proper. Lazar Fleishman patiently guided this project from inception to completion, sacrificing his own research time to give detailed and illuminating answers to my endless inquiries. Irina Reyfman and Sergei Davydov, the outside readers selected by the University of Wisconsin Press, went far beyond the call of duty in their careful readings of my commentaries and in their willingness to field subsequent questions. Daria Solodkaia meticulously proofread the manuscript, saving me from countless errors and making suggestions that led to substantial improvements.

At the University of Wisconsin Press, I am indebted to Marlyn Miller for superlative copyediting and Adam Mehring for patience and understanding.

Finally, I thank David Bethea and Caryl Emerson for their encouragement over many years.

Reader's Guide

Most readers will use this book to learn about individual poems. Since I do not expect them to read consecutively, I have made no assumptions about what they might have encountered elsewhere in the commentary. However, in order to avoid potential misunderstandings, I strongly urge the first-time user to begin by reading the following explanatory information.

This commentary does not include the texts of the Russian poems. It did not seem worth the production costs to do so, since Pushkin's lyric poetry can be easily found in any Russian bookstore or on the internet.

The commentary follows the Academy edition (Полное собрание сочинений, т. 3, кн. 1, 1948), which is generally agreed to be the most reliable Pushkin edition to date. This edition is now accessible on the internet. (Go to http://feb-web.ru/feb/pushkin/default.asp, then to "Произведения Пушкина," then to "Собрания сочинений Пушкина," then to "Полное собрание сочинений в шестнадцати томах," then to "том третий: стихотворения 1826–1836. Сказки," then to "стихотворения 1826–1836," where the poems can be found by year.) As in the Academy edition, I follow the convention of putting the Russian title in angular brackets (< >) when that title was supplied by the editors. Likewise, I follow their convention for untitled poems of using the first line (in quotation marks) as a title. However, I do not retain their use of square brackets around individual words to indicate things Pushkin himself crossed out in draft. Such editorial details are essential for textologists, but they would be unnecessarily confusing to my probable readership. In the case of obscene words (which the Academy edition regularly omitted), I follow the texts given at http://www.rvb.ru/pushkin/tocv012.htm.

Readers consulting other editions should have no problem using the commentary, because the texts rarely vary. (Some editions omit poems or change the dates, but – with minor exceptions in cases of modernization of spelling – none change the actual words.)

The present volume contains commentary to every lyric poem Pushkin wrote from 1826 to his death in early 1837. Specific poems can be found in the index of titles and first lines at the back of the volume. (Titles of poems do occasionally change from edition to edition, so first lines are generally the safest way to search.)

The commentary is geared toward the level of an advanced American undergraduate or beginning graduate student. If a word can unambiguously be found in a standard Russian–English dictionary, I have not glossed it. However, I have tried to cover all instances where a seemingly familiar word has changed meaning since Pushkin's day. For example, when Pushkin uses the word "язык" to mean "a people," I gloss it. When it means "language," I do not.

Since Pushkin wrote poetry to be heard (and not only to be read silently), it is essential that one understand where the stresses fall. I mark the accents on all words that I gloss. (I do not mark the stress in passages from Pushkin's prose or in verse citations from other Russian poets.) The convention followed is that no stress is marked on monosyllabic words or on polysyllabic words where the stress falls on the first syllable. There are, however, a few exceptions to this practice. I mark the stress on the first syllable of a word where a student would logically expect it to fall elsewhere, for example, in folkloric passages, where the expected "деви́ца" becomes "де́вица." I mark the stress on monosyllabic prepositions in the rare instances when the stress shifts onto them rather than falling on the noun that follows. I mark the "ё" to distinguish it from "é," so, for example, the stress on "чернь" is not marked, but the stress on "чёрный" is indicated by the two dots over the vowel.

When Pushkin uses a form that might strike a student as unfamiliar, I place that word in the standard modern form in an adjacent parenthesis, putting an equal sign in front of it, for example, оспо́ривай (=оспаривай) глупца́. It is crucial that readers recognize this convention, lest they think that Pushkin himself gave such alternate forms. In fact, if they scan correctly, some of these alternate forms can be found in less scholarly editions. However, in many cases, the parenthetical form does not scan, as in чредо́ю (=чередой) незаме́тной, in which case, of course, no editor would include it. Students should be aware that Pushkin frequently uses the "неполногасие" (non-pleophonous) form of words that are now more common in "полногласие" (pleophony). In cases where the definition seems obvious (e.g., "младой" instead of "молодой"), I do not gloss it. In slightly more complicated cases ("глас" instead of "голос"), I do. Likewise, I ordinarily do not give the modern versions of older feminine endings (e.g., "большо́й" when Pushkin writes "большо́ю"), though if I am glossing a passage for other reasons, I give the modern form even of relatively obvious words such as these.

Pushkin read in several foreign languages, and I have taken considerable effort to cite these texts in the form he probably encountered them. When the passage is brief (a word, a phrase, or even a sentence), I translate it into English. When quotations are lengthy, I do not. My logic is that long citations (e.g., entire poems in French or Polish) will be of interest only to readers who actually know those languages and that English translations may not be able to convey the qualities of the original that attracted Pushkin in the first place. The same policy holds with Russian quotations. My task is limited to glossing Pushkin's verse; I do not gloss any of the Russian poets he cites, even when – as in the case of eighteenth-century poets – their poetic idiom is more complicated than his.

The bibliography gives full references to secondary works that are cited only by author, date (when multiple works of the same scholar have been used), and page number in the commentary. Primary sources (i.e., the works Pushkin himself read) are cited in full in the commentary and are therefore not included in the bibliography.

Occasional references to classic Russian novels that postdate Pushkin (e.g., Tolstoy, Dostoevsky, Turgenev) are primarily intended for the student who may not be aware of the extent of Pushkin's influence on later Russian literature.

A COMMENTARY TO *Pushkin's Lyric Poetry, 1826–1836*

1826

<К Бараты́нскому> – To Baratynskii

Pushkin was a great admirer of the poetry of Evgenii Abramovich Baratynskii (1800–1844). The present epigram concerns Baratynskii's narrative poem "Эда," set in Finland, in which the innocent eponymous heroine falls for a Russian soldier. The work was attacked by several critics whom Pushkin detested and distrusted (see line 5).

The poem is written in a five-line stanza of iambic tetrameter rhyming a-B-a-a-B.

---

2 черво́нец – a golden coin
3 Чухо́ночка – diminutive of чухонка, a Russian word for Finn. Pushkin refers to Eda, the beautiful bucolic heroine of Baratynskii's poem.
ей-ей – truly
4 Греча́нок Байрона миле́й (=милее) – dearer than Byron's Greek women. The allusion is to Byron's poem *The Corsair,* which features a number of Greek women slaves.
5 твой Зо́йл прямо́й чухо́нец – Your Zoilus is a real "chukhonets." Zoilus was a philosopher and literary critic in the fourth century BCE. His works do not survive, but his reputation as a harsh (and petty) critic does. Here the name refers to Faddei Bulgarin (see commentary to "На Булгарина"), who had published what Pushkin considered an "indecent" review of Baratynskii's poem. The "joke" of the final line is that, in Russian, "chukhonets" was often used as a pejorative term for an uncultured person.

<Из письма́ к Великопо́льскому> – From a letter to Velikopol'skii

Ivan Ermolaevich Velikopol'skii (1797–1868) was a minor but prolific poet and a compulsive gambler. In 1820, he lost 30,000 rubles (a huge sum) in the provinces and then still more in Petersburg, where he attempted recoup his losses. He and Pushkin exchanged a number of poems; not surprisingly, they are all devoted to gambling. (See also "Послание к Великопольскому" and "На Великопольского"). Though Velikopol'skii wrote poetry about the evils of gambling, he was unable to refrain from this vice. Worse still, as this poem makes clear, he usually lost.

It is written in iambic pentameter with a caesura after the second foot, with the rhyme scheme a-B-B-a-C-d-C-d.

---

1 мне вновь счита́ться довело́сь – Again I had occasion to settle accounts
2 Пе́ве́ц любви́ – Singer of love. Quite possibly a reference to a "romance" that

Velikopol'skii had penned in 1824, which began with the exclamation "Певец любви!" (The entire poem is cited in Modzalevskii 1999, 354.)

4 штос – Shtoss (from Austrian-German "Stoß"). A card game, related to Faro (also: Pharaoh), one of the most popular among gamblers in Pushkin's day.

5 Пять сот (= Пятьсот) – Five hundred

6 Нали́чные свиде́тели тому́ – Clear witnesses to this. There is a pun here: in addition to the fixed phrase "Наличный свидетель" (literally: a witness who is present) the word "наличные" was commonly used as a substantivized adjective, a shortened version of the phrase "Наличные деньги" (cash on hand, ready money).

7 Сейча́с, мой друг, уви́дишь почему́ – Now, my friend, you will see why. According to Modzalevskii (1999, 362), this poem ended not with a period, but with a colon, which led directly to a brief prose passage that concluded the letter: "Сделайте одолжение, пятьсот рублей, которые вы мне должны, возвратить не мне, но Гавриилу Петровичу Назимову, чем очень обяжете преданного Вам душевно *Александра Пушкина*." ("Do me a favor: do not return to me the 500 rubles that you owe me; <send them> to Gavriil Petrovich Nazimov. In doing so you will greatly oblige your sincerely devoted *Aleksandr Pushkin*.") In other words, Pushkin had already managed to gamble away the money he had won from Velikopol'skii. Nazimov (1794–1850) was a landowner in the Pskov region.

Literature: Modzalevskii 1999, 339–64.

К Е. Н. Вульф – To E. N. Vul'f

Evpraksiia Nikolaevna Vul'f (1809–1883), a member of the Osipov family, lived at Trigorskoe while Pushkin was in exile at the neighboring village of Mikhailovksoe. "Pushkin's relations with the Osipov family, his country neighbors, are not easily duplicated in the annals of literary amours. During his years of enforced rustication [...] and later on visits to the Vulfs in their province-of-Tver lands, he courted five or six members of the clan." (Nabokov, 2:534). Little is known of the precise nature of Pushkin's relationship to Evpraksiia Nikolaevna (as part of her last will and testament she apparently ordered Pushkin's letters to her destroyed). It is probable that Pushkin only flirted with her at this time, since his more serious attentions were directed to slightly older members of her family.

This light and witty poem is written in iambic tetrameter with the rhyme scheme A-A-b-A-b.

---

1 Зина – Pushkin called her both "Zina" and "Zizi" (e.g., in a famous passage in *Eugene Onegin* 5:XXXII)

4 И впредь у нас не разрыва́йте – And in the future do not tear up

5 Ни мадрига́лов, ни серде́ц – Madrigals or hearts. In the usage of Pushkin's day, a madrigal was a brief poem of flattery addressed to a woman. This line is a classic example of a zeugma, when a single verb is "yoked" to two nouns, either of which would be an appropriate complement, but which together

produce a strange (often comic) effect. In this case, Pushkin plays on two meanings of "разрывать" – first literal and then figurative. When questioned about this passage by an editor long after the poet's death, Pushkin's erstwhile friend, the rake Aleksei Nikolaevich Vul'f, explained that his sister "ненавидела мадригальные стихи и весьма мало отвечала на любезности своих собеседников" ("hated madrigals and barely responded to the compliments of her <male> interlocutors"). Of course, Vul'f could easily have invented this explanation to fit the poem. It is equally plausible that Pushkin was simply teasing young Zina, since at this point in her life she was unlikely to have attracted the numerous admirers implicit in her brother's statement.

<Из Ариóстова „Orlando Furioso"> – From Ariosto's *Orlando Furioso*

Ludovico Ariosto (1474–1533) published his enormous mock-epic *Orlando Furioso* (*Mad Orlando*) in its entirety in 1532. The work was extremely influential in European literature. Pushkin himself admitted that he borrowed one episode from it in his first narrative poem "Ruslan and Liudmila."

These free translations come from canto 23 (the entire work has 46 cantos). The scene describes how the hero goes mad when he learns that his beloved Angelica has married Medor.

It is difficult to determine what language(s) Pushkin was translating from. He could read Italian to some extent, using his perfect French as a crutch, but it is not obvious that he could handle a text of the complexity of *Orlando Furioso*. Aside from the original and numerous French translations, he surely knew Batiushkov's Russian prose rendition of this particular passage (which, however, according to Lo Gatto [8] is more distant from the original than Pushkin's own version).

100
Lo strano corso che tenne il cavallo
Del Saracin pel bosco senza via,
Fece ch' Orlando andò duo giorni in fallo,
Nè lo trovò, nè potè averne spia.
Giunse ad un rivo che parea cristallo,
Nelle cui sponde un bel pratel fioria,
Di nativo color vago e dipinto,
E di molti e belli arbori distinto.

101
Il merigge facea grato l' orezzo
Al duro armento ed al pastore ignudo;
Sì che nè Orlando sentia alcun ribrezzo,
Che la corazza avea, l' elmo e lo scudo.
Quivi egli entrò, per riposarvi, in mezzo:
E v' ebbe travaglioso albergo e crudo,
E più che dir si possa empio soggiorno,
Quell' infelice e sfortunato giorno.

102
Volgendosi ivi intorno vide scritti
Molti arbuscelli in su l' ombrosa riva.
Tosto che fermi v' ebbe gli occhi e fitti,
Fu certo esser di man della sua diva.
Questo era un di quei lochi già descritti,
Ove sovente con Medor veniva
Da casa del pastore indi vicina
La bella donna del Catai regina.

103
Angelica e Medor con cento nodi
Legati insieme, e in cento lochi vede.
Quante lettere son, tanti son chiodi
Coi quali Amore il cor gli punge e fiede.
Va col pensier cercando in mille modi
Non creder quel ch' al suo dispetto crede:
Ch' altra Angelica sia, creder si sforza,
Ch' abbia scritto il suo nome in quella scorza.

104
Poi dice: conosco io pur queste note:
Di tal' io n' ho tante vedute e lette.
Finger questo Medoro ella si puote:
Forse ch' a me questo cognome mette.
Con tali opinion dal ver remote
Usando fraude a se medesmo, stette
Nella speranza il mal contento Orlando,
Che si seppe a se stesso ir procacciando.

105
Ma sempre più raccende e più rinnova,
Quanto spenger più cerca, il rio sospetto:
Come l' incauto augel che si ritrova
In ragna o in visco aver dato di petto,
Quanto più batte l' ale e più si prova
Di disbrigar, più vi si lega stretto.
Orlando viene ove s' incurva il monte
A guisa d' arco in su la chiara fonte.

106
Aveano in su l' entrata il luogo adorno
Coi piedi storti edere e viti erranti.
Quivi soleano al più cocente giorno
Stare abbracciati i duo felici amanti.
V' aveano i nomi lor dentro e d' intorno,
Più che in altro dei luoghi circostanti,
Scritti, qual con carbone e qual con gesso;
E quel con punte di coltelli impresso.

107
Il mesto conte a piè quivi discese;
E vide in su l'entrata della grotta
Parole assai, che di sua man distese
Medoro avea, che parean scritte allotta.
Del gran piacer che ne la grotta prese,
Questa sentenzia in versi avea ridotta.
Che fosse culta in suo linguaggio io penso;
Ed era ne la nostra tale il senso:

108
Liete piante, verdi erbe, limpide acque,
Spelunca opaca e di fredde ombre grata,
Dove la bella Angelica che nacque
Di Galafron, da molti invano amata,
Spesso nelle mie braccia nuda giacque;
Della commodità che qui m' è data,
Io povero Medor ricompensarvi
D' altro non posso, che d' ogni or lodarvi:

109
E di pregare ogni signore amante,
E cavalieri e damigelle, e ognuna
Persona, o paesano o viandante,
Che qui sua volontà meni o fortuna;
Ch' all' erbe, all' ombre, all' antro, al rio, alle piante
Dica: benigno abbiate e sole e luna,
E delle Ninfe il coro che proveggia
Che non conduca a voi pastor mai greggia.

110
Era scritto in arabico che 'l conte
Intendea così ben, come latino.
Fra molte lingue e molte ch' avea pronte,
Prontissima avea quella il paladino;
E gli schivò più volte e danni ed onte,
Che si trovò tra il popol saracino:
Ma non si vanti, se già n' ebbe frutto;
Ch' un danno or n' ha, che può scontargli il tutto.

111
Tre volte e quattro e sei lesse lo scritto
Quello infelice, e pur cercando in vano,
Che non vi fosse quel che v' era scritto;
E sempre lo vedea più chiaro e piano:
Ed ogni volta in mezzo il petto afflitto
Stringersi il cor sentia con fredda mano.
Rimase al fin cogli occhi e colla mente
Fissi nel sasso, al sasso indifferente.

112

Fu allora per uscir del sentimento,
Sì tutto in preda del dolor si lassa.
Credete a chi n' ha fatto esperimento,
Che questo è 'l duol che tutti gli altri passa.
Caduto gli era sopra il petto il mento,
La fronte priva di baldanza, e bassa;
Nè potè aver (che 'l duol l' occupò tanto)
Alle querele voce, o umore al pianto.

This is how the passage reads in Pushkin's edition, *L'Orlando Furioso di Lodovico Ariosto* (Paris: Publicato da A. Buttura, 1825), 4:174–79; however, the relevant passage is in a volume in which the pages are uncut. Hence it is not possible to establish precisely what Italian edition Pushkin used, if he indeed was looking at the Italian original. Pushkin also owned a French translation of the work, in which all the pages were cut. The relevant passage is in *Œuvres du Comte de Tressan* (Paris, 1822), 6:194–99.

Il les pria seulement de dire à Mandricard, si le hasard le leur faisait rencontrer avant lui, qu'il resterait encore trois jours dans le même lieu, et que, passé ce temps, il irait joindre l'armée de Charlemagne. Roland prenait ainsi ses mesures, pour que le Sarrasin pût le trouver quand il voudrait le chercher. Tous les deux le lui promirent, et, de nouvelles assurances d'amitié ayant accompagné leurs adieux, ils se séparèrent.

Le comte d'Angers reprit Durandal à l'arbrisseau et marcha du côté où il crut pouvoir trouver le Sarrasin; mais le cheval de Mandricard, n'ayant eu pour guide que sa frayeur, avait tellement égaré son maître, que Roland ne fit pendant deux jours qu'une vaine recherche.

Ce fut vers le milieu du troisième, que le paladin arriva sur le rivage agréable d'une belle fontaine qui serpentait dans une prairie émaillée de fleurs; de grands arbres dont le faîte s'unissait en berceaux ombrageaient cette fontaine, et la défendaient des rayons du soleil. L'ardent midi faisait desirer la fraîcheur du zéphir aux durs troupeaux, aux pâtres demi-nus: Roland, couvert de sa cuirasse, de son casque et de son écu, n'éprouvait pas moins de chaleur. Il s'arrêta sous ce berceau délicieux où tout semblait l'inviter au repos: mais il ne pouvait choisir un plus funeste asyle; il y vit luire le plus malheureux jour de sa vie.

Le comte d'Angers tourne les yeux de tous côtés: il admire tout ce qui contribue à rendre cette solitude agréable; il voit que presque tous les arbres qui l'entourent sont couverts de chiffres et de lettres entrelacées; il s'approche, il attache ses yeux sur ces lettres: mais quelle est sa surprise! il reconnaît les traces de la main de celle qu'il adore.

Ce lieu était en effet un de ceux où la charmante reine du Cathay venait souvent avec Médor, parcequ'il était voisin de la maison du pasteur chez lequel l'hymen avait couronné leur amour. Les noms d'Angélique et de Médor sont gravés sur ces arbres, noués, entourés par des chiffres de fleurs; Roland peut les trouver en cent endroits différents, et ces chiffres sont autant de blessures mortelles pour son cœur. Il s'agite, il ne peut en croire ses yeux; mille soupçons s'élèvent en son ame, et s'y détruisent tour-à-tour; il rejette ceux qui nourrissent son désespoir; quelquefois même il croit que c'est d'une autre Angélique qu'il voit le nom gravé sur ces arbres.

Le moment d'après il se disait à lui-même: Non, je ne peux méconnaître les traits d'une main si chère: ces caractères sont en effet de celle d'Angélique; j'en ai vu trop souvent pour m'y méprendre; peut-être a-t-elle imaginé ce nom de Médor pour cacher celui dont son cœur est occupé: j'ose espérer que c'est de moi seul que ma divine Angélique a voulu parler en confiant le secret de son ame à cette solitude. C'est ainsi que Roland se plaisait à se tromper lui-même; flottant sans cesse entre la crainte et l'espérance, plus il se formait d'idées nouvelles, plus son cœur était déchiré. Ce paladin si renommé n'était plus alors que le plus faible et le plus malheureux des amants; il ressemblait à l'oiseau qui vient de donner dans un filet, ou de s'abattre sur des gluaux; plus il bat des ailes pour se dégager, plus il s'embarrasse et se lie.

Roland suit le cours du ruisseau, et parvient à l'un de ses détours, où les roches de la montagne semblaient s'être exprès recourbées pour former une grotte agréable et profonde, dont l'eau pure de la fontaine baignait l'entrée. Les tiges rampantes et tortueuses du lierre et celles d'une vigne sauvage tapissaient le portique rustique de cet asyle creusé par la main de la nature. C'est là que les deux amants fortunés avaient si souvent fui les regards importuns et les rayons brûlants du milieu du jour; c'est là que, leurs bras étant unis par l'amour, un doux silence succédait aux serments mutuels de s'aimer toujours: les murs de cette grotte étaient encore plus couverts de leurs noms et de leurs chiffres qu'aucune autre partie des environs; la craie, la pointe de leurs couteaux, le charbon même, avaient été employés pour les multiplier.

Le triste comte, dès l'entrée de la grotte, aperçut un assez long écrit d'une autre main que celle d'Angélique, et qui paraissait gravé depuis peu; c'étaient des vers que l'heureux Médor avait écrits dans sa langue asiatique, en mémoire du bonheur qui comblait si souvent ses desirs dans cette paisible grotte; et c'est ainsi qu'il s'était exprimé: Arbrisseaux fleuris, gazons naissants, onde transparente, grotte obscure où la fille de Galafron oubliait tant d'amants qu'elle avait toujours méprisés, vous l'avez vue souvent cette charmante Angélique dans les bras de l'heureux Médor; nul de ses charmes alors n'était voilé pour vous que par les ailes de l'amour. Ah! que votre silence et votre asyle nous furent agréables, et que la mémoire en sera chère à ce Médor, qui ne peut les reconnaître qu'en vous célébrant et qu'en formant des vœux pour vous!

Tendres amants, fiers chevaliers, villageois, voyageurs altérés que le hasard conduira dans cette délicieuse retraite, respectez ces gazons, cet ombrage, cette grotte, cette fontaine et ces arbrisseaux; jouissez de leurs charmes, et répétez tous avec moi:

Lieu charmant, puisse le soleil entretenir toujours pour toi la fécondité!

Que les rayons de l'astre de la nuit te prêtent leur douce lumière, et que les nymphes viennent ici danser en rond à leur clarté!

Que le pasteur grossier ne laisse jamais fouler ce gazon, et troubler la pureté de ces eaux par les pieds poudreux de son troupeau!

Ces vers étaient écrits en langue arabe; cette langue était familière à Roland, et de toutes les langues qu'il avait apprises, c'était celle qu'il parlait le

> plus facilement: elle lui fut souvent très utile pendant son séjour parmi les Sarrasins: mais si la pratique de cette langue le garantit de quelques périls et de quelques peines, il lui fut bien cruel de l'entendre si bien, lorsqu'elle servit à confirmer son malheur.
>
> L'infortuné paladin lit et relit plusieurs fois ce fatal écrit; il voudrait bien encore répandre quelque illusion sur cette évidence si cruelle. Ses efforts sont inutiles; tout se réunit pour constater cette affreuse vérité. Son cœur se glace; il lui semble qu'une main froide le lui presse et le déchire; il reste les yeux fixes, et comme privé de toute idée; ses regards sont attachés sur ce rocher: mais que peut-il y voir encore! il paraît être immobile, insensible comme lui. Dès ce moment, l'intelligence du paladin commence à s'altérer. En pourrez-vous douter, amants infortunés, qui n'avez jamais connu de malheur plus cruel que l'infidélité d'une maîtresse adorée! Sa tête tombe sur sa poitrine; son front et ses regards ont perdu l'audace qui les animait; sa voix arrêtée ne forme point de plaintes; ses yeux ardents ne répandent point de pleurs; sa douleur, en voulant s'exhaler avec trop d'impétuosité, reste concentrée en lui-même: c'est ainsi que nous voyons l'eau fixée dans un vase, dont la vaste capacité se termine par un goulot étroit; on ne parvient point à la vider en retournant le vase; la colonne du liquide se presse, se concentre dans cet étroit passage, de telle sorte qu'à peine elle peut s'échapper goutte à goutte.

A comparison suggests that Pushkin was not only using the French translation. However, if he consulted the original, he gave no thought to retaining its form. The Italian poem is in octaves (which Pushkin had used as early as the 1821: "Кто видел край, где роскошью природы," and would again turn to in "Осень" and the narrative poem "Домик в Коломне"), but Pushkin's translation is in freely rhymed iambic tetrameter, with stanzas of varying lengths.

---

2 Ручéй прозрáчнее стеклá – a brook more transparent than glass
4 убралá – decorated
5 обсади́ла древесáми – planted with trees
11 нашёл несчáстный – the unfortunate one found
13 на деревáх – on the trees. In modern Russian, the standard form would be "на дерéвьях."
17 Невóльный страх егó влечёт – an involuntary terror leads him on
19 в жар полднéвный – in the noontime heat. In poetry "полдневный" often has the figurative meaning of "southern," but here it most likely has the literal meaning.
22 Сам друг – as a twosome
24 Соединённы вензелóм – united in a monogram. In modern Russian, the form would be "вензелём."
25 гвоздём – like a nail
30 силится вообрази́ть – tries to imagine
33 Другóй, не этой Анджели́кой – By another Angelica, not this one
35 черты́ – marks
41 Он мыслит, что судьбé помóжет – He thinks that he will help <his> fate
42 чем он более – the more he

43 утуши́ть – (archaic) to allay
44 тем пуще – the more. The “тем” is parallel to the “чем” in line 42. The same construction is found in lines 47–48.
49–50 где своды / Гора́ склони́ла на ручей́ – where the mountain bent its arch over the brook. The brook seems to flow into (or out of) the mountain.
51 Криво́й, бродящей павили́кой (=повиликой) – By a crooked, wandering dodder. Dodder is a parasite that winds around other plants.
73 С преле́стной дщерью Галафро́на – With Galafron’s charming daughter
75 уте́хи Купидо́на – Cupid’s pleasures
76 Чем, бедный, вас я награжу́ – With what, poor man <that I am> shall I reward you
80 Госпо́д любо́вников молю́ – I beseech noble lovers
83 в сторону сию́ – to this place
92 от злых прока́з – from evil tricks
94 три раза́ – three times. In modern Russian the stress falls on the first syllable (ра́за).
99–101 И нестерпи́мая тоска́, / Как бы холо́дная рука́, / Сжима́ет сердце в нем ужа́сно – And an unbearable anguish, Like a cold hand, Presses terribly on his heart. Nabokov (3:5–6) sees this passage as proof that Pushkin was using the French translation by Tressan rather than the Italian original. Cf. “Son cœur se glace; il lui semble qu’une main froide le lui presse.”
104 в горести безгла́сной – in silent grief
111 Ни вопля, ни слезы́ одно́й – Neither a scream nor a single tear

„Криста́л, поэ́том обновле́нный“ – “A crystal <glass>, initiated by the poet”

In this unfinished poem, Pushkin apostrophizes a wineglass that the poet Nikolai Mikhailovich Iazykov (1803–1845) had used, presumably as the poets consumed “жжёнка” together at Trigorskoe (see commentary to “К Языкову,” line 14). As in that poem, Pushkin shows particularly high regard for Iazykov’s talent.

The poem is written in iambic tetrameter quatrains, though the manuscript is in such a chaotic state that even the ordering of the stanzas is open to debate. The lines following “В тебе таится жар целебный” are missing; part of the manuscript page was torn out.

---

1 обновле́нный – initiated; used for the first time. In modern Russian, the word would be “обновлённый.”
6–7 Една́ уста́ красноречи́вы (=красноречивые) / Тебя́ косну́лися (=коснулись), и вмиг – Hardly have his eloquent lips touched you, when suddenly. There is a curious echo (or play) on the lexicon and grammatical constructions of “Пророк,” which was written at approximately this time – “Моих ушей коснулся он […] И он к устам моим приник” (cf. the final word in the present poem, “проник”).

„Под небом голубы́м страны́ своéй роднóй“ – “Under the blue sky of her native land”

The poem is dedicated to the memory of Amalia Riznich, née Ripp (1803?–1825). The daughter of an Austrian father and an Italian mother, Riznich was living in Odessa because her husband – more than a decade older than she – was a wealthy local merchant, one of the directors of a bank (and also of the local theater). Amalia arrived in Odessa soon after her wedding in the spring of 1823 and immediately attracted a swarm of admirers. Pushkin arrived soon after and fell passionately in love with her. She became consumptive in late 1823, and her condition deteriorated considerably after she gave birth to a son on 1 January 1824. In May of that year she left for Italy, where she died in early 1825.

Vasilii Ivanovich Tumanskii (1800–1860), a poet who knew Pushkin from Odessa, wrote a sonnet on the subject of Riznich's death and dedicated it to Pushkin. In that poem, he bemoaned that fact that none of her admirers now remembered her. The sestet begins: "И где ж теперь поклонников твоих / Блестящий рой? Где страстные рыданья?" ("And where now is the brilliant swarm of your admirers? Where are the passionate sobs?") Veresaev (1993, 1:398–99) suggests that Pushkin's poem was a response to this reproach.

The form of Pushkin's poem is alternating iambic hexameter and tetrameter, with the hexameter lines ending in masculine rhymes and the tetrameter in feminine rhymes. This exact form is found in two other Pushkin poems on the subject of recollection ("Воспоминание" and "На холмах Грузии"). The metrical and semantic model is probably Batiushkov (Proskurin 1999, 197–203).

---

1 страны́ своéй роднóй – of her native land. Pushkin considered Riznich's native land to be Italy. Proskurin notes two Batiushkov passages that Pushkin appears to draw on: "Под небом сладостным отеческой земли" (from "Тень друга") and "Под небом сладостным Италии моей" (from "Умирающий Тасс").

2 Онá томи́лась, увядáла … – She was languishing, she was withering. The use of the verb "увядать," repeated in the next line in perfective aspect (the only instance of a perfective verb in the entire poem), is common in Russian elegiac verse as a euphemism for "to die."

4 Младáя тень – the young shade. The shade is "young" either because she died at such a young age or because she has so recently joined the world of the dead.

5 недосту́пная чертá – an inaccessible border. Cf. "Между протекшего есть вечная черта" ("Between that which has passed there is an eternal border") from Batiushkov's elegy "Воспоминание," a poem written between 1807 and 1809 that contains numerous interesting parallels.

6 Напрáсно чувство возбуждáл я – In vain I tried to awaken my feeling

7 Из равноду́шных уст – from indifferent lips. It is not known who told Pushkin of Riznich's death.

8 ей внимáл я – I heard it. The antecedent of "ей" is "смерти весть" ("news of her death"). The use of "внимать" with dative case is standard.

10 С таки́м тяжёлым напряже́ньем – with such difficult tenseness. Pushkin was not alone in vying for Riznich's affections; this line (and the next few) reflects his mood of the time.

14 Для бедной, легкове́рной тени – For the poor, gullible shade. There is a curious temporal shift between adjective and noun; in death, Riznich would presumably no longer be gullible. Note also the subtle contrast between lightness (the "легко" in "легковерной") and the heaviness of "тяжёлым напряженьем" in line 10. According to Ginzburg (1997, 191) the surprising word "легковерной" replaces the expected elegiac "легкокрылой" (already suggested in the imagery of line 4: "младая тень уже *летала*").

16 Не нахожу́ ни слёз, ни пени – I find neither tears nor lament. Cf. the final line of "Из Ариостова 'Orlando Furioso'."

К Вяземскому – To Viazemskii

This poem was inserted in a letter that Pushkin wrote to Prince Pavel Andreevich Viazemskii (1792–1878) on 14 August 1826. It is a polemic reaction to Viazemskii's poem "Море" (sent to Pushkin on 31 July 1826). In that poem, commenting on the reprisals against the Decembrists, Viazemskii had praised the sea as an alternative to the injustice of the land. Pushkin's poem is generally considered a response to the following stanza (though other passages were probably in his mind as well):

> В вас нет следов житейских бурь,
> Следов безумства и гордыни,
> И вашей девственной святыни
> Не опозорена лазурь.
> Кровь ближних не дымится в ней;
> На почве, смертным непослушной,
> Нет мрачных знамений страстей,
> Свирепых в злобе малодушной.

> (In you there are no traces of life's storms, / Traces of madness and pride, / And the azure of your virginal sacred place is not disgraced. / The blood of neighbors does not billow in it; / On ground that is not obedient to mortals, / There are no dark signs of passions, / Fierce in their cowardly malice.)

Pushkin himself spelled out the reasons for his attack on the sea in his letter: "Правда ли, что Николая Т.<ургенева> привезли на корабле в П<етер>Б<ург>? Вот каково море наше хваленое!" ("Is it true that they have brought Nikolai Turgenev to Petersburg by ship? So much for our highly touted sea!") Nikolai Turgenev (see commentary to "Стансы," line 8), then living in England, was wanted for interrogation in connection with the Decembrist rebellion. Knowing that he was innocent of complicity but also that he would be judged severely (and probably put to death), he refused to return to Russia. The rumor at the basis of Pushkin's poem – that Turgenev had been brought to Russia against his will – proved to be untrue. (Turgenev first returned to Russia two decades after Pushkin's death.)

The poem is in iambic tetrameter. The two stanzas use different rhyme schemes: first a ring structure, then alternating.

---

1 древний душегу́бец – ancient killer of souls. The reference to antiquity is perhaps suggested by Viazemskii's poem:

> Так! Древности постиг теперь
> Я баснословную святыню:
> О волны! Красоты богиню
> Я признаю за вашу дщерь!
>
> (So, I have now understood the legendary sacred place of antiquity, O waves, I recognize the goddess of beauty as your daughter!)

2 Воспламеня́ет гений твой – Inflames your spirit

4 Непту́на грозного трезу́бец – the trident of dread Neptune. Neptune, god of the waters in Roman mythology, is traditionally portrayed with a trident in hand. The line is possibly a phonetic echo of "Ни рока грозного перуны" ("Not the lightning bolts of dread fate") from Viazemskii's poem, cf. *Нептуна* / *перуны*.

7 На всех стихи́ях – On all the elements. The reference is to the four elements: earth, air, fire, and water. In his poem, Viazemskii had written (about the sea): "В стихии светлой чистоты" ("In the element of light purity"). In his earlier poem "К морю," Pushkin himself had addressed the sea as "свободная стихия" ("the free element"), hence the reference in the letter to "*our* highly touted sea."

Literature: Nemirovskii, 269–70.

К Язы́кову – To Iazykov

Pushkin first met the poet Iazykov (see commentary to "Кристал, поэтом обновленный") in the summer of 1826, when the latter was visiting friends at Trigorskoe, the village next to Mikhailovskoe. (Pushkin was still in exile; his unexpected call to the capital occurred on 4 September 1826.) Iazykov then returned to Dorpat (Tartu), and on 19 August he sent Pushkin a friendly epistle beginning "О ты, чья дружба мне дороже" ("Oh, you, whose friendship is dearer").

> О ты, чья дружба мне дороже
> Приветов ласковой молвы,
> Милее девицы пригожей,
> Святее царской головы!
> Огнём стихов ознаменую
> Те достохвальные края
> И ту годину золотую,

Где и когда мы: ты да я,
Два сына Руси православной,
Два первенца полночных муз,
Постановили своенравно
Наш поэтический союз.
Пророк изящного, забуду ль,
Как волновалася во мне,
На самой сердца глубине,
Восторгов пламенная удаль,
Когда могущественный ром
С плодами сладостной Мессины,
С немного сахара, с вином,
Переработанный огнём,
Лился в стаканы-исполины?
Как мы, бывало, пьём да пьём,
Творим обеты нашей Гебе,
Зовём свободу в нашу Русь,
И я на вече, я на небе
И славой прадедов горжусь?
Мне утешительно доселе,
Мне весело воспоминать
Сию поэзию во хмеле,
Ума и сердца благодать.
Теперь, когда Парнаса воды
Хвостовы черпают на оды,
И простодушная Москва,
Полна святого упованья,
Приготовляет торжества
На светлый день царевенчанья, –
С челом возвышенным стою,
Перед скрижалью вдохновений,
И вольность наших наслаждений,
И берег Сороти пою!

Pushkin responded on 28 August with his own poem. Like Iazykov's (and many other Russian friendly epistles), it is in astrophic iambic tetrameter with an unpredictable rhyme scheme. The jocular tone and familiar language spiced with (fairly uncomplicated) allusions to Greek mythology, are all typical of the genre. In several places, Pushkin makes specific reference to Iazykov's poem. However, these allusions would only have been recognizable to Iazykov himself (or to a small group of initiates), since Pushkin's poem was published in 1827, while Iazykov's first appeared in print in 1866, long after both poets had died.

---

2 Твоё посла́нье удало́е – Your daring epistle. The "daring" quality of Iazykov's poem may concern the overall tone or more specifically the pointedly political conclusion, with its unfavorable comparison of Moscow's celebrations (the coronation of Nicholas took place on 22 August 1826) to Iazykov's songs about the more mundane pleasures of country life. It should be noted that

Iazykov had used the word "у́даль" in rhyming position (cleverly paired with "забу́ду ль"), a freedom that surely amused Pushkin, who would not tolerate such a rhyme in his own practice. Pushkin "corrects" it here with his own clever rhyme "удало́е/молодо́е" (note how the "л" and "д" of "удалое" shift positions), which then leads to the next rhyming word "водо́й."

6 каста́льскою водо́й – With Castalian water. The Castalian spring, near Delphi, is traditionally associated with poetic inspiration. This reference (and that of lines 8–9) is inspired by Iazykov's mention of "Парнаса воды."

7 Ты воспои́л свою́ Каме́ну – You nurtured your Muse. The verb "воспоить" may recall a different verb that would be more appropriate in conjunction with a muse: "воспеть" (to sing, to laud).

8–9 Пега́с ину́ю Иппокре́ну / Копы́том вышиб – Pegasus knocked open another Hippocrene with his hoof. According to Greek myth, Pegasus created the Hippocrene (favored well of the Muses) with a single kick of his hoof.

11 пенится хмельно́ю брагой – froths in an intoxicating brew

12 разы́мчива, пьяна́ – potent, intoxicating

14 Слия́нье рому и вина́ – A mixture of rum and wine. The ending on "ром" is an old genitive. This "noble" drink was called "жжёнка" (from "жечь" [to burn], because caramelized sugar – not mentioned by Pushkin – was an important ingredient). Iazykov's poem gives a more detailed recipe: "могущественный ром / С плодами сладостной Мессины, / С немного сахара, с вином" (powerful rum / Together with the fruits of sweet Messina [either lemons or oranges] / With a little sugar, with wine).

16–17 жаждою свобо́дной / Откры́тый в наши времена́ – Discovered in our times by a free thirst. The phrase "в наши времена" is synonymous with "в наше время," but stylistically more elevated. The beverage in question was indeed a recent discovery, and not only in Trigorskoe; it had appeared in Russia only after the Napoleonic wars. Though presumably first appreciated by Russian soldiers, it quickly became a drink of choice among students. In a draft Pushkin had written "лирою свободной / Воспетый" ("sung by a free lyre") rather than "жаждою свободной / Открытый." The fact that the adjective "свободный" occurs in both versions points to its centrality. It clearly responds to Iazykov's poem, both the line "Зовем свободу в нашу Русь" ("We summon freedom to our Rus'") and the closing passage: "И вольность наших наслаждений / И берег Сороти пою" ("and I sing the freedom of our pleasures and the shore of the Sorot' [the river at Trigorskoe]"). Iazykov's use of the word "вольность" had pointed to Pushkin's poem of that name, which – unpublished but widely circulated – gave Pushkin the reputation of a political troublemaker and (at least indirectly) led to his exile. Using the innocuous synonym "свободный," Pushkin signals his awareness of that political subtext. However, rather than following Iazykov's lead and closing his poem on the expected image of singing (the "воспетый" would have nicely echoed "воспоил" – after all, the петь/пить pun was a favorite of Iazykov's [see commentary to the 1828 poem "К Языкову"]), Pushkin chooses the word "открытый." In the context of the poem, "открытый" suggests an opened bottle, recalling the more general theme of drinking as well as Pegasus's opening up the Hippocrene by stamping with his hoof.

Песни о Стеньке Разине – Songs about Sten'ka Razin

Pushkin was fascinated by bandits and pretenders: Sten'ka Razin and (later) Emilian Pugachev. Razin was the leader of a peasant uprising from 1668 to 1670. Though put to death in Moscow in 1671, he lived on in various folk songs and poems dedicated to his daring and often bloodthirsty exploits. In a letter written from Mikhailovskoe, Pushkin asked his brother to send him historical material on Razin, "единственн<ая> поэтическ<ая> личность в русской истории" ("the only poetic character in Russian history").

The three songs are stylizations, relying on fokloric verse for lexicon, syntactic constructions, and meter. (These songs are among the first poems in which Pushkin uses accentual rather than syllabo-tonic verse. They represent various types of what in Russian folklore is called "песенный стих" or "sung verse"). The first two are based on well-known stories about Razin; the last is Pushkin's invention, but it also draws on known folkloric conventions and material (though not specifically about Razin). All three revolve around the quintessentially folkloric motif of gift-giving (Bethea 2009, 289–90).

Pushkin attempted to publish these songs in 1827, but was not granted permission. Count Benkendorff (the head of the secret police and Pushkin's de facto censor) wrote: "Песни о Стеньке Разине, при всем поэтическом своем достоинстве, по содержанию своему неприличны к напечатанию. Сверх того церковь проклинает Разина, равно как и Пугачева." ("The songs about Sten'ka Razin are, nothwithstanding their poetic worth, inappropriate for publication on account of their content. Besides, the church has cursed Razin, just like Pugachev.")

1. „Как по Во́лге реке́, по широ́кой" – "Along the broad Volga"

This song uses a three-stress accentual meter (in lines like "В волны бро́сил кра́сную деви́цу," the stress on syllable one is omitted, and in "Сам хозя́ин, гро́зен Стенька Ра́зин," stress is omitted on "сам" and "Стенька"), with frequent stress on the third syllable of the line and fixed stress on the penultima. The one stress that falls between these two positions is separated from the others by anywhere from one to three unstressed syllables. This type of verse anticipates that of the majority of the "Песни западных славян." Those poems, however, do not rhyme, whereas here Pushkin does, albeit only intermittently and unpredictably.

The precise source for the plot of this poem was most likely the journal "Северный архив" of April 1824, which included an article by A. O. Kornilovich, in which he wrote at length about a book by a Dutch sailor who had personally encountered Razin.

> В другой раз он [the Dutch sailor] видел его [Razin] на шлюпке, раскрашенной и отчасти покрытой позолотою, пирующего с некоторыми из своих подчиненных. Подле него была дочь одного персидского хана, которую он с братом похитил из родительского дома во время своих набегов на Кавказ. Распаленный вином, он сел на край шлюпки и, за-

думчиво поглядывая на реку, вдруг воскликнул: „О Волга славная! ты доставила мне золото, серебро и разные драгоценности, ты меня взлелеяла и вскормила, а я, неблагодарный, ничем еще не воздал тебе. Прими же теперь достойную тебя жертву". С сим словом схватил он несчастную персиянку, которой все преступление состояло в том, что она покорилась буйным желаниям разбойника, и бросил ее в волны. Впрочем, Стенька приходил в подобное исступление только после пиров, когда вино затемняло в нем рассудок и воспламеняло страсти. Вообще он соблюдал порядок в своей шайке и строго наказывал прелюбодеяние. (cited in Fomichev 1989, 10)

---

1 Как по Волге – Along the Volga. A standard opening of a "былина" (Russian heroic folk verse), cf. "Как во городе было во Казани" (sung by the monk Varlaam in *Boris Godunov*). In these instances "Как" is simply a particle that indicates that a song is beginning.

7 красная деви́ца – beautiful maiden. The standard folkloric form would be "кра́сна де́вица" (Pushkin opts for a literary version of the phrase).

12 Ой ты гой еси – (folk poetic) a formal greeting, something along the lines of "Hail"

13 С глупых лет – from my earliest youth; from childhood

14 В долгу (=долгую) ночь – during the long night (here the adjective is truncated in accordance with folkloric practice, cf. "В долгу ночь на ветке дремлет" in the interpolated folksong in the 1824 narrative poem "Цыганы" ["The Gypsies"]).

15 волнову́ю – stormy

16 мо́лодца – (folk poetic) a strapping lad. It is possible that the stress here falls on молодца́, the standard literary accentuation, so that there would not be more than three unstressed syllables between the ictuses in the line (and in the entire poem).

2. „Ходи́л Стенька Разин" – "Sten'ka Razin Went"

This song is written in two-stress accentual verse with exclusively feminine cadences and occasional (unpredictable) rhyme. Intervals between stresses are usually one or two syllables, but occasionally three. Most of the lines have six syllables, though some have five. Because the lines are so short, one can also conceive of the meter as a mixture of syllabo-tonic lines (iambs, trochees, amphibrachs). Bondi (428–31) views the poem this way and suggests a metrical source in folklore. The motif of stealing coats is often found in Russian folklore.

The meeting depicted in the poem can be traced to 1669. On his way home to the Don region, Razin needed to go through Astrakhan. The local governor Prozorovskii offered to give Razin free passage in exchange for booty. Razin agreed, as his rather unheroic behavior at the end of this poem suggests. However, the story does not end where the poem does. The following year Razin conquered Astrakhan and executed the governor.

2 Астрахань – Astrakhan is located on the Volga River, very close to where it meets the Caspian Sea.
4 воевóда – (here) governor. In working with folkloric texts of uncertain provenance in 1824, Pushkin attempted to discern the original text from beneath later emendations. In doing so, he repeatedly replaced the modern "губернатор" with the historically accurate "воевода" (Bondi, 398–99).
7 Камкú хрущатые – rustling damask cloth
9 Парчú – brocades
13 Пóлы – flaps of a garment (plural of полá)
14 бобрóва – of beaver fur
15 собóлья – of sable fur
19 Отдáй с плеча шýбу – Give the coat from you shoulder. The normal stress on "плеча" is omitted in accordance with standard practice of folklore (and spoken Russian), where stress on two adjacent syllables results in one stress being lessened or altogether omitted.
22 Что во чистом поле – in the open field; the "что" here is a marker of folk style and need not be translated.
26 Думати думу – to think a thought; pleonasm is typical of folkloric texts (думати is archaic for думать).
27 Добрó – all right; ok
30 Да нé было б шýму – so that there won't be a fuss

3. „Что не конский топ, не людскáя молвь" – "It's not a horse's clatter, not people's talk"

The third song uses masculine and dactylic cadences. Most lines have three ictuses, though some have four. The verse form recalls the "былина" (heroic song), a major genre of Russian folklore, though the tendency for entire lines to read as anapests is not typical of folklore and is presumably to be understood as the influence of literary verse (Bondi, 431–32).

1 Что не – It's not. Here "Что" stands in for "То" as part of a broader construction, "not this … but that."
"Топ" is short for "топот" ("clatter"), молвь is short for "молва" ("talk"). These are examples of apocope (cutting off the final syllable of words). When Pushkin used the lines "Лай, хохот, пенье, свист и хлоп, / Людская молвь и конский топ" in *Eugene Onegin*, he was taken to task by critics. In footnote 31 of *Eugene Onegin*, Pushkin defended these lines and explained the source of the unfamiliar words: "В журналах осуждали слова: *хлоп*, *молвь* и *топ* как неудачное нововведение. Слова сии коренные русские: 'Вышел Бова из шатра прохладиться и услышал в чистом поле людскую молвь и конский топ' (*Сказка о Бове Королевиче*)." ("In journals the words 'khlop,' 'molv'' and 'top' were criticized as unsuccessful neologisms. These words are native Russian: 'Bova left his tent to cool off and heard in the open field

people's talk and horses' clatter' [The Tale of Bova the Prince].") On Pushkin and "The Tale of Bova," see commentary to "Гнедичу" (1832), line 24.

1–2 It is typical of Russian folklore to describe what something is not before explaining what it is.

5 Зазыва́ет меня́ – urges me

6 Погуля́ть по морю, по синему – To wander (sail) on the blue sea. The repeated preposition is typical of folk style.

7 лихо́й – daring

15 душа-де́вица – (folk poetic) girl of one's dreams; beloved. The stress on де́вица falls on the first syllable in folkloric texts (in modern Russian it is деви́ца), the stress on the preceding syllable (душа́) is omitted.

Literature: Blagoi 1950, 521–27; Salupere.

„Будь подо́бен полной чаше" – "Be like a full cup"

This unfinished poem is somewhat mysterious. Presumably it was written for a light dramatic work along the lines of a vaudeville. Pushkin received a request for precisely this type of work from the poet Pavel Aleksandrovich Katenin (1792–1853) in a letter of 6 June 1826. However, the plot that Katenin sketched – though concerning a wedding – differs in obvious ways from Pushkin's text.

> Молодой Floridor (по-русски Владимир) случайно заперт в комнате своей кузины, молодой вдовы, ночью на новый год, и не теряет времени с нею; пока они разнеживаются, под окном дается серенада, в конце второго куплета бьет полночь, l'heure du berger; старики входят, застают молодых, и остается только послать за попом, ибо все прочее готово. Французские куплеты дурны, но я прошу тебя мне сделать и подарить хорошие. Ты видишь по ходу сцены, что они должны означать.

If this is indeed a response to Katenin, Pushkin alters the plot and omits most of the details Katenin mentions.

The first twenty lines are in trochaic tetrameter, largely based on two rhymes (-а́ша, -его́), with a refrain on the word "ничего." It is clearly not spoken by one character, but it is difficult to say with certainty how many speakers there are. (Conceivably, each stanza represents a new speaker.) The final six lines switch to iambic tetrameter. Presumably Masha speaks lines 21–24, while the final two lines belong to different characters.

---

1 подо́бен полной чаше – like a full cup. This is an idiom that means to live a carefree, financially secure existence.

5 что за каша – what confusion

7 воля ваша – as you wish

9 То-то праздник мне да Маше – It's a real holiday for me and Masha

13 Стойте – Wait

26 И этой свадьбе не быва́ть – And this wedding must not take place

Признáние – A Confession

Unpublished in Pushkin's lifetime, this poem was written to Aleksandra Ivanovna Bekleshova (1805 [or 1806]–1863). At the time of this poem, she was unmarried (and presumably unattached) and with the maiden name Osipova. As the stepdaughter of Praskov'ia Aleksandrovna Osipova (1781–1859), she lived at Trigorskoe, the neighboring estate to Pushkin's Mikhailovskoe. The poem reflects Pushkin's jealousy (cf. line 27), as he observed Osipova's preference for his friend and rival A. N. Vul'f. It contains numerous biographical references (some of which remain obscure), but it also reads like a "dry run" for Eugene Onegin's letter to Tatiana in chapter 8 of the novel in verse.

The poem is written astrophically, which makes it appear on the page like a letter. The meter is iambic tetrameter and the rhyme scheme unpredictable. The dating of the poem is uncertain; it could have been written at any point between 1824 and 1826.

---

1 хоть я бешýсь – even though I'm in a state of fury

5 Мне не к лицý и не по лéтам ... – It's inappropriate for me and for someone my age. Pushkin was in his mid-twenties at the time of composition.

21 за пяльцами – behind the tambour. A tambour was a frame used for embroidery.

24 в умилéньи (= в умилении or в умиленье) – in a state of tender emotion.

29 собирáетеся в даль (= собираетесь вдаль) – you get ready <to take a walk> far away. Since it is unlikely that Osipova would have set off for a long walk in inclement weather, the line is probably meant ironically.

30 И ваши слёзы в одинóчку – And your tears when you are alone. These tears are presumably noticed by the eavesdropping speaker.

31 речи в уголкý вдвоём – tête-à-tête conversations in the corner. As in the previous line, the speaker is probably not a participant in these discussions, but a jealous observer.

32 путешéствия в Опóчку – trips to Opochka. Opochka was the name of the district where Mikhailovskoe was located, but also (relevant to this passage) of a specific town in that district.

33 вечеркóм – in the evening

34 Али́на – Alina was at the time a fashionable diminutive for Aleksandra (Nabokov, 2:291).

38 Но притвори́тесь – But pretend

Literature: Berezkina 1991.

Прорóк – The Prophet

One of Pushkin's most famous works, this poem has been read as a political statement (about the Decembrist uprising) and a poetic manifesto (the poet as God's mouthpiece). However, it should be emphasized that neither of these readings can be derived from the text itself. Kiukhel'beker (see below) calls his prophet a "певец" ("singer"), perhaps drawing on a lengthy tradition in French poetry that identified the poet as prophet; for examples see Kahn, 189 (from a poem by André Chénier that Pushkin had translated in 1823, where Homer is called "prophète eloquent"), and Kahn, 206 (in French critical prose). Pushkin was obviously aware of this tradition: in *Boris Godunov* his imposter states: "Я верую в пророчества пиитов" ("I believe in the prophecies of poets"). Yet Pushkin does not make this connection explicit in "Пророк." It is true that this poem shares some essential vocabulary with the 1827 "Поэт," but this may tell us more about the latter poem than about the former. As concerns the political reading: it was once fashionable to claim that Pushkin had written an additional stanza that he intended to read to Nicholas if their famous meeting of September 1826 went badly. That supposed final stanza so appealed to Soviet scholars that they included it in the Academy edition, albeit separated from the poem itself. It is still cited by scholars who would like to see Pushkin as part of a "revolutionary" tradition.

> Восстань, восстань, пророк России,
> В позорны ризы облекись,
> Иди, и с вервием на выи
> К убийце гнусному явись.

However, claims for the authenticity for these lines rest on very unstable foundations and should be taken with a pillar of salt. The stanza is out of keeping with the poem and poetically inferior. It is highly unlikely that Pushkin wrote it (Nemirovskii, 226–27; Esipov 2009). Similarly fanciful are claims about the poem being written on a specific date that had political significance (Esipov 2005).

There are two essential subtexts. The first is the book of Isaiah, 6:1–10.

> В год смерти царя Озии видел я Господа, сидящего на престоле высоком и превознесенном, и края риз Его наполняли весь храм. Вокруг Него стояли Серафимы; у каждого из них по шести крыл: двумя закрывал каждый лице свое, и двумя закрывал ноги свои, и двумя летал. И взывали они друг ко другу и говорили: Свят, Свят, Свят Господь Саваоф! вся земля полна славы Его! И поколебались верхи врат от гласа восклицающих, и дом наполнился курениями. И сказал я: горе мне! погиб я! ибо я человек с нечистыми устами, и живу среди народа также с нечистыми устами, – и глаза мои видели Царя, Господа Саваофа. Тогда прилетел ко мне один из Серафимов, и в руке у него горящий уголь, который он взял клещами с жертвенника, и коснулся уст моих и сказал: вот, это коснулось уст твоих, и беззаконие твое удалено от тебя, и грех твой очищен. И услышал я голос Господа, говорящего: кого Мне послать? и кто пойдет для Нас? И я сказал: вот я, пошли меня. И сказал Он: пойди и скажи этому народу: слухом услышите – и не уразумеете, и очами смотреть будете – и не увидите. Ибо огрубело сердце народа сего, и ушами с трудом слышат, и очи свои сомкнули, да не узрят очами, и не услышат ушами, и не уразумеют сердцем, и не обратятся, чтобы Я исцелил их.
>
> (In the year that king Uzziah died I saw also the LORD sitting upon a throne, high and lifted up, and his train filled the temple. Above it stood the seraphim:

> each one had six wings; with twain he covered his face, and with twain he covered his feet, and with twain he did fly. And one cried unto another, and said, Holy, holy, holy, is the LORD of hosts: the whole earth is full of his glory. And the posts of the door moved at the voice of him that cried, and the house was filled with smoke. Then said I, Woe is me! for I am undone; because I am a man of unclean lips, and I dwell in the midst of a people of unclean lips: for mine eyes have seen the King, the LORD of hosts. Then flew one of the seraphim unto me, having a live coal in his hand, which he had taken with the tongs from off the altar: and he laid it upon my mouth, and said, Lo, this hath touched thy lips; and thine iniquity is taken away, and thy sin purged. Also I heard the voice of the Lord, saying, Whom shall I send, and who will go for us? Then said I, Here am I; send me. And he said, Go, and tell this people, Hear ye indeed, but understand not; and see ye indeed, but perceive not. Make the heart of this people fat, and make their ears heavy, and shut their eyes; lest they see with their eyes, and hear with their ears, and understand with their heart, and convert, and be healed.)

The second is the 1822 poem "Пророчество" ("Prophecy") by Vil'gel'm Karlovich Kiukhel'beker (1797–1846), Pushkin's friend from the Lyceum. Kiukhel'beker participated in the Decembrist uprising and was sentenced thereafter to lifelong Siberian exile. If there is any political element to Pushkin's poem, it may be a coded message of approval directed to this friend. Curiously, Kiukhel'beker's own poetics were diametrically opposed to Pushkin's. When he first encountered Kiukhel'beker's poem, Pushkin could barely contain his mirth. In a letter to his brother of 4 September 1822, Pushkin wrote:

> Читал стихи и прозу Кюхельбекера – что за чудак! Только в его голову могла войти жидовская мысль воспевать Грецию, великолепную, классическую, поэтическую Грецию, Грецию, где всё дышит мифологией и героизмом, – славянорусскими стихами, целиком взятыми из Иеремия. Что бы сказал Гомер и Пиндар? – но что говорят Дельвиг и Баратынский?

> (I was reading Kiukhel'beker's poetry and prose – what an eccentric! Only he would come up with the Yid idea to sing Greece – glorious, classical, poetic Greece, where everything breathes myth and heroism! – in Slavono-Russian verses taken completely from Jeremiah. What would Homer and Pindar say? – But what do Del'vig and Baratynsky say?)

Kiukhel'beker's poem (and Pushkin's as well) borrows some of its imagery from Derzhavin's ode "На взятие Измаила" ("On the Taking of Izmail"), see Ram, 166–68.

⇜ПРОРОЧЕСТВО

Глагол господень был ко мне
За цепью гор на бреге Кира:
"Ты дни влачишь в мертвящем сне;
В объятьях леностного мира:
На то ль тебе я пламень дал
И силу воздвигать народы? –

Восстань, певец, пророк Свободы!
Вспрянь, возвести, что я вещал!

Никто – но я воззвал Элладу;
Железный разломил ярем:
Душа ее не дастся аду;
Она очистится мечем,
И, искушенная в горниле,
Она воскреснет предо мной:
Ее подымет смертный бой;
Она возблещет в новой силе!"

Беснуясь, варвары текут;
Огня и крови льются реки;
На страшный и священный труд
Помчались радостные греки;
Младенец обнажает меч,
С мужами жены ополчились,
И мужи в львов преобразились
Среди пожаров, казней, сеч!

Костьми усеялося море,
Судов могущий сонм исчез:
Главу вздымая до небес.
Грядет на Византию горе!
Приспели грозные часы:
Подернет грады запустенье;
Не примет трупов погребенье,
И брань за них подымут псы!

Напрасны будут все крамолы;
Святая сила победит!
Бог зыблет и громит престолы;
Он правых, он свободных щит! –
Меня не он ли наполняет
И проясняет тусклый взор?
Се предо мной мгновенно тает
Утесов ряд твердынь и гор!

Блестит кровавая денница;
В полях волнуется туман:
Лежит в осаде Триполицца
И бодр, не дремлет верный стан!
Священный пастырь к богу брани
Воздел трепещущие длани;
В живых молитвах и слезах
Кругом вся рать простерлась в прах.

С бойниц неверный им смеется,
Злодей подъемлет их на смех:
Но Кара в облаках несется;

Отяжелел Османов грех!
Воспрянул старец вдохновенный,
Булат в деснице, в шуйце крест:
Он вмиг взлетел на вражьи стены;
Огонь и дым и гром окрест!

Кровь отомстилась убиенных
Детей и дев, сирот и вдов!
Нет в страшном граде пощаженных:
Всех, всех глотает смертный ров! –
И се вам знаменье Спасенья,
Народы! – близок, близок час:
Сам Саваоф стоит за вас!
Восходит солнце обновленья!

Но ты, коварный Альбион,
Бессмертным избранный когда-то,
Своим ты богом назвал злато:
Всесильный сокрушит твой трон!
За злобных тайный ты воитель!
Но будет послан ангел-мститель;
Судьбы ты страшной не минешь:
Ты день рожденья проклянешь!

Тебя замучают владыки;
И чад твоих наляжет страх;
Во все рассыплешься языки,
Как вихрем восхищенный прах.
Народов чуждых песнью будешь
И притчею твоих врагов,
И имя славное забудешь
Среди бичей, среди оков!

А я – и в ссылке, и в темнице
Глагол господень возвещу:
О боже, я в твоей деснице!
Я слов твоих не умолчу! –
Как буря по полю несется,
Так в мире мой раздастся глас
И в слухе Сильных отзовется:
Тобой сочтен мой каждый влас!

Kiukhel'beker was an "archaist," a poet who sought to revivify the eighteenth-century odic tradition. "Пророчество" draws on lexical, formal, and stylistic conventions that, for Pushkin in 1822, could only ring false. By 1826, however, Pushkin no longer rejected elevated style out of hand. Biblicisms made sense for biblical content, and "Пророк" is brimming with Slavonicisms and, of course, with biblical allusions (for additional possibilities beyond Isaiah, see Surat 2000, 93 and Stennik, 185–88). It is characteristic of Pushkin's development that he reevaluated his views, introducing into his poetry elements that he had once mocked.

Kiukhel'beker was not the only poet to evince interest in the book of Isaiah. In 1822, Fedor Glinka published "Призвание Исайи" ("The Calling of Isaiah"), a fifty-seven-line poem in iambic tetrameter. It is not clear whether the poem predates or postdates the Kiukhel'beker, but the opening passage shows striking similarities. It surely would have been known to Pushkin, as would other Glinka poems on the subject of prophets. See Gukovskii, 268–72.

Иди к народу, мой Пророк!
Вещай, труби слова Еговы!
Срывай с лукавых душ покровы
И громко обличай порок!
Иди к народу, мой Пророк!

Pushkin's poem exemplifies the notion of kenosis, the emptying out of the human body to allow it to be filled with a divine essence. Compared to the biblical passage (and the Kiukhel'beker poem), it is considerably more violent and less specific. It is striking that Pushkin focuses on the moment of inspiration, ending his poem where Kiukhel'beker and Glinka begin – with God's words to the prophet.

1 томи́м – tormented, exhausted (a present passive participle).
2 В пусты́не мрачной – In a dark wilderness. If this is to be taken literally (and it may just be a spiritual wilderness), it should be noted that the Isaiah passage lacks a desert landscape.
влачи́лся – dragged myself along. Cf. Kiukhel'beker's poem, where the same word is used in the idiom "влачить дни" ("to drag out one's days").
5 перста́ми – with fingers ("перст" is the older word for "палец")
6 зени́ц – eyes (genitive case because governed by the verb "коснуться")
7 отве́рзлись – opened (archaic for "открылись")
вещие – prophetic
10 шум и звон – note that the two nouns take a singular verb because they have essentially the same meaning. This type of agreement is typical of the eighteenth-century ode.
At this point the lengthy anaphora on "И" begins, a stylistic allusion to biblical diction ("polysyndeton" is the rhetorical term).
11 внял – perceived. The word usually takes dative case, but sometimes (as here) accusative; it governs all of the phrases up until line 15. The prophet perceives everything – the heavens (lines 11–12), the earth (line 14), the water's depths (line 13).
13 гад – (here) creatures. This is an archaic genitive plural; the modern Russian form would be "гадов."
14 прозяба́нье – vegetation (archaic)
17 празднoсло́вный и лука́вый – idle-speaking and crafty (both adjectives are associated with sin, the latter often an epithet of the devil)
18 жало мудрыя змей – the tongue of the wise snake. "Мудрыя" is an archaic genitive (and was archaic in Pushkin's day as well), a clear stylistic allusion to the language of the Bible (and perhaps, from there, to the poetry of the eighteenth century). The reference is probably to Matthew 10:16 ("будьте мудры, как змии, и просты, как голуби," a passage that influenced the

Kiukhel'beker poem), itself going back to an ancient (pre-Christian) belief of the snake as a bearer of wisdom. This has nothing to do with the tempter of Eve (the nominative case of which would be "змей" [or "змий"] not "змея").

20 десни́цею крова́вой – with his bloody right hand (cf. the "кровавая денница" ["bloody dawn"] in the first line of stanza 6 and the "десница" of stanza 7 in Kiukhel'beker's poem)

21 рассе́к – cut open

23 пыла́ющий огнём – burning with fire

24 Во грудь – into my chest. The preposition "Во" is used instead of "В." Strictly speaking, it is unnecessary, but it adds to the elevated tone and adumbrates the verb "водви́нул"

26 Бога глас (=голос) – God's voice. Contrary to the practice of Soviet editions, "Бога" should of course be written with a capital letter.

27 виждь – archaic imperative of видеть

28 Испо́лнись волею (=волей) мое́й – Fill yourself with my will

29 зе́мли – lands (plural). Ram (116) notes that the rhyme внемли/земли echoes a similar passage in Derzhavin's poem "Видение мурзы" ("The Vision of the Murza"). Curiously, Derzhavin had stressed the second syllable of each word (using "земли́" as a locative singular and taking advantage of an alternate stress on "внемли́").

30 Глаго́лом жги сердца́ люде́й – Burn the hearts of men with the word; that is, God's word, or logos. (In modern Russian "глагол" means only "verb.") B. Gasparov (239–40) traces the origin of this famous closing line to Derzhavin's "Цыганская пляска" ("Gypsy Dance"): "Жги души, огнь бросай в сердца" ("Burn souls, throw fire into hearts").

К. А. Тима́шевой – To K. A. Timasheva

This poem was written by Pushkin in the album of the poet Ekaterina (presumably he called her "Katerina," hence the confusion of initials) Aleksandrovna Timasheva (1798–1881). It begins with high praise and ends with an unexpected "prosaism" (and witticism).

The poem is a response to Prince Viazemskii's recently published poem "Запретная роза." The eponymous "rose" was Elizaveta Petrovna Lobanova-Rostovskaia (1805–1854), Timasheva's niece, who was in the process of divorcing Prince Lobanov-Rostovskii in order to remarry.

Запретная роза

Прелестный цвет, душистый, ненаглядный,
Московских роз царица и краса!
Вотще тебя свежит зефир прохладный,
Заря златит и серебрит роса.
Судьбою злой гонимая жестоко,
Свой красный день ты тратишь одиноко,
Ты про себя таишь дары свои:

Румянец свой, и мед, и запах сладкой,
И с завистью пчела любви, украдкой,
Глядит на цвет, запретный для любви.
Тебя, цветок, коварством бескорыстным
Похитил шмель, пчеле и розе враг;
Он оскорбил лобзаньем ненавистным,
Он погубил весну надежд и благ!
Счастлив, кто, сняв с цветка запрет враждебный,
И, возвратив ее пчеле любви,
Ей скажет: цвет прелестный! цвет волшебный!
Познай весну и к счастью оживи!

Pushkin responds to this poem in several ways, though not in terms of form. Both poems are written as a single stanza, but Pushkin's clearly breaks into three iambic tetrameter quatrains, the first and third rhyming in a ring construction (sharing the rhyme word "идеал"), the middle quatrain alternating.

---

2 Сии́ преле́стные созда́нья – these charming creations (i.e., the poems). The word "сии" is high style. Note that "прелестный" appears twice in Prince Viazemskii's poem (as the first word and in the penultimate line).
4 Боготворя́т – praise, idolize
5 пил отра́ву – drank poison. The phrase is being used figuratively, suggesting a dangerous beauty.
6 В душо́й испо́лненных черта́х – In your features that are filled with your soul, that is, your physical expression reflects your spirit.
9 Сопе́рницы *запре́тной розы* – of the rival *of the forbidden rose*. The "forbidden rose" is in italics to signify that it is a quotation, a reference to Viazemskii's poem about Lobanova-Rostovskaia. Timasheva was presumably her "rival" in terms of beauty.
10 идеа́л – model
11 Стокра́т блаже́н, кто – A hundred times blessed is he who. The construction occurs frequently in poetry, but it is worth noting that Prince Viazemskii's poem concludes with a similar construction: "Счастлив, кто" (Happy is he who).
12 много прозы – much prose. This presumably refers to (love) letters.

Literature: Tsiavlovskii 1930.

<Няне> – To My Nanny

This unfinished and untitled poem was written to Pushkin's nanny Arina Rodionovna Iakovleva (1758–1828), also known by the married name Matveeva. Uneducated and illiterate, she spoke a colorful and expressive peasant dialect. Pushkin's genuine fondness for her is beyond doubt, and it contrasts greatly with his cold attitude toward his parents. (At the beginning of his exile in Mikhailovskoe, Pushkin was watched over by his father. After constant quarrels, the father departed together with Pushkin's brother and sister, leaving him alone in the house with Arina Rodionovna.) Arina Rodionovna may well have aroused Pushkin's interest in folk poetry by reciting fairy tales to him during the Mikhailovskoe exile, but her influence was wildly exaggerated by Soviet scholars, eager to show the poet's closeness to the people. With one exception, the sources of Pushkin's fairy-tales are to be found in Western literature, not in the tales of his nanny (Azadovskii 1936).

The verses are written in iambic tetrameter with alternating rhymes, breaking off suggestively at the beginning of what would presumably have been a new quatrain. The fragment is interesting stylistically, in that it combines Pushkin's elegiac style (тоска, чудится) with the folklorically-tinged words that presumably recall the speech of Arina Rodionovna (голубка, горюешь, светлица).

---

1 дней моих суро́вых – of my bleak days. (The reference is to Pushkin's exile in Mikhailovskoe, which had ended shortly before this poem was written.)

2 голу́бка дряхлая моя́ – my decrepit darling (a striking combination of adjective and noun)

9 воро́ты – gates. In standard modern Russian "воро́та"

<Из письма́ к Соболе́вскому> – From a letter to Sobolevskii

Sergei Aleksandrovich Sobolevskii (1803–1870) was a poet of humorous (sometimes obscene) verse, a bibliophile, and a great admirer and friend of Pushkin. This poem genuinely was part of a private letter and was published only after Pushkin's death, when Sobolevskii made it available to scholars. Pushkin sent it from Mikhailovskoe to Moscow on 9 November 1826, after spending an unpleasant eight days on the road. The poem is largely gastronomical, poking fun at Sobolevskii's fondness for food.

The tone is light and familiar, though according to the ingenious reading of Kunin (47–59), it has a serious subtext. The towns that Pushkin mentions are all on the road from Moscow to Petersburg, but they are also literary, being chapter titles in Aleksandr Radishchev's forbidden *Путешествие из Петербурга в Москву* (*Journey from Petersburg to Moscow*). This book, which survived in only a few copies after Catherine the Great declared it subversive and packed its author off to Siberia, was one of the jewels of Sobolevskii's collection, and it is known that Pushkin borrowed it from him at some point. It is possible that in his references to these specific places and in some of the details (see, for example, commentary below to line 23) he was signaling to his friend – in a way that third parties would never recognize – that he was studying Radishchev's work.

The poem is written in trochaic tetrameter quatrains with alternating rhymes, though it is "interrupted" once by the absurdly long line 7 (note that the rhyme comes not at the end of this line, but at the appropriate place, on the eighth syllable) and once by a brief prose passage. (The letter itself begins and ends in prose, but these passages are omitted from most editions of the verse. On their significance, see Brown, 484–85). The logic behind the choice of meter is clarified by a marginal note in Pushkin's letter, where he explains that the song should be sung to the tune of "Жил да был петух индейской" ("There once was a turkey-cock"). That poem, otherwise known as “Цапли” (“Herons”), was authored by none other than Sobolevskii himself (together with Baratynskii) on the subject of one of Pushkin’s relatives and his travails in trying to marry off his daughters. While Pushkin’s theme is unrelated, his poem has the same jocular quality, and it is written in the identical meter and rhyme scheme.

---

1 У Галья́ни иль Кольо́ни – At Gagliani’s or Coglioni’s. Paolo Dem’ianovich and Sharlotta Ivanovna Gagliani were the owners of a popular inn in Tver’. The name Coglioni echoes Gagliani in an obscene way, since it is the plural of the Italian word “coglione,” which means either “testicle” or, figuratively, “idiot.”

3 С пармаза́ном макаро́ни – macaroni with parmesan <cheese>

4 Да яйшницу (=яичницу) свари́ – And make an omelette. After the exoticism of the Italian words of the previous line, this phrase sounds incongruous. In Pushkin’s day, the spelling “яишница” (rather than “яичница”) was standard. As noted by Iu. A. Batalin (in Bukalov, 40), Pushkin is probably making an obscene pun: the Russian word for “testicles” is “яички,” so the motif of “coglioni” resurfaces.

6 У Пожа́рского в Торжке́ – At Pozharskii’s in Torzhok. Evdokim Dmitrievich Pozharskii and his wife and daughter had a famous hotel (with dining establishment and stores) in Torzhok, where Pushkin stayed numerous times on his travels.

7 Жареных котле́т отве́дай (именно котле́т) – Try the fried meat patties (absolutely the meat patties). Russian “котлеты” have nothing to do with what in America are known as “cutlets,” but are closer to meatballs: they are made of chopped meat, onion, and small pieces of bread. The word “жареных” nicely echoes the name “Пожарский,” but the details of the line truly reflect Pushkin’s culinary tastes, judging from a later letter (of 21 August 1833, to his wife), in which he praises “M-lle Pojarsky” (apparently the daughter) who “жарит славные котлеты” (“makes glorious meat patties”).

8 И отпра́вься на легке́ (=налегке) – And set off without taking any extra baggage. Presumably the extra baggage meant is food for the road (rendered unnecessary by the meat patties consumed earlier).

9–10 Как до Яжельбиц дота́щит / Колыма́гу мужичо́к – When your coachman drags your beat-up carriage to Iazhel’bitsy

11–12 То-то друг мой растара́щит / Сладостра́стный свой глазо́к! – Then my friend will really open wide his lustful little eye!

13 форе́ли – trout (plural)

15–16 Как уви́дишь: посине́ли, / Влей в уху́ стака́н шабли́ – When you see that they’ve turned blue / Pour a glass of Chablis into the soup. “Уха” is broad term for Russian fish soups; trout makes a particularly tasty variety. Sometimes a dry white wine is added (hence Pushkin’s Chablis) to give a certain bitterness to the flavor. Russian cooks used to add vinegar or sulfites to the boiling water in order to make the fish look blue (and therefore more appetizing).

17 по сердцу – to your liking

20 Луку маленькой (=маленький) кусо́к – A little piece of onion. The ending on “луку” is an old genitive (as in перцу of the previous line).

21 У пода́тливых крестья́нок – From the obliging peasant girls
22 Чем и славится Валда́й – for which Valdai is famous
23 накупи́ бара́нок – buy up some "baranki." Baranki are ring-shaped small breads, similar in shape to bagels. Like the traditional bagel, they are quickly boiled before being baked. Lines 21–23 are all meant to recall a passage at the beginning of the chapter entitled "Valdai" in Radishchev's *Путешествие (Journey)*: "Кто не знает валдайских баранок и валдайских разрумяненных девок? Всякого проезжающего наглые Валдайские и стыд сотрясшие девки останавливают, и стараются возжигать в путешественнике любострастие, воспользоваться его щедростью, на счет своего целомудрия." ("Who does not know the baranki of Valdai and the rouge-cheeked lasses of Valdai? Those base shameless Valdai lasses stop every [male] who arrives and try to inflame lust in the traveler, to take advantage of his generosity at the expense of their chastity.")
24 И скоре́е поезжа́й – And set off faster.

„Как счастлив я, когда́ могу́ поки́нуть“ – "How happy I am when I can abandon"

This somewhat mysterious and probably unfinished lyric monologue was not published in Pushkin's lifetime. The "rusalka" theme connects it to later works such as the unfinished drama of that name as well as to "Яныш королевич," the fifteenth of the "Песни западных славян."

Above the text Pushkin wrote the date and place of composition (a village on the way from Mikhailovskoe to Moscow), followed by the Latin letters "EW." The initials would suggest that the poem was connected either to Evpraksiia Vul'f (Wulf) or Elizaveta Vorontsova (Worontsova), but the relevance of this biographical reference remains obscure.

The poem is written in blank verse that looks back to *Boris Godunov* rather than forward to the *Little Tragedies*, in that Pushkin maintains a caesura after the second foot. With the exception of a few folkloric references, the lexicon is largely that of Pushkin's elegies and love lyrics.

---

2 столи́цы и двора́ – of the capital and the court
3 пусты́нные дубро́вы – the uninhabited groves
6 как рыбка золота́я – like a golden little fish. The phrase has folkloric associations (cf. Pushkin's later "Сказка о рыбаке и рыбке").
19 мед – mead
24 Томи́тельно любо́вью замира́я – stopping in torment with love
29 майской (=майский) шум небе́с – the sound of the heavens in May
30 Иль (=Или) звонкие Боя́на Славья (=соловья) гусли – Or the sonorous "gusli" of Boian the Nightingale. Pushkin uses the name Boian as a general term for a Russian singer of antiquity (Tsiavlovskii 1962, 208–9). It is appropriate that he play the "gusli" – an ancient Russian many-stringed plucked instrument (akin to the lyre).

<Из письма́ к Алексе́еву> – From a letter to Alekseev

Nikolai Stepanovich Alekseev (1788–1854 according to Chereiskii; elsewhere given as 1789–1850) was a veteran of the war with Napoleon who later served in Kishinev, where he met Pushkin. The two became close friends, and their friendship continued long after Pushkin left Kishinev.

These verses come at the end of a friendly and jocular letter of 1 December 1826, which Pushkin wrote in response to a letter from Alekseev of 30 October 1826. The poem obviously plays with adjectives based on geographical names (lines 1, 3, 4), but too little is known of the context to allow us to understand precisely the references that required no elaboration for Pushkin and his correspondent.

The poem is written in iambic tetrameter (iambic hexameter in the third line) with alternating rhymes.

---

1 отше́льник бессара́бской (= бессарабский) – Bessarabian hermit. Bessarabia was then the standard term for the region where Moldavia was located (where Pushkin met Alekseev). The notion of a hermit, not associated with the life that Alekseev led when Pushkin was present, perhaps refers to a line in Alekseev's above-mentioned letter: "Теперь сцена кишеневская опустела, и я остался один на месте" ("Now the Kishinev scene has emptied and I remain alone in place").

2 лука́вый друг – crafty friend. The adjective and noun combination is odd, since лукавый is usually associated with the devil. Alekseev's letter provides an explanation: "Я имел многих приятелей, но в обществе с тобою я себя лучше чувствовал, и мы кажется оба понимали друг друга; несмотря на названии: *лукавого соперника* и *черного друга* я могу сказать, что мы были друзья-соперники, – и жили приятно!" ("I had many acquaintances, but felt best in your company, and we seem to have understood each other; in spite of the names 'crafty rival' and 'dark friend' I can say that we were friendly rivals – and we lived well.") Since "dark friend" clearly refers to Pushkin (as is made explicit in Pushkin's letter to Alekseev of 26 December 1830), "crafty rival" was surely the nickname for Alekseev. In the present case, Pushkin conflates the two nicknames.

3 не сказочкой ара́бской – not with an Arabian fairy-tale. The reference is presumably to the *One Thousand and One Nights*.

<И. И. Пущину> – To I. I. Pushchin

On 11 January 1825, while Pushkin was in exile at Mikhailovskoe, his classmate from the Lyceum, Ivan Ivanovich Pushchin (1798–1859), visited him unannounced. Shortly thereafter, Pushkin began drafting a poem celebrating the event, writing five and a half five-line stanzas. (He also commemorated the event in the poem "19 октября 1825.") Less than a year after this meeting in Mikhailovskoe, Pushchin was sentenced to lifetime exile in Siberia for his participation in the Decembrist uprising. On the eve of the first anniversary of the uprising, Pushkin returned to the poem he had abandoned, taking almost verbatim the first stanza from his earlier draft, rejecting the others, and composing a new second stanza that reflected the recent turn of events (and gave a clear structure to what had earlier been a meandering poem).

The finished poem consists of two five-line stanzas of iambic tetrameter rhymed A-b-A-A-b. The stanzas are clearly contrastive: in the first, Pushchin brings unexpected joy to the exiled Pushkin, in the second, Pushkin – now a free man – attempts to do the same for the exiled Pushchin.

The poem could not be published in Pushkin's lifetime, but it did reach its addressee. According to his memoirs, Pushchin received this poem (in a handwriting he did not recognize, i.e., not Pushkin's) from the wife of another Decembrist on his first day in Chita (the city in Eastern Siberia where he was exiled).

---

1 Мой первый друг – My first friend. The phrase is meant literally. On 12 August 1811 the two met at the entrance exam for the Lyceum. It turned out that they were living near each other, and when Pushchin learned that they both had been accepted, he sought out his future classmate. The two became friends immediately and remained so.

3 двор уедине́нный – isolated courtyard. In modern Russian, the stress is "уединённый."

4 печа́льным снегом занесе́нный – covered with sad snow. In the original 1825 version of this line, Pushkin had written "пустынным" rather than "печальным" (an adjective he had used twice in the second stanza). Both of these adjectives are examples of transferred epithets. There is nothing inherently sad (or empty) in the snow, but it reflects the mood of the observer (the poet). The snow is not symbolic, but simply Russian realia. Pushchin's visit took place on 11 January 1825 – as his memoirs make clear, it was bitter cold, and the courtyard had not been cleared of snow. In modern Russian, the stress is "занесённый."

5 Твой колоко́льчик огласи́л – the bell of your carriage filled with sound

6 Молю́ свято́е провиде́нье – I beg holy providence

7 Да голос мой – May my voice

9 Да озари́т он заточе́нье – May it <my voice> illuminate the imprisonment

Стансы – Stanzas

A politically complicated poem, which has been interpreted as shameful flattery (cf. commentary to "Друзьям" and to "Ответ Катенину") or subtle admonition. The "Stanzas" are addressed to Nicholas, but this only becomes clear in the final stanza. Most of the poem concerns Peter the Great, a subject of endless fascination for Pushkin. Pushkin's relationship to Nicholas would become extremely difficult, but in 1826 it was too soon to tell which of the contradictory paths the new tsar would follow: vengeance (he had dealt brutally with the Decembrists) or forgiveness (he had allowed Pushkin to return to the capital after years of exile). Pushkin's strategy – which was not unique to him (Al'tshuller, 27) – was to draw numerous parallels between Nicholas and Peter, suggesting that the difficult beginnings of his reign would ultimately lead to glory. Al'tshuller (27–35) argues that Pushkin is simultaneously setting the positive pairing of Nicholas/Peter against a negative pairing of Catherine (the Great)/Alexander.

The poem is written in iambic tetrameter with alternating rhymes. The title is not a genre designation, but merely describes a relatively short poem in which each stanza is a complete thought. (For Pushkin, such poems are in iambic tetrameter with alternating rhymes; in drafts he used the term "Стансы" to designate the poems "В часы забав иль праздной скуки" and "Брожу ли я").

---

4 мятежи́ и казни – rebellions and executions. The initial years of Peter the Great's reign were indeed full of rebellions and executions. In particular, Pushkin is thinking of the "streltsy" (Palace Guard or literally, the musketeers). In 1698, when Peter was abroad, these regiments rose up against him. Peter rushed back to Russia and, though the rebellion had already been crushed, meted out brutal punishments, torturing and then executing the rebels by the hundreds.

6 нау́кой – through learning. Russian "наука" is a much broader term than English "science."

7 от буйного стрельца́ – from a rebellious "strelets"

8 отли́чен Долгору́кой – Dolgorukoi <was> different. Iakov Fëdorovich Dolgorukii (1639–1720). In Pushkin's day (and earlier), the ending on this surname could be written either as ой or ий. (In general, these adjectival endings were frequently interchangeable for masculine nominative singular.) Renowned for his daring, Dolgorukii was the subject of numerous anecdotes. The one referred to here is discussed at some length in Pushkin's "Table Talk" (the title is in English), where he notes that he heard it from Prince A. N. Golitsyn:

> "Славный анекдот об указе, разорванном князем Яковом Долгоруким, рассказан у Голикова ошибочно и не вполне. Долгорукий после дерзкого своего поступка уехал домой из сената. Государь, узнав обо всем, очень прогневался и приехал к нему. Князь Яков стал перед ним на колени и просил помилования. Государь, побранив его, стал с ним рассуждать о сущности разорванного указа. Долгорукий изложил ему свое мнение. 'Разве не мог ты то же самое сказать, – заметил ему Петр, – не раздирая моего указа?' – 'Правда твоя, государь, – отвечал Долгорукий, – но я знал, что если я его раздеру, то уже впредь таковых подписывать не станешь, жалея мою старость и усердие'. – Государь с ним помирился, но, приехав к себе, приказал царице, которая к князьям Долгоруким была особенно милостива, призвать князя Якова и присоветовать ему на другой день при всем сенате просить прощения у государя. Князь Яков начисто отказался. На другой день он, как ни в чем не бывало, встретил в сенате государя и более чем когда-нибудь его оспоривал. Петр, видя, что с ним делать нечего, оставил это дело и более о том уже не упоминал."
>
> ("The well-known story about the decree that Prince Iakov Dolgorukii tore up is recounted by Golikov inaccurately and incompletely. After his

bold act Dolgorukii went home from the Senate. The tsar, having heard about it, got extremely upset and went to see him. Prince Iakov got on his knees and asked for mercy. After scolding him, the tsar started to discuss the essence of the decree that had been torn up. Dolgorukii explained his opinion. 'Couldn't you have said the same thing,' noted Peter, 'without tearing up my decree?' 'You're right, my lord,' answered Dolgorukii, 'But I knew that if I tore it up, you wouldn't sign such things in the future, taking pity on my age and zeal.' The tsar made peace with him, but returning home, ordered the empress, who was particularly well-disposed to the Dolgorukii family, to summon Prince Iakov and advise him to ask for forgiveness before the Senate the next day. Prince Iakov simply refused. On the next day, as if nothing had happened, he met the tsar in the Senate and argued with him more than ever. Peter, seeing that nothing was to be done with him, left the matter at that and never mentioned it again.")

Similar brief references to Dolgorukii's bold character can be found in "Мордвинову" and "Моя родословная." There is a curious echo in lines 7–8 of a passage in "О народном просвещении" ("On the Enlightenment of the People"), an internal memo that Pushkin had written just before this poem in response to the tsar's request (i.e., command). In a rather daring passage, Pushkin had defended the liberal thinker Nikolai Turgenev (who was sympathetic to many of the Decembrists' aims, though against armed revolt). Turgenev, Pushkin wrote, "отличался посреди буйных своих сообщников нравственностию и умеренностию" ("differed from his rebellious comrades through morality and moderation"). On the implications of this parallel, see Nemirovskii 243–46 and Proskurin 2006, 112–13. On Turgenev, see commentary to "К Вяземскому."

13 то … то … – at times … at times
академик – an academic. Peter founded the Academy of Sciences.

14 мореплáватель – a sailor. Peter's love for all things naval was well known.
плотник – a carpenter. From his earliest years Peter loved carpentry.

16 рабóтник – a worker. The peasants were claimed to have said of Peter that "He works harder than any *muzhik.*"

17 Семéйным сходством – family resemblance. Nicholas was related to Peter, both being members of the Romanov dynasty.

20 Памятью … незлобен – Not rancorous (merciful) in his memory, that is, not holding grudges. The rather unusual collocation is derived from the common Russian adjective "злопамятный." This is a character trait commonly attributed to Tsar Alexander (Al'tshuller, 13), and it is possible that Pushkin was setting up a contrast between the late tsar he detested and the new tsar, from whom he expected significant improvement. It should be noted that Peter was not necessarily remembered for his foregiveness, but Pushkin noted it elsewhere (see "Пир Петра Первого") and in any case wished to impress on Nicholas its importance. (The political "subtext" is that Pushkin is asking him to be merciful to the exiled Decembrists.)

Отве́т Ф. Т*** – An Answer to F. T***

The initials F. T. refer to the minor poet Fedor Antonovich Tumanskii (1799–1853), who had written the following album verses in praise of Sof'ia Fedorovna Pushkina (1806–1862).

Она черкешенка собою,
Горит агат в ее очах,
И кудри черные волною
На белых лоснятся плечах.
Любезна в ласковых приветах,
Она пленяет простотой,
И живостью в своих ответах
И милой резвой остротой.
В чертах лица ее восточных
Нет красоты – видна душа
Сквозь пламень взоров непорочных
Она как радость хороша.

Pushkin met Sof'ia Fedorovna (who was apparently unrelated to him, though some sources claim her to have been a very distant relative) almost immediately after being freed from his Mikhailovskoe exile. He proposed to her within a matter of days, but she rejected him, preferring – to Pushkin's amazement – a man who had been assiduously courting her for two years. Pushkin's poem, presumably written before the rejection, shows him at the height of his infatuation.

The poem is clearly a polemic response to Tumanskii's rather formulaic model. It is conceivable that Pushkin simply disagrees with his fellow poet's depiction, but it is also possibly a rejection of the Circassian "type" of woman, made famous by Pushkin's narrative poem "Кавказский пленник" ("The Prisoner of the Caucasus"). Both Tumanskii's poem and Pushkin's response are written in iambic tetrameter with alternating rhymes, though with a different sequence (in Pushkin, feminine follows masculine). Pushkin's feminine rhymes are curiously linked: века/Казбека/Востока/ока. The first and fifth lines of Pushkin's poem are connected syntactically and rhythmically, with the first stress of the iambic line occurring on the first syllable of the line.

---

2 от века – since the world began
4 угрю́мого Казбе́ка – from sullen Kazbek. Kazbek is a mountain in Georgia.
5 ага́т – agate. Agates, known for their brightness of color, sometimes resemble eyes.
7 Не стоят сладостных луче́й – Are not worth the sweet rays
8 полу́денного – southern. Judging from portraits and contemporary memoirs, Sof'ia Fedorovna had strikingly dark eyes. From the geographical standpoint of a Russian, this represents southern beauty.

Зимняя доро́га – Winter Journey

This meditation, with its uncharacteristically frequent and expressive use of ellipsis, reflects a passenger's melancholy (note how often forms of "грустно" and "печально" appear) as he travels the vast expanses of the Russian landscape. In numerous ways, the poem anticipates the much darker "Бесы" of 1830.

As Gasparov (1990, 8) notes, virtually all of Pushkin's lyric poems connected to the subject of travel are written in trochaic tetrameter. In this case, the quatrains have alternating feminine and masculine rhymes.

---

1 волни́стые – wavy
2 Пробира́ется – moves with difficulty
4 льёт печа́льно – sadly pours. Throughout this stanza the moon is personified, and the poet projects his own feelings onto it.
6 Тройка борзая – a fleet troika. A troika was a carriage led by three horses.
7 Колоко́льчик – Little bell. This was the bell on all carriages that warned oncoming traffic.
10 В долгих песнях ямщика́ – in the lengthy songs of the coachman
11 То разгу́лье удало́е – Now wild merry-making
12 То серде́чная тоска́ – Now a heartfelt melancholy. Nabokov (4:98) describes the indefinable Russian "тоска" as "boredom, yearning, nostalgia, heartache, dull anguish" and as being "between 'скука' (ennui) and 'мука' (torment)."
15 вёрсты полоса́ты – striped mileposts. A verst was a measure of distance in prerevolutionary times slightly greater than a kilometer.
16 одне́ (=одни) – alone. "Одне" is an archaic plural that reflects the feminine gender of the noun (i.e., "верста").
17 Нина – The name "Nina" is not connected to any woman in Pushkin's biography. It is either a complete fiction or a name chosen to hide the identity of a love interest.
20 Загляжу́сь не наглядя́сь – I will fasten my gaze, not getting enough <of you>
23 доку́чных удаля́я – sending off the dull <people>
28 Отума́нен лунный лик – The face of the moon is covered with fog

„В евр<е́йской> хижине лампа́да" – "In a Jewish hut a lamp"

These verses are clearly the introduction to an unfinished narrative poem on a Jewish theme. According to a diary entry of 19 February 1827 of Franciszek Malewski (1800–1870), a Pole and friend of Mickiewicz, Pushkin claimed to be writing a poem about the wandering Jew. This legend, dating from the Middle Ages but popular among the European Romantics (see Nabokov 2:354–57), concerned a Jew who had taunted Christ and was as a result condemned to walk the earth forever. Kiseleva (94–95) argues that Pushkin's probable source was a French version of the tale related in the multi-volume *Bibliothèque universelle des romans* that was in Pushkin's library in Mikhailovskoe.

Shvartsband (475–89) disputes Malewski's story and contends that Pushkin probably began work on this poem in 1822.

Pushkin wrote constantly in iambic tetrameter, but this use of unrhymed (i.e., blank) iambic tetrameter is unique in Pushkin's work and highly unusual in Russian poetry generally. The striking enjambments (lines 4, 8, 23) further estrange the meter. Pushkin's repeated use of the word "еврей" (and various forms thereof) rather than "жид" suggests a more sympathetic treatment of the characters than is met with in his other depictions of Jews (though these are admittedly stylized). The exception is presumably the wandering Jew himself (in Russian "вечный жид"), the "unknown wanderer" who appears just as the poem breaks off.

---

2 бледна́ (=бледная) – pale
12 трапе́зу – food. Strictly speaking, the word means a table (with food on it), but by metonymy it often means simply "food."
14 Засте́жки медные сомкну́л – closed the brass hasps
17 Никто́ нейдёт (=не идет) – No one comes
28 доро́жный посох – wanderer's staff

К *** – To ***

This love poem – the addressee is unknown – humorously plays the profane (or pagan) against the sacred (Christian), with an obvious preference for the former. The tone and theme recall the narrative poem "Гавриилиада" ("The Gabriliad"), though it is not as outspokenly blasphemous.

While written as a single stanza of iambic tetrameter, it clearly breaks down into quatrains, the first two with a ring rhyme, the final one alternating. The lexicon, whether describing Christian or erotic love, is fully within the canons of secular love poetry. The tone is colloquial.

The poem was unpublished (and – given the sensitivity of religious censorship – unpublishable) in Pushkin's lifetime.

---

1 богома́терь – mother of god. In Russian, this is the standard epithet of the Virgin Mary. (One does not think of Venus, for example, as a "богоматерь.")
2 красо́й – with her beauty
3 дух свято́й – the holy spirit
7 не спрося́сь супру́га – not asking her husband for permission
9 Он бог Парни́, Тибу́лла, Мура – He is the god of Parny, Tibullus, Moore. Pushkin's admiration for the minor French poet Évariste-Désiré de Forges, Vicomte de Parny (1753–1814) is well documented (among other things, he was an important source for the "Gabriliad"). Pushkin's interest in the love poetry of Tibullus (first century BCE) was kindled by Batiushkov, while his knowledge of the Irish poet Thomas Moore (1779–1852) was largely due to Zhukovskii's translations. Pushkin often combines the names of Tibullus and Parny (see Tomashevskii 1960, 147), but the addition of Moore (whom Pushkin generally disliked) was probably for the convenience of rhyme.
10 Им мучусь, им уте́шен я – I'm tormented by him, I'm consoled by him

11 Он весь в тебя́ – ты мать Аму́ра – He looks exactly like you – you are Amor's mother. In Roman mythology, Venus was the mother of Amor (more commonly known as Cupid).

<Мордви́нову> – To Mordvinov

Nikolai Semënovich Mordvinov (1754–1845) was a well-educated, honest, and independent statesman, the only member of the High Court (Верховный суд) who did not sign the death sentence for the Decembrist leaders. He was a military hero with close ties (both personal and professional) to the West, especially England. Pushkin, like most liberal (and even radical) thinkers of the time, had immense respect for him. This poem was not published in Pushkin's lifetime.

It is written in four-line stanzas with alternating masculine and feminine rhymes. The first three lines are in iambic hexameter, the fourth in iambic tetrameter. The form is unusual in Pushkin; it can be found again in "Памятник" ("Я памятник себе воздвиг нерукотворный"), though there the alternating rhymes begin with feminine rhymes. In both cases the stanzaic form appears to connote for Pushkin elevated subject matter. In this poem (about a hero so closely linked to the glory of eighteenth-century Russia), Pushkin relies repeatedly on archaisms (e.g., the word "пиит," found also in "Памятник").

---

2 Еди́ный из седы́х орло́в Екатери́ны – One of Catherine's gray eagles (favorites). The word "eagle" calls to mind the Orlov (from "орёл" or "eagle") brothers, who helped bring Catherine to the throne. The specific reference, though, is to the eighteenth-century poet Vasilii Petrov (1736–1799), named explicitly in line 9. Petrov endeared himself to Catherine and became her court poet (as well as her translator and librarian). His highly rhetorical odes were in the style of Lomonosov, with a lexicon and syntax no less archaic, which particularly stood out in the latter half of the eighteenth century. He is described as "gray" because the Age of Catherine has ended, and he is old and dying (cf. line 1). As becomes clear in line 9, Pushkin is writing about 1796, the year Petrov penned an ode to Mordvinov, with the characteristically florid title "Его высокопревосходительству черноморского флота господину вице-адмиралу и орденов Св. Александра Невского, Св. Князя Владимира первой степени и Св. Анны кавалеру Николаю Семеновичу Мордвинову." Petrov's ode is written in unusual eight-line iambic stanzas of hexameter (lines 1 and 3), tetrameter (lines 2 and 4), and trimeter (lines 5–8), with rhyme scheme A-b-A-b-C-C-d-d.

4 Пинда – of Pindus. This Greek mountain range is traditionally associated with poetic inspiration.

7 взыгра́л – became excited, enthused, inspired. The verb "взыграть" is common in the eighteenth-century ode, but the specific reference here is to Petrov's ode to Mordvinov: "Свершение надежды / Моими зря днесь вежды / И славу сбытия, / Не возыграю ль я?" ("Seeing with my own eyes today the fulfillment of hope and the glory of the event, do I not now become inspired?").

Vinogradov (1941, 495–98) cites passages from eighteenth-century odes showing that this verb is often paired with the image of an eagle.

8 Во сретенье твое́й денни́цы – to meet your morning star. In the draft Pushkin had used the stylistically neutral "На встречу." The archaic word "сретенье" has religious connotations. It can designate the holiday that celebrates the meeting of Jesus and Mary with Simeon and Anna (which corresponds – inexactly – to Candelmas Day in the Western Church).

9 Петро́в – the reference is to the poem discussed above (commentary to lines 2 and 7).

10 Коци́та – of Cocytus, the river leading to the land of the dead in Greek mythology (the presumed location of the now deceased Petrov).

12 вещего пии́та – of the prophetic poet (i.e., Petrov).

16 Долгору́кой (=Долгорукий) – See commentary to line 8 of "Стансы." Once again, Dolgorukoi represents bravery and independence, the ability to stand up to a powerful ruler.

17–20 – an extended (or epic) simile, rare in Pushkin's verse, but common in the eighteenth-century ode. The basic comparison is of the (now elderly) Mordvinov to a gray cliff, not bothered by the roaring elements that surround him. (The steadfast cliff amidst the battering elements was itself a topos of the eighteenth-century ode, cf. Vinogradov 1941, 497–98.)

20 увива́ются – wind around
плещут – splash

21 рамена́ – (archaic) shoulders

22 казно́ю – the treasury (from 1821 Mordvinov's official post was closely linked to the Treasury).

23 лепт – penny (from the Greek "lepton," the coin with the lowest value). Pushkin alludes to the two "widow's mites" in Mark 12:42. In Russian, the standard form is feminine ("лепта"), but the use of the masculine had a precedent in Zhukovskii's "Императору Александру," in the line "Последний бедный лепт за лик твой отдает."

дань сиби́рских руд – tribute of Siberian (iron) ore. The reference is to the mineral wealth in Siberia. In March of 1826, Mordvinov had pushed to increase the yield of gold and iron from Siberia. One wonders if Pushkin is subtly recalling the fate not only of the biblical widow, but also the poor Decembrists, given that the exact phrase reappears in the opening line of "Во глубине сибирских руд," written in January 1827.

~1827

„Во глубине́ сиби́рских руд“ – “In the depths of Siberian mines”

This famous civic poem is addressed to the Decembrists. After the uprising five of their leaders were executed and their bodies buried in anonymous graves (a fact that would disturb Pushkin to the end of his days). More than a hundred others were jailed (see line 14) or exiled to Siberia, where they were forced to work at hard physical labor, such as mining (see line 1).

The poem was not published (and not publishable) in Pushkin's lifetime, though it was circulated and known to the Decembrists themselves. It is written in iambic tetrameter with alternating rhymes (first stanza) and ring rhymes (other stanzas). Note how the first rhyme (руд/труд) echoes with the final rhyme (падут/отдадут).

---

1 Во глубине́ сиби́рских руд – In the depths of Siberian mines. Ordinarily one would say “в глубине.” The additional syllable creates the expectation of a high style (appropriate for civic poetry). Strictly speaking, “руда” means “ore.” It is used here as a metonymy for “mines.”

2 Храни́те гордое терпе́нье – Maintain your proud endurance. Lotman (1997, 34–35) notes that this line echoes a song that Del'vig had written for the Lyceum graduation (“Прощальная песнь воспитанников Имп. Царскосельского лицея,” 1817), a work that was rehearsed and sung – and presumably would have been remembered years later – by those students (who included two Decembrists). The relevant excerpt is cited below; the italics are *not* in the original.

> Простимся, братья! Руку в руку!
> Обнимемся в последний раз!
> Судьба на вечную разлуку,
> Быть может, здесь сроднила нас!
>
> Друг на́ друге остановите
> Вы взор с прощальною слезой!
> *Храните*, о друзья, *храните*
> Ту ж дружбу с тою же душой,
> То ж к славе сильное стремленье,
> То ж правде – да, неправде – нет,
> В несчастье – *гордое терпенье*,
> И в счастье – всем равно привет!
>
> (Let us part, brothers! Hand in hand! Let us embrace for a final time! Fate has brought us together perhaps for an eternal separation. / Fix your glance on one another with a farewell tear! Maintain, o friends, maintain that same friendship with that same soul, that same powerful aspiration for glory, that same “yes” to truth, “no” to falsehood, in unhappi-

ness <that same> proud endurance, and in happiness a greeting to all equally.)

Note also that Pushkin repeats Del'vig's rhyme (стремленье/терпенье).

3 the singular verb has two subjects: "труд" and "стремленье"

5 Несча́стью верная сестра́ – The faithful friend to misfortune

9 дружество – (archaic) friendship

11 каторжные норы – penal burrows. The noun "каторга" means "penal servitude, hard labor."

12 свобо́дный глас (=голос) – free voice. It should be kept in mind that at this point Pushkin was convinced that Tsar Nicholas, by ending his exile, had set him free. (Cf. "Друзьям," line 18.)

14 свобо́да – freedom. A personification.

16 отдаду́т – There is some ambiguity here: it means either "will give" or "will give back." This line has often been interpreted as a call for revolution. It was understood as such by the Decembrist Aleksandr Ivanovich Odoevskii, who – having read Pushkin's poem in a handwritten copy that reached him in his Siberian exile – wrote a spirited poetic response. Odoevskii's poem, frequently and fervently cited in Soviet Pushkin editions, spoke of forging swords out of fetters. However, it has been argued (Al'tshuller, 36–37) that Odoevskii misunderstood Pushkin's poem, that Pushkin's final image of the sword was meant not literally, but symbolically (as an emblem of aristocracy). In other words, Pushkin was not calling for rebellion, but for patience (cf. line 2 above), in the hope that the Decembrists would ultimately be pardoned and allowed to rejoin society in the same capacity as before.

Солове́й и роза – The Nightingale and the Rose

The nightingale and the rose are associated with Eastern poetry (hence Pushkin's "восточный соловей"), where they commonly appear as symbols of the poet and his beloved. In Pushkin's earlier narrative poem "Бахчисарайский фонтан," the pairing occurs, presumably to underline the exoticism of the southern (Crimean) locale: "И, с милой розой неразлучны, / Во мраке соловьи поют" ("And, inseparable from the dear rose, the nightingales sing in the darkness"). Pushkin's treatment of the theme in this later lyric poem includes a motif that will become increasingly common in his poetry (e.g., "Эхо") – the poet's inability to achieve the desired effect on his audience. It has been suggested that this poem reflects Pushkin's recent rejection by Sof'ia Fedorovna Pushkina. If so, the hurt was apparently not so great, since Pushkin published it shortly after writing it.

Pushkin relates his "Eastern" allegory in alexandrines, with the caesura marked syntactically in every line. Though written as a single stanza, it breaks logically into two parts of four lines each. The first introduces the nightingale and rose; the second explicitly "explains" them as the poet and his beloved.

---

4 под влюблённый гимн – to the accompaniment of the hymn of love. Strictly speaking, this is a transferred epithet. It is the nightingale who is "влюблённый" (in love), not his song.

6 Опо́мнись – Stop and think
8 взыва́ешь – нет отве́та – When you call, there is no answer

Эпигра́мма (Из Антоло́гии) („Лук звени́т, стрела́ трепе́щет") – Epigram (From the Anthology) ("The Bowstring sounds, the arrow quivers")

This epigram is directed at Andrei Nikolaevich Murav'ev (1806–1874), a fledgling poet then close to the philosophically-minded "Liubomudry" ("Wisdom Lovers"). While the "Liubomudry" admired Pushkin, he maintained a skeptical attitude toward them. At a salon in the home of Zinaida Volkonskaia (see commentary to "Княгине З. А. Волконской"), Murav'ev happened (through sheer clumsiness) to break the arm of a plaster-of-Paris statue of Apollo. He responded by writing a poem on the pedestal of the statue commemorating the event. Inscriptions of this type were not unprecedented (see Vatsuro 1989, 234–35).

О Аполлон! поклонник твой
Хотел померяться с тобой,
Но оступился и упал,
Ты горделивца наказал:
Хотел пожертвовать рукой,
Чтобы остался он с ногой.

(Oh, Apollo! Your admirer wanted to measure himself against you [i.e., to challenge you], but he took a false step and fell; You punished the proud one: you were ready to sacrifice your arm so that he could keep his leg [i.e., so that he could remain unharmed].)

These verses were surely meant to be ironic and even self-deprecating. Pushkin had been quite friendly to this young poet, and his response was surprising in its nastiness, especially since he chose to publish it, rather than simply allowing it to be passed around in manuscript form or repeated orally.

The epigram is written in trochaic tetrameter with alternating rhymes (note how the first masculine rhymes change case to become the second feminine rhymes, allowing the "punch line" of the epigram stand out for its novelty).

Subtitle: Из Антологии – From the <Greek> Anthology.
The Greek Anthology was the term used for a number of multi-authored collections of verses from antiquity. They were mainly composed of brief and epigrammatic verse. Pushkin's reference here is either a mystification or a joke.
2 И клубя́сь издо́х Пифо́н – writhing in circles, Python died. In Greek mythology, Python was a serpent slain by Apollo.
3 лик – (arch.) face (often of a god); note here the echo of "лук."
4 Бельведе́рский Аполло́н – The Apollo Belvedere. Considered one of the masterworks of antiquity (see commentary to line 21 of "Поэт и толпа"), this statue depicts Apollo shortly after the arrow has left his bow in its course to

slay Python. It is called "Belvedere" because it was initially exhibited in the courtyard of the Belvedere villa in Rome.

8 Бельведéрский Митрофáн – The Mitrofan Belvedere. Mitrofan was the lazy and dim-witted protagonist of Fonvizin's comedy "Недоросль" ("The Minor," 1782). The play was so successful that the name Mitrofan was applied to any stupid and self-satisfied young person.

„Есть роза дивная; онá" – "There is a wonderful rose; it"

Not published in Pushkin's lifetime, the poem is a mystery. It belongs to a subgenre of poems on the subject of withered and withering roses ("увядать" is the key verb), begun in the Lyceum, to which Pushkin returned at various points in his life (see Alekseev 1972). Despite the ellipsis at the end, it appears to be complete. It also appears to be serious, even philosophical, an uncharacteristic hymn to an immortal ideal.

However, this impression is somewhat undone by certain formal features and by the drafts. It is written in Pushkin's standard iambic tetrameter with alternating rhymes (a-B-a-B-c-D-c-D), yet in the draft it is labeled "Sonnet." Since the poem bears no formal resemblance to a sonnet, it is either a translation of a sonnet or a joke. The draft is dated 1 April – for evidence that this date had the same unserious associations then as today, see Pushkin's humorous poem of 1825, "Брови царь нахмуря," and note that the narrator of "История села Горюхина" (probably Ivan Petrovich Belkin) was born on 1 April. Moreover, in a stanza of *Eugene Onegin* (4:XLII) written at approximately this time, Pushkin mocks the rhyme of мороза/роза (the concluding rhyme of "Есть роза дивная") as being hackneyed.

Blagoi (1967, 148–49) reads the poem's irony as being directed against the recently deceased Venevitinov, whose poem "Три розы" ("Three Roses") was published posthumously, shortly before Pushkin wrote this poem. Vatsuro (1989, 239–40) reads Pushkin's poem as part of a larger and more serious dialogue with Zinaida Volkonskaia and her salon. He argues that the date of 1 April was not written by Pushkin, but was a deliberate mystification on the part of Pushkin's friend Sobolevskii.

---

2 Пред изумлённою (=изумлённой) Кифéрой – Before the amazed Cythera. Cythera, a Greek island, was famed in antiquity for its temple to Aphrodite and is often used in poetry metonymically to name Aphrodite.

3 румя́на и пышнá – red and splendid. These are truncated adjectives agreeing with "она" (line 1).

4 Благословéнная Венéрой – Blessed by Venus. Venus (Roman name of Aphrodite) was often associated with roses.

5–6 Вотщé Кифéру и Пафóс / Мертви́т дыхáние морóза – The breath of frost (i.e., winter) deadens Cythera and Pafos in vain. Pafos (also spelled Paphos), a city in Cyprus, was likewise associated with the cult of Aphrodite.

7 между минýтных роз – among the momentary roses. The preposition "между" can be followed by the genitive case.

<Ек. Н. Ушакóвой> – To Ek. N. Ushakova

After seeing Ekaterina Nikolaevna Ushakova (1809–1872) at a ball at the end of 1826, Pushkin fell madly in love with her. He was a frequent guest at her parents' house, where he constantly sought her out. This poem, written for her album on the occasion of her eighteenth birthday, was not published in Pushkin's lifetime. It was apparently requested by Ushakova, who complicated the task by giving him the key phrase "Аминь, аминь, рассыпься." In Pushkin's poem, this folkloric formula is used twice, first addressed to demons, then to the poet's "internal demons" (i.e., his infatuated heart or, more precisely, the dream within it).

It is written in free iambs (iambic lines of various lengths without any discernable pattern). Eleven lines are in tetrameter, three are in hexameter, and the two containing the key phrase are in pentameter (these are obviously parallel, with the second serving as a refrain). The rhyme scheme alternates masculine and feminine until the final four, which shift to a ring pattern (a not unusual means of emphasizing closure).

---

1 Когдá, бывáло, в старинý – When it happened in the olden times
3 сатанý – In Russian, Satan is grammatically feminine, but logically masculine. Hence it requires masculine verb endings (as in "Подражание италиянскому," line 9).
5 Ами́нь, ами́нь, рассы́пься! – Amen, amen, disappear! As Pushkin notes, this truly was a folk incantation used to drive away an evil spirit or demon.
7 Бог ведает, кудá девáлися они́ – God <only> knows where they've gone. Both parts of this phrase are strikingly colloquial, with the first part a play on words. ("God knows" is a fixed expression, but "God" is also highly relevant in the context of demons.)
8 злой иль (=или) добрый гений – evil or kind spirit
13 очарóван – enchanted. The word's etymological connection to magic (чары=charms) is significant here.
15 сердцу, полному мечтóю (=мечтой) – to my heart, full of a dream.

Княги́не З. А. Волкóнской – To Princess Z. A. Volkonskaia

Zinaida Aleskandrovna Volkonskaia (1789–1862) was a poet, singer, and composer, whose Moscow salon attracted the city's cultural elite. In the first few years after his return from exile, Pushkin was a frequent visitor. (See "Эпиграмма" ["Лук звенит"] for one event that took place there.)

The meter is iambic tetrameter with a fairly complicated rhyme scheme: a-B-a-B-c-c-D-e-e-D-f-G-f-G-f. (The first ten lines, formally an odic stanza, are devoted to praise of the addressee; these are followed by a five-line humility topos.) The lexicon, however, recalls the language of the salon rather than that of the eighteenth-century ode.

---

1 Среди́ рассе́янной Москвы́ – Amidst absent-minded Moscow. Either a personification or a metonymy (with the epithet transferred from the inhabitants to the city itself).

2 При толках виста и босто́на – During talks of whist and boston (two popular card games of the time)

3 молвы́ – of rumor

4 игры Аполло́на – the games of Apollo

7 Волше́бный скипетр вдохнове́ний – The magical sceptre of inspirations. The cacophonous consonantal cluster "скипе*тр вд*охновений" is unusual in Pushkin's verse.

9 Двойны́м уве́нчанным венко́м – Crowned with a double wreath. There are two different instrumental cases in this line; "увенчанным" is an instrumental in agreement with челом (forehead) of the previous line, while "двойным венком" is the agent of the passive participle. The "double" wreath refers to Volkonskaia's double talents – music and poetry, both traditionally associated with Apollo (cf. line 4).

10 гений – the spirit <of creativity>

12 смире́нной дани – humble tribute (i.e., the present poem)

14 Катала́ни – Catalani. The Italian soprano Angelica Catalani (1780–1849), one of the most celebrated opera singers of the age, performed to great acclaim throughout Europe until her retirement in 1828. Pushkin here refers to a story according to which Catalani, during a tour in Moscow, heard a Gypsy chorus and gave her shawl to the soloist as a sign of her delight and astonishment. According to some versions, the Gypsy in question was Tat'iana Dmitrievna Dem'ianova (1810–1876 [1877?]), whose voice Pushkin himself particularly admired. (In Dem'ianova's own memoirs of Pushkin, however, the incident is attributed not to her, but to Stesha [surname unknown], who died when Dem'ianova was fourteen years old. Moreover, there is no mention of a shawl.) Pushkin appears to embellish the story, emphasizing the coincidental nature of this meeting with the word "мимоездом" ("while riding past") and describing the Gypsy herself as nomadic ("кочевой"). (These Gypsies seem to have lived permanently in Moscow.)

<Кн. П. П. Вяземскому> – To Prince P. P. Viazemskii

This humorous poem owes its existence to Prince Viazemskii's young son Pavel (1820–1888), who proffered his newly acquired album to Pushkin during one of the poet's visits to his parents. Pushkin apparently took the album and returned it a few days later with this poem inscribed.

It is written in amphibrachic dimeter in couplet rhymes. Because all rhymes are feminine, the amphibrachic pulse runs uninterruptedly through the entire poem. The rhymes are all noteworthy. The first is enriched (моя Павел/моих правил) and therefore clever, the second (то-то/того-то) is almost infantile, while the third (ясно/прекрасный) is clearly intended for comic effect. (Pushkin's otherwise strict attitude toward rhyme would not allow him to use rhymes with such jarringly differing syllables after the stress.)

---

1 Душá моя Павел – my dear friend Pavel

5 Кажи́сь – it would seem. This is (substandard) colloquial for "кажется." Pushkin uses it not only to set an informal tone, but also to create an additional rhyme (with "Держись" of line 2).

6 Прощáй – farewell

<Ек. Н. Ушакóвой> – To Ek. N. Ushakova

Pushkin wrote this poem in the album of Ekaterina Nikolaevna Ushakova (see "Ек. Н. Ушаковой" ["Когда, бывало, в старину"]) shortly before his departure from Moscow. It is unclear how to account for the fact that Pushkin uses the formal "вы" rather than the "ты" that he had used in the poem to her written a few months earlier in that same album. Either the "вы" is a plural here, referring to Ushakova and her younger sister, or – more probably – it can be explained by genre, this poem being a different type of album verse with more formal expectations. The themes of parting and memory are, of course, standard fare in album poetry.

The poem is written in trochaic tetrameter with alternating rhymes.

3–4 Томных уст и томных глаз / Буду памятью размýчен – I will be tormented by the memory of <your> sweetly languorous lips and sweetly languorous eyes. In modern Russian, one would say "измучен" rather than "размучен."

5 Изнывáя – Languishing

6 утéшен – consoled. This seems more logical than the definition given for this passage in the *Словарь языка Пушкина* as "pleased" or "joyful."

7 Вы ж – But will you

8 повéшен – hung. The line need not be understood biographically, though Soviet commentators suggested that Pushkin was referring to the continuing repercussions over his poem "André Chénier." It is no less probable that Pushkin was simply joking, making the sort of darkly prophetic statement expected from a Romantic poet. Such a reading is supported by the fact that he apparently wrote in the margin next to this line: "Автор ехал на Кавказ" ("The author was going to the Caucasus") or, according to other versions "Писано перед отъездом на Кавказ" ("written before departure for the Caucasus"). (The manuscript of the poem has not survived – the marginalia and the text are known through contemporary copies.) In any case, the point to be emphasized here is that Pushkin included the Caucasus reference to add dramatic flair. As Ushakova surely knew, he had no intention of traveling to the Caucasus; he was in fact leaving for Petersburg.

„В степи́ мирско́й, печа́льной и безбре́жной" – "In the world's steppe, sad and endless"

This brief and very dark poem was not published in Pushkin's lifetime. It is sometimes referred to as "Три ключа" ("Three Streams"), though there is no reason to think that Pushkin used this title. Blagoi (1967, 148) sees the poem as a response to Venevitinov's allegorical "Три розы" ("Three Roses"), which begins with the line "В глухую степь земной дороги" ("Onto the empty steppe of the earth's path").

The meter is iambic pentameter with a caesura after the second foot. The rhymes alternate feminine, then masculine. Each two-line segment ends with a full stop, with the semantics following the syntactic breaks.

1 В степи́ мирско́й – In the world's steppe. The word "степь" is not to be taken literally, but rather as an endless empty expanse. Proskurin (2007, 334–35) traces the expression to the common Christian image of "пустыня мира" ("the desert of the world").

2 пробйлись – forced their way through

5 Каста́льский ключ – The Castalian Spring. The Castalian Spring, located in Delphi, is traditionally associated with poetic inspiration.

Ари́он – Arion

The story of Arion is familiar from Herodotus's *Histories* 1.23–24. Pushkin knew it either from there or from subsequent retellings, none of which differed substantially (for an overview, see Glebov, 296–98). According to Herodotus, Arion was a famous singer. After winning a competition in Sicily, he was traveling home to Corinth when the sailors on board decided to kill him and steal his riches. Arion was given the following unappealing choice: either he could commit suicide on deck (in which case he would receive a funeral on land) or he could be thrown alive into the sea. Arion asked permission to sing one final song, then leapt overboard. He was saved by one of the dolphins that had gathered to hear his music. The dolphin brought him to safety, and the evil sailors were eventually punished.

Since the poem is so distant from the source, it is commonly agreed that Pushkin was using the classical allusion as a smokescreen to hide his own agenda. In other words, the poem was not a retelling of a story from antiquity, but rather a commentary on contemporary Russian events. Accordingly, the sailors – comrades of the poet – represent the Decembrists. After a sudden storm shipwrecks them, Pushkin alone survives and continues to sing his old songs.

However, it should be emphasized that this "obvious" allegorical reading did not occur to contemporaries; it first became popular in the Soviet period, where Pushkin's ties to the Decembrists were particularly valued.

The publication history of the poem is odd. Pushkin wrote it in 1827, but – uncharacteristically – seems not to have shown it to anyone. He first published it anonymously in 1830 (and republished it anonymously a year later). None of these publications attracted any notice, and it was not until decades after his death that the poem began to be included in editions of his work. There is no question of Pushkin's authorship, since a draft version of the poem exists and since he included it in a list of poems that he intended to publish in an unrealized collection of his verse (Nemirovskii, 276). The draft is interesting for several reasons, the most significant being that Pushkin at one point changed the first-person pronouns ("I" and "we") to third-person pronouns ("he" and "they"). He also included a reference to being saved by a dolphin (in all probability a reference to Tsar Nicholas, which complicates the "Decembrist" reading considerably), which then disappeared from the final version.

Poems on the subject of shipwrecks and storms at sea were not uncommon in Russian and Western literature. However, one particular poem by Horace, as translated by Pushkin's uncle Vasilii L'vovich, has a strikingly similar choice of words as well as theme:

> От гибели спасенный,
> Богам коварных волн
> Я ризу омоченну
> В восторге посвятил.
>
> (Saved from death, I enthusiastically dedicated my wet garment to the gods of the nefarious waves.)

These are the concluding lines of the poem "К Пирре" ("To Pyrrha").

Formally, of course, Vasilii L'vovich's Horace translation is unrelated to "Arion." Its unrhymed iambic trimeter lines (common in imitations of antiquity) are distant from the rhymed iambic tetrameter of "Arion" (in which the rhyme scheme is unusual: A-b-b-A-c-D-D-D-c-E-E-f-G-G-f). The lexicon of "Arion" is at times archaic, presumably to reflect the ancient setting.

---

2 Ины́е парус напряга́ли – Some tightened the sails

3 Други́е дружно упира́ли – Others simultaneously pressed

4 мощны (=мощные) вёслы – powerful oars. "Вёслы" is an archaism; in contemporary Russian, the standard plural form is "вёсла." The truncated adjective amplifies the archaist qualities of the line.

5 кормщик – helmsman

8–9 Вдруг лоно волн / Измя́л с налёту вихорь шумный – Suddenly a noisy whirlwind unexpectedly churned up the depths of the waves. The word "лоно" has positive connotations, suggesting comfort (e.g., "на лоне природы" – "in the open air"). The use of "лоно" in connection with water is not rare in Russian poetry – Pushkin had used the phrase "на лоне тихих вод" in the poem "Приметы" ("Signs") of 1821 and "по лону вод" in *Eugene Onegin* (Nabokov the literalist renders it "upon the bosom of the waters" – Nabokov, 1:194). A similar usage ("Из лона чистой глубины") can be found in Viazemskii's "Море" of 1826.

10 Поги́б и кормщик и плове́ц – The helmsman and the sailor perished. The use of a singular verb with two singular subjects is not uncommon in Russian poetry. Note also that singular "пловец" is being used to connote plural "пловцы."

14–15 ризу влажную мою́ / Сушу́ на солнце – I dry my wet garment in the sun. The elevated word "риза" usually refers to a priest's garment. Together with the word "гимны" ("hymns") of line 13, it endows the poet with sacerdotal qualities.

Literature: Nemirovskii, 262–80; Vickery 1976, 71–84; Davydov 2005, 295–306.

Ангел – The Angel

The subject – the power of goodness to affect evil – is treated with laconicism and simplicity. The poem revises the image of the demon as treated in the 1823 lyric "Демон."

It is written in three stanzas of iambic tetrameter with alternating rhymes. The rhymes are exclusively grammatical, with all even-numbered lines rhyming with each other (including the key word "сиял" twice). There are a number of subtle acoustical echoes (e.g., "*не*бе *нена*видел" "*мир*е през*ир*ал").

---

1 эде́ма – of heaven. When capitalized (which it is not in the present passage), it means "Eden."

2 Главо́й пони́кшею (= поникшей) – With a bowed head

7 жар нево́льный умиле́нья – the involuntary heat of tender emotion. Cf. Nabokov, 3:71 (on "умиление"): "The word can be accurately rendered only by the French *attendrissement*, for which the horrible 'inteneration' has been suggested in English. It can be paraphrased by 'melting mood,' 'softheartedness,' 'tender emotion,' and the like. It is related to compassion as charm is to beauty or a dewy eye to one brimming with tears." See also Nabokov, 2:213 and the chapter "Умиление" (focusing on this poem) in Gershenzon 1919, 69–80.

9 Прости́, он рек – Forgive <me>, he said. The word "рек" is archaic, often used as a biblicism.

„Кака́я ночь! Моро́з треску́чий" – "What a night! The hard frost"

This unfinished text, probably intended as part of a narrative poem, reflects Pushkin's interest in Russian history and, more specifically, in its more brutal moments. The peaceful night scene depicted in the first few lines contrasts with the horrific events that occurred earlier in day, when numerous people were tortured by Ivan the Terrible's ruthless henchmen.

The poem is written in iambic tetrameter with unpredictable rhyme scheme.

---

2 На небе ни еди́ной тучи – There's not a single cloud in the sky. Strictly speaking, the word "нет" belongs before "ни," but this is sometimes omitted in colloquial speech.

3 Как шитый полог – Like an embroidered curtain

6 Затво́ры с тяжкими замка́ми – bolts with heavy locks
7 поко́ится наро́д – the people are sleeping
9 лает страж дворо́вый – the yard guard barks. Pushkin plays on the fixed phrase "дворовая собака," a dog that stands guard outside.
16 Где труп, разру́бленный с разма́ха – Here there is a corpse, split apart with a powerful blow
17 Где столп, где вилы; там котлы́ – Here there is a post, here there are pitchforks; there there are cauldrons
18 Осты́вшей полные смолы́ – full of pitch that has gone cold
19 Здесь опроки́нутая плаха – Here an executioner's block is overturned
20 Торча́т желе́зные зубцы́ – The iron teeth stick up
21 С костя́ми груды пепла тлеют – Piles of ash smolder with bones
22 На кольях, скорчась – On pointed poles, fixed in contorted poses. The singular form is "кол."
23 Оцепене́лые – Benumbed
25 Струёю тощей – In a thin stream
26 подыма́лся томный стон – an anguished moan arose
30 По грозной площади несётся – Rushes across the dread square. The word "грозной" is surely meant to recall "Иван Грозный" (Ivan the Terrible or, more poetically, John the Dread).
31 свист – whistling sound. This is either a whistle that a person makes (perhaps to hurry the horse along) or a sound produced by rapid movement.
33 Кто сей? – Кроме́шник удало́й. – Who is this? The daring oprichnik. An "oprichnik" was a member of the secret police established by Ivan the Terrible, notorious for its cruelty. Since "опричь" is a synonym for "кроме," the common people substituted "кромешник" for "опричник" in order to emphasize its infernal essence (the phrase "тьма кромешная" means "hell"). In vol. 9, ch. 2 of his *History of the Russian State* (a work Pushkin read with particular attention and which may have been the source for this poem), Karamzin writes: "Скоро увидели, что Иоанн предает всю Россию в жертву своим опричным: они были всегда правы в судах, а на них не было ни суда, ни управы. Опричник или *кромешник* – так стали называть их, как бы извергов тьмы *кромешней* <sic> – мог безопасно теснить, грабить соседа, и в случае жалобы брал с него пеню за бесчестье." ("They soon saw that Ivan was sacrificing all of Russia to his oprichniki; they were always in the right in the courts, and there were no legal proceedings or justice against them. The 'oprichnik' or 'kromeshnik' – thus they began to be called, like monsters from hell – could oppress, rob his neighbor and in the case of a complaint fined him for dishonor.")
37 лети́ стрело́й – fly like an arrow
39 размахну́л плетёной гривой – shook its braided mane
44 под плетью – under the whip
51 Лихи́х изме́нников царя́ – the evil traitors to the tsar. Despite the genitive case, there is no ambiguity here: the line refers to those who betray the tsar.
53 була́тные копы́ты – steel hooves. A paraphrase for horseshoes.
56 Неси́сь – rush (an imperative)

„Весна́, весна́, пора́ любви́" – "Spring, spring, the time of love"

This unfinished piece, in a later redaction, ended up as the second stanza of the seventh chapter of *Eugene Onegin*:

> Как грустно мне твое явленье,
> Весна, весна! пора любви!
> Какое томное волненье
> В моей душе, в моей крови!
> С каким тяжелым умиленьем
> Я наслаждаюсь дуновеньем
> В лицо мне веющей весны
> На лоне сельской тишины!
> Или мне чуждо наслажденье,
> И всё, что радует, живит,
> Всё, что ликует и блестит,
> Наводит скуку и томленье
> На душу мертвую давно,
> И всё ей кажется темно?

However, the earlier version presents several mysteries. Its final two lines (which never found their way into *Onegin*) suggest that, in its original form, the poem was intended to undermine the traditional poetic associations of spring, showing instead a typically Russian preference for winter. (This was the strategy of Prince Viazemskii's "Первый снег" ["First Snow"], a poem much admired by Pushkin.) However, too little of Pushkin's poem exists to allow for any sense of where the poem was to lead (and how seriously to take the speaker).

Formally, beyond the iambic tetrameter meter, the verses do not resemble an *Onegin* stanza. Pushkin perhaps intended to write eight-line stanzas with the unusual rhyme scheme a-B-B-a-B-c-B-c. If that is the case, the final line of the first stanza is missing (there is no rhyme for "блестит"). It is not obvious how the existing final two lines (clearly part of another section) fit in with the rest of the poem. Logically, they sound like the opening of the second stanza, but it would be odd for the first stanza to begin with a masculine rhyme and the second to begin with a feminine rhyme.

---

3 томное волне́нье – tormented agitation. Note how the two words are combined in the rhyme "томленье."

8 мете́ль и вьюгу – blizzard and snowstorm. The words are synonymous.

<Кипре́нскому> – To Kiprenskii

In May or June of 1827 Orest Adamovich Kiprenskii (1782–1836) painted what is generally considered the most successful portrait of Pushkin. The work was commissioned by Pushkin's friend Anton Del'vig, who owned it until his death. Pushkin subsequently purchased it from Del'vig's widow, and it hung in his study until his own death. It is now in Moscow's Tretiakov Gallery, which obtained it in 1916 from the poet's grandson.

The poem is in iambic tetrameter in six-line stanzas rhyming A-b-A-b-A-b.

---

1 Люби́мец моды легкокры́лой – darling of fleeting fashion

3 вновь – again. The idea is presumably that God created him once, and now the artist has created him for a second time.

5 смеюся (=смеюсь) – laugh. Note the echo of "муз" from the previous line.

6 Ушёд на век от смертных уз – Having escaped forever from the mortal bonds

10 Пристра́стья важных Аони́д – the favor of the solemn Muses. Kiprenskii's portrait of Pushkin includes in the background (upper right) a statue of Erato, the muse of poetry. Note that the rhyme word "Аонид" occupies the parallel position of the synonymous "Муз" (line 4 in both stanzas).

11 Риму, Дрездену, Пари́жу – Rome, Dresden, Paris. This is not hyperbole; Kiprenskii had achieved a truly international reputation, especially in Italy, where he had spent a considerable amount of time.

12 вид – face; likeness

Ака́фист Екатери́не Никола́евне Карамзино́й – An Acathistus to Ekaterina Nikolaevna Karamzina

The present poem was written in the album of Ekaterina Nikolaevna Karamzina (1806–1867), the daughter of the great historian and writer Nikolai Mikhailovich Karamzin and his second wife Ekaterina Andreevna. The opening image of a sailor miraculously saved from a storm recalls "Арион," (written two weeks earlier). Here, however, the lines serve as the "vehicle" of a simile, rather than the theme of the poem. Like much album verse, the poem sings the praises of the recipient's beauty and kindness.

The meter is iambic tetrameter, with the somewhat unusual rhyme scheme a-B-a-B-B-a-C-d-C-d.

Title: Ака́фист – Acathistus. A hymn in the orthodox church, originally to Mary, but later to various holy personages.

5 с умиле́ньем – with tender emotion. The word is often used in a sacred context. See commentary to "Ангел," line 7.

10 Для наших набожных оче́с – for our pious eyes. "Очес" (rather than "очей") is markedly archaic (and biblical).

Поэ́т – The Poet

One of Pushkin's most famous poems. The contrast of the petty poet of everyday life (first stanza) with the inspired poet who flees human contact (second stanza) carries through much of Pushkin's work, providing a curious gloss on "Пророк" (with which it shares several key words and images) and culminating in the unfinished story "Египетские ночи" ("Egyptian Nights").

Pushkin published this poem in the journal *Московский вестник*, where a few issues earlier a poem with the same title had appeared. That poem, written by the short-lived philosophical poet Dmitrii Vladimirovich Venevitinov (1805–1827), is a straightforward hymn to the poet, who is notably distant from worldly cares and devoted entirely to his art.

Тебе знаком ли сын богов,
Любимец муз и вдохновенья?
Узнал ли б меж земных сынов
Ты речь его, его движенья?
Не вспыльчив он, и строгий ум
Не блещет в шумном разговоре,
Но ясный луч высоких дум
Невольно светит в ясном взоре.
Пусть вкруг него, в чаду утех,
Бушует ветреная младость,
Безумный крик, нескромный смех
И необузданная радость:
Всё чуждо, дико для него,
На всё спокойно он взирает,
Лишь редко что-то с уст его
Улыбку беглую срывает.
Его богиня – простота,
И тихий гений размышленья
Ему поставил от рожденья
Печать молчанья на уста.
Его мечты, его желанья,
Его боязни, упованья –
Всё тайна в нем, всё в нем молчит:
В душе заботливо хранит
Он неразгаданные чувства …
Когда ж внезапно что-нибудь
Взволнует огненную грудь –
Душа, без страха, без искусства,
Готова вылиться в речах
И блещет в пламенных очах …
И снова тих он, и стыдливый
К земле он опускает взор,
Как будто слышит он укор
За невозвратные порывы.
О, если встретишь ты его
С раздумьем на челе суровом –
Пройди без шума близ него,
Не нарушай холодным словом
Его священных, тихих снов;
Взгляни с слезой благоговенья

И молви: это сын богов,
Любимец муз и вдохновенья.

It has been convincingly argued (Smirnov, 52–54; Rodnianskaia, 33–34) that Pushkin's poem was intended as a polemical response.

The fact that both poems are written in iambic tetrameter is, however, hardly a sign of their closeness, given the frequency with which this meter was used. Moreover, Venevitinov's poem is astrophic (and rhymed unpredictably), whereas Pushkin creates two stanzas of uneven length that are set off from each other through rhyme. The first rhymes alternately, the second rhymes in a ring pattern (lines 9–12 and 17–20), while lines 13–16 alternate, recalling the opening stanza (and even repeating one of the rhyme words). The closing ellipsis is not a sign of an unfinished poem, but a powerful poetic effect.

---

2 Аполло́н – Apollo, god of poetry.
3 суетного света – of the vain world. Pushkin repeats this exact phrase in another metapoetic poem, "Сонет" (1830).
6 Душа́ вкуша́ет хладный сон – His soul experiences a cold sleep. In other words, his soul (his true self) is absent.
8 всех ничто́жней (= ничтожнее) он – his is the lowliest of all
9 Но лишь боже́ственный глаго́л – But as soon as the divine word
10 До слуха чуткого коснётся – Touches his sensitive ear. Cf. "Египетские ночи" ("Egyptian Nights"), chapter 2: "Чужая мысль чуть коснулась вашего слуха и уже стала вашею собственностию [...] Итак, для вас не существует ни труда, ни охлаждения, ни этого беспокойства, которое предшествует вдохновению?"
12 Как пробуди́вшийся орёл – Like an awakened eagle. The line recalls "Как у испуганной орлицы" in "Пророк." In fact, Pushkin's draft here was even closer: "Как испугавшийся орел."
14 Людско́й чужда́ется молвы́ – He avoids the people's talk
19 На берега́ пусты́нных волн – To the shores of empty waves. This is a transferred epithet; "empty" logically refers to the shores, but grammatically to the waves. The image clearly appealed to Pushkin, who recycled it in the first line of "Медный всадник."
20 В широкошу́мные дубро́вы – To wide-sounding groves

„Близ мест, где царствует Вене́ция злата́я" – "Near the places, where golden Venice reigns"

These verses, first published by Pushkin under the title "Перевод неизданных стихов Андрея Шенье" ("A Translation of Unpublished Verses of André Chénier"), are precisely that. Pushkin learned of this poem's existence from a copy that had made its way to Russia – he himself copied it out in pencil into his (published) edition of Chénier's poetry. By a curious quirk of fate, Pushkin's translation and the Chénier original first appeared in print at almost exactly the same time.

Pushkin's translation is unusually accurate, but he changes the emphasis several times and transposes the order of the final lines. In both the original and the translation, the gondolier who sings Tasso (a cliché, see Nabokov, 2:182–84) serves as the vehicle (lines 1–8) in a simile where the poet himself is the tenor (lines 9–12). Given the closeness of translation and original, it is remarkable that one hears several striking echoes also from Pushkin's own "Арион" (in the drafts this is still more pronounced, e.g., the draft has "по лону волн" rather than "над бездной волн").

Chénier's poem is written in French alexandrines, and Pushkin renders them in the standard Russian equivalent – iambic hexameter couplets.

The Chénier poem that reached Pushkin differs considerably from the version that was then published (among other things, it is six lines shorter). Modzalevskii (1910, 192) includes a facsimile of Pushkin's autograph, as well as his own (not always accurate) transcription thereof. The version below takes into account the facsimile as well as the later transcription of it by L. B. Modzalevskii [in Tsiavlovskii, Modzalevskii, and Zenger, 503–4]. The missing accents and circumflexes are either the result of haste or are simply no longer visible. (Pushkin wrote in pencil, which has become less visible over the years.)

Près des bords, où Venise est reine de la Mer,
Le gondolier nocturne, au retour de Vesper
d'un leger <sic> aviron bat la vague aplanie,
Chante Renaud, Tancrede <sic> et la belle Herminie.
Il aime les chansons, il chante sans désir,
Sans gloire, sans projets, sans craindre l'avenir,
Il chante – et plein du Dieu qui doucement l'anime
Sait égayer du moins sa route sur l'abime <sic> –
Comme lui, sans echo je me plais à chanter –
Et les vers inconnus que j'aime à méditer
Adoucissent pour moi la route de la vie
Où de tant d'Aquilons ma voile est poursuivie.

---

2 Оди́н, ночно́й гребе́ц – Alone, a night oarsman. (The punctuation makes clear that it cannot mean "One night oarsman.")
3 При свете Веспера – By the light of Venus (i.e., the planet)
4 Рина́льда, Годфреда, Эрми́нию поёт – He sings Rinaldo, Tancredi, Erminia. These are the main characters of Tasso's epic *Gerusalemme liberata* (*Jerusalem Liberated*).
6 Без дальных умыслов – without far-reaching plans
11 утёшно я пою́ – I sing happily

Literature: Sandomirskaia 1978.

Из Alfieri – From Alfieri

The passage Pushkin chose to translate is the opening soliloquy of the tragedy *Filippo*, by Vittorio Alfieri (1749–1803). As his first published tragedy, *Filippo* is invariably printed as the first work in any edition of Alfieri's dramas. It is therefore possible that Pushkin did not seek out a particularly important passage, but simply started from the beginning. However, the plot of *Filippo*, drawn from a well-known incident in sixteenth-century European history (and recounted in later European literature), may well have attracted Pushkin. The eponymous hero is Philip II of Spain, who by his first wife fathered Don Carlos. This son was betrothed to Elizabeth of France; however, political expedience caused the widower Philip to alter this plan and marry her himself. A similar familial love triangle (with the inevitable tragic outcome) can also be found in Byron's "Parisina," a poem that Pushkin greatly admired and that influenced his own narrative poems "Цыганы" ("The Gypsies") and "Poltava." In the "Advertisement" (opening statement) to his poem, Byron explicitly praises Alfieri and Schiller for treating such plots and thus alludes to *Filippo* and *Don Carlos* (albeit without naming them).

The Italian tragedy begins with Elizabeth (whom Alfieri renames Isabella) admitting her true feelings for Don Carlos.

In the Italian edition that Pushkin owned (*Tragedie scelte di Vittorio Alfieri* [Paris: A. Buttura, 1825], 7–8), the relevant passage reads as follows:

> Desio, timor, dubbia ed iniqua speme,
> Fuor del mio petto omai. Consorte infida
> Io di Filippo, di Filippo il figlio
> Oso amar, io? … Ma chi 'l vede, e non l' ama?
> Ardito umano cor, nobil fierezza,
> Sublime ingegno, e in avvenenti spoglie
> Bellissim' alma; ah! perchè tal ti fero
> Natura e il cielo? … Oimè! che dico? imprendo
> Così a strapparmi la sua dolce imago
> Dal cor profondo? Oh! se palese mai …
> Fosse tal fiamma ad uom vivente! Oh! s' egli
> Ne sospettasse! Mesta ognor mi vede …
> Mesta, è vero, ma in un dal suo cospetto
> Fuggir mi vede; e sa che in bando è posta
> Da ispana reggia ogni letizia. In core
> Chi legger puommi? Ah! Nol sapess' io, come
> Altri nol sa! così ingannar potessi,
> Sfuggir così me stessa, come altrui! …
> Misera me! sollievo a me non resta
> Altro che il pianto; ed il pianto è delitto.
> Ma, riportare alle più interne stanze
> Vo' il dolor mio; più libera … Che veggio?
> Carlo? Ah! si sfugga: ogni mio detto o sguardo
> Tradir potriami: oh ciel! Sfuggasi.

The extent of Pushkin's knowledge of Italian remains unclear. However, there is ample evidence that his translation of this passage reflects an acquaintance with the Italian text. Not only does Pushkin follow the blank verse of the original; he even repeats the frequent interjections and the striking use of enjambment. (Pushkin enjambs lines 11–18, which if anything exaggerates Alfieri's usage of this same device.)

The poem was not published in Pushkin's lifetime.

---

2 не в силах я – I do not have the strength. (The use of the plural here is standard Russian.)

3 Невéрная супрýга я Фили́ппу – I am an unfaithful wife to Philip

9 таки́м тебя́ создáли – created you this way

10 Ах! – note that the force of this interjection is heightened since it falls on a weak syllable in the iambic line (the technical term for this is "hypermetrical stress"). The same technique is used in line 17.

12 пламень мой – my flame (a standard metaphor for "my love")

13 станет – will. In the future tense, the verb "стать" is often the equivalent of "быть" (for another example, see line 19).

17–18 и самóй / Не можно мне – Even I myself cannot. "Не можно мне" is archaic.

20 Увы́, мне, бедной – alas, poor me

23 Идý к себé – I <will> go to my room

24 Уйдём – Let's get away. Despite the plural form, the comment is directed by the speaker to herself, not to Karl. (This is presumably Pushkin's rendering of the impersonal Italian "si sfugga.")

мне измени́ть – to betray me

Послáние Дельвигу – An Epistle to Del'vig

This lengthy epistle is a comic tribute to Pushkin's friend Anton Antonovich Del'vig (1798–1831), who was indeed descended from German (Baltic) nobility. Del'vig was by nature a phlegmatic dreamer – the opposite of the "heroic" forebear whom Pushkin depicts.

The poem is written in iambic tetrameter with an unpredictable rhyme scheme and features a fairly lengthy prose insert. The combination of poetry and prose within a single work was a possibility that fascinated Pushkin, beginning in *Boris Godunov* and culminating in "Египетские ночи" ("Egyptian Nights"). This poem reads as if it was part of a genuine letter, but no such letter is known. More importantly, it was written with an eye to publication, and was indeed published by Pushkin himself shortly after its composition.

---

2 по праву – by right

3 Тебé повéдаю – I will make known to you

4 готи́ческую славу – Gothic fame. The adjective "Gothic" suggests both the genre of the "Gothic novel" (i.e., the morbid theme suggested in the prose passage after line 126) as well as the "Gothic" in the sense of "ancient" (i.e., going back to the Middle Ages).

5 не раз – more than once

6 Парáми Вакха нагревáлся – was heated by the steam of Bacchus. The reference

is to the fixed expression “винные пары” (always plural), meaning “wine” or “alcohol” generally.

7 Лито́вский меч в недо́брый час – A Lithuanian sword at an unfortunate hour

15 Нае́здник, чаши друг испра́вный – A horseman, a meticulous friend of the drinking cup. The adjective “исправный” ordinarily modifies a noun such as “чиновник”; the usage here is comic.

16 Гроза́ – Scourge

19 рыцарской душо́й – in his knightly soul

22 С главо́ю (=головой), миртами венча́нной – With a head wreathed in myrtle. A myrtle wreath is traditionally associated with poetry. (In pictorial representations, it is often worn by Erato, the muse of lyric poetry.)

23 В очка́х – in glasses. Del’vig indeed wore glasses.

24 Поко́йником в церко́вной книге – As a corpse in the Church book. In Pushkin’s day (and earlier), church records were the primary source of information on births and deaths.

27 Вкуша́л непробуди́мый сон – He tasted eternal sleep

30 Пасто́ра лестью погреба́льной – With the funerial flattery of the pastor. This paraphrastic line refers to the (presumably boilerplate) eulogy pronounced by the priest after the baron’s death. Ordinarily, the stress on “пастор” falls on the first syllable.

34 Поко́йникам поко́я нет – There’s no peace for the deceased. The line puns on the etymology of “покойник” (literally: peaceful one).

35 Косма́тый баловень приро́ды – Nature’s shaggy favorite. A paraphrase for a student, recognizable by his long and unkempt hair.

39 Идеоло́г и филоло́г – Ideologue and philologist. Like the word “физиолог” in the previous line, the stress falls on the final syllable (as against the penultimate, which is standard in modern Russian). The monotonous rhymes of физиоло́г, идеало́г, and филоло́г mirror the vapidity of the student being described.

40 Коро́че вам – студе́нт прися́жный – To be brief for you – a classic student

43 спеси́во – arrogantly

44 пенить пиво – to froth beer, that is, to drink beer

47 Лотхен – Lottchen. Riga being a German town, Pushkin chooses a typical German name (short form of Charlotte, though Pushkin himself – in the story “Гробовщик” [“The Coffin Maker”] – appears to have thought that it came from the name Luise).

48 Стихи́ писа́ть, да бить жидо́в – To write verses and beat the Yids. Picking on Jews was a standard form of entertainment for provincial philistines. (Cf. a similar passage in the first chapter of *Капитанская дочка* [*The Captain’s Daughter*].)

50 В камо́рке – a tiny room (the traditional housing for impecunious students)

55 Фихте и Плато́на – of Fichte and Plato. Johann Gottlieb Fichte (1762–1814), a German philosopher known for his abstract and often obscure speculations.

62 Почте́нный мыслитель – the esteemed thinker. The standard stress would be “мысли́тель,” which Pushkin shifts to the first syllable, perhaps to emphasize the irony.

73 слова нет – there is no word <to say about this> (i.e., that’s for certain)

76 с кистером градски́м – with the town sexton. The Russian word "кистер" (from German "Küster") is used only in connection with the non-Orthodox (here Lutheran) church, where it denotes a low-ranking assistant who helps with practical things (such as upkeep of the church and occasionally in burials). Lutheranism was brought to the Baltics by German barons; hence it is logical that Del'vig's ancestor would have been buried in a Lutheran church.

82 Не льзя ли (=Нельзя ли) – Would it not be possible

88 Кляну́сь тебе айде́сским богом – I swear to you by the god of Hades

94 Итти (=Идти) – To go

Prose passage:

Брать с собо́ю *будущего* – to take with him a traveling companion. "Будущий" was a technical term used in official documents of the time for an as yet unnamed person who would accompany a traveler on a journey.

Мой прия́тель Вульф – My friend Vul'f. Aleksei Nikolaevich Vul'f (1805–1881), Pushkin's sometime neighbor in Mikhailovskoe. Vul'f was a student at Dorpat (now Tartu) University from 1822–1826, but often returned home to Trigorskoe on vacations. He took his studies about as seriously as Pushkin's hero does, and the proximity of Dorpat to Riga makes his appearance in the poem entirely plausible.

132 Вино́м кипя́щим освяти́ – Consecrate <it> with bubbly wine. This wine is either champagne or (if кипящий is taken literally as "boiling") punch, a potent hot brew much loved by students (and by Pushkin), see commentary to "К Языкову" (1826).

133 Да запива́й уху́ да кашу – Use it to wash down fish soup and kasha

134 Певцу́ Корса́ра подража́й – Imitate the singer of "The Corsair." Byron, author of the celebrated narrative poem *The Corsair*, also wrote a brief lyric poem called "Lines Inscribed upon a Cup Formed from a Skull" (1808).

135 скандина́вов рай – Scandinavians' paradise. According to Norse legend, dead warriors ended up in Valhalla, where they drank heavily (just as they had done in life). Pushkin here refers to a widespread misconception (that can be traced to a mistranslation by the physician and scholar Olaus Wormius in the seventeenth century) that these warriors drank from the skulls of their enemies.

137 Гамлет-Бараты́нской (=Баратынский) – Hamlet-Baratynskii. Pushkin's friend and fellow poet Evgenii Baratynskii had written a poem in 1824 called "Череп" ("The Skull"). The poem, which features the poet's meditations on mortality while gazing at a skull, is linked in Pushkin's mind with Hamlet's famous lines about Yorick.

„Всем красны́ боя́рские коню́шни" – "Everything about the boyars' stables is good"

This unfinished poem clearly owes its existence to Pushkin's interest in Russian folklore, which leaves its mark on the subject matter, the meter, the lexicon, and numerous grammatical constructions. Some of the details in this poem (e.g., the house spirit's treatment of the horse) appear to have been taken from M. D. Chulkov's *Словарь русских суеверий* (*Dictionary of Russian Superstitions*), a work that Pushkin also consulted for the folkloric episodes of *Eugene Onegin*. Curiously, Pushkin, having decided to abandon this project in an almost complete form, "gave" the plot to a genuine peasant poet of the day, Fedor Nikiforovich Slepushkin (1787 [or early 1788]–1848), who wrote and published a (far less interesting) poem on the identical subject called "Конь и домовой" ("The Horse and the House Spirit").

Ironically, Slepushkin wrote his poem in iambic tetrameter (i.e., the standard literary meter of the day), while Pushkin opted for an accentual meter, one of his first attempts to capture the sound of genuine folk poetry. In this sense, the poem anticipates the "Песни западных славян" (see commentary to those poems). The basic line has three stresses, and the unstressed intervals between them range from one to three syllables. Fixed stresses occur on the third syllable of each line and – with the exception of the unfinished line 24 – the penultima (i.e., all cadences are feminine). The poem is unrhymed. The break into two stanzas is clearly motivated, setting the seemingly supernatural events (first part) against a logical explanation thereof (second part).

---

1 Всем красны́ боя́рские коню́шни – Everything about the master's stables is good. More literally: The master's stables are good in all respects. The adjective "боярские" comes from "boyar," the noble class in pre-Petrine Russia. However, the word continued to be used among the serfs to refer to their wealthy landowners.

5 Сбруя блещет на стойках дубо́вых – The harness shines on the oak stands

6 борзые – fleet

7 Лишь одни́м коню́шни неприго́жи – Only in one respect are the stables bad

8 Домово́й пова́дился – A house spirit kept visiting. The belief in house spirits goes back to pagan times, but uneducated classes managed to find room for them within Russian Orthodoxy. House spirits were not necessarily evil, but tended to be mischievous, and it behooved the peasant to mollify rather than challenge them.

10 холит коне́й боя́рских – cares for the master's horses

11 в коси́чки – into little pigtails

13 Как не взлюбит он вороно́го – How he dislikes the black <horse>

14 с водопо́ю – from the watering hole

17 испра́вен – well-appointed

19 весь <в> мыле, жаром пышет – completely foaming, all ablaze

24 До зака́та месяца – Until the moon goes down

26 зага́дку – riddle. It is worth recalling that riddles were a significant genre of Russian folklore.

27 Полюби́л красну де́вку младой ко́нюх – The young groom has fallen in love with a beautiful lass. (The stress on младо́й would be lessened because of the stress on the subsequent syllable.)

28 разгу́льный парень – rakish lad

30 Потихо́нько – Quietly. In modern Russian, this would be "потихо́ньку."

31 Полего́нько – Easily. In modern Russian, this would be "полего́ньку."

32 На коня́ на борзого сади́тся – mounts the fleet horse. The repeated preposition is typical of Russian folkloric style.

Literature: Iezuitova 1979.

„Блаже́н в злато́м кругу́ вельмо́ж" – "Blessed in the golden circle of grandees"

The poem, not published in Pushkin's lifetime, is one of a series devoted to the theme of the poet. As so often, it is difficult to determine where Pushkin himself stands. Here the poet is pictured as universally popular – beloved by the tsars and grandees as well as by the common folk. However, the poet seems more an obsequious entertainer than a force of genuine moral improvement. And the banishment of the common man at the end reads like an early version of "Мирская власть."

The poem is written in iambic tetrameter, but the rhyme scheme is highly unusual. It is composed of three different types of quatrains, first a ring construction, then couplets, then alternating. Assuming that this was the form the entire poem was to take (and this is indeed an assumption, as the poem may be incomplete), the formal structure vaguely recalls either the *Onegin* stanza (upside down, without the closing couplet and with masculine and feminine rhymes reversed) or – probably more relevant – an odic stanza (upside down, with an extra couplet in the middle). The rhyme пиры/хвалы is not pure (there is no supporting consonant, though "r" and "l" are related consonants [liquids]).

---

1 Блаже́н – Blessed <is>. See Nabokov, 2:213: "All these 'happy he,' 'blessed he,' 'blest he,' and so forth stem (through the French, *heureux qui*) from the *felix qui* or *beatus ille qui* of the ancient poets (e.g., Horace, *Epodes*, 2, 1)."

2 Пии́т – poet. The word was archaic (and therefore elevated style) already in Pushkin's time.

4 Припра́вя горькой правдой ложь – Seasoning falsehood with bitter truth. The verb "приправить" is ordinarily used in connection with things culinary. It seems to pick up on the adjective "горькой" in this line and the word "вкус" in the following one. In the draft Pushkin originally wrote: "Сливая с горькой правдой ложь" ("Pouring falsehood together with bitter truth").

5 Он вкус приту́пленный щеко́тит – He arouses their dulled taste. In modern Russian, the standard form would be щеко́чет.

6 И к славе спесь боя́р охо́тит – And urges the boyars' arrogance to glory (i.e., he urges the arrogant boyars on to glory). The word "boyar" probably marks the action historically as belonging to the pre-Petrine period (though it was occasionally used by peasants in later periods, cf. commentary to "Всем красны боярские конюшни," line 1). The presence of "boyar" ("боярин") and "grandee" ("вельможа") in the same poem is not an anachronism, as both words can be found in Old Russian documents.

10 у чёрного крыльца́ – at the back exit. The word "черного" recalls the key word "чернь" from "Поэт и толпа."

11 Нарóд – the <common> people
12 Пóбдаль – At a distance

Literature: Rodnianskaia.

„В роще карúйской, любéзной ловцáм, тайтся пещéра“ – “In the Carian grove, beloved to hunters, a cave is hidden”

This unfinished piece was intended to be part of a lengthy work on an ancient theme. Given the dearth of myths connected with Caria, one may assume that the poem was to be devoted to the myth of the beautiful youth Endymion, who slept eternally in a cave on Mount Latmos in Caria (Gasparov 1997, 65). The form is a Russian imitation of Greek hexameters, which Pushkin associated primarily with the genre of the idyll (Gasparov 1986, 34). Pushkin used this form so rarely that he apparently felt the need to remind himself of its peculiarities: he drew its scheme (with an inaccuracy! – see Gasparov 1997, 63) above these verses in his notebook.

In antiquity, at certain points in the line, poets could substitute a spondee for a dactyl. Given the difficulty of creating spondees (two consecutive stresses) in the Russian language, Russian poets adapted this freedom, allowing a trochee to substitute for a dactyl. Such substitutions were infrequently used, but Pushkin takes advantage of this possibility here in almost every line. It is likewise noteworthy how often Pushkin uses enjambment, in this regard anticipating his 1832 “Из Ксенофана Колофонского” (“From Xenophanes of Colophon”).

---

1 карúйской – Carian. Caria was the name of a region in Western Anatolia (now Turkey) that was at various times part of Greece (and later part of the Roman Empire).

2–4 и тенью / Вход её заслонён на воле бродя́щим в изви́вах / Плющём – And by a shadow / Its entrance is covered by the ivy that wanders in circles at will. Gasparov (1997, 62) points to this passage as proof that the poem is unfinished, since Pushkin would never have published a sentence with such clumsy syntax (two instrumental cases serving the identical grammatical function are separated by an entire line).

4 любóвником скал и рассéлин – lover of crags and fissures. This phrase, in apposition to “плющем” (“ivy”), is a personification, yet it also hints at the central role that love plays in the myth of Endymion (who is visited by the moon goddess every night.) Note in this regard also “любезной” in line 1.

5 Звонкой струи́тся дугóй – It flows in a sonorous arc

6 виётся (= вьётся) – twists

7 веселя́ её сладким журча́ньем – bringing joy to it with a sweet babbling. The antecedent of “её” is “роща” (“grove”).

Literature: Gasparov 1997.

„Сводня грустно за сто́лом“ – “At the table the madame sadly”

Pushkin never made any effort to publish this poem. The subject matter (which ensured that it was unpublishable) is most directly connected to “Опасный сосед” (“The Dangerous Neighbor”), the hugely popular (but likewise unpublished and unpublishable) poem by Pushkin’s uncle Vasilii L’vovich. In that work, the eponymous hero invites the narrator to a bordello. Their visit ends when the narrator’s tryst is interrupted by a drunken brawl instigated by the infamous neighbor. In the present work, Pushkin plays off (deflates) the reader’s expectation that the visit will end in a brawl.

In his choice of meter, Pushkin alludes to another classic text, this one not only published, but canonical. Rejecting the formal model of “The Dangerous Neighbor” (iambic hexameter couplets), he parodies Zhukovskii’s celebrated ballad “Svetlana” (Tomashevskii 1958, 104). Though Zhukovskii’s stanzas are fourteen lines long, their first eight lines coincide exactly with Pushkin’s stanza: alternating trochaic tetrameter with trimeter, with the tetrameter lines rhyming masculine and trimeter lines feminine. Zhukovskii’s poem, a Russian variation of Bürger’s popular ballad “Lenore,” also begins with fortune-telling and features the arrival of a mysterious guest.

---

1 Сводня – a procuress or madame (of a brothel).

2 Карты разлага́ет – sets out cards. Divining by cards is part of a folkloric matchmaking ritual.

3 барышни – young ladies. This was the standard prerevolutionary term for unmarried women of the gentry class. However, in the context of this poem the young ladies are prostitutes. (The word is also used ironically in conjunction with prostitutes in “Опасный сосед.”)

5 туз черве́й – the ace of hearts

6 коро́ль бубно́вый – the king of diamonds

8 И при то́м обно́вы – And moreover the new dresses

9–10 А по картам – ждать госте́й / Надобно сего́дня – But according to the cards <we> should expect guests today

14 Все толкну́ли <- - -> – the line should read: Все толкну́ли целку – Everyone pushed the virgin. “Целка” is much lower stylistically than “девственница.”

19 Он с б<- - -> целый век – the line should read: Он с бля́дями целый век – He has spent his whole life with whores

21 Б<- - -> в кухню руки мыть – the line should read: Бляди в кухню руки мыть – the whores <rushed> into the kitchen to wash their hands

23 пукли (=букли) взбить – to fluff up their curls

24 Прыскаться духа́ми – to spray themselves with perfume

30 Барыше́й дово́льно – Are there sufficient profits? There is probably a pun here on the барышни of lines 3 and 12.

31 Сводня за́ щеку взяла́сь – The madame reached for her cheek. This is a common Russian gesture aimed at eliciting pity. The ordinary stress on “щеку́” here switches to the preposition that precedes it.

37 с Петро́ва дня – Since Saint Peter’s day. Celebrated on 12 July, the traditional

holiday in honor of the saints Peter and Paul (commonly known as "Петров день") was a time of great festivities. The Orthodox Church forbade sex on major holidays, which could explain the dearth of clients. There is a comic effect in the fact that the madame's frame of reference is the church (see also line 48), though it should be noted that the common people marked the passing of days in terms of church holidays.

43 Я б<- - - > им вывожу – the line should read: Я бляде́й им вывожу́ – I lead my whores to them.

45 Занима́ются всю ночь – They make love all night

53 поцалу́й (=поцелуй) – kiss <me>

54 Выбрать, так оби́дишь – By choosing I would insult <them>. The use of second-person pronoun here is semantically equivalent to English "one" (though far more conversational) or "I," cf. the same technique in the rhyme word of line 56.

55 Так на всех и <- - - > – The line should read: Так на всех и <встанет хуй> – From each of them I'll get an erection

56 Только вас уви́дишь – As soon as I see you

58 Хо́чете ль Жане́ту? – Do you want Jeanette? "Хочете" is substandard Russian for "Хотите." The prostitute's name (like all the others) is Western, presumably to give her a more exotic status.

59 В деле так у ней (=у нее) гори́т – she's truly aflame. Given the stylistic register of the poem, the line probably implies the noun "пизда" (i.e., her cunt is on fire).

63 Мне охо́ты что-то нет – Somehow I don't feel like it

Literature: Mikhailova 2004.

19 октября́ 1827 – 19 October 1827

Pushkin read this poem at the anniversary meeting of his Lyceum class in 1827. This was the first of these festivities he had attended since his exile. Some of his listeners appear to have thought the poem to be an improvisation, but such a carefully structured work could only have been the result of concentrated prior effort. The poem speaks in generalities in the first stanza and the first half of the second; the final two lines shift almost imperceptibly to specific biographical references. Indeed, the closing allusion to the Decembrists appears to have eluded the censor, since the poem was published more than once in Pushkin's lifetime.

The poem is written in iambic tetrameter with ring rhyme. Because lines 1 and 5 are identical, the final word of each stanza (the "a" rhymes) stands out in stark contrast: "И в сла́дких та́инствах люби́" becomes "И в мра́чных про́пастях земли́" (note the identical syntax, stress pattern, and punctuation of these lines).

---

1 Бог по́мочь вам – Good luck to you (literally: "may God give help to you"). The archaic noun по́мочь (in the drafts it is written as the standard "помощь") should not be confused with the infinitive, which takes stress on the second syllable ("помо́чь").

3 разгу́льной дружбы – of wild friendship. The adjective implies drinking and other forms of dissipation.

7 В краю́ чужо́м, в пусты́нном море – In a foreign land, in an empty sea. The first part of this line is most likely a reference to Pushkin's classmates who had become diplomats (Sergei Grigor'evich Lomonosov and Aleksandr Mikhailovich Gorchakov), the second part to the sailor Fedor Fedorovich Matiushkin.

8 И в мрачных пропастях земли́ – And in the dark abysses of the earth. The final line refers (probably metaphorically rather than literally) to the Decembrists in the Lyceum class, Vil'gel'm Karlovich Kiukhel'beker and Ivan Ivanovich Pushchin. Cf. the latter's memoirs: "И в эту годовщину, в кругу товарищей-друзей Пушкин вспомнил меня и Вильгельма, заживо погребенных, которых они не досчитывали на лицейской сходке." ("At that anniversary, in the circle of his friends and <school> comrades, Pushkin remembered me and Wilhelm, buried alive, absent at the Lyceum gathering.") It is not surprising that Pushkin should have been thinking about Kiukhel'beker at precisely this time. By an incredibly odd coincidence, Pushkin had encountered him five days earlier, on his return to Petersburg from Mikhailovskoe. At a way station, while waiting for his horses to be changed, Pushkin looked up at a group of convicts and recognized among them his old friend. They embraced but were soon separated by policemen who were accompanying Kiukhel'beker (and some other Decembrists). They were being transferred from Schlüsselburg (Шлиссельбург) prison to their next destination.

Рефута́ция г-на Беранже́ра – Refutation of Monsieur Béranger

This poem parodies a patriotic French song that begins "T'en souviens-tu, disait un capitaine" ("Do you remember, a captain said"), in which a soldier reminisces about the glory days under Napoleon. The Russian poem, which was sung at Lyceum meetings and was also known outside of the Lyceum circle, makes light of the French by recalling their defeat at the hands of the Russians.

There are probably two misattributions involved in this poem. The first is that, contrary to the implication in the Russian title, the French text was not written by Pierre-Jean de Béranger (1780–1857), but by a lesser-known contemporary, Paul Emile Debraux (1796–1831). More important is the second misattribution: it is highly probable that the Russian poem was *not* written by Pushkin. On the dubiousness of his authorship and the reasons for its inclusion in (most) Pushkin editions, see Nemirovskii, 281–88.

As in most parodies, the form is borrowed from the target text. The French poem (with the exception of the first stanza) is written in eight-line stanzas of alternating feminine/masculine rhymes. It is written in lines of 10 syllables, which in syllabo-tonic verse corresponds most closely to iambic pentameter. Like the French model, the Russian poem has pronounced lexical repetitions: in addition to the first words of each stanza's opening line, a refrain runs through the entire poem.

---

2 Мусье́ францу́з, г<- - -> (=говённый) капита́н – Monsieur Frenchman, <you> shitty captain

4 Над нехристем побе́ды россия́н – The victories of the Russians over the heathen

5 Хоть это нам не составля́ет много – Though we don't much care

6 Не из ины́х мы прочих, так сказа́ть – We are, so to speak, not like some others

8 <- - -> = <ебёна твоя мать> – your mother is fucked

9 Суво́ров – Aleksandr Vasil'evich Suvorov (1729–1800), celebrated Russian general. The reference in this stanza is to 1799, when Suvorov successfully led the Russians against the French in Italy and then, trapped in Switzerland, led his troops across the Alps. These lines exaggerate Suvorov's successes; in fact, these campaigns – while in many ways impressive – were marked by terrible losses on the Russian side.

11 Как наш стари́к трепа́л вас, живодёров – How our old man beat you up, you skin-flayers

17 всю пригна́л Евро́пу – drove all of Europe (to Russia). By the time of the Russian campaign, Napoleon's army was composed of soldiers from all the countries he had conquered.

19 <- - -> = <жопу> – ass

25 от уга́ра – from the fumes (the reference is to the burning of Moscow, cf. line 27)

26 как бубен гол и лыс – naked and bald as a tambourine. "Гол как бубен" is an idiom to describe someone who has thrown (or gambled) away his fortune. The "лыс" is apparently added for emphasis (and rhyme).

35 батаре́й задо́рный подогре́вец – the enthusiastic shooting of our battalions. Подогревец is a diminutive.

43 к винцу́ подсе́в побли́же – have seated themselves closer to the wine. "Винцо" is a diminuitive of "вино."

44 похва́ливал да <- - -> (= <ёб>) – praised and fucked

Талисма́н – The Talisman

From a biographical point of view, the poem is connected to Elizaveta Ksaver'evna Vorontsova (1792–1880), whom Pushkin wooed in Odessa. Pushkin's superior, who happened to be her husband, responded to this provocation by having the poet exiled to Mikhailovskoe. Upon parting, Vorontsova presented Pushkin with a ring inscribed with mysterious cabalistic writing. The highly superstitious Pushkin believed in the ring's magical powers, preserving it like a relic and putting it on for protection only for the most important events in his life. He wore it for the final time at his last duel; it was still on his finger at the time of his death.

However, the poem is not simply autobiographical. Pushkin stylizes the scene, placing it in an eastern – or conceivably southern – locale. (The opening four lines could be understood as a reference to Odessa, but the harems and Muslims of the next lines point to a still more distant setting.)

The poem clearly echoes the 1825 poem on the same subject "Храни меня, мой талисман," likewise with a refrain on the key word "талисман." However, while the earlier poem is in quatrains of iambic tetrameter, this one is in eight-line stanzas of trochaic tetrameter. This meter is often associated in Pushkin's poetry with eastern exoticism (see Gasparov 1990, 9).

---

1 Там, где море вечно плещет – There, where the sea eternally splashes. The line recalls the second line of the unfinished "Я знаю край" of the same year.

12 Он тебе́ любо́вью дан – It is given to you by love. Cf. "Ты в день печали был мне дан" in "Храни меня, мой талисман."

19–20 И покло́нников проро́ка / Он тебе́ не покори́т – It will not subdue for you the admirers of the prophet (i.e., of Mohammed).

21 на лоно друга – to your friend's breast. The word "лоно" should be understood abstractly. In citing this passage, the *Словарь языка Пушкина* defines it as "грудь," but then adds the following gloss, "как символ духовного прибежища, того, где можно найти сочувствие, поддержку" ("the breast as a symbol of spiritual refuge, where one can find sympathy, support").

22 От печа́льных чуждых стран – From sad foreign countries. Cf. "В уединеньи чуждых стран" in "Храни меня, мой талисман."

25 кова́рны (=коварные) очи – nefarious eyes

26 Очару́ют – charm. Note the enjambed sound orchestration: очи/очаруют.

28 Поцалу́ют (=Поцелуют) – will kiss

30 От серде́чных новых ран – from new wounds of the heart (i.e., wounds inflicted by [unhappy] love). The word "сердечных" here does not mean "sincere," but instead refers to the heart, a standard metaphor for love. The phrase "сердечных ран" (in the same meaning) also appears in rhyming position in "Храни меня, мой талисман."

<Бараты́нскому> – To Baratynskii

It is presumed that these unfinished verses were written to Baratynskii to congratulate him on the publication of his collected poetry. Baratynskii's book appeared approximately two months before Pushkin wrote this.

The lines are written in iambic tetrameter, but given the brevity of the excerpt, it is difficult to say with certainty what the precise form would have been. The rhyme scheme of the existing passage is a-B-B-a-B-a, which suggests either an unusual and virtuoso stanzaic form or (more likely) a freely rhymed astrophic poem.

---

6 мадрига́л – madrigal. In Pushkin's day, this was a brief poem of flattery addressed to a woman.

„Я знаю край: там на брега́“ – "I know a land: there onto the shores"

One can only speculate on where this fragment was to lead. The bare southern landscape (seascape) may suggest Odessa.

The meter is iambic tetrameter with rhyme scheme a-B-B-a-C-d. The connection of rhyme words in lines four and five (лугá/нагáя) is striking, but perhaps coincidental.

---

1 Я знаю край – I know a land. The phraseology echoes Goethe's famous "Mignon-Lied" from *Wilhelm Meister*. See notes to the epigraph of "Кто знает край" (1828).
4 опалённые лугá – singed meadows
5 дубрáв не видно – no groves (i.e., trees) are visible

1828

Друзья́м – To My Friends

Pushkin's poem to Tsar Nicholas of 1826 ("Стансы") was first published in January 1828, and it was immediately attacked as being disingenuous. Pushkin responded with the present poem, in which he defends himself against such criticisms, insisting that his statements were motivated not by flattery, but by conviction. The friends in the title included Katenin (see commentary to "Ответ Катенину") and probably Prince Viazemskii (see Nemirovskii, 241–42). It has been argued that this poem (like "Стансы") is in fact more complex politically than it may seem. According to such a view, the praise is only superficial and the two "hypothetical" stanzas (about the flatterer) should be taken as a subtle critique of present conditions. Such an interpretation is appealing, but unlikely. It is more probable that Pushkin was attempting to influence Tsar Nicholas insofar as he could by highlighting the aspects of his policies that seemed to be taking a new and decisive course (see Proskurin 2006, 113). If the poem was truly meant to be a critique, then the authorities failed to detect it. When Pushkin submitted the poem to censorship, he received the reply (from the tsar, via Benkendorff) that it could circulate but not be published. Presumably Nicholas wanted the sentiments known, but felt that an "official" imprimatur would lessen its effect.

The poem is written in iambic tetrameter quatrains in either ring rhymes (stanzas 1, 3, 4) or alternating rhymes (2, 5–8). Except for the fifth stanza, the opening rhyme of each stanza is masculine.

---

1 Не́т, я не льсте́ц – No, I am not a flatterer. Note the way the stress is placed on the first and fourth syllables, a striking rhythmical means of drawing attention to the first word. Cf. similar sentiments in the closing passage of Derzhavin's "Видение мурзы" ("The Murza's Vision"): "Что я не из числа льстецов" and "Не лесть я пел и не мечты." Derzhavin's broader subject is relevant to Pushkin's poem: whether a panegyric is written out of conviction or out of sycophancy.

4 Язы́ком сердца – in the language of the heart. The stress in modern Russian would be "языко́м."

8 Войно́й, наде́ждами, труда́ми – by means of a war, of hopes, and of works. Russia was at war with Persia from 1826 to 1828 and had a brief skirmish with Turkey in 1827.

9 юность в нём кипи́т – youth seethes in him. Nicholas was born in 1796, three years before Pushkin.

11–12 Тому́, кого́ кара́ет явно, / Он втайне милости твори́т. Whomever he punishes publicly, he secretly treats well. It is mysterious whom Pushkin has in mind here; perhaps it expresses his hopes about the Decembrists (cf. line 24). "Милость" can mean a pardon or any type of benefaction. Irina Reyfman has suggested to me that the use of "милость" in this poem may be meant to recall Karamzin's 1792 poem "К Милости," addressed to Catherine the Great in an attempt to inspire her to pardon the recently arrested Novikov.

17 почти́л – respected

18 Освободи́л он мысль мою́ – He freed my thought. This is a reference to the "special" arrangement Nicholas created for Pushkin, whereby the tsar himself was to serve as censor. It was to prove disastrous, but at this point Pushkin was optimistic. K. Ospovat notes (134) that Pushkin borrows the sentiment (and the words) from Derzhavin's poem in praise of Catherine "Изображение Фелицы" ("The Depiction of Felitsa"): "Я вам даю свободу мыслить." ("I give you the freedom to think.")

22 Он горе на царя́ накли́чет – He will bring grief to the tsar

23–24 Он из его́ держа́вных прав / Одну́ лишь милость ограни́чит – Of all his (the tsar's) autocratic rights / He (the flatterer) will limit only forgiveness. In other words, the flatterer feels that the tsar's ability to show mercy should be curtailed. For Pushkin, of course, mercy is the highest virtue, the right that the tsar should exercise most freely. Pushkin (obliquely) urges Nicholas to display this royal prerogative and pardon the Decembrists. Blagoi (1967, 167) claims that the line is a direct reference to a report by the Supreme Court (Верховный суд) that warned the tsar against showing excessive kindness to the Decembrists. Al'tshuller (46–47) sees this as a reference to A. A. Arakcheev's relationship to Tsar Alexander.

27 просвеще́нья плод – the fruit of enlightenment. This demonization of enlightenment does appear to be polemical, though it would have gone unnoticed to Pushkin's readers. In "О народном воспитании" ("On National Education"), an internal memo that Pushkin was "asked" (i.e., obliged) to write for the tsar in 1826, he had stressed the value of true enlightenment, noting that the Decembrist revolt was a result of a "недостаток просвещения" ("deficiency of enlightenment"). In response to this memo Benkendorff had informed Pushkin that, according to the tsar, "принятое Вами правило, будто бы просвещение и гений служат исключительным основанием совершенству, есть правило опасное для общего спокойствия, завлекшее вас самих на край пропасти и повергшее в оную толикое число молодых людей. Нравственность, прилежное служение, усердие предпочесть должно просвещению неопытному, безнравственному и бесполезному." ("The principle that you have argued for – that enlightenment and genius supposedly serve exclusively as the basis for perfection – is a principle dangerous for the general tranquility; it led you yourself to the edge of a precipice and cast a considerable number of young people into it. Morality, diligent service, and zeal are to be preferred to inexperienced, immoral, and useless enlightenment.")

32 Молчи́т, поту́пя очи долу – Is silent, casting his glance downwards. Al'tshuller (47), continuing his argument that the criticism of the final stanzas is directed at Tsar Alexander, suggests that the poet Pushkin has in mind is Zhukovskii. In January 1826 Pushkin had written to Zhukovskii: "Говорят, ты написал стихи на смерть Александра – предмет богатый! – Но в течение десяти лет его царствования лира твоя молчала. Это лучший упрек ему." ("I'm told that you have written verses on the death of Alexander – a rich sub-

ject! – But in the course of ten years of his reign your lyre was silent. That is the best reproach to him.")

Посла́ние к Великопо́льскому, сочини́телю „Сати́ры на игроко́в" – Epistle to Velikopol'skii, the Author of "A Satire on Gamblers"

In 1828 Ivan Ermolaevich Velikopol'skii published his first book of poetry, a twenty-four-page work in freely rhymed iambic hexameters called "Сатира на игроков." The plot, to a significant extent autobiographical, centered on the dangers of gambling. The protagonist Arist loses in a single evening his fortune, his honor, and his sanity to Damon, an unscrupulous opponent. Pushkin, an inveterate gambler who had won 500 rubles from Velikopol'skii in 1826 (see "Из письма к Великопольскому"), responded to Velikopol'skii's didactic verse tale with this witty (and surprisingly nasty) poem, which was published anonymously in Faddei Bulgarin's journal *Северная пчела* (*The Northern Bee*) with the tag *ex ungue leonem* (<One can tell> a lion from its claw). The Latin idiom was common (Pushkin himself wrote a poem with this title), but it also recalls Pushkin's famously long fingernails, which Velikopol'skii himself referred to as "когти длинные поэта" ("the poet's long claws") in an epistle to Pushkin of 1826 (cited in Modzalevskii 1999, 363). Pushkin's poem is written in freely rhymed iambic tetrameter.

1 элеги́ческую лиру – elegiac lyre. Velikopol'skii wrote in many genres, among them (as Pushkin was obviously aware) elegies.
3 На благочи́нную сати́ру – For a decorous satire
4 Хвалю́ поэ́та – дельно миру! – I praise the poet – it's good for the world!
5 Ему поле́зен розги свист – The whistle of the rod is good for it (the world)
10 Проду́лся весь и так пропа́л! – He gambled away all his money and thus was ruined!
20 А то, уча́ безу́мный свет – But then again, teaching the crazy world
22 Пе́рсиев насле́дник – descendent of Persius. Persius (full name: Aulus Persius Flaccus) was a Roman satirist of the first century. He is mentioned (together with Boileau, the neoclassical satirist) in Velikopol'skii's poem.
24 Некто мой сосе́д – a certain neighbor of mine
25 Хлебну́в каста́льских вод бока́л – Having downed a goblet of Castalian waters. Castalia is a spring on Mount Parnassus, long associated with the Muses and thus with poetic inspiration. In this particular line, the combination of colloquial verb and elevated object creates a comic effect.
30 молча стасова́л – silently shuffled <the cards>
31 Дал снять – let him cut the deck
32 понтирова́л – placed his bets
38 И проигрыш его писа́ть – And write down his loss(es). In the gambling of Pushkin's time, rather than exchanging money constantly, the dealer kept a running tally of wins and losses.

Literature: Mozdalevskii 1999, 365–71.

„Сто лет мину́ло, как тевто́н“ – “One hundred years passed, since the German”

This is the first of Pushkin’s three translations (see also “Будрыс и его сыновья” and “Воевода”) from the great Polish poet Adam Mickiewicz (1788–1855). It comes from the verse introduction to the lengthy Byronic poem *Konrad Wallenrod*, a patriotic Lithuanian saga very loosely based on historical events of the fifteenth century. In 1827 Pushkin heard Mickiewicz read from this (as yet unpublished) work and expressed interest in translating it. However, Pushkin’s knowledge of Polish was inadequate to the task; in addition to the Polish text, he had at his disposal a literal French prose translation (now lost) prepared especially for him by a mutual friend, Apollon Aleksandrovich Skal’kovskii (1808–1898). Pushkin’s text renders 38 of the 51 lines of Mickiewicz’s introduction. By omitting the last lines, he changes the tone of the whole, concluding it with an image of harmony at odds with Mickiewicz’s poem. He published this version under the title “Отрывок из поэмы Мицкевича: Конрад Валленрод” (“Fragment of a Narrative Poem by Mickiewicz: Konrad Wallenrod”).

Pushkin probably had sufficient Polish to determine the versification of the original. It is written in syllabic verse typical of Polish poetry, with 11 syllables per line and exclusively feminine rhymes. Pushkin rendered this into his standard iambic tetrameter with both masculine and feminine rhymes, which come unpredictably (though the scheme follows the Polish for the first 11 lines). Pushkin apparently sought out an equivalent meter; he took a Polish Byronic poem and translated it into the verse form that (thanks to his own narrative poems of the early 1820s) had become the standard for Russian Byronic poems. In the Polish edition that subsequently appeared (*Poezye Adama Mickiewicza,* Saint Petersburg, Drukiem Karola Kraya 1829), vol. 1, pp. 3–5, the passage reads as follows:

Sto lat mijało, jak Zakon krzyżowy
We krwi pogaństwa północnego brodził;
Już Prusak szyję uchylił w okowy,
Lub ziemię oddał, a z duszą uchodził;
Niemiec za zbiegiem rozpuścił gonitwy,
Więził, mordował, aż do granic Litwy.

Niemen rozdziela Litwinów od wrogów:
Po jednéj stronie błyszczą świątyń szczyty,
I szumią lasy, pomieszkania bogów;
Po drugiéj stronie, na pagórku wbity
Krzyż, godło Niemców, czoło kryje w niebie,
Groźne ku Litwie wyciąga ramiona
Jak gdyby wszystkie ziemie Palemona
Chciał z góry objąć i garnąć pod siebie.

Z téj strony, tłumy litewskiéj młodzieży,
W kołpakach rysich, w niedźwiedziej odzieży,
Z łukiem na plecach, z dłonią pełną grotów,
Snują się, śledząc niemieckich obrotów.

Po drugiej stronie, w szyszaku i zbroi,
Niemiec na koniu nieruchomy stoi;
Oczy utkwiwszy w nieprzyjaciół szaniec,
Nabija strzelbę i liczy różaniec.

I ci, i owi pilnują przeprawy.
Tak Niemen, dawniej sławny z gościnności,
Łączący bratnich narodów dzierżawy,
Już teraz dla nich był progiem wieczności;
I nikt, bez straty życia lub swobody,
Nie mógł przestąpić zakazanej wody.
Tylko gałąska litewskiego chmielu,
Wdziękami pruskiej topoli nęcona,
Pnąc się po wierzbach i po wodnym zielu,
Śmiałe, jak dawniej, wyciąga ramiona,
I rzekę kraśnym przeskakując wiankiem,
Na obcym brzegu łączy się z kochankiem.
Tylko słowiki kowieńskiej dąbrowy,
Z bracią swoimi zapuszczańskiej góry,
Wiodą, jak dawniéj, litewskie rozmowy,
Lub, swobodnymi wymknąwszy się pióry,
Latają w gości na spólne ostrowy.

---

1 тевтóн – the German. The reference is to the Teutonic Order of the Knights of the Cross, which had been brought into East Prussia at the beginning of the thirteenth century. It devastated Poland and Lithuania for much of the fourteenth century. In this poem, Pushkin uses "тевтон," "германец," and "немец" interchangeably.

2 В кровú невéрных окупáлся – bathed in the blood of the unfaithful (i.e., non-Christians)

3 Странóй полнóчной – the northern country. (In Polish this is the "pagan north," i.e., ancient Lithuania.)

4 прусáк в окóвы вдался – the Prussian gave himself up in chains. The Teutonic order had been invited to East Prussia by a Polish prince in order to protect himself against the Lithuanians and Prussians. However, the order soon subjugated the Prussians and menaced Poland and Lithuania.

6 Понёс изгнáнную главý – Brought his exiled head. In modern Russian, the word "изгнанную" is stressed on the first syllable.

8 Немен – The Nemen River flows into the Baltic Sea; it forms (in places) the southern border of Lithuania.

на однóм – on one <shore>

11 рощи вековы́е – ancient groves

12 Духóв пристáнища святы́е – Holy refuges of spirits. In modern Russian, the word "духов" (in the sense of "spirits") is stressed on the first syllable.

13 Симвóл гермáнца – The symbol of the German. In modern Russian "символ" is stressed on the first syllable.

15 Свои́ объя́тия грозя́щи (=грозящие) – their menacing embraces

16 свыше захвати́ть – to grab from above

17 область Палемóна – the realm of Palemon. According to a legend (dreamed up by the Lithuanians during the fifteenth or sixteenth centuries), Palemon was the leader of a group of Roman families who in ancient times settled the area of Lithuania. The story was invented to claim for the Lithuanians a blood relationship to the Roman Empire.
18 племя чуждого закóна – the tribe of a foreign law. At this point in history, the Lithuanians were still pagans (in contrast to the "Christian" Knights).
19 привлачи́ть – to drag
21 рысьей – made of lynx
22 Калёных стрел – of arrows forged by fire. The phrase "каленые стрелы" occurs frequently in Russian folklore.
26 покры́тый шишакóм – covered by a spiked helmet
27 В бронé закóванный – bound in armor
28 На страже – on guard
30 Пищáль – harquebus. These were long guns, state of the art military equipment in the fifteenth century.
31 Всяк перепрáву охраня́л – Everyone guarded the crossing
34 прагом вечности – the threshold of eternity. ("Праг" is an archaism for "порог.")
39 Немéцкой тополью пленéнный – captivated by the German poplar. In modern Russian "тополь" is masculine. Pushkin uses an archaic form, perhaps to suggest through grammatical gender its love relationship to the masculine "хмель" of the previous line.
42 Брегóв (=берегов) проти́вных достигáл – Reached the opposite shore. As in line 38, the plural form "shores" refers to a single side of the river. In modern Russian, "противный" can only mean "disgusting."

Literature: Levkovich 1974, 1983b; Weintraub, 115–33.

Эпитáфия младéнцу – Epitaph for an Infant

Epitaphs were a standard eighteenth-century genre. Pushkin turned to it here not as an exercise in stylization, but out of necessity. The infant in question was the son of the Decembrist Sergei Grigor'evich Volkonskii (1788–1865) and his wife Mariia Nikolaevna, née Raevskaia (1805 or 1807–1863). Upon departing to join her exiled husband in Siberia, she left her son in the care of his grandparents. Pushkin knew the Raevskii family well, having spent extremely happy times traveling with them during the early part of his southern exile. Mariia's father, N. N. Raevskii (1771–1829), asked Pushkin to write the epitaph and had it chiseled onto the tombstone. Though the Academy edition dates the poem as 1828 (the year of the death), correspondence of the Raevskii family suggests that it was written in 1829.

The poem is written in free iambs (pentameter, tetrameter, and two lines of hexameter) with alternating rhymes.

---

3 изгнáние земнóе – earthly exile. The phrase has a double meaning (metaphysical and political).

„Кто знает край, где небо блещет" – "Who knows the land, where the sky shines"

After a long introduction, the subject of the poem turns out to be Mariia Aleksandrovna Musina-Pushkina, née Urusova (1801–1853), considered one of the great beauties of the day. After her marriage in 1822, she had traveled to Italy. Pushkin's poem sings the beauty of Italian art, but extols with still more fervor the beauty of a Russian woman.

The poem is written in iambic tetrameter in stanzas of uneven length with unpredictable rhyme scheme. It is unfinished and was first published posthumously (with the censor removing the final six lines, presumably considering them blasphemous).

First epigraph: Kennst du das Land … – Do you know the land … The opening of Goethe's "Mignon-Lied," which expresses a yearning for Italy, from the novel *Wilhelm Meisters Lehrjahre*. Pushkin's knowledge of German was almost non-existent, but the poem he quotes was so celebrated that even he seems to have known this phrase in the original. (The manuscript shows that he wrote the impossible and ungrammatical "Könnst" instead of "Kennst.")

Second epigraph: По клюкву, по клюкву, по ягоду, по клюкву – <Let's go pick> a cranberry, a cranberry, a berry, a cranberry. According to the recollections of Prince Viazemskii, Musina-Pushkina amused Russian high society by explaining how much she missed cranberries in Italy. The lines that Pushkin chooses were apparently not simply a folk stylization, but an actual quotation. An early folklorist and Pushkin scholar (Shein, 10–11) recalls how in 1846 he heard a young berry salesman ("клюквенник") sing the following:

По клюкву, по клюкву!
По ягоду, по клюкву
    По кр-р-рупну!
Э! эй … клюква!
Приехала клюква,
Приехала красна
Из города Володимира
    Э! эй … клюква!
    Кр-р-р-рупна!
Брали бабушки,
Звали их наташки.
    Э! эй … клюква!
    Кр-р-р-рупна!
Господа сенаторы
Из банковой конторы.

Shein follows this quotation with the comment: "Дальше не припомню. Но впечатление осталось такое, что о сенаторах было упомянуто в сатирическом смысле. Из слов моего клюквенника, сколько помню, можно было догадаться, что клюквенных выкриков существует несколько вариантов."

7 Торквáто величáвый – The majestic Torquato. Torquato Tasso (1544–1595),

one of Italy's great poets. The theme of Tasso's octaves being sung by boatmen can already be found in the first chapter of *Eugene Onegin.* According to Nabokov, "allusions to gondoliers and Tasso's octaves belong … to the tritest commonplaces of Romanticism" (Nabokov, 2:181). In the present poem, the octaves are repeated by the waves (which may simply be a metonymy for sailors, since a draft version has them sung by a "ночной пловец" in a gondola).

11 Где Рафаэ́ль живописа́л – Where Raphael painted. Raphael (1483–1520) was in Pushkin's day considered the greatest of the Italian painters. The Russian verb "живописать" is high style and rarely used.

12 резе́ц Кано́вы – the chisel of Canova. Antonio Canova (1757–1822), a much-admired sculptor.

15 Страда́л, люби́л и проклина́л – Suffered, loved, and cursed. In Italy Byron met the great love of his life, Teresa Guiccioli, who left her (much older) husband for him.

20 <Людми́ла> – The etymology of "Людмила" ("людям мила" – "dear to the people") may be relevant, given the broad adoration she receives in this poem. The name was not traditional, but invented in the late eighteenth century and popularized in literature, especially by Zhukovskii's ballad of that name and Pushkin's own "Ruslan and Liudmila." (See Proskurin 2007, 82–83.) Drafts of the poem show that Pushkin was considering more exotic names: Глицера, Эльвина, Леила, Рогнеда.

28 Сыно́в Авзо́нии – Sons of Ausonia. Ausonia, a poetic name for Italy, is derived from Auson, who according to Vergil was the patriarch of a southern Italian clan.

30 Их пёстры (= пестрые) волны за собо́й – their many-colored waves after her

31 полу́денной – southern

38 Себя́ прекра́сней – more beautiful than herself

40 Пред флорентинскою Кипри́дой – In front of the Florentine Venus. The Medici Venus, a first-century copy of a Greek statue, is the oldest sculpture in the Uffizi Gallery in Florence. The name "Киприда" refers to Cyprus ("Кипр"), where a cult of Aphrodite (Venus in Roman mythology) flourished in antiquity. According to Greek myth, Aphrodite was born from the foam of the sea near Cyprus and soon after reached that island.

41 Их две … – There are two <Florentine Venuses>. That is: the Russian beauty as well as the statue of Venus.

45 Форнари́ны – of the Fornarina. For obscure reasons, eighteenth-century scholars began to refer to Raphael's mistress as "La Fornarina" ("The Bakeress"). In the Uffizi Gallery there is a painting by this name by Sebastiano del Piombo. Pushkin probably assumed that this was Raphael's mistress and he may have assumed (as was common at the time) that the painter was not Sebastiano, but Raphael himself.

46 Мадо́ны молодо́й – of the young Madonna. Even if we assume that Pushkin is still writing about Raphael, it is hard to say which of his Florentine Madonnas is meant.

54–55 Ва́ятель безымя́нный / Боги́ни вечной красоты́ – Anonymous sculptor of the goddess of eternal beauty. Another reference to the Medici Venus (cf. commentary to line 40).

56 Хари́тою (= Хари́той) венча́нный – crowned by one of the Graces

58 Забу́дь евре́йку молоду́ю – Forget the young Jewess (i.e., the Virgin Mary).
62 Пиши́ Мари́ю нам другу́ю – Paint for us another Mary. The reference is presumably to Mariia Musina-Pushkina. The imperative, addressed to Raphael, recalls a similar apostrophe in Derzhavin's "Изображение Фелицы" ("Depiction of Felitsa").
63 С други́м младе́нцем на рука́х – With another child in her arms. Mariia Musina-Pushkina had given birth to her second son (Aleksandr) on 10 June 1827.

Literature: Tsiavlovskii 1962, 369–78.

В. С. Филимо́нову – To V. S. Filimonov

Vladimir Sergeevich Filimonov (1787–1858) was a minor poet, whose work and hedonistic personality were appreciated by Pushkin and his friends. On 22 March 1828 Filimonov sent Pushkin a copy of his new long poem "Дурацкий колпак" ("The Dunce Cap"), with an inscription (facsimile in Modzalevskii 1910: non-numbered page between 264 and 265):

> А. С. ПУШКИНУ
> Вы в мире славою гремите;
> Поэт! В лавровом вы венке.
> Певцу, безвестному, простите:
> Я к вам являюсь – в колпаке.
>
> (You sound forth in glory in the world; O, poet! You are <wearing> a laurel wreath. Forgive an unknown singer: I come to you – in a cap.)

Pushkin's verse epistle (apparently penned that very day) not only responds to this inscription, but also to the poem itself (especially to the opening "Посвящение").

---

2 Колпа́к связа́ли в добрый час – They <the Muses> wove you a cap just at the right time. The line echoes Filimonov's opening line of "Дурацкий колпак": "Вы мне давно колпак связали." Moreover, in line 7 Filimonov refers to his poem as a "стихотворное вязанье" ("weaving of verse").
3 грему́шки – little bells
4 Феб – Phoebus Apollo
9 Но старый мой колпа́к изно́шен – But my old cap is worn out
12 красный цвет – red color. Red caps were placed on the heads of new members at the meetings of Arzamas, a poetry society to which the young Pushkin and many of his friends belonged. In a poem of 1817 called "Товарищам" ("To my comrades"), addressed to his friends shortly before graduation from the Lyceum, Pushkin had written "Оставьте красный мне колпак" ("Leave me my red cap").
14 бью чело́м – I make obeisance (literally: I beat my head). This phrase refers to

the traditional low bow, a sign of great respect, archaic already in Pushkin's day.

Literature: Vatsuro 1994, 91–99.

„Увы́! Язы́к любви́ болтли́вой" – "Alas! The garrulous language of love"

The poem, clearly unfinished (line 18 is missing altogether), was addressed to Anna Alekseevna Olenina (1808–1888), whom Pushkin was assiduously courting at this time.

It is written in astrophic iambic tetrameter, but it clearly breaks down into quatrains, both through rhyme (alternating) and syntax (up until the final quatrain, which breaks the pattern in a semantically significant way). The shift in pronouns (from "тебе" to "ей") in lines 4–8 (and back again beginning in line 9) is striking.

---

1 Язы́к любви́ болтли́вой – of garrulous love. In the Academy edition (1948), the word is incorrectly given as "болтливый." It was corrected in the 1959 volume (Additions and Corrections) of the same edition. The semantic difference is minimal, especially since Pushkin often used "-ой" endings instead of "-ый" for masculine nominatives. Even if the "-ой" ending is meant as a genitive singular (in agreement with "любви"), the meaning does not change, since it would surely be a transferred epithet – though grammatically in agreement with "love," it logically refers to "language."

2 Язы́к и тёмный <?> и просто́й – A language both dark (i.e., inscrutable) and simple. The combination of adjectives creates an oxymoron. In the Academy edition (1948), this line originally read "Язык неполный <?> и простой." It was corrected in the 1959 volume (Additions and Corrections) of the same edition.

3 Свое́ю (=Своей) прозой ндради́вой – With its careless prose

4 Тебе́ доку́чен – is tiresome to you

6 Честолюби́вый Аполло́н – Honor-seeking Apollo. The Russian word "честолюбие" can have either positive or negative connotations. Here it presumably is positive (wishing to be honored) rather than negative (vain, ambitious).

14 Судьбо́ю (=Судьбой) вверенный мне дар – The gift entrusted to me by fate

15 Досе́ле <в> жизненной пусты́не – Until now in life's desert

17 Мне навлека́л одно́ гоне́нье – Has brought me only persecution. The subject is дар (line 14).

To Dawe, Esqr.

The only one of Pushkin's poems with an English title, it was written to the British portrait painter George Dawe (1781–1829), who had achieved great fame in Russia thanks to Tsar Alexander's patronage (see commentary to "Полководец"). There is no record of Pushkin meeting Dawe until the date of this poem (9 May 1828), when the two were (coincidentally) on the same boat to Kronstadt. Pushkin was participating in an excursion organized by Prince Viazemskii. Dawe was leaving Russia permanently, having fallen out of favor with Tsar Alexander's successor Nicholas; from Kronstadt he would continue his journey to England. This is an occasional poem, a verbal response to Dawe's spontaneous pencil drawing (which has never been located).

The poem is written in iambic tetrameter with alternating rhymes.

---

1 дивный карандáш – wondrous pencil. Nabokov (3:205) detects in this locution a phonetic and semantic echo of the French "crayon divin" (a phrase used in a poem by Voltaire).

2 мой арáпский профиль – my Negroid profile

3 Хоть ты векáм егó предáшь – Even if you pass it on to the centuries. The antecedent of "его" is "профиль," which Dawe would pass on in the form of his drawing.

4 Его осви́щет Мефистóфиль – Mephistopheles will hiss it. Aside from the demon made famous in Goethe's *Faust*, this may be an allusion to Ivan Sergeevich Mal'tsov (1807–1880), known by the nickname Mephistopheles, who had in early 1828 written critically about Dawe's work.

5 Олéниной черты́ – Olenina's features. The reference is to A. A. Olenina, who was also on the boat as a guest of Prince Viazemskii.

Воспоминáние – Recollection

Scholarship on this important poem has been dominated not by the poem proper, but by numerous drafts, which include a continuation lengthier than the poem itself. However, since Pushkin excluded that (personal and highly interesting) passage, it seems sensible to limit the present commentary to the finished poem that Pushkin chose to present to the world.

The meter is alternating iambic hexameter and iambic tetrameter with alternating masculine/feminine rhymes. The most likely metrical model is Batiushkov's "К другу" (with which Pushkin's poem intersects thematically in several ways), though Baratynskii's "Зачем, о Делия! Сердца младые ты" was probably also influential. (See Proskurin 1999, 205–7).

---

1 для смертного – for a mortal

умóлкнет – falls silent. Pushkin uses perfective not as future tense, but as repetitive present.

2 стогны града (=города) – the squares of the city. The phrase is distinctly archaic.

3 Полупрозрáчная наля́жет ночи тень – The half-transparent shadow of night spreads out. Once again Pushkin uses perfective as repetitive present. This line has generally been understood as a reference to Petersburg's white nights. (Pushkin dated the draft as 19 May.) It may also emphasize the liminal quality of the scene (Liapunov 1976, 36).

4 И сон, дневны́х трудо́в награ́да – And sleep, the reward for the day's labors, <descends>. This phrase is in nominative case, with the verb supplied from the previous line.
5 влача́тся – drag on
6 томи́тельного бденья – of tortuous wakefulness
7 живе́й (=живее) горя́т – burn more vividly. Such metaphorical use of "burning" is not uncommon in Russian poetry, but may be a Gallicism (Liapunov 1976, 37).
8 Змей серде́чной угрызе́нья – the gnawings of the snake of the heart. The passage may draw on Derzhavin's "Евгению. Жизнь званская" ("To Evgenii. Life at Zvanka"): "Чтоб черная змия мне сердце угрызала" – "That the black snake does <not> gnaw my heart." (Proskurin 1999, 204).
9 пода́вленном тоско́й – oppressed by sorrow. The nuance of "тоска" is difficult to convey in English. See Nabokov's attempt at a definition (4:98): "'boredom,' 'yearning,' 'nostalgia,' 'heartache,' 'dull anguish'; between *skuka*, 'ennui,' and *muka*, 'torment.'"
10 Тесни́тся тяжких дум избы́ток – An overabundance of heavy thoughts crowd together
12 Свой длинный развива́ет свиток – Unfurls its long scroll
16 Но строк печа́льных не смыва́ю – But I don't remove the sad lines. Strictly speaking, the verb "смывать" means "to remove by washing" or "to wash away." Both the literal and figurative uses may be relevant here, for example, "смывать чернила" "to wash away ink" or "смывать позор," "to wash away a disgrace." Commentators have expended considerable energy over this last line because it can mean two very different things – either "I do not want to remove the sad lines" or "I am incapable of removing the sad lines." The overall tone of the poem seems to favor the former reading: the poet chooses not to change the past, painful as it may be.

Literature: Liapunov 1976; Proskurin 1999, 203–18.

Ты и вы – You <informal> and you <formal>

An occasional poem written to A. A. Olenina, after she mistakenly used the informal "ты" rather than the formal "вы" in conversation with the poet. Pushkin's poem plays brilliantly off of the difference, where Olenina's error leads to the poet's deliberate confusion of the same pronouns.

The poem is written as a single eight-line stanza with alternating rhymes in the first four lines and a ring rhyme in the last four. The feminine rhymes are all connected (заменила/возбудила/силы/милы), but the change in rhyme scheme underlines the semantic structure, setting the first four lines off against the second four.

---

1 серде́чным *ты* – with a sincere "ты"
2 обмо́лвясь – misspeaking
6 Свести́ оче́й с неё нет силы – <I have> no power to take my eyes off her

7 как *вы* ми́лы – how kind you ("вы") are. Despite the italics, the word вы does not take stress.
8 мыслю – I think

„Дар напра́сный, дар случа́йный" – "Vain gift, chance gift"

Pushkin includes the date because it is his birthday, for him a time of reckoning. Though the poem passed through censorship and was published in 1829, it was considered by some almost blasphemous in its questioning of providence. (See commentary to "В часы забав иль праздной скуки.")

The meter is trochaic tetrameter with alternating feminine and masculine rhymes.

1 дар – gift (in the sense of "present"; in modern Russian "дар" generally means "gift" only in the sense of "talent")
6 Из ничто́жества воззва́л (=вызвал) – called me out of nothingness (ex nihilo). Ivanov (1987, 31) suggests that this line is an echo of "Je ne sais qui m'a mis au monde" ("I don't know who put me in the world") from Pascal's "Pensées."
11 томи́т меня́ тоско́ю – torments me with anguish. In this passage "тоска" could also mean "boredom."

И. В. Слёнину – To I. V. Slenin

Ivan Vasil'evich Slenin (1789–1836) was a minor poet, but an important publisher. His fame resided primarily in the bookstore that he owned, which was located on Nevskii Prospekt. Its excellent stock of French books ensured that Pushkin was a frequent visitor.

For the poets of Pushkin's age, albums were a fact of life, and Pushkin generally writes about them with a certain resignation or even exasperation (see, for example, *Eugene Onegin* 4:XXVIII–XXX or the second paragraph of "Египетские ночи" ["Egyptian Nights"]). This poem discusses various types of album verse, creating a hierarchy at which Slenin's own occupies a uniquely high position.

The poem is written in iambic tetrameter with alternating rhymes. Though astrophic, it breaks down both logically and syntactically as quatrains. The sole exception is the third (middle) quatrain, which logically breaks in the middle, dividing the poem into two sections of ten lines each.

2 ослепи́тельная смесь – dazzling variety. Daria Solodkaia has suggested to me that this passage (including the rhyme смесь/спесь) borrows from Prince Viazemskii's poem of 1825 (published 1826) "Альбом," which begins: "Альбом, как жизнь, противоречий смесь, / Смесь доброго, худого, пустословья: / Здесь дружбы дань, тут светского условья, / Тут жар любви, там умничанья спесь."

3 Аспáзий – of Aspasias. Aspasia (470?–400 BCE), mistress (and perhaps wife) of Pericles, was known for her beauty, intelligence, and interest in the arts, as well as for her "immoral" behavior. In this case, it is a backhanded compliment, since they are associated with arrogance ("спесь"). These "Aspasias" – patronesses of the arts of Pushkin's day – keep albums as a means of advertising their own glory.
7 Милéй (=Милее) – is dearer (i.e., than the "fashionable albums" of line 1).
9 Ни здесь, ни там – Neither here nor there. These two "places" refer to the two types of albums named in lines 5–6.
13 питóмцам Аполлóна – to Apollo's pupils.
15 Цари́ц ты любишь Геликóна – You love the queens of the Helicon (i.e., the Muses).
17 Вхожу́ в негó прямы́м поэ́том – I enter it as a true poet. The antecedent of "it" is "your album" (line 11).
20 лар – Lares. The Lares, Roman household gods. The word is in accusative (genitive) plural, following the verb "почтив" ("having shown respect for") in the previous line.

„Ещё дуют холóдные ветры" – "The cold winds are still blowing"

These unpublished and unfinished verses about the coming of spring reflect Pushkin's interest in folk themes and style (note the frequent repetitions, the diminutives, the truncated adjectives).

The verse form is accentual. Lines vary in length from 9–11 syllables, usually 10. The passage is unrhymed, but has exclusively feminine cadences. As if to offset the lack of rhyme, Pushkin includes anaphora (скоро) and parallelism (вылетала/полетела) at the line beginnings, and usually puts the first stress on the third syllable. The form is essentially that of the majority of the "Песни западных славян" and, as in those poems, most lines have three stresses, separated by intervals of one, two, and occasionally three unstressed syllables.

5 Как из чудного царства восковóго – As if from a wondrous wax kingdom. The simile looks forward to line 6.
6 Из души́стой келéйки медóвой – From a fragrant little cell of honey
7 Вылетáла – In the Academy edition (1948), the word is given incorrectly as "Вы́летела." It is corrected in the 1959 volume (Additions and Corrections) of the same edition.
9 О красной веснé поразвéдать – To find out about the beautiful spring. "Красная весна" is a standard expression in folk poetry.
10 гостья дорогáя – the dear guest. This is a metaphor for the spring ("красная весна," feminine gender).
12 у кудря́вой у берёзы – of the leafy birch. The repeated preposition is typical of folk style. "Кудрявая" is a traditional folk epithet for a birch tree.
13 Распу́стятся клейкие листóчки – The sticky little leaves will open up. Note how the adjective "клейкие" picks up on the diminutive "келейки" of line 6.
14 Зацветёт черёмуха души́ста (=душистая) – The fragrant bird cherry will

<soon> blossom. The “soon” is elliptical, carrying over from the anaphora lines 10–12. See Nabokov 3:11: “Dictionaries usually translate the ‘черемуха’ as ‘bird cherry,’ which is so vague as to be practically meaningless. Specifically, ‘черемуха’ is the ‘racemose old-world bird cherry,’ Fr. *putier racémeux, Padus racemosa* Schneider <sic>. The Russian word, with its fluffy and dreamy syllables, admirably suits this beautiful tree, distinguished by its long racemes of flowers, giving the whole of it, when in bloom, a gentle pendulous appearance. A common and popular woodland plant in Russia, it is equally at home among the riverside alders and on the pine barren; its creamy-white, musky, Maytime bloom is associated in Russian hearts with the poetical emotions of youth.”

„Кобыли́ца молода́я“ – “Young mare”

Pushkin’s initial publication of the poem bore the subtitle “Подражание Анакреону” (“An Imitation of Anacreon”), in reference to Anacreon’s ode “To a Thracian Filly.” Horses are not an important theme in Anacreontic poetry, and readers (even in antiquity) interpreted this ode as a masked love poem, with the mare representing a young woman. Pushkin’s poem loosely follows Anacreon, in that it borrows its main conceit. With this in mind, one may conjecture that underneath its patina of antiquity (and apparently unbeknownst to his contemporaries and his addressee), Pushkin’s poem is actually addressed to A. A. Olenina.

The poem is written in trochaic tetrameter (typical of Russian Anacreontic odes) with alternating rhymes; the syntactic breaks and rhyme scheme indicate that the poem consists of three quatrains, but it is printed as one continuous stanza.

2 Честь кавка́зского тавра́ – pride of the Caucasian breed. Strictly speaking, a “тавро” is a mark branded onto a horse that indicates to whom it belongs. Here it is used figuratively as a type of horse.
5 Не коси́сь пугли́вым оком – Don’t look askance at me with a scared eye
6 Ног на воздух не мечи́ – Don’t fling your legs in the air
12 Укоро́ченной уздо́й – with a shortened bridle

Её глаза́ – Her Eyes

The title of the poem is deliberately misleading, as the possessive pronoun ultimately refers to two sets of eyes belonging to two “competing” Petersburg beauties: A. O. Rosset (1809–1882) and A. A. Olenina (1808–1888). Pushkin was madly in love with the latter at the time (he soon proposed to her, but was rejected), so it is hardly surprising that the poem shows him partial to her. The competition of Russian beauties is supplemented by a competition of poets. Pushkin’s poem is a response to “Черные очи” (“Dark Eyes”), Prince Viazemskii’s paean to A. O. Rosset. As her name suggests, Rosset was of French descent; Viazemskii’s poem places her fiery “southern” beauty (for which Italy and France become synonymous) in the context of the cold north. In the first publications of his own poem, Pushkin spelled out the literary allusion by calling the poem first "К приятелю, сравнивавшему глаза одной девицы с южными звездами" ("To a Friend Who Compared the Eyes of One Maiden to Southern Stars") and later "Ее глаза (В ответ на стихи князя В–го)" ("Her Eyes [In Response to Verses of Prince V<iazemskii>]").

Черные очи

Южные звезды! Черные очи!
Неба чужого огни!
Вас ли встречают взоры мои
Нá небе хладном бледной полночи?

Юга созвездье! Сердца зенит!
Сердце, любуяся вами,
Южною негой, южными снами
Бьется, томится, кипит.

Тайным восторгом сердце объято,
В вашем сгорая огне;
Звуков Петрарки, песней Торквато
Ищешь в немой глубине.

Тщетны порывы! Глухи напевы!
В сердце нет песней, увы!
Южные очи северной девы,
Нежных и страстных, как вы!

Viazemskii's poem is written in quatrains of dactylic tetrameter (with caesura that omits a syllable) alternating with dactylic trimeter. Pushkin's poem, in iambic tetrameter with alternating rhymes (the first five lines are exceptional in this respect) is formally unrelated. However, Pushkin borrows much of the imagery and lexicon from Viazemskii.

---

1 скажý меж нами – <Just> between you and me I'll say it

2 Придвóрных витязей грозá – the scourge of court warriors. This bombastic phrase ("витязь" is a legendary hero) has a comic effect, especially coming after the innocuous introductory "Она мила."

3 с южными звездáми – with the southern stars (cf. first line of Viazemskii's poem). In modern Russian, the stress falls on the first syllable of "звёздами."

4 осóбенно стихáми – especially in verses. There is a certain irony in this phrase, suggesting that the comparison is rather absurd, but it works if you do it in verse.

5 Её черкéсские глазá – Her Circassian eyes. Viazemskii had turned Rosset's French ancestry into Italian (Petrarch and Tasso), so Pushkin pushes the comparison still further, making her a Circassian. (One thinks of Pushkin's narrative poem "Кавказский пленник" ["The Prisoner of the Caucasus"], which features a passionate Circassian woman. See also commentary to "Ответ Ф. Т***" of 1826.)

7 огня́ живе́й (=живее) – more lively than fire. A reference to the Viazemskii poem, where the word "огонь" occurs twice.

8 сам призна́йся, то ли дело – You yourself must admit, how different (i.e., how much better) <are>. The address to Viazemskii comes as a surprise, since he has not been invoked directly up to this point. The phrase "то ли дело" is colloquial.

10 гений – spirit. This word, in conjunction with the "детской простоты" (child-like simplicity) of the next line, echoes with the famous phrase "гений чистой красоты" ("spirit of pure beauty"), which appears in Pushkin's famous 1825 poem to Anna Petrovna Kern, "К***" („Я помню чудное мгновенье"). Pushkin found this formula in two poems by Zhukovskii, and also in his prose, in a description of the Sistine Madonna (Blank, 86). See commentary below to lines 16–17.

14 Поту́пит их с улы́бкой Леля – When she lowers them with a smile of Lel'. Lel' is a Slavic god of love and the grove, whom Pushkin sometimes associates with sleep (see *Eugene Onegin* 5:X). Nabokov (2:501) argues that the name is "probably derived from a mere refrain: comparable to the *leli, leli, leli* and *ay lyuli lyuli* of Russian songs." (For a variation of this folkloric motif, see "Колокольчики звенят," line 4).

16–17 Подни́мет – ангел Рафаэ́ля / Так созерца́ет божество́ – <When she> raises <them> – this is the way Raphael's angel looks at the divinity. The reference is to the so-called Sistine Madonna in Dresden, in which two angels (at the base of the painting) look upward at the Virgin and child. One of the most celebrated works of the Italian Renaissance, Pushkin would have known it through numerous reproductions as well as written accounts by his friends Zhukovskii and Kiukhel'beker (Koka 1962, 22,106). It is noteworthy that Pushkin, like Viazemskii before him, concludes his poem with a reference to Italian culture.

„Не пой, краса́вица, при мне" – "Don't sing, beauty, in my presence"

The poem is addressed to A. A. Olenina, who – aside from being the object of Pushkin's admiration at this time – was a singer and a student of M. I. Glinka. Though Pushkin mentions songs (plural), there is reason to believe that the specific melody in question was written down by Griboedov (himself a talented pianist until a dueling injury limited his dexterity) and arranged by Glinka. One occasionally encounters the unlikely and illogical argument that this poem was intended to be sung to that melody.

The poem is written in quatrains of iambic tetrameter with alternating rhymes: a-B-a-B. Only in the third stanza does the "a" rhyme vary. An earlier version of the poem has a different second stanza, emphasizing the Caucasian background: "Напоминают мне оне / Кавказа гордые вершины, / Лихих чеченцев на коне / И закубанские равнины." It, too, uses the same "a" rhyme. The final stanza is, of course, a refrain; its effect depends on the knowledge imparted in the second and third stanzas.

---

1 An earlier version has “волшебница” instead of “красавица.”

2 Ты песен Грузии печáльной – songs of sad Georgia. The inclusion of the preposition “ты” softens the imperative. In his narrative poem “Кавказский пленник,” (“The Prisoner of the Caucasus”) Pushkin had described how the Circassian maiden visits the eponymous Russian prisoner and sings him “песни Грузии счастливой.” He appended the following footnote to that line: “Счастливый климат Грузии не вознаграждает сию прекрасную страну за все бедствия, вечно ею претерпеваемые. Песни грузинские приятны и по большей части заунывны. Они славят минутные успехи кавказского оружия, смерть наших героев: Бакунина и Цицианова, измены, убийства – иногда любовь и наслаждения.”

3 онé – They. This archaic plural form refers only to feminine nouns (in this case “песни”).

4 Другýю жизнь – Another life. Pushkin presumably recalls his trip to the Caucasus in the summer of 1820 with the Raevskii family.

8 Черты далёкой, бедной девы – The features of a distant, poor maiden. This is generally assumed to refer to Mariia Raevskaia, now “distant” and “poor” because she has joined her Decembrist husband in Siberia. (See commentary to “Эпитафия младенцу.”)

Literature: Tsiavlovskii 1962, 381–83; Tsiavlovskaia, 256.

К Язы́кову – To Iazykov

This is Pushkin’s third and final epistle to Nikolai Mikhailovich Iazykov (see also “К Языкову” of 1826). Iazykov was a student at the University of Dorpat (today Tartu, Estonia) from 1822–1829, where he wrote hedonistic poetry that Pushkin admired. The wordplay in Pushkin’s poem between “петь” and “пить” draws on Iazykov’s own verse, for example, “Мы пьем – так рыцари пивали, / Поем – они так не певали.”

Pushkin’s poem is written in iambic tetrameter with an unpredictable rhyme scheme. The two stanzas of unequal length are divided according to theme, the first about the poet himself, the second directed to the addressee.

---

1 сбирáлся (=собирался) – intended <to go>

2 В немéцкий град (=город) – To the German city. Dorpat was part of the Russian empire, but the city’s culture (and language) was German.

4 Тобóй воспéтое винó – The wine that has been sung by you. In his epistle to Pushkin of 1825 (“А. С. Пушкину”), Iazykov had described himself as “Певец единственной забавы, / Певец вакхических картин, / И <дерпт>ских дев, и <дерпт>ских вин.” Though it is unclear which of the (mainly unpublished) poems Pushkin would have known, Iazykov wrote frequently in praise of wine, for example, “Душа героев и певцов, / Вино любезно и студенту” or “Счастлив, кому судьбою дан / Неиссякаемый стакан,” which concludes with the passage (the antecedent of “Он” is “студент”):

Вином и весел и счастлив,
Он – для одних восторгов жив.
И меж его и царской долей
Не много разницы найдем:
Царь почивает на престоле,
А он – забывшись – под столом.

5 зазыва́л меня́ – urged me to come; invited me
6 Киселёв – Nikolai Dmitrievich Kiselev, see "Н. Д. Киселеву"
9 Нево́лю – Servitude; lack of freedom. Pushkin often equates Petersburg with a spirit of slavery (see "Город пышный"), but in this poem the chains are also financial (see lines 12–13).
10 И что́ ж? Гербо́вые забо́ты – But what happened? Concerns about debts. "Герб" means a "coat of arms," but accounts of debts were written on official stationery (which would feature a coat of arms).
11 за́ полы – by the flaps <of my coat>
14 О юность, юность удала́я – O youth, wild youth. Pushkin associated the adjective "удалой" with Iazykov (see commentary to line 2 of "К Языкову" of 1826), but here the most prominent echo is from Pushkin's own unfinished narrative poem "Братья-разбойники" ("Brigand Brothers") of 1821–1822. The line "Ах, юность, юность удалая" is spoken by one of the eponymous brothers describing the carefree days of yore when they would pillage and murder without a second thought.
17 Заимода́вцев убега́я – avoiding creditors
22 тяжесть денег и годо́в – the weight of money and years. In rhetoric, this is an example of a zeugma (often, as here, a comic device).
23 Прости́, певе́ц! игра́й, пиру́й – Farewell, singer! Play, revel. The intonation of this line (and the next) recalls the concluding injunction of "Пророк."
24 С Кипри́дой, Фебом – With Aphrodite, Apollo
25 сия́тельного чванства – radiant arrogance. The adjective would presumably call to mind a high rank of Russian society ("Ваше сиятельство" ["Your Radiance"] was an official term of address for princes and counts).
26 любе́зных должнико́в – courteous debtors, that is, people who will borrow (and presumably not return) your money.
27 не плати́ свои́х долго́в – don't pay your debts. Iazykov (like Pushkin himself) was constantly in debt. The miserable state of Iazykov's finances (mentioned in several of his poems) would have been known to Pushkin through their mutual friend, the rake A. N. Vul'f. (See Brown, 360–61.)

<Н. Д. Киселёву> – To N. D. Kiselev

Nikolai Dmitrievich Kiselev studied (together with the poet Iazykov, who introduced him to Pushkin) at the university in Dorpat. Kiselev was by profession a diplomat, but judging from this poem, he was about to go abroad for health reasons. Pushkin wrote these occasional (and perhaps impromptu) verses in Kiselev's notebook, where he included a sketch of himself. Pushkin and Kiselev shared an interest not only in wine, but also in gambling (see Pushkin's letter to Prince Viazemskii of 1 September 1828). On Kiselev and Pushkin, see Tsiavlovskaia, 263–64.

The poem is written in iambic hexameter alternating with iambic tetrameter with rhyme scheme a-B-a-B.

---

3 карлсба́дские пить воды – to drink the Karlsbad waters. Karlsbad (Carlsbad, Karlovy Vary), located not far from Prague, was one of the spas for the rich and famous of the nineteenth century.

Портре́т – A Portrait

The poem is devoted to Agrafena Fedorovna Zakrevskaia (née Tolstaia, 1799–1879), a passionate woman with little interest in her husband (who was a dozen years her senior). Pushkin, who had a short-lived affair with her in the summer of 1828, published the poem that same year.

It is written in iambic tetrameter with rhyme scheme a-B-B-a-C-d-C-d.

---

3 О жёны Севера – Oh, women of the North. The use of "жёны" rather than "женщины" is high style.
5 света – of society
8 В кругу́ расчи́сленном свети́л – In the calculated orbit of the stars

Напе́рсник – The Confidant

Another poem dedicated to Zakrevskaia (see commentary to "Портрет"), again bearing witness to her emotional nature. The poem seems to intersect with Pushkin's letter to Prince Viazemskii of 1 September 1828: "Но она утешительно смешна и мила. Я ей пишу стихи. А она произвела меня в свои сводники." ("But she [Zakrevskaia] is consolingly amusing and sweet. I write verses to her. And she has raised me to the ranks of her panderers.")

There is some uncertainty as to whether the following thematically and formally related verses represent a continuation of the same poem or a different poem altogether:

Счастлив, кто избран своенравно
Твоей тоскливою мечтой,
При ком любовью млеешь явно,
Чьи взоры властвуют тобой;
Но жалок тот, кто молчаливо,
Сгорая пламенем любви,
Потупя голову, ревниво
Признанья слушает твои.

In any case, Pushkin published the poem without them. The Academy edition treats them as a variant.

As Pushkin published it, the poem is in iambic tetrameter with alternating rhymes. Structurally, syntactically and logically, it is divided into two quatrains, but it is written as a single stanza.

---

4 упойтелен – intoxicating
7 их пламенной зара́зы – their fiery infection (i.e., their infectious quality)

Кирджали – Kirdzhali

These twelve lines were apparently intended as an introduction to a lengthy poem about Georgii Kirdzhali, a Bulgarian who fought against the Turks and escaped to Moldavia after the disastrous defeat at Skulian in June of 1821. (This is the battle where Pushkin's Silvio, in the story "Выстрел" ["The Shot"] meets his death.) Pushkin had mentioned Kirdzhali in the poem "Чиновник и поэт" of 1823. In 1834 he would write (and publish) an excellent short story about him with a surprising and wholly fictive conclusion. The historical Kirdzhali (as against the one in Pushkin's story) was handed over to the Turks by the Russians in 1824 and put to death soon thereafter.

This unfinished fragment is written in iambic tetrameter with unpredictable rhyme scheme (the final line is an orphan). This was the standard form of Pushkin's narrative poems before 1830.

Title: In Bulgarian, the name Kirdzhali is stressed on the first syllable (on a back vowel that does not exist in Russian). Pushkin never indicated where he placed the stress (the poetic usage is ambiguous), so there is no consensus on this question.
1 Буджака́ – of Budzhak (sometimes spelled Budjak). Budzhak is a steppe region between the Prut and the Dniester rivers, located today in Moldova.
2 Прут, заветная река – Prut, the forbidden river. The Prut was the border between Turkish and Russian dominion. Pushkin's choice of modifier presumably reflects the river's role as boundary between the historical antagonists.
11 ратобо́рствуют – do battle. The word is distinctly high style.

Literature: Trubetskoi 1983, 317–19.

„А в нена́стные дни" – "And on gloomy days"

Originally included in a letter to Prince Viazemskii of 1 September 1828, the poem is famous because Pushkin would later use it as the first epigraph to his story "Пиковая дама" ("The Queen of Spades").

Metrically it is sufficiently unusual that one can point to a specific source: a humorous underground song by the Decembrist Kondratii Fedorovich Ryleev (1795–1826) that first appeared in print (abroad, no less) in 1865. (In underground copies of the 1850s Ryleev's poem was combined with Pushkin's, as if they were part of the same text.) Ryleev's verses begin:

> Ах, где те острова,
> Где растет трынь-трава <sic>,
> Братцы!
> Где читают Pucelle,
> И летят под постель
> Святцы.
>
> (Oh, where are those islands / Where it doesn't matter / Brothers! / Where *Pucelle* [Voltaire's popular blasphemous epic about Joan of Arc, a work banned in Russia] is read / And where under the bed / The Church Calendar flies.)

Pushkin's poem is thematically unrelated, but borrows the jocular tone (in addition to the distinctive meter). Formally it is somewhat more complicated. Ryleev's poem is in three-line stanzas of anapestic dimeter followed by a line of trochaic monometer, rhyme scheme a-a-B-c-c-B. Pushkin more or less follows this, but lines 7 and 8 are in anapestic monometer with hyperdactylic endings (i.e., the stress occurs four syllables from the end of the line). Strictly speaking, these lines do not rhyme, but they nonetheless are perceived as rhymes because of the lengthy identity of syllables following the same stressed vowel. Throughout Pushkin's poem, all of the masculine rhymes are on the vowel "и."

---

4 Гнули, <---> их <--->. Pushkin apparently wrote: "Гнули, мать их ети" ("They doubled the stakes, fuck their mother"). When he published the verses, he replaced these unprintable words with the more decorous: "Гнули, Бог их прости!" – ("They doubled the stakes, God forgive them"). "Гнуть" normally means "to bend," but in card playing it has the special meaning relevant here.

9 мелом – with chalk. Chalk was used in Russian card games to record the wins and losses after each hand.

12 делом – <their> business. The word usually means "work." There is some irony here, but the point is that, for serious card players, this is not pleasure, but business.

Literature: Oksman 1934, 509–10.

Предчу́вствие – A Foreboding

A very personal and agitated meditation. The cause of alarm, unclear in the poem, was actually unclear to Pushkin himself. Unbeknownst to him, his poem "Андрей Шенье" had recently come to the attention of the authorities, who viewed it as a statement of allegiance to the revolutionary aims of the Decembrists. (In fact, the poem predated the Decembrist rebellion and hence had no "topical" allusions.) Though unaware of the precise nature of the accusations leveled against him, Pushkin could not have failed to see that officials were eyeing him with suspicion. (One of the members of the government commission that evaluated the poem and recommended that Pushkin be placed under surveillance was Aleksei Nikolaevich Olenin. This incident was surely one of the factors that explain why Pushkin's marriage proposal to his daughter was rejected.)

The poem is written in eight-line stanzas of trochaic tetrameter, with alternating feminine/masculine rhymes. It is the identical form as "Утопленник." Salient differences in genre and style notwithstanding, the poems are linked in curious ways: the theme of impending doom, the return of punishment, the storm imagery (which is surprisingly common in Pushkin poems in this meter).

---

3 Рок зави́стливый – envious fate
7 Непрекло́нность – firmness
15 мой ангел – my angel. This is generally understood to be A. A. Olenina. The focus on her gaze (line 20) is strikingly reminiscent of the conclusion of "Ее глаза."
18 *прости́* – farewell. The italics are here the equivalent of putting the word in quotation marks.
19 Опеча́лься – grieve
21 твоё воспомина́нье – your recollection. What is presumably meant is "my recollection of you" rather than "your recollection of me." If it is the latter, then the poem adumbrates the later "Что в имени тебе моём?"
23 упова́нье – hope

Уто́пленник – The Drowned Man

The poem reflects Pushkin's interest in incorporating the simplicity of folk style into poetry, which he understood – mainly from his readings of French sources – to be the tendency in recent English Romantic verse (e.g., Wordsworth and Coleridge). In an unpublished essay of the time he complained about the backwardness of Russian taste: "Прелесть нагой простоты так еще для нас непонятна, что даже и в прозе мы гоняемся за обветшалыми украшениями … Поэзию же, освобожденную от условных украшений стихотворства, мы еще не понимаем." There is no direct folkloric source of "Утопленник," but subject matter, lexicon, and style place it squarely in the tradition of the ballad. Publications that appeared during Pushkin's life included subtitles that pointed directly at its folkloric qualities: "Простонародная песня" ("folk song") and "Простонародная сказка" ("folk tale").

The form is trochaic tetrameter, used often by Pushkin in folkorically stylized poems (cf. "Бесы" and "Зимний вечер," both of which also feature storms). The eight-line stanzas alternate feminine and masculine rhymes. The rhymes of the final two stanzas are carefully chosen for emphasis. The second masculine rhyme in the penultimate stanza carries through the entire final stanza. The rhyme word in the penultimate line of the penultimate stanza ("стучались") recurs in a different tense as the rhyme word of the penultimate line of the last stanza ("стучится").

---

2 В торопя́х (= Второпя́х) – hurriedly
3 Тятя! – Dad. (This is the way Russian peasant children addressed their father.)

5 Врите, врите, бесеня́та – You're talking nonsense, you little devils

7 Ох, уж эти мне робя́та! – Oh, how these kids <exhaust> me (i.e., I'm sick and tired of these kids). Note the substandard peasant speech variant "робята" instead of "ребята."

8 Будет вам ужо́ мертве́ц! – Just you wait and you'll really get a corpse!

9 Суд нае́дет, отвеча́й-ка – The law <officer> will show up, and we'll have to answer for it (a murder). The particle "-ка," is colloquial and modifies the force of an imperative.

10 С ним я век не разберу́сь – I'll never be able to clear myself

11 хозя́йка – wife

12 уж поплету́сь – I'll go drag myself along

19 Горемы́ка – wretch. The word is distinctly common, not literary.

20 Погуби́л свой грешный дух – killed himself

22 Али (= Или) хмельный молоде́ц – Or a drunken lad. The forms "али" (and "аль") are substandard folk forms inadmissible in traditional Russian verse. In modern Russian, the adjective would be stressed "хмельно́й."

23 Аль (= Иль) – Or

24 Недога́дливый – Slow-witted

25 Мужику́ како́е дело? – What does it matter to a peasant (i.e., to me)?

31–32 по́плыл снова / За моги́лой и кресто́м – again sailed off for his grave and his cross. The verb "по́плыл" (in modern Russian the stress is on the second syllable) does not necessarily imply volition, but it can have this meaning ("swam off"), which Pushkin plays on in line 34.

34 Плыл кача́ясь, как живо́й – Sailed (swam), rolling around, as if alive

38 Будет вам по калачу́ – Each of you will get a kalach. A kalach is a traditional round white bread. (Note the homophonic rhyme on "поколочу.")

39 Да смотри́те ж, не болта́йте – And look out, don't talk <about what you've seen>

40 А не то – Or else

43 лучи́на – a poor man's candle made of a long wood splinter

46 На пола́тях – on his bed. "Полати" refers to a specific type of raised bench in peasant huts that was used as a bed.

51 Каин – Cain. The name is presumably used as a curse word, but it of course calls to mind the archetypal fratricide in the Bible.

52 Чорт (= Чёрт) – The Devil

53 Где вози́ться мне с тобо́ю? – Why should I be bothering myself with you?

61 Всё в нем страшно онеме́ло – Everything went terribly numb in him. This line (like the others in this stanza) describes the drowned man, but in such a way as if he were not dead. Cf. commentary to lines 31–34.

63 распу́хнувшее тело – swollen body. In modern Russian, the form would be "распухшее."

65 захло́пнул – slammed shut

67 Так и обмер: „Чтоб ты лопнул!" – He became motionless: "A pox on you!" (The "muzhik" wishes that his [dead] visitor will die.) Note that the verb "лопнуть" ("to explode") can connote a body swollen from drowning that can literally burst.

70 Трясся ночь он напролёт – He trembled the night through

71 И до у́тра всё стуча́лись – And a knocking continued all night until morn-

ing. The grammatical construction avoids any indication of who is knocking (though we – and the protagonist – presume it is the drowned man). In modern Russian, the stress would be "до утрá."

72 под окнóм – at the window (the preposition "под" need not be understood literally as "under")

76 В день урóчный – On the appointed day (i.e., on the anniversary)

„Рифма, звучная подрýга" – "Rhyme, sonorous friend"

This is the first of two poems – the other being "Рифма" (1830) – devoted to a mythological figure named Rhyme. Both poems describe the birth of Rhyme in Greek antiquity. Such a genealogy is anachronistic, since classical poetics did not know rhyme (which first became an organizing principle of European verse in the medieval period). Pushkin introduces his fanciful genealogy in subjunctive (lines 25–33), but cleverly removes the subjunctive beginning in line 34.

While the mythological setting is entirely Pushkin's invention, the idea of addressing Rhyme comes from Sainte-Beuve, in a poem first published in 1828 called "À la rime." Pushkin's poem departs in obvious ways from that of Sainte-Beuve, but he borrows several elements – most notably, the eroticized treatment of the masculine poet and feminine Rhyme. (Conveniently, the word "rhyme" is of feminine gender in both French and Russian.) Still more important: Pushkin borrows the unusual six-line stanza of a-a-b-c-c-b (this was a common form in French Renaissance poetry; one of Sainte-Beuve's goals was revive such "fixed forms"). Instead of the exclusively masculine rhymes of the French, Pushkin alternates feminine and masculine rhymes (A-A-b-C-C-b). He also changes the alternating line lengths of the French, using trochaic tetrameter throughout. Both poets, in keeping with the subject, use great ingenuity in producing clever and unexpected rhymes (at times more than the rhyme scheme demands). Pushkin structures his poem in two groups of four stanzas each: the first is a lover's plaint that concerns the recent past and present, the second the "genealogy" of rhyme set in hoary antiquity.

Pushkin owned the book *Œuvres choisies de Pierre de Ronsard avec notice, notes et commentaires, par C. A. Sainte-Beuve* (Paris, 1828), where Sainte-Beuve published "À la rime" under his own name as an "homage" on pp. 50–52.

Rime, qui donnes leurs sons
    Aux chansons;
Rime, l'unique harmonie
Du vers, qui, sans tes accents
    Frémissants,
Serait muet au génie;

Rime, écho qui prends la voix
    Du hautbois,
Ou l'éclat de la trompette;
Dernier adieu d'un ami,
    Qu'à demi
L'autre ami de loin répète;

Rime, tranchant aviron,
  Éperon
Qui fends la vague écumante;
Frein d'or, aiguillon d'acier
  Du coursier
A la crinière fumante;

Agrafe, autour des seins nus
  De Vénus
Pressant l'écharpe divine,
Ou serrant le baudrier
  Du guerrier
Contre sa forte poitrine;

Col étroit, par où saillit
  Et jaillit
La source au ciel élancée,
Qui, brisant l'éclat vermeil
  Du soleil,
Tombe en gerbe nuancée;

Anneau pur de diamant,
  Ou d'aimant,
Qui, jour et nuit, dans l'enceinte
Suspends la lampe, ou le soir
  L'encensoir
Aux mains de la Vierge sainte;

Clé qui, loin de l'œil mortel,
  Sur l'autel
Ouvres l'arche du miracle,
Ou tiens le vase embaumé
  Renfermé
Dans le cèdre au tabernacle;

Ou plutôt, Fée au léger
  Voltiger,
Habile, agile courrière,
Qui mène le char des vers
  Dans les airs
Par deux sillons de lumière;

O Rime! qui que tu sois,
  Je reçois
Ton joug; et, longtemps rebelle,
Corrigé, je te promets
  Désormais
Une oreille plus fidèle.

Mais aussi devant mes pas
  Ne fuis pas;

Quand la Muse me dévore.
Donne, donne par égard
    Un regard
Au poète qui t'implore!

Dans un vers tout défleuri,
    Qu'a flétri
L'aspect d'une règle austère,
Ne laisse point murmurer,
    Soupirer,
La syllabe solitaire.

Sur ma lyre, l'autre fois,
    Dans un bois,
Ma main préludait à peine;
Une colombe descend,
    En passant,
Blanche sur le luth d'ébène.

Mais au lieu d'accords touchants,
    De doux chants,
La colombe gémissante
Me demande par pitié
    Sa moitié,
Sa moitié loin d'elle absente.

Ah! plutôt, oiseaux charmants,
    Vrais amants,
Mariez vos voix jumelles;
Que ma lyre et ses concerts
    Soient couverts
De vos baisers, de vos ailes;

Ou bien, attelés d'un crin
    Pour tout frein
Au plus léger des nuages,
Traînez-moi, coursiers chéris
    De Cypris,
Au fond des sacrés bocages.

In addition, "Рифма" has sources in German literature that Pushkin had recently encountered in translation: Goethe's *Faust* (the "rhyming scene," where Faust meets Helen of Troy) as well as Schiller (Khitrova, 86–91). Pushkin's poem is also connected to his own *Eugene Onegin* (6:XLIII, lines 6–8), written at the end of 1826.

---

6 Измени́ла – you betrayed [me]
7 прежни дни (=прежние дни)
8 серде́чный – amorous
18 С нею (=с мечто́й) – like "рифма," "мечта" is personified
26 на́ небе – in heaven (the stress falls on the preposition)

27 Олимпи́йская – of [Mount] Olympus, home of the gods according to Greek mythology
28 с нею (=с семьёй)
32 пове́дали – made known
33 Гезио́д – Hesiod – traditionally viewed as being in competition with Homer – was, like Homer, one the earliest Greek poets whose work has survived.
Оми́р – one of the possible renderings of the name Homer in Russian. Proskurin (2007, 124–25) points out that in the years before 1820, battles had raged as to whether the name should be transcribed as the Europeanized "Омер" or the "Church Slavic" variant "Омир." By the 1820s, thanks to Gnedich's translation of the *Iliad*, "Гомер" became the standard form. Pushkin's use of "Омир" in a poem of 1828 would thus have sounded archaic. (On a strictly poetic level, it also picks up the "rhyme" from ми́ру in the previous line).
The names of Hesiod and Homer were probably linked in Pushkin's mind because of Batiushkov's poem "Гезиод и Омир, соперники" (1816–1817), a translation of Charles Millevoye's "Combat d'Homère et d'Hésiode."
34 Феб – Phoebus Apollo, "god of the lyre and reed pipe, god of light and verse" (as he is described in lines 41–42)
Адме́та – Admetus. The mythological basis of this section is an episode where Apollo fell out of favor with Zeus, who transformed him (for one year) into a mortal and forced him to tend the flocks of King Admetus.
35 Тайге́та – Taygetus (a mountain range in Southern Greece)
38 страша́сь Зеве́са (=Зевса) – fearing Zeus
45 Мнемози́на притекла́ – Mnemosyne (mother of the Muses) approached. Pushkin uses "течь" in the archaic sense, meaning "идти," to give his myth the appropriate stylistic coloration.
46 в тихой роще – in a quiet grove (cf. the "sacrés bocages" ["sacred groves"] in the final line of Sainte-Beuve's poem)
Гелико́на – of Helicon (the Greek mountain associated with Apollo and the Muses)

Literature: Achinger 2000, 47–48; Khitrova.

<Б. М. Фёдорову> – To B. M. Fedorov

Boris Mikhailovich Fedorov (1798–1875) was a significant figure in the Russian literary world whom Pushkin met on many occasions, but a poet and critic of modest talents. It is not known whether Pushkin refers here to a specific incident or to his work in general. The poem was not published in Pushkin's lifetime.

It is composed of two iambic hexameter (alexandrine) lines. The caesura after the third foot is in both cases a syntactic break.

---

1 Полжа́луй, Федоров, ко мне – Be so kind, Fedorov, to my house. The opening words sound like a friendly welcome until they are ironically undercut by "не приходи́."
2 иль (=или) после не буди́ – or don't wake <me> up afterwards

„Ворон к ворону лети́т" – "A raven flies to a raven"

In 1802, Sir Walter Scott published under the title *Minstrelsy of the Scottish Border* a collection of "historical and romantic ballads" that he himself had collected. Among them was a poem called "The Twa Corbies" ("corbie" is Scottish for "raven").

As I was walking all alane,
I heard twa corbies making a mane;
The tane unto the t'other say,
"Where sall we gang and dine to-day?"

"In behint yon auld fail dyke,
I wot there lies a new-slain knight;
And naebody kens that he lies there,
But his hawk, his hound, and lady fair.

"His hound is to the hunting gane,
His hawk to fetch the wild-fowl hame,
His lady's ta'en another mate,
So we may mak our dinner sweet.

"Ye'll sit on his white hause-bane,
And I'll pike out his bonny blue een;
Wi' ae lock o' his gowden hair,
We'll theek our nest when it grows bare.

"Mony a one for him makes mane,
But nane sall ken where he is gane;
O'er his white banes, when they are bare,
The wind sall blaw for evermair."

Scott glosses some words (though not as many as one might wish):
Fail – Turf
Hause – Neck
Theek – Thatch

Pushkin surely could not have understood the English original without the aid of his French prose translation. In the edition in Pushkin's library (*Chants populaires des frontières méridionales de l'écosse*, Paris, 1826), the following translation is found in volume 3, pages 216–17.

⇴Les deux corbeaux

Comme je me promenais tout seul, j'entendis deux corbeaux se parler; l'un dit à son camarade: "Où irons-nous dîner aujourd'hui."

– "Derrière ce vieux mur en terre, gît un chevalier nouvellement tué, et personne ne sait qu'il gît en ce lieu, excepté son épervier, son chien et sa dame.

Son chien est allé à la chasse; son épervier lie pour un autre maître les oiseaux sauvages; sa dame a pris un autre serviteur; ainsi, nous pourrons faire un bon dîner.

Toi, tu te percheras sur sa blanche poitrine; moi, je lui arracherai avec mon bec ses beaux yeux bleus, et des boucles de ses cheveux blonds nous boucherons les fentes de nos nids.

De ses amis plus d'un mène grand deuil, mais nul ne saura jamais où il est tombé; et sur ses os dépouillés et blanchis, les vents souffleront toujours."

As usual, Pushkin adapted (and truncated) his source. Moreover, he viewed it through the prism of Russian folklore, using trochaic tetrameter with pair rhymes alternating masculine and feminine (cf. his later "Сказка о царе Салтане" ["Tale of Tsar Saltan"]), simple syntax, numerous lexical repetitions, and a host of words (e.g., "хозяйка" for "wife") and phrases (e.g., "в чистом поле") distinctive to Russian folklore. Pushkin's poem itself influenced later Russian translations of Scott's ballad (see Oksman 1922, 34).

---

7 В чистом поле под раки́той – In the open field under a willow

8 Богаты́рь – warrior (hero of Russian folklore)

11 Да кобы́лка ворона́я – and <his> black mare. Note the diminutive ("кобы́лка" for "кобы́ла"), typical of Russian folklore, which is not related to size, but rather reflects tenderness in the attitude of the speaker toward the object. The adjective "вороно́й," meaning "black" (and etymologically related to ворон) is used exclusively about horses.

15 А хозя́йка ждёт мило́го – But <his> wife awaits her beloved. In modern Russian, the stress would fall on the first syllable of "милого."

16 Не уби́того, живо́го – Not murdered, but alive. Phrases such as this (a negative, followed by its opposite) are common in Russian folklore.

Literature: Lobanova; Oksman 1922.

„Город пышный, город бедный" – "Splendid city, poor city"

The eponymous city of contradictions is Petersburg, but the emphasis of the poem is on a single inhabitant, A. A. Olenina. In this spirit of synecdoche, she is not named, but represented only by a single foot and a single curl of her hair.

The poem is written in trochaic tetrameter with alternating rhymes. The tone changes markedly in the final four lines (the diminutives and verbs stand out against the severe and monumental setting of the verbless opening).

---

2 дух нево́ли – spirit of servitude. Pushkin often used this epithet in connection with the capital city, for example: "Оставить был совсем готов / Неволю невских берегов" (from "К Языкову," a poem that predates "Город пышный" by a few months).

4 грани́т – granite. Granite is a fundamental feature of the Petersburg cityscape, as it was used to create the embankments. "В гранит оделася Нева" ("The Neva clothed itself in granite") as Pushkin writes in "Медный всадник" ("The Bronze Horseman").

5 вас – the antecedent is plural, including all of the nouns in the first four lines
7 ножка – foot. The word can also mean "leg," but Pushkin appears to have used it only in the sense of "foot." See Nabokov's comments (2:115–16) on the "pedal digression" in the first chapter of *Eugene Onegin*.
8 Вьётся локон золотóй – A lock of golden hair curls. One assumes that Olenina had blonde hair (cf. Rice, 20–21).

Literature: Rice, 18–24.

<Из альбóма А. П. Керн> – From the Album of A. P. Kern

Not all Pushkin editions group these five poems under this heading, and there is good reason to question such editorial practice. The first three probably were indeed written in the (long-lost) album of Anna Petrovna Kern, née Poltoratskaia (1800–1879). The other two are connected to Kern, but their provenance and even – in the case of the final poem – authorship is disputed. Anna Petrovna Kern was in her youth an extraordinary beauty, who was forced to marry a man much older, for whom she had little interest. She was immortalized in Russian cultural history as the dedicatee of Pushkin's celebrated 1825 love poem "Я помню чудное мгновенье," in which she appears as a muse and almost a goddess. However, in his letters, a different picture emerges. Writing to A. K. Vul'f on 7 May 1826 Pushkin calls Anna Petrovna "наша Вавилонская блудница" ("our whore of Babylon") and, a few years later, in February of 1828, he comments to his friend Sobolevskii: "Ты ничего не пишешь мне о 2100 р., мною тебе должных, а пишешь мне о M-me Kern, которую с помощию божией я на днях уеб." ("You aren't writing me about the 2100 rubles that I owe you, but you write me about Mme Kern, whom a few days ago with God's help, I fucked.") The seeming contradiction can be explained; for Pushkin a love poem and a personal letter were two completely different genres, each of which depended on the addressee for its tone and style.

The first three poems are known only from Kern's memoirs, which were published in 1859. In them she explains that Pushkin once took her album and began translating the poems in them from French to Russian and vice versa.

1. „Если в жизни поднебéсной" – "If in earthly life"

Pushkin was responding to the following lines:

Oh, si dans l'immortelle vie
Il existait un être parfait,
Oh, mon aimable et douce amie,
Comme toi sans doute il est fait – etc. etc.

(Oh, if in the immortal life / There exists a perfect being, / O, my dear and sweet <woman> friend, / It would be without doubt like you – etc. etc.)

The French text is in eight-syllable lines with alternating rhymes. Pushkin translates this into trochaic tetrameters with couplet rhymes, which become increasingly ridiculous and which end with an unrhymed fifth line.

---

4 Я скажу́ тебе́ резо́н – I will tell you the reason. "Резон" is a Gallicism.

2. „Amour, exil" – "Love, exile"

Another (mediocre) poem in Kern's album apparently had the phrase "Ecrit dans mon exil" ("Written in my exile") written beneath it, and Pushkin created out of it a two-line iambic dimeter couplet. The rhyme of French and Russian creates a comic effect, especially given the Romantic associations of exile (thanks in large part to Pushkin's own lyrics from the southern period).

---

2 гиль – nonsense. The word is rarely used and distinctly unpoetic. (This is the only instance in all of Pushkin's work.)

3. „Не смею вам стихи́ Барко́ва" – "I do not dare <to translate> for you Barkov's verses"

The third poem had been written by an acquaintance of Pushkin, the minor poet Dmitrii Nikolaevich Barkov (1796–1855). Rather than responding to that, Pushkin focuses on the poet's surname; a different Barkov (Ivan Semenovich, 1732–1768) was widely known for his pornographic verse. Pushkin's horror at the mention of Barkov's name is of course feigned; he was thoroughly familiar with these works and may have been the author of a pornographic poem entitled "Тень Баркова" ("Barkov's Shade") while still at the Lyceum. (On this controversy, see Tsiavlovskii 1993 and Esipov 2005). Pushkin's poem to Kern is in iambic tetrameter with alternating rhymes. The rhyme pair перевесть/произнесть (rather than перевести/произнести) is probably intended to recall eighteenth-century usage.

---

2 Благопристо́йно – decorously; decently

4. „Когда́, стройна́ и светлоо́ка" – "When, slender and fair-eyed"

The fourth poem is known only through the memoirs of the minor poet Andrei Ivanovich Podolinskii (1806–1886), which were published in 1872. He explains that the first two lines of the poem were a citation (hence the italics) from his own poem "Портрет," dedicated to Anna Petrovna Kern. (Strictly speaking, the first two and a half lines are cited, and other things are borrowed or developed.) Podolinskii's poem was published – without dedication – in 1829 in the almanac "Подснежник"

("Snowdrop") on pages 257–58. The date of Pushkin's poem is uncertain; he might have known Podolinskii's poem from an album copy or from a recitation before it appeared in print.

Когда, стройна и светлоока,
Передо мной стоит она,
Я мыслю: гурия пророка
С небес на землю сведена.
Коса и кудри темнорусы,
Наряд небрежный и простой,
И на груди роскошной бусы
Роскошно зыблются порой.
Весны и лета сочетанье
В живом огне ее очей,
И тихий звук ее речей
Раждает <sic> негу и желанье
В груди тоскующей моей.

---

3 в день Ильи́-проро́ка – On the day of Il'ia the Prophet. The day of Il'ia the Prophet is celebrated on 2 August. A Christian holiday with obvious links to pagan traditions, the day is accompanied by all sorts of prohibitions; none, however, concern marriage or divorce.

4 Она́ была́ разведена́ – She was divorced. Anna Petrovna Kern and her husband were estranged, but not divorced. The fact that she received her husband's pension after his death (she forfeited it only when she remarried) indicates that they did not divorce. (Veresaev, 2:46).

5. „Вези́, вези́, не жале́й" / „Мне изю́м" – "Give <me> a ride, Give <me> a ride, you won't regret it" / "A raisin for me"

This final poem, which is composed of two parts, but is treated as two separate poems in the Academy edition, is mysterious. It is the only one in this group that exists in Pushkin's own hand, written on the back of the first (blank) page of a French translation of the first-century Latin poet Publius Papinius Statius. However, under the verses are Anna Petrovna Kern's initials (*not* Pushkin's) and, in her hand, the date of 19 October 1828. This suggests either that Kern added the dedication to herself at the end of the poem (an unconventional practice, to say the least) or, as Berezkina (1995, 120) hypothesizes, that Kern herself composed at least some of these lines.

The poem is in two parts, and in the absence of context, it is difficult to see a precise link (beyond their flirtatious tone). Both parts draw on folk culture. The first two lines echo a common saying of the time: "Купи, денег не жалей – Со мной ездить веселей" ("Buy <it>, don't regret the cost – It's more fun to go with me.") The fact that these lines (and Pushkin's imitation) are not written in a syllabo-tonic meter further suggests that the origin is folkloric (rather than literary). This couplet is followed by a straight line (presumably written by Pushkin) that separates it from the second part. That next passage (if rearranged slightly) scans as four lines of iambic tetrameter couplets. These are borrowed from a traditional popular song (note the metrical irregularities in the first two lines that Pushkin smoothed out):

> Ходи, миленькой, почаще,
> Носи пряничков послаще,
> Винограду,
> Хоть для взгляду,
> А изюму –
> Ради уму!

---

2 Нейдёт на ум – doesn't come to mind (i.e., I can't think about it)
3 Цуккербро́д – sugar bread (from the German "Zuckerbrot")
4 Не лезет в рот – does not enter my mouth
5 Пастила́ – a confection made of fruit
6 Без тебя́, моя́ душа́ – Without you, my dear. The phrase is a direct address (vocative case). The point is that nothing tastes good if Kern is absent.

<19 октября́ 1828> – 19 October 1828

One of Pushkin's less serious anniversary poems, it is based on the principle of anticlimax. The first two celebratory lines are undercut by the conclusion. One frequently encounters the claim that this was the first reunion that Pushkin attended since his exile; however, he had also attended the event in 1827.

The poem consists of a single quatrain of iambic tetrameter with alternating feminine/masculine rhymes.

---

2 Лице́ю прокрича́в *ура́* – Having shouted "Hurray" to the Lyceum. The word "ура" is in italics as the equivalent to quotation marks.
3 Проща́йте, братцы: мне в доро́гу – Farewell, friends, <it's time> for me to set off. In contrast to the other festivity participants, who, as line 4 suggests, were planning to go home to sleep, Pushkin set off that same evening (after the anniversary celebration) on a trip to Mikhailovskoe.

„Уроди́лся я, бедный недоно́сок" – "I was born a wretched, premature baby"

An unfinished fragment of folkloric stylization, the text looks ahead to the "Песни западных славян" ("Songs of the Western Slavs"), and it recalls one of the Russian folksongs that Pushkin took down and ultimately gave to P. V. Kireevskii, a collector of folklore. (There is some dispute as to whether that particular text is a genuine folksong or an invention of Pushkin; see Tomashevskii 1926, 41–42 and Speranskii 1930, 97n2). Regardless of its status, the poem clearly shares its theme and, in places, its lexicon with this fragment.

Уродился я несчастлив, бесталанлив:
Приневолили меня, малёшенька женили;
Молода была жена, я глупенек,
Стал я молодцем – жена стала старенька.
Полюбилась мне молодка молодая,
Иссушила мое сердце ретивое.
Как вечёр меня молодка огорчила,
Мне несносную насмешку насмеяла:
– Отступися, мне сказала, отвяжися,
У тебя своя жена, с ней и целуйся! –
Во бору-ли, во сыром-ли стук, треск:
Бурлачки сосну подрубливают,
Подрубливают, поваливают;
Из сыра бора по лугу́ волокут,
По крутому бережку покатывают,
Середь лодочки устанавливают,
Тонкий парус навешивают,
Уплывают вниз по Волге по реке.
Вы постойте, добры молодцы, погодите,
Вы с собой меня возьмите, посадите,
Разлучите с опостылой со женою.

Like the folk song, Pushkin's poem is a three-ictus "тактовик" without rhyme. The lines in his "Уродился я, бедный" all end in a feminine cadence, while the folkloric model "Уродился я несчастлив" is more varied in its line endings.

---

1 Недоно́сок – a baby born premature. The word "Недоносок" appears in genuine folkloric texts. See Lerner's footnote in Tomashevskii 1926, 41.
2 С глупых лет брожу́ я сирото́ю – From my earliest years I wander as an orphan. The expression "с глупых лет" is found in another folkloric stylization, the first of the "Песни о Стеньке Разине" („Как по Волге реке, по широкой"), line 13.
3 Недорослем – While a minor (i.e., not yet of age)
5 Суда́рыня жена́ не приласка́ла – My wife, the mistress, didn't caress <me>. In this line "сударыня" is more or less equivalent to "жена" (such a repetition is typical in Russian folklore). The line itself is an example of litotes (understatement).

Literature: Tomashevskii 1926, 41–42.

„В прохла́де сладостной фонта́нов" – "In the sweet coolness of the fountains"

This poem, not published in Pushkin's lifetime, is somewhat mysterious. It contrasts "Eastern" poets with a still greater poet from another land. The latter poet is described briefly and hence not obviously identifiable. However, the most probable candidate is Adam Mickiewicz, whose presence is hinted at by a complicated series of references to the Crimea. Pushkin had put the Crimea on the literary map in the early 1820s with his narrative poem “Бахчисарайский фонтан” (“The Fountain of Bakhchisarai”). Mickiewicz developed the tradition with a cycle of “Crimean Sonnets” in 1826, which, when translated into Russian prose by Prince Viazemskii, contributed towards establishing his fame in Russia. In those sonnets, Mickiewicz had included a note in praise of Pushkin’s Crimean poem.

---

3 Поэ́т быва́ло тешил ханов – The poet used to amuse the khans

4 Стихо́в гремýчим жемчуго́м – With the resounding pearl of his verses. The comparison of poetry to precious stones (as again in line 7) is probably a stylization of Eastern poetry. A similar image can be found in the closing lines of the eighth (final) chapter of Saadi’s *Gulistan*: “it is, however, not concealed from enlightened men … that pearls of curative admonition are strung upon the thread of explanation.” It is not known what (French) edition of this work Pushkin consulted. In modern Russian the stress falls on the first syllable of “жемчугом.”

5 нити – threads

6 Низа́л – threaded

7 Прозра́чной лести ожере́лья – necklaces of transparent flattery

8 чётки – beads

9 сыны́ Саа́ди – the sons of Saadi. The plural form “сыны” is high style and is to be understood metaphorically, as followers of Saadi, poets in Saadi’s tradition.

10 краснoба́й – rhymester. The word is usually pejorative, suggesting empty rhetoric.

12 Бахчисара́й – Bakhchisarai, the Crimean setting of Pushkin’s famous narrative poem

14 эрива́нские ковры́ – carpets of Erevan, presumably what we would now call “Persian carpets.” In modern Russian “Эриван” is spelled “Ереван.”

16 Гире́ев – of Gireis. Girei (or Girai) was a standard name of Crimean khans (Proskurin 2007, 309–10).

21 прозорли́вый <и> крыла́тый – far-sighted and inspired

22 Поэ́т той чудной стороны́ – Poet of that wondrous land. Assuming the poet to be Mickiewicz, the wondrous land would be Lithuania.

23 мужи грозны и косма́ты – the men are fearsome and shaggy. Pushkin had used the unusual epithet “косматый” to describe the helmets made of lynx fur worn by Lithuanian warriors in his 1828 translation of Mickiewicz (see “Сто лет минуло,” line 21). In modern Russian, the stress would be “мужи́.”

24 А жёны гуриям равны́ – And the women are equal to huris. A huri is a beautiful maiden who awaits the devout Muslim in paradise.

Literature: Izmailov 1975, 125–73.

Клеопа́тра – Cleopatra

This poem is well known because editors traditionally place it at the end of the (unfinished) story “Египетские ночи” (“Egyptian Nights”). Though Pushkin did not explicitly indicate that this was his intent, it certainly is logical that some version of this poem was to be recited by the Italian *improvisatore*. See commentary to "Сонет," line 11.

The source of Pushkin's Cleopatra story is the book *De viris illustribus urbis Romae* (*Of Illustrious Men of the City of Rome*), usually ascribed to Sextus Aurelius Victor, an obscure fourth-century historian. As Lotman has noted (1997, 362–64), Pushkin's awareness of this author and his retelling of this striking episode from Cleopatra's life almost certainly comes from the brief reference to it in Rousseau's *Emile*. Once Pushkin came across that passage, he surely looked up the original source.

In an unfinished story called "Мы проводили вечер на даче" (written in 1835), Pushkin explicitly discussed this subject:

> Надобно знать, что в числе латинских историков есть некто Аврелий Виктор, о котором, вероятно, вы никогда не слыхивали.
> – Aurelius Victor? – прервал Вершнев, который учился некогда у езуитов, – Аврелий Виктор, писатель четвертого столетия. Сочинения его приписываются Корнелию Непоту и даже Светонию; он написал книгу de Viris illustribus – о знаменитых мужах города Рима, знаю …
> – Точно так, – продолжал Алексей Иваныч, – книжонка его довольно ничтожна, но в ней находится то сказание о Клеопатре, которое так меня поразило. И, что замечательно, в этом месте сухой и скучный Аврелий Виктор силою выражения равняется Тациту: *Haec tantae libidinis fuit ut saepe prostiterit; tantae pulchritudinis ut muiti noctem illius morte emerint* (<She was known for such vice that she often sold herself; such was her beauty that many purchased a night with her at the cost of their lives>) …
> – Дело в том, что Клеопатра торговала своею красотою, и что многие купили ее ночи ценою своей жизни.

Pushkin had first written a poem on this theme in 1824; the version under consideration here represents a revision, in which the free iambs of 1824 are rejected in favor of strict iambic tetrameter (though in sections of uneven length). Until line 36, the rhyme scheme alternates feminine and masculine; after that point, it becomes unpredictable. Cleopatra's final speech (lines 58–73) is marked by an incredibly consistent realization of the iambic tetrameter; with one exception, all lines have an identical stress pattern (in which the first, second, and fourth ictuses are always stressed). In the exceptional line, only the first and fourth bear stress. The function of this repetition is open to interpretation, but there can be no doubt that it was done intentionally. (See Kolmogorov and Rychkova, 382.)

---

1 Греме́ли хором – sung out in chorus

5 Сердца́ несли́сь к её престо́лу – hearts rushed to her throne (i.e., everyone was attracted by her)

7 долу – downwards

8 Пони́кла дивною главо́й (=дивной головой) – <she> lowered her beautiful head

15 раве́нство – equality. In modern Russian, the stress is on the first syllable.

17 Кто к торгу страстному присту́пит – Who is ready to take on this passionate trade

20 Цено́ю (=Ценой) жизни – at the price of <his> life
21 Рекла́ – и ужас всех объе́млет – She spoke – and horror envelops everyone
29 Смела́ их поступь – Their gait is daring (i.e., they walk forward without fear)
36 Выхо́дят жребии чредо́й (=чередой) – The lots come out in order
38 В дружи́нах римских поседе́лый – having grayed in the Roman battalions
39 от жены́ – from a woman (i.e., from Cleopatra). The editors of the *Словарь языка Пушкина* understand this to mean "from <his> wife," which would introduce a domestic motivation for his acceptance of Cleopatra's offer.
45 в рощах Эпику́ра – in the groves of Epikouros. The Greek philosopher Epikouros (fourth and third centuries BCE) was the founder of Epicureanism, the philosophy of hedonism. He is not ordinarily associated with groves.
47 Хари́т, Кипри́ды и Аму́ра – of the Graces, of Aphrodite and of Cupid. Pushkin mixes Greek and Roman mythology. Aphrodite will be invoked by Cleopatra herself in line 62.
49 Как вешний цвет – Like a vernal flower
50–51 После́дний имени века́м / Не переда́л – The last <of the three> did not leave his name to the ages (i.e., his name has been forgotten).
51–52 Его лани́ты / Пух первый нежно отеня́л – The first fluff <of hair> delicately shaded his cheeks
58 Кляну́сь, о матерь наслажде́ний – I swear, o mother of pleasures
59 неслы́ханно – in an unprecedented way
60–61 На ложе страстных искуше́ний / Просто́й наёмницей всхожу́ – As a simple bought woman I enter the bed of passionate temptations
64 О боги грозного Аида – O gods of dread Hades
70 Но только утренней порфи́рой – But as soon as with its morning porphyry
71 Авро́ра – Aurora, goddess of dawn
72 под смертною (=смертной) секи́рой – under the fatal axe
73 Глава́ (=Голова) – the head
74 сокры́лся день – day <light> has hidden itself
75 Восхо́дит месяц златоро́гий – the golden-horned moon ascends. A "horned moon" ("рогатый месяц") is a standard Russian expression, depicting the shape of a new moon. The epithet "златорогий" is a consciously archaic word formation, recalling Homeric epithets (e.g., "rosy-fingered dawn").
76 Александри́йские – of Alexandria
78 Фонта́ны бьют – the fountains splash
79 Кури́тся лёгкий фимиа́м – the light (i.e., weightless) incense smokes
81 Земны́м гото́вятся бога́м – Are prepared for the earthly gods
82 В роско́шном сумрачном поко́е – In the luxurious dark room
84 Под сенью пурпурных заве́с – Under the cover of purple curtains. In modern Russian, the stress is "пурпу́ных."

Анча́р – The Upas-Tree

This dark poem reflects Pushkin's thoughts on the origin of evil. The title is mysterious even to Russians; it would appear that this was the first time the word "анчар" was used in Russian. Pushkin himself felt it necessary to gloss it as "Древо яда" –

literally: "Tree of Poison." (Actually, in the first publication it was not a gloss, but simply a part of the title: "Анчар, древо яда.") Readers familiar with English poetry will note striking similarities to Blake's "A Poison Tree" (from *Songs of Experience*, 1794), but it is highly unlikely that Pushkin was aware of its existence. Yet the English tradition is relevant: first of all, the upas tree appears in the fourth canto, stanza CXXVI, of Byron's *Childe Harold*, a work that Pushkin knew well:

Our life is a false nature – 'tis not in
The harmony of things, – this hard decree,
This uneradicable taint of sin,
This boundless upas, this all-blasting tree,
Whose root is earth, whose leaves and branches be
The skies which rain their plagues on men like dew –
Disease, death, bondage – all the woes we see –
And worse, the woes we see not – which throb through
The immedicable soul, with heart-aches ever new.

In the Pichot translation that Pushkin was likely to have read, the passage reads as follows:

Notre vie est une fausse nature ... elle n'est pas dans l'harmonie universelle ... Pourquoi ce terrible décret porté contre nous? pourquoi cette tache ineffaçable du péché? Nous sommes sous un arbre destructeur, sous un Upas aux vastes rameaux: sa racine est toute la terre; ses branches et ses feuilles sont les cieux, qui distillent sur l'homme, comme une rosée, leurs intarissables fléaux; la maladie, la mort, l'esclavage, tous les maux que nous voyons, et, plus funestes encore, ceux que nous ne voyons pas, assiégent l'âme par des tortures renouvelées sans cesse.

In the manuscript copy of the poem, there is an epigraph (in English) from Coleridge's tragedy *Remorse*: "It is a poison-tree that pierced to the inmost / Weeps only tears of poison." In some Coleridge editions these lines serve as the epigraph to that play; Pushkin would not have had to read the play to discover them. (Gustafson, 104). Regardless of the edition he read, however, it would not have required much persistence to happen on this passage, as it appears very early in the first act (lines 21–25):

Remorse is as the heart in which it grows:
If that be gentle, it drops balmy dews
Of true repentance; but if proud and gloomy,
It is a poison-tree, that pierced to the inmost
Weeps only tears of poison!

Coleridge's poison tree is not explicitly an upas, and the broader context of his quote (the theme of remorse) has no significance for Pushkin's poem. This may explain why Pushkin ultimately opted to omit the Coleridge epigraph.

In any case, the primary source for Pushkin's interest in the upas tree was a work of a far lesser English poet, Erasmus Darwin (1731–1802), also a botanist (grandfather of Charles Darwin), who in his long poem "The Loves of the Plants" (published 1789) had popularized views purportedly by a Dutch surgeon named N. P. Foersch. This "scholarly" tract was in fact a deliberate mystification created by the Shakespearean scholar and practical joker George Steevens (1736–1800). (See the entry for "upas" in the *Oxford English Dictionary*.) Steevens' alter ago Foersch had a lively and sadistic imagination (he gives "eyewitness" accounts of people being tortured by this devastating poison and claims to have used it himself to administer grisly experiments on numerous animals). Darwin was apparently skeptical of Foersch's account, but nonetheless took it seriously enough to include it in its entirety as an appendix to his poem (which was retained in the French translation that Pushkin read).

The relevant passage in Darwin is in canto 3, lines 219–58:

Where seas of glass with gay reflections smile
Round the green coasts of Java's palmy isle;
A spacious plain extends its upland scene,
Rocks rise on rocks, and fountains gush between;
Soft zephyrs blow, eternal summers reign,
And showers prolific bless the soil, – in vain!
– No spicy nutmeg scents the vernal gales,
Nor towering plaintain shades the mid-day vales;
No grassy mantle hides the sable hills,
No flowery chaplet crowns the trickling rills;
Nor tufted moss, nor leathery lichen creeps
In russet tapestry o'er the crumbling steeps.
– No step retreating, on the sand impress'd,
Invites the visit of a second guest;
No refluent fin the unpeopled stream divides,
No revolant pinion cleaves the airy tides;
Nor handed moles, nor beaked worms return,
That mining pass the irremeable <sic> bourn. –
Fierce in dread silence on the blasted heath
Fell UPAS sits, the HYDRA-TREE of death.
Lo; from one root, the envenom'd soil below,
A thousand vegetative serpents grow;
In shining rays the scaly monster spreads
O'er ten square leagues his far-diverging heads;
Or in one trunk entwists his tangled form,
Looks o'er the clouds, and hisses in the storm.
Steep'd in fell poison, as his sharp teeth part,
A thousand tongues in quick vibration dart;
Snatch the proud Eagle towering o'er the heath,
Or pounce the Lion, as he stalks beneath;
Or strew, as marshall'd hosts contend in vain,
With human skeletons the whiten'd plain.
– Chain'd at his root two scion-demons dwell,
Breathe the faint hiss, or try the shriller yell;
Rise, fluttering in the air on callow wings,

And aim at insect-prey their little stings.
So Time's strong arms with sweeping scythe erase
Art's cumberous works, and empires, from their base;
While each young Hour its sickle fine employs,
And crops the sweet buds of domestic joys!

To this description Darwin appended a note:

> Upas. 1. 238. There is a poison-tree in the island of Java, which is said by its effluvia to have depopulated the country for 12 or 14 miles round the place of its growth. It is called, in the Malayan language, Bohun-Upas; with the juice of it the most poisonous arrows are prepared; and, to gain this, the condemned criminals are sent to the tree with proper direction both to get the juice and to secure themselves from the malignant exhalations of the tree; and are pardoned if they bring back a certain quantity of the poison. But by the registers there kept, not one in four are said to return. Not only animals of all kinds, both quadrupeds, fish, and birds, but all kinds of vegetables also are destroyed by the effluvia of the noxious tree; so that, in a district of 12 or 14 miles round it, the face of the earth is quite barren and rocky, intermixed only with the skeletons of men and animals; affording a scene of melancholy beyond what poets have described or painters delineated. Two younger trees of its own species are said to grow near it. See London Magazine for 1784 or 1783. Translated from a description of the poison-tree of the island of Java, written in Dutch by N. P. Foersch. For a further account of it, see a note at the end of the work.

Especially when read in conjunction with Foersch's own text (which Darwin – as promised in his footnote – cited in an appendix), "Loves of the Plants" explains an overwhelming number of details in Pushkin's poem, a fact that is still more obvious if one examines his drafts (as Gustafson does). Foersch even supplies the religious rationale, changed by Pushkin from a Muslim to a Christian context. He writes: "all the Malayans consider this tree as an holy instrument of the great prophet to punish the sins of mankind."

Gustafson (103) notes that the word "анчар" is one of the few details that cannot be explained by Darwin (who uses only "upas"). However, it is referred to as "antiar" and "antschar" with some frequency in French and English "scientific" publications of the time. Inessa Medzhibovskaya has pointed out to me that, to a Russian ear, it has a distinctly exotic and Eastern ring, calling to mind words like "чары" ("intoxications") and "янычар" ("Janissary"). Ronen (64) argues that "анча́р" may have appealed to Pushkin as an anagram for "саранча́" (locusts), a word with important biblical connotations (one of the plagues in Exodus). Moreover, locusts had a biographical connection for Pushkin. In his exile in Odessa, he was forced as part of his duties to accompany a group of government officials on an extended trip into the countryside to determine the extent of locust devastation. The trip appears to have made a lasting impression on him: the word "саранча" appears in another text of 1828, the narrative poem "Poltava": "И падшими вся степь покрылась / Как роем черной саранчи" ("And the entire steppe was covered with the dead / Like a swarm of black locusts").

The biblical significance of locusts is particularly apt because the most important source for the deeper meaning of the poem is the Bible. Pushkin rewrites Genesis, turning a creation myth into a destruction myth.

The poem is written in Pushkin's beloved iambic tetrameter quatrains, with alternating masculine and feminine rhymes. The diction, much more archaic than in most of the poetry of this period, harks back to the Bible. Biblical influence can also be noted in the numerous lines beginning with "И" (see "Пророк," where this technique is still more emphatic).

---

2 зноем раскале́нной – parched by intense heat. In modern Russian, the pronunciation would be "раскалённой."

4 оди́н – alone. Cf. Foersch: "It is surrounded on all sides by a circle of high hills and mountains; and the country round it, to the distance of ten or twelve miles from the tree, is entirely barren. Not a tree, nor a shrub, nor even the least plant or grass is to be seen."

5 жаждущих степе́й – of the thirsting desert<s>. Pushkin uses the word "степь" in a very broad sense. See Nabokov, 3:178–79. Pushkin's word choice is surely connected to Lomonosov's famous "Ode on the Taking of Khotin" (Berkov, xix): "И персы в жаждущих степях / Не сим ли пали пораженны?" ("And did the Persians in the thirsting deserts / Not fall, defeated by this man?"). The man in question is Peter the Great.

6 день гнева – day of wrath. A direct translation of Latin *Dies irae*, a traditional part of a requiem mass. Cf. Foersch: "We are told in our new Alcoran, that, above an hundred years ago, the country around the tree was inhabited by a people strongly addicted to the sins of Sodom and Gomorrha; when the great prophet Mahomet determined not to suffer them to lead such detestable lives any longer, he applied to God to punish them: upon which God caused this tree to grow out of the earth, which destroyed them all, and rendered the country for ever uninhabitable."

11 ввечеру́ = вечером

12 смоло́ю – in a resin. Cf. Foersch: "The poison which is procured from this tree is a gum that issues out between the bark and the tree itself."

14 нейдет = не идёт. Pushkin elides the words, saving a syllable for metrical purposes, but also creating a more archaic coloration. Note also the consonant cluster in "тигр нейдет," highly uncharacteristic of the mature Pushkin, but here recalling the cacophonous sound fabric of the eighteenth-century ode. Cf. Foersch: "This however is certain, though it may appear incredible, that from fifteen to eighteen miles round this tree, not only no human creature can exist, but that, in that space of ground, no living animal of any kind has ever been discovered. I have also been assured by several persons of veracity, that there are no fish in the waters, nor has any rat, mouse or any other vermin, been seen there; and when any birds fly so near this tree that the effluvia reaches them, they fall a sacrifice to the effects of the poison."

15 древо (= дерево) смерти – tree of death, an allusion to the "древо жизни" that appears numerous times in Genesis 2. Also relevant are the biblical "древо познания добра и зла" ("tree of the knowledge of good and evil") and Darwin's "hydra-tree of death."

18 дрему́чий – thick (as in foliage).

21 челове́ка челове́к – After surveying the "natural" scene, two men enter: "человека человек." The syntax here is telling: the fact that one man is in nominative case (the master, later called "владыка") and the other in accusative case (the slave, later called "раб") indicates that man is not equal to man. In Foersch's account the emperor sends criminals to harvest the poison: "Malefactors, who for their crimes are sentenced to die, are the only persons who fetch the poison; and this is the only chance they have of saving their lives. After sentence is pronounced upon them by the judge, they are asked in court, whether they will die by the hands of the executioner, or whether they will go to the Upas tree for a box of poison? They commonly prefer the latter proposal, as there is not only some chance of preserving their lives, but also a certainty, in case of their safe return, that a provision will be made for them in future by the Emperor [...] The worthy old ecclesiastic has assured me, that during his residence there, for upwards of thirty years, he had dismissed above seven hundred criminals in the manner which I have described; and that scarcely two out of twenty have returned."

23 поте́к – set off. An archaism synonymous with "пошёл," but more in keeping with the biblical tone. Curiously, the more common meaning ("flowed"), while by no means the primary connotation here, recalls the many images of liquid in this poem. In modern Russian, the word is pronounced "потёк."

26 Да – and

28 хладными = холодными (meaning is identical, but Pushkin chooses the more archaic form)

30 шалаша́ на лыки – of a hut on bast matting. The language here is not at all biblical, but rather recalls the poverty of the archetypal Russian peasant. The prepositional phrase "на лыки" is in accusative case because it is governed by the verb of motion "лег" in the previous line.

33 князь – prince. In the first publication Pushkin wrote "царь," but changed it subsequently because of censorship demands. (On the unexpected reasons for those demands, see the ingenious reconstruction of events in Dolinin 2007, 75–83.) While "царь" can be a general term ("Цари" is the book "Kings" in the Bible), it would also give the poem a specifically Russian reference (see the comments on line 30). Note also the acoustic echo in "царь/анчар."

33–34 напита́л / Свой послу́шливые – The words here are carefully chosen: "напитал" recalls "напоила" of line 8; in both cases the ordinarily positive connotation of the verb is overturned. "Послушливые" recalls "послушно" (line 23). At the crux of Genesis is a story about disobedience ("Of man's first disobedience," as Milton has it in the opening line of *Paradise Lost*). In Pushkin's revision it is obedience that leads to doom.

36 К сосе́дям – to his neighbors. Cf. Foersch: "I have been convinced that the gum of the Upas is the most dangerous and most violent of all vegetable poisons; and I am apt to believe that it greatly contributes to the unhealthiness of that island. Nor is this the only evil attending it: hundreds of the natives of Java, as well as Europeans, are yearly destroyed and treacherously murdered by that poison, either internally or externally. Every man of quality or fashion has his dagger or other arms poisoned with it; and in times of war the Malayans poison the springs and other waters with it; by this treacherous practice

the Dutch suffered greatly during the last war, as it occasioned the loss of half their army."

Literature: Gustafson.

Отве́т Кате́нину – An Answer to Katenin

This poem was long considered completely obscure until Tynianov came up with an ingenious interpretation that neatly (perhaps too neatly) resolves its numerous mysteries. Pavel Aleksandrovich Katenin (1792–1853) had a difficult character, but was a talented poet and literary critic, whose severe judgments Pushkin generally respected. He was an army officer who retired in 1820 and was exiled to his estate in 1822 for questionable political sympathies. In 1828 he wrote the poem "Старая быль" ("A True Story of Old"), set in the times of Vladimir, which featured a singing competition between a skillful yet servile Greek and a Russian, who ultimately follows Vladimir's own advice and chooses not to compete. The Greek wins a horse and suit of armor while the Russian gets the consolation prize of a goblet. Several elements of the Greek's song may have been intended as a parody of Pushkin's stanzas to Tsar Nicholas (e.g., the Greek explains that he will praise Vladimir's ancestors and thus indirectly praise Vladimir himself). Such criticism (if criticism it is) is further complicated because Katenin sent this poem directly to Pushkin together with a poem called "А. С. Пушкину." In this second poem, Katenin states that the goblet discussed in the first poem (i.e., the prize associated not with the Greek, but with the Russian) now belongs to Pushkin himself. The goblet, he notes, is enchanted and can only be used by a true poet. According to Tynianov, this second poem was meant to be tongue-in-cheek and was thus part and parcel of the same polemic. For reasons of his own and to Katenin's fury, Pushkin chose to publish "Старая быль" together with his own "Ответ Катенину," omitting from publication "А. С. Пушкину." The result must have mystified readers, since Pushkin's poem responds not to "Старая быль," but to "А. С. Пушкину."

Pushkin's poem is written in iambic tetrameter with unpredictable rhyme scheme; Katenin's "А. С. Пушкину" is written in the same form, as is the interpolated song of the Greek in "Старая быль." (The remainder of that poem is in six-line stanzas of alternating amphibrachic tetrameter and trimeter, a form strikingly reminiscent of Pushkin's 1822 "Песнь о вещем Олеге.")

---

2 чудный кубок – miraculous goblet. A reference to the line "Он, я слыхал, заворожен" ("I heard it is bewitched") in "А. С. Пушкину."

3 И выпить за здоро́вье просишь – And you ask to drink to <our> health. A reference to the concluding lines of "А. С. Пушкину":

> Налив, тебе подам я чашу,
> Ты выпьешь, духом закипишь,
> И тихую беседу нашу
> Бейронским пеньем огласишь.

(Having poured it, I will give you a glass, / You will drink, your spirit will heat up, / And you will drown out with Byronic song / Our quiet conversation.)

The reference to Byron should, according to Tynianov, be understood politically (i.e., the Byron who supported the cause of Greek independence). In other words, Katenin urges Pushkin to return to the type of poetry that got him exiled.

4 *Не пью, любе́зный мой сосе́д* – I will not drink, my dear neighbor. The line is italicized because it is a quote from Derzhavin's "Философы, пьяный и трезвый," a conversation between the two eponymous "philosophers." The former expresses a hedonistic world-view and urges his comrade to join him in drinking; the latter counters the arguments of the first with strict morality. Each of his replies ends with the line "Не пью, любезный мой сосед." In other words, Pushkin casts himself in the role of the sober neighbor, giving the role of the carefree drunk to Katenin (who, according to Tynianov, was known to have a drinking problem). Proskurin (1999, 230) notes that the rhymes in the following passage (-а́вый/-а́вой/-о́м) are all borrowed from Derzhavin's poem.

9 Тебе́ во след опя́ть за славой – <to follow> you again for glory. The "опять" refers not to following Katenin again, but to searching for glory again and (elliptically) to the exile that resulted from this search.

12 Вакха дар – gift of Bacchus (i.e., wine)

13–14 Пока́ войнственный уга́р / Его́ на месте не подко́сит? – Until the martial intoxication lays him low (i.e., until he gets too drunk to remain standing)

15 служи́вый – soldier

16 Пора́ убра́ться на поко́й – It's time (for me) to retire

17 Оста́нься ты в строя́х Парна́сса – It's you who should remain in the formations of Parnassus. The verb form is an imperative; including the "ты" makes it more emphatic. The word "строй" is a military image (in keeping with the previous lines).

19 лавр Корне́ля или Тасса – the laurel of Corneille or Tasso. Katenin translated from these (and many other) writers. According to Tynianov (84), Pushkin chooses these two because – after their initial successes – they encountered misfortunes; Corneille had severe financial difficulties and Tasso went insane.

20 Оди́н с похме́лья пожина́й – Harvest <the laurel> alone when you have a hangover.

Literature: Tynianov, 74–85.

Отве́т А. И. Гото́вцевой – An Answer to A. I. Gotovtseva

Anna Ivanovna Gotovtseva (1799–1871) published poetry in the journals of the 1820s and 1830s. Pushkin did not know her, but his friend Prince Viazemskii did. In a letter of 18 and 25 September 1828, Viazemskii wrote from his estate Ostaf'evo:

Ты, неблагодарный, не отвечаешь мне на мои письма, а я по всем великороссийским губерниям сводничаю для тебя и горячу воображение и благородные места молодых дворянок. Вот тебе послание от одной костромитянки, а ты знаешь пословицу про Кострому. Только здесь грешно похабничать: эта Готовцева точно милая девица телом и душою. Сделай милость, батюшка Александр Сергеевич, потрудись скомпоновать мадригалец в ответ, не посрами своего сводника. Нельзя ли напечатать эти стихи в 'Северных Цветах': надобно побаловать женский пол, тем более, что и он нас балует, а еще тем более, что весело избаловать молодую девицу. Вот и мои к ней стихи: мы так и напечатали бы эту Сузану между двумя старыми прелюбодеями.

The poem Viazemskii mentions is Gotovtseva's "А. С. Пушкину" ("To A. S. Pushkin"), which begins with fulsome praise of Pushkin's accomplishments (his "southern poems," which belonged to an earlier phase of his writing, but continued to enjoy immense popularity), then suddenly shifts to a critical position, using two lines of dots to indicate a transition (a Pushkinian device).

О Пушкин, слава наших дней,
Поэт, любимый небесами!
Ты век наш на заре своей
Украсил дивными цветами:
Кто выразит тебя сильней
Природы блеск и чувства сладость,
Восторг любви и сердца радость,
Тоску души и пыл страстей?
Кто не дивится вдохновеньям,
Игривой юности мечтам,
Свободных мыслей выраженьям,
Которые ты предал нам?
В неподражаемой картине
Ты нам Кавказ изобразил,
И деву гор, и плен в чужбине,
Черкесов жизнь в родной долине
Волшебной кистью оживил.
Дворец и сад Бахчисарая,
Фонтан любви, грузинки месть
Из края в край, не умолкая,
Гласят поэту славы весть.
Одно … Но где же совершенство?
В луне и солнце пятна есть!
…………………………………………
…………………………………………
Несправедлив твой приговор, –
Но порицать тебя не смеем:
Мы гению простить умеем –
Молчанье выразит укор.

Pushkin claimed not to understand her accusation about his "unfair judgment" (see his letter to Del'vig of 16 November 1828), though it surely was connected to some of the less charitable passages he had recently written about Russian women and their attitudes to poetry. For example, his "Отрывки из писем, мысли и замечания" (published in *Северные цветы* of 1828) contained the following diatribe:

> Жалуются на равнодушие русских женщин к нашей поэзии, полагая тому причиною незнание отечественного языка: но какая же дама не поймет стихов Жуковского, Вяземского или Баратынского? Дело в том, что женщины везде те же. Природа, одарив их тонким умом и чувствительностию самой раздражительною, едва ли не отказала им в чувстве изящного. Поэзия скользит по слуху их, не досягая души; они бесчувственны к ее гармонии; примечайте, как они поют модные романсы, как искажают стихи самые естественные, расстраивают меру, уничтожают рифму. Вслушивайтесь в их литературные суждения, и вы удивитесь кривизне и даже грубости их понятия … Исключения редки.

Pushkin not only wrote the poetic response (which, in the above-mentioned letter to Del'vig he called, citing Voltaire's 1768 poem to Madame de Saint-Julien, "petits vers froids et coulants" ["little cold and smooth verses"]), but even allowed it to be published in *Северные цветы* together with the poems of Viazemskii and Gotovtseva (as Viazemskii had suggested in his letter).

Gotovtseva's poem was written in iambic tetrameter with unpredictable rhymes. Pushkin's answer is likewise written in iambic tetrameter, but with an alternating rhyme scheme (feminine/masculine). Judging from Pushkin's poem, he clearly understood Gotovtseva's criticism to be directed at his attitude towards women. The "legalistic" terminology at the conclusion of Pushkin's poem (опроверженьем, клеветы) presumably picks up from Gotovtseva's "приговор."

---

2 на твой цветы́ – at your flowers. In keeping with a metaphor of antiquity (and present in the very name of the almanac *Северные цветы*), Pushkin uses the word "flower" as a synonym for poetry.

3 строгий стоик – strict stoic. The Stoics believed that one should accept fate and remain unemotional. In this line, the phrase is not in vocative (it is not an address to Gotovtseva), but in nominative (i.e., "Who is the strict Stoic who can accept …")

4 хари́т – of the Graces.

6 недоска́занный упрёк – reproach not fully expressed. Pushkin alludes to the dots that precede the final four lines of Gotovtseva's poem.

10 Краса́виц ветреный зои́л – The empty-headed Zoilus (i.e., critic) of beautiful women

Цвето́к – The Flower

A poem based on metonymy, in which a forgotten flower calls forth a host of possible associations in the mind of the poet. It has been suggested, on the basis of

Pushkin's drawing on the manuscript copy, that the poem is connected to the love affair of A. I. Osipova (Bekleshova) and A. N. Vul'f (Pushkin's longtime rival). See Berezkina 1991, 136, n23.

The poem is written in iambic tetrameter quatrains with alternating rhymes.

---

1 безухáнный – without fragrance
6 сорван – plucked
15 увя́ли – withered. The word is used literally about flowers and figuratively (poetically) about people.

„Брадáтый староста Авдéй" – "The bearded village elder Avdei"

This unfinished poem was probably intended to be a Russian version of "Vert-vert," a comic poem by Jean-Baptiste-Louis Gresset (1709–1777) that Pushkin greatly admired. The plot of Gresset's work concerns a parrot who repeats pious sayings but, after falling in with a profane crowd, changes his vocabulary and utters obscenities to the horror of the nuns who are accustomed to his earlier self. Pushkin apparently was so taken by the idea that, during his southern exile, he taught a parrot to swear in Moldavian, causing some embarrassment to his kindhearted supervisor General Ivan Nikitich Inzov, who first discovered his parrot's ability during a priest's Easter visit (Liprandi, 302–3).

The poem is written in iambic tetrameter. So little exists that it is impossible to speak with certainty about the rhyme scheme. The ten lines begin with a couplet and then shift to alternating rhyme; most likely the rhyme scheme would have been unpredictable, as in all of Pushkin's narrative poems before 1830.

---

2 барыне своéй – to his lady
3 Замéсто красного я́ичка – Instead of a red egg. A red egg is the traditional symbol of Easter. "Заместо" is colloquial for "вместо" or "взамен."
4 учёного скворцá – a learned starling. Starlings are mimics and in captivity can be taught to repeat words.
6 Умнéй инóго мудрецá – is smarter than some wise men
7 надýвшись величáво – having puffed himself up majestically
9 картáво – in guttural style. The verb "картавить" refers to the inability to pronounce either the letters "r" or "l." In the present case, Pushkin has in mind the "r" sound, which is used four times in line 10.
10 Хр<истóс> в<оскрéсе>! – Christ is risen! The traditional Russian Easter greeting.

„За Netty сердцем я летáю" – "With my heart I fly after Netty"

A humorous poem reflecting annoyance with recent rejections rather than true love. (True love poems generally do not mention other love interests.) It was not published in Pushkin's lifetime.

The poem is written in lines of iambic tetrameter (with feminine rhyme) alternating with iambic dimeter (with masculine rhyme). The grammatical first rhyme contrasts with the striking second one.

It is possible that the poem has been incorrectly dated and that it was written in 1829 rather than 1828. (See Berezkina 1993, 130–32.)

---

1 Netty – the nickname of Anna Ivanovna Vul'f (1799 [according to Chereiskii, after 1800 according to other sources]–1835). Pushkin first met her in 1825 when he was in exile in Mikhailovskoe. He flirted with her then and at various points in his life, but was never seriously in love with her.

2 В Твери́, в Москве́ – In Tver', in Moscow. Tver' was both a city and a region. Malinniki (estates of various members of the Vul'f family) were located there.

3 И *R* и *O* позабываю – And I forget "R" and "O." It is presumed that "R" stands for "Rosset" and "O" for "Olenina," two beauties of the capital. If the poem was indeed written in 1829, Berezkina (1993, 132) argues that "O" should stand for "Ouchakoff" (i.e., "Ушакова").

4 *N* и *W* – N. W. are the initials of Netty Wul'f (transliterated in the German style). "W" should be pronounced "вэ" so that it rhymes with "Москве."

„Как быстро в поле, вкруг откры́том" – "How quickly in the field, open on all sides"

The poem is unfinished, but anticipates later poems such as "Зима. Что делать нам в деревне?" and "Осень" (especially stanza 9), written five years later.

Judging from the extant twelve lines, it seems that Pushkin intended to write the poem in eight-line stanzas; however, unlike the iambic hexameter octaves of "Осень," it uses iambic tetrameter in a stanza of two different types of quatrains (A-b-A-b-C-d-d-C).

---

2 Подко́ван – shod

4 промёрзлая – frozen through

7 Лани́ты, ярче вешних роз – Cheeks that are brighter than spring roses. The роз/мороз rhyme was already a cliché (cf. *Eugene Onegin* 4:XLII), but this does not prevent Pushkin from using it without irony here (or, for that matter, later, in the famous hymn to Petersburg in "Медный всадник" ["The Bronze Horseman"]: "Люблю зимы твоей жестокой / Недвижный воздух и мороз, / Бег санок вдоль Невы широкой, / Девичьи лица ярче роз"). See also commentary to "Зима. Что делать нам в деревне?" line 47.

8 Игра́ют холодом и кровью – Play with cold and blood. The reference to blood emphasizes health (red cheeks), cf. the Russian expression "кровь с молоком" (a description of a young woman brimming with health).

9 завя́лый – faded

10 Проглянет день – и уж темно – Day shows, and it is already dark. (In other words, daylight lasts for a very brief time.)

Literature: Berezkina 1993, 127–30.

Поэт и толпа – The Poet and the Crowd

One of Pushkin's most celebrated poems on the subject of the poet and his audience, it takes the form of a dialogue with introduction. As usual in such instances, it is probably incorrect to equate Pushkin with the poet, though the views expressed here undoubtedly reflect his annoyance with the public's expectations. In the first publication Pushkin called the poem "Чернь" ("The Rabble"), a word that appears in line 6.

The poem is written in iambic tetrameter with unpredictable rhyme scheme. Each segment of the poem is marked off by rhymes – the rhymes never continue beyond their respective stanza.

Epigraph: Procul este, profani – Keep away, profane ones! These are the words that the Cumean sybil utters in Vergil's *Aeneid* (6:258) before beginning her prophecy.

6 толковала – spoke. The word can also be translated as "to interpret," a second meaning that may be ironically relevant here.

7 звучно – sonorously

13 песнь (=песня) – song

15 Какая польза нам от ней (=неё)? – What use do we get from it?

17 Подёнщик – Day worker

19 червь – worm. Note the echo with "чернь" (line 6).

20–21 на вес / Кумир ты ценишь Бельведерской (=Бельведерский) – You value the Belvedere idol for its weight. The reference is to the Apollo Belvedere, widely considered the epitome of classical beauty, for example, Byron's famous description of it in *Childe Harold* (canto 4, stanzas CLXI–CLXIII):

> Or view the Lord of the unerring bow,
> The God of life, and poesy, and light –
> The Sun in human limbs array'd, and brow
> All radiant from his triumph in the fight;
> The shaft hath just been shot – the arrow bright
> With an immortal's vengeance; in his eye
> And nostril beautiful disdain, and might
> And majesty, flash their full lightnings by,
> Developing in that one glance the Deity.
>
> But in his delicate form – a dream of Love,
> Shaped by some solitary nymph, whose breast
> Long'd for a deathless lover from above,
> And madden'd in that vision – are exprest

All that ideal beauty ever bless'd
The mind within its most unearthly mood,
When each conception was a heavenly guest –
A ray of immortality – and stood,
Starlike, around, until they gather'd to a god!

And if it be Prometheus stole from Heaven
The fire which we endure, it was repaid
By him to whom the energy was given
Which this poetic marble hath array'd
With an eternal glory – which, if made
By human hands, is not of human thought;
And Time himself hath hallow'd it, nor laid
One ringlet in the dust – nor hath it caught
A tinge of years, but breathes the flame with which 'twas wrought.

23 Но мрамор сей ведь бог! – But this marble is a god
24 Печнóй горшóк – a cooking pot
32 Мы сердцем хладные скопцы́ – In our heart we are cold eunuchs
35 ближнего любя́ – loving your neighbor
40 каменéйте смело – boldly turn to stone. This command echoes the reference to the marble statue in lines 21 and 23.
41 лиры глас – the voice of the lyre. Note the archaic (elevated) "глас" rather than "голос."
46 рабóв безýмных – mindless slaves
51 Жрецы́ ль у вас метлý берýт? – Should the priests take a broom from you?

„Какóв я прежде был, такóв и ныне я" – "As I was before, so am I now"

The epigraph, rendered fairly exactly in the first line of Pushkin's poem, is taken from an elegy by André Chénier. In the edition that Pushkin owned, this is the first elegy in the section called "Fragments" (*Oeuvres complètes de Chénier* [Paris, 1819], 171). However, beyond the alexandrine meter and the patina of antiquity, Pushkin borrows little from the French poet. Though Pushkin himself dated the poem 1828, it was written mainly (and perhaps entirely) in 1826. It is conceivable that the date of 1828 was intended to distract attention from the real message of the poem – that the poet was unchanged despite years of exile. However, nothing in the poem proper would suggest such an "allegorical" reading.

The poem is written in iambic hexameter with couplet rhymes and a caesura after the third foot (the traditional Russian rendering of the French alexandrine). The fact that it closes with an "orphan" (unrhymed) line suggests that it is unfinished, but the fragmentariness is deliberate. Pushkin published the poem in 1832.

Epigraph: Tel j'étais autrefois et tel je suis encor – As I was formerly and as I still am.
2 влюбчивый – given to falling in love; falling in love easily
6 бился – struggled

7 сетя́х, раски́нутых Кипри́дой – < in > nets set by Kypris (Aphrodite). While the most famous reference to Aphrodite and nets is the scene in the *Odyssey* where she is trapped by her husband during a tryst with Ares, nets are also a traditional attribute of Aphrodite herself.

8 не испра́вленный стокра́тною оби́дой – not improved through hundredfold insult

„Лищи́н < ский > околе́л – оте́честву беда́“ – "Lishchinskii has croaked – a calamity for the fatherland"

This mysterious two-line epigram was written in the margins of a manuscript page that contains the drafts of a very different type of poem about death – "Ворон к ворону летит." Since it was discovered and deciphered long after Pushkin's death, no contemporary remained who might have been able to elucidate it. No Lishchinskii is known, unless this refers to Stanisław Leszczyński (1677–1766), the last of a long line of Polish nobility and the king of the Polish-Lithuanian Commonwealth. A Polish connection is suggested by the manuscript, which shows that in the second line Pushkin initially wrote the name "Потоцкий," another aristocratic Polish clan. However, Pushkin then crossed out "Потоцкий," and replaced it with the wholly obscure "Князь Сергий." It is equally possible that Pushkin simply used the name "Лищинский" to stand in for someone who really did die in 1828.

The poem consists of a rhymed couplet of iambic hexameter where the caesura is marked in each line by a strong syntactic break (underscored by the presence of a hyphen). The form may be intended to recall (and parody) the alexandrines of eighteenth-century poetics.

1 околе́л – croaked. The word is strikingly unpoetic, used about animals and (pejoratively) about people.

„Поко́йник, автор сухоща́вый“ – "The deceased, a lean author"

This mysterious epigram was written by Pushkin in the margins of the fair copy of the poem "Поэт и толпа" (at that point entitled "Чернь") and was obviously not intended for publication. It apparently reflects in satirical form the same questions about the poet's calling that are raised in the more famous poem.

It consists of two lines of iambic tetrameter with a feminine couplet (the rhyme, by Pushkin's standards inexact, creates a comic effect).

2 пил из славы – drank from fame

~1829

Е. Н. Ушако́вой – To E. N. Ushakova

Pushkin spent considerable time at the Ushakov household, flirting with Ekaterina Nikolaevna (1809–1872) and, somewhat less seriously, with her younger sister Elizaveta (1810–1872). The latter kept an album, in which Pushkin left his notorious "Don Juan list" (a list of women he had wooed – both successfully and unsuccessfully), numerous drawings, as well as this poem. Taking advantage of the conventions of album poetry and a remarkable poetic economy, he appears to have taken the first lines of this piece verbatim from an (unpublished) 1828 poem dedicated to another woman (probably Olenina).

The poem is written astrophically, in freely-rhymed iambic tetrameter.

---

1 избало́ваны приро́дой – spoiled by nature. The English translation is ambiguous, but the Russian is not. This is clearly a compliment (i.e., nature has endowed generously), not an insult (that she is spoiled and that this is her nature).

4 доку́чной одой – an annoying ode. The ode was associated with eighteenth-century panegyrics.

7 Арми́да – Armida is the beautiful sorceress in Tasso's epic *Jerusalem Delivered*. Pushkin's broad use of the name as a synonym for a beautiful young woman follows French practice (see Nabokov, 2:140).

8 Сильфи́да – a Sylph, a mythological creature akin to a fairy. It is unclear why Pushkin capitalizes the word.

17 Аво́сь – Perhaps. The colloquial quality of this word is striking against the rather formulaic sentiments that have been expressed earlier.

18 пева́л – used to sing

19 Пресненское поле – Presnia field. The Ushakovs lived in the Presnia section of Moscow, at that time the outskirts of the city.

~

<Е. П. Полтора́цкой> – To E. P. Poltoratskaia

These verses are known only from the memoirs of Anna Petrovna Kern (née Poltoratskaia), set down many years after Pushkin's death. Apparently, Kern was writing a letter to her younger sister Elizaveta Petrovna (dates unknown) in Ukraine, and Pushkin added these lines as a jocular improvisation.

The poem takes the form of a quatrain of iambic tetrameter with alternating rhymes. The comic effect is lies in the contrast in tone between the first two lines and the last two, with the rhymes playing a particularly significant role in deflating the seriousness of the opening.

4 В тенѝ укра́инских чере́шен – in the shadow of Ukrainian cherry trees. In modern Russian, the stress would be "украйнских."

„Подъезжа́я под Ижо́ры" – "Driving up towards Izhory"

The poem was written to Ekaterina Vasil'evna Vel'iasheva (1813–1865), whose picture Pushkin drew on the manuscript page. She was the granddaughter of P. A. Osipova (Pushkin's neighbor when he lived in Mikhailovskoe) and the cousin of Pushkin's friend, the rake A. N. Vul'f. Pushkin met her when visiting her relatives at their estate in the Tver' district (see commentary to line 8). In a letter to Vul'f of 16 October 1829, Pushkin quotes the first four lines of this poem, referring to them as "наши общие стихи" ("our common verses," i.e., verses we wrote together) and noting that Vul'f's uncle Pavel Ivanovich "corrected" ("исправил") lines 2 and 3. No existing draft makes clear how those lines originally read or precisely which lines Pushkin and A. N. Vul'f composed collectively. The poem is written in trochaic tetrameter with alternating rhymes.

1 Ижо́ры – Izhory was the last stop before Petersburg when traveling from Torzhok. The name is chosen not simply as realia, but also because it creates an almost comic soundplay with the verb and preposition that precede it.

3 воспо́мнил (=вспомнил) ваши взоры – I remembered your glances. Взоры can also mean simply "eyes."

6 Вашей девственной красо́й – by your virginal beauty. In the above-mentioned letter to Vul'f, Pushkin reports that Vel'iasheva (whom he calls "Gretchen," alluding to the heroine of Goethe's *Faust*) "хорошеет и час от часу делается невиннее" ("becomes prettier and more innocent by the hour").

7 Хоть вампи́ром имено́ван – though I am called a vampire. Drafts indicate that Pushkin took a while to settle on this noun; he first tried "повесой" ("a rake"), then "ловласом" ("a Lovelace," the villain of Samuel Richardson's once popular novel of 1748 *Clarissa*, whose name, when written, as here, in lower case is simply a synonym for "rake"). It may be relevant that in the letter to Vul'f, Pushkin addresses him as "Любезный Ловлас Николаевич" ("my dear Lovelace Nikolaevich"). Pushkin mentions the Vampire (upper case) in *Eugene Onegin* (3:XII) as one of the Romantic heroes who trouble the sleep of adolescent girls.

8 в губе́рнии Тверско́й – in the Tver' district. Prerevolutionary Russia was divided into districts. The Tver' district was east of the Pskov district (where Mikhailovskoe was located) and north of the Moscow district.

12 Вас трево́жить не хоте́л – I did not want to agitate you. Cf. "Я не хочу печалить вас ничем" (from "Я вас любил").

13–14 Упива́ясь неприя́тно / Хмелем светской суеты́ – Unpleasantly filling myself with the hops of high society's vanity. The verb, often used in poetry in the sense of "being inspired," is here used literally. It also develops the vampire theme of line 7.

21 по прежню (=прежнему) следу – along my earlier track

22 мирные края́ – peaceful realms. The Russian use of plural here is standard.

24 И влюблю́сь до ноября́ – And will fall in love until November. According to Levkovich (1986, 276), the poem was written somewhere between 16 October and 8 November. Presumably the idea is that the poet will return the next summer and fall in love with her again, but only until November, when it will be time for him to return to Saint Petersburg.

Приме́ты – Portents

An unusual poem, in that what first appears to be a love lyric is transformed into a poem about poets (and, presumably, poetry). Pushkin was highly superstitious, but here he is well aware of his penchant for projecting his own feelings onto his surroundings. Insofar as this poem was inspired biographically (and this is not necessarily the case), scholars have been unable to identify the addressee, who – it should be noted – is mentioned directly only in the first line.

In Russian folklore, it was indeed significant which side the (new) moon was viewed from: the right side was a good omen, whereas the left side was not. In *Eugene Onegin* (5:V–VI), Pushkin – using a striking interstanzaic enjambment – describes Tatiana's superstitious nature (which, as scholars have shown, parallels his own): "Вдруг увидя / Младой двурогий лик луны / На небе с левой стороны, / Она дрожала и бледнела." ("Suddenly seeing / The two-horned face of the new moon / In the sky on her left, / She shuddered and turned pale.")

The poem is written in iambic tetrameter quatrains; the first two, clearly parallel, use the identical rhyme scheme (and even repeat the same rhymes in lines two and four), whereas the third stanza changes to a ring rhyme.

---

1 живы́е сны – vivid dreams
2 За мной вили́сь – swirled behind me
3 месяц – the <new> moon
4 бег рети́вый – swift run. This epithet has a folkloric quality; it is often paired with "конь" (which is here implied by the verb "ехал").

Литерату́рное изве́стие – Literary News

This poem was written in 1825, but first published in 1829 in the heat of the polemics of that year between Pushkin and Mikhail Trofimovich Kachenovskii (1775–1842). Pushkin held a grudge against him from his student days (see Tsiavlovskii 1962, 359–64), but the flurry of epigrams in 1829 concern Kachenovskii's role as publisher of the journal *Вестник Европы* (*The European Herald*). The title "Литературное известие" refers to the genre of advertising; under this rubric announcements appeared for journals soon to be published, listing contributors, and so on. Pushkin squarely situates Kachenovskii with the ridiculous figures of eighteenth-century literature.

The poem is written in iambic pentameter with caesura after the second foot. The rhyme scheme begins A-b-b-A-b, then switches to couplets. The lexicon mixes old-fashioned words ("сей") and forms ("муж" in the meaning of "man") reminiscent of eighteenth-century verse with words that would never be found in an eighteenth-century poem (e.g., сотрудники, хлопочет).

---

1 В Эли́зии – In Elysium. In Greek mythology this was the resting place of the dead. Such references were common in the neo-classical poetry of eighteenth-century Russia.

Васи́лий Тредьяко́вский – Vasilii Kirillovich Trediakovskii (1703–1769) was a resourceful and erudite poet, but Pushkin, like most of his contemporaries, considered him the quintessential pedantic buffoon (cf. *Капитанская дочка* [*The Captain's Daughter*], where Shvabrin likens Grinev's clumsy verses to Trediakovskii's). The standard spelling is Тредиаковский; Pushkin replaces the "и with "ь" for metrical reasons.

2 Пре́бстрый муж – a most clever man

4 сам вызвался Попо́вский – Popovskii himself volunteered. Nikolai Nikitich Popovskii (1730–1760), poet and translator, remembered for his lengthy and complicated odes. He originally studied for the priesthood, but – on Trediakovskii's recommendation – was selected for study at the university.

5 Ела́гин – Ivan Perfil'evich Elagin (1725–1794), poet and translator. He is mentioned in this context not for his poetry, but for his prose works (e.g., his "Опыт повествования о России"), which were written in a complicated "Slavonic" idiom.

6 Курга́нов – Nikolai Gavrilovich Kurganov (1725 [or 1726] – 1796), author of *Российская универсальная грамматика или всеобщее писмословие, предлагающее легчайший способ основательного учения русскому языку, с седьмью присовокуплениями разных учебных и полезнозабавных вещей.* This work (which contained among its seven supplements a poetry anthology) went through numerous editions, but by the nineteenth century it was considered old-fashioned and distinctly low-brow.

7 "Письмо́вник" – "Manual of Writing" or, in this context, "Grammar." This was the short name for Kurganov's work. In this line it is in nominative case, presumably a metonymy for Kurganov himself.

8 на-днях (= на днях) – soon

9 преполе́зный – most useful

11 Чтоб подоспе́л Миха́йло Качено́вский – For Mikhailo Kachenovskii to arrive. In the first publication the name did not appear, but the rhyme made it obvious. The use of "Михайло" rather than "Михаил" is modeled on eighteenth-century usage (e.g., Михайло Ломоносов).

Эпигра́мма („Журна́лами оби́женный жесто́ко") – Epigram ("Cruelly insulted by journals")

Another epigram directed against Kachenovskii. The circumstances alluded to in the present poem are explained by a fairly long prose piece entitled "Отрывок из литературных летописей" ("An Excerpt from Literary Chronicles") that Pushkin published in the almanac *Северные цветы на 1830 год* (a first attempt to publish it in 1829 was rejected by the censor). The situation may be summarized as follows: after reading an unfavorable piece about himself written by Nikolai Alekseevich Polevoi, Kachenovskii had complained to the censor for allowing its publication. Kachenovskii argued that he had been attacked personally (rather than for his literary work). The censor ruled in favor of Polevoi.

Pushkin's poem is written in iambic pentameter with an unpredictable rhyme scheme. (The final ten lines, perhaps coincidentally, follow the rhyme scheme of an odic stanza.)

---

2 Зойл Пахóм – Pakhom the Zoilus. In this poem, the word "Zoilus" is synonymous with petty critic. On the historical Zoilus, see commentary to "К Бараты́нскому" (1826). In Pushkin's day, the Russian name Pakhom had low-class associations.

4 нам смех, зóйлу нос – We are amused, the Zoilus is left with nothing. The idiom implied here is "остаться с носом," to be left with nothing, to end up looking like a fool.

5 Инáя брань конéчно неприли́чность – Some cursing, of course, is an indecency (i.e., some types of criticism are indeed inadmissable).

6 Не льзя (=Нельзя)

де – short for "дескать." A colloquial particle indicating direct speech, it adds a slight irony to the statement. The use of italics in lines 6–8 is the equivalent of quotation marks.

7 *плюгáвый* – despicable

8 личность – an ad hominem attack

10 парнáсский старовéр – the Parnassian conservative. Strictly speaking, "старовер" connotes the religious sect of Old Believers, but here it is used more broadly. Parnassus is the mountain in Greece traditionally associated with the Muses.

11 *(В свои́х статья́х)* – In his essays. The italics (and parenthesis) are used to emphasize that this is not a direct attack on his person, but only on his published work.

12 отмéнно скучновáт – especially rather dull. Ordinarily "отменно" is followed by positive attributes. In correct speech, it should not be followed by an adjective with the suffix "-оват." (It would be the equivalent of putting "very" and "slightly" before the same adjective.)

14 Тут не лицó, а только литерáтор – Here it is not <a question of> the person (i.e., an ad hominem attack), but only the writer.

<На Великопóльского> („Поэ́т-игрóк о Беверлей-Горáций") – On Velikopol'skii ("Poet-gambler o Beverly-Horace")

Another of Pushkin's poems about the unfortunate Ivan Ermolaevich Velikopol'skii (see commentary to "Из письма к Великопольскому"), who seems never to have lost his high regard for Pushkin, though he certainly had sufficient reason to.

The poem is written in iambic pentameter with caesura after the second foot and rhyme scheme A-A-b-b-C-b-C.

---

1 Поэ́т-игро́к – Poet-gambler. This opening conceivably echoes Velikopol'skii's 1826 poem to Del'vig which begins "Поэт-ленивец" ("Poet-lazybones"). Cited in Modzalevskii 1999, 359.

Беверлей-Гора́ций – Beverly-Horace. Horace is the Roman poet, Beverley the protagonist of *The Gamester*, a domestic tragedy by the English dramatist Edward Moore (1712–1757). After gambling away all his money and possessions to a dishonest opponent, Beverley goes mad and commits suicide. Pushkin knew the work through a popular French verse translation ("Béverlei, tragédie bourgeoise") by Bernard-Joseph Saurin (1706–1781). This plot, incidentally, recalls Velikopol'skii's own 1828 "К Эрасту (Сатира на игроков)" (see commentary to "Послание к Великопольскому").

5 на злоде́йку – on the little villain. The phrase is in apposition to "на карту" ("on a card").

7 Когда́ б твой стих ходи́л хотя в копе́йку – If your verse would even go for a kopeck. This nasty jab alludes to a passage in Velikopol'skii's 1828 rejoinder to Pushkin's "Послание к Великопольскому." In that poem Velikopol'skii drew attention to an unfortunate moment in Pushkin's own gambling career, when Pushkin supposedly bet and lost a chapter of his own *Eugene Onegin*. Velikopol'skii had written: "Глава 'Онегина' вторая / Съезжала скромно на тузе" ("The second chapter of Onegin / Modestly slid away on an ace"). Strictly speaking, at least according to Pushkin, this was false: Pushkin had not gambled away the second chapter of *Onegin*, but had used the printed version to pay off a (gambling) debt. Pushkin had successfully intervened at the time to prevent Velikopol'skii's poem from being published; here he recalls that passage and rewrites it in a way most unflattering to Velikopol'skii.

Literature: Modzalevskii 1999, 363–69.

Эпигра́мма („Там, где древний Кочерго́вский") – Epigram ("There, where the ancient Kochergovskii")

Another of Pushkin's many epigrams directed at Kachenovskii (see commentary to "Литературное известие"), this poem takes aim at Kachenovskii's sympathies with the "archaists," who advocated returning poetry to eighteenth-century norms.

The poem is written in trochaic tetrameter with alternating rhymes. The "elevated" lexicon of the opening lines is used parodically, undercut by words like "дурень."

---

1 Кочерго́вский – Pushkin slightly alters his target's name, but in a way that would have been transparent to his readers. The new name recalls, in the first place, the rather undignified "кочерга" (a poker, i.e., the instrument used to stoke fires).

2 Над Ролле́нем опочи́л – fell asleep above Rollin. In poetic style, "опочил" can also mean "died." (See Ivanova, 351, who notes the comic contrast of this Slavonicism with the colloquial verbs of line 4.) The reference is to the

French historian Charles Rollin (1661–1741), author of a sixteen-volume history of antiquity. History was one of the many subjects about which Pushkin and Kachenovskii disagreed. (Pushkin's high opinion of Karamzin's *History of Russia* was not shared by Kachenovskii.)

3 Дней нове́йших Тредьяко́вский – The Trediakovskii of the most recent days. The indefatigable Trediakovskii translated all sixteen volumes of Rollin's *History* twice; the first completed version was consumed by a fire before it had been readied for publication. On Trediakovskii and Kachenovskii, see commentary to "Литературное известие," line 1.

6 Вестник свой – His "Herald." The reference is to *Вестник Европы*, the journal Kachenovskii published.

7 мёртвою водо́ю (=мертвой водой) – water of death. This dread potion frequently appears in Russian fairy tales, as does its life-bringing opposite, "живая вода" (see line 8).

8 Прыскал ижицу живо́й – He sprinkled the "izhitsa" with the water of life. The "izhitsa" (**ѵ**), the final letter in the Old Church Slavonic alphabet, was obsolete in the Russian of Pushkin's day. As part of his program, Kachenovskii had tried in his journal to revive the use of this and other archaic letters. Such ideas were viewed by Pushkin and his friends as pedantic and hopelessly anachronistic.

„Кто на снега́х возрасти́л Феокри́товы нежные розы?" – "Who cultivated Theocritus's tender roses on the snows?"

According to the introductory parenthetical phrase ("При посылке бронзового Сфинкса"), the poem was sent with a statue of the sphinx. The legend of the sphinx (i.e., a combination of various things) and, in particular, the notion of its riddle is developed in this poem. The solution to the riddle is Anton Del'vig, whose first (and only) collection of poetry had recently been published. Pushkin greatly admired Del'vig's idylls (written in an imitation of ancient hexameter, see the commentary to "Сонет"). Del'vig also wrote elegiac distichs, another form from antiquity (of which the odd-numbered lines are hexameters). This poem, Pushkin's first in elegiac distichs, is thus a tribute to his friend, written in a form borrowed from that friend. Even the idea of sending a present with an accompanying poem in distichs appears to have been inspired by Del'vig's example. In 1821, Del'vig wrote a poem entitled "Ф. Н. Глинке. (Присылая ему греческую Антологию)," in which he plays on the double meaning of "anthology" as flowers and poems (a traditional conceit that Pushkin draws on in the "roses" of his first line).

---

1 Феокри́товы нежные розы – Theocritus's tender roses. Theocritus, a Greek poet of the third century BCE, is considered the first bucolic poet and the "inventor" of the genre of the idyll. The roses probably refer to the almanac *Северные цветы*, which Del'vig had founded in 1825.

2 золото́й – golden. This adjective agrees with the implied "век" ("age").

3 родом германец – a German by heritage. Del'vig came from a family of (Russified) Baltic Germans.
4 хитрый Эдип, разреши! – Solve <it>, crafty Oedipus.

„На холмах Грузии лежит ночная мгла" – "The night's haze lies on the hills of Georgia"

The addressee of this this famous and laconic love lyric remains disputed (see Zinger, 128–31). Logic suggests that Pushkin would have written the poem to his fiancée Natalia Goncharova. However, a draft version of the poem (entitled "Отрывок") includes the lines "Я твой попрежнему <sic> тебя люблю я вновь / И без надежд и без желаний." The words "попрежнему," "вновь," and "без надежд" simply do not fit that biographical scenario. Either Pushkin changed his addressee in the course of moving from draft to final version or the poem must have been dedicated to someone else. Candidates for this other addressee include Mariia Raevskaia (in Siberia with her exiled husband) or Amalia Riznich (who had died in 1825 and whose death Pushkin had already commemorated in the same meter though in very different tones in "Под небом голубым" of 1826).

The form, alternating iambic hexameter and tetrameter with alternating rhymes, links it to two other "memory" poems (Proskurin 1999, 218–21). It is written as one continuous stanza, with the key word (тобою, тобой) straddling the boundary between the two parts. The simple lexicon is complicated by a number of paradoxes (most striking in line 3).

---

1 На хóлмах – on the hills. In modern Russian the stress falls on the second syllable (на холмáх), but both stresses can be found in Pushkin's poetry (depending on metrical convenience).
2 Арáгва – the Aragva (in English more commonly "Aragvi") River in Georgia.
3 Мне грустно и легкó; печáль моя светлá – I am sad and light <in spirit>; my sadness is radiant. Both of the hemistichs are marked by oxymoron.
5–6 Уны́нья моегó / Ничтó не мучит, не тревóжит – Nothing torments or troubles my melancholy.
8 не люби́ть онó не может – It <the heart> cannot not love (i.e., it must love).

Калмы́чке – To a Kalmyk Woman

In Pushkin's day, the Kalmyk people were some of the exotic inhabitants one might encounter in southern Russia (more precisely: the area near the Caspian Sea that in Russian is called the "Нижнее Поволжье"). Originally from Mongolia and China, they have distinctly Asiatic features (see lines 6–7).

The interest in non-European peoples was part and parcel of the Orientalism favored by European Romantics. Pushkin inherited this fascination most directly from Byron, and it is reflected particularly strongly in his work of the early 1820s (the "southern poems" and short poems such as "Черная шаль"). In keeping with the Romantic notion that life and art were inseparable, Pushkin supposedly joined a band of Gypsies and traveled with them for a few weeks, drawing material for his narrative poem "Цыганы" (for more on this, see the notes to the lyric "Цыганы" of 1830). By the late 1820s, Pushkin had a more detached and less infatuated approach toward southern cultures, but the "похвальная привычка" mentioned in the third line of "Калмычке" refers to his earlier "habit" of spending time with his ethnographical subjects.

In the first chapter of his *Путешествие в Арзрум во время похода 1829 года* (*Journey to Arzrum during the Campaign of 1829*), Pushkin describes a meeting of this type. This episode is best understood as a parody of the cross-cultural love story Pushkin treated seriously in earlier works like "Кавказский пленник" ("The Prisoner of the Caucasus"). In that narrative poem, the Russian captive is rejuvenated by a pretty Circassian maiden who gives him – among other things – mare's milk ("кумыс") to drink. Pushkin even interrupts that passage with a footnote on the virtues of mare's milk: it is "довольно приятен вкусу и почитается весьма здоровым" ("rather pleasant to the taste and considered quite healthy"). In the scene in the *Journey*, he enters the camp of a very pretty but laconic eighteen-year-old Kalmyk maiden, who proffers him tea mixed with lamb fat ("Не думаю, что народная кухня могла произвести что-нибудь гаже" – "I do not think that an ethnic cuisine could produce anything more disgusting"), followed by a chaser of dried mare's meat. Pushkin is not capable of bringing this potential romance to its logical conclusion: "Калмыцкое кокетство испугало меня; я поскорее выбрался из кибитки и поехал от степной Цирцеи" ("The Kalmyk coquetry frightened me; I quickly hurried out of the camp and set off away from my Circe of the steppes"). The poem "Калмычке" offers another take on that same situation, though its irony is directed less at the indigenous woman than at Russian society belles.

The poem is astrophic, written in iambic tetrameter with an unpredictable rhyme scheme that presumably reflects the informal and jocular treatment of the theme. Note, for example, the "surprising" fifth line, which instead of beginning a new thought (as one would expect), returns both in subject and rhyme to the passage that preceded it.

---

4 не – after чуть-чуть, the не is simply an intensifier; it does not make the sentence negative (i.e., "this praiseworthy custom almost led me after your kibitka")

5 киби́ткою – ordinarily a conveyance (see notes to "Дорожные жалобы"), but here (as in the final line of this poem and the prose passage cited above) meaning a temporary shelter or camp that the Kalmyks would set up and then take down as they continued their wanderings.

8 лепе́чешь – you prattle

9 Ты шелком не сжима́ешь ног – You don't squeeze your legs with silk (i.e., you don't wear silk stockings). The device is "остранение" (defamiliarization), whereby the "civilized" and aristocratic clothing is made to seem strange.

10 По-а́нглийски – in contemporary Russian, "по-англи́йски"

11 Узо́ром хлеба не кроши́шь – You don't break your bread into patterns. Presumably this refers to a current culinary fashion of shaped cookies or biscuits.

12 Сен-Маром – a reference to *Cinq-Mars*, an 1826 novel by Alfred Victor de Vigny (1797–1863) on the subject of court intrigue during the time of Louis XIII. Pushkin complained about the "нелепые несообразности" ("absurd incongruities") of Vigny's novel in an essay of 1836 published posthumously as "О Мильтоне и переводе 'Потерянного рая' Шатобриана" ("On Milton and Chateaubriand's Translation of 'Paradise Lost'"). It is safe to assume that Pushkin had the same low opinion of that work when he wrote "Калмычке."

16 Ma dov'è – But where is (Italian). A reference to the aria in act 1, scene 9, from Rossini's 1819 opera *La Donna del Lago* (*The Lady of the Lake*): "Ma dov'è colei, che accende / Dolce fiamma nel mio seno? / De' suoi lumi un sol baleno / Fa quest'anima bear! / Fausto amor se a me sorride, / Io non so che più bramar! / Ed allor, qual nuovo Alcide, / Saprò in campo fulminar." ("But where is she who lights / A sweet flame in my breast? / A single flash from her light / Fills this soul with heavenly bliss! / If propitious love smiles on me, / I know not what more to wish! / And, therefore, like a new Hercules, / I'll know how to strike in the field.") The final image recalls a lightning bolt on the field of battle. The aria is sung by a man. This reference was first recognized by I. A. Pil'shchikov (Shapir 2006, 414). In all Pushkin commentaries the line is absurdly misattributed to the opera *Didone abbandonata* (*Dido Abandoned*, 1741) by Baldassarre Galuppi (1706–1785).

17 Гало́п – a fast dance in 2/4 time (the name is derived from the movement of horses). The "galop" had become popular in Vienna in the early 1820s, in Paris and London (and presumably Russia) in 1829.

19 Пока́ коне́й мне запряга́ли – while my horses were being harnessed (a traveler's horses would need to be changed at certain points along a road)

24 The "зала" suggests a ball, the "ложе" (in nominative case "ложа") a theater. Pushkin uses the now obsolete feminine form "зала"; only "зал" is used in modern Russian.

<Фази́ль-хану> – To Fazil-Khan

During his journey in the Caucasus, Pushkin met the Persian court poet Fazil-Khan Shaida (1783 [or 1784]–1852), who was on his way to Saint Petersburg in an official capacity. Pushkin briefly discusses their meeting (and his unexpectedly positive impressions thereof) in the first chapter of *Путешествие в Арзрум* (*Journey to Arzrum*).

This unfinished poem, clearly inspired by that meeting, was abandoned in its very early stages; it is hard to say much about its formal qualities except that it was written in iambic tetrameter.

---

1 подвиг новый – new heroic deed. Pushkin presumably has in mind his pilgrimage to the north.

4 Гафи́за и Саа́ди – of Hafiz and Saadi. The two famous Persian poets, from the fourteenth and twelfth century respectively.

6 край полно́чный – northern land

9 Рассы́пь на северных снега́х – Strew on the northern snows. The image of

flowers on snow was used by Pushkin in his poem on Del'vig, "Кто на снегах возрастил Феокритовы нежные розы."

„Жил на свете рыцарь бедный" – "There lived a poor knight"

An unusual poem in the Russian tradition, since Russian Orthodoxy did not know the cult of the Virgin Mary as it was developed in the West. As the references to the crusades make clear, it is medieval in spirit, though filtered through Romanticism. (On the possible influence of German Romanticism – via Zhukovskii – see Vatsuro 1994, 186). Though not labeled as such, its plot-oriented nature makes it close to a ballad. One suspects a Western source, but none has been discovered. Intended to be part of Pushkin's unfinished prose drama *Сцены из рыцарских времен* (*Scenes from the Time of Chivalry*), the poem is far better known than the rest of that work (perhaps because of the prominent role it plays in Dostoevsky's novel *The Idiot*). Neither the play nor the poem was published during Pushkin's lifetime. The drafts to this poem are extensive; one has the title "Легенда" ("A Legend"), suggesting a connection to a religious genre that is refracted through folk belief.

The poem is written in four-line stanzas of trochaic tetrameter with alternating rhymes. Pushkin keeps the lexicon and syntax simple; the numerous truncated adjectives suggest a folk style.

---

1 на свете – the phrase need not be taken literally ("in the world"); it sometimes just has the sense of "once"

3 С виду – Of countenance ("у" is an archaic genitive ending for masculine nouns). In modern Russian the expression "с виду" has an entirely different meaning ("seemingly").

4 Духом – in spirit

5 виде́нье – a vision

10 На доро́ге у креста́ – At a cross in the road. The reference is presumably to crosses that were placed along the roads (away from churches) in medieval times for the convenience of travelers who wished to pray.

11 Мари́ю деву – a literal translation into Russian of "Virgin Mary" (as against the standard Russian appellation of Mary as "Богоматерь")

19 чётки – prayer beads (the rosary)

21 Отцу – One must assume a "ни" before "Отцу" – he prayed not to the Father, not to the Son, not to the Holy Ghost

22 ввек – never

25 целы ночи (=целые ночи) – entire nights

26 Перед ликом пресвято́й – before the face of the most holy <woman>. "Лик" refers to the face of an icon, "пресвятой" (in genitive case here) to the Virgin Mary.

27 скорбны очи (=скорбные очи) – grieving eyes

28 лья – pouring (from лить)

31 *Ave, Mater Dei* – (Latin) Hail, Mother of God

34 Ввстречу – when meeting. The word is an archaism even in Pushkin, who elsewhere uses "Навстречу" (the form still in use in modern Russian).
37 Lumen coelum, sancta Rosa! – (Latin) Light of the sky, holy Rose! If this phrase is a quotation, its source has yet to be discovered.
40 со всех сторон – from everywhere
41 за́мок – castle (not to be confused with замо́к, lock)
46 Дух лука́вый подоспе́л – the crafty spirit (i.e., the devil) appeared
48 преде́л – realm
49 Он-де Богу не моли́лся – "He didn't pray to God," he said. The particle "де" indicates reported speech. All Soviet editions wrote "Бог" with a small letter, but in this instance it obviously should be capitalized.
51 Не путём-де волочи́лся – He inappropriately ran after. The word is usually used to describe a love interest. See Blank (140): "It is virtually impossible to provide an adequate English translation of the words *volochilsia* and *matushka*, used here in reference to the Mother of God. In Russian the last two lines of this stanza (i.e., lines 51–52) sound both courtly and scandalous – or rather, scandalous because of their courtly tone."
53 пречи́стая – the most pure <one> (i.e., Mary)
55 вечно – a truncated adjective here, not an adverb, thus "into the eternal kingdom," *not* "eternally into the kingdom"

Из Гафи́за – From Hafiz

Pushkin's knowledge of the fourteenth-century Persian poet Hafiz was limited. This poem is not a translation, but a stylization. It appears to be addressed from a male to another male, and such an overt homosexual theme was something Pushkin associated with "Eastern" poetry and mores (cf. "Подражание арабскому"). However, there are other possible explanations for this mystification. The fact that Pushkin indicates that the poem was written in a military camp (the parenthetical "Лагерь при Евфрате" [Camp near the Euphrates]) suggests that he wanted the reader to understand the poem as a comment on the present military campaign. It is conceivable that Pushkin used the veil of Hafiz to make publishable his own antiwar sentiment. (If so, it worked; the poem was published twice in his lifetime.)

Like "Подражание арабскому," the poem is written in trochaic tetrameter with alternating rhymes. Both poems are written astrophically, yet syntax and logic clearly break them into quatrains.

1 Не пленя́йся бранной славой – Do not be captivated by military glory
4 С караба́хскою толпо́й – With the crowd from Karabakh. Karabakh was famed for its horses (and, by extension, its warriors).
6 Азраи́л – Azrail (according to Islamic belief, the angel of death)
8 И поща́да будет ей – And there will be mercy to it (i.e., it will be spared). The antecedent is "красота" of the previous line.

„Критóн, роскóшный граждани́н“ – “Crito, citizen of luxury”

So little of the poem exists that one can only speculate as to how it might have developed. According to an ingenious hypothesis of Levkovich, these lines are connected to Pushkin’s own experiences at the Tiflis baths, as related at the beginning of the second chapter of *Путешествие в Арзрум* (*Journey to Arzrum*). Pushkin visited the baths on a day reserved for women and was delighted to be allowed in and to have the opportunity to admire their beauty. (They paid no attention whatsoever to him.) However, such a reading does not easily account for the ancient Greek setting. Taking this as his starting point, Fomichev argues that Pushkin planned to set the poem in the time of the Athenian plague in the age of Pericles. That subject, however, is not easily reconciled with what is a clearly comic tone.

The meter is iambic tetrameter with an unpredictable rhyme scheme.

---

1 Критóн – The name Crito is generally associated with wealth because of the eponymous hero of Plato’s dialogue. (Pushkin had also used the name in “Клеопатра,” admittedly without this association.)
3 Во цвете жизни – in the prime of life
4 Всем упоéньям бытия́ – to all the pleasures of life
6 по Керáмику – in Ceramic. The name of the northwestern part of ancient Athens.
7 из рощи вековóй – from an ancient grove
11 пред банею (=перед баней) – in front of the baths
15 сокры́лась (=скрылась) – disappeared

Literature: Levkovich 1983a, 10; Fomichev 2001.

<На карти́нки к „Евгéнию Онéгину“ в „Невском альманáхе“> – On the Illustrations for “Eugene Onegin” in the “Nevsky Almanac”

Pushkin wrote a number of epigrams on the illustrations for *Eugene Onegin* published by the artist Aleksandr Vasil’evich Notbek (1802–1866) in the *Nevsky Almanac* of 1829. He made no effort to publish these poems; they were written in a copy of the almanac for the amusement of his friend Mikhail Ivanovich Pushchin (1800–1869), who subsequently lost the almanac but reconstructed two of the poems from memory.

Curiously enough, the poems are not in Onegin stanzas, but in iambic tetrameter with alternating rhymes. The lexicon ranges from poetic to substandard.

1. „Вот перешéд чрез мост Кокýшкин“ – “Here, having crossed Kokushkin Bridge”

The first illustration was to chapter 1, stanza XLVIII.

1 мост Кокýшкин – Kokushkin Bridge, a Saint Petersburg landmark
2 Опéршись <- - -> о гранúт (= Опершись жопой о гранит) – Leaning his ass against the granite. The line is an auto-parody of the already bathetic passage in *Onegin*: “С душою, полной сожалений, / И опершися на гранит, / Стоял задумчиво Евгений, / Как описал себя Пиит.” In the novel in verse, Pushkin had put a footnote after these lines and quoted a passage from the little-known poem “Богине Невы” (“To the Goddess of the Neva”) by Mikhail Nikitich Murav’ev (1757–1807): “Въявь богиню благосклонну / Зрит восторженный пиит, / Что проводит ночь бессонну, / Опершися на гранит.” In fact, the reference is really to Batiushkov (who cited Murav’ev’s poem) and who himself used the image of a poet leaning against a rock in a translation from Petrarch. (See Rossi 2007.)
3 Сергéич (= Сергеевич) – Sergeevich (son of Sergei). Pushkin’s spelling reflects the actual pronunciation rather than the correct orthography.
4 мосьё – Monsieur
6 Тверды́ню власти роковóй – The fortress of fateful power. This is the Peter and Paul Fortress (also a prison), the “крепость” of the next line. In Pushkin’s conception of the scene (which is known less from the novel in verse than from a sketch he himself drew), Pushkin and his friend Onegin have crossed the bridge and are leaning on the granite embankment, looking away from the viewer in the direction of the famous fortress.
8 Не плюй в колóдец, милый мой – Don’t spit in the well, my dear. The idiom “Не плюй в колодец” is frequently used in Russian. The point is that one should not spit in a well because one will later need to drink that very water. In this line, Pushkin addresses the saying to himself. In other words, one shouldn’t show disrespect for the prison, as one might well end up there.

2. „Пупóк чернéет сквозь рубáшку“ – <Her> navel shows darkly through her chemise

The second illustration was to chapter 3, stanza XXXII, when Tat’iana finishes writing her impassioned letter to Onegin. The relevant passage reads:

Татьяна то вздохнет, то охнет;
Письмо дрожит в ее руке;
Облатка розовая сохнет
На воспаленном языке.
К плечу головушкой склонилась.
Сорочка легкая спустилась
С ее прелестного плеча …

Но вот уж лунного луча
Сиянье гаснет.

According to Pushchin, the text of this epigram consisted of twelve lines, but he could not remember the first four.

---

1 Пупо́к черне́ет – <Her> navel shows darkly. Some editions give the more logical "Сосок чернеет" ("A nipple shows darkly"). This is listed as a variant in the Academy edition.
2 Нару́жу титька – <Her> tit is fully visible (i.e., uncovered)
3 мнёт – folds
4 Зане живо́т у ней (=у неё) боли́т – Because her tummy aches. The word "Зане" was already archaic in Pushkin's time; its presence in this lexical context creates a humorous effect.
7 И на подти́рку изорва́ла – And tore up for purposes of wiping (i.e., toilet paper)
8 „Невский альмана́х" – *Nevsky Almanac*. This was, of course, the periodical that printed these pictures.

Literature: Nabokov, 2:177–79.

Оле́гов щит – Oleg's Shield

The title refers to a passage related in the history of Kievan Rus' known as the *Повесть временных лет* (*Primary Chronicle*). In 907 Oleg defeated the Greeks in Constantinople and hung his shield on the city's walls to signify his victory. Pushkin's poem compares that ancient conquest with recent events. In 1828–1829, Russia was at war with Turkey; after many missteps and miscalculations, the Russian army made a quick push towards Constantinople, forcing the Turks to agree to the Adrianople Peace Treaty on 2 September 1829. The results were beneficial for Russia, but not overwhelmingly so. Pushkin's poem, written shortly after the peace treaty was concluded, appears to cast doubt on Russia's accomplishments. It is, however, peculiar that the two fragments on the same subject (see "Восстань, о Греция, восстань" and "Опять увенчаны мы славой") present a much more favorable view of the results of the war.

The poem is written in iambic tetrameter. The eight-line stanzas use alternating rhymes. The bipartite structure of the poem (then versus now) is reflected in the two stanzas. The somewhat archaic lexicon recalls in places the eighteenth-century ode.

---

1 ко граду Константи́на – to the city of Constantine. The city, originally Byzantium, was renamed Constantinople in the fifth century AD after Constantine (who had conquered it in the fourth century AD). The "modern" name Istanbul was already attested in the tenth century and in common usage by the fall of Constantinople in 1453 (an event not mentioned but possibly relevant to the present poem).

2 вои́нственный варя́г – martial Varangian. The phrase is in vocative case, addressed to Oleg. The Varangians were Scandinavian (Viking) colonists who came to Russia beginning in the ninth century.

3 славя́нская дружи́на – a Slavic (as opposed to Varangian) army

4 развила́ побе́ды стяг – unfurled the banner of victory

6 Стропти́ву (= строптивому) греку в стыд и страх – To the shame and fear of the obstinate Greek. As often in Pushkin's verse, the singular is used in place of the logical plural. Cf. "Отсель грозить мы будем шведу" ("From here we will threaten the Swede") in "Медный всадник" ("The Bronze Horseman").

7 була́тный – steel

8 царегра́дских – of Constantinople. "Царьград" was the Old Russian name for Constantinople. (It is the word used in the account of Oleg in the *Primary Chronicle*.)

11 днесь – now

12 К Стамбу́лу грозно притекли́ – We menacingly came to Istanbul. "Течь" is archaic for "идти."

13 Твой холм – Your hill. "Твой" here and in the next lines refers to Oleg. What hill Pushkin has in mind is unclear. Like Rome, Istanbul is famed for its seven hills. Leibov and Ospovat (82) argue that it is the burial mound mentioned in "Песня о вещем Олеге."

14 стон ревни́вый – jealous moan. Presumably Oleg is jealous of the Russian army because it is in a position to take over the city he once defeated.

16 Твой старый щит останови́л – Your old shield stopped <our army>.

Literature: Leibov and Ospovat 2007.

„Как сати́рой безымя́нной" – "When with an anonymous satire"

Afer Pushkin wrote two parodies on Kachenovskii (see commentary to "Журналами обиженный жестоко" and "Там, где древний Кочерговский"), a response appeared in *Вестник Европы*. In an essay purportedly on "Полтава," the critic complained that Pushkin recently "ударился в язвительные стишонки и ругательства" ("became keen on nasty little verses and curses"). Since the journal in question was edited by Kachenovskii, Pushkin attributed the sentiment to him (though the article in question was in fact written by Nadezhdin).

The poem is in trochaic tetrameter with alternating rhymes.

1 безымя́нной – anonymous. The point is not that the satire was authored anonymously, but rather that the target of the satire was not directly named.

2 Лик зойла я пятна́л – I sullied the face of the Zoilus. The fact that Pushkin writes "зоил" with a small letter indicates that he does not use it as a proper noun, but rather as a synonym for "petty critic."

3 бранный – martial

8 Расписа́лся – acknowledged; signed off on

„Опя́ть уве́нчаны мы славой“ – “Again we are crowned with glory”

The poem, like “Восстань, о Греция восстань,” is clearly inspired by recent political events, but it celebrates Russia’s gains rather than those of Greece.

The poem is written in iambic tetrameter. The two quatrains, if treated as an eight-line unit, would form a truncated odic stanza (cf. Pushkin’s early ode “Вольность,” but with the masculine and feminine lines reversed). The same form (though again beginning with a masculine rhyme) can be found in “Восстань, о Греция восстань.”

---

3 Решён в Арзру́ме спор крова́вый – In Arzrum the bloody quarrel is decided. A reference to General Paskevich’s military victories.

4 В Эды́рне мир провозглашён – In Edirne peace has been proclaimed. Edirne is another name for Adrianople (the reference is to the peace treaty that was ratified there).

6 облегла́ – surrounded

7 пол-Эвкси́на – half of the Euksin. “Pont Euksin” is the Greek name for the Black Sea. It is archaic in Russian, but is found in odic poetry (e.g., Derzhavin’s “Осень во время осады Очакова”). As part of the Adrianople peace treaty, Russia gained most of the Eastern shore of the Black Sea.

„Восста́нь, о Греция восста́нь“ – “Rise up, O Greece, rise up”

One of the results of Russia’s 1828–1829 war with Turkey was that Turkey agreed to grant autonomy to Greece, an issue that had exercised Europeans (Pushkin included) for some time. Though unfinished, one can assume that Pushkin’s broad strategy in this poem was to connect the contemporary battles of Greece with its glorious past.

The poem is written in iambic tetrameter. The four-line stanzas use different rhyme schemes; the first and third alternating, the second a ring structure. It is tempting to read the first eight lines as an abbreviated odic stanza (reminiscent of Pushkin’s own “Вольность”) and the final four as the opening of another such stanza. However, the quatrain form makes this unlikely.

See also commentary to “Опять увенчаны мы славой.”

---

2 напряга́ла силы – strained <your> nerves; made great efforts. The subject is presumably “Греция.”

3 потряса́ла брань – the battle shook

4 Оли́мп и Пинд и Фермопи́лы – Olympus and Pindus and Thermopolae. Mount Olympus and the Pindus mountain range, traditionally associated with the “klephts” (patriotic Greek outlaws who hid there to avoid the Turks), were the scene of battles during the Greek war for independence. The reference to Thermopolae recalls the 1821 Battle of Alamana (fought nearby), in which a small number of Greeks attempted to block the advance of a much larger

group of Turkish soldiers. The Greeks lost, and their leader was martyred, but their daring and patriotism became a rallying point for the Greek cause.

5 их верши́н – their heights

7 Пери́кла – of Pericles. Pericles (495–429 BCE), the great Athenian general and statesman.

8 мраморных Афи́н – of marble Athens. The great buildings of Athens were made of marble (e.g., the Acropolis). Athens ("Афины") is plural in Russian.

10 вери́ги – fetters

12 Тиртея, Байрона, и Риги – Tyrtaeus, Byron, and Rhigas. Tyrtaeus was a Greek poet who lived in the seventh century BCE. Little is known of him, and his work survives only in fragments. He was the author of patriotic political poetry in which he urged the Spartans to fight for their country.

Lord Byron (1788–1824) is mentioned in this context because he made the Greek war for independence his personal crusade and died in Greece (admittedly not on the battlefield), furthering this cause.

Konstantinos Rhigas (1757–1798), was a Greek poet and revolutionary who devoted his life (and lost it) waging war against the Turks. His "Greek Marseillaise" was particularly famous and translated into English by Byron. That translation begins: "Sons of the Greeks arise! / The glorious hour's gone forth, / And, worthy of such ties, / Display who gave us birth." This is followed by a chorus: "Sons of Greeks! let us go / In arms against the foe, / Till their hated blood shall flow / In a river past our feet." The poem proper continues with references to antiquity ("Hellenes of past ages, / Oh, start again to life!") and to Thermopolae.

„Зорю бьют … из рук мои́х" – "Reveille sounds … from my hands"

The poem consists of a brilliant series of echoes and contrasts (sound vs. silence, poetry vs. reality, now vs. then). The poet's reading of Dante is interrupted by martial sounds; he recalls similar interruptions from long ago. Biographically, the two temporal references are the present (when Pushkin accompanied the Russian army in the Caucasus) and his time at the Lyceum, where he would have heard reveille from the nearby military barracks.

The poem is written in trochaic tetrameter with rhyme scheme a-B-a-a-B-c-D-D-c. The fact that lines 1, 3, and 4 rhyme could perhaps be understood as a distant echo of Dante's terza rima. The French edition that Pushkin was probably reading (see commentary to line 2) did not retain this form, but Pushkin was obviously aware of it, judging from his Dante stylization written the following year (cf. "В начале жизни школу помню я"). The period at the end of line 5 marks the logical break of the poem into two parts. The drafts indicate that Pushkin initially planned to write the poem in iambic tetrameter. His decision to switch to trochees can probably be explained by the poem's exoticism (both in terms of the place of composition and "ancient" source, see Gasparov 1990, 9–10). According to Lotman (1997, 162–63), Pushkin's trochaic verse in this period – in contrast to his iambic verse – is consistently marked by a transition from reality to some sort of hypothetical state (whether expressed as desire or, as in this poem, recollection). See Belousov, 29.

1 Зорю бьют – Reveille sounds. Literally: "<they> beat reveille." In Pushkin's time, reveille took the form of beating a drum. Lotman claims that this could refer to morning or evening reveille, but the former seems more plausible.

2 Ветхий Данте выпада́ет – Ancient Dante falls out. The adjective has a number of possible meanings. It could simply refer to the fact that Dante lived long ago. More probable is that it describes a specific edition of Dante's works. Such a reading is supported by the draft version, which reads "Мой ветхий Дант." If this is the case, it could mean either "worn out" or, as Vatsuro (2000, 245) argues, "ancient." Pushkin may well refer to a specific edition that he owned, which happened to be the first complete translation of the *Divine Comedy* ever published (it was also the oldest book in Pushkin's library): *La comedie de Dante, de l'Enfer, du Purgatoire & Paradis, mise en ryme françoise et commêtée par M. B. Grangier Conseiller & Aulm-er du Roi; & Abbé de S. Barthelemi ne Noyon* (Paris, 1596). This would mean that the verse that he never finishes reading (lines 3–4) was in French, not Italian.

5 Дух дале́че улета́ет – The spirit flies far away. The "spirit" in question is presumably either the spirit of Dante's time (or work) or the poet's thoughts about Dante.

7 Сколь ты часто раздава́лся – How often you sounded

8 тихо развива́лся – quietly developed

9 давни́шнею поро́й – at a time long ago

„Счастлив ты в преле́стных дурах" – "You are fortunate in charming fools"

This epigram was conceivably addressed to Rufin Ivanovich Dorokhov (who died in 1852 doing battle with Chechens). The prototype for Dolokhov in Tolstoy's *War and Peace*, Dorokhov was a career officer who was repeatedly demoted for participating in duels. Pushkin met him in the Caucasus in August of 1829.

The poem is written in trochaic tetrameter with alternating rhymes. Though astrophic, it divides logically into two parts. As so often in epigrams, strong repetition is interrupted by an unexpected conclusion. Note, for example, the string of anaphora from lines 3 to 6. Also remarkable is the use of prepositional case in every line except the last one (where "вполне" hints at the preposition "в," but changes the emphasis; "вполне" is also the only rhyme that is not grammatical).

1 в преле́стных дурах – in charming fools. The usually literal Nabokov (3:198) renders this as "foolish charmers." Neither translation really conveys the essential point: that the male addressee is successful with pretty, but vapid, women.

3 Ты St.-Priest в карикату́рах – You are Saint-Priest in caricatures, that is, when it comes to caricatures, you are another Saint-Priest. Emmanuil Karlovich Saint-Priest (1806–1828), an eccentric famed for his caricatures (none of which seem to have survived).

4 Неле́динский – Iurii Aleksandrovich Neledinskii-Meletskii (1752–1829), a poet

known for his folkloric stylizations. The stress on the name is dictated by the meter.

5 простре́лен на дуе́ле (=дуэли) – shot through in a duel

6 разру́блен – cut up; chopped up

7 Хоть геро́й ты в самом деле – Even if you're truly a hero

8 Но пове́са ты вполне́ – But you're quite the rake

<На Надеждина> („Наде́ясь на моё презре́нье") – On Nadezhdin ("Hoping for my Disdain")

One of several epigrams aimed at Nikolai Ivanovich Nadezhdin (1804–1856), a literary critic who at this time was publishing screeds against Pushkin's work in the journal *Вестник Европы* (*The European Herald*).

The poem is written in iambic tetrameter with alternating rhymes. The rhyme scheme follows the syntax, structuring the poem in three four-line segments.

---

2 Седо́й зо́йл – the gray-haired Zoilus. A reference to M. T. Kachenovskii, publisher of the journal *Вестник Европы* (*The European Herald*), who was in his mid-fifties at the time.

4 Я эпигра́ммой отвеча́л – I answered with an epigram. Pushkin had written (and published) numerous epigrams on Kachenovskii (see "Литературное известие," "Журналами обиженный жестоко" and "Там, где древний Кочерговский"), so it is difficult to say which one in particular he refers to.

5 Уку́шенный – stung; bitten

6 наде́ясь на отве́т – hoping for a response. There may be a pun intended in this repeated "надеясь" and the never explicitly mentioned "Надеждин." (The poem's title was supplied by the editors, not by Pushkin.) This line apparently alludes to the concluding sentence in Nadezhdin's (negative) review of "Poltava" in *Вестник Европы*, no. 9 (1829): "Утешаюсь, по крайней мере, тою мыслию, что ежели певцу 'Полтавы' вздумается швырнуть в меня эпиграммой – то это будет для меня *незаслуженное* удовольствие!"

7 холо́п – lackey

8 Руга́ть бы также стал – Would also begin to curse

9 перед обе́дней – before mass

11 сиди́ себе – sit quietly. "Себе" is a particle here (as against line 10, where it is a pronoun).

12 будет с барином расчёт – There will be an accounting with the master

„Был и я среди́ донцо́в" – "I too was among the Don Cossacks"

The poem appears to be based on a conversation that Pushkin overheard on his journey to the Caucasus. In a passage that never made its way into the *Путешествие в Арзрум* (*Journey to Arzrum*), he recounts the following discussion:

Мы ехали из Арзрума в Тифлис. Тридцать человек линейских казаков нас конвоировали, возвращающихся на свою родину. Перед нами показался линейский полк, идущий им на смену. Казаки узнали своих земляков и поскакали к ним навстречу, приветствуя их радостными выстрелами из ружей и пистолетов. Обе толпы съехались и обнялись на конях при свисте пуль и в облаках дыма и пыли. Обменявшись известиями, они расстались и догнали нас с новыми прощальными выстрелами.
– Какие вести? – спросил я у прискакавшего ко мне урядника, – все ли дома благополучно?
– Слава богу, – отвечал он, – старики мои живы; жена здорова.
– А давно ли ты с ними расстался?
– Да вот уже три года, хоть по положению надлежало бы служить только год …
– А скажи, – прервал его молодой артиллерийский офицер, – не родила ли у тебя жена во время отсутствия?
– Ребята говорят, что нет, – отвечал веселый урядник.
– А не б<лядова>ла ли без тебя?
– Помаленьку, слышно, б<лядова>ла.
– Что ж, побьешь ты ее за это?
– А зачем ее бить? Разве я безгрешен?
– Справедливо; а у тебя, брат, – спросил я другого казака, – так ли честна хозяйка, как у урядника?
– Моя родила, – отвечал он, стараясь скрыть свою досаду.
– А кого бог дал?
– Сына.
– Что ж, брат, побьешь ее?
– Да посмотрю; коли на зиму сена припасла, так и прощу, коли нет, так побью.
– И дело, – подхватил товарищ, – побьешь, да и будешь горевать, как старик Черкасов; смолоду был он дюж и горяч, случился с ним тот же грех, как и с тобой, поколотил он хозяйку, так что она после того тридцать лет жила калекой. С сыном его случись та же беда, и тот было стал колотить молодицу, а старик-то ему: "Слушай, Иван, оставь ее, посмотри-ка на мать, и я смолоду поколотил ее за то же, да и жизни не рад." Так и ты, – продолжал урядник, – жену-то прости, а выб<ляд>ка посылай чаще по дождю.
– Ладно, ладно, посмотрим, – отвечал казак уряднику.
– А в самом деле, – спросил я, – что ты сделаешь с выб<ляд>ком?
– Да что с ним делать? Корми да отвечай за него, как за родного.
– Сердит, – шепнул мне урядник, – теперь жена не смей и показаться ему: прибьет до смерти.
Это заставило меня размышлять о простоте казачьих нравов.

By writing the poem in the first person (in a way that recalls the much earlier "Черная шаль"), Pushkin significantly complicates the moral certainty of the speaker's position. This stylized quality of this poem is also reflected in the formal choices. The poem is in trochaic tetrameter, using simple syntax and lexicon. The rhymes alternate masculine and feminine. All feminine rhymes are on the same vowel, with the fourth line of each stanza ending on the key word "нагайку."

---

1 среди донцóв – among the Don Cossacks. The Cossacks were employed by the Russians as soldiers in their wars against the Turks.
2 осмáнов шайку – the band of Osmans. Already in eighteenth-century Russian poetry, Osman had become a general (pejorative) term for Turk.
4 нагáйку – a whip (made of horsehair)
6 балалáйку – <my> balalaika. The balalaika was a folk instrument; no sophisticated Russian would ever have played one.
9 Что таи́ться от друзéй – Why should I hide <this> from my friends
10 свою́ хозя́йку – my wife
12 И берёг свою́ нагáйку – And I kept my whip

Сапóжник (Притча) – The Cobbler (A Parable)

Pushkin's poem (first stanza) retells the story – recounted by Pliny the Elder in his *Natural History*, 35 – of the painter Apelles and a shoemaker who criticized his depiction of a shoe. Apelles altered the painting in accordance with the expert's opinion. However, when the shoemaker, emboldened by the painter's acceptance of his first criticism, claimed to detect an inadequacy in the rendering of the leg, Apelles told him that he should limit his judgments to shoes. In the second stanza, Pushkin applies this story to Nadezhdin, who had recently attacked Pushkin's work.

The poem is written in iambic pentameter with caesura after the second foot. The first stanza rhymes A-b-A-b-C-d-C-d, the second rhymes E-E-f-E-f. The lexicon reflects an interesting mix of the bookish and the colloquial.

---

1 раз – once. Pushkin has in mind Pliny's account.
6 А эта грудь не слишком ли нагá? – Is that breast not too naked? Pushkin here obviously departs from Pliny's story. Clearly, he was annoyed by the "moralistic" tone of Nadezhdin's criticisms.
7 Апеллéс – Apelles (fourth century BCE), reputed to be the greatest painter of antiquity (none of his work survives)
8 "Суди́, дружóк, не свыше сапогá!" – "My friend, you should not judge above the shoe." The line in quotation marks is indeed a quote, a Latin "familiar quotation" that Pushkin had probably learned in school. In Pliny, the line reads: "Ne supra crepidam judicaret" ("Let him not judge above the shoe").
12 Но чорт (= чёрт) его несёт суди́ть о свете – But why the devil is he making judgments about high society (and its ways)
13 Попрóбуй он – Let him try

<На Надéждина> („В журнáл совсéм не европéйский“) – On Nadezhdin ("To a journal not at all European")

Another attack on Nadezhdin, this one written in iambic tetrameter (and, in the second line, iambic pentameter).

---

1 совсéм не европéйский – Not at all European. Nadezhdin published his essays in *Вестник Европы* (*The European Herald*), but Pushkin, associating the word "European" with openness to new ideas and approaches, points out that this journal – its name notwithstanding – is xenophobic and conservative.

2 Над коим чахнет старый журналúст – Over which an old journalist withers away. Pushkin has in mind Kachenovskii. See commentary to line 2 of "На Надеждина" ("Надеясь на моё презренье").

4 Взошёл болвáн семинарúст – A dolt-seminarian entered. Nadezhdin was educated at a seminary.

Дон – The Don

Pushkin returned home from his visit to the Russian army before the campaign was concluded, thus reaching the Don River before the soldiers did. In this poem, Pushkin greets the Don River while the Don Cossacks are still engaged in battle. One need not insist on the identity of the speaker with the biographical Pushkin. The language and the form are stylized.

The poem is written in trochaic tetrameter with alternating rhymes, which recalls the highly stylized "Был и я среди донцов," except that the order of feminine and masculine rhymes is reversed. Both poems use emphatic repetition in the rhymes. Here the Дон/поклон rhyme of the first two stanzas resurfaces in the feminine rhyme of stanza 3 – as погони/кони – then is hinted at again in the fourth with the appearance of the word "Дон" on the third foot of the first line.

---

1 Блеща – Shining. In modern Russian, the stress is on the second syllable: блещá.

3 От сынóв – From your sons. The use of "сынов" (rather than "сыновей") is a stylization.

6 тихий Дон – the quiet Don. The epithet is folkloric.

7 От Арáкса и Евфрáта – From the Araz and the Euphrates. In modern Russian, the Euphrates is spelled "Эфрат." The Russian army (with Pushkin in tow) had recently encountered both of these rivers. In 1814, the Araz (also called Aras) River was the border between the Russian Empire and Persia. The army's camp near the Euphrates figures as the place of composition of the poem "Из Гафиза."

8 поклóн – a bow. It is a standard Russian expression to send a bow ("передать поклон") as a sign of respect.

9 от злой погóни – from quick pursuit

10 Чуя – Smelling; sensing

12 Арпача́йскую струю́ – The Arpa-Chai stream. The Arpa-Chai River was the border that separated Turkey and Russia. During the campaign that Pushkin witnessed, the Russians pushed beyond it. Cf. *Путешествие в Арзрум* (*Journey to Arzrum*), chapter 2.
15 Сок кипу́чий, искромётный – the foaming, sparkling juice
16 Виногра́дников твои́х – of your vineyards

Доро́жные жалобы – Traveling Complaints

The poem reflects a traveler's musings on mortality and is surely influenced by the lengthy travels that Pushkin undertook in 1829. Though Pushkin himself dated the poem 1829, a reference in the drafts to an acquaintance of Pushkin's who died on the road in 1830 suggests that the poem was begun in 1829, but completed later. (The first publication was in 1831.)

The poem is written in trochaic tetrameter with alternating rhymes. Gasparov (1990, 8) notes that this is the standard form for Pushkin's poems on the subject of travel. The lexicon is striking for its conversational tone.

---

1 гуля́ть на свете – to wander about the world
2 То в коля́ске, то верхо́м – At times in a carriage, at times on horseback. A "коляска" was not quite as solid as a "карета" (see line 3), but still quite comfortable and fashionable. The carriage was open, with a roof that could be folded up or down, and it was usually pulled by two or three horses (a "пара" or a "тройка").
3 То в киби́тке, то в каре́те – At times in a covered cart, at times in a carriage. A "кибитка" was a partially covered wagon, not particularly expensive or luxurious. At the beginning of the novel *Капитанская дочка* (*The Captain's Daughter*), the hero Grinev leaves his home in a "кибитка." A "карета" was the most luxurious means of travel in Pushkin's day. It was fully covered, had cushioned seats, and was ordinarily pulled by three or four horses. At the conclusion of Pushkin's story "Станционный смотритель" ("The Station Master"), we learn that the fabulously wealthy Dunia came to visit her father in a "карета" pulled by six horses.
4 в теле́ге – in a cart. This was the simplest wheeled conveyance in Pushkin's day.
5 в насле́дственной берло́ге – in my inherited den
6 отческих (=отеческих) – ancestral
7–8 На большо́й мне, знать, доро́ге / Умере́ть госпо́дь суди́л – On the highway, it seems, the Lord judged that I should die.
9 На каме́ньях – on the stones. Presumably Pushkin has in mind the stones lying in the road. In modern Russian, the form would be "на камня́х."
12 Под разо́бранным мосто́м – under a bridge that has fallen apart (or, conceivably, a bridge that has been taken down, e.g., to prevent it from being destroyed by inclement weather).
13 подце́пит – will grab hold of. Pushkin uses this verb in an unusual way. Ordinarily one says this of a non-serious disease, for example, "он подцепил

простуду," ("he caught a cold"), but not "простуда его подцепила." If used about a more serious disease (e.g., syphilis), it suggests recklessness.

14 окостени́т – will ossify

15–16 Иль (=Или) мне в лоб шлагба́ум влепи́т / Непрово́рный инвали́д – Or a clumsy invalid smacks a wooden barrier into my forehead. In Russian (as in French), an "инвалид" is simply an old (retired) soldier, infirm, but not necessarily injured. In this poem, he is apparently employed as a guard who uses a wooden turnstile to stop traffic and (presumably) to collect a tax. Pushkin (perhaps unknowingly) plays on the German origin of the word "шлагбаум" (schlagen = to hit; to strike). Like the German equivalent, the word has two (not three) syllables.

19 со скуки околе́ю – I'll croak from boredom

20 в карантине́ – in quarantine. During his travels in the Caucasus in 1829, Pushkin had spent three days in quarantine in Gumri, Armenia, mentioned briefly in chapter five of *Путешествие в Арзрум* (*Journey to Arzrum*). In modern Russian the stress would be "в каранти́не."

22 Пост нево́льный – an involuntary fast

24 Трюфли Яра – Truffles from "Iar." The restaurant "Iar" (named after its owner, Trankel' Petrovich Iar) was opened in Moscow in 1826 and quickly became popular among literati (and many others). Pushkin first dined there within a week of his return from exile in 1826. This was the restaurant where, on 27 January 1831, Pushkin and his friends (Viazemskii, Baratynskii, and Iazykov) held a memorial dinner for the recently deceased Del'vig.

25 То ли дело быть на месте – How much better it is to be in one's place (i.e., to stay in one's home town)

26 По Мясни́цкой разъезжа́ть – To travel about on Miasnitskaia Street. Miasnitskaia is an old street in the center of Moscow. (In a draft version, Pushkin had named another Moscow street: "По Никитской разъезжать.") After five months in the Caucasus, Pushkin returned to Moscow on 20 September 1829 and spent the next month there. The streets in question both were significant for Pushkin. Natalia Goncharova lived on Nikitskaia, while Anna Petrovna Malinovskaia (who interceded on Pushkin's behalf with the Goncharov family) lived on Miasnitskaia.

31 То ли дело, братцы, дома – How much better it is, friends, to be home

32 Ну, пошёл же, погоня́й – Well, let's go, whip <the horses>. The final line is addressed by the passenger to the driver.

Ме́док. (Ме́док в Уа́ллах). – Madoc. (Madoc in Wales).

A translation of the opening of Robert Southey's narrative poem "Madoc." In characteristic fashion, Southey begins this lengthy poem with a preface (in the edition Pushkin owned, *The Poetical Works of Robert Southey* [Paris, 1829], the passage is on page 196):

> The historical facts on which this Poem is founded may be related in few words. On the death of Owen Gwyneth, king of North Wales, AD 1169, his

children disputed the succession. Yorwerth, the elder, was set aside without a struggle, as being incapacitated by a blemish in his face. Hoel, though illegitimate, and born of an Irish mother, obtained possession of the throne for a while, till he was defeated and slain by David, the eldest son of the late king by a second wife. The conqueror, who then succeeded without opposition, slew Yorwerth, imprisoned Rodri and hunted others of his brethren into exile. But Madoc, meantime, abandoned his barbarous country, and sailed away to the West in search of some better resting-place. The land which he discovered pleased him: he left there part of his people, and went back to Wales for a fresh supply of adventurers, with whom he again set sail, and was heard of no more. Strong evidence has been adduced that he reached America, and that his posterity exist there to this day, on the southern branches of the Missouri, retaining their complexion, their language and, in some degree[1] their arts. <…>

Note

1. That country has now been fully explored, and wherever Madoc may have settled, it is now certain that no Welsh Indians are to be found upon any branches of the Missouri. – 1815 (Southey's note).

The poem proper begins on the next page:

PART I – Madoc in Wales
I. The Return to Wales

Fair blows the wind, – the vessel drives along,
Her streamers fluttering at their length, her sails
All full, – she drives along, and round her prow
Scatters the ocean spray. What feelings then
Filled every bosom, when the mariners,
After the peril of that weary way,
Beheld their own dear country! Here stands one
Stretching his sight toward the distant shore,
And as to well-known forms his busy joy
Shapes the dim outline, eagerly he points
The fancied headland and the cape and bay,
Till his eyes ache o'erstraining. This man shakes
His comrade's hand, and bids him welcome home,
And blesses God, and then he weeps aloud:
Here stands another, who in secret prayer
Calls on the Virgin and his patron Saint,
Renewing his old vows of gifts and alms
And pilgrimage, so he may find all well.
Silent and thoughtful and apart from all
Stood Madoc; now his noble enterprise
Proudly remembering, now in dreams of hope,
Anon of bodings full and doubt and fear.
Fair smiled the evening, and the favouring gale

Sung in the shrouds, and swift the steady bark
Rushed roaring through the waves.
The sun goes down.

Pushkin's translation closely follows the blank verse of the original.

---

1 Попу́тный веет ветр – A favorable wind blows. Note that this translation exactly follows the syntax of Southey's English (adjective – verb – noun), at least insofar as Pushkin understood it.
4 Многим – with much; with many things. This is an instrumental case governed by the verb "напо́лнилася" (=наполнилась), "was filled" – in the following line.
5 у всех пловцо́в – of all the sailors
11–12 пока́ недви́жны (=недвижные) очи / Не заболя́т – until his motionless eyes begin to hurt
14 господа (=Господа) – the Lord; God. Note that the stress falls on the first syllable of this word.
17 дальних поклоне́ний – of distant worships. Presumably Pushkin's rendering of "pilgrimages."
25 меж ве́рвей – among the ropes. (Pushkin accurately renders the English "shrouds," a nautical term for tight ropes.)

„Стрекоту́нья белобо́ка" – "White-sided chirrer"

Pushkin completed very little of this poem, so it is difficult to determine where it was leading. However, an ingenious reading of the surviving text together with a rejected – and quite different – draft version suggests striking similarities with the later "Бесы" (Berezkina 1991, 132–35). Both poems rely on folklore; both are winter scenes narrated in the first person. Formally, the poems are in the identical meter and stanza (assuming these eight lines to be the first stanza of the larger work).

---

1 Стрекоту́нья белобо́ка (=белобо́кая) – White-sided chirrer. "Стрекотунья" is a feminine form of "стрекотун," which is anything that makes a chirring or chattering sound ("стрекотать"). In this case, as line three makes clear, it is a magpie (which has a white underside and shoulder feathers).
3 Скачет пёстрая соро́ка – The pied magpie hops. Strictly speaking, magpies are not multicolored, but two-colored (black [or dark blue] and white).
4 проро́чит – prophecies. According to a Russian superstition (and Pushkin was fascinated by superstitions, cf. *Eugene Onegin* 5:V), a magpie by a window signifies that guests will soon arrive.
5 Колоко́льчик небыва́лый – an unheard-of bell. The "колокольчик" refers to the little bell on carriages and other wheeled conveyances in Pushkin's time. Note that both of the words occur in "Бесы."
8 снежный прах – snowy dust (i.e., powdery snow)

„Зимá. Что делать нам в дерéвне? Я встречáю" – "Winter. What is there for us to do in the village? I meet"

One of the rare instances where Pushkin appended a date to the published version of his poem, though it is unclear whether the poem was fully written or only completed on that day. Pushkin, travelling from Moscow to Petersburg, was either in Pavlovskoe or Malinniki (both places associated with the Vul'f family), and this poem certainly reflects scenes from rural life. However, the events recounted in the poem may be less autobiographical than fictional and literary.

The poem is striking for its combination of a fairly stolid form (alexandrines) with prosaic lexicon and content. Even potentially elevated themes (e.g., poetry) are treated with an almost comic choice of words. The tone changes noticeably beginning at line 30, where Pushkin's erotic imagination takes over, with exclamation points "answering" the question marks of the opening.

Pushkin's use of the alexandrine is experimental; in many lines, he avoids the temptation of a syntactic break at the caesura by displacing it. This is particularly pronounced in the first line, where the syntactic breaks after the first and fourth feet are supplemented by an enjambment that extends the expected final syntactic break to the end of the first foot of the next line. Pushkin even plays with the predictability of rhymed couplets by ending the poem on an odd-numbered line (i.e., without its rhymed pair). This "unfinished" quality notwithstanding, the poem is complete.

Pushkin draws both lexically and formally on Viazemskii's "Первый снег" ("First Snow"), a celebration of winter written in iambic hexameter (with rhymes often, though not always, coming in couplets).

---

2 Слугý, несýщего – a servant who is bringing. "Слуга" is feminine in form, but designates a male servant, hence the masculine ending in несущего.

4 Порóша – powder (i.e., fresh snow)

7 Мы встаём – We get up. It is somewhat mysterious who is meant by "we."

9 Арáпники – riding whips

10 прилéжными глазáми – with diligent eyes. The speaker is carefully looking for footprints of his prey.

11 Кружи́мся, рыскаем – We go in circles, we search. The standard conjugation of рыскать is now рыщем.

12 Двух зайцев протрави́в – Having failed to hunt down two hares

13 Кудá как весело – How very joyful

14 стесня́ясь, сердце ноет – feeling constrained, the heart aches

15 По капле, медленно глотáю скуки яд – I swallow the poison of boredom slowly, by the drop

18–19 наси́льно вырывáю / У музы дремлющей несвя́зные словá – with great effort I tear away disjointed words from <my> dozing muse

20 нейдёт (= не идет) – doesn't go

21 Над рифмой, над моéй прислýжницею (= прислужницей) странной – Over rhyme, over my strange servant. The personification of rhyme as a woman has numerous precedents in Pushkin's poetry. See commentary to "Рифма, звучная подруга."

23 с лирою (= лирой) я прекращáю спор – I cease my quarrel with the lyre

24–25 разгово́р / О близких выборах, о сахарном заво́де – A conversation about the imminent elections, about the sugar factory. The passage recalls similar lists of unexciting conversation topics in *Eugene Onegin*, for example, "Их разговор благоразумный / О сенокосе, о вине, / О псарне" (2:XI) or "вечный разговор / Про дождь, про лён, про скотный двор" (3:I).

26 Хозя́йка хмурится в подо́бие пого́де – The mistress of the house frowns like the <inclement> weather

28 Иль про черво́нного гада́ет короля́ – Or tells fortunes about the king of hearts

29 Тоска́ – Boredom

30 по́д вечер – towards evening

39 вечерко́м – in the evening

40 вальсы резвые – lively waltzes

43 крыльцо́ – porch. A крыльцо could also be the steps leading up to a house. The precise meaning here is unclear.

44 вьюга ей в лицо́ – the snowstorm <blows> into her face

45 русской розе – to the Russian rose

46 Как жарко поцалу́й (=поцелуй) пыла́ет на моро́зе – How a kiss burns hotly in the frost.

47 Как дева русская свежа́ в пыли́ снего́в – How a Russian girl is fresh in the dusting of snow. Note how the cold snowy "пыль" emerges from the burning image of "пылает" in the previous line. This line and the preceding two recall a couplet from Viazemskii's "Первый снег," about a love tryst in a snowy landscape: "Презрев мороза гнев и тщетные угрозы, / Румяных щек твоих свежей алеют розы" ("Having scorned the anger and vain threats of frost / The roses of your rouge cheeks redden more freshly"). Pushkin had already borrowed from this passage in *Eugene Onegin* (1:XXXIII) – "розы пламенных ланит" ("roses of fiery cheeks").

Literature: Briggs, 27–43.

Зимнее утро – Winter Morning

It has been argued (Briggs, 41) that this is a companion piece to "Зима. Что делать нам в деревне?" That poem is dated 2 November (and the date was included in the publication); this one is dated 3 November, thereby suggesting that the amorous tryst in the earlier poem ended successfully. However, the date of the second poem is only to be found in Pushkin's notebooks, not as part of the published text. Moreover, if this poem really does continue the poem of the previous day, one wonders where all the other people disappeared to – especially the second "девица." The fact that no one has ever identified the woman in question suggests that the entire love affair described is a fiction rather than a recounting of an autobiographical encounter.

The poem is written in six-line stanzas of iambic tetrameter, rhymed A-A-b-C-C-b. Particularly striking is the play of color.

4 сомкну́ты (=сомкнутые) негой взоры – eyes closed in bliss

5 Навстре́чу северной Авро́ры – To meet the northern Aurora. Aurora, goddess

of dawn in Roman mythology, is often used as a paraphrase for dawn. The use of the preposition "навстречу" with a genitive complement is a Gallicism. (Ordinarily it takes dative.)

6 Звездо́ю севера яви́сь – Appear as a star of the north

7 Вечо́р – yesterday evening

8 мгла носи́лась – darkness rushed

10 желте́ла – showed yellow. This is presumably the effect of the moon filtered through the dark storm clouds. (A draft had the more expected "бледнелась," which was probably rejected because of the "бледная" in the previous line.)

14 Великоле́пными ковра́ми – Like magnificent carpets, in the form of magnificent carpets. This instrumental case is not parallel to line 13, but rather connected to the expanse of snow of the following line.

16 Прозра́чный лес оди́н черне́ет – Only the transparent forest shows black. The image seems paradoxical, but presumably the forest is transparent because it is leafless; hence one sees only the dark trees without foliage.

17 ель сквозь иней зелене́ет – the spruce shows green through the hoarfrost. The spruce (in contrast to the trees in the previous line) is an evergreen.

19 янта́рным блеском – by an amber glow

22 у лежа́нки – at the bench by the <heating> stove. This was the warmest part of the room.

24 Кобы́лку бурую запре́чь – to harness the brown filly

„Заче́м, Еле́на, так пугли́во" – "Why, Elena, so timorously"

This clearly incomplete love poem exists only in rough draft. The variants indicate that Pushkin began with unsurprising word choices and gradually changed them (in lines 2 and 4) to less expected lexical combinations. In his notorious "Don Juan list," a list of love interests that he composed for the Ushakova sisters in 1829, the name Elena appears twice. The first one has been identified, but nothing is known of the second (presumably this one).

The lines are written in iambic tetrameter with rhyme scheme A-b-b-A-b. It is impossible to say whether this represents a stanzaic unit or simply the opening of a longer astrophic (and perhaps freely rhymed) poem.

2 ревни́вой быстрото́й – jealous speed

4 надзира́ешь торопли́во – hastily watch over

Эпигра́мма („Седо́й Свисто́в!") – Epigram ("Grey-haired Svistov!")

This epigram is directed not at Nadezhdin the critic, but at Nadezhdin the poet, who had recently published his first verses.

The poem is written in iambic pentameter with caesura after the second foot and alternating rhymes. The exclamatory tone and markedly archaic lexicon serve to recall (and mock) elevated style.

1 Свисто́в – The name is transparently derived from Хвосто́в. Dmitrii Ivanovich Khvostov (1757 [in Chereiskii 1756]–1835) had been a constant target for Pushkin and his friends because of the quality and quantity of his verse. He championed Nadezhdin as a young poet with similar archaist principles.

5 Се: внемлет мне масти́тый собесе́дник – Behold: the venerable interlocutor harkens to me

6 Сверша́ется (= Совершается) судьби́ны произво́л – The whim of fate is complete

8 Свистов II – Svistov the Second. ("II" should be read as "второ́й.")

Эпигра́мма („Мальчи́шка Фебу гимн поднёс") – Epigram ("A young lad brought a hymn to Apollo")

Another epigram directed at Nadezhdin. The point of departure is Nadezhdin's essay in *Вестник Европы* purportedly on Pushkin's narrative poem "Poltava," but really a discussion of Pushkin's recent poetry, which is treated as being vastly inferior to his previous work. Early in the essay (which takes the form of a dialogue), one of interlocutors dismisses the idea that Pushkin is a genius because of his early success. He does so by referring to Vasilii L'vovich Pushkin (Pushkin's uncle), who had written (actually, translated from the French) a tale of Apollo and a "precocious" youth:

> Какой-то стихотвор (довольно их у нас!)
> Послал две оды на Парнас.
> Он в них описывал красу природы, неба,
> Цвет розо-желтый облаков,
> Шум листьев, вой зверей, ночное пенье сов
> И милости просил у Феба.
> Читая, Феб зевал и наконец спросил:
> "Каких лет стихотворец был
> И оды громкие давно ли сочиняет?"
> "Ему 15-ть лет," – Эрата отвечает.
> "Пятнадцать только лет?" – "Не более того."
> "Так розгами его!"

Pushkin's first four lines neatly summarize his uncle's poem. He then turns the tables on his critic by likening Nadezhdin to the fifteen-year-old. Pushkin's poem is written in iambic tetrameter. The structure follows the rhyme scheme, dividing the poem into three four-line units. The first and third use alternating rhymes, the middle section a ring structure. The lexicon mixes archaisms and colloquialisms.

2 Охо́та есть, да мало мозгу – He has the desire, but not much brains

3 А сколько лет ему́, вопро́с? – The question is: how old is he?

4 Только-то? Эй, розгу! – That's all? Hey, <get the> rod! Note the jarring intonation (a spondee) in "э́й, ро́згу!"

5 За сим – After this
семинари́ст – the seminarian. Pushkin's nickname for Nadezhdin, who had studied in a seminary.
6 Тетра́дь лаке́йских диссерта́ций – A notebook of lackey's dissertations. Pushkin has in mind the lengthy essays Nadezhdin published in *Вестник Европы.*
7 Гора́ций – Horace (65–8 BCE), the Roman poet, probably mentioned here because he could be seen as a "lackey" to Augustus.
9 как от дурма́на – like from a narcotic
12 Поста́вить в палки приказа́л – Ordered him to be caned

„Я вас люби́л, любо́вь ещё, быть может" – "I loved you, love still perhaps"

One of Pushkin's most celebrated poems, it is a model of concision and balance. Most likely the addressee of the poem is A. A. Olenina, whom Pushkin had unsuccessfully wooed the previous year (Chereiskii 1973). Be that as it may, the poem is so unspecific in its depiction of the beloved and so universally applicable that the biographical prototype is hardly significant. The final line has been understood as resignation or reproach – quite possibly it is both at once.

It has been suggested that the poem is a radically truncated version of two Sainte-Beuve poems (Vickery 1972) or a variation of a Del'vig poem (the first stanza of "За ваше нежное участье," as Igor' Smirnov has pointed out to me).

It is written in iambic pentameter with caesura after the second foot and alternating rhymes. The final rhyme is complicated by a "false" rhyme that anticipates the real one: томи́м – люби́мой – други́м.

---

5 безнаде́жно – hopelessly. In modern Russian the stress would be безнадёжно.
6 томи́м – tormented. This is a present passive participle that agrees with "я."
8 Как дай вам Бог люби́мой быть други́м – That may God grant you to be loved by another. The word "как" finishes the construction begun with the repeated "так" in he previous line. All Soviet editions give "бог" rather than "Бог."

Воспомина́ния в Царском Селе́ – Recollections in Tsarskoe Selo

The poem has the same title (and is written in precisely the same form) as the famous poem of 1814 that Pushkin read at the Lyceum exam in front of the aged Derzhavin. That meeting of two poetic generations had great significance for Pushkin (who recalls it in *Eugene Onegin* 8:II).

Tsarskoe Selo (The Tsar's Village) was the town outside of Petersburg that housed the summer palace and, in the adjacent building, the Lyceum. The students were free to roam about the magnificent gardens, which were full of statues and monuments commemorating Russia's history. (The 1814 poem focused on several of these, as does the present one.) In coming back to the same subject fifteen years later, Pushkin was inevitably comparing his present thoughts to his schoolboy impressions.

The poem is written in a highly unusual eight-line iambic stanza, with lines 1, 2, 4, and 8 in tetrameter and the others in hexameter. As Tomashevskii (1958, 93) has shown, this form is derived from Batiushkov's elegy "На развалинах замка в Швеции" ("On the Ruins of a Castle in Sweden").

The last lines of this unfinished draft are, even by the standards of Pushkin's manuscripts, very difficult to decipher. Editors of the Academy edition considered many words illegible; later editors have filled them in based on additional study and logical guesses. Formal considerations make clear that the last eight lines of the poem do not constitute a full stanza, but rather the second half of two different stanzas.

---

1 Воспомина́ньями смуще́нный – Stirred by memories. In modern Russian, the form would be "смущённый."

2 сладкою (=сладкой) тоско́й – with sweet yearning

3–4 Сады́ прекра́сные, под сумрак ваш свяще́нный / Вхожу́ с пони́кшею главо́й (=поникшей головой) – <Oh> beautiful gardens, I enter under your sacred twilight with a bowed head

5 Отрок библии – The youth of the Bible. The reference is to the prodigal son, as related in Luke 15:11–32 (a parable Pushkin would develop in 1830 in the story "Станционный смотритель" ["The Station Master"]).

6 До капли истощи́в раска́янья фиа́л – Having drained the goblet of remorse to the <last> drop

9 В пылу́ – In the heat

10 В беспло́дном вихре суеты́ – In the fruitless whirlwind of vanity

16 Вообража́л сии́ сады́ – I imagined these gardens. "Сии" is markedly high style.

22 тая́ – hiding

24 Поэ́том забыва́юсь я – I forget myself as a poet (i.e., in poetry)

25 въявь – in reality

27 Вели́кою Жено́ю (=Великой женой) – by the Great Woman. The allusion is to Catherine the Great, who loved to wander in the gardens (see line 28) that adjoined her summer palace.

29 населены́ черто́гами, врата́ми – inhabited by palaces, gates

30 куми́рами бого́в – <by> statues of gods

32 Екатери́нинских орло́в – of Catherine's eagles. The *Словарь языка Пушкина* notes that the word "орел" can have a figurative meaning: "о выдающемся деятеле" ("about an outstanding individual"). In this poem the word may be a pun on the Orlov brothers (see lines 37 and 39). See commentary to "Перед гробницею святой" (1831), lines 11–12.

34 У посвящённых им столпо́в – At the columns dedicated to them

35 стесни́тель ратных строев – the conqueror of military formations. As the *Словарь языка Пушкина* explains, a "стеснитель" is one who constrains the enemy, who forces him to retreat. The reference here (and in the next line) is to Rumiantsev's victory over the Turks on 21 July 1770.

36 Перу́н кагу́льских берего́в – Perun of the Kagul (Kartal) shores. Perun was the god of thunder and war in Russian (pagan) mythology.

37 вождь полу́нощного (=полуночного) флага – leader of the northern (i.e., Russian) flag. Pushkin alludes to Graf Aleksei Grigor'evich Orlov and his vic-

tory against the Turks at the fort of Chesme off the Anatolian coast on 24 June 1770.

38 морéй пожáр – the fire of the seas. This apparent oxymoron probably refers to the circumstances of the battle, when the burning mast of a Turkish ship fell onto a Russian vessel, leading to an explosion that killed the Turkish leader.

39 герóй Архипелáга – hero of the archipelago Fedor Grigor'evich Orlov. The reference is to an episode in the Russo-Turkish war (known in English as the "Orlov Revolt," but in Russian as the "Первая Архипелагская экспедиция") in which Orlov daringly saved much of his boat's crew before it exploded.

40 навари́нский Ганнибáл – the Gannibal of Navarino. The line refers to Pushkin's great uncle, who defeated the Turks at Navarino. Pushkin may be playing on the name of Hannibal, the historical namesake of his ancestor (see Nabokov, 3:432–33). The column in Tsarskoe Selo that bore the inscription "Победам Ганнибала" ("<Dedicated> To <H>annibal's victories") was a source of great pride for Pushkin.

43 потóк нарóдной брани – the flood of peoples' fighting

45 <Отчи́зну> обнялá кровáвая забóта – A bloody agitation (i.e., caused by war) enveloped the fatherland. In the Academy edition, the first word of this line was deemed illegible; later scholars have suggested this emendation.

46 мимо нас <летя́т> – fly past us. The Academy edition omits the final word of this line as illegible, probably because of their error in transcribing line 48 (see below).

47 тучи конные, бородáтая пехóта – the cavalry clouds, the bearded infantry. This infantry was a "people's army," composed not of clean-shaven regulars, but of unshaven "muzhiki."

48 пушек светлый ряд – The bright row of canons. The Academy edition has the plural ("светлые ряды"), which would complicate the rhyme choice. Later editors' suggestions of "светлый ряд" make rhyming considerably easier. However, if this is correct, it is the only instance of iambic trimeter in the entire poem. More recent editions, recognizing this problem, have altered the line to read: "И медных пушек светлый ряд" ("And the bright row of copper [bronze] cannons").

51–52 И, негоду́я, мы и детство проклинáли / И узы строгие нау́к – And, indignant, we cursed both our childhood and the severe bonds of the sciences. In other words, the Lyceum students were upset that their age (and schoolwork) prevented them from participating in the battles. "Негодуя" is a verbal adverb from the verb "негодовать." "Наука" has a broader meaning in Russian than in English; it means any field of learning, not only the natural or social sciences. The editors of the Academy edition could not agree on a reading of line 51 and left it incomplete (И детство [missing word] негодуя проклинали).

53 многих не пришлó – many did not return.

54 Бородинá – of Borodino. Borodino was the scene of a massive battle that took place on 7 September 1812, the final stand of the Russians as Napoleon marched towards Moscow. Though Russian historians generally view it as a turning point in the war, there were enormous casualties on both sides.

55 На кульмских вы<сотáх>, в лесáх Литвы́ суровых – On the heights of Kulm, in the severe forests of Lithuania. Kulm (Chlumec, Bohemia) was the

site of a lengthy and bloody battle on 29–30 August 1813. The reference to the Lithuanian forests (assuming the reading is correct: the word "Литвы" does not appear in the Academy edition) probably concerns the attempts of the Russians in the brutally cold month of December 1812 to reach and retake Vilnius. In modern Russian, the stress would be "высóтах."

56 Вблизи́ Монма́р<тра> – Near Montmartre. Montmartre was the scene of one of the final battles (30 March 1814) of the war against Napoleon. It led directly to the taking of Paris by the Russians and their allies.

„Поéдем, я готóв; кудá бы вы, друзья́" – "Let's go, I am ready; wherever you, friends"

This poem must be understood biographically. At this time Pushkin had begun wooing Natalia Goncharova, but had met with a cold reception. This love theme coincides in the poem with another preoccupation: travel abroad. The three specific places mentioned (France, Italy, China) are repeated in a letter written to Benkendorff shortly thereafter (the poem is dated 23 December 1829, the letter 7 January 1830): "Tandis que je ne suis encore ni marié, ni attaché au service, j'aurais désiré faire un voyage soit en France, soit en Italie. Cependant s'il ne me l'était pas accordé, je demanderais la grâce de visiter la Chine avec la mission qui va s'y rendre." ("Since I am not yet married nor bound by service, I would like to take a trip either to France or to Italy. If this is not be allowed, I would ask the favor of visiting China with the <diplomatic> mission that is going there.") Permission was denied; Pushkin was never to leave the borders of the Russian Empire.

Strangely enough, the poem also has a literary source: André Chénier. In the Chénier edition owned by Pushkin, the section called "Elegies" concludes with short pieces under the rubric "Fragments." Curiously, in the initial publication, Pushkin entitled his own poem "Элегический отрывок" ("An Elegiac Fragment"). Like Pushkin's poem, Chénier's concerns the poet's wish to take a journey in an attempt to forget a woman.

Partons, la voile est prête, et Byzance m'appelle.
Je suis vaincu; je suis au joug d'une cruelle.
Le temps, les longues mers peuvent seuls m'arracher
Ses traits que malgré moi je vais toujours chercher;
Son image partout à mes yeux répandue,
Et les lieux qu'elle habite et ceux où je l'ai vue.
Son nom qui me poursuit, tout offre à tout moment,
Au feu qui me consume un funeste aliment.
Ma chère liberté, mon unique héritage,
Trésor qu'on méconnaît tant qu'on en a l'usage,
Si doux à perdre, hélas! et si-tôt regretté,
M'attends-tu sur ces bords, ma chère liberté?

From *Oeuvres complètes de Chénier* (Paris, 1819), 174.

Chénier's poem is written in alexandrines, and Pushkin's poem takes the equivalent Russian form (couplets of iambic hexameter), with the caesura after the third foot usually serving as a syntactic boundary. The fact that Pushkin's poem ends on an "orphan" (unrhymed) line and is followed by a series of dashes lends it a fragmentary quality.

---

3 надме́нной убега́я – avoiding the haughty <woman>.
4 К поднóжию ль стены́ – At the foot of the wall
6 Где Тасса не поёт уже ночнóй гребéц – Where the night gondolier no longer sings Tasso. This was a comonplace of the period (see Nabokov, 2:182–83), but the specific allusion in this case is probably Byron: "In Venice Tasso's echoes are no more / And silent rows the songless gondolier" (from *Childe Harold's Pilgrimage*, 4:3). In Pichot's translation: "Les échos de Venice ne répètent plus les poésies du Tasse; le gondolier ne chante plus en parcourant L'Adriatique."
7 Где древних городóв под пеплом дремлют мощи – Where the relics of ancient cities slumber under ash. Probably a reference to Pompei and Herculaneum.
8 Где кипари́сные благоуха́ют рощи – where the cypress groves are fragrant

Literature: Grombakh 1983.

„Ещё однóй, высóкой важной песни" – "Yet one more high and solemn song"

A translation of the beginning of Robert Southey's lengthy "Hymn to the Penates." Pushkin read the poem in *The Poetical Works of Robert Southey* (Paris, 1829), 689–90 (cited below). Pushkin's interest in the poem appears to be based on the theme of exile, which – barely present in the original – is quite emphatic in the otherwise faithful translation. (The few inaccuracies, it would appear, stem from misunderstandings of English grammar and usage, not from willful departures.)

Following Southey's example, Pushkin's poem is written in blank verse.

Yet one Song more! one high and solemn strain,
Ere, Phoebus! on thy temple's ruin'd wall
I hang the silent harp: there may its strings,
When the rude tempest shakes the aged pile,
Make melancholy music. One Song more!
Penates! hear me! for to you I hymn
The votive lay; whether, as sages deem,
Ye dwell in inmost Heaven,[1] the Counsellors[2]
Of Jove; or if, Supreme of Deities,
All things are yours, and in your holy train
Jove proudly ranks, and Juno, white-arm'd Queen,
And wisest of Immortals, the dread Maid
Athenian Pallas. Venerable Powers!
Hearken your hymn of praise! Though from your rites

Estranged, and exiled from your altars long,
I have not ceased to love you, Household Gods!
In many a long and melancholy hour
Of solitude and sorrow, hath my heart
With earnest longings pray'd to rest at length
Beside your hallow'd hearth – for Peace is there.

Yes, I have loved you long! I call on you
Yourselves to witness with what holy joy,
Shunning the common herd of human kind,
I have retired to watch your lonely fires
And commune with myself. Delightful hours,
That gave mysterious pleasure, made me know
Mine inmost heart, its weakness and its strength,
Taught me to cherish with devoutest care
Its strange unworldly feelings, taught me too
The best of lessons – *to respect myself.*
Nor have I ever ceased to reverence you,
Domestic Deities! <…>

Notes

1. Hence one explanation of the name Penates, because they were supposed to reign in the inmost heavens. (Southey's note.)

2. This was the belief of the ancient Hetrusci, who called them Concertes and Complices. (Southey's note.)

---

1 песни – song. An unusual case of "внимать" taking genitive case. Usually it takes dative (as in line 7) or accusative.

2 внемли́ – Hear! (Note that Pushkin has misunderstood the meaning of the English "ere")
Феб – Phoebus Apollo

4 да издаёт <онá> – Let it sound forth. (The object – "печáльный звук" – comes two lines later.)

8 обéтный – votive
Зевéса – of Zeus

9 в небéсной глубинé – in heaven's depths. Pushkin freely renders Southey's "inmost Heaven" and clearly ignores the note, in which Southey explains the etymology of the word "Penates" ("the inner ones").

13 Вели́кой (=Великий) Зевс – Great Zeus. Зевс and Зевéс (cf. line 8) are interchangeable in Russian.

15 Афи́нская Паллáда – Pallas Athena

18 тихих воз<лия́ний> – quiet libations

28 Бесéдуя с сами́м собóю – Conversing with myself

30 сердéчну (=сердечную) глубь – the heart's profundity

„Брожу́ ли я вдоль улиц шумных“ – “Whether I wander along noisy streets”

One of Pushkin’s greatest poems, this meditation reveals his obsession with death, place of burial, and the afterlife. The theme of “guessing” the moment of one’s death reflects Pushkin’s fascination with fatidic dates. It is revealing that the draft of this poem concludes with an extremely precise recording of the time of its completion: 26 Дек<абря> 1829 С.П.Б. 3 часа 5 м<инут> (26 December 1829 S<aint> P<eters>b<urg> 3:05). The draft also includes the rejected title “Stanzas” (alternately spelled “Станцы” and “Стансы”). On the significance of this designation, see commentary to “Стансы” (1826).

The poem is in Pushkin’s beloved iambic tetrameter quatrains with alternating rhyme. Most of the masculine rhymes have the same stressed vowel (“а”), and several stanzas are linked by infinitive rhymes on “-ать.” The use of pronouns is particularly effective; note how the overwhelming emphasis on the self (first-person singular) gradually shifts from nominative to dative case, then disappears entirely in the final stanza with the imagined death of the speaker (and the attendant decomposition of the ego).

---

3 меж юношей безу́мных – among mad (wild) youths

4 мои́м мечта́м – to my thoughts, to my imaginings. In Pushkin’s day, “мечта” was any kind of thought, not necessarily (as in contemporary Russian) about something desirable.

6 сколько здесь ни видно нас – however many of us are visible here

7 Мы все сойдём под вечны (=вечные) своды – we will all descend under the eternal vaults

10 патриа́рх лесо́в – patriarch of the forests. As a metaphor (personification) of the oak tree (“дуб”), the word “patriarch” connotes veneration generally, not necessarily religious. However, it also picks up the religious motif already found in the “храм” of line 2.

11 переживёт – will outlive

14 прости́ – farewell. In modern Russian, this word can only mean “forgive.”

16 Мне время тлеть, тебе́ цвести́ – It is time for me to decay, <it is time> for you to bloom

17 каждую годи́ну – each year

18 думой провожда́ть (=провожать) – accompany with the thought. The objects of this verb are in line 17.

19 Гряду́щей смерти годовщи́ну – the anniversary of <my> future death

20 Меж их (=них) – Among them. The antecedent is not a plural noun, but a combination of singular nouns (день, година).

21 судьби́на – fate

24 Мой примет охладе́лый прах – will accept my dust that has grown cold

25 И хоть бесчу́вственному телу – And though a non-sentient body

27 к милому преде́лу – to my dear border (i.e., to the area [land] dear to me)

28 почива́ть – to rest. The word is commonly used as a euphemism for death.

30 Млада́я будет жизнь игра́ть – Young life will play. Presumably a reference to children.

31 И равноду́шная приро́да – And indifferent nature. Note how the conspicu-

ously absent concept of “душа” sneaks into the poem this way. The word “равно” had appeared in the previous stanza in connection with the body (“тело”). The phrase “равнодушная природа” was sufficiently memorable to be cited by Ivan Turgenev in the final line of the novel *Fathers and Sons*.

32 Красóю вечною сия́ть – Shine in eternal beauty

Кавка́з – The Caucasus

One of several poems written during Pushkin’s visit to the Caucasus in 1829, where he went to witness the Russo-Turkish war. In its depiction of natural forces battling with each other, it resembles “Обвал.”

The poem is written in amphibrachic tetrameter with rhyme scheme a-B-B-a-C-C. This is not a meter one would expect in a nature poem, but Pushkin was to use it again in “Туча.”

---

2 у края стремни́ны – at the edge of a precipice. (The same word appears in plural in line 14.)

3 с отдалённой подня́вшись верши́ны – having ascended from a distant peak. The construction (with the verbal adverb coming between adjective and noun) is bookish.

4 наравне́ – on the same level

5 Отсе́ле я вижу пото́ков рожде́нье – From here I see the birth of streams (i.e., where the mountain streams originate)

9 утёсов наги́е грома́ды – bare masses of cliffs

10 мох тощий, куста́рник сухо́й – sparse moss, arid shrubbery

11 зелёные сени – green canopies

14 по злачным стремни́нам – along the lush precipices

15 пастырь – a shepherd

16 Ара́гва – The Aragva River (in Georgia)

17 нае́здник – horseman

18 Где Терек игра́ет в свире́пом весе́льи (=веселье) – Where the Terek River plays in its fierce gaity. The adjective/noun combination is striking.

20 Зави́девший пищу из клетки желе́зной – having espied food from <his> iron cage

24 Тесня́т его грозно немы́е грома́ды – The mute masses (of mountains) constrain it menacingly

Обва́л – The Avalanche

On the one hand, the poem appears to reflect Pushkin’s experience of an avalanche when he was traveling in the Caucasus in 1829, as reported in the first chapter of his *Путешествие в Арзрум* (*Journey to Arzrum*):

> Дорога шла через обвал, обрушившийся в конце июня 1827 года. Таковые случаи бывают обыкновенно каждые семь лет. Огромная глыба, свалясь, засыпала ущелие на целую версту и запрудила Терек. Часовые, стоявшие ниже, слышали ужасный грохот и увидели, что река быстро мелела и в четверть часа совсем утихла и истощилась. Терек прорылся сквозь обвал не прежде, как через два часа. То-то был он ужасен! <…> В это время услышал я глухой грохот. "Это обвал," – сказал мне г. Огарев. Я оглянулся и увидел в стороне груду снега, которая осыпалась и медленно съезжала с крутизны. Малые обвалы здесь не редки. В прошлом году русский извозчик ехал по Крестовой горе. Обвал оборвался; страшная глыба свалилась на его повозку, поглотила телегу, лошадь и мужика, перевалилась через дорогу и покатилась в пропасть с своею добычею.

See also the first stanza of the poem "Кавказ," which features avalanches, an eagle, and a cliff. On the other hand, the poem's form has a distinctly literary source: Barry Cornwall's "A Sea-Shore Echo," which likewise focuses on a threatening natural phenomenon. (For the full text of this poem, see commentary to "Эхо," which draws on it even more extensively.) The six-line iambic stanzas all have masculine rhymes (a-a-a-b-a-b), with four lines in tetrameter lines and two (indented) lines in dimeter. This form, sometimes mixing masculine and feminine rhymes, is not uncommon in English literature (where it is sometimes referred to as the "Burns stanza," after the Scottish poet Robert Burns [1759–1796], who was probably Cornwall's source). However, it is rare in Russian. See Tomashevskii 1958, 82.

The poem has been incorrectly dated in all Pushkin editions; the correct date should be 1830. (See Rak, 317–29.)

---

1 Дробя́сь о мрачные скалы́ – Beating against the gloomy crags. In modern Russian, the stress would be "ска́лы."

2 пенятся валы́ – waves froth

5 средь волни́стой мглы – amid the wavelike haze. The adjective here is not entirely clear; it could refer to the wavelike contour of the mountains, to undulant clouds or, more literally, to the water that has been thrown into the air after the waves strike against the crags.

7 Отто́ль – from there

11 Терека – of the Terek River (in the Caucasus)

12 Останови́л – Stopped. Note how the syntax makes this one-word final line more emphatic.

15 Но задних волн упо́рный гнев – But the stubborn wrath of the back waves

16 Проши́б снега́ – Broke through the snow(s)

17 затопи́л – flooded

18 брега́ (=берега́) – shores

19 прорванный – torn; with a hole in it

20 Нета́лой грудою (=грудой) – in an unthawed (frozen) mass

22 И пылью вод – And with the spray of its water(s)

24 Ледя́ный свод – the icy vault. This is synonymous with the "прорванный

обвал," under which the Terek flows. In modern Russian, the form would be "ледяно́й."

25 И путь по нём широ́кий шел – And a long path went along it. The point is that the avalanche thus becomes part of the path itself, cf. the quote above from the *Путешествие*: "Дорога шла через обвал" ("The path went through the avalanche").

26 влёкся вол – the ox dragged itself along. In a poem rich with soundplay, the "вал" of the opening stanzas becomes a "вол" in the final stanza (cf. "вод" in the penultimate stanza).

28 Степно́й купе́ц – the merchant of the steppe (presumably from the Caucasian steppe)

29 Эо́л – Aeolus, god of the winds in Greek mythology

Делиба́ш – The Delibash

Under the text of this poem in the manuscript version Pushkin wrote "Сыганлу," a location in the Caucasus where on 13 June 1829 he witnessed part of the Russo-Turkish campaign. Pushkin writes about that battle in the third chapter of *Путешествие в Арзрум* (*Journey to Arzrum*), though – beyond specific lexical items (such as "делибаш") – there is little overlap with the poem. Indeed, the ambiguity of perspective in the poem contrasts sharply with the jingoistic tone of the prose account.

The exotic word "делибаш" is of Turkish origin. Literally "deli" means "daring" and had been used since the fifteenth century to designate soldiers; "bash" means "head." While many Turks seem to understand "delibash" as "head (i.e., leader) of the daring ones," Pushkin obviously translated it as "daring head" or, in Russian, "удалая башка" (see line 12). The claim in Kalinowska (161) that the word can also refer to the hats worn by Turkish soldiers appears not to be true; I have found no native speakers who confirm this.

The poem is written in trochaic tetrameter with alternating rhymes (beginning with a feminine rhyme). As often in Pushkin, the trochaic meter is used to convey exotic subject matter (Gasparov 1990).

---

1 Перестре́лка – exchange of gunfire. The word frequently appears in *Путешествие в Арзрум* to describe the skirmishes between the Russians and Turks.

2 Смотрит лагерь их и наш – Their camp and our camp look (i.e., both camps are at the ready)

3 пред казака́ми – in front of the Cossacks. The Cossacks traditionally served as special units in the Russian army.

4 Вьётся красный делиба́ш – A red delibash weaves his way. The verb suggests that the delibash is on horseback. Cf. the third chapter of *Путешествие в Арзрум*, where Pushkin emphasizes the contrast of the Turkish and Cossack soldiers. "Их высокие чалмы, красивые доломаны и блестящий убор коней составляли резкую противуположность с синими мундирами и простою сбруей казаков." ("Their <the Turks'> tall turbans, beautiful

robes, and gleaming horse armor supplied a sharp contrast to the dark blue uniforms and simple harnesses of the Cossacks.")

5 не суйся к *лаве* – don't go toward the Cossack formation. The word "лава" is a specific Cossack military term; Pushkin italicizes it to emphasize its foreignness. (It also appears in the third chapter of *Путешествие в Арзрум*.)

6 Пожале́й своё житье́ – Spare your life

7 Вмиг ами́нь лихо́й заба́ве – Suddenly <your> daring pleasure will be over

9 Эй, каза́к! не рвися к бою – Hey, Cossack! Don't hurry into battle. Note how the intonation and grammatical construction parallels line 5.

11 Срежет саблею криво́ю (=саблей кривой) – will cut off with a curved saber. Turks were famed for their curved swords.

12 башку́ – head. The word is Turkish in origin, though commonly (colloquially) used in Russian. It is etymologically related to "делибаш," though few readers would have had the linguistic knowledge to appreciate Pushkin's clever translation of that word as "удалую башку."

13 сшиблись – they have clashed (i.e., started fighting)

14 каковы? – How are they? How have they fared?

15 на пике – on a lance

16 без головы́ – without a head. Cf. *Путешествие в Арзрум*, chapter 3: "Турки отсеченные головы отсылают в Константинополь." ("The Turks send the heads they chop off to Constantinople.")

Literature: Kalinowska, 160–63.

Монасты́рь на Казбе́ке – The Monastery on Kazbek Mountain

Perched atop a mountain peak near Kazbek Mountain (the highest peak in Georgia) is the picturesque Tsminda Sameba (Holy Trinity) church, generally agreed to be the subject of this poem. Pushkin mistakenly calls it a monastery, probably conflating it with the nearby Betlemi (Bethlehem) Monastery complex. In the fifth chapter of *Путешествие в Арзрум* (*Journey to Arzrum*), Pushkin writes again about the subject of this poem: "Утром, проезжая мимо Казбека, увидел я чудное зрелище. Белые оборванные тучи перетягивались через вершину горы, и уединенный монастырь, озаренный лучами солнца, казалось, плавал в воздухе, несомый облаками."

The poem is written in iambic tetrameter, in two stanzas of unequal length with a rhyme scheme that spans the two stanzas: a-a-B-B-c-B-c-D-e-D-e.

---

1 над семьёю гор – above the family of mountains. There are many mountains in the area, but Kazbek is the highest.

2 шатёр – tent. The word is used here to signify the shape of the mountain peak.

5 Как в небе реющий ковче́г – Like an ark hovering in the sky

8 сказа́в прости́ – having said farewell

11 скрыться мне – I would like to take refuge. The same expression, with an implied "мне," governs line 9 (i.e., "I would like to ascend")

„Меж горных <стен?> несётся Терек“ – “The Terek rushes among the mountain walls”

In the first chapter of *Путешествие в Арзрум* (*Journey to Arzrum*), Pushkin left a prose description of his impressions of the Terek river.

> Кавказ нас принял в свое святилище. Мы услышали глухой шум и увидели Терек, разливающийся по разным направлениям. Мы поехали по его левому берегу. Шумные волны его приводят в движение колеса низеньких осетинских мельниц, похожих на собачьи конуры. Чем далее углублялись мы в горы, тем уже становилось ущелие. Стесненный Терек с ревом бросает свои мутные волны чрез утесы, преграждающие ему путь. Ущелие извивается вдоль его течения. Каменные подошвы гор обточены его волнами. Я шел пешком и поминутно останавливался, пораженный мрачною прелестию природы.

This unfinished poem is likewise connected to those impressions. The personification of the Terek recalls the final stanza of "Кавказ" ("Играет и воет, как зверь молодой").

The meter is iambic tetrameter; the rhyme scheme is unusual since it is different in each of the stanzas. The first stanza rhymes A-A-b-C-C-b, the second A-b-A-b-C-d. The fact that the final two lines of the poem do not rhyme reflects the unfinished nature of the work; Pushkin surely would have altered one (or both) of them had he continued.

---

2 точит – grinds down
3 вкруг (=вокруг) – around
4 доро́гу роет – rips up the path
9 истоща́ясь – becoming exhausted
12 кремни́стое русло́ – stony riverbed. In modern Russian, the stress is "ру́сло."

„И вот уще́лье мрачных скал“ – “And here the ravine of dark crags”

Another unfinished poem, clearly connected to "Меж горных <стен?> несется Терек." It is in iambic tetrameter with rhyme scheme a-B-B-a.

---

2 станови́тся – becomes. In modern Russian the stress falls on the second syllable: "стано́вится."
3 Но тише Терек злой стреми́тся – But the angry Terek rushes more quietly
4 Луч солнца ярче засия́л – The sun's ray has shone more clearly.

„Страшно и скучно" – "Terrifying and boring"

This unfinished poem appears to be linked to Pushkin's overnight at the Dar'ial Ravine. The corresponding prose passage in *Путешествие в Арзрум*, with its comparison to Rembrandt's chiaroscuro technique, is in many ways more "poetic" than the poem:

> В семи верстах от Ларса находится Дариальский пост. Ущелье носит то же имя. Скалы с обеих сторон стоят параллельными стенами. Здесь так узко, так узко, пишет один путешественник, что не только видишь, но, кажется, чувствуешь тесноту. Клочок неба как лента синеет над вашей головою. Ручьи, падающие с горной высоты мелкими и разбрызганными струями, напоминали мне похищение Ганимеда, странную картину Рембрандта. К тому же и ущелье освещено совершенно в его вкусе.

The poem is in the unusual meter of dactylic dimeter, with rhyme scheme A-B-c-A-B-c. Given that the second stanza is incomplete, it is difficult to interpret the rhyme scheme. Most likely it would have followed this same pattern except that the "b" rhyme is masculine. It is unlikely that the second and third lines were conceived as a rhyme (тюрьмы/шумит), since rhymes of this type are rare in Pushkin. The language of the poem is remarkably simple, with strikingly "prosaic" words (скучно, обидно).

2–3 Здесь новосе́лье, / Путь и ночле́г – Here is a new place to stay, a path, and a night's shelter

7 чуть видно – barely visible

8 Как из тюрьмы́ – As from a prison. The image of a prisoner and the weak ray of light he sees was a Romantic commonplace that can be traced to Byron's "The Prisoner of Chillon" (translated into Russian by Zhukovskii):

> There are seven pillars of Gothic mould,
> In Chillon's dungeons deep and old,
> There are seven columns massy and grey,
> Dim with a dull imprison'd ray.
> A sunbeam which hath lost its way,
> And through the crevice and the cleft
> Of the thick wall is fallen and left.

Собра́ние насеко́мых – The Insect Collection

A parody on contemporary poets. Pushkin used asterisks rather than names, leaving considerable uncertainty to this day as to whom he had in mind.

The poem is written in iambic tetrameter with couplet rhymes. The epigraph is taken from a fable of Pushkin's friend Ivan Andreevich Krylov (1768 [or 1769]–

1844), "Любопытный" ("The Curious One"), about a visit to Peter the Great's *Kunstkammer*, the famous collection of freaks of nature and other curiosities. Like most fables, "Любопытный" is written in free iambs (i.e., iambs of varying length) and an unpredictable rhyme scheme. However, the two lines that Pushkin borrows create the impression of couplet rhymes and thus set his rhyme scheme in motion.

Epigraph: Какúе крохотны корóвки! / Есть, право, менее булáвочной голóвки. – What tiny ladybugs! Truly, some are smaller than the head of a pin.

4 За ними где ни рылся я! – I dug everywhere to find them!

5 Затó какáя сортирóвка! – But then, what a variety!

6 <Глинка> – Fedor Nikolaevich Glinka (1786–1880), a military man and poet whom Pushkin genuinely liked, but whose poetry he found uninspired

7 <Каченóвский> – See commentary to "Литературное известие"

8 <Свиньúн> – Pavel Petrovich Svin'in (1787–1839), a writer, especially of travelogues, and the editor of the journal *Отечественные записки* (*Notes of the Fatherland*). He was an admirer of Pushkin's talent, but the admiration was not reciprocated.

9 <Олин> – чёрная мурáшка – Olin is a tiny black ant. Valer'ian Nikolaevich Olin (1788 [?] – 1841). A writer and editor of various journals and almanacs. Like Svin'in, an admirer of Pushkin's talent, who wrote perceptively about his southern poems. In 1828, Pushkin wrote (but did not publish) a negative review of Olin's tragedy *The Corsair* (after Byron).

10 <Раич> – мелкая букáшка. Raich is an insignificant insect. Semen Egorovich Raich (1792–1855), a poet, translator, and editor of various journals and almanacs.

11 Кудá их много набралóсь! – How very many of them have been collected! "Куда" in this context is an ironic intensifier.

12 Опрятно – in a neat and tidy fashion

13 пронзённые насквóзь – stabbed through

14 Рядкóм торчáт – stick up side by side

„Когдá твой младые лета" – "When your young years"

Poetically speaking, this poem looks back to "Поэт и толпа" (though here the crowd is high society rather than philistines) and anticipates "Что в имени тебе моем?" both thematically (the speaker in contrast to the rest of society) and even in its grammatical constructions (e.g., the repeated imperatives at the end).

It is usually assumed that this poem was written to the flamboyant Agrafena Fedorovna Zakrevskaia (see commentary to "Портрет").

The poem is written in Pushkin's favorite meter of iambic tetrameter quatrains with alternating rhyme.

---

2 Позóрит шумная молвá – Noisy rumor defames

3 по приговóру света – according to the verdict of society (the beau monde)

8 Куми́р бесчу́вственный молю́ – I entreat the unfeeling idol
9–10 Но свет … Жесто́ких осужде́ний / Не изменя́ет он свои́х – But society … It doesn't change its cruel condemnations
12 Но тайны требует для них – But demands secrecy for them. The antecedent is "заблуждения" (errors). In other words, society doesn't care about morality, but it wants people to commit their sins in private.
13 Досто́йны равного презре́нья – Are worthy of the same disdain
14 тщесла́вная любо́вь – vain love
15 лицеме́рные гоне́нья – hypocritical attacks
17 Не пей мути́тельной отра́вы – Don't drink the poison that agitates

К бюсту завоева́теля – To the bust of a conqueror

The bust in question was the work of the celebrated Danish sculptor Bertel Thorvaldsen (1770–1844), from whom Alexander I commissioned a bust in 1820. It was one of very few times in his life that Alexander sat for an artist. Pushkin wrote a very brief prose piece on this subject: "Торвальдсен, делая бюст известного человека, удивлялся странному разделению лица, впрочем прекрасного – верх нахмуренный, грозный, низ же выражающий всегдашнюю улыбку. – Это не нравилось Торвальдсену. Questa è una bruta figura." ("Thorvaldsen, making the bust of a famous person, was surprised at the strange division of the face, which was incidentally beautiful – the top part was frowning, menacing, but the bottom expressed a constant smile. This did not please Thorvaldsen: What an ugly image <he said>".) No source confirms that Thorvaldsen actually made such a comment. If he did, he must have said it to one of the many Russian artists visiting Rome (where Thorvaldsen spent most of his life, hence the Italian phrase). Conceivably, the anecdote is apocryphal, but someone clearly had passed it on to Pushkin.

The tsar himself was delighted with the bust; he rewarded the artist with a diamond ring and recommended him highly to others. The original bust has apparently been lost, but a copy done by Thorvaldsen himself is to this day on display in the Hermitage Museum. The expression of the mouth does indeed seem to contradict that of the brow.

Pushkin's dislike of Tsar Alexander is well known, but it is somewhat mysterious why he should have turned to this subject in 1829, long after the tsar's death. The probable explanation is that, precisely at this time, there was a debate in artistic circles about the appropriate way to portray Alexander. Nicholas himself participated in these discussions and criticized the likeness of Thorvaldsen's bust. Pushkin's opening statement is presumably not addressed to Nicholas, but to an unspecified person who holds that same opinion.

It will be noted that Pushkin mentions Tsar Alexander neither in the poem nor in the prose piece. Early drafts of the poem have the title "Кумир Наполеона" ("The Statue of Napoleon") and "Бюст Наполеона" ("The Bust of Napoleon"), but these were probably chosen to mislead readers rather than inform them.

The poem is written in a single eight-line stanza with alternating feminine and masculine rhymes. The lexicon shifts from conversational (opening line) to lofty – as befits a subject of historical importance. The final word functions almost as in an epigram, suddenly lowering the tone.

---

2 рука́ иску́сства – the hand of art (i.e., the artist's hand)

4 хладный (= холодный) лоск чела́ – the cold lustre of the forehead

5 лик сей двуязы́чен – this face is two-tongued. According to the *Словарь языка Пушкина*, "двуязычен" means that the face expresses two (mutually exclusive) feelings.

7 К противочу́вствиям привы́чен – accustomed to contradictory feelings. This is the only time Pushkin ever uses the word "противочувствие." In his famous dictionary, Dal' defines the word as "antipathy," but Pushkin clearly means it differently, hence the *Словарь языка Пушкина* glosses it as "чувство, настроение, противоположное, несовместимое с другим чувством" ("a feeling <or> mood that is contradictory to or irreconciliable with another feeling").

8 В лице́ и в жизни арлеки́н – In his face and in his life <he was a> harlequin. Harlequin was originally a figure in Italian commedia dell'arte, a clown who wore a black half-mask and a many-colored costume.

Literature: Koka 1958; Al'tshuller, 50–53.

~1830

<Циклóп> – Cyclops

An occasional poem, written for a masquerade ball where the participants, costumed as personages from Greek mythology, were supposed to address verses to the tsar and his wife. Pushkin's poem was written for Countess Ekaterina Fedorovna Tizengauzen (granddaughter of Kutuzov, daughter of E. M. Khitrovo), who dressed as a Cyclops. Pushkin sent the poem to her in a letter of 1 January 1830, where he wrote: "Acceptez cette platitude comme une preuve de ma parfaite soumission à vos ordres" ("Accept this platitude as a proof of my complete submission to your orders"). It was declaimed with other poems of this type (mostly written in French) a few days later at the ball, though Pushkin himself was probably not in attendance.

The poem is in iambic tetrameter with rhyme scheme A-A-b-C-b-C.

---

1 разом – at once
2 еди́ным глазом – with a single eye.
4 Судьбы́ – the Fates

~

„Что в имени тебé моём?“ – "What is my name to you?"

A classic example of Pushkin taking a rather formulaic genre (album verse) and producing a masterpiece. The poem was written for Karolina Adamovna Soban'skaia (in Polish Sobańska, 1794–1885), whom Pushkin had first met in 1821 in Odessa, unaware that she was acting as a government spy. Talented, beautiful, and scandalous, she went through numerous husbands (Soban'skii, more than three decades her senior, was the first of four) and lovers (including Mickiewicz). She collected autographs in an album and, when she requested Pushkin to sign, he produced (presumably with considerable preparation) this poem.

The key images of Pushkin's poem appear to be borrowed from Byron's "Lines written in an album, at Malta" (1809, published 1812). It is likely that Pushkin would have known this poem in French prose translation rather than in the original (though by this time he was capable of making his way through an English text).

> As o'er the cold sepulchral stone
> Some name arrests the passer-by;
> Thus, when thou view'st this page alone,
> May mine attract thy pensive eye!
>
> And when by thee that name is read,
> Perchance in some succeeding year,

Reflect on me as on the dead,
And think my Heart is buried here.

In French editions of Byron, this small poem would have been particularly visible because it begins the section of "Poésies diverses" ("Miscellaneous poems"). Pichot's translation (which appears to have remained unchanged from edition to edition) reads:

> Vers écrits sur un album.
> I. De même que sur la froide pierre d'un tombeau, un nom arrête parfois le passant, puisse le mien fixer un moment ton oeil pensif lorsque tu verras cette page isolée!
> II. Peut-être dans quelques années liras-tu ce nom oublié: alors pense à moi comme à ceux qui ne sont plus; et persuade-toi que c'est ici que mon coeur est enseveli. (From *Oeuvres de Lord Byron* [Paris, 1822], 2:411)

Pushkin's poem is written in iambic tetrameter quatrains; the first two stanzas use a ring rhyme (a-B-B-a) and the second two alternate (a-B-a-B).

2–3 Davydov (2008, 165) notes that the surname "Pushkin" is anagramatically encrypted in these lines twice (backwards, then forwards, where the "г" is pronounced as "к" in accordance with standard rules of Russian pronunciation):

О*Н*о умрет, ка*К* *Ш**У*м *П*ечальный (н.к.ш.у.п.)
Волны, *П*лесн *У*в*Ш*ей в береГ(*К*) даль*Н*ый, (п.у.ш.к.н.)

4 в лесу́ глухо́м – in a dense forest. This is a standard expression (cf. "Эхо"), but note that the adjective "глухо́й" has a secondary meaning connected to sound (conceivably relevant to both poems).

5 на памятном листке́ – on the memory page (i.e., a page of an album). Pushkin uses a similar paraphrase in *Eugene Onegin* 4:XXVII: "на листках воспоминанья" (rendered as "leaves of remembrance" in Nabokov, 1:187).

15–16 Скажи́: есть память обо мне́ / Есть в мире сердце, где живу́ я – Say: "There is a memory of me. There is in the world a heart where I am alive." In other words, the poet tells his addressee to pronounce his name. This name will in turn remind her that there is someone who remembers and loves her. The Byron poem ends in a similar way.

Literature: Il'in-Tomich 1987.

Отве́т („Я вас узна́л, о мой ора́кул") – An Answer ("I recognized you, o my oracle")

The poem, addressed to Ekaterina Nikolaevna Ushakova (1809–1872), is a response to a letter that has been lost. At the time this poem was written, she lived with her parents in a highly cultured atmosphere in the Presnia area of Moscow (see line

16). Her beauty, wit, and playful nature (e.g., the "ветреность" of line 15) made Pushkin a frequent guest.

A good example of Pushkin's comic style (note, for example, the opening and closing rhymes and the mixed lexicon throughout), the poem is written in iambic tetrameter with alternating rhymes, breaking logically (and, in the first part, syntactically) into two sections of eight lines each, which are nonetheless connected by an internal rhyme (живо́й/тоско́й).

---

1 ора́кул – oracle. It is unclear what precisely she was predicting, though the word may also refer simply to the obscurity of an anonymous letter (see line 3).

3 Сих неподпи́санных кара́кул (= каракуль) – of these unsigned scratches. Apparently Ushakova's letter was unsigned.

13 город чопорный, уны́лый – a mannered, melancholy city (he is speaking about Petersburg)

16 Ни муз, ни Пресни, ни хари́т – neither the Muses, nor Presnia, nor the Graces. The sequence of nouns (with the street address sandwiched between the goddesses of antiquity) produces a humorous effect. The plurals (Muses, Graces) probably refer to Ekaterina and her sister Elizaveta, who was one year younger.

„В часы́ заба́в иль праздной скуки" – "In hours of amusements or idle boredom"

First published under the title "Станцы" <sic>, this poem is a response to a response. Pushkin wrote "Дар напрасный, дар случайный" on his birthday in 1828, but first published it in late December of 1829. Shortly thereafter, the metropolitan of Moscow, Filaret (Drozdov) (1782–1867) became acquainted with it and wrote a rejoinder (palinode) in the same meter and using the same rhymes, taking issue with Pushkin's despair and lack of faith. Since the poem was not published in Filaret's lifetime, there are numerous variants, but the text most probably read as follows (Al'tshuller, 239):

Пушкин
От мечтания перешедший к размышлению

Не напрасно, не случайно
Жизнь судьбою мне дана,
Не без правды ею тайно
На печаль осуждена.

Сам я своенравной властью
Зло из темных бездн воззвал,
Сам наполнил душу страстью,
Ум сомненьем взволновал.

Вспомнись мне забвенный мною!
Просияй сквозь сумрак дум –
И созиждется Тобою
Сердце чисто, светлый ум.

The last two lines draw heavily on Psalm 50 (in the English bible, Psalm 51): "сердце чисто созижди во мне Боже, и дух прав обнови во утробе моей." ("Create in me a clean heart O God and renew a right spirit within me.") To preserve the rhyme, Filaret substitutes "ум" for "дух." This psalm is known as the primary penitential psalm; Filaret was writing from Pushkin's perspective, as it were repenting for the blasphemous sentiments in the earlier poem.

A letter of Pushkin to E. M. Khitrovo (who had acquainted Filaret with "Дар напрасный"), written sometime in the first half of January 1830, indicates that he had just learned of the metropolitan's verses. On 19 January, he wrote "В часы забав иль праздной скуки" in acknowledgment and appreciation of Filaret's "answer."

It would probably be overhasty to read this poem as a sign of pure religious devotion. Such a turn toward religion does occur emphatically in the poetry of 1836, but there is little evidence to suggest a fervent religiosity in 1830 (and even less earlier). More probably, Pushkin was genuinely touched that such an eminent figure would take the time to write such verses, and he responded in language appropriate to the situation.

Pushkin's poem is written in iambic tetrameter with alternating feminine and masculine rhymes. This is hardly unusual for Pushkin, but it is noteworthy that it breaks the formal expectations (trochees) created by the previous poems. The lexicon is relatively simple, but features a number of words with obvious religious connotations, both negative (праздной, лукавый) and positive (кроткой, чистый).

Years after Pushkin's death, his younger contemporary Mikhail Danilovich Delariu (1811–1868) insisted that the final four lines had originally read as:

Твоим огнем душа согрета,
Отвергла мрак земных сует,
И внемлет арфе Филарета
В священном ужасе поэт.

There is little reason to believe that Pushkin wrote these lines. However, in recent years this (probably false) version has been cited with increasing frequency.

---

1 праздной скуки – of idle boredom

3 изнéженные – pampered, spoiled

5 и тогдá – even then. It is unclear precisely what events Pushkin refers to when he heard Filaret's "голос величáвый" ("stately voice"). He had first encountered Filaret at the annual exams in religion at the Lyceum. (Filaret had been the rector of the Petersburg Religious Academy since 1812. He became the metropolitan of Moscow in 1826.)

11 Твои́х речéй благоухáнных – of your fragrant speeches. The word "благоухание" has liturgical associations. It occurs in the prayer for the blessing of the incense, which the priest says several times during most ser-

vices: "Кадило Тебе приносим, Христе Боже наш, в воню благоухания духовнаго." ("Incense do we offer unto Thee O Christ our God as an odor of spiritual fragrance.") In Pushkin's poem, "благоуханных" is probably a transferred epithet, logically (though not grammatically) referring to "елей" (which can be scented).

12 еле́й – oil (in religious ceremonies). In biblical times, "елей" was also used medicinally. For example, the Good Samaritan rubs it on the wounds of the man robbed and beaten by thieves (Luke 10:34).

13 И ныне – And again today. Pushkin is here referring to Filaret's poem, which he has presumably just received.

17–18 Твои́м огнём душа́ пали́ма / Отве́ргла мрак земны́х суе́т – Singed by your fire, my soul / Renounced the darkness of earthly vanities

20 в свяще́нном ужасе – in sacred horror. Striking as it may seem, the phrase was not uncommon in poetry of this period, cf. Del'vig's "Видение" and Gnedich's "Рождение Гомера." However, Pushkin combines the figurative and literal meanings of "священный" in a way that his predecessors do not.

Literature: Liapunov 2003.

„Не́т, я не дорожу́ мяте́жным наслажде́ньем" – "No, I do not value riotous pleasure"

Unique among Pushkin's love poems and probably among love poems generally, its subject is the sexual act. Pushkin apparently wrote it to his wife (a variant – though not in Pushkin's hand – bears the title "К жене"), which makes its technique of praise through comparison even more bizarre. (He made no efforts to publish it in his lifetime.) Later editors are hesitant to date the piece as 1830, noting that it could easily have been written later. It is possible (see Vickery 1983, 145–46) that the poem reworks elements of Batiushkov's "К постарелой красавице" ("To an aged beauty").

The poem is also unusual formally, written in the alexandrines ordinarily reserved for elevated subject matter or stylization (e.g., "К вельможе," also of 1830). The key images of the two stanzas contrast the pagan with the Christian. The fact that the second stanza is two lines longer is semantically significant. (Note in this regard the enjambment in line 11 and the hesitation written into the dash at the end of line 13.) It is striking that the stanzaic form (and rhyme scheme) of this poem coincides exactly with "Элегия" ("Безумных лет"), though the latter is in pentameter rather than hexameter. If this poem really was written in 1830, it would indicate that Pushkin was experimenting with a variety of fourteen-line forms at that time (his only sonnets date from this same year).

---

1 Не́т, я не дорожу́ – Note how the poem begins with a stress on the first syllable, a striking effect in iambic tetrameter. Cf. "Поэт, не дорожи" from "Поэту," a poem in the same meter (and without the initial rhythmic variation), with a more "appropriate" theme for iambic hexameter.

2 чувственным – sensual

3 Стена́ньем, криками вакха́нки молодо́й – the moaning, the shrieks of the young Bacchante. A Bacchante is a maenad, a woman follower of the god Bacchus (Dionysus).

4 вия́сь в мои́х объя́тиях змиёй – writhing in my embraces like a snake. This is not the biblical serpent of Genesis ("змей"), but a snake ("змея́," modern Russian instrumental singular would be "змеёй"). As Lerner (152) notes, the reference is to Alfred de Musset, who writes in "Madrid" about his Spanish lover: "Il faut voir, dans nos grands combats, / Ce corps si souple et si fragile, / Ainsi qu'une couleuvre agile / Fuir et glisser entre mes bras!" ("One should see in our great struggles, this so supple and so fragile body, that like an agile <grass> snake, flees and slips amid my arms!") In the edition that Pushkin owned (Alfred de Musset, *Contes d'Espagne et d'Italie* [Paris, 1830]), this passage is on page 173.

5 язвою лобза́ний – With the wounds of kisses. The sound repetition is striking (зв/бз), but the image is peculiar. Etymologicallly "язва" is connected to "острие, жало" (the latter can be either an insect's stinger or a snake's tongue, hence the potential connection to a snakebite). However, this is not a common Russian usage. In poetic or archaic Russian, it means "wound," but in a very precise sense (usually "язва чести," a wound received in battle, see the epilogue to Pushkin's "Кавказский пленник" ["The Prisoner of the Caucasus"]). More abstractly and poetically it can mean any sort of pain. In modern Russian "язва" means "ulcer." When Pushkin used this same image in describing the kisses of his Georgian woman in "Кавказский пленник," his friend Prince Viazemskii suggested that he change it. Pushkin's reply, in a letter of 1–8 December 1823, is worth quoting, since it has relevance to the present poem as well: "Дело в том, что моя Грузинка кусается, и это непременно должно быть известно публике." ("The fact is that my Georgian woman bites, and this must definitely be known to the public"). Proskurin (2007, 326) sees this word combination as a development of the "baisers acres" ("acrid kisses") from Rousseau's *Nouvelle Héloïse*, an unusual expression that had provoked considerable discussion in France.

7 смире́нница – modest, humble woman. The adjective has strong Christian connotations (humility).

8 мучи́тельно тобо́ю счастлив – painfully (tormentedly) happy with you. An oxymoron.

13 боле = более = больше

14 по нево́ле (in some variants written as one word: понево́ле) – involuntarily (*not* "against your will")

Соне́т („Суро́вый Дант не презира́л соне́та") – Sonnet ("Stern Dante did not scorn the sonnet")

This is the first sonnet that Pushkin ever wrote. Like all of Pushkin's sonnets – and the vast majority of Russian sonnets – it is Petrarchan rather than Shakespearean. None of Pushkin's sonnets are "canonical" examples. In this case, Pushkin repeats the "b" rhyme (изливал/облекал, etc.) in the sestet (заключал/забывал), a glaring departure from the norm. This "extra" rhyme seems to suggest that Pushkin understood the sonnet as a virtuoso exploitation of rhyme (and sound play in general); hence one finds clever and unexpected sound repetitions such as жар/Петрарка, суетного/рисует and девы/Дельвиг.

The title is both a form and a theme; it could be rendered as "A Sonnet" (a genre description) and "The Sonnet" (a poem on the subject of sonnets).

Structurally and thematically, it is closely modeled on the Wordsworth sonnet cited in the epigraph. Both are metapoetic (i.e., sonnets on the sonnet) and both move from the Renaissance to modernity and from Italy to the poet's native country. However, given Pushkin's imperfect knowledge of English, it is not clear that he had read Wordsworth's sonnet in the original. If so, he most likely used the cheap (but accurate) pirated edition *The Poetical Words of William Wordsworth* (Paris: A. and W. Galignani, 1828, p. 119), according to which the poem is cited below. At precisely this time, Pushkin was reading Sainte-Beuve's *Vie, poésies et pensées de Joseph Delorme* (Paris, 1829), where Wordsworth's sonnet is rendered into French on page 193. (In the 1830 edition, which Pushkin also owned, the identical text appears on pages 275–76.) In many respects, the Russian poem is closer to the French "imitation" than to the English original. Even the epigraph (which Pushkin quotes in English) departs in punctuation and therefore meaning from the original. However, it coincides exactly with a back-translation from the French.

The Wordsworth sonnet and its translation by Sainte-Beuve follow:

Scorn not the Sonnet; Critic, you have frowned,
Mindless of its just honours; – with this Key
Shakspeare <sic> unlocked his heart; the melody
Of this small Lute gave ease to Petrarch's wound;
A thousand times this Pipe did Tasso sound;
With it Camoens soothed an Exile's grief;
The Sonnet glittered a gay myrtle Leaf
Amid the cypress with which Dante crowned
His visionary brow: a glow-worm Lamp,
It cheered mild Spenser, called from Faery-land
To struggle through dark ways; and, when a damp
Fell round the path of Milton, in his hand
The thing became a Trumpet; whence he blew
Soul-animating strains – alas, too few!

SONNET
Imité de Wordsworth

Ne ris point des sonnets, ô critique moqueur!
Par amour autrefois en fit le grand Shakspeare;
C'est sur ce luth heureux que Pétrarque soupire,
Et que le Tasse aux fers soulage un peu son coeur;

Camoens de son exil abrège la longueur,
Car il chante en sonnets l'amour et son empire;
Dante aime cette fleur de myrte, et la respire,
Et la mêle au cyprès qui ceint son front vainqueur;

Spencer, s'en revenant de l'île des féeries,
Exhale en longs sonnets ses tristesses chéries;
Milton, chantant les siens, ranimait son regard;

Moi, je veux rajeunir le doux sonnet en France;
Dubellay, le premier, l'apporta de Florence,
Et l'on en sait plus d'un de notre vieux Ronsard.

---

1 Суро́вый Дант – Stern Dante. Dante Alighieri (1265–1321). Vatsuro (2000, 236) traces this phrase to Batiushkov's 1816 "Речь о влиянии легкой поэзии на язык" ("Speech on the Influence of Light Poetry on Language").

2 Петра́рка – Francesco Petrarca or, more commonly in English, Petrarch (1304–1374).

3 творе́ц Макбе́та – the creator of "Macbeth," a paraphrastic naming of Shakespeare (1564–1616).

4 Камо́энс – Luiz Vaz de Camoens (1524?–1580), Portuguese poet.

6 Вордсво́рт – William Wordsworth (1770–1850). As the stress indicates, Pushkin had little idea of English pronunciation.

7 от суетного света – from the bustling (or conceivably: from the vain) world. Pushkin had used this same phrase in line 3 of his poem "Поэт" of 1827.

9 Тавриды – of Tauris (archaic for Crimea). The ninth line, the traditional "turn" in the sonnet, moves to the Slavic countries, with a reference to Adam Mickiewicz (named paraphrastically in line 10 as "Певец Литвы" ["Singer of Lithuania"]), whose "Crimean Sonnets" had achieved great popularity. Despite Pushkin's reference to the "размер его стесненный" ("its constraining measure"), Mickiewicz's sonnets were structurally much looser than the canonic sonnet. (It is not clear whether Pushkin knew them in the original Polish or in Russian translation.)

11 мгнове́нно – suddenly. One ordinarily would not apply this word to a form as strict as the sonnet, which does not lend itself to spontaneous composition. But Mickiewicz was also famed as an improviser, and this epithet undoubtedly reflects Pushkin's admiration for the virtuoso displays he had personally witnessed (where the Polish poet had improvised in French). A reflection of this theme can be found in Pushkin's prose work "Египетские ночи" ("Egyptian Nights"), where the interpolated poems are the work of such an "improvisor."

12–14 Pushkin sets the final tercet off from the preceding one, moving within the Slavic world from Poland to Russia. (Admittedly, Pushkin tended to view Poland as part of Russia.) Anton Del'vig (1798–1831) was Pushkin's best friend from the Lyceum. He had written a number of sonnets in 1823. While these were not the first Russian sonnets (several eighteenth-century poets had pioneered the form, but their efforts had been forgotten), they were largely responsible for a sonnet renaissance. Before turning to sonnets, Del'vig had favored the genre of the "idyll," an imitation of antiquity written in Russian hexameters (unrhymed dactyls, with occasional substitutions of trochaic feet for dactylic feet). In this closing passage, Pushkin implies a number of oppositions (unrhymed/rhymed, idyll/sonnet, ancient/modern).

Literature: Achinger 2000; Surat 1998, 211–15.

<На Булга́рина> – On Bulgarin

This epigram is one of Pushkin's numerous attacks on Faddei Venediktovich Bulgarin (1789–1859), the writer, editor, and government spy. As is often the case in such poems, a series of repetitions is created and then broken in the final line. In a curious defensive reflex, Bulgarin himself first published the poem under the title "Epigram" in his journal *Сын отечества*, but changed the last words to "Фаддей Булгарин," making it less insulting and thus removing much of the sting.

The poem is in iambic tetrameter, with rhyme scheme A-A-b-C-C-b, the same form as in "Рифма, звучная подруга" (though the forms are probably unrelated because in this case the entire poem consists of a single stanza).

See also commentary to "Эпиграмма" ("Не то беда, Авдей Флюгарин").

---

2 Костю́шко лях, Мицке́вич лях! – Koscuisko is a Pole, Mickiewicz is a Pole!
Thaddeus Kosciusko (1746–1817), Polish general; Adam Mickiewicz (1798–1855), Polish poet
лях – Pole (archaic)

3 будь себе тата́рин – You can even be a Tatar. In this context "себе" is an unstressed particle (not a pronoun), reflecting an attitude of acceptance.

5 жид – Jew. While by no means a compliment, the word did not have the strong anti-semitic overtones in Pushkin's day that it has now. (It is also a cognate of the neutral Polish word for Jew.)

6 Видо́к Фигля́рин – Видок is Eugène François Vidocq (1775–1857), a French criminal who became a government spy and private detective. He is often credited as being the father of modern criminology. While numerous subsequent writers (Victor Hugo, Edgar Allan Poe) found his story inspirational, Pushkin considered him beneath contempt, writing a damning review of his four volumes of memoirs (1828–1829) that he published anonymously in *Литературная газета*. Strictly speaking, the piece was about Vidocq, but Pushkin implicitly (and – for readers of the time – transparently) compared him to Bulgarin. After all, Bulgarin was the government's cultural spy and, like the Vidocq of Pushkin's article, was "married to one of those unfortunate creatures whom his office obliges him to keep under surveillance" (Binyon 318).
Фигля́рин – a transposition of the name "Булгарин," based on the word "фигляр" ("joker, fool"). This insulting nickname first appeared in an 1825 poem by Viazemskii (see notes to "Эпиграмма" ("Не то беда, Авдей Флюгарин").

„Шуми́т кустáрник … На уте́с" – "The bushes make a sound … Onto the cliff"

An unfinished fragment that appears to have its origin in the stag hunt of the first canto of Sir Walter Scott's *Lady of the Lake*. Entitled "The Chase," this section describes a hunter and his dogs in (vain) pursuit of a deer. The most relevant lines seem to be from the fifth section:

The noble stag was pausing now,
Upon the mountain's southern brow,
Where broad extended, far beneath,
The varied realms of fair Menteith.
With anxious eye he wander'ed o'er
Mountain and meadow, moss and moor [...]
Fresh vigour with the hope return'ed
With flying foot the heath he spurn'd,
Held westward with unwearied race,
And left behind the panting chase.

Pushkin had Scott's works in English (Walter Scott, *The Lady of the Lake* [Edinburgh, 1810], the passage above is on pages 8–9) as well as French translation. The (unfinished) Russian text is distant from both the English and the French. Moreover, the setting is changed from Scotland to the Dnieper region (line 7).

Pushkin's poem, like the English original, is in iambic tetrameter, though the meter is so common in Pushkin's verse that it would be hard to say that he was following Scott's example. Moreover, his rhyme scheme departs from Scott's rhymed couplets. On the basis of the fourteen extant lines, one may surmise that he planned to write in ten-line stanzas with rhyme scheme a-B-a-B-c-D-c-D-e-e. However, this may not be the case, since the English has stanzas of differing lengths. It is nonetheless possible that Pushkin took his cue from the English in the sense that the first stanza of Scott's poem is indeed composed of ten lines:

The Stag at eve had drunk his fill,
Where danced the moon on Monan's rill,
And deep his midnight lair had made
In lone Glenartney's hazel shade;
But, when the sun his beacon red
Had kindled on Benvoirlich's head,
The deep-mouthed blood-hound's heavy bay
Resounded up the rocky way,
And faint, from farther distance borne,
Were heard the clanging hoof and horn.

---

1 утéс – cliff (normally "утёс," but here rhyming with "лес")
3 поднóжный лес – the forest beneath his feet
8 Венчáнны чащею древéсной – crowned with a grove of trees
11 незáпный (= внезапный) – sudden
14 прянул – jumped down

Literature: Iakubovich; Kulagin.

К вельмо́же – To a Grandee

This unusually lengthy poem was written to the wealthy Prince Nikolai Borisovich Iusupov (1751–1831), owner of a splendid mansion outside of Moscow and a living link to the age of Catherine the Great. In his youth, Iusupov had been one of Catherine's favorites, and he had traveled widely in Europe bearing diplomatic dispatches and meeting with the luminaries of European culture. Such a figure could only fascinate Pushkin.

The poem is written in alexandrines, a form Pushkin had used with frequency in his Lyceum poetry (see, for example, the epistle "К другу стихотворцу" or "Александру"), but which was rapidly becoming old-fashioned. In 1830, Pushkin was experimenting with it again, often – as here – to take advantage of this "archaicizing" aura. (He would turn to it again in his profound philosophical and religious poems of 1836.) In the present case, the meter, combined with the length, clearly recalls the eighteenth-century epistle. Pushkin's contemporary A. F. Voeikov, who republished the poem (probably without permission) added a note in which he stated that the poem reminded him of Batiushkov's epistle to I. M. Murav'ev-Apostol (1816). However, Batiushkov himself – in his choice of meter – was simply following the eighteenth-century tradition (Stennik, 309–11). A more likely metrical (and semantic) source is Baratynskii's 1824 "Богдановичу" ("To Bogdanovich"), with its outspoken praise of the eighteenth century.

---

1 An interesting opening line in that the lexicon (in conjunction with the title) suggests that we are dealing with a poem on a civic theme. That this is not the case only becomes apparent in line 2.

2 зефи́р – zephyr (a gentle breeze). The three opening lines are periphrastic, describing the arrival of spring.

4 пото́мок Аристи́ппа – descendent of Aristippus. Another periphrastic expression. Aristippus, a philosopher of antiquity (flourished around 400 BC), was an advocate of hedonism. His writings have been lost.

6 циркуль зодчего, пали́тра и резе́ц – the architect's compass, the palette and the chisel. The passage is based on metonomy, spelled out in the case of the first noun, but not in the others. Each type of art (architecture, painting, sculpture) is named by the instrument through which it is created.

7 Учёной прихоти – to <your> learned whim (the phrase borders on the oxymoronic)

8 вдохнове́нные – inspired. This plural adjective agrees with the three singular nouns (ци́ркуль, палитра и резец) of line 6.

14 Посла́нник молодо́й уве́нчанной Жены́ – The young envoy of the Woman who was crowned (a paraphrase for Catherine the Great).

15 Яви́лся ты в Ферне́й – You appeared at Ferney (Voltaire's estate, where he spent the last two decades of his life). Note the parallel with line 5: "К тебе явлюся я." The notion of the older generation greeting the younger was dear to Pushkin, cf. "… Вновь я посетил" or *Eugene Onegin* 8:II.

16 проны́рливый – crafty. According to the *Словарь языка Пушкина*, this is the only usage of this word in all of Pushkin's works.

17 Своё влады́чество на Севере любя́ – Loving his dominion in the North. The

line refers to Russia, where Voltaire was revered by readers and especially beloved by Catherine (who would later obtain his library, which remains in Russia to this day).

18 моги́льным голосом – with a voice from the grave. This is not a metaphor, but rather a Russian translation of "une voix sépulcrale," a common French idiom that Stéphanie Félicité, comtesse de Genlis, had used to describe Voltaire's loud voice in memoirs that Pushkin undoubtedly knew: *Mémoires inédits de madame la comtesse de Genlis, sur le dix-huitième siècle et la révolution française, depuis 1756 jusqu'à nos jours.* (Vatsuro 1994, 108). See also Vinogradov 2000, 279.

22 Проро́ческих оче́й не простира́я вдаль – Not extending <their> prophetic eyes far. The allusion is to the French revolution that was imminent, but unnoticed.

23 Арми́да – Strictly speaking, the enchantress in Tasso's *Jerusalem Delivered*, but here a periphrastic naming of Marie Antoinette. The usage of "Armida" in the more general sense of a beautiful temptress comes from the French (Nabokov, 2:140).

27 Триано́н – Most likely a reference to the "Petit Trianon," the retreat of Marie Antoinette; possibly the "Grand Trianon" is meant.

31 чтитель промысла – someone who respects Providence. In this line the epithets become increasingly godless.

32 Дидеро́т – Denis Diderot (1713–1784), Enlightenment philosopher. Pushkin here retains the spelling of the French (and, according to the meter, gives the name three syllables), though elsewhere (in his prose) he writes "Дидрот." Modern Russian renders this name only as "Дидро."

Трено́жник – see commentary to "Поэту," line 14.

35 афе́ю иль деисту – <to> an atheist or a deist

36 Как любопы́тный скиф афи́нскому софи́сту – As a curious Scythian <listened to> an Athenian Sophist. Note the extraordinary sound repetitions in this line.

The source of this comparison is Voltaire's satire in alexandrines "Le Russe à Paris" ("A Russian in Paris," 1760): "C'est un Scythe grossier voyageant dans Athène / Qui vous conjure ici, timide et curieux; / De dissiper la nuit qui couvre encore ses yeux" ("It is a coarse Scythian voyaging in Athens / Who begs you here, timid and curious, / To dissipate the night that still covers his eyes"). The historical model is Anacharsis, a Scythian philosopher of the sixth century BC who visited Greece.

38 двойственный собо́р – a double assembly (the two houses of British parliament)

39 Здесь натиск пламенный, а там отпо́р суро́вый – Where the one side's fiery attack is met with the other's stern rebuff (this translation is taken from Mirsky, 133).

41 Темзою (=Темзой) скупо́й – by the restrained Thames. The Thames is used metonymically for London (or England), which could not offer Iusupov the sumptuous pleasures of France or Spain.

44 Бомарше́ – Pierre-Augustin Caron de Beaumarchais (1732–1799), author of the comedies *The Barber of Seville* (1775) and *The Marriage of Figaro* (1778).

(Figaro is the "hero" mentioned in the previous line.) The details here are historically accurate: Iusopov met Beaumarchais in London.

49 Как пылкой (=пылкий) отрока востóргов полный сон – like an adolescent's passionate dream, full of raptures. The complicated syntax makes the phrase grammatically ambiguous, but this seems the most logical reading.

50 жёны – women

59 как падает письмó из-за решётки – how a letter falls from behind the grate. This could be a topos of comic opera, but it is conceivably a specific reference to the first act of Beaumarchais' drama *The Barber of Seville*, where Rosine drops a letter from the window to Count Almaviva, who, in disguise outside her window (cf. line 62), has come to woo her. (Vol'pert, 197).

62 Трепéщет и кипи́т – shudders and seethes. Gershenzon (1926, 22) traces this phrase to Batiushkov's "кипел и трепетал" (from "На развалинах замка в Швеции").

64 сою́з умá и фурий – the union of reason and the Furies (a reference to the savagery of the French Revolution and its "logical" origins in Enlightenment thought)

67 И мрачным ужасом сменённые забáвы – And amusements are replaced by a dark terror. The word "ужас" is here most likely a direct translation of French "terreur" (i.e., the "Reign of Terror" of 1793–1794 is known in French as "la Terreur").

72 Доны́не странствует с кладби́ща на кладби́ще – To this day wander from graveyard to graveyard. Though he died in Paris, Voltaire's friends (who feared that he would not receive a Christian burial because of his anticlerical writings) spirited his body one hundred miles away to the Abbey of Scellières (Province of Champagne) and buried him there before the church had time to forbid it. In 1791, during the time of the French Revolution, his remains were returned to Paris and, with much fanfare, interred in the Pantheon. According to persistent rumors (which Pushkin seems to refer to here), his remains were later disinterred by religious fanatics. In modern Russian, the stress is on the first syllable of "кладбище."

73 Барóн д'Ольбáх – Paul-Henri Thiry [Paul Heinrich Dietrich], baron d'Holbach (1723–1789), prolific writer and bon vivant. His wealth allowed him to maintain the most brilliant salon in Paris, which attracted a wide range of European (and American) intellectuals, both Enlightenment figures and genuine radicals.

Морлé – Abbé André Morellet (1727–1819), author of articles on theology and metaphysics for the Encyclopedia (see line 74).

Гальяни – Abbé Ferdinando Galiani [sometimes spelled "Gagliani"] (1728–1787), writer and economist, spent almost a decade in Paris where he became friendly with Diderot, with whom he later corresponded. Pushkin owned a volume of his letters and cited them in his own correspondence.

74 Энциклопéдии скепти́ческой причóт – the congregation of the skeptical Encyclopedia. Given the freedom with which Pushkin interchanges the masculine adjectival endings "-ий" and "-ой," it is conceivable that the translation should read "the skeptical congregation of the Encyclopedia." *The Encyclopedia* (*Encyclopédie*), one of the great achievements of French Enlightenment thought, was edited by Diderot, with articles written by a host of luminaries.

The first volume appeared in 1751, the seventeenth and “final” in 1765 (even this was followed by supplementary volumes). The term “причот” is usually associated with the church; its use here is ironic, given the *Encyclopedia*’s hostile stance toward organized religion. In modern Russian, the word is either “причт” or, colloquially, “при́чет.”

75 бесно́сый Касти – Giambattista Casti (1724–1803), Italian poet and libretto author, served at Catherine the Great’s court from 1778–1781. One may safely assume that Iusopov was acquainted with Casti, though nothing is known of their meeting(s). The epithet “noseless” refers to syphilis, which Casti apparently contracted during his stay in Russia. Contemporary Italians repeatedly commented on the irony that such a libertine would have the name “Casti” (“chaste”). Pushkin seems to be aware of this incongruity, in that he rhymes “Касти” with “страсти” (See Gardzonio).

79 быв = having been (in modern Russian only the present tense form “будучи” is used)

82 с расхо́дом свесть прихо́д – to balance credit and debit

83 Теми́ра – Temira. A standard female name in poetry of the time. According to Nabokov, it came to Russia from the French Arcadians, who frequently wrote about “Thémire” (Nabokov, 2:416).

88 куми́ры – statues (Iusupov had an extensive art collection, see note to line 96)

95 Аля́бьевой – Aleksandra Vasil’evna Aliab’eva (1812–1891), a famous Moscow beauty

Гончаро́вой – Natalia Nikolaevna Goncharova (1812–1863), another beauty, soon to be Pushkin’s wife

96 Корре́джием – Antonio da Correggio (1489–1534), Italian Renaissance painter

Кано́вой – Antonio Canova (1757–1822), sculptor. The works of these artists were indeed on display at Iusopov’s estate. Iusupov had been friendly with Canova and had an entire room of his works (now on display at the Hermitage).

97 мирски́х – worldly, profane (usually this word is opposed to “sacred,” but here its opposite is not religion, but art)

105 день-друго́й – for a day or two

Literature: Vatsuro 2000, 179–216.

Новосе́лье – Housewarming

The poem is addressed to Mikhail Petrovich Pogodin (1800–1875), a writer and critic, at the time the editor of the journal *Московский Вестник*. Pogodin had just purchased a house in Moscow.

The poem is written in iambic tetrameter with alternating rhymes.

---

2 дома́шний свой куми́р – your domestic idol (presumably a paraphrase of the Penates, the household gods).

3 ты перенёс – you transferred. There is perhaps a pun here: “перенос” is the Russian term for “enjambment.”

5 домик малый – little house (the diminutive "домик" denotes an emotional closeness rather than the actual size, which is suggested by "малый"). In fact, the house was large, but Pogodin rented out much of it to lodgers, so Pushkin presumably refers to the part that Pogodin actually inhabited.
8 как от огня́ – as <you insured it> against fire. The house that Pogodin bought was made of stone.

Literature: Tsiavlovskii 1962, 394–96.

„Когда́ в объя́тия мои́" – "When in my embraces"

Like "Нет, я не дорожу," a highly unconventional love poem, which addresses the present beloved and contrasts her to her predecessors. Among other things, it is fascinating for the various types of speech it includes (from whispers to curses).

The entire poem is structured around a "when/then" construction, with the "then" section beginning at line 13. Written in iambic tetrameter, it breaks down into four-line units, with one rhyme (преданья/вниманья/staранья/ожиданья) connecting the first part of the poem with the second. It is not divided into stanzas, perhaps because two different rhyme schemes (alternating and ring rhyme) are employed.

Not published in Pushkin's lifetime, the poem is always dated as 1830, though close textological study done since the Academy edition was prepared suggests that it probably was written in 1828 and edited slightly in 1830 (Sandomirskaia 1962). This raises complicated issues about whether Pushkin changed the addressee. (It was generally assumed to be his future wife Natalia Goncharova, but this could not have been the case if the poem was written in 1828.)

2 стройный стан – slender figure
4 расточа́ю – spend profligately (a wonderful metaphor)
5 от стесне́нных рук – from <my> tightly-clasped arms. Strictly speaking, "руки" could also mean hands, but in the present context it seems unlikely.
6 гибкой (=гибкий) – supple
10 преда́нья – legends; stories

Поэ́ту – To the Poet

This is the second of Pushkin's three sonnets. Once again, Pushkin is free with the form. Here the second quatrain uses a different rhyming pattern than the first, a glaring departure from the canon. The poem is written in iambic hexameter (with the expected caesura after the third foot), a meter not uncommon in Russian sonnets and which Pushkin generally reserves for elevated subjects.

The poem's theme recalls "Поэт и толпа," though stylistically it is very different. Rather than a conversation between antagonists, the poet here addresses another poet (or quite possibly himself).

---

7 Усоверше́нствуя – Perfecting. In modern Russian, present verbal adverbs are not made from perfective verbs, but Pushkin does this with some frequency.
8 подвиг – a heroic deed of a spiritual nature
9 Они́ – the antecedent is the награ́д(ы) of the previous lines
13 плю́ет – spits (stress on the first syllable rather than in the modern "плюёт"). Together with брани́т of the previous line, it marks a sudden shift in tone.
13 где твой ого́нь гори́т – the fire imagery contrasts to the "смех толпы холодной" of line 3.
14 трено́жник – tripod. The reference is to Pythia, the (pagan) priestess who sat upon a tripod at the Oracle of Apollo in Delphi.

Мадо́на – Madonna

Pushkin's third sonnet, written a day after "Поэту." Like the others, it is formally unusual. The rhyme scheme of the two quatrains changes (i.e., the first quatrain is a ring construction, the second quatrain alternates) and the "turn" expected after the octet occurs late, after the first tercet. The meter is iambic hexameter, with the caesura falling in the expected place in the middle of the line.

If Pushkin's first two sonnets are poetic (and metapoetic), this one is a love poem, though a curious one. It combines sacred and secular imagery, moving from a description of an artistic work (ekphrasis) to a living person. Accordingly, the title plays on two meanings of "Madonna" – the first is religious, while the second goes back to troubadour poetry and the literal translation of "madonna" as "my lady." Pushkin addresses the poem to Natalia Goncharova, soon to be his wife.

The poem intersects with a letter from Pushkin to Goncharova written from Petersburg to Moscow on 30 July 1830. "Les belles dames me demandent à voir votre portrait, et ne me pardonnent pas de ne pas l'avoir. Je m'en console en passant des heures entières devant une madone blonde qui vous ressemble comme deux gouttes d'eau, et que j'aurais achetée, si elle ne coûtait pas 40000 roubles." ("The ladies are asking to see your portrait and they do not forgive me for not having it. I console myself passing entire hours in front of a blonde Madonna that resembles you as two drops of water [resemble each other], and I would buy it if it didn't cost 40,000 rubles.") In many commentaries, the precise picture Pushkin so admired is wrongly identified as a Perugino. In fact, it was a copy of Raphael's "Bridgewater Madonna." Though Raphael's painting lacks the palm tree mentioned in line 11, the (unknown) copyist replaced the niche in the right of the background of the original with an open window that looked out onto a tree. See Tsiavlovskii (1962, 396–403) and especially Koka 1967.

Butakova (130) draws attention to a passage in Karamzin's celebrated *Письма русского путешественника* (*Letters of a Russian Traveler*) that gives an appreciation of a picture of Mary Magdalene in strikingly similar terms: "Всё прелестно в Магдалине [...] Я видел много славных произведений живописи, хвалил, удивлялся искусству; но эту картину желал бы иметь; был бы счастливее с нею; одним словом люблю ее! Она стояла бы в моем уединенном кабинете, всегда перед моими глазами.” (“Everything is beautiful in the Magdalena […] I have seen many glorious paintings, I have praised and been amazed at [their] art; but this picture I would like to own; I would be happier with it; in a word, I love it! It would be in my solitary study, always before my eyes.”).

The poem was published more than once in Pushkin’s lifetime, which indicates that the censor was not bothered by the conflation of the Virgin Mary with the beloved. The fact that Pushkin was describing a Western painting (rather than an icon) presumably made the poem unproblematic for the authorities.

Title: Мадóна – in modern Russian the word is spelled “Мадонна.” According to Averintsev, the spelling with one “n” reflects French usage. Such a spelling appears to have been widespread in Pushkin’s day.

1–4 A classic example of preterition

1 стари́нных мастерóв – of the old masters

2 Укрáсить я всегдá желáл свою́ оби́тель – I always wanted to decorate my abode. The word “обитель” often has a religious connotation. Gershenzon (1926, 119) contends that Pushkin adapted the line from a 1798 poem of Ivan Ivanovich Dmitriev (entitled “К гр. Н. П. Румянцеву”), likewise about a portrait. Dmitriev writes “Украшу им свою смиренную обитель.”

4 знатокóв – of experts. Koka (1962, 132) notes a similarly ironic (or pejorative) use of this word in Pushkin’s unfinished story *Dubrovskii* (chapter 13): “Он говорил о картинах не на условленном языке педантического знатока, но с чувством и воображением.” (“He spoke about the pictures not in the conventional language of the pedantic expert, but with feeling and imagination.”)

5 В простóм углý моём – in my simple corner. The word “угол” can mean “corner” in the literal sense or, more broadly, “the place where one lives.” It is worth recalling that, in traditional Russian homes, an icon was always located in the corner (the so-called “красный угол”).

медленных трудóв – works that are produced slowly (presumably poetry)

6–7 the anaphora on “Одной” agrees grammatically with “картины,” but also emphasizes the feminine gender as such.

8 пречи́стая – literally: the most pure. The word is a standard epithet of the Virgin Mary. Cf. “Жил на свете рыцарь бедный,” line 53. Curiously, that poem is also about the power of an artistic representation of the Virgin Mary. Note how the sounds of the word “пречистая” will be echoed in the final line: *Чист*éйшей *пре*лести *чист*éйший.

11 Сиóна – of Zion

12 Творéц – the creator. Coming at the beginning of a sentence (and end of the line, making a striking enjambment), the word must of course be capitalized, thus allowing a pleasant – though only momentary – ambiguity of whether this is an artist or God.

14 Чистéйшей прелести чистéйший образéц – The purest example of the purest charm. The word “образец” contains within itself “образ” (icon). Averintsev notes that “прелесть” also has religious overtones, albeit strongly negative. In Church Slavonic usage, “прелесть” is a vice (cf. modern Russian “лесть”). However, it is not obvious that Averintsev’s observation is relevant; Pushkin may have been using the word only in its modern (worldly) sense.

„Полюбу́йтесь же вы, дети" – "Go and admire, guys"

This jocular poem was inspired by an incident that Pushkin himself witnessed. At an evening of gambling, Pushkin's friend Sergei Grigor'evich Golitsyn (1803–1868) appeared unexpectedly and placed a large bet with a dealer who owed him money from a previous evening. The dealer asked him what money he was betting ("да ты на какие деньги играешь? на эти или на те?"), and Golitsyn answered "это все равно: и на эти, и на те, те, те." Pushkin, amused by the reply, composed these verses, basing all the rhymes on the words "эти" and "те." The key to the poem is that the refrain is literally the same, but the antecedent for the pronouns shifts in each stanza. In keeping with the convention, Pushkin marks the quotation by using italics. The meter is trochaic tetrameter.

---

1 дети – a familiar form of address to friends
3 Длинный Фирс – Tall Firs. "Firs" was Golitsyn's nickname. He was indeed tall.
5 Черно́кая Россе́ти – dark-eyed Rosseti. Aleksandra Osipovna Rosset, later Smirnova (1809–1882) was a Petersburg beauty (see commentary to "Ее глаза") renowned also for her wit and intelligence. Here her name is Italianized for purposes of rhyme.
6 самовла́стной – all-powerful
10 стелет – spreads out (from the verb "стлать")

Literature: Khodasevich, 1:150–51.

Бесы – The Demons

This famous poem marks the beginning of the incredible stream of masterworks that Pushkin composed at his estate in Boldino, where he was unexpectedly quarantined for three months (early September to late November) due to a cholera outbreak. In this poem, Pushkin develops the quintessentially Russian topos of a sudden snowstorm, which he also used to great (though different) effect in prose works like the story "Метель" ("The Blizzard," written in Boldino six weeks after this poem) and in chapter two of the novel *Капитанская дочка* (*The Captain's Daughter*). Here folkloric elements combine with realistic depiction to create a scene of physical and metaphysical despair. The meter is trochaic tetrameter with alternating rhymes. In Russian versification, trochees are often used to approximate folklore (a trochaic tendency of folk verse was already recognized by Trediakovskii in his theoretical writings of the early eighteenth century). To see how strongly Pushkin associated poetic form with themes and styles, it is instructive to compare "Бесы" with "Зимний вечер" (1825). Both poems use precisely the same meter, stanza, and rhyme scheme, both have numerous folk elements (specific vocabulary, a refrain), both are night poems and storm poems. However, "Бесы" is a much darker work.

Curiously, when Pushkin commenced work on the poem, he apparently intended to write something comic. The initial subtitle (or perhaps even title) was "Шалость" ("A prank"), which recalls the first of the two key subtexts to his poem. In 1828, Pushkin's friend Prince Viazemskii had authored a cycle of comic poems called "Зимние карикатуры" ("Winter Caricatures"), one of which was called "Метель" ("The Blizzard," the precise word that Pushkin uses for the above-mentioned short story). In that poem, a sudden snowstorm portends disaster, but the conclusion undercuts the seriousness. In the course of his poem, Viazemskii includes in italics the unusual phrase "мерзлый пар" ("frozen steam"). This marks it as a quotation: in fact, it is a reference to one of the most famous works of eighteenth-century Russian poetry, Mikhailo Lomonosov's "Вечернее размышление о Божьем величестве при случае великого северного сияния" ("Evening Meditation on God's Greatness on the Occasion of the Great Northern Lights," 1743). This is in turn Pushkin's second subtext. Lomonosov's poem describes and attempts to understand the aurora borealis, a phenomenon that fascinated numerous scientists of the age (including Lomonosov himself). The poem reviews various scientific theories, but ultimately explains it in terms of God's benevolent design, inscrutable to man's limited understanding. Viazemskii completely reverses Lomonosov's poem (in Lomonosov night turns suddenly to day; in Viazemskii day turns suddenly to night). But Viazemskii draws no profound conclusions; his poem, relying on anticlimax, takes a potentially grave situation and renders it a joke. Pushkin goes further, replacing Lomonsov's Enlightenment belief in cosmic order with a Romantic view of demonic nature.

Pushkin's poem furnishes one of two epigraphs to Dostoevsky's novel *Бесы* (*The Demons*; sometimes freely translated as *The Possessed*).

Below the Viazemskii and Lomonosov poems are cited in their entirety.

Метель

День светит; вдруг не видно зги,
Вдруг ветер налетел размахом,
Степь поднялася мокрым прахом
И завивается в круги.

Снег сверху бьет, снег веет снизу,
Нет воздуха, небес, земли;
На землю облака сошли,
На день насунув ночи ризу.

Штурм сухопутный: тьма и страх!
Компас не в помощь, ни кормило:
Чутье заглохло и застыло
И в ямщике и в лошадях.

Тут выскочит проказник леший,
Ему раздолье в кутерьме:
То огонек блеснет во тьме,
То перейдет дорогу пеший,

Там колокольчик где-то бряк,
Тут добрый человек аукнет,

То кто-нибудь в ворота стукнет,
То слышен лай дворных собак.

Пойдешь вперед, поищешь сбоку,
Все глушь, все снег, да *мерзлый пар.*
И божий мир стал снежный шар,
Где как ни шаришь, все без проку.

Тут к лошадям косматый враг
Кувыркнется с поклоном в ноги,
И в полночь самую с дороги
Кибитка на бок – и в овраг.

Ночлег и тихий и с простором:
Тут тараканам не залезть,
И разве волк ночным дозором
Придет проведать – кто тут есть?

Вечернее размышление о Божьем величестве при случае великого северного сияния

Лице свое скрывает день;
Поля покрыла мрачна ночь;
Взошла на горы черна тень;
Лучи от нас склонились прочь;
Открылась бездна звезд полна;
Звездам числа нет, бездне дна.

Песчинка как в морских волнах,
Как мала искра в вечном льде,
Как в сильном вихре тонкий прах,
В свирепом как перо огне,
Так я, в сей бездне углублен,
Теряюсь, мысльми утомлен!

Уста премудрых нам гласят:
Там разных множество светов;
Несчетны солнца там горят,
Народы там и круг веков:
Для общей славы божества
Там равна сила естества.

Но где ж, натура, твой закон?
С полночных стран встает заря!
Не солнце ль ставит там свой трон?
Не льдисты ль мещут огнь моря?
Се хладный пламень нас покрыл!
Се в ночь на землю день вступил!

О вы, которых быстрый зрак
Пронзает в книгу вечных прав,
Которым малый вещи знак

Являет естества устав,
Вам путь известен всех планет, –
Скажите, что нас так мятет?

Что зыблет ясный ночью луч?
Что тонкий пламень в твердь разит?
Как молния без грозных туч
Стремится от земли в зенит?
Как может быть, чтоб мерзлый пар
Среди зимы рождал пожар?

Там спорит жирна мгла с водой;
Иль солнечны лучи блестят,
Склонясь сквозь воздух к нам густой;
Иль тучных гор верьхи горят;
Иль в море дуть престал зефир,
И гладки волны бьют в эфир.

Сомнений полон ваш ответ
О том, что окрест ближних мест.
Скажите ж, коль пространен свет?
И что малейших дале звезд?
Несведом тварей вам конец?
Скажите ж, коль велик творец?

Analysis of the drafts of the poem reveals that Pushkin was probably responding to Katenin as well (Proskurin 1999, 224–29), though few of these echoes remain in the final version.

---

1 тучи – not just clouds, but "storm clouds"
2 невиди́мкою луна́ – Russians generally gloss this simply as "the invisible moon" or "the moon, seemingly invisible." However, the word "невидимка" has a folkloric ring to it (e.g., шапка-невиди́мка, a hat that makes the wearer invisible), the first of many folkloric touches in the poem.
5 в чистом поле – in an open field (a common phrase in folk poetry)
6 Колоко́льчик – this is the little bell that was attached to carriages, presumably so that their approach could be heard at a distance (see, for example, "И. И. Пущину" ["Мой первый друг"] or the narrative poem "Граф Нулин" ["Count Null"]). The bell will fall silent in line 30.
дин-дин-дин – onomatopoeia. This is the sound the little bell makes.
7 понево́ле – involuntarily (not to be confused with "against one's will")
9 At this point a dialogue ensues between the driver (ямщи́к) and his master (барин)
Эй – "Hey" – a striking colloquialism for Russian poetry of this period
пошёл – a command, spoken by the "барин" (who we later realize is the narrator): "Move it!" or "Get going!"
Нет мочи – literally: "there is no <more> strength" (i.e., the horses are exhausted)
11 слипа́ет о́чи – (colloquial) forces my eyes to close

12 доро́ги занесло́ – The paths have been covered by snowdrifts. An impersonal construction often used with weather (i.e., about something one has no control over). The subject is omitted.

13 хоть убе́й – Even if you kill me. This is of course simply an idiom (meaning approximately "no matter what you do"), though the dark hint of murder is relevant to the end of the poem.

13 следа́ не ви́дно – no trace (i.e., hoofprint, footprint) is visible. "След" is in the genitive case because of negation.

14 Сбились мы – We've gotten lost

16 Да кружи́т по сторона́м – And makes <us> go in circles. Circularity is a frequent and essential motif in the poem.

18 дует, плюет – blows, spits (in modern Russian the stress would be "плюёт"). According to Russian folk belief, one is supposed to "дуть" and "плевать" in order to get rid of the devil. Pushkin reverses the practice; the demons are the ones engaged in these activities. According to Vatsuro (1986, 305–8), the source of these verbs is a fable by Sumarokov, where the subject is the fierce north wind: "Борей мой дует, / Борей мой плюет, / И сильно под бока проезжего он сует" (from "Феб и Борей," the first fable in his book).

19 cf. the "овраг" at the end of Viazemskii's poem

21 версто́ю небыва́лой – like a fantastic (unbelievable) milepost. A "verst" was a prerevolutionary Russian measurement for distance, slightly more than a kilometer. Posts were set up at various distances along a road. In this construction (common in Russian poetry), instrumental case is used as a simile.

23 искрой малой – like a small spark. Another instrumental used as simile. This comparison is chosen to link the poem to Lomonosov (see line 8: "Как мала искра в вечном льде" – "like a small spark in eternal ice").

32 пень иль волк? – Is it a tree stump or a wolf? (cf. the wolf in the penultimate line of the Viazemskii poem, combined with the interrogative intonation)

33 Вьюга злится, вьюга плачет – The storm is angry, the storm cries. The parallel construction recalls the opening line (repeated in line 25), with "вьюга" acoustically recalling "вьются," but now the storm is personified.

35 дале́че = далеко (NB: this is *not* a comparative!)

37 понесли́ся (= понеслись) – rushed off. The prefix по- is inceptive (i.e., they have set off).

39 духи – spirits; ghosts

40 беле́ющих – from белеть ("to turn white," or simply "to show white"), presumably the effect of the moonlight and the snow

41 Pushkin initially wrote another four lines here, but as usual he was a brilliant editor, replacing them with far better ones. Note the way the key word "бес" resounds in the etymologically unrelated "бесконечны" and "безобразны" (the latter brought out by the enriched rhyme "бесы разны").

42 месяца – of the moon. In meaning "месяц" is the same as "луна," but the Slavic word adds a folk quality particularly appropriate for the stanza (the specific demons in lines 47 and 48).

43 разны (= разные) – various

44 Будто листья в ноябре́ – this phrase draws on an entire epic tradition of leaf similes (Homer, Vergil, Dante, Milton), where leaves are compared to dead people.

47 Домово́го ли хоро́нят, / Ведьму ль замуж выдаю́т? – Is a house spirit being buried, / Is a witch getting married? Davydov (2003, 89) notes that the line combines in a folkloric key Pushkin's two obsessions during the Boldino autumn (the three months of extraordinary creativity spent on his estate in 1830): death (from the cholera epidemic) and marriage (related to his imminent marriage to Natalia Goncharova).

45–48 the insistent questions are reminiscent of the end of the Lomonosov poem

53–54 note the play on "бесы" and "беспредельной"

56 надрыва́я – tearing. The noun "надрыв" ("laceration") will become a key term in Dostoevsky.

Literature: Smirnov, 46–51.

Эле́гия („Безу́мных лет уга́сшее весе́лье") – Elegy ("The extinguished happiness of wild years")

The elegy was the favored genre of the 1810s and early 1820s, but by 1830 it was essentially the province of epigones. Pushkin himself had mocked it in the figure of Lensky in *Eugene Onegin* and even "killed it off" with the elegy Lensky pens on the eve of his death. Thus, to entitle a poem "Элегия" in 1820 was barely necessary (it was expected); for a poet as conscious of literary development as Pushkin, to do so in 1830 was surprising. This elegy features the melancholy tone characteristic of the genre, but it takes remarkable freedoms, changing the usually predictable metaphors and breaking the lexical norms.

Pushkin writes the poem in iambic pentameter, retaining the (by then old-fashioned) caesura after the second foot. Though fourteen lines in length, it has nothing to do with a sonnet. (See also commentary to "Нет, я не дорожу.") The rhymes come in couplets, alternating masculine and feminine. The two stanzas are in opposition (as the "Но" at the beginning of the second indicates), yet each statement of the second part is qualified, so that even the hopes of the future are judged as fleeting at best.

---

2 похме́лье – hangover. A very odd word in a traditional Russian elegy.

4 старе = старше

чем старе, тем сильне́й – the older, the stronger. Oenophiles might wonder about this claim.

6 волну́емое – shaking, moving. (The word "волна" [wave], suggested by sound, is encouraged by the proximity of "море.")

7 дру́ги – archaic for "друзья"

11 гармо́нией упью́сь – I will become intoxicated by harmony. "Упиться" can be used literally and figuratively. The second usage is primary here, but the former is also relevant, given the wine similes early in the poem.

12 Над вымыслом – over the creation of <my> imagination

Отве́т анони́му – An Answer to an Anonymous <Writer>

In June of 1830 Pushkin received an unsigned poem congratulating him on his engagement (about which rumors were circulating) and expressing the certainty that marriage would give him new poetic inspiration. Pushkin was pleased to receive this, since it was commonly believed that marriage would destroy him as a poet (see the reflection of this problem in the description of Lensky's potential future in *Eugene Onegin* 6:XXXIX: "Расстался б с музами, женился" ["He would have parted with the Muses <and> gotten married"]). The author of this poem was Ivan Aleksandrovich Gul'ianov (1789–1841), a leading Egyptologist and acquaintance of Chaadaev. Pushkin subsequently met and befriended him.

The poem is one of many Pushkin devotes to the theme of the poet and his audience; the image of the "заезжий фигляр" (line 15) anticipates the improviser in "Египетские ночи" ("Egyptian Nights"), and the attitude of the masses toward the poet recalls the narrator's thoughts in that same work.

Gul'ianov's poem was in iambic tetrameter, so it is noteworthy that Pushkin responds with the somewhat old-fashioned alexandrines that he was experimenting with at this time. Pushkin himself published the poem without citing the text he was responding to, as was (and remains) the custom. The poem breaks off abruptly after the first line of a new couplet. The effect is striking particularly since the final verb is "безмолвствует" (cf. "народ безмолвствует" at the end of *Boris Godunov*). In short, the poem is *intentionally* unfinished.

---

3 Чья скрытая рука́ мне крепко руку жмёт – Whose hidden hand firmly shakes my hand ("hidden" because Pushkin does not know to whom it belongs)

8 Иль (= Или) пола кроткого стыдли́вый херуви́м – Or a bashful cherub of the meek sex. In the Bible, cherubim are hybrid winged creatures, often having the faces of lions or cows, sometimes having four legs. In Renaissance art, they are usually depicted as chubby children. For reasons not entirely clear, cherubs (and angels in general) were often considered to be androgynous. (Pushkin chooses the word "кроткого" also for reasons of euphony: отрок … храним / кроткого … херувим.)

9 умиле́нный – overcome by sweet emotion. In modern Russian, the form would be "умилённый."

10 Внима́нья слабого предме́т уедине́нный – A solitary subject of weak attention. In modern Russian, the form would be "уединённый."

13 Смешо́н, уча́стия кто требует у света! – Ridiculous is he who demands sympathy from (high) society. The archaic syntax (ordinarily it would read Смешон, кто …) is reminiscent of eighteenth-century verse.

15 Как на зае́зжего фигля́ра – As at a wandering player. The word "фигляр" was very much on Pushkin's mind at this point (see his epigram on Bulgarin, "На Булгарина," and "Моя родословная"). However, here (as in *Mozart and Salieri*), he uses it in its dictionary meaning: a (bad) actor.

16 выразит – should express. (The many perfective verbs that follow create a modal sense, i.e., of possibility.)

19 Она́ в ладо́ни бьёт – It (the crowd ["толпа"]) claps its hands

21 неза́пное (= внезапное) – sudden
22 изгна́нье, заточе́нье – exile, incarceration. These are both words that Pushkin used elsewhere in his poetry to describe his southern exile.
26 меж ими = между ними
27 оно = счастие

Труд – Labor

This brief poem reflects Pushkin's ambivalent mood after completing *Eugene Onegin*, the novel in verse begun in 1823. Interestingly, it is written in elegiac distichs rather than in an *Onegin* stanza.

Tomashevskii (1939, 484) has found the source of this poem in the memoirs of the English historian Gibbon, who describes similar feelings after completing his monumental *Decline and Fall of the Roman Empire*. The passage in English reads:

> It was on the day, or rather night, of the 27th of June 1787, between the hours of eleven and twelve, that I wrote the last line of the last page in a summer-house in my garden. After laying down my pen, I took several turns in a berceau or covered walk of acacias, which commands a prospect of the country, the lake, and the mountains. The air was temperate, the sky was serene, the silver orb of the moon was reflected from the waters, and all nature was silent. I will not dissemble the first emotions of joy on the recovery of my freedom, and perhaps the establishment of my fame. But my pride was soon humbled, and a sober melancholy was spread over my mind by the idea that I had taken an everlasting leave of an old and agreeable companion, and that, whatsoever might be the future fate of my history, the life of the historian must be short and precarious.

Pushkin owned two French editions of Gibbon. In the version of Guizot (*Histoire de la Décadence et de la chute de l'Empire Romain*, vol. 1 [Paris, 1728], 40) the key passage reads: "mais les mouvemen<t>s de mon orgueil se calmèrent bientôt, et des sentimen<t>s moins tumultueux et plus mélancoliques s'emparèrent de mon âme lorsque je songeai que je venais de prendre congé de l'ancien et agréable compagnon de ma vie."

In the other version (*Mémoires de Gibbon*, [Paris, 1793], translator unnamed), the passage is rendered as "Mais mon orgueil fut bientôt humilié, et une mélancolie pensive s'empara de mon esprit, à l'idée que j'avais pris un congé eternel d'un vieux et agréable compagnon, et que, quelle que pût être la durée future de mon histoire, la vie précaire de l'historien ne pouvait plus être longue."

---

1 вожделе́нный – desired. In modern Russian, the word has exclusively sexual connotations, but in eighteenth-century literature it was used much more broadly. Pushkin clearly wants the archaic coloration in this poem.
3 подвиг – glorious deed
поде́нщик – day laborer

5 жаль мне трудá – I am sorry <to part with> my work
6 Друга Аврóры златóй, друга пенáтов святы́х – friend of the golden Aurora, friend of the holy Penates.
Аврóра – goddess of the dawn
Пенáты – household gods (in Roman mythology)

Царскосéльская статуя – The Statue in Tsarskoe Selo

The statue in question, which can still be found in the park of Tsarskoe Selo, is a work by the sculptor Pavel Petrovich Sokolov (1764–1835). The subject is taken from La Fontaine's fable about a peasant girl who drops a jug of milk on her way to market while daydreaming about what she will do with the money she earns from selling it. Pushkin ignores this moral and draws a much broader meaning from the statue. The statue actually contained (and to this day contains) a fountain, with water flowing from the jug. Pushkin's contemporary Mikhail Danilovich Delariu wrote a poem on the same statue (clearly inspired by Pushkin's, also in elegiac distichs), which explicitly commented on this transformation: "Но молоко, пролиясь, превратилось в журчащий источник" ("But the milk, spilling out, turned into a gurgling stream" [Kibal'nik, 159]).

As often in his unrhymed poems, Pushkin takes advantage of other types of sound repetition (e.g., урну/уронив).

---

1 урну – jug. This is an unusual use of this word; ordinarily it is a decorative vase at a gravesite. See commentary to "Когда за городом, задумчив, я брожу," line 12.
об утёс – against the cliff. The statue sits on a large rock pedestal.
3 сякнет – (archaic) dries out

Literature: Loseff, 40–41; Kibal'nik.

„Глухóй глухóго звал к судý судьи́ глухóго" – "A deaf man summoned a deaf man before a deaf judge"

A free translation of the poem "Les trois sourds" ("The Three Deaf Men") that Pushkin found in the book *Anthologie Française, ou choix d'épigrammes, madrigaux, portraits, épitaphes, inscriptions, moralités, couplets, anecdotes, bons-mots, réparties, historiettes*, vol. 1 (Paris, 1816), 10, where it was attributed (wrongly, as Tomashevskii shows) to Mellin de Saint-Gelais (1491–1558).

Un Sourd fit un Sourd assigner
Devant un Sourd dans un village,
Puis s'en vint son droit entonner;
La demande était d'un fromage:

L'autre répond du labourage;
Le juge étant sur ce suspens,
Déclara bon le marriage,
Et les renvoya sans dépens.

(A deaf man hauled up another deaf man before a deaf elder in his village and tried thumping out his rights in the case. His plea concerned a cheese, but the defendant mentioned a field; the judge having no view on the matter declared the marriage valid and dismissed the case without costs.)

The original is in eight-syllable lines with alternating rhymes (with lines 2, 4, 5, and 7 all on the same rhyme). Pushkin departs from the form of the original, using rhymed iambic couplets (all lines hexameter except the fifth, which is pentameter). In keeping with the subject matter, Pushkin produces a wonderful cacophonic effect by word and sound repetition.

---

1 Глухóй – A deaf man. Throughout the poem, this word (whether in nominative or accusative) is a substantivized adjective.
2 „Моя им сведенá корóва!“ – My cow was stolen by him
4 пустошью – undeveloped, empty parcel of land

Literature: Tomashevskii 1917, 61–64.

Прощáние – Farewell

An extremely dark love poem, written to Elizaveta Ksaver'evna Vorontsova (1792–1880), whom Pushkin had met (and fallen in love with) during his southern exile. The form is precisely that of "Паж или пятнадцатый год," but the tone is portentous and troubled. Behind the deceptively simple language one finds unusual and surprising word combinations.

---

1 Note the soundplay in "раз" and "образ" (and "дерзаю" in line 2)
2 мысленно ласкáть – to caress in my thoughts. The elegiac cliché "образ милый" (see Proskurin 2007, 226–27) is put in a new and surprising context by the physicality of "ласкать."
3 сердéчной силой – through the power of <my> heart (i.e., through love)
4 с негой робкой и уны́лой – with timid and melancholy languor. All of these words are standard elegiac vocabulary, but ordinarily "нега" and "унылая" would not appear together, the former being positively charged and the latter negative.
5 воспоминáть = вспоминать
13 Как овдовéвшая супрýга – like a wife who has been widowed
15 Пред заточéнием егó – before his incarceration. In the drafts, the line read "Перед изгнанием его" ("before his exile"). On the nouns "заточение" and "изгнание," see commentary to line 22 of "Ответ анониму."

Паж или пятна́дцатый год – The Page or The Fifteenth Year

The poem, a dramatic monologue from the perspective of the title character, intersects with many of the concerns of the *Маленькие трагедии* (*Little Tragedies*), which were written contemporaneously. For example, the poison reference (line 24) recalls an important and enigmatic motif in *Mozart and Salieri*. In general, though, the poem picks up the "Spanish" theme of *Каменный гость* (*The Stone Guest*). The epigraph refers to Cherubino, the adolescent in Beaumarchais's drama (and Mozart's opera) *The Marriage of Figaro*, who is in love with every woman he sees and, in this sense, represents another version of Don Juan. From a psychological perspective, it is noteworthy that this poem was composed shortly before Pushkin's marriage.

The poem is written in iambic tetrameter in an unusual five-line stanza based on two rhymes: A-b-A-A-b (the same form as the love poem "Прощание," though worlds apart in terms of content and tone). In this case, the model was undoubtedly Alfred de Musset. In his *Contes d'Espagne et d'Italie* (Paris, 1830 – though it actually appeared at the end of 1829), there is a section called "Chansons à mettre en musique" ("Songs to put to music"). The first poem in this section (on pages 163–66) is called "Barcelone" ("Barcelona"); in later publications it was called "L'Andalouse" ("The Woman from Andalusia"). Aside from the formal resemblances (including the placement of masculine and feminine rhymes), Musset's poem is devoted to the praise of a dark Spanish beauty. Note that the final stanza includes an address to the speaker's page.

Avez-vous vu, dans Barcelone,
Une Andalouse au sein bruni?
Pâle, comme un beau soir d'automne!
C'est ma maîtresse, ma lionne!
La marquesa d'Amaëgui.

J'ai fait bien des chansons pour elle,
Je me suis battu bien souvent.
Bien souvent j'ai fait sentinelle,
Pour voir le coin de sa prunelle,
Quand son rideau tremblait au vent.

Elle est à moi, – moi seul au monde –
Ses grands sourcils noirs sont à moi!
Son corps souple et sa jambe ronde,
Sa chevelure qui l'inonde,
Plus longue qu'un manteau de roi!

C'est à moi son beau corps qui penche
Quand elle dort dans son boudoir,
Et sa basquina sur sa hanche,
Son bras dans sa mitaine blanche,
Son pied dans son brodequin noir!

Vrai Dieu, lorsque son oeil pétille
Sous la frange de ses réseaux,
Rien que pour toucher sa mantille,
De par tous les saints de Castille,
On se ferait rompre les os.

Qu'elle est superbe en son désordre,
Quand elle tombe, les seins nus,
Qu'on la voit, béante, se tordre
Dans un baiser de rage, et mordre
En criant des mots inconnus!

Et qu'elle est folle dans sa joie!
Lorsqu'elle chante le matin,
Lorsqu'en tirant son bas de soie,
Elle fait sur son flanc qui ploie,
Craquer son corset de satin!

Allons! mon page, en embuscades!
Allons! la belle nuit d'été!
Je veux ce soir des sérénades
A faire damner les Alcades
De Tolose au Guadalété.

Lerner (151–53), the first to recognize the significance of this poem, notes the relevance of yet another Musset poem, "Madrid" (in the same section of Musset's book, pages 171–74). Though formally different, "Madrid" also praises a beautiful Spanish woman (perhaps the same one): "Car c'est ma princesse andalouse! / Mon amoureuse! ma jalouse!" ("For she is my Andalusian princess! / My beloved! My jealous one!")

Epigraph: C'est l'âge de Chérubin – It is the age of Cherubino. This phrase does not occur in Beaumarchais. The French "âge" rhymes with Russian "паж." It is perhaps relevant that in yet another love poem to his Andalusian beauty ("Madame la Marquise"), Musset addresses cherubs: "Gais chérubins! veillez sur elle!" (176).

1 Пятна́дцать лет мне скоро минет – I'll soon be fifteen

3 Как он вперёд меня́ подви́нет! – How it will push me forward! (Less literally: What a step forward it will be!). The antecedent of "он" is "день."

10 Попро́буй кто меня толкну́ть – Just somebody try to push me

12 между ими = между ними

15 Что жизни мне миле́й (= милее) она́ – That she's dearer to me than my own life

21 вечо́р – yesterday (or yesterday evening)

27 молву́ – rumor

29 мою́ севи́льскую графи́ню – my countess of Seville. In the Beaumarchais play (and the Mozart opera) the action takes place in Seville, where Cherubino is particularly smitten by the countess Almaviva. Note also that Seville is the capital of Andalusia (cf. the Musset poem).

A draft of this line reads “мою́ варша́вскую графи́ню” (“my Warsaw countess”). Combined with some other passages that Pushkin crossed out, commentators have been encouraged to see prototypes for these characters in Iosif Osipovich Rosset (1812–1854), who had recently graduated from the “пажеский корпус” (“Corps de Pages”), an educational institute open only to the highest ranks of the social elite. He was the brother of Aleksandra Osipovna Rosset, whose close school friend was the Polish countess Stephanie Radziwill (1809–1832), generally thought to be the “Warsaw Countess” of Pushkin’s draft.

„Румя́ный критик мой, насме́шник толстопу́зый“ – “My rosy critic, my potbellied scoffer”

Since the poem was not published in Pushkin’s lifetime, it is not certain that its two parts were intended to comprise one work, but the tone, the form, and even the lexicon (e.g., the relatively unusual verb “трунить” [“to mock”] in lines 2 and 29) suggest that they are related.

The critic who is being mocked is probably Bulgarin, who, in reviews of 22 March and 1 April 1830, had criticized Pushkin’s recent work (chapter 7 of *Onegin*) for its “томление” (Bulgarin had even italicized the word).

The poem is a remarkable depiction of a rural scene, drawn as a contrast between a traditionally poetic idealization of the bucolic life (such as would appeal to the apostrophized “critic”) and the prosaic reality (boring and even horrifying).

Pushkin experiments with form, taking the staid tradition of the alexandrine and investing it with everyday intonations and “inappropriate” thematic material. The use of diminutives is particularly interesting.

---

1 Румя́ный критик мой, насме́шник толстопу́зый – My rosy critic, my potbellied scoffer. If describing a woman, “румяная” is a compliment; when describing a man, it is an insult, suggesting “well-fed” and “pampered.” The word “пузо” (“paunch”) is flagrantly unpoetic.

2 над нашей томной музой – at our tormented muse. The *Словарь языка Пушкина* glosses this usage of “томной” as “шутливо об элегической поэзии” (“jokingly about elegiac poetry”).

3 Поди́-ка … прися́дь-ка – Just come … come on and sit down. The colloquial particle “-ка” is used to “soften” imperatives, creating a sense of familiarity.

4 с прокля́тою хандро́й – with the accursed spleen. Nabokov renders the word as “chondria” (see his lengthy note in 2:151–56). As a psychological condition somewhere between “melancholy” and “ennui,” this was a ubiquitous ailment of the rich and aimless in the late eighteenth and early nineteenth centuries. Onegin (1:XXXVIII) suffered from it. On 22 July 1831 Pushkin would write to Pletnev: “хандра хуже холеры, одна убивает только тело, другая убивает душу” (“‘Chondria’ is worse than cholera, the one kills only the body, the other kills the soul”).

5 убо́гой = убо́гий

6 равни́ны скат отло́гой (= отлогий) – sloping incline of the plain. This does not sound as tautological (or paradoxical) in Russian as in English translation.

8–9 Где … где … где – these are things the critic would expect to see in a poem about the countryside

11 И то – and even then (a qualifier)

14 Чтоб лужу засори́ть, лишь только ждут Боре́я – They (the leaves) are only waiting for Boreas, in order to litter the puddle. Boreas is the north wind that brings cold winter air. It is an unusual word choice in that it recalls eighteenth-century poetics, particularly jarring in the lexical context of this line.

15 И только – And that's it. A rhythmical echo of line 9 (with the somewhat unusual pause after the second foot, since the alexandrine would ordinarily have the logical break coincide with the caesura after the third foot) and a semantic echo of lines 9 and 11.

17 подмы́шкой – under his arm; in his armpit. The word is strikingly unpoetic in Russian.

18 кличет издали лени́вого попёнка – calls from afar <to> the priest's lazy <young> son. "Кличет" (from "кликать") is colloquial rather than poetic. This son is the antecedent of "тот" in the following line.

20 давно́ бы схорони́л – he should have buried him long ago

21 Что ж ты нахму́рился? – Нельзя́ ли блажь оста́вить? – Why are you frowning? – Can't you leave aside this whim? In the first part of the line the poet again addresses the critic. In the second part, the critic responds to the poet. (One of the functions of a dash in Russian is as a quotation mark, indicating a new speaker.)

24 Мне здесь не прогуля́ть – so I don't miss <the name-day party> by goofing around here

Посто́й – а каранти́н! Wait – what about the quarantine! The entire area in Boldino (where Pushkin was writing this poem) was under quarantine because of an outbreak of cholera.

25 инди́йская зара́за – the Indian infection. The source of the nineteenth-century cholera epidemics was the Ganges delta.

26–27 Сиди́, как у воро́т угрю́мого Кавка́за / Быва́ло сиживал поко́рный твой слуга́ – Wait, like at the gates of the lugubrious Caucasus / Your humble servant once had to wait around. The reference is to 1829, when Pushkin, who had traveled to the Caucasus to witness the Russian army in battle, had to spend three days in quarantine in Gumri, Armenia (mentioned briefly in *Путешествие в Арзрум* [*Journey to Arzrum*], chapter 5).

Literature: Meilakh 1962, 151–55; Khodasevich, 1:212–18.

К перево́ду Илиа́ды – On the Translation of the Iliad

This epigram is characteristic of Pushkin in that it reveals a tendency to take mutually exclusive positions on a given issue. In this case, we see a completely different attitude towards Gnedich's accomplishment than in the other distich on the subject, "На перевод Илиады" (written at approximately the same time). However, it should be emphasized that Pushkin chose to publish that other poem. He not only refrained from publishing this one; he crossed it out in his notebook so thoroughly that it took the efforts of the greatest Russian textologists of the early twentieth century to decipher it.

The form is that of "На перевод Илиады," but here the elegiac distich is used for parodic purposes.

---

1 Крив – one-eyed (Gnedich had lost an eye in his youth in an accident)
Преложи́тель – transposer; translator
2 схож – similar

„Я здесь, Инези́лья“ – "I'm here, Inesilla"

The impulse (and several lexical items) for this "Spanish" poem comes from a poem of the minor English Romantic Barry Cornwall, pen name of Bryan Waller Procter (1787–1874). However, the rather sinister additions (e.g., lines 11–12, the refrain "мраком и сном") align it with another Spanish work written at this same time – the little tragedy *Каменный гость* (*The Stone Guest*). Indeed, it reads almost as if it were an interpolated song from the drama.

The meter, unrelated to Cornwall's poem, is amphibrachic dimeter with alternating feminine and masculine rhymes. Because the amphibrachic rhythm continues across the line wherever there are feminine cadences, the lines sound like (and could be rearranged as) amphibrachic tetrameter masculine couplets, a typical ballad meter (cf. Pushkin's own "Черная шаль" of 1820). Arranged as it is, the rhymes are much more apparent, and they are even augmented, for example, when "окном" is used as a rhyme word in the first two stanzas and "здесь" (emphatically repeated in the first lines) becomes a rhyme word in the penultimate stanza.

Serenade

Inesilla! I am here:
Thy own cavalier
Is now beneath thy lattice playing:
What art thou delaying?

He hath riden <sic> many a mile
But to see thy smile:
The young light on the flowers is shining,
Yet he is repining.

What to him is a summer star,
If his love's afar?
What to him the flowers perfuming,
When his heart's consuming?

Sweetest girl! why dost thou hide?
Beauty may abide
Even before the eye of morning
And want no adorning.

Now, upon their paths of light,
Starry spirits bright
To catch thy brighter glance are staying:
Why art thou delaying?

From *The Poetical Works of Milman, Bowles, Wilson, and Barry Cornwall* (Paris: A. and W. Galignani, 1829), 4:177–78.

---

11 старый – the old man (husband or, conceivably, father)
12 Мечо́м уложу́ – I'll fell him with my sword
13 Шелко́вые петли – silk cords. These cords, when hung from the windows, would allow the speaker to clamber up to the woman's room.

Рифма – Rhyme

This is the second poem that treats Rhyme as a personage of Greek mythology (see commentary to "Рифма, звучная подруга"). Once again, she is the daughter of Apollo, though this time her mother is the nymph Echo, who entered this poem either through Ovid's *Metamorphoses* or conceivably through some of the other treatments of this text, for example, Barry Cornwall's "A Sea-Shore Echo" (see commentary to "Эхо") or Jacques Charles Louis Clinchamp de Malfilâtre's *Narcisse*, the source of Pushkin's epigraph to the third chapter of *Eugene Onegin*: "Elle [refers to Nymph Echo] était fille; elle était amoureuse" – "She was a young girl; she was in love."

The paradox of this poem is both semantic (like "Рифма, звучная подруга," it anachronistically sets the birth of rhyme in antiquity) and formal. It is written in elegiac distichs (a stylization of antiquity) and, as such, without rhyme. However, Pushkin compensates for lack of rhyme with assonances and off-rhymes at the line endings and partial anagrams (e.g., рифма/нимфа, резвая дева) throughout.

In keeping with a stylization of antiquity, Pushkin uses numerous archaic forms (e.g., брегу, страстию, воспылал).

---

1 бессо́нная – sleepless. The nymph Echo is traditionally depicted as sleepless after having been rejected by Narcissus.
Пене́я – of Peneus. Peneus can be either the name of a specific river (near Mount Olympus) or the name of a river god. Insofar as the latter is evoked, it is worth remembering that he was the father of Daphne, a nymph pursued by Apollo. This myth is recounted in Ovid's *Metamorphoses* (for more on possible Ovidian references, see Kibal'nik, 160).
3 плод понесла́ – bore (became pregnant with) the fruit

5 прия́ла – acted as midwife. The verb "приять" is in modern Russian replaced by "принять."
Мнемози́на – Memory (mother of the Muses)
6 в хоре – either "in the chorus" or "in the group" (the latter meaning an eighteenth-century usage)
боги́нь-аони́д – of the goddess-muses

Отрок – The Youth

In elegiac distichs, the poem is devoted to a "mythical" treatment of the biography of Mikhailo Lomonosov (1711–1765), the poor fisherman turned poet and scholar. (Actually, Lomonosov was a merchant's son and not particularly poor, but legend had it that he rose from destitution.) Pushkin presents Lomonosov's story through a biblical prism ("fisher of souls").

The main influence on this poem is Batiushkov's "Послание И. М. Муравьеву-Апостолу" (1816), which contains a lengthy passage on Lomonosov:

Близ Колы пасмурной, средь диких рыбарей,
В трудах воспитанный уже от юных дней
Наш Пиндар чувствовал сей пламень потаенный [...]
Он сладко трепетал, когда сквозь мрак тумана
Стремился по зыбям холодным океана
К необитаемым, бесплодным островам
И мрежи расстилал по новым берегам.
Я вижу мысленно, как отрок вдохновенной
Стоит в безмолвии над бездной разъяренной

Near the bleak Kola River, among the uncivilized fishermen,
Already from his young days experienced in work,
Our Pindar felt that secret flame [...]
He trembled sweetly when through the fog's gloom
He rushed along the ripples of the cold ocean
To uninhabited and barren islands
And he spread nets along the new shores.
I see in my thought how the inspired youth
Stands in silence above the furious abyss

---

3 мрежи (=мере́жи) – (archaic) nets. This is the only time in all of Pushkin's work where this word appears. Aside from its presence in the Batiushkov poem cited above, the word appears in Matthew 4:18–22 in the Slavonic Bible (Kibal'nik, 162).
4 будешь помо́щник царя́м – you will be a helper to the tsars. This is a bit of an exaggeration, but in keeping with the myth of Lomonosov popular in Pushkin's day and, to a large extent, to the present time. Lomonosov held no high rank, but he was indeed in favor at the court of Elizabeth, where he advised on subjects as varied as geology, education, and art. Perhaps the phrase has

less to do with the historical Lomonosov than with the position of authority that Pushkin felt was due to any great poet, himself included (Proskurin 1999, 298).

„Два чувства дивно близки нам“ – “Two feelings are wondrously dear to us”

An unfinished meditation on a subject close to Pushkin’s heart (see “Брожу ли я вдоль улиц шумных” and the translation from Southey, “Hymn to the Penates” [“Еще одной высокой, важной песни”]).

The poem is written in iambic tetrameter, the first stanza in ring rhyme, the second stanza alternating. (A variant version has the third and fourth lines of the first stanza reversed, which would make the rhyme scheme of both stanzas identical.)

---

3 к родно́му пепели́щу – to our native hearth
4 к отече́ским гроба́м – to our ancestral graves
5 святы́ня – a holy place
6 без них – refers to the two feelings
7 Recent manuscript study suggests that the line should probably read: Как <без?> <оазиса?> пустыня – Like a desert without an oasis (Arinshtein 1989, 298).

„Когда́ поро́й воспомина́нье“ – “When at times a recollection”

An unfinished and somewhat mysterious composition. The poem borrows from earlier poems and anticipates later ones. The basic contrast drawn is between the *locus amoenus* of the south (Italy) and the cold and forbidding north (Russia). Scholars have speculated on what precise island Pushkin has in mind. Hypotheses range from “Golodai” (the island where the hanged Decembrists were rumored to be buried) to the Solovetsky Islands (where the young Pushkin was supposed to be exiled before numerous influential friends interceded to have him sent to the south instead). In its barrenness, the island anticipates the empty island at the end of “Медный всадник” (“The Bronze Horseman”). The text breaks off before one can make any precise identification, but the sense of foreboding is unmistakable.

The poem is written in iambic tetrameter with unpredictable rhyme scheme, a common form in lyric meditations. The opening sentence is eighteen lines long – rarely does Pushkin use such lengthy syntactic periods.

---

2 Грызёт мне сердце – gnaws at my heart. Cf. the “Змеи сердечной угрызенья” in “Воспоминание.”
7 возненави́дя – despising. A present verbal adverb formed from a perfective verb.
9 не в светлый кр<ай>, где н<ебо блещет> – from this point on (for ten

lines), the poem borrows extensively from another unpublished fragment "Кто знает край" with its invocation of Italy. (See the commentary to that poem.)

12 ветхой = ветхий

17 далéче – far away; in the distance. (NB: this is *not* a comparative)

23 дикой – дикий

24 брусни́кой – red whortleberry (a bitter-tasting berry that grows in harsh climates)

29 рыбарь – fisherman. The word is now obsolete.

Эпигрáмма („Не то бедá, Авдéй Флюгáрин") – Epigram ("The problem is not, Avdei Fliugarin")

A second epigram on Bulgarin, which clearly builds on his earlier one ("На Булгарина") in lexicon, tone, and meter. Since Bulgarin had himself managed to "defang" the earlier epigram by changing the final words, Pushkin appears to structure this poem in such a way that the insults come in several places, making similar defensive strategies impossible (Grekhnev, 336–38).

This poem is one line shorter than the other, but the rhyme scheme is similar: A-A-b-A-b.

---

1 Авдéй – Avdei. The name is chosen both because it rhymes with Фаддей (Bulgarin's first name) and because it was a distinctly lower-class name.

Флюгáрин – the word is derived from "флюгер," which technically means a "weather vane" or "pennant" that indicates which way the wind is blowing. However, it has a secondary meaning of someone who frequently changes his views, a person without true convictions. This moniker was first used to describe Bulgarin in Prince Viazemskii's 1825 poem "Семь пятниц на неделе" ("Seven Fridays in a Week"):

> Устроив флюгер из пера,
> Иной так пишет, как подует!
> У тех, на коих врал вчера,
> Сегодня ножки он целует.
> Флюгарин иль Фиглярин, тот
> Набил уж руку в этом деле,
> Он и семь совестей сочтет,
> Да и семь пятниц на неделе.

> Making a pennant from his pen
> Some person writes whichever way the wind blows!
> Those people whom he lied about yesterday,
> Today he kisses their feet.
> Fliugarin or Figliarin, he
> Is experienced in such things,
> He can even count seven consciences,
> And also seven Fridays in a week.

(The Russian expression "У него семь пятниц на неделе" is said about someone who constantly changes his positions or intentions.)
2 Another reference to Bulgarin's Polish roots.
4 Видóк Фиглярин – see "На Булгарина"
5 твой ромáн – Bulgarin had recently published the historical novel "Дмитрий Самозванец," which Pushkin justifiably contended had been plagiarized from his own still unpublished *Boris Godunov.* (See Dunning, 105–7.)

Заклинáние – An Incantation

In terms of theme (the death of a beloved and the hope for a meeting after death), this poem is linked to "Для берегов отчизны дальной" (and it is sometimes thought to be dedicated to the same woman – Amalia Riznich). However, it is much more stylized. If the other poem is pensive and restrained, this one is exclamatory and full of Romantic graveyard imagery. Some of that imagery (as well as the poem's title and opening intonation) can be traced to Barry Cornwall's "An Invocation."

Pushkin's poem is written in iambic tetrameter, but the stanzaic form is odd, being a common variant of the odic stanza (as in Pushkin's own "Вольность"). Given the clearly Romantic origins and qualities of this poem, one must presume another source. Tomashevskii (1958, 87–88), pointing to the refrain, notes that this form was also common in (French) romances, and that Pushkin was probably drawing on that tradition.

The poem was first published after Pushkin's death by Zhukovskii. In his edition and in all editions thereafter, it consists of three stanzas. However, Mikhailova (1995) argues that Pushkin himself crossed out the middle stanza. According to her, the poem should be published as sixteen lines, with the middle eight lines being a variant.

Pushkin read Cornwall's "Invocation" in the *The Poetical Works of Milman, Bowles, Wilson, and Barry Cornwall* (Paris: A. and W. Galignani, 1829), 4:145.

I.
If, at this dim and silent hour,
Spirits have a power
To wander from their homes of light,
And on the winds of night
To come, and to a human eye
Stand visible, like mortality –

II.
Come thou, the lost Marcelia, thou –
And on thy sunny brow
Bear all thy beauty as of old,
For I dare behold
Whatever sights sublime there be,
So I may once more look on thee.

III.
Or be thou like a daemon <sic> thing,
Or shadow hovering,
Or like the bloody shapes that come
With torch and sound of drum,
Scaring the warrior's slumbers, I
Will welcome thee, and wish thee nigh.

IV.
And I would talk of the famous brave,
Of the dead, and their house the grave,
And feel its wondrous silentness,
And pity those whom none may bless,
And see how far the gaping tomb
Stretches its spectral arms – and hear my doom.

V.
And I would know how long they lie
On their dark beds who die,
And if they feel, or joy, or weep,
Or ever dare to sleep
In that strange land of shadows. Thou
Whom I do call, come hither – now.

VI.
But there thou art, a radiant spirit,
And dost inherit
Earlier than others thy blue home,
And art free to roam
Like a visiting beam, from star to star,
And shed thy smiles from skies afar.

VII.
Then, soft and gentle beauty, be
Still like a star to me;
And I will ever turn at night
Unto thy soothing light,
And fancy, while before thine eyes,
I am full in the smile of Paradise.

Bitsilli (1929) suggests additional sources in Parny's "Le Revenant" ("The Ghost"), Batiushkov's translation of it entitled "Привидение" ("The Apparition") and Derzhavin's "Призывание и явление Плениры" ("The Summoning and Appearance of Plenira").

---

2 Когда́ поко́ятся живы́е – when the living are sleeping

7 я жду Лейлы – I wait for Leila. Pushkin ignores the name of Cornwall's heroine ("Marcelia"), probably because it would have no associations for a Russian reader. Instead, he chooses a markedly Byronic name (Leila is the female protagonist of *The Giaour*, who appears as a shade to the hero).

8 сюда́, сюда́ – to here, to here. This refrain is reminiscent of the refrain "dahin, dahin" ("to there, to there") of Goethe's famous "Mignon-Lied" ("Kennst du das Land?"), which Pushkin – despite his very poor German – used as an epigraph in "Кто знает край," and again referenced in "Когда порой воспоминанье."

9 Яви́сь, возлю́бленная тень – Appear, beloved shade. Mikhailova argues that this is an allusion to the song of the protagonist of Karamzin's Gothic short story "Bornholm Island," which he addresses to his beloved Lila: "Явися мне, явися / Любезнейшая тень!"

18 According to Anna Akhmatova, these lines are borrowed from André Chénier's elegy "O Muses, accourez": "A vos persécuteurs il reproche leur crime" ("he reproaches your persecutors for their crime"). In the edition of Chénier in Pushkin's library (*Oeuvres complètes de Chénier* [Paris, 1819]), this passage is on page 108. The shared context (an address to deceased women) makes the claim plausible, though the sentiment is not so very rare in Romantic literature.

Literature: Iakovlev 1917.

„Стамбу́л гяу́ры нынче славят" – "Today the Giaours praise Istanbul"

Pushkin published the first thirty lines of this poem (with minor variations) in the fifth chapter of *Путешествие в Арзрум* (*Journey to Arzrum*), where he called it "начало сатирической поэмы, сочиненной янычаром Амином-Оглу" ("the beginning of a satirical narrative poem, written by the Janissary Amin-Oglu"). This is undoubtedly a mystification: the poem is written by Pushkin himself, though from the perspective of a Janissary. It does indeed appear to be the opening of a longer work, but too little exists to allow much speculation about where it was leading.

The poem is written in iambic tetrameter, with a complicated rhyme scheme. In each of the stanzas up until line 30 – whether of five or of seven lines – one of the rhymes repeats three times. (There are also numerous internal rhymes.) This pattern changes at line 30, where it shifts to an unpredictable rhyme scheme typical of Pushkin's southern poems. In these final lines, a plot begins to emerge, and the change in rhyme scheme seems to reflect the tradition of Pushkin's narrative poems (exoticism, local color). However, the narrator's voice reflects a conservative (fundamentalist, as we might say today) Muslim perspective, which distinguishes it from that of the southern poems.

---

1 гяу́ры – Giaours. The word was familiar to all readers because of Byron's immensely popular poem of this name. In Arabic it is a pejorative word denoting people who do not believe in Islam, "infidels" (usually Christians). In English, "Giaour" rhymes with "power."

2 кованой пято́й – with a steel heel

3 Как змия спящего, разда́вят – they'll crush it like a sleeping serpent

5 Стамбу́л засну́л – Istanbul has fallen asleep (a personification as well as an

internal rhyme). The image of sleeping Istanbul may have been influenced by Victor Hugo's poems in the collection *Orientales* (see Achinger 1991, 149).

10 измени́л – betrayed

11 от по́ту – from sweat (an archaic genitive)

16 харе́мы (= гаремы) – harems

17 подку́пленный евну́х – a bribed eunuch. Pushkin's "Бахчисарайский фонтан" ("Fountain of Bakhchisarai") had featured a severe, uncorruptible eunuch who guarded the harem.

18 Арзру́м – Arzrum (or Erzerum), now in Turkey. Pushkin traveled there in 1829, having left Petersburg without permission, in order to experience first-hand the Russians' war with the Turks.

21 Не черплем – we don't extract (from the verb "черпать," to scoop out, draw out [as water from a well])

22 В вине́ – in wine

23 Пости́мся – we observe the fasts (in Muslim tradition, fasting allows for the drinking of water)

26 Джиги́ты – horsemen (of Caucasian origin)

30 Алла́ – Allah. In modern Russian "Алла́х."

31 гони́мый яныча́р – a persecuted Janissary. Formed in the fourteenth century, the Janissaries were special Turkish troops who guarded the sultan. They became increasingly powerful and corrupt, and in 1826 Sultan Mahmud II disbanded them. They then mutinied, but were forced to retreat to Thessaloniki, Greece, where their barracks were set on fire. The surviving Janissaries were treated brutally.

32 Тогда́ нас буря долу гнула – Then a storm pushed us downwards

34 От Рущука́ – from Rushchuk. A port city on the Danube (today in Bulgaria); in Pushkin's day it was part of the Russian Empire, but the scene of frequent attacks by the Turks.

до старой Смирны – to old Smyrna. Smyrna was an ancient Greek port city on the Aegean Sea (in Pushkin's day [and today] Izmir, Turkey).

35 От Трапезу́нда до Тульчи́ – From Trapezund to Tulcea. Trapezund (also called Trabzon) is a city on the northeast coast of Turkey. Tulcea is located on the Danube, now in Rumania. It had been under Ottoman rule since the fifteenth century.

36 Склика́я – calling together

39 до́мы – in modern Russian "дома́"

40–44 These lines represent an excellent example of Pushkin's poetic economy. He borrows them almost entirely from another scene of slaughter – lines 20–24 of the unfinished "Какая ночь. Мороз трескучий" (1827).

40 зубцы́ – the top parts of a fortress wall (which look like teeth, hence the connection to "зуб")

41 у́гли – coals

42 На ко́льях скорчась – on pointed poles, fixed in contorted poses

43 Оцепене́лые – Benumbed

<Дельвигу> – To Del’vig

Though nowhere stated explicitly, this unfinished poem (reconstructed by scholars from a messy draft) appears to be addressed to Anton Del’vig (1798–1831), Pushkin’s best friend from the Lyceum, poet and publisher of the almanac *Северные цветы* (*Northern Flowers*). Critics (among them Bulgarin) had recently written a number of attacks (and parodies, see line 22) on the two of them.

The poem is written in four-line stanzas of iambic tetrameter with alternating feminine/masculine rhyme.

---

1 брат назва́ный – soul brother (based on an old Slavic ritual of “побратимство,” in which two people celebrate their friendship by considering themselves brothers)

3 Кипри́да – Aphrodite
Феб – Phoebus Apollo
Вакх румя́ный – red-faced Bacchus (i.e., red from drink)

6 На ипподро́м, а не на торг – To the hippodrome, not to the market. Presumably a reference to *otium* (pleasure) rather than *negotium* (business). Pushkin here takes aim at the “торговое направление в русской литературе” (“mercantile movement in Russian literature”), represented by Grech and Bulgarin.

7 Вблизи́ Держа́винского гроба – Next to Derzhavin’s grave. The echo with *Eugene Onegin* (8:II) is obvious. As in that reference, the phrase probably should be understood as a statement of solidarity and continuity.

10 в гордой лености – in proud indolence. As a schoolboy Del’vig was famed for his laziness.

16 хитрых торгаше́й – of sly salesmen. Pushkin compares Del’vig (who did not depend on his poetry for his livelihood) with himself.

19–20 Мы любим славу <?> да в б<ока́ле> / Топи́ть разгу́льные умы́. – We love glory and <we love> to soak our wild minds in the wine glass. These are presumably the reproaches that are directed at them.

Стихи́, сочинённые ночью во время бессо́нницы – Verses Composed at Night during a Time of Sleeplessness

Written at Boldino and not published in the poet’s lifetime, this strange, laconic, and highly emotional poem reflects Pushkin’s fascination with pattern and meaning. The poem’s title, carefully recording the circumstances of composition (“Стихи́, сочинённые” is a formula of eighteenth-century poetry, though it would be followed by something more precise, e.g., the city where the poem was written), contrasts with the urgency of the poem proper. Though it trails off at the end (perhaps signifying that the author has fallen asleep), it is surely a complete poem, not an unfinished work.

There are several striking shifts in the poem. The intonation moves from statement to question back to statement. The first-person pronouns shift from oblique cases to nominative, while the second-person pronouns do the opposite.

The poem is written in trochaic tetrameter with an unpredictable rhyme scheme (see comments to line 5).

---

1 Мне не спится, нет огня́ – I can't sleep, there is no light. There is no causal relationship between these phrases. (The lack of light is not the reason why the speaker cannot sleep.) The line simply establishes the setting (complete darkness) and explains why the central images of the poem all pertain to sound, not vision.

2 доку́чный – annoying

3 Ход часо́в – the movement of time, but probably more specific: a ticking clock that is either in the room or nearby ("близ меня")

5 Парки – genitive of "Парка," Fate. Ordinarily a threesome, these goddesses are depicted spinning, measuring, and cutting thread. English is "Parcae," but it is rarely used. The line has nothing to do with parks, though the words are homonyms. In the draft of the poem, Pushkin had supplemented the Parca with a biblical image of apocalypse (cf. Revelation 6:8): "Топот бледного коня." The number of variants is sufficiently large to make it difficult to know precisely how Pushkin originally envisioned the poem, but this line would presumably have supplied the "missing" rhyme and led to a more traditionally structured poem (two groups of eight lines, each ending with ellipsis). However, in the final version there is no trace of the Bible, and the poem is oddly unbalanced (presumably a reflection of the troubled state of the speaker rather than the unfinished state of the poem).

бабье – adj. formed from "баба" ("hag"). The word is pejorative in this context, radically lowering the standard mythological reference. Drafts indicate that Pushkin began with more traditional depictions of the Fates and only gradually arrived at this striking image (Grigor'eva, 204–5).

7 мышья – modern Russian would be "мыши́ная." Note how a mouse (rushing about the house at night, apparently part of the poem's realia) becomes a crucial metaphor.

8 There is nothing in the poem that would allow the reader to anticipate the appearance of the pronoun "ты." Its exact identity remains a mystery, though it is surely connected to the sounds of the previous lines.

13 проро́чишь – make prophecies. Recall the Parca in line 5.

15 When Zhukovskii prepared this poem for publication after Pushkin's death, he was bothered by the impure rhyme (хочу́/ищу́) and took the liberty of rewriting the final line, making it "Темный твой язык учу." This (excellent) emendation was not written by Pushkin, but gained currency and was quoted enthusiastically by poets like Andrei Belyi long after it was shown to be incorrect.

Геро́й – The Hero

One of Pushkin's most extended meditations on history and truth, it has important implications for Pushkin's later historical fiction – *Капитанская дочка* (*The Captain's Daughter*) – and method – "Table Talk" (Pushkin's title is in English), as well as *История Пугачева* (*History of the Pugachev Rebellion*). Since the poem is framed as a dialogue between friends, the reader cannot distinguish exactly where Pushkin himself stands. (It would surely be overhasty to identify the poet with Pushkin.) The issue under discussion is heroism, with Napoleon the exemplary figure. (Throughout his life, Pushkin reevaluated his attitude toward Napoleon; this poem is not consistent with the demonic image one finds of him in much of the early poetry and, for example, in the brief allusion in “Пиковая дама” [“The Queen of Spades”].)

As part of his Egyptian campaign of 1799, Napoleon captured the city of Jaffa. According to legend, he visited a military hospital there, shaking the hands and even touching the wounds of his soldiers who were dying from the plague. This story was widely known (in 1804, it inspired a famous painting by Antoine-Jean Gros). Shortly before Pushkin wrote his poem, a certain Louis-Antoine de Bourrienne published his memoirs about Napoleon, where he claimed eyewitness status and debunked numerous myths, including the one about the hospital in Jaffa. (De Bourrienne’s claims themselves were later challenged, but only after this poem was written.)

Pushkin was fascinated by patterns and repetitions, and he used the date and place at the end of the poem to create another layer of meaning. The poem was composed not in Moscow in September, but in Boldino in October, where Pushkin was waiting out the cholera epidemic that is reflected in this work and others of the period (e.g., the drama *Пир во время чумы* [*Feast in the Time of the Plague*]). However, on 29 September 1830, Nicholas (probably conscious of the Napoleonic precedent) had visited Moscow during a cholera epidemic. (Admittedly, there is no record of his meeting with cholera victims.)

Published anonymously in 1831, the poem first appeared under Pushkin’s name in the posthumous volume of Pushkin’s own journal *“Современник”* (*“The Contemporary”*) 5, no.1 (1837). There the editors included the following footnote:

> Редакция получила это стихотворение от М. П. Погодина при следующем письме: “посылаю вам стихотворение Пушкина ‘Герой.’ Кажется, никто не знает, что оно принадлежит ему. Пушкин прислал мне оное во время холеры в 1830 году из нижегородской своей деревни, и вот что писал об нем: … Посылаю вам из моего Патмоса апокалиптическую песнь. Напечатайте где хотите, хоть в ‘Ведомостях’, но прошу вас и требую именем нашей дружбы не объявлять никому моего имени. Если Московская ценсура не пропустит, то перешлите Дельвигу, но также без моего имени, и не моей рукою переписанную.” Я напечатал стихи тогда в “Телескопе” и свято хранил до сих пор тайну. Кажется, должно перепечатать их теперь. Разумеется никому не нужно припоминать, что число, выставленное Пушкиным под стихотворением, после многозначительного *утешься*, 29 сентября 1830, есть день прибытия государя императора в Москву во время холеры.

The epigraph introduces a New Testament element and may indirectly invoke other biblical scenes (e.g., Christ healing the lepers).

The meter is iambic tetrameter with unpredictable rhyme scheme. The poem breaks off conspicuously at the beginning of a line, creating a fragmentary impression. In many respects (e.g., the meter, the presence of an epigraph from antiquity, the dialogue with a poet, the low opinion of the masses, cf. the "народ бессмысленный" of line 7), "Герой" recalls "Поэт и толпа," though the speakers are not antagonists here.

Epigraph: John 18:38 (Pilate's words to Christ)

1 Да, слава в прихотях вольна́ – Yes, fame is free in its caprices (i.e., it is unpredictable)

2 язы́к – the tongue (of a flame)

10 на крова́вом поле – on the bloody field (i.e., on the field of battle)

11 на чреде́ ино́й – in a different position/post/occupation

12 избра́нных – the second time this religiously-tinged word has been used, here with the archaic stress to give it an elevated tone (cf. "и́збранным" in line 2)

14–17 These lines represent a reworking of a passage about Napoleon from the fragmentary tenth chapter of *Eugene Onegin* (stanza VIII): "Сей муж судьбы, сей странник бранный, / Пред кем унизились цари, / Сей всадник, папою венчанный, / Исчезнувший, как тень зари."

14 пришле́ц (=пришелец) сей бранный – this martial newcomer. According to the dictionary definition, "someone who arrived," but Pushkin uses it here and elsewhere to mean Napoleon, with the implication that he was an "outsider." In other words, he was not a person of royal blood, but someone who came from without, willing himself into the center of things. ("Пришлец" is contrasted to the "цари" of line 15.)

15 смири́лися – note the curious echo with "смиренно" in line 6

16 вольностью венча́нный – crowned by freedom. The freedom Pushkin has in mind is the French Revolution. The word "вольностью" echoes with "вольна" of line 1.

18 Когда ж – But when

19 Свое́ю чудною (=своей чудной) звездо́й – By its miraculous star. The star, drawing on the celestial imagery of lines 2–5, serves as a metaphor for Napoleon's good fortune.

21 Ита́лии свято́й – of holy Italy. Napoleon became "king" of Italy in March 1805.

23 жезл дикта́торский – the dictator's scepter (in 1804, Napoleon had himself declared emperor)

25 Войны́ стреми́тельное пламя – the flame of war that spreads quickly. (The image emphasizes the elemental quality of the war; it picks up on the fire imagery of lines 2 and 9.)

27 Над ним – above the flame (the antecedent is "пламя," not Napoleon)

28 Как рать геро́я плещет – When the army of the hero applauds

29 грома́дой – "громада" was used by Pushkin to mean any enormous building or construction project (cf. the "спящие громады" in the famous invocation of Petersburg in "Медный всадник" ["The Bronze Horseman"]). In this case in this case it refers to the pyramids (the historical background is Napoleon's campaign in Egypt).

30 пусты́нно – emptily, because Moscow had been abandoned before Napoleon's arrival

34 зятем кесаря – the son-in-law of the Kaiser. Napoleon's father-in-law (the father of his second wife) was Franz II, the last emperor (Kaiser) of the Holy

Roman Empire, which was dissolved after Napoleon routed his forces in the battle of Austerlitz. Even afterwards, Franz remained Kaiser, since in 1804 he had been crowned Kaiser of Austria (a title he retained until his death). Napoleon married his daughter in 1806.

35–36 an enjambment that emphasizes motion downwards (in this case, taking one's seat or place)

36 казнию (=казнью) поко́я – by the execution of peace/stillness (an oxymoron). The reference is to Napoleon's exile on Elba, the scene of his enforced inactivity (temporary, as it turned out).

41 одро́в – of beds. This is both a literal description of hospital beds and a metaphorical reference to death (the standard Russian phrase for on one's deathbed is "на смертном одре").

42 труп живо́й – a living corpse (another oxymoron)

45 Не бранной смертью – Not by the death one encounters in battle

47 чуме́ – the plague (here personified)

48–49 в погиба́ющем уме́ / Рожда́ет бодрость – in the dying mind <he> gives birth to courage

49–50 another enjambment, particularly effective because the word "Небесами" is only understood after the first word of the next line, "Клянусь." ("By the heavens … I swear.")

52 уга́сший взор – exhausted (literally: burned out) gaze. The phrase suggests the face of someone about to die.

55 Земли́ слепо́й – of the blind earth. A metonymy for the unenlightened people who inhabit the earth (the "наро́д бессмы́сленный" of line 7)

55 Мечты́ поэ́та – the (naïve) dreams of a poet

59 правды свет – the light of truth. (Note that the other meaning of "свет" has been used in the previous line.)

63–64 Тьмы низких истин мне доро́же / Нас возвыша́ющий обма́н – A deception that elevates us is dearer to me than a multitude of low truths. The most famous lines of the entire poem. The passage is striking because "истина" (a word which harks back to the epigraph) is generally an unambiguously positive term in Russian, while "обман" is ordinarily strongly negative. Note also how the two lines are contrasted rhythmically, with the heavily stressed first line leading to a line with two unstressed feet (pyrrhics).

Literature: Evdokimova, 107–35.

„В нача́ле жизни школу помню я" – "I remember school at the beginning of life"

One of Pushkin's most enigmatic poems, it is hard to know whether one should read it as a (radical) rewriting of Dante or as a disguised autobiography. If the former, it must be admitted that very few passages have obvious relevance to the *Divine Comedy*. If the latter, it is tempting to read it as a poem about the Lyceum (and the adjacent park with statues), though some have argued that it describes the park at the Iusupov mansion, where Pushkin spent time as a child. It is sufficiently distanced that one cannot point with certainty to any obvious prototypes for the people or the specific statues mentioned.

The poem is written in terza rima (a-B-a-B-c-B-c-D-c etc.), a form rare in Russian (first introduced in the 1820s) and indelibly connected in European poetic history (and cultural memory) to Dante's *Divine Comedy*. In Russian versification, the iambic pentameter is the closest approximation to Dante's *endecasillabo* (eleven-syllable) line. By 1830, Pushkin had come to appreciate Dante and to associate him with Romanticism (as he did earlier in regard to Shakespeare). However, Pushkin's language is not Romantic (i.e., that of his Byronic southern poems), but consciously archaic.

---

1 В нача́ле жизни – In the beginning of life. Cf. the opening line of Dante's *Inferno*: "Nel mezzo del cammin di nostra vita" ("In the middle of the path of our life"). The *Inferno* could also supply a logic for the "demons" in line 36.

5 Велича́вая жена́ – majestic woman. Pushkin used the phrase "великая жена" in the 1829 "Воспоминания в Царском Селе" to describe Catherine the Great, but that would be an anachronism here. The art historian Gerda Panofsky has suggested to me that this refers to Empress Elizaveta Alekseevna (1779–1826), wife of Alexander I. Pushkin saw her at the opening of the Lyceum and at the annual exams. She apparently dressed modestly, though "убого" would be a distinct exaggeration. (On Pushkin's admiration for her, see Shebunin.) The image of a woman who guides the poet recalls Beatrice, though she, in contrast to the "majestic woman" of Pushkin's poem, is younger than her poet.

15 словеса́ – (archaic) words, modern Russian plural would be "слова́."

28 циркули – compasses. This is not the kind of compass that tells direction, but the kind used to draw circles in geometry lessons.

30 порфи́ры – porphyry (the color of royalty). Here presumably a metonymy for royal robes or mantles.

32 Мне на́ сердце – Into my heart

36 То были двух бесо́в изображе́нья – These were the depictions of two demons. Pushkin presumably means not "devil" (as in the poem "Бесы"), but rather "daemon" (supernatural beings of antiquity, who could be either good or bad).

37 Оди́н (Дельфи́йский идол) лик младо́й – One youthful countenance (the Delphic idol). This is usually understood to be Apollo.

40 Друго́й женообра́зный – the other in the form of a woman. This is generally agreed to be Aphrodite. (Женообразный should not be confused with женоподобный [a man who looks like a woman], see "Сафо" of 1825.)

На перево́д Илиа́ды – On the Translation of the Iliad

Nikolai Gnedich (1784–1833) worked for more than two decades on his translation of the *Iliad*, which he completed in 1829. Pushkin repeatedly urged him on, convinced that this work would have a beneficial influence on the development of Russian literature. When it first appeared, he wrote an enthusiastic note in *Литературная газета* praising it as a "подвиг" ("heroic feat").

Gnedich's translation is written in the Russian imitation of ancient hexameters (unrhymed dactylic hexameters with feminine cadences and occasional substitutions of dactylic feet by trochaic feet). Pushkin's poem takes the form of another stylization of antiquity, the elegiac distich, in the Russian tradition usually reserved for poetic miniatures. As so often in poems without rhyme, Pushkin compensates by taking advantage of other elements of sound (in this case the assonance on "y").

By looking at the drafts, Lotman (1997, 373) has shown that the initial impetus for the first line came from La Harpe's tragedy *Philoctete*.

See also "К переводу Илиады."

---

1 Слышу умо́лкнувший звук – I hear the sound that has become silent. A paradox to be explained by the fact that Homer is long gone and ancient Greek is a dead language, but it has been resurrected by Gnedich.

эллинской – Hellenic (used in Pushkin's time to describe the Greece of antiquity, as against "Греция" [modern Greece])

2 Старца вели́кого – of the great old man (i.e., of Homer)

„Для берего́в отчи́зны дальной" – "For the shores of your distant homeland"

A sort of companion poem to "Заклинание," clearly dedicated to the same former love (now deceased). Most scholars assume that this was Amalia Riznich, who had died in 1825 (see commentary to "Под небом голубым" of 1826). Evidence suggests that Pushkin wrote this poem in 1828 and revised it in 1830.

It is written in iambic tetrameter, in eight-line stanzas with alternating feminine and masculine rhymes. Only one feminine rhyme is used in the second stanza, and it repeats again in the final rhymes of the third stanza, connecting many of the key words of the poem: лобзанья/изгнанья/свиданья/страданья.

---

1 отчи́зны дальной (=дальней) – of a distant homeland. Riznich was actually from Vienna (she was half Austrian, half Italian), but for Pushkin her native land was Italy. This phrase originally read "чужбины дальной" ("of a distant foreign land"); Pushkin's decision to alter the noun reflects a fascinating shift in perspective.

5 хладе́ющие – becoming cold. A curious transferred epithet, in that the word often is used to describe death.

7–8 Томле́нье страшное разлу́ки / Мой стон моли́л не прерыва́ть – My moan begged you not to interrupt the terrible torment of parting. In other words: he begged her to prolong the moment of parting (not to leave).

11 Из края мрачного изгна́нья – From the dark realm of exile. Pushkin was in his southern exile in 1824, when Riznich left for Italy (via Austria). Shortly thereafter he was forced to leave the South for Mikhailovskoe.

14 Под небом вечно голубы́м – Under the eternally blue sky. Cf. the earlier poem on Riznich's death "Под небом голубым."

15 В тени́ олив – in the shadow of olive trees. The olive trees are a metonomy for Italy. The idea of a meeting in Italy with Riznich was not simply a poetic conceit, but had been a genuine obsession for Pushkin. (See Kogan.)
17 неба своды – the vaults of heaven (i.e., the sky)
23 поцалу́й = поцелу́й
24 Но жду его́; он за тобо́й – But I await it (i.e., the kiss); you owe it to me

Отры́вок ("Не розу Пафо́сскую") – Fragment ("Not the rose of Paphos")

Though Pushkin himself entitled the poem "Fragment," it is not the type of Romantic fragment one might expect (cf. "Осень"), but rather a truly unfinished work (as the three unrhymed lines at the end suggest). Formally, it is unusual: amphibrachic dimeter with rhyme scheme: A-B-c-A-B-c-D-E-f (where capital letters are dactylic rhymes and small letters masculine). The poem is Anacreontic in spirit, but not in form.

The final image of the poem (of the wilted rose on the bosom of the beloved) is hardly original, and its origin therefore not easy to trace. However, given Pushkin's interest in Barry Cornwall, it is noteworthy that his beloved British poet devoted an entire poem to this theme. In the Cornwall edition Pushkin owned, it appears two pages after "Here's a health to thee, Mary" (see commentary to "Из Barry Cornwall"). Moreover, Pushkin began translating the Cornwall poem at precisely this time (see Dovgii and Kulagin). Admittedly, the Cornwall poem lacks all references to antiquity and is written in an unrelated form. It is found in *The Poetical Works of Milman, Bowles, Wilson, and Barry Cornwall* (Paris: A. and W. Galignani, 1829), 4:154.

On A Rose

Oh! thou dull flower, here silently dying:
And wilt thou never, then, – never resume
Thy colour or perfume?
Alas! and but last night I saw thee lying
Upon the whitest bosom in the world,
And now thy crimson leaves are parch'd and curl'd.

Is it that Love hath with his fiery breath
Blown on thee, until thou wast fain to perish
(Love, who so strives to cherish),
And is the bound so slight 'tween life and death –
A step but from the temple to the tomb?
Oh! where hath fled thy beauty – where thy bloom?

For me, last night I envied thee thy place,
So near a heart which I may never gain,
And now, perhaps in pain,
Thou 'rt losing all thy fragrance – all thy grace.
– And yet, it was enough for thee to lie
On her breast, for a moment, and then – die.

1 ро́зу Пафо́сскую – the rose of Paphos. Paphos (on the west coast of Cyprus) was known for its cult of Aphrodite.
4 ро́зу Фео́сскую – the rose of Theos (an Ionian city on the coast of what is now the Aegean Sea), the birthplace of Anacreon.
8 на персях – (poetic) on the bosom
9 Эли́зы мое́й – of my Elise. This may refer (playfully) to Elizaveta Mikhailovna Khitrovo (1783–1839), daughter of General Kutuzov. Pushkin regarded her passionate affection with irony, but appreciated her friendship.

Из Barry Cornwall – From Barry Cornwall

Pushkin's poem, despite the title, is an adaptation rather than a translation. It retains the five-line stanzas, but with each stanza takes increasing liberties with the text itself. (Even the first line departs from the original, since Cornwall addresses Mary, whereas Pushkin only does so in the third stanza.) It is free also in regard to form, with the anapestic meter derived from the first line of the English ("Here's a héalth to thee, Máry") and the rhyme scheme only vaguely echoing that of Cornwall. Pushkin's epigraph, besides pointing to the Cornwall text, appears to echo Cornwall's own epigraph from Burns. Pushkin read it in *The Poetical Works of Milman, Bowles, Wilson, and Barry Cornwall* (Paris: A. and W. Galignani, 1829), 4:152.

Song

Here's a health to thee, Jessy.
– BURNS

Here's a health to thee, Mary,
Here's a health to thee;
The drinkers are gone,
And I am alone,
To think of home and thee, Mary.

There are some who may shine o'er thee, Mary,
And many as frank and free,
And a few as fair,
But the summer air
Is not more sweet to me, Mary.

I have thought of thy last low sigh, Mary,
And thy dimm'd and gentle eye;
And I've call'd on thy name
When the night winds came,
And heard my heart reply, Mary.

Be thou but true to me, Mary,
And I'll be true to thee;

And at set of sun,
When my task is done,
Be sure that I'm ever with thee, Mary.

---

6 краше = красивее

8 пéри – usually "Пери." A figure in Eastern mythology, a kind spirit in the form of a beautiful winged woman. She figured prominently in *Lalla Rookh: An Oriental Romance* (1817) by Thomas Moore (1779–1852), particularly the second part, "Paradise and the Peri," which became widely known in Russia thanks to the translation of Vasilii Zhukovskii.

„Пред испáнкой благорóдной" – "Before the noble Spanish woman"

An apparently unfinished poem, since a very rough draft of the opening lines of a third stanza exists. However, the two completed stanzas make a striking composition, building to a climax, but cutting off before the resolution. Pushkin loved the genre of love confessions (chapter 8 of *Eugene Onegin*, the False Dimitri and Marina in *Boris Godunov*). The closest parallel to this scene is in "Сказка о мертвой царевне" ("Fairy Tale of the Dead Princess"), where seven warriors pose this very same question to the princess. As in that tale, the suitors are (to the reader) completely indistinguishable; here they are always named simply as "оба."

The poem is written in trochaic tetrameter with alternating rhymes. The rhyme scheme is complicated by virtue of rhymes that cross the stanzas (i.e., lines 2 and 4 rhyme with lines 14 and 16, lines 5 and 7 with lines 13 and 15). As often in Pushkin, a trochaic meter is used to create a "foreign" quality (here Spanish [cf. "Родриг"], elsewhere Russian folk style [cf. "Утопленник"]). The form also recalls Pushkin's other poem about a knight, "Жил на свете рыцарь бедный."

---

13 люби́м тобóю – loved by you

Моя родослóвная – My genealogy

Another installment of Pushkin's bitter quarrel with Faddei Bulgarin, who had recently published a piece attacking the "aristocratic party" of Russian literature and mocking Pushkin's origins (Binyon, 319–21). This was particularly galling to Pushkin, who prided himself on his family history. He struck back with this lengthy – and deeply felt – polemic on heredity and class, concluding it with an unusually nasty – and undisguised – ad hominem shot at Bulgarin. Pushkin never published the poem, but it circulated widely in copies and was therefore well-known in Pushkin's day.

Pushkin's concern with his own lineage comes through in many works, including "Арап Петра Великого" ("The Blackamoor of Peter the Great") and *Boris*

Godunov. Despite an abiding respect for Peter the Great, Pushkin was always troubled by Peter's poor treatment of the hereditary nobility ("дворяне"), whose decline coincided with the rise of a new type of "service" nobility, for which he pejoratively used the term "аристократия" (see Driver, 10–11). Thus, in a prose piece of 1830 (part of the unfinished story "Гости съезжались на дачу" ["Guests Gathered at the Dacha"]), a visiting Spaniard asks about the Russian aristocracy and learns that: "Настоящая аристократия наша с трудом может назвать и своего деда. Древние роды их восходят до Петра и Елисаветы. Денщики, певчие, хохлы – вот их родоначальники." These thoughts are echoed in the third stanza of "Моя родословная."

Pushkin's specific references to his family history are based on Karamzin's *History* (which he studied with great care), on family papers, and on family legend. Pushkin was not above suppressing and altering some aspects of this history when they did not conform to his broader conception of his place in the world.

The poem is written in eight-line stanzas of alternating feminine and masculine rhymes. In the "post scriptum" section the rhyme scheme is the same, but the eight-line stanzas are broken into four-line stanzas (possibly to avoid an "orphan" stanza of four lines at the end).

In a draft version the poem had an epigraph from the poem "Le Vilain" by the songwriter Pierre Jean de Béranger (1780–1857): "Je suis vilain et très vilain / Je suis vilain, vilain, vilain." ("I am ignoble and very ignoble / I am ignoble, ignoble, ignoble.") The relevance of the poem is evident from the tone and content of the opening stanza.

> Hé quoi! J'apprends que l'on critique
> Le *de* qui précède mon nom.
> Êtes-vous de noblesse antique?
> Moi, noble? oh! Vraiment, messieurs, non.
>
> (Hey! I hear that the "de" that precedes my name is being criticized. Are you of the ancient nobility? Me, noble? Oh! Certainly not, good sirs.)

Unlike Pushkin, Béranger was telling the truth here. He really was *not* a noble (the "de" in his name had been added by his father to disguise his modest origins). If Pushkin was aware of this fact, it would perhaps explain why he ultimately rejected the epigraph. In any case, Pushkin's few references elsewhere to Béranger indicate a low regard for his poetry. (See Tomashevskii 1960, 162, 452–53.)

---

2 Писáки – scribblers

5 асéссор – a "collegiate assessor" was the eighth rank in the prerevolutionary table of ranks. It was the threshold rank that gave the right of hereditary nobility.

6 по кресту – by a medal. The point is that Pushkin was born into the (old) nobility; he did not have to eke out the title through service and medals (such as the "владимирский крест"), as was often the case for the new nobility.

7 Не акадéмик, не профéссор – Not an academician, not a professor. These were usually either foreigners (often Germans) or Russians not of noble origin.

Aristocrats looked at them with suspicion. As Botvinnik (1979, 153) notes, this passage was probably influenced by Batiushkov's words to Fate in the brief poem "Меня преследует судьба":

> Оставь меня, я не поэт,
> Я не ученый, не профессор,
> Меня в календаре в числе счастливцев нет,
> Я – отставной асессор.

8 русской (= русский) мещани́н – A Russian bourgeois (a man not of noble birth)

11 нова́ рожде́ньем знатность – our hereditary aristocracy is new

12 чем нове́е, тем знатне́й – the newer, the more aristocratic (i.e., the "new" nobility is more powerful than the old). Pushkin is not so much ironic here as bitter.

13 Родо́в дряхле́ющих обло́мок – a broken piece from decrepit clans

15 Боя́р – of boyars. Peter the Great's reforms had weakened the boyars' position in society.

16 братцы – guys (vocative case)

17–22 These lines are all barbs aimed at the new aristocracy, who had risen to prominence from undistinguished (and therefore, for Pushkin, undeserving) origins. Aleksandr Danilovich Menshikov (1673–1729), who worked closely with Peter the Great and essentially governed the country during the reign of Catherine I (Peter's widow), had supposedly once been a pie salesman in Moscow. Ivan Pavlovich Kutaisov (1759–1834) began as the valet of Paul I, but was later entrusted with important state positions. Aleksei Grigorievich Razumovskii (1709–1771) was Elizabeth's lover and held important positions in her reign, but began his career as a court singer. Prince Aleksandr Andreevich Bezborodko (1747–1799) was of Ukrainain origin ("хохол" is a pejorative term for a Ukrainian). The deserter from the Austrian army alludes to the grandfather of Count Petr Andreevich Kleinmikhel' (1793–1869), a favorite of Nicholas.

25 Рача – in one of several autobiographical passages (all of which are relevant to the present poem) of the essay "Опровержение на критики" ("Objections to my critics"), Pushkin wrote: "Род мой один из самых старинных дворянских. Мы происходим от прусского выходца Радши или Рачи, человека знатного (мужа честна, говорит летописец), приехавшего в Россию во время княжества святого Александра Ярославича Невского." ("My lineage is one of the oldest of the nobility. We come from a Prussian émigré Radsha or Racha, a noble (as the chronicler says, an honorable man), who came to Russia in the time of the principality of Saint Aleksandr Iaroslavich Nevskii.")

It has been argued (Ronen, 64) that this line reflects a phonological transposition (either conscious or subconscious) of a passage in a prayer – "притекающе к *раце мощей*" ("coming to the shrine of relics").

27 гнев венча́нный – crowned wrath. A metaphor, it stands in apposition to Ivan the Terrible in the next line.

28 Ива́н IV – this should be read as "Ива́н четвёртый" so that the line scans correctly. Ivan IV (1530–1584), known to posterity as "Иван Грозный" ("Ivan

the Terrible" or, more poetically, "John the Dread"). What Pushkin really knew about these distant ancestors is not clear; while some indeed served as "oprichniki" (warriors in Ivan's service), others were punished (Eidel'man, 315).

29 (in the online Academy edition, this line is incorrectly numbered as 30) Води́лись Пушкины с царя́ми – Pushkins were acquaintances of the tsars. It is not entirely clear who is meant. When writing his play *Boris Godunov*, Pushkin included two ancestors who interact with Boris. (One of these never existed, but even he was based on a clear historical prototype; see Virolainen and Dolinin, 264.) The tsar, fearing their treachery, at one point exclaims: "Противен мне род Пушкиных мятежный" ("I hate the rebellious clan of Pushkins").

30 не оди́н – more than one. Once again, it is difficult to know precisely whom Pushkin has in mind. One member of this group, however, can be clearly identified. Gavrila Grigor'evich Pushkin (died in 1638), who is depicted as a cunning opportunist in *Boris Godunov*, later in life became a true Russian patriot, a comrade-in-arms of Minin (see next note). As Pushkin wrote about Gavrila Pushkin in a draft of a 1829 letter (probably from 30 January) to N. N. Raevskii, "Il a eu de grands talents, homme de guerre, homme de cour, homme de conspiration surtout." ("He had great talents – as a warrior, as a courtier, and especially as a conspirator.")

32 Нижегоро́дский мещани́н – The bourgeois from Nizhni Novgorod. During the Time of Troubles, Nizhnii Novgorod was one of the few places that retained its allegiance to Moscow. Kuz'ma Minin (the person alluded to by the sobriquet) headed the army known as the "нижегородское ополчение," which spearheaded an uprising that drove the Poles away and reinstated Moscow's power. His origins are obscure, but certainly not noble (hence Pushkin's "мещанин"). Concerning a statue then in Red Square that bore the inscription "Гражданину Минину и князю Пожарскому," Pushkin wrote a footnote in 1836:

> Надпись Гражданину Минину, конечно, не удовлетворительна: он для нас или мещанин Косма Минин по прозванию Сухорукий, или думный дворянин Косма Минич Сухорукий, или, наконец, Кузьма Минин, выбранный человек от всего Московского государства, как назван он в грамоте о избрании Михаила Федоровича Романова. Всё это не худо было бы знать, так же как имя и отчество князя Пожарского. Кстати: недавно в одной исторической статье сказано было, что Минину дали дворянство и боярство, но что спесивые вельможи не допустили его в думу и принудили в 1617 году удалиться в Нижний Новгород – сколько несообразностей! Минин никогда не бывал боярином; он в думе заседал, как думный дворянин; в 1616 их было всего два: он и Гаврило Пушкин. Они получали по 300 р. окладу. О годе его смерти нет нигде никакого известия; полагают, что Минин умер в Нижнем Новегороде, потому что он там похоронен, и что в последний раз упомянуто о нем в списке дворцовым чинам в 1616.

34 бранных непого́д – of battle [literally: of military storms]

35–36 Когда́ Рома́новых на царство / Звал в грамоте свое́й наро́д – When the people summoned in a document the Romanovs to rule. The first Romanov was elected by the Земский собор in 1613. This event was marked by a couple of official documents (грамоты).

37 Мы к оной руку приложи́ли – We signed it. The antecedent of "оной" is "грамота" (document). The reference is probably to the "Грамота Земского собора на Двину об избрании Михаила Федоровича царем," dated 25 February 1613, which begins with a list of important people that includes the "воевода [commander] Никита Михайлович Пушкин." Strictly speaking, the idiom "руку приложить" originally meant "to put one's fingerprint" on a document, though later it became synonymous with a signature. The distinction may be significant, judging from Pushkin's letter of early June, 1825 to Del'vig: "Видел ли ты Н.<иколая> М.<ихайловича>? идет ли вперед История? где он остановится? Не на избрании ли Романовых? Неблагодарные! 6 Пушкиных подписали избирательную грамоту! да двое руку приложили за неумением писать! А я, грамотный потомок их, что я? где я." ("Have you seen Nikolai Mikhailovich Karamzin? Is his *History* progressing? Where does he plan to stop? Not at the election of the Romanovs? Those ingrates! Six Pushkins signed the election document. And two of them put their fingerprints on it because they were illiterate! And I, their literate descendent, what am I? Where am I?"). In fact, seven members of the Pushkin clan participated in the election (Eidel'man, 319).

38 Нас жаловал страда́льца сын – The son of the sufferer treated us favorably. The line refers to Tsar Mikhail Fedorovich Romanov (1596–1645), founder of the Romanov dynasty (elected in 1613). His father, Fedor Nikitich (1553–1633), had been forced to take monastic vows and was essentially imprisoned by Boris Godunov. After a few transfers of power, which briefly gave him a position of authority, he was again imprisoned for eight years by the Polish King Sigismund III.

42 В родню́ свою́ – like his kin

43 С Петро́м мой пращур не пола́дил – My ancestor did not hit it off with Peter

44 Fedor Pushkin was executed in 1697 for his role in a conspiracy against Peter. In fact, he was beheaded, not hanged. (Eidel'man, 324).

45 The line is strikingly close to line 5 of the opening stanza of *Eugene Onegin*.

47 Яков Долгору́кой – see notes to "Стансы," line 8

49 Мой дед – Lev Aleksandrovich Pushkin (1723–1790)

Когда́ мяте́ж подня́лся – When the rebellion arose. In a palace coup of 1762, Catherine II (later known as Catherine the Great) took power from her husband Peter III.

51 Миних – In 1762, the then seventy-eight-year-old Fieldmarshal Burkhard Christoph Graf von Münnich (1683–1767) was pardoned (after spending twenty years in Siberia on false charges) by the Germanophile Peter III. Not surprisingly, Münnich came out on Peter's side in the palace coup of that year, though he (in contrast to Pushkin's claim about his grandfather, see commentary to line 54) was soon forgiven. In the beginning of *Капитанская дочка* (*The Captain's Daughter*), it is noted that Grinev's father served under Münnich, a detail that may explain his retirement far from the capital.

53 Орло́вы – Grigorii Grigor'evich Orlov (1734–1783), lover and favorite of Catherine, was a major force behind the coup that brought her to power. His

brother Aleksei Grigor'evich Orlov (1737–1807) was entrusted with guarding the disgraced Peter III, who died in his care under mysterious and suspicious circumstances a few months after being forced to abdicate in favor of his wife.

54 в крепость – into prison. Pushkin claims that his grandfather was imprisoned for two years because of his loyalty to Peter III. In reality, Lev Aleksandrovich Pushkin was sentenced to two years of house arrest for a crime unrelated to politics – for beating up a defenseless servant. By the time the palace coup occurred, he had retired to his Boldino estate on account of poor health. The only ancestor serving in the guards at that time was Lev's cousin Mikhail Alekseevich, who is never mentioned by the poet. Though apparently brilliant, Mikhail Alekseevich distinguished himself during the coup only through his cowardice. Later he was sentenced to death (commuted to permanent exile in Siberia) for attempting to counterfeit ruble notes together with his brother Sergei (whose death sentence was commuted to lifelong imprisonment on the Solovetsky Islands). See Al'tshuller, 188–96.

55 присмирéл наш род – our clan quieted down

59 якшáюсь – (pejorative) I hang around with

60 крови спесь – the arrogance of my blood (i.e., my inherited arrogance)

61 грамотéй – (archaic) writer

62 Пушкин просто, не Мусúн – the Pushkins and the Musin-Pushkins were descended from the same ancestor, but the latter had remained wealthy, titled aristocracy, while the former had lost their wealth and stature.

64 Я сам большóй – I'm my own master; I'm independent. The reference, which Pushkin repeats at greater length in the "Onegin's Journey" section of *Eugene Onegin*, is to line 719 of Antiokh Kantemir's "Fifth Satire."

65 Фигля́рин – see commentary to "Эпиграмма" ("Не то беда"), line 1.

66 дед мой Ганнибáл – my grandfather Gannibal. Strictly speaking, it is the great-grandfather who is meant (see lines 77–78).

67 за буты́лку рома – for a bottle of rum. This story was, as Pushkin notes in line 65, an invention of Bulgarin. See Nabokov, 3:436.

69 Сей шкипер – This skipper. An allusion to Peter the Great, lover of all things nautical and captain of the ship of state.

74 сходно – at a reasonable price

77 отéц он Ганнибáла – the father of <that> Gannibal. One of the sons of Abram Gannibal was Ivan Abramovich Gannibal (1731–1801), the uncle of Pushkin's mother.

78 средь чесменских пучúн – Among the depths of Chesma. Ivan Abramovich Gannibal was one of the heroes in the battle against the Turks at the Bay of Chesma in 1770 (see "Воспоминания в царском селе").

80 Навари́н – the fortified Turkish port that Gannibal conquered in 1770.

83 в семьé своéй почтéнной – in his respected family. According to rumors, Bulgarin married a former prostitute.

84 он в Мещáнской дворяни́н – He's the nobleman on Meshchanskaia Street. The street was famous for its brothels. Cf. "Тень Баркова" ("Barkov's Shade"), an obscene poem often attributed to the schoolboy Pushkin, which begins: "Однажды зимним вечерком / В бордели на Мещанской" ("Once on a winter evening / In a bordello on Meshchanskaia Street").

Цыга́ны – The Gypsies

The exact date of this poem is unknown, but in spirit it closes the miraculously productive three months Pushkin spent at Boldino (see commentary to "Бесы"); one senses the poet taking leave of his estate and moving on to a new phase of life.

Gypsies had been part of the Russian literary landscape since Derzhavin's poem "Цыганская пляска" (1805), but Pushkin's narrative poem "Цыганы" (begun in October 1824, published 1827) was – and remains – the most celebrated Russian text about them. The short poem of 1830 is a type of valedictory statement both to the Gypsies themselves and to an earlier period of Pushkin's creative and personal life.

According to memoirs, Pushkin spent about two weeks in 1821 with a Gypsy tribe before writing his narrative poem. The memoirs (which were published long after Pushkin's death) dovetail so neatly with this poem that one has to wonder about their reliability. In any case, the issue is not so much whether the episode in fact occurred as reported, but the way Pushkin's contemporaries judged it to be true (with Pushkin's encouragement, cf. the epilogue to the narrative poem "Цыганы" and *Eugene Onegin* 8:V).

Curiously enough, this lyric poem may have a literary source. Pushkin initially published it with the subtitle "С английского" ("From the English"), and it is not clear if this was a mystification or an acknowledgment (for a similar problem, see the commentary to "Из Пиндемонти"). While no obvious source has been adduced, Iakovlev (1923) cites two admittedly distant poems by Wordsworth and William Bowles (1762–1850) on the subject of Gypsies. The Bowles poem seems more relevant, if only because his verses were included in the same book as Pushkin's beloved Barry Cornwall. Pushkin had repeatedly turned to this book for inspiration during the preceding three months.

The Gipsy's <sic> Tent

When now cold winter's snow is fled,
    And birds sing blithe again,
Look, where the gipsy's tent is spread,
    In the green village-lane.

Oft by the old park-pales, beneath
    The branches of the oak,
The watch-dog barks, when in slow wreath
    Curls o'er the woods the smoke.

No home receives the wandering race,
    The pannier'd ass is nigh,
Which patient bears, from place to place,
    The infant progeny.

Lo! houseless o'er the world they stray,
    But I at home will dwell,
Where I may read my book and pray,
    And hear the Sabbath-bell.

From *The Poetical Works of Milman, Bowles, Wilson, and Barry Cornwall* (Paris: A. and W. Galignani, 1829), 2:184.

Unlike Bowles' poem, Pushkin's is written in four-line stanzas of trochaic tetrameter (cf. the narrative poem "Цыганы" written in freely rhymed iambic tetrameter with an inserted folk song in trochaic tetrameter). The lexicon of Pushkin's short poem is reminiscent of his narrative poem (not only "ethnographic" details like "шатры" and "костры," but also the philosophical word "вольный").

---

4 огни́ разложены́ – the campfires are set

5 Compare this to the concluding section of the epilogue of Pushkin's narrative poem (addressed to the Gypsies): "Но счастья нет и между вами" ("But even among you there is no happiness").

8 провожда́л (= провожал) сии́ шатры́ – accompanied those tents. The high-style "сии" gives the quotidian tents an elevated quality.

14 прока́зы старины́ – pranks of the old days

15–16 для сельской неги / И дома́шней тишины́ – for rustic languor and domestic tranquility. Pushkin presumably looks ahead (idealistically) to his life as a family man.

1831

„Перед гробни́цею свято́й“ – “Before the revered tomb”

The tomb in question is that of General Mikhail Illarionovich Kutuzov (1745–1813), who is widely credited with having saved Russia in the war against Napoleon. Kutuzov was interred in the Kazan Cathedral in Petersburg. The poem first appears in Pushkin's letter to E. M. Khitrovo (Kutuzov's daughter) from the middle of September 1831. Russia had at this point successfully squelched the Polish uprising, and Pushkin explains: "Ces vers ont été écrits dans un moment où il était permis d'être découragé. Grâce à Dieu, ce moment n'est plus. Nous avons repris l'attitude que nous n'aurions pas dû perdre. Ce n'est plus celle que nous avait donnée le bras du prince votre père, mais elle est encore assez belle." ("These verses were written in a moment when it was permissible to be discouraged. God be thanked, that moment is no more. We have again taken the position that we could not lose. It is no longer that which the hand of your father the prince would have given us, but it is still quite good.")

Pushkin's choice of subject may have been influenced by a poem that had appeared in *Литературная газета* at about this time by Dmitrii Iur'evich Struiskii (1806–1856), who published under the pseudonym of Trilunnyi. (Beliaev, 286).

The poem is written in iambic tetrameter with the rhyme scheme a-a-B-c-B-c. Tomashevskii (1958, 80) traces the form to French poetic tradition: Malherbe used it in a number of poems addressed to eminent statesmen. Pushkin's frequent use of paraphrase, archaism (сей, днесь, година), and his almost aggressive alliterations (грани́тные грома́ды, страж страны́, остально́й из стаи, etc.) recall the eighteenth-century ode.

---

3 лампа́ды – icon lamps

4 золотя́т – make golden

5 Столбо́в грани́тные грома́ды – the granite masses of columns

6 их знамён нави́сший ряд – the hanging row of their banners

8 дружи́н – of troops. The word originally referred to the tsar's retinue of warriors in ancient Rus', but was also used in a broader sense. The archaic coloration fits in neatly with the lexicon and tone of this poem.

11–12 остально́й из стаи славной / Екатери́нинских орло́в – the last remaining of the glorious flock of Catherine's eagles. On this figurative use of "eagle," see commentary to "Воспоминания в Царском Селе," line 32. Cf. Derzhavin's poem "На кончину графа Орлова" ("On the Death of Count Orlov") where, punning on the name of the deceased, Derzhavin calls him "Орел из стаи той высокой" ("An eagle from that lofty flock"). Additional support for the claim that Pushkin is alluding to this poem comes in the rhyme pair "славной" and "державной" (which through paronomasia suggests the name Derzhavin).

15 о той годи́не – about that time

16 наро́дной веры глас (=голос) – the voice of people's belief (vox populi).

People were annoyed with Kutuzov's predecessor, Barclay de Tolly (see commentary to "Полководец"), who had chosen to retreat rather than face Napoleon's army in a major battle.

19 днесь – (archaic) now

25 дланию (=дланью) своéй – (archaic) with your hand

29 твоéй моги́лы бранной – of your military grave

Клеветника́м Росси́и – To the Slanderers of Russia

One of Pushkin's most jingoistic poems, a defense of Russia's brutal response to the recent Polish uprising and a saber-rattling rant against the French, whose free thinkers (e.g., Lafayette), had spoken out on behalf of the Poles. (For a detailed summary of French political opinion in prose and verse, see Frantsev, 71–79.) Pushkin defends Russia by appealing to history. In his view, the relationship of Russia and Poland is a family feud that goes back centuries, and France harbors malice against Russia because of its defeat in 1812. There is every indication – for example, his correspondence, especially the letter to Prince Viazemskii of 1 June 1831, which echoes this poem ("для нас мятеж Польши есть дело семейственное") – that Pushkin was not writing these verses to curry favor with the authorities, but was expressing his own political convictions.

The poem is written in a mixture of iambic hexameter and tetrameter with a markedly elevated lexicon. The numerous rhetorical questions recall the intonations of the eighteenth-century ode. (As Stennik [313] notes, Pushkin explicitly refers to the poem as an ode in a letter to E. M. Khitrovo of September or October of 1831, where he thanks her for "L'élégante traduction de l'ode.") The rhyme scheme is unpredictable, with the final ten lines forming a reverse odic stanza (perhaps a coincidence).

---

1 вити́и – orators

3 Литвы́ – of Lithuania. Pushkin here uses the word as a synonym for Poland.

5 взвешенный судьбóю – weighed by fate (the metaphor is presumably of the "scale" of justice)

12 Кичли́вый лях – (archaic) haughty Pole
росс – (archaic) Russian

16 сии́ крова́вые скрижа́ли – these bloody tablets. Pushkin himself, in the above-mentioned letter to Khitrovo, translated "скрижали" into French as "tables, chroniques."

19 Прага – an eastern suburb of Warsaw (not to be confused with Prague). The word also appears in "Бородинская годовщина," there – as here – in a rhyming position. The storming of Praga was the scene of Suvorov's brutal suppression of the Warsaw Uprising of 24 October/4 November 1794, celebrated by Russian patriots, but viewed with horror by Poles (and much of Western Europe) because of the indiscriminate killing of civilians.

24 на разва́линах пыла́ющей Москвы́ – on the ruins of burning Moscow. The line refers to the burning of Moscow in the war with Napoleon. Hokanson (151–52), citing Karamzin's detailed and indignant description in his *His-*

tory, argues that the line also calls to mind a parallel scene that occurred two centuries earlier, when Polish invaders burned Moscow during the Time of Troubles.

26 Тогó, под кем дрожáли вы – of him before whom you trembled (i.e., Napoleon)

29 нашей кровью искупи́ли – absolved with our blood (note the religious lexicon)

32 старый богаты́рь – the old warrior (here a personification of Russia)

33 завинти́ть свой измáйльский штык – to screw on its Izmail bayonet. A reference to Suvorov's victory against the Turks in December of 1790, when the Russians stormed the fortress of Izmail.

37 от Перми до Таври́ды – from Perm to Tauris. (Perm is at the foot of the Urals, Tauris is the old term for Crimea). This type of "от … до" construction was a topos in Russian odic poetry of the eighteenth century. For numerous examples, see Stennik (312). In modern Russian, the stress would be "от Перми́."

38 до пламенной Колхи́ды – to the fiery Kolchis. Kolchis was the archaic (Greek) name of Abkhaziia, today a self-styled independent region on the southeastern shore of the Black Sea. By Russian standards, it is a hot climate.

39 От потрясённого Кремля́ – from the shaken Kremlin (cf. "Бородинская годовщина," line 67)

40 до стен недви́жного Китáя – to the walls of unmoving China. This is probably best understood as a transferred epithet ("the unmoveable walls of China"). The same phrase appeared in a draft to "Поедем, я готов." In that poem it was then changed (apparently by Pushkin himself) to "стены спокойного Китая" and then again to the more straightforward "стены далекого Китая."

41 Стальнóй щети́ною сверкáя – sparkling with a steel bristle. A rather roundabout way of referring to Russia's bayonets.

44 сынóв – (archaic) of sons

46 Среди нечýждых им гробóв – Among graves not foreign to them. Pushkin refers to the enormous losses the French suffered in Napoleon's disastrous Russian campaign.

<Из письмá к Вяземскому> – From a letter to Viazemskii

These verses opened up a letter from Pushkin to his friend Prince Viazemskii of 14 August 1831. Viazemskii had received the title of "камергер" (Kammerherr, gentleman of the chamber) on 5 August.

The poem is written in iambic hexameter couplets, with the second couplet rhyme (itself based on the key word "камергер" of the first) identical to that of the final couplet.

2 Васи́лья Львовича – of Vasilii L'vovich <Pushkin>. V. L. Pushkin (1766–1830) was the poet's uncle, a minor poet, known to posterity primarily for

his obscene narrative poem “Опасный сосед” (“The Dangerous Neighbor”). Like Viazemskii and Pushkin himself, Vasilii L’vovich had been a member of the literary society Arzamas. Pushkin was thinking about Vasilii L’vovich at precisely this time because he and his friends were about to commemorate the first anniversary of his uncle’s death (20 August). In the present poem, Pushkin has a specific work of his uncle’s in mind, an epistle to P. N. Priklonskii of 1812, which begins: “Любезный родственник, поэт и камергер, / Пожалуй, на досуге / Похлопочи о друге! / Ты знаешь мой манер.” (“Dear relative, poet and gentleman of the chamber, / Please, at your leisure / Take care of your friend! / You know my manner.”) Hence the “manner” that Pushkin mentions has a double meaning: “my uncle’s ways” and “the way my uncle rhymed the word ‘камергер’.”

4 Укра́шенну ключо́м – who was decorated with a key. The uniform had a symbolic key which was worn on the back near the rear pocket (see line 6). The word “украшенну” is a truncated form of the dative case (in agreement with “камергеру” of the preceding line).

5 Так солнце и на нас взгляну́ло из-за туч! – So the sun has glanced from behind the storm clouds even on us! Judging from Pushkin’s letter to Viazemskii from the end of January 1929, Viazemskii (and Pushkin) had been out of favor.

8 поздра́вь княги́ню Веру – Congratulate Princess Vera. The name of course comes from the noun “вера” (“faith”), with which it rhymes. Viazemskii’s wife Vera (1790–1886) was a princess not only by virtue of her marriage to Prince Viazemskii; she was born Princess (“княжна”) Gagarina. (In Russia, such ranks were social titles independent of government positions.)

<Из запи́ски к А. О. Россе́т> – From a note to A. O. Rosset

This brief poem is connected to the recent political events. Together with the note, Pushkin sent her the booklet of poems about the Warsaw Uprising (which contained “Клеветникам России,” “Бородинская годовщина,” as well as a no less enthusiastic poem on the same subject by Zhukovskii).

On Rosset, see the notes to “В альбом А. О. Смирновой.” As far as the present poem is concerned, several documents confirm that Rosset was, if not the first, one of the first to give Pushkin the news that Warsaw had surrendered (Beliaev, 284–85).

In her memoirs, Rosset refers to the poem as a “quatrain,” but it is unclear whether Pushkin actually completed the second line. This poem is in iambic tetrameter with alternating rhymes (it is safe to assume that the second and fourth lines would have rhymed).

---

1 плен Варша́вы – the capture of Warsaw

Бороди́нская годовщи́на – The Anniversary of Borodino

Pushkin, who was fascinated by the possibility of a hidden order that governed events both personal and historical, saw a certain providence in the fact that the taking of Praga (a suburb of Warsaw across the Vistula River that was of great strategic importance, see line 89) occurred on the anniversary of the battle of Borodino (26 August/7 September). At Borodino, sixty miles west of Moscow, Kutuzov had made his stand against Napoleon, with horrific losses on both sides. Nonetheless, the battle has traditionally been considered the turning point in the war and therefore celebrated as a great Russian victory. To compare Russia's war of self-defense against Napoleon to its brutal treatment of the Polish uprising was offensive to many liberal thinkers of the time (and of later times). As in "Клеветникам России," Pushkin's anger is directed less at the Poles (as he seems to consider rebellion in their blood) than at the French, who considered intervening in the "fraternal quarrel."

In form, style, and subject matter, the poem is probably the closest thing Pushkin ever wrote to an eighteenth-century solemn ode. It is written in iambic tetrameter in a ten-line stanza very close to – though not coinciding with – that of the standard eighteenth-century ode. The stanza used by Pushkin is a-B-a-B-c-c-D-e-D-e, while the traditional odic stanza would be the same until the final four lines, which would end D-e-e-D. The lexicon and locutions are clearly reminiscent of eighteenth-century odes celebrating military victories.

---

2 Мы братской тризной помина́я – We, recalling <the great day of Borodino> in a fraternal funeral feast. Logically, there should be a comma after "Мы."

5 Не вся ль Евро́па тут была́? – Was not all of Europe here? By the time Napoleon marched on Russia, his French army had been joined by a host of armies of other nations (including Poles, see line 23).

10 И равен был нера́вный спор – The unequal quarrel was equal. That is, many nations ganged up on Russia, but Russia was equal to the task. (Pushkin frequently uses the word "спор" as a metaphor for battle. See Grigor'eva, 101.)

11 свой бедственный побе́г – their disastrous flight. Pushkin has in mind Napoleon's retreat from Moscow.

12 Кича́сь – In their arrogance. Strictly speaking, the word is a verbal adverb from "кичиться."

13 русской (=русский) штык и снег – The Russian bayonet and snow. The Russian army (represented metonymically here by the bayonet) and the cold weather were the two factors credited for Napoleon's defeat.

15 Знако́мый пир их манит вновь – A familiar feast beckons them again. The line is directed to the French who advocate intervening in Russia's war with Poland.

16 Хмельна́ для них славя́нов кровь – Slavic blood is intoxicating for them. The standard form would be "славян," not the archaic "славянов."

20 Под злаком – under the grass

21 Русь – Pushkin opts for the historical and patriotic term rather than the more imperialist "Россия."

22 прошеные гости – (ironic) invited guests

23 Уж Польша вас не поведёт – Poland won't lead you any more. (In the Napoleonic wars the Poles had joined France in attacking Russia. This time, Pushkin points out, the Poles have already been defeated.)

26–27 Вновь наши вторглись знамена́ / В проло́мы падшей вновь Варша́вы – Once again our banners pushed their way into Warsaw, which has fallen once again. Pushkin says "again" because the celebrated Russian general Aleksandr Vasil'evich Suvorov (1729–1800) had so brutally taken the outlying district Praga in 1794 that Warsaw surrendered without a fight (see lines 79–80). In modern Russian, the stress would be "знамёна."

29 стяг крова́вый – bloody banner. Pushkin either means that the banner is covered with blood or perhaps simply refers to the Polish flag of the time, which was half red (and half white).

33 Мы не напо́мним ныне им – We won't remind them today. A classic example of preterition. The next lines are devoted precisely to the subject that will supposedly not be raised.

34–35 Того́, что старые скрижа́ли / Храня́т в преда́ниях немы́х – That which the old tablets preserve in mute legends. As the next line makes clear, Pushkin (with apparent belief in Russian magnanimity) points out that Russia will not burn Warsaw, the way the Poles burned Moscow (in 1611).

37 Немези́ды – Nemesis (Greek goddess of retribution).

41 мути́тели пала́т – inciters of the chambers. The French Parliament of 1830 was composed of two chambers. It was there that support of Poland – and of military intervention – was discussed.

42 легкоязы́чные – light-tongued. The idea is that these orators speak without thinking about the consequences. This is the only usage of the word in all of Pushkin's writings.

43 черни бедственный наба́т – the calamitous alarm of the rabble

44 клеветники́ – slanderers. Pushkin recalls his earlier "Клеветникам России."

45 Что взяли вы? – What have you gained?
росс = русский

46 *Больной, расслабленный колосс* – A sick, weakened colossus. The use of italics, according to a convention of the time, marks it as a quotation, but no such quotation has been found. Lednicki (1928, 123) argues that Pushkin is rewriting a passage of anti-Russian propaganda from the manifesto of the French-Polish Committee in Paris: "Quelle est donc cette puissance colossale qui prétend vous anéantir? Tout s'agite et s'ébranle autour d'elle: le sol tremble sous ses pieds." ("What is then this colossal power that intends to annihilate you? Everything is agitated and collapses around it: the ground shakes under its feet.") However, Pushkin's allusion may not be so precise. The image of Russia as a weak colossus was widespread at the time (McNally, 179).

50 предпи́шет – will dictate; will impose

51 Куда́ отдви́нем строй тверды́нь? – To where should we withdraw the line of our fortresses? Pushkin opts for the more archaic "отдвинуть" over "отодвинуть."

52 За Буг, до Ворсклы, до Лима́на? – Beyond the Bug, up to the Vorskla, up to Liman? The Bug River (in Ukraine, Belorussia, and Poland). Pushkin considered this river the ethnographic border between Russia and Poland. The

Vorskla River was the site of a Polish defeat in 1399. The Liman was an area on the western and northern shores of the Black Sea that once belonged to the Polish-Lithuanian Commonwealth.

53 За кем оста́нется Волы́нь? – Whom will the Volyn' belong to? Volyn' is the name of a large territory in northwestern Ukraine (its western border is the Western Bug River), which became part of the Russian Empire as a result of the second partition of the Polish-Lithuanian Commonwealth in 1793.

54 Насле́дие Богда́на – the legacy of Bogdan (i.e., Ukraine). Bogdan Khmel'nits'kii (approximately 1595–1657), a Cossack leader, led a rebellion against the Poles to free Ukraine from Polish dominion. In search of support, he joined forces with Moscow.

60 Святы́ню всех свои́х гробо́в – in the original publication, a printer's error changed "гробов" into "градов." In a letter to E. M. Khitrovo from mid-September 1831 Pushkin corrected this mistake, explaining that "Il s'agit des tombeaux de Ярослав et de ceux des saints de Печора" ("It concerns the tombs of Iaroslav and those of the saints of the Cave Monastery"). Iaroslav (978–1054), grand prince of Novgorod and Kiev, was buried in the Saint Sophia Cathedral in Kiev. The Kiev Monastery of the Caves is considered one of the holiest places in Eastern Christianity.

65 Война́, и мор – war and pestilence. The former refers to the war with Turkey in 1828–1829, the latter to the cholera epidemic of 1830–1831, which felled, among others, the commander in chief of the Russian army, Hans Karl von Diebitsch (Иван Иванович Дибич-Забалканский).

66 И бунт, и внешних бурь напо́р – rebellion and the pressure of external storms. The former is probably the Polish uprising, the latter a metaphor for the threats of intervention from France.

67 потряса́ли – shook (Russia)

69 А вкруг её волне́нья пали – But around it (Russia) the disturbances subsided

71–73 These exclamations might be found in any patriotic ode of the eighteenth century.

75 он – General Ivan Fedorovich Paskevich (1782–1856) was wounded in battle as he led the Russian troops against the Poles.

77 вершины Тавра – the peaks of the Taur, a mountain range in Turkey. Paskevich had led the Russian troops in the 1829 war with Turkey.

78 Эрива́нь – Erevan, the capital of Armenia (in modern Russian "Ереван"). As the general in the Persian campaign of 1827–1828, Paskevich had taken much of present-day Armenia, earning him the official title of "Граф Эриваньский" (sometimes spelled "Эриванский").

79–80 Кому́ суво́ровского лавра / Вено́к сплела́ тройна́я брань – For whom the triple battle wove the wreath of Suvorov's laurel. The "triple battle" refers to the three wars that Paskevich directed as a general: with Persia (line 78), with Turkey (line 77), and, of course, with Poland.

81–90 The image of a deceased warrior leaving his grave to bless his successors is a topos of the solemn ode (cf. Lomonosov's ode on the battle of Khotin, where Peter the Great and Ivan the Terrible make cameo appearances to express their delight at the recent Russian victory).

89–90 И с ней летя́щего за Прагу / Младо́го внука своего́ – And his young grandson who rushes beyond Praga (i.e., towards Russia) with it (i.e., the news). Word of Russia's victory was brought to Petersburg by A. A. Suvorov (1804–1882), grandson of the general. That Suvorov's grandson should bear the good tidings was apparently the idea of Tsar Nicholas (Beliaev, 284).

Эхо – Echo

A virtuoso exploitation of all aspects of Russian (sound, syntax, stanza) to create a labyrinth of echoes. The meta-poetic conclusion may well reflect Pushkin's own frustrations with his audience. In any case, it is the most obvious departure from its source.

The unusual six-line stanza (iambic tetrameter in lines 1, 2, 3, 5 and iambic dimeter in the others, with all masculine rhymes, the tetrameter lines all on the same rhyme) comes from English literature. Pushkin had used it earlier (see commentary to "Обвал"). The semantics of this poem make it clear that Pushkin had a very specific source: Barry Cornwall's "A Sea-Shore Echo."

I stand upon the wild sea-shore –
I see the screaming eagle soar –
I hear the hungry billows roar,
    And all around
The hollow answering caves out-pour
    Their stores of sound.

The wind, which moaneth on the waves,
Delights me, and the surge that raves,
Loud-talking of a thousand graves –
    A watery theme!
But oh! those voices from the caves
    Speak like a dream!

They seem long hoarded, – cavern-hung, –
First uttered ere the world was young,
Talking some strange eternal tongue
    Old as the skies!
Their words unto all earth are flung:
    Yet who replies?

Large answers when the thunders speak
Are blown from every bay and creek,
And when the fire-tongued tempests speak
    The bright seas cry,
And when the seas *their* answer seek
    The shores reply.

But Echo from the rock and stone
And seas earns back no second tone;
And Silence pale, who hears alone
    Her voice divine,

Absorbs it, like the sponge that's thrown
On glorious wine!

– Nymph Echo, – elder than the world,
Who wast from out deep chaos hurl'd,
When beauty first her flag unfurl'd,
And the bright sun
Laugh'd on her, and the blue waves curl'd,
And voices run.

Like spirits on the new-born air,
Lone Nymph, whom poets thought so fair,
And great Pan wooed from his green lair,
How love will flee!
Thou answeredst *all*; but none now care
To answer thee!

None, – none: Old age has sear'd thy brow;
No power, no shrine, no gold hast thou:
So Fame, the harlot, leaves thee now,
A frail, false friend!
And thus, like all things here below,
Thy fortunes end!

From *The Poetical Works of Milman, Bowles, Wilson, and Barry Cornwall* (Paris: A. and W. Galignani, 1829), 4:176–77.

1 в лесу́ глухо́м – in a deep forest
6 Роди́шь ты вдруг – You suddenly give birth to. The poet addresses the echo.
11 Тебе́ ж нет отзыва – But for you there is no response. Cf. "без отзыва утешно я пою" in the 1827 poem "Близ мест, где царствует Венеция златая."

„Чем чаще празднует лице́й" – "The more frequently the Lyceum celebrates"

Arguably the greatest of Pushkin's "October 19" poems (the manuscript bears the date 19 October 1831), the poem mixes the expected genre of celebratory drinking song with that of elegy (or eulogy). This paradoxical mix of genres (note the striking shifts between "мы" and "я") is marked by a number of oxymorons. The poem is brilliant in its exploitation of grammatical necessity (comparatives) for poetic purpose.

It is composed of eight-line stanzas of alternating rhymes: a-B-a-B-c-D-c-D. In principle, one could see this as two quatrains of alternating rhyme, but the syntax does not allow such a clear demarcation. The punctuation indicates that Pushkin wants each eight-line stanza to function as a unit, making the thought process more complicated and less predictable. The lexicon ranges from middle to markedly high style reminiscent of the ode, for example, “закланья,” “узрим,” “утекший.” (Zhukovskii was so uncomfortable with this last archaism that he replaced it with “ушедший” in the initial posthumous publication.) Originally, Pushkin had written another stanza (which came between what is now printed as the first and the second) devoted to political and world-historical events that had occurred in the previous twenty years. He presumably discarded it as being out of keeping with the personal and intimate tone elsewhere.

---

1 чаще – more frequently. The poem begins with a paradox (or, at the least, a semantic tension). The Lyceum celebrates its anniversary once a year, hence it does not celebrate “more frequently.” Pushkin is well aware of this, of course, and his word choice is psychologically significant (i.e., it *seems to the speaker* that it is occurring more frequently).

2 святу́ю – holy (a clear use of a religious word in a secular context to indicate a reverential attitude)

4 В семью́ стесня́ется еди́ну – Crowds together in a single family. “Едину,” a truncated adjective, is used non-predicatively (in modern Russian this is impossible). Note how the common meaning of “стесняться” (“to be bashful, uncomfortable”) – while not relevant to the line per se – resonates with “робче” of line 3.

5 Тем реже он – The sparser it (“круг друзей”) is. Note the tension between “чаще” (line 1) and “реже” here.

6 В своём весе́лии мрачне́е – Darker in its joy. Pushkin uses syntax to allow the oxymoron to stand out more emphatically.

7 заздра́вных чаш – of congratulatory cups. There is an echo of “чаще” (line 1) in “чаш” (which then supplies an internal rhyme in “наши” of line 8).

9 бурь земны́х – of earthly storms. As so often in Pushkin, “буря” is used metaphorically.

10 неча́янно – unexpectedly

14 жите́йски = житейские

16 закла́нья – (archaic) sacrifices

17 упра́здненных – made idle (empty). Note the oxymoronic echo of “празднует” of line 1 and “праздник” of line 5. In modern Russian, the stress is different: “упразднённых.”

20–23 Pushkin enumerates the “six” places, each one getting either a “кто” or a “кого.” These did indeed correspond to the circumstances of death of six classmates. S. S. Esakov died on the field of battle, N. A. Korsakov and P. F. Savrasov died abroad, N. G. Rzhevskii and K. D. Kostenskii died of illness. Pushkin apparently attributed Del’vig’s unexpected death (line 26) to “sadness.”

25 И, мнится, очередь за мной – And it seems it’s my turn. The line proved prophetic; Pushkin was the next Lyceum graduate of his class to die.

26 Дельвиг – Anton Del’vig, Pushkin’s best friend in the Lyceum, publisher of the almanac *Северные цветы* (*Northern Flowers*). He had died unexpectedly in January 1831, shortly after a run-in with the spy and censor Benkendorff. Many people viewed this meeting as precipitating Del’vig’s death.

28 Това́рищ юности уны́лой – Comrade of melancholy youth. On first glance an obvious oxymoron, given that it repeats the previous line, changing “живой”

to "унылой." The explanation is probably to be sought in the elegy, the defining genre of Pushkin's youth, which favored words like "унылый," and which colored the early poetry of both Pushkin and Del'vig.

31 Тудá, в толпý тенéй родны́х – To there, to the crowd of kindred shadows (i.e., dead people). The entire line is in accusative case, governed by "Зовёт" ("calls") of line 26.

32 Навéк от нас утéшкий гений – A spirit who has departed from us forever

33 Теснéй – More tightly. The return to a comparative recalls the opening stanza; phonetically, the word recalls "теней" of line 31.

35 Почи́вшим песнь окóнчил я – I have finished my song to the departed (literally: to those who are resting)

37 нéкогда – at some point in the (distant) future

1832

„И дале мы пошли́ – и страх обня́л меня“ – "And we went further – And I was possessed by fear"

Like "В начале жизни школу помню я," this is a work in terza rima, though here Pushkin uses a longer line (iambic hexameter rather than iambic pentameter). In this poem, the connection to Dante's *Divine Comedy* is considerably clearer. Pushkin's verses are not a translation, but an amplification. He draws on Dante much as he drew on Goethe in his "Сцена из Фауста" ("Scene from Faust") of 1825, using familiar characters, but putting them in a new situation.

At the beginning of canto 9 of *The Inferno*, Dante and his guide Vergil encounter a foul smell rising from the lower circles of Hell. While they accustom themselves to the stench, Vergil explains the structure of Hell, that each of the bottom rungs is composed of a number of smaller circles. Moneylenders (in Russian: "ростовщики") are found in the third round of circle 7. Procuresses are in the next circle, and it appears that these are the women whose punishment is described in the second part of Pushkin's poem.

It is not surprising that Pushkin should have chosen to focus on the sin of usury in his foray into Dantesque poetry. An inveterate gambler, he was frequently at the mercy of moneylenders; cf. his treatment of the subject in the little tragedy *Скупой рыцарь* (*The Covetous Knight*).

The two sections of the work should be understood as two brief cantos, not as separate poems. In neither part do the punishments correspond to specific scenes in Dante.

---

2 Бесёнок, под себя́ поджа́в своё копы́то – a little demon, tucking its hoof under itself

3 Крути́л ростовщика́ – turned a moneylender. The moneylender is presumably being roasted on a spit.

5 лопал – was bursting; was splitting up

6 Пове́дай мне: в сей казни что сокры́то – Tell me (literally: Make known to me): what is the meaning of this punishment (literally: execution)

7 Вирги́лий мне – Vergil <said> to me

8 Одно́ стяжа́ние име́в всегда́ в предме́те – Having always only thought about possessions

10 крути́л – twirled around (took advantage of)

12 в холо́дной Лете – in cold Lethe. In ancient Greek mythology, Lethe was the river of oblivion that one crossed after dying.

14 Сто на́ сто я терплю́: проце́нт неимове́рный – I'm suffering one hundred on one hundred; unbelievable interest. The moneylender understands his punishment in the same monetary terms that he used when alive.

15 Тут звучно лопнул он – Then he burst with a loud sound. The manuscript has a parallel passage here: "И с горя пернул он" ("And he farted from grief"). It has been argued (Shapir 2003, 150) that this latter variant, which conceivably contains an allusion to Dante (*Inferno* 21, 139), should be treated as pri-

mary. (Since the poem was not published in Pushkin's lifetime, the question is necessarily decided by editorial discretion.)

16 услы́шал … запах скверный – I smelled a nasty smell. ("Слышать запах" is not a metaphor, but a standard Russian expression.)

18 Иль (= Или) каранти́нный страж кури́л жаро́вней серной – Or a guard on quarantine duty was making smoke on a sulphuric brazier

21 камень приподня́в за медное кольцо́ – Having slightly lifted a stone by a copper handle. This (heavy) stone presumably serves as the doorway to the next rung of hell, to which the speaker and Vergil descend.

22 узре́л – saw. (This is high style for "увидел.")

24 вата́ге муравьи́ной – a mass of ants

25 тешились – amused themselves

28 разлега́лася (= разлегалась) – stretched out

29 раскали́в как жар чугу́н ядра́ – having heated up like embers the cast iron of a cannonball

32 растре́скалась колю́чими звезда́ми – cracked into prickly stars (into star-shaped splinters)

35 жену – a woman. Note the elevated lexicon.

36 заголи́ли их, и вниз пихну́ли – lifted their skirts (i.e., exposed their bare bottoms), and shoved them down

37 сидючи пусти́лись вниз стрело́й – sitting, set off downwards with the speed of an arrow

Мальчику (Из Кату́лла) – To <my servant> boy (from Catullus)

Pushkin had at his disposal two editions of Catullus, one in the original and one a bilingual Latin-French facing-page edition. His Latin was not good enough to allow him to understand the text without the aid of a pony, but he obviously worked with both texts, using the French whenever the Latin proved too difficult.

Pushkin chose a trochaic tetrameter meter, probably because it was for him the standard form of Anacreontic poems (which this resembles in obvious ways). In this context, his use of rhyme is unusual (see commentary to "Рифма"); lines 1 and 3 rhyme, as do lines 5 and 7; however, the even-numbered lines do not rhyme (though all lines have masculine cadences).

Pushkin almost certainly used the facing-page edition in his library: *Traduction complète des Poésies de Catulle*, vols. 1–2 (Paris, 1806). The Latin text appears in volume 1, page 48, with the French translation on page 49.

AD PUERUM SUUM.

Minister vetuli puer Falerni,
Inger mî calices amariores,
Ut lex Posthumiae jubet magistrae,
Ebriosâ acinâ ebriosioris.
At vos, quò lubet, hinc abite, lymphae,
Vini pernicies, et ad severos
Migrate: hic merus est Thyonianus.

⇝A SON ESCLAVE.

Esclave, verse-nous le vieux Falerne. Je veux le boire à longs traits, selon les statuts de la bacchante Posthumia, législatrice des orgies. Coule à grands flots, vin délicieux, et vous, ennemies de la joie, eaux insipides, fuyez, allez abreuver nos Catons. Ici l'on se garde bien de corrompre les dons de Bacchus. Ici Bacchus réprouve ce perfide mélange.

This brief translation was followed in volume 2 with lengthy explanatory footnotes (157–59).

v. 1. *MINISTER*, échanson. Les Latins appelaient encore ces sortes d'esclaves, qui étaient ordinairement dans la fleur de l'âge et chers à leurs maîtres à plus d'un titre, *pocillator*, de *poculum*, *pincerna*, *puer ad Cyathum*, et *servus à potione*, comme le portent d'anciennes inscriptions.

Ibid. *Falerni*. Le Falerne était très-estimé chez les Romains. On en distinguait trois sortes, le rude, le doux, et le délicat.

v. 2. *Amariores*. Ce vin, en vieillissant, devenait amer. Cette amertume en faisait le prix. On y mêlait même de l'eau de mer, pour l'accélérer.

v. 3. *Posthumiae*. C'était une fameuse biberonne, qui avait rédigé une espèce de code pour les festins. Un des statuts était de vider d'un trait de larges coupes de vin, ce qu'on appelait *amystis*. Il paraît que la législatrice prêchait d'exemple.

Ibid *Magistrae*. C'est ce qu'Horace appelle *arbiter bibendi* et *regna vini*; Cicéron, *magister* et *magisterium*; Varron, *modiperator*; Catulle lui-même, *coenae pater*; et d'autres, *strategi, dictatores, parochi, etc.*

v. 6. *Vini pernicies*. Cette injure est très-convenable dans une orgie, et rappelle celle qu'un ivrogne en colère croyait la plus outrageante de toutes, lorsqu'il disait: "Va, je te méprise, comme un verre d'eau." Mais les anciens ont souvent préconisé le mélange de l'eau et du vin. Plutarque dit poétiquement qu'il faut tempérer Bacchus en l'unissant avec les Nymphes, et l'on trouve à ce sujet dans l'Anthologie une épigramme ingénieuse qu'on me pardonnera sans doute de citer. Je me sers de la version de Grotius, que vient de publier Hieron. de Bosch, savant distingué d'Amsterdam, avec qui je m'honore d'avoir eu des relations durant le cours da ma mission en Hollande.

Ignibus enatum Nymphae lavêre Lyaeum:
    Multus erat circum fumida membra cinis.
Nunc quoque cum Nymphis Liber bonus: absit ab illis:
    Fervet adhuc, venas imbuet igne suo.

v. 7. *Thyonianius*. De Thyonius, surnom de Bacchus. Sémélé, sa mère, s'appelait aussi Thyoné. Suivant d'autres, c'était sa nourrice.

Au reste, cette petite pièce vaut à Catulle, dans l'esprit de Corradini, un brevet de sagesse; car, si l'on en croit Plaute:

Qui utuntur vino vetere, sapientes puto.

A l'exemple de Catulle, Horace et Martial ont adressé des vers à leur échanson. La brièveté de ces deux espèces de couplets permet de les insérer ici.

Persicos odi, puer, apparatus;
Displicent nexae phylirâ coronae:
Mitte sectari, rosa quo locorum
Sera moretur.

Simplici myrto nihil allabores
Sedulus curo: neque te ministrum
Dedecet myrtus, neque me sub arctâ
Vite bibentem.

Le C. Daru a traduit ainsi cette ode, qui est la trente-huitième du premier livre.

Je hais du Perse barbare
Le faste trop orgueilleux,
Et ces couronnes qu'on pare
D'un tilleul voluptueux.
Ne va point chercher des roses
Après la saison écloses:
Cueille le myrte amoureux;
Lorsque je bois sous la treille,
Et que tu tiens la bouteille,
Le myrte sied à nous deux.

Epigraph: Minister vetuli, puer. The first three words of the Latin original, but Pushkin's punctuation differs from the text cited above and also from the other Latin edition he had in his library. Conceivably he was misled by the Horace poem cited in the footnote to line 7 (i.e., "Persicos odi, puer, apparatus"). Pushkin's punctuation is odd, since the whole phrase is in vocative case, but it is not unprecedented. There were editions of Catullus that punctuated the line as Pushkin writes it.

1 Пьяной горечью Фалéрна – With the drunken bitterness of Falerno. Falerno (or Falernus), the favorite wine of the Roman Empire, is mentioned in numerous texts of antiquity. The notion of bitterness appears to come from the note to *Amariores*.

3 Постýмия – Posthumia. The name comes from the Latin (and French).

7 Строгих постников пойте – Give drink to those strict ones who are observing the fasts. In other words, water (as against wine) is appropriate only for ascetics.

8 Бахус – Bacchus, god of wine. In choosing this form of the name, Pushkin clearly follows the French (rather than Latin). Bacchus here appears to be a metonymy for wine. In the online version of the Academy edition, the entire final line is inadvertently omitted.

Literature: Faibisovich 1980.

<В альбóм А. О. Смирнóвой> – In the album of A. O. Smirnova

Pushkin greatly admired Aleksandra Osipovna Smirnova, née Rosset (1809–1882). At the time he wrote this poem (18 March 1832), she was a newlywed, having married on 11 January of that same year. Throughout that year, Pushkin visited Smirnova frequently; impressed by her powers of observation, he encouraged her to write memoirs. Turning the etiquette of album poetry on its head, he presented her with an album on which he wrote "Исторические записки А. О. С." ("Historical Notes of Aleksandra Osipovna Smirnova") and supplied this poem as a motto of sorts. In terms of album poetry (admittedly, the album in question was not the standard type), these verses represent a play with convention, since they are not addressed to her, but rather written from her perspective.

The poem is written in iambic tetrameter with an unusual rhyme scheme: A-b-A-A-A-b-C-d-C-d.

---

10 набелó – cleanly, without changes or corrections. In modern Russian, the stress usually falls on the first syllable (нáбело).

<В альбóм кж. А. Д. Абамелéк> – In the album of Princess A. D. Abamelek

Anna Davydovna Abamelek (1814–1889) had already translated Pushkin's "Талисман" into French and would subsequently translate other works of his.

The poem is written in iambic tetrameter and breaks down into two parts, the first of five lines (A-A-b-A-b), the second with alternating rhyme. The poem is remarkable in its sudden shifts of feeling: from religious admiration to erotic attraction to a nanny's pride.

---

1 с умилéньем – with tender emotion

2 Я смел вас няньчить – I dared to take care of you. Pushkin recalls that Abamelek's family had visited the Lyceum in July 1815, when she was still an infant. Presumably Pushkin had done something to amuse the baby (or at least he pretends that this was the case). The verb "няньчить" will be picked up again in the simile of the final line.

5 Вам ныне поклоня́юсь я – today I worship you. The word "ныне" is chosen partially for its acoustical qualities, since it echoes the key words "няньчить" (line 2) and "нянька" (line 9).

7 ношу́сь – I fuss over

<Гнедичу> – To Gnedich

In late 1832 Gnedich published a collection of his poetry which included a brief poem called "А. С. Пушкину, по прочтении сказки его о царе Салтане и проч."

("To A. S. Pushkin on Reading The Tale of Tsar Saltan and others"). Though Pushkin had received the poem in a private letter of April 1832, it appears that he only began his response after it appeared in print. Drawing less on that particular poem than on other poems in the collection, Pushkin combines themes of Gnedich's own poetry with two of his own: the wide and unexpected range of a true poet's interests (in his epistle, Gnedich had addressed Pushkin as "Proteus") as well as the "poet and the crowd" ("поэт и толпа"). He puts all of this in the context of the biblical story of Moses.

The genre of epistle was predicated on an intimate personal connection between poet and addressee. After Gnedich died in early 1833, Pushkin made no effort to publish his poem, though he appears to have returned to it at some point in 1834.

"Гнедичу" is written in alternating lines of iambic hexameter (masculine rhymes) and iambic tetrameter (feminine rhymes). The stanzaic form came to Russian poetry from a celebrated elegy of the French poet Nicolas Joseph Florent Gilbert (1751–1780), which Gnedich had translated in 1819 as "К провидению" ("To Providence"). Pushkin's poem has the identical form as this Gnedich translation. (See Tomashevskii 1958, 70.)

---

1 Gnedich worked for more than two decades on his translation of the *Iliad* before publishing it (see notes to "На перевод Илиады"). The word choice of this line is probably dictated by Gnedich's poem "Иностранцам гостям моим" ("To my foreign guests") where he wrote about himself: "Беседовал с Гомером и Природой."

4 скрижáли – tablets

7 буйну песнь (= буйную песню) – wild song

кругóм – around (a preposition followed by a genitive, i.e., "кумира")

8 От нас создáнного кумúра – an idol created by us. This is a very unconventional use of the preposition "от" to express agency. The stress on "создáнного" is likewise a poeticism; ordinarily it would be "сóзданного."

14 Скрывáться в тень долúны малой – To hide yourself in the shadow of a humble vale

17 Такóв прямóй поэ́т. Он сетует душóй – Such is the true poet. He laments in his soul

18 На пышных играх Мельпомéны – at the splendid games of Melpomene (the muse of tragedy). Pushkin often uses the word "игра" in the context of artistic performance.

20 лубóчной сцены – of the folk stage

21 Рим … Илиóн – Rome … Troy. Given Gnedich's connection to the *Iliad*, it is obvious why Troy appears, but there is little (beyond a brief "Imitation of Horace") in Gnedich's work to justify the allusion to Rome. Pushkin appears to have borrowed the reference from Gnedich's "К К. Н. Батюшкову." Batiushkov was particularly close to Italy, and in his epistle, Gnedich invites Batiushkov to his house so that they can travel together in spirit:

> Над всей подлунною страною
> Мечты промчимся на крылах.
> Туда, туда, в тот край счастливый,
> В те земли солнца полетим,

Где Рима прах красноречивый
Иль град святой, Ерусалим.

The "туда, туда" is the clear marker of Italy (see notes to "Кто знает край"). Perhaps to reflect the "musicality" of Italian verse (and Batiushkov's imitations thereof), Gnedich uses the word "Rome" in an internal rhyme: полети́м/Ри́ма/Ерусали́м. Jerusalem, a reference to Tasso, has no relevance to Gnedich, so Pushkin omits it. Curiously, however, "Ерусалим" seems to have echoed in Pushkin's mind and appears in his own poem – acoustically transformed – in the final word: "Еруслана."

22 скалы старца Оссиа́на – the cliffs of old man Ossian. In the 1760s, the Scotsman James Macpherson claimed to have discovered manuscripts of the ancient bard Ossian. The fact that Macpherson had actually authored them was subsequently revealed, but not before his mystification had created an enormous vogue throughout Europe and in Russia. Gnedich wrote repeatedly about Ossian, including numerous stanzas in the poem to Batiushkov.

24 Бовы́ иль (=или) Ерусла́на – of Bova or Eruslan. Bova and Eruslan were heroes of Russian folklore. (Strictly speaking, Bova was a chivalric romance of Western origin, but his tale had become sufficiently domesticated that he was considered by Pushkin (Gasparov 1990, 7) and most Russians of his time to be a Russian hero. Derzhavin, for example, had called "The Tale of Bova" an "известная старинная русская повесть.") This final line refers more to the work of Pushkin than to that of Gnedich. The young Pushkin started writing a poem about Bova that scholars usually date as 1814. Given the opening of the present poem, it is worth citing the first two lines of Pushkin's "Bova": "Часто, часто я беседовал / С болтуном страны Эллинския." ("Often, often I conversed / With the chatterbox of the Hellenic land"). The name Eruslan is connected in folklore with the warrior Eruslan Lazarevich, whose name, in slightly altered form, may have provided Pushkin with the hero of "Ruslan and Liudmila," a narrative poem in a faux-folkloric style (see Proskurin 2007, 81–82). "Еруслан" also rhymes with another of Pushkin's heroes – "Салтан," which brings us full circle (back to Gnedich's poem in praise of that work). Indeed, Pushkin's drafts reveal that his poem to Gnedich originally ended with the words "царя Салтана." He most likely rejected that variant as immodest and inappropriate in a poem celebrating another poet.

Literature: Vatsuro 1991.

Краса́вица – The Beauty

The poem was written in the album of Countess Elena Mikhailovna Zavadovskaia (1807–1874), considered one of the most beautiful women of the time. According to some scholars, Zavadovskaia was the true identity of "Nina Voronskaia," the "Cleopatra of the Neva" mentioned in *Eugene Onegin* (8:XVI), whose "мраморная краса" ("marble beauty") seems to parallel the type of beauty described in this poem.

Pushkin plays with the conventions of album verse by addressing not the woman herself, but another (male) admirer. The effect is thus not one of intimacy, but rather admiration from a distance.

"Красавица" is composed in iambic tetrameter with rhyme scheme A-b-A-b-C-d-d-C. Tomashevskii (1958, 88) insists that the generic source is the romance (see notes to "Заклинание"), rather than the ode (as in Pushkin's own "Вольность"). However, both of these traditions may have come together here, as the poem combines the language of a love lyric (the lexicon belongs to the expected "middle" style) with an attitude of reverence and solemnity one expects in an ode ("в красе торжественной").

---

2 выше мира – above things earthly
6 Ей нет сопéрниц, нет подрýг – She has no rivals, no friends.
12 сокровéнное мечтáнье – cherished dream
15 Благоговéя богомóльно – showing reverence like a pilgrim

K*** („Нет, нет, не должен я, не смею, не могý") – To *** ("No, no, I musn't, I don't dare, I can't")

Another unusual Pushkin love poem, generally agreed to be addressed to Nadezhda L'vovna Sollogub (1815–1903).

Written in iambic hexameter and beginning with "Нет," one cannot help but think of "Нет, я не дорожу мятежным наслажденьем." This poem is astrophic with alternating rhymes that would suggest syntactic groups of four lines. Pushkin often violates this expectation, reflecting highly-charged emotion. Like "Нет, я не дорожу," this poem has a clear bipartite structure. The tone of resignation at the end recalls "Я вас любил" and is probably similarly ambiguous as far as the sincerity of that sentiment is concerned. It comes as no surprise to learn that Pushkin's wife greatly disliked Sollogub.

---

6 минýтное мечтáнье – a momentary reverie
7 нечáянно пройдёт – by chance passes. (The perfective here does not have any meaning of futurity; rather it suggests a repeated action in the present tense. For other examples, see line 9.)
9 не можно – is it not possible?
10 в печáльном сладострáстье – in sad ecstasy. The expression verges on the oxymoronic and well expresses the speaker's state of mind. In a draft Pushkin had written the less surprising "в томленье сладострастья" ("in the torment of ecstasy").

В альбóм – In an Album

A mysterious poem from the biographical point of view, in that nothing is known of the circumstances of its composition. Stylistically, it is interesting in that Pushkin sets the first two lines (lexically and syntactically) against the rest of the poem. As often in album verse, the poem ends with the theme of memory.

It is written in iambic tetrameter with alternating feminine/masculine rhymes, with the word "Moscow" (in different cases) providing two sets of rhymes.

---

1 Гони́мый рока самовла́стьем – Pursued by the inexorable power of fate.
2 От пышной далеко́ Москвы́ – Far from splendid Moscow. The placement of "далеко" creates a Latinate syntax and therefore a bookish effect.
7 ваша память – the memory of you (i.e., the thought of you)
8 Одна́ – alone. The word modifies "память"

Из Ксенофа́на Колофо́нского – From Xenophanes of Colophon

The title of this poem is somewhat misleading. These verses are indeed a (free) translation of a poem by the pre-Socratic philosopher Xenophanes (approximately 570–480 BCE), but Pushkin's direct source was not Xenophanes, but the Greek writer Athenaeus, who – approximately seven centuries later – cited Xenophanes's poem in a work called *The Deipnosophists* (*The Banquet of the Learned*). Pushkin owned a French translation of Athenaeus, lavishly illustrated in five volumes: *Banquet des savans, par Athénée, Traduit, tant sur les Textes imprimés, que sur plusieurs Manuscrits, Par M. Lefebvre de Villebrune* (first four volumes 1789, fifth volume 1791). As a quotation from Pierre Bayle's *Dictionnaire historique et critique* cited on the title page of Villebrune's translation indicates, *The Deipnosophists* is prized less on its own merits than as a compendium of earlier Greek texts, many of which were subsequently lost and are therefore known only through their presence in this later work. There is no question that this work (in French translation) influenced Pushkin's conception of the ancient world. Pushkin initially published this and the following poem ("Из Афенея") under the title "Подражание древним" ("Imitation of the Ancients").

In contrast to his other renderings from Athenaeus, which were in elegiac distichs, Pushkin wrote this poem in dactylic hexameter with unrhymed masculine endings – the Russian equivalent of the ancient hexameter. The inspiration for the meter was most likely Gnedich's *Iliad* (see "На перевод Илиады") and perhaps Del'vig's extended "idylls" (themselves influenced by Gnedich). For Pushkin, the distinction between the distich and the hexameter appears to have been length (see also his 1823 poem "Внемли, о Гелиос"). In the original Greek (which Pushkin could not read), the meter is elegiac distich. Pushkin's extended use of enjambment in the Russian hexameter is unusual.

Villebrune's translation (4:192–94) reads as follows:

> Déjà le sol de la salle est propre, chacun a les mains bien nettes, les *gobelets, kylikes,* sont rincés: tous les convives ont leurs couronnes sur la tête. L'un présente dans une coupe un parfum d'une odeur exquise: le cratère est là rempli de la source de la joie. Un autre tient le vin tout prêt, et dit qu'il ne le quittera pas sans y faire raison; c'est un vin délicat qui parfume par son bouquet tous les pots. Au milieu de tout ceci, l'encens flatte l'odorat par les émissions

de sa vapeur naturelle; il y a de l'eau fraîche d'une saveur agréable et pure; des pains d'une couleur dorée sont sous la main; la table riante est chargée de fromage et de miel pur: l'autel qui est au milieu même de la salle, est paré de fleurs de tous côtés. La musique et les chants retentissent dans toute la maison; mais il faut que des gens sages commencent par célébrer les louanges de la divinité, et ne fassent entendre alors que des paroles saintes et de bon augure. Ils doivent demander, en faisant des libations, de pouvoir toujours se maintenir dans les termes de la justice; d'ailleurs cela est plus facile que d'*être injuste*. Ce n'est pas un crime que chacun boive autant de vin qu'il peut en prendre, pour s'en retourner chez lui sans être accompagné d'un serviteur, lorsqu'il n'est pas trop âgé; mais louons l'homme qui en buvant communique des choses dignes d'être retenues, et celui qui fait sentir le prix de la vertu. Laissons-là ces combats des Titans et des géans, de même que ces rixes sanguinaires des anciens Centaures, autres inepties, dont on ne tire aucun avantage; mais usons toujours de cette prévoyance dont les suites sont si heureuses.

---

2 Все уж увéнчаны гости – The guests are already wreathed

3 открывáет амфóру – opens an amphora. In antiquity, amphorae were vessels with a thin neck that held wine (and, at times, other things).

4 разливáя далёче – spreading in the distance

7 Но в начáле трапéзы, о други – But at the beginning of our festive meal, O friends. Note the archaisms: "трапеза" (instead of "стол"), "други" (instead of "друзья"). "Трапеза" is used as a metonymy for the feast that takes place around it.

8 благовéщие – portending good things. The word is not nearly as common as its opposite (зловещий = ominous).

9–10 да сподóбят нас чистой душóю (= душой) / Правду блюсти́: ведь онó ж и легче – may they consider us worthy to preserve justice with a pure soul. After all, it's easier that way.

Literature: Gasparov 1986.

Из Афенéя – From Athenaeus

This is a much shortened translation of a tombstone inscription by the minor poet Hedylus that Pushkin found in his French edition of *The Deipnosophists*, 2:178–79.

Théon, le monaule agréable, gît sous ce monument, lui qui faisoit même tous les charmes des Mimes aux orchestres. Skirpalus (son père) ayant déja perdu la vue de vieillesse, l'eut pour fils. Il se fit présenter cet enfant, célébrant le jour de la naissance de *lui, qui eut la main si habile*, et lui donna ce nom (Théon), pour indiquer par-là quelle seroit la douceur de ses accens. Théon célébra sur sa flûte les jeux des Muses, animés de la liqueur bachique: que dis-je, au milieu des cratères de vin pur il célébra Battalus, cet agréable buveur, cet enjoué Battalus, ce beau Battalus. Dites donc, *en passant*, au *Calamaulète* Théon, bonjour, Théon!

(Theon, the pleasing reedpipe <player>, lies under this monument, he who made all the charms of the Mimes of the theaters. Skirpalus (his father), who had already lost his vision from old age, had him as a son. He presented this child, in celebration of his birthday, who had such an agile hand, and gave him this name (Theon) to indicate thus the sweetness of his songs. Theon celebrated on his flute the Muses' games, animated by the Bacchic liquor: what am I saying, in the midst of bottles of pure wine he celebrated Battalus, that pleasing drinker, that playful Battalus, that beautiful Battalus. Say therefore, *in passing*, to the *reedpipe player* Theon: Hello, Theon!)

The passage is accompanied by a lengthy footnote in which the editor, evaluating previous readings of the poem, insists that Skirpalus must be the father of Théon, who chose his son's name as an allusion to the Greek word "Theios" (godlike, divine).

Pushkin renders the French prose in elegiac distichs.

---

1 флейта – flutist. Normally the word means "flute" – here by metonymy the person who played the flute.
3 нарéк – (archaic) named

„Бог весёлый виногрáда" – "The joyous god of the grape"

This is a free translation (or adaptation) of a fragment from Athenaeus's *The Deipnosophists* (see commentary to "Из Ксенофана Колофонского") that Pushkin read in French. He takes only the beginning of the poem in question, focusing on the therapeutic value of the first three glasses of wine and omitting the increasingly dire effects recorded about glasses four through ten.

The relevant passage, a speech of Bacchus himself, reads in the French translation of Lefebvre de Villebrune (1:130–31): "Pour les sages, je ne mêle que trois cratères; un pour la santé, et c'est celui qu'ils boivent le premier; le second est pour l'amour et pour le plaisir; le troisième pour le sommeil. Quand ils ont bu ce troisième verre, ils s'en vont chez eux, en gens sages." ("For wise men I only mix three glasses; the first for health, and that is the one they drink first; the second is for love and for pleasure; the third is for sleep. When they have drunk this third glass, they betake themselves to their homes, among wise men.")

Pushkin renders the French prose as unrhymed trochaic tetrameter (with exclusively masculine endings). The meter indicates that he reads the passage as a type of Anacreontic ode. (This may also explain why he chooses to eliminate the warnings about drinking to excess, though similar omissions can be found in "Из Ксенофона Колофонского.")

---

10 Все венкѝ с главы́ слагáет – Removes all wreaths from his head
11 возлия́нья – libations
12 Благодáтному Морфéю – beneficial Morpheus. (Morpheus was the Greek god of sleep and dreams.)

В альбóм („Долго сих листóв завéтных“) – In an Album (“For a long time these cherished pages”)

Like “В альбом” (“Гонимый рока самовластьем”), an album poem about which the circumstances of composition are unknown. While some album poetry was meant to be improvised, other albums were given to a houseguest, who was to write something in it during the course of his stay. This poem is clearly of the second type, and it shows Pushkin once again playing with expectations, emphasizing how he is tormented by having to prepare an “impromptu” genre. His only hope is that the addressee will never have an album “on his conscience” (“на совести” – a phrase usually used in conjunction with crimes or moral lapses).

The poem is written in trochaic tetrameter, with an interesting and unusual rhyme scheme, which breaks the poem into a pattern of five lines plus four lines plus five lines. Each of the five-line sections is based on two rhymes (with the first and fourth feminine, the others masculine), while the four-line middle section uses alternating rhyme. The key word “альбом” is featured in both five-line sections, the first time in nominative case, the second time in genitive.

---

1 завéтных – The *Словарь языка Пушкина* defines this usage as “connected with a vow,” because (as becomes apparent in the next few lines) the poet had promised to write in the album. However, another meaning of the word (“dear”) may also be possible here.

3 Виновáт, в столé моём – it’s my fault; in my desk

5 Залежáлся – Lay idle for a long time. (The word is a partial anagram for “пожелать” in line 7.)

6 В именúны, очень кстати – On your name day, very timely. In prerevolutionary Russia name days (the church holiday celebrated on the day of the saint with your name) were more important than birthdays.

8 Много всякой благодáти – much of every type of happiness

10 На Парнáсе – On Parnassus (the Greek mountain associated with poetic inspiration)

13 Ни едúного альбóма – not a single album

1833

„Юноша! скромно пиру́й, и шумную Вакхову влагу" – "Youth, celebrate modestly, and <mix> the noisy liquid of Bacchus"

Burgi (268) contends that this brief poem is a free translation of a passage in *The Deipnosophists* that comes directly after the fragment "Вино," which Pushkin had translated on the same day that he wrote this piece. The passage in question is a citation from the Athenian physician Mnesitheus, who states, in the edition that Pushkin owned (*Banquet des savans*, 1:130):

> Les dieux ont fait connoître le vin aux hommes, comme un très-grand bien pour ceux qui en usent avec raison, mais comme très-pernicieux pour ceux qui en usent sans discrétion. Il nourrit, fortifie le corps et l'ame, et devient très-utile pour la médecine; car on en fait entrer le mélange dans les médicamen<t>s. On ne le trouve pas moins avantageux pour les plaies. Il met dans une assiette tranquille l'esprit de ceux qui en boivent modérément, et étendu, dans les repas ordinaires. Si l'on passe la juste mesure, il causera des querelles: si l'on en boit avec moitié eau, il rend fou;[1] mais pris pur, il abat tout le corps. Voilà pourquoi Bacchus est invoqué par-tout comme médecin. La Pythie a même ordonné à quelques-uns d'invoquer Bacchus comme dieu de la santé.

Note

1. C'est à-peu-près ce que l'on trouve dans les problèmes d'Aristote, sect. III, no. 18; mais l'assertion n'en est pas plus vraie. (Note by Villebrune, the French editor of *The Deipnosophists.*)

> The gods made wine known to men as a great good for those who use it with reason, but as very ruinous for those who use it immoderately. It nourishes, fortifies the body and soul and is very useful for medicine; because one can mix it with medicines. One finds it no less advantageous for wounds. It puts in a tranquil pose the spirit of those who drink it moderately and diluted in ordinary meals. If one goes beyond the appropriate measure it causes quarrels; if one mixes it by half with water, it makes one insane;[1] but taken pure, it destroys the entire body. This is why Bacchus is invoked everywhere as a doctor. Pythius has even enjoined some people to invoke Bacchus as the god of health.

Note

1. This is approximately what one finds in the problems of Aristotle, section III, no. 18; but the assertion there is no more true.

In short, one finds in this passage a good deal more than Pushkin uses; but one also finds numerous key points: mixing wine with water, moderation. It should be noted, however, that this is hardly the only possible source. Pushkin had presumably read a disquisition on the subject in his edition of Catullus. (See commentary to "Мальчику (Из Катулла)," in particular the French footnote to "*Vini pernicies.*")

Like many of Pushkin's short works on themes of antiquity, the poem takes the form of an elegiac distich.

---

2 С трезвой струёю – with a sober stream

Винó (Иóн Хиóсский) – Wine (Ion of Chios)

A (free) translation of a passage cited in *The Deipnosophists*, which is found on the same page as the piece Pushkin translated as "Бог веселый винограда." In the Villebrune translation that Pushkin owned the relevant passage reads:

> ⇴Mais Ion de Chio appelle
>
> Le vin un enfant indomptable, à l'œil de taureau, un jeune vieillard, l'aimable entremetteur des bruyantes amours, un maître qui donne de la fierté. (1:130)

> ⇴But Ion of Chios calls
>
> wine an indomitable child, glaring like a bull, a young old man, an amiable mediator of noisy loves, a master who gives <you> pride.

Typical of his treatment of miniatures from antiquity, Pushkin uses an elegiac distich to render the French prose.

---

1 властели́н добронра́вный – a well-disposed ruler

„Царéй потóмок Меценáт" – "Maecenus, descendent of tsars"

In this fragment, Pushkin translates the opening eight lines of the first poem of the first book of Horace's poetry. It is tempting to view the poem's theme (the relationship of the poet and the ruler) through the lens of Pushkin's biography.

Pushkin probably used the bilingual facing-page Horace edition in his library, which offered him the Latin original (with French glosses) as well as a French prose translation: *Traduction des oeuvres d'Horace; par M. René Binet* (Paris, 1816), 1:2–5.

> ⇴I. Ad Maecenatem
>
> *Alios aliis rebus duci; se Lyrici carminis palmam Maecenatis judicio velle consequi.*
>
> Maecenas,[1] atavis edite regibus,
> O et praesidium et dulce decus meum,

Sunt quos curriculo pulverem Olympicum,
Collegisse juvat; metaque[2] fervidis
Evitata rotis, palmaque nobilis
Terrarum dominos evehit ad Deos:
Hunc,[3] si mobilium turba Quiritium[4]
Certat tergeminis[5] tollere honoribus

Notes

1. *Maecenas*, simple Chevalier Romain, Favori et principal Ministre d'Auguste, étoit d'une très-ancienne famille de Toscane; ses ayeux pouvoient y avoir tenu, sinon le sceptre, au moins le premier rang.

2. *Meta*, petite colonne placée au bout de la carrière, autour de laquelle il falloit tourner le plus court possible pour perdre moins de tems, sans cependant la toucher, ce qui n'eût point manqué de renverser et de briser le char.

3. Sous – entendu les deux verbes précédens, *juvat* et *evehit ad Deos*.

4. *Quirites*, nom que l'on donnoit aux Romains dans les assemblées, soit comme descendans de Romulus, autrement *Quirinus*; soit à cause de la ville de *Cures* au pays des Sabins, d'où une partie des Romains tiroient leur origine.

5. *Tergeminis*, id est, *congestis*, *cumulatis*, accumulés.

I. A Mécène

Le Poète fait entendre que comme tous les hommes ont leur passion, la sienne est de mériter une place entre les Poètes lyriques, sur-tout s'il a le suffrage de son illustre ami.

Vous qui comptez des rois parmi vos ayeux, Mécène, ô mon appui et ma gloire la plus chère; il en est qui s'applaudissent de s'être couverts de poussière dans la lice olympique; et qui, fiers d'avoir su de leurs roues brûlantes raser la borne sans la toucher, se croient élevés, par l'honneur de la palme, au rang des Dieux maîtres de l'univers. L'un est au comble de ses vœux, si la foule inconstante des enfans de Romulus s'empresse d'accumuler les honneurs sur sa tête.

Pushkin's poem, like the Latin text cited above, is astrophic. Rather than using an unrhymed meter or a distich (Pushkin's usual form for stylizations of antiquity), he writes in his standard rhyming iambic tetrameter.

---

3 Ины́е – Some people. These people are set off against the "другие" in line 9.
4 риста́лище – stadium; hippodrome
5 запове́данной огра́ды – established boundary (i.e., the finish line, the mark that indicates the endpoint of a race)
10 титла знамени́ты (=знаменитые) – important titles
11 Непостоя́нные квири́ты – Inconstant Roman citizens. The fact that Pushkin used the word "квирит" strongly suggests that he was cognizant of the Latin.
12 Им предаю́т молву́ – Lend them notoriety. All editions give "предают" rather than "придают," but according to Arinshtein (1989, 299) this is a misreading of the manuscript.

Гуса́р – The Hussar

The precise source of this poem is unknown, but there is no question that it is drawn from Ukrainian folklore, which abounds in tales of Witches' Sabbaths. While Pushkin's knowledge of the original folkloric texts was probably limited, he was definitely aware of several literary treatments of the theme. In particular, he would have known Gogol's early tales *Вечера на хуторе близ Диканьки* (*Evenings on a Farm near Dikanka*) and a story by Orest Mikhailovich Somov (1793–1833 – he died suddenly about a month after Pushkin wrote this poem) called "Киевские ведьмы" ("The Kiev Witches"), which first appeared in the very same almanac as Pushkin's narrative poem "Домик в Коломне" ("The Little House in Kolomna").

The genre is a ballad (a tale, often supernatural, featuring uneducated or lesser educated characters who act impulsively), but lacks the ternary meter commonly associated with Russian ballads (cf. "Будрыс и его сыновья") or even the trochaic meter that Pushkin tended to use in folkloric stylizations thereof (cf. "Утопленник" of 1828). Rather, we find Pushkin's standard iambic tetrameter quatrains with alternating rhyme. The poem's distinctive flavor, then, is not due to the meter, but to the "skaz" (oral) narration. The speaker and protagonist is a hussar, a cavalry soldier, and his colloquial speech (including at times specific Ukrainianisms) colors the entire tale. (It is important not to equate the crass, sexist, and racist sentiments expressed in the poem with Pushkin's own views.)

---

1 Скребни́цей – with his horse-comb. The opening image of the hussar tending to his horse is at once a realistic detail and a curious echo of the tale he is about to relate.

2 не в меру – excessively

3 вражий дух – hostile spirit (i.e., the devil)

4 На распрокля́тую кварте́ру (=квартиру)! – To this most cursed apartment

5 челове́ка берегу́т – they take care of a person

7 Наси́лу щей пусты́х даду́т – they barely give you cabbage soup without meat

8 А уж не думай о горе́лке – And don't even think about vodka

9 как лютый зверь – like a wild animal (note that this agrees with "хозяин" in the next line, not "тебя")

11 Не бось (=Небось) – I dare say

12 ни честью, ни нага́йкой – neither with honor (i.e., claims of honorable intentions) nor with a whip

13 То ль (=ли) дело Киев! – Kiev is completely different!

14 галу́шки – dumplings

15 Вино́м – хоть пару поддава́й – And there's so much wine that you could use it to make steam in the bathhouse. (In the traditional Russian bathhouse, one throws water on the hot coals to produce steam.)

16 А молоди́цы-молоду́шки! – And the young (married) women! The standard stress would be "моло́душки."

17 Ей-ей, не жаль отда́ть души́ – Indeed, you're not sorry to give up your soul (i.e., to die). The word choice may also hint at a pact with the devil.

18 красо́тки *чернобри́вой* – of a dark-browed beauty. The normal (folklori-

cally tinged) word would be “чернобровой.” Pushkin italicizes it as a Ukrainianism.

19 Одни́м, одни́м не хороши́ – They (the women) are bad only in one respect

20 служи́вый – military man; soldier

22 Молвить без оби́ды – If I may say without insulting you

23 хлопец – my lad

24 мы вида́ли виды – We (i.e., I) have seen quite a bit in life (i.e., I am experienced)

26 моя хозя́йка – my landlady

28 помер – died. The word is colloquial for “умер.”

30 Живём согласно, так что любо – We live so harmoniously that it is a pleasure to see

31 Прибью́ – Мару́синька моя́ – When I beat her, my Marusinka. The perfective is used here to emphasize repeated action, not the future tense. The name “Марусинька” is a diminutive form of “Маруся,” itself a diminutive form of “Мария.”

32 Слове́чка не промо́лвит грубо – she doesn’t say a coarse word. The word “грубо” is technically an adverb, but is difficult to translate as such.

33 Напью́сь – уло́жит – When I get drunk, she puts me in bed

34 Опохмели́ться пригото́вит – prepares a drink to ease my hangover (a time-honored Russian remedy)

35 Мигну́ быва́ло: “Эй, кума́!” – It used to be that I’d signal: “Hey, my sweetie.”

37 Кажи́сь – It would seem. This is a colloquialism for the standard “кажется.”

38 Живи́ в дово́льстве – Live happily

39 Да нет: я вздумал ревнова́ть – But no: I got it into my head to become jealous

40 Что делать? враг попу́тал, видно – What can you do? Clearly the devil led me astray.

42 до петухо́в – Before the cocks <crow>
кто просит – Who’s asking <her to do this>

44 лука́вый – the devil. As an adjective, the word means “crafty, sly,” but it is often (as here) used as a noun, a euphemism for the devil.

46 Раз я лежу́, глаза́ прищу́ря – Once I’m lying down, squinting

47 тюрьмы́ черне́й (= чернее) – blacker than a prison

48 буря – storm. In Pushkin’s texts, storms are often the scenes of mistaken or false identities (see “Бесы,” the story “Метель” [“The Snowstorm”], chapter 2 of the novel *Капитанская дочка* [*The Captain’s Daughter*]).

49 кумушка – diminutive of кума (see line 35)

50 тихо́хонько – a folk diminutive of “тихо” (standard diminutive would be “тихонько”)

51 Слегка́ обша́рила меня́ – touched me a bit. She is either searching for something or (more probably) checking if he is asleep.

52 уголь вздула – lit a coal

55 с полки скляночку взяла́ – took a little vial from the shelf

56 сев на веник – having sat down on a broom. A “веник” is a coarse broom made of sticks.

58 три раза́ хлебну́ла – she drank three times (in quick succession). Normally, the stress should fall on “ра́за.” The shifted stress is substandard.

60 Взвила́сь в трубу́ – и улизну́ла – She flew up into the chimney – and disappeared.

61 Эге́! смекну́л в мину́ту я – Aha! I figured it out immediately

62 басурма́нка – an infidel (i.e., a witch). The word is usually used about Muslims.

62 голу́бушка моя́ – my darling (literally: my little dove)

64 И с печки слез – I got down off the stove. In traditional Russian (and Ukrainian) houses people slept on top of the large stove, since it was the warmest part of the house.

66 Плесну́л я на́ пол – I splashed (the liquid) on the floor.

67 Прыгну́л ухва́т, за ним лоха́нь – The oven fork jumped up, <and> the washtub went after it. An "ухват" is a traditional implement used to remove hot pots from an oven. It has a wooden handle and rounded metal tips that fit snugly under the lip of the pot. In modern Russian, the stress on the verb would be "пры́гнул."

68 худо! – Uh, oh! (Literally: That's bad!)

71 Как фыркнет он! я: брысь – How he snorted! And I <said>: "shoo"

73 Я ну кропи́ть во все углы́ – Well, I <started> to spray in all corners (i.e., everywhere) "Ну" is a colloquial particle that emphasizes the inception of an action.

74 С плеча́, во что уж ни попа́ло – Not thinking, onto whatever was there

76 Марш! марш! всё в печку поскака́ло – One after another! Everything jumped up into the stove.

77 Кой чорт (=чёрт)! – What the devil!

78 и духом – and in one gulp

79 верь не верь – believe it or not

80 Но к верху вдруг взвился́ я пухом – But I suddenly flew up like a feather

81 Стремгла́в – headlong

84 Праве́й! (=правее) – <Move> further to the right!

88 Жида́ с лягу́шкою венча́ют – They're marrying a Yid to a frog

89 плюнул – spat. Spitting is a traditional way to rid oneself of the devil.

91 Домо́й! кто звал тебя, постре́л? – "Go home <she said>"! "Who called you, you rascal?"

92 Но я, не струся – But I responded fearlessly

93–94 чорта (=чёрта) с два! почём / Мне знать доро́гу – Doubly damned! How can I find the right way?

94 Ах, он странный! – Oh, he's so odd! Marusia addresses the hussar, but speaks to him in the third person.

95 Вот кочерга́, сади́сь верьхо́м – There's a poker, sit down on it. In modern Russian, the form would be "верхом" (same stress, but no soft sign).

96 И убира́йся, окая́нный – And scram, cursed one. The irony is that the witch is addressing the hussar as if *he* is the demon.

97 Чтоб я – So you want me …

98 Гуса́р прися́жный! – A hussar by oath (i.e., a real hussar)

99 врагу́ – to the enemy (i.e., the devil)

100 Иль (=Или) у тебя́ двойна́я шкура? – Or do you have a double skin? The hussar addresses Marusia, asking if she has a demonic side as well as her ordinary appearance.

101 Коня́! – На́, дурень, вот и конь – <Give me> A horse! – Here, you idiot, here's a horse.
104 Дуго́ю шея, хвост трубо́ю – His neck like an arch, his tail up like a funnel (or, conceivably, like a chimney)
112 Вот что случа́ется поро́ю – That's what happens sometimes
113–116 A refrain is a standard balladic technique.

„Царь уви́дел пред собо́й" – "In front of himself the tsar saw"

The form of this unfinished piece (trochaic tetrameter couplets) coincides exactly with that of Pushkin's "Сказка о золотом петушке" ("Fairy Tale of the Golden Cockerel"), which is based on Washington Irving's "Legend of the Arabian Astrologer." Akhmatova (2002, 20–21) has argued that this passage is taken from that same Irving tale and thus was probably part of Pushkin's initial plan for his own "сказка." The simple syntax and numerous diminutives certainly support the claim that this was intended to be part of a fairy tale.

The textology of this fragment is highly disputed; no two editions are exactly alike. For a thorough discussion of the difficulties of establishing a definitive text, see Rak, 343–77.

4 из во́ску – of wax (an old form of the genitive)
6 куколки – little statuettes (here: chess pieces)
8 коленко́ровых – calico
9 В опере́нных шишачка́х – In feathered helmets
10 с палаша́ми – with broadswords
11 лоха́нь – a wash tub
12 Приказа́л нали́ть водо́ю (= водой) – He ordered to be filled with water
14 тьму – a multitude
15 каторог – (archaic) of rowboats
19 ветри́льцы – little sails
20 крильцы – little wings. In modern Russian, the form would be "крыльца."

„Францу́зских рифмаче́й суро́вый судия́" – "Strict judge of French rhymers"

This unfinished poem is addressed to Boileau (1636–1711), a figure Pushkin had at times treated with derision (see his early "Сравнение"), but whose opinions about literature he always respected. In the present context, Boileau is only a smokescreen, since the poem is ultimately concerned with Russian literature of the present, not French literature of the past.

The poem is written in alexandrines, closely associated with the French neoclassicists, and a form which the French Romantics were in the process of revolutionizing (though Pushkin thought little of their innovations, see Achinger 1991, 120–21). Lexically, the poem is remarkable; Pushkin often uses high style and then undercuts it with low (e.g., лавры precedes парик in line 6, восчувствовав of line 19 is followed by the internal rhyme хватаете/мараете in line 20).

---

2 классик – A classic. Here probably in the sense of the movement of neoclassicism.
Депрео́ – Boileau's full name was Nicolas Boileau-Despréaux.
4 преста́л (=перестал) – ceased. The lines plays on Matthew 13:57 ("A prophet is not without honour, save in his own country, and in his own house"). In Russian: "Несть пророка в отечестве своем."
5 дерзких умников – of bold know-it-alls. Pushkin refers to the French Romantics (Sainte-Beuve and Victor Hugo).
6 лавры твоего́ густо́го парика́ – the laurels of your thick wig. In antiquity laurel wreaths were given to great poets. Pushkin conflates ancient Greece and French neoclassicism in a somewhat comic way.
7 растрёпанный нове́йшей вольной школой – disheveled by the most recent free school (i.e., the French Romantics)
10 вожа́таем – (archaic) leader. In modern Russian, the noun "вожатай" has been replaced by the substantivized adjective "вожатый."
11 Заня́ть кафе́дру ту, с кото́рой в прежни (=прежние) лета – to occupy the tribune from which in earlier years. In modern Russian the stress is on the first syllable: "ка́федру."
12 Ты слишком превознёс досто́инства соне́та – You too much extolled the virtues of the sonnet. In a famous line in his poem "L'art poétique" ("The Art of Poetry"), Boileau had written: "un sonnet sans defauts vaut seul un long poëme" ("a flawless sonnet is even as good as a long poem") (Canto 2, line 94). In 1828, Pushkin had published "Отрывки из писем, мысли и замечания" ("Excerpts from Letters, Thoughts, and Observations"), among which one finds the following: "Un sonnet sans defauts vaut seul un long poëme. Хорошая эпиграмма лучше плохой трагедии … Что это значит? Можно ли сказать, что хороший завтрак лучше дурной погоды?" ("Un sonnet sans defauts vaut seul un long poëme. A good epigram is better than a bad tragedy … What does that mean? Can one say that a good breakfast is better than bad weather?") Despite his three sonnets of 1830 Pushkin remained skeptical about the sonnet as a poetic form.
14 вранью́ – about the nonsense (the dative case follows "приговор" ["sentence; judgment"])
15 Нове́йшие врали́ врале́й стари́нных стоят – Our most recent chatterers are equal to the ancient chatterers. (Note the way Pushkin places emphasis on the repetitive nature of this activity through word order: "врали вралей.")
18 одна́жды за всегда́ (=завсегда) – once and for all
19 восчу́вствовав отва́гу – having felt courage. The word is archaic for "почувствовав."
21 Тисне́нью – To press (i.e., publication)
23 прямы́м ли вдохнове́ньем – with true inspiration
24 Иль необду́манным одни́м пополznове́ньем – Or only with an overhasty impulse
26 Иль (=Или) вам не верят в долг – or your credit is not good (i.e., no one will lend you money)

29 С хвалёным Ж<уковым> таба́чный торг заве́сть (=завести) – To start a tobacco business with the much-vaunted Zhukov. Vasilii Grigor'evich Zhukov (1795–1882) was a wealthy Moscow tobacco merchant.
30 снискивать <…> бары́ш и честь – to gain <…> profit and honor. The expression verges on a zeugma.
31 Чем объявле́ния сова́ть – than to shove announcements
32 кропа́я мадрига́лы – scribbling madrigals. According to the usage of Pushkin's time, a madrigal was a brief poem of flattery.
33 Над меньшей собратье́й – Over your lesser colleagues. Собратья (sometimes spelled "собратия") is a collective noun.
34 выше мнения отва́жно вознеся́сь – courageously raising yourself above (common) opinion. Note the lexical echoes with line 19.
35 С опло́шной публики (как некие писа́ки) – From a mistaken public (as some scribblers)
36 Подпи́ску собира́ть – на будущие враки – To gather subscriptions for future nonsense. This is a reference to Nikolai Alekseevich Polevoi (1796–1846), who announced a subscription for his twelve-volume *History of the Russian People* when he had only written the first volume (the publication ceased after the sixth). Polevoi was the son of a merchant, and he himself had considerable experience in the world of business. The polemics that developed between him and Pushkin reflect Polevoi's distaste for the "literary aristocracy" and Pushkin's disdain for the inadequate education (and bad breeding) of the merchant class.

„В поле чистом серебри́тся“ – "In the open field <the snow> shows silvery"

A fragment celebrating the Russian winter. In setting, spirit, form, and specific lexical items, it can be usefully contrasted to the nightmarish visions of "Бесы."

Like many of Pushkin's foklorically stylized texts, it is written in trochaic tetrameter. The quatrains have alternate feminine-masculine rhymes; in the first three stanzas, only one masculine rhyme is used, but the final line suggests that the pattern would stop there. The language and syntax are simple and direct.

---

2 волни́стый и рябо́й – in waves and ripples. This is not a terrifying blizzard, but a picturesque snowscape.
3 Светит месяц – the moon shines
4 По доро́ге столбово́й – along the high road. This is the main road between cities that would have distance markers along it.
8 песни удало́й – of a daring song. This could either mean the type of song or the type of performance.
13 Лучи́нушка, лучи́на – A "лучина" was a poor-man's candle, used for lighting in a peasant's house. It was simply a strip of dry wood that, when lit, supplied a meager light until it burned out. "Лучинушка" is the diminutive. Pushkin here either cites (or perhaps slightly varies) a genuine folksong. One ver-

sion (from the Kireevskii edition of Russian folklore) goes: “Ты лучина-ль, лучинушка, лучина моя! / Что-ж ты, лучинушка, не ясно горишь?”

„Сват Ива́н, как пить мы станем“ – “Ivan the in-law, when we begin to drink”

A folk stylization. In the manuscript next to this piece, Pushkin sketched a tipsy “muzhik” sitting at a table, presumably the “сват” of this poem.

The form is trochaic tetrameter, often used in folkloric stylizations (Gasparov 1990: 8–9). Rhyme pairs, the simplest form of rhyming, encourage the listener to guess the final word of the even-numbered lines as soon as the odd-numbered line finishes. The language and style, borrowed from the folk genres mentioned in lines 21–23, feature frequent word and sound repetition (e.g., *трё*х Ма*трё*н. Пет*ро́м*, Па*хо́м*овну по*то́м*).

The work is probably incomplete; it exists only in rough draft.

---

1 сват – in-law. In the complicated lexicon of Russian kinship, this was the term with which relatives of the bride (or groom) would address certain members of the family their children had married into.

2 помя́нем – let’s drink to the memory of

3 Трех Матрён, Луку с Петром – Three Matrenas, Luke and Peter. This combination of names was commonly found in “прибаутки” (see line 22) of various regions of Russia (Shein, 17–18).

4 Да Пахо́мовну – and Pakhomovna (daughter of Pakhom). In uneducated circles, it was common to name people only by their patronymic. Pakhomovna, as we learn in lines 19–35, was herself a performer of numerous folk genres.

5 жива́ли – lived <for a long time>

6 Уж как хочешь – будь что будь – However you want, whatever might happen. The line is composed of phrases with little semantic significance.

7 Этих – those (i.e., them, the people mentioned in lines 3–4)

9 Помина́ть, так помина́ть – If we’re to drink to them, let’s drink

11 Лить так лить, разли́в разли́вом – If we’re to pour, let’s pour, in an enormous flood <of wine>

12 Начина́й-ка – So go ahead and begin

18 Сказки сказывать – to tell (fairy) tales

20 отку́да что брала́ – she took material <for her stories> from everywhere. This is an idiom used to express admiration for inventiveness in storytelling.

21 А куды́ (=куда) разу́мны шутки – And how clever were <her> jokes

22 Пригово́рки, прибау́тки – proverbs, (humorous) sayings. In both of these folkloric genres the wordplay is often more important than the semantics.

23 Небыли́цы, былины́ – nonsense stories, heroic tales. The standard stress would be “были́ны,” but folkloric stress is free.

24 Правосла́вной старины́ – of Russian times of old. In this context, the adjective does not have any religious connotations.

25 Слушать, так душе́ отра́дно – listening makes one’s soul happy

27 Всё бы слушал да сиде́л – I would just listen and sit

28 ладно – harmoniously, smoothly
33 начну́ перво́й – I'll start. "Перво́й" is probably nominative masculine here (with free folkloric stress).
34 Сказка будет за тобо́й – It will be your turn to tell a story. In modern standard Russian, this is the only possible meaning, but it may have an alternate folkloric meaning of "this story is for you."

„Чу, пушки грянули! крыла́тых корабле́й" – "Hark, cannons have sounded! Of the winged ships"

This unfinished poem was apparently dedicated to a military ceremony of 1833 when a new battleship was first displayed (to the accompaniment of cannon shots). Pushkin also commemorated this event in two lines that he eventually removed from the introduction to "Медный всадник" ("The Bronze Horseman") – "Или крестит средь невских вод / Меньшого брата русский флот" ("Or when among the Neva's waves the Russian fleet christens its youngest brother").

The poem is written in four-line stanzas of iambic hexameter with alternating rhymes. The hemistich is marked not only by caesura, but in most cases also by a syntactic break.

1–2 крыла́тых корабле́й / Покры́лась облаком стани́ца боева́я – The military flock of winged ships has been covered by a cloud. Note the repeated "к" and "р" sounds. Comparisons of ships to birds (which continue in line 4 with the swan simile) go back to Homer. The cloud of line 2 is presumably the gunpowder from the cannon shots.
3 среди́ зыбе́й – among the ripples
4 как лебедь молода́я – like a young swan. Ordinarily, the word "лебедь" is masculine. This line, and this passage generally, calls to mind a one-line fragment (iambic pentameter, insofar as it is complete) that the editors of the Academy edition date to September of 1835: "Плывёт кора́бль как лебедь громове́ржец" ("The boat sails like a thunder-hurling swan"). "Громовержец" is the traditional epithet for Zeus.
6 взволнова́лась – has become agitated

Будрыс и его сыновья́ – Budrys and his sons

A translation of Mickiewicz's poem "Trzech Budrysów" ("The Three Brothers Budrys"), which the poet designated a "Lithuanian ballad." Mickiewicz's poem is written in syllabo-tonics, very unusual for Polish poetry but standard in the Russian poetry of Pushkin's day. The basic foot is the anapest. The odd numbered lines have fourteen syllables, the even-numbered lines ten. The odd-numbered lines do not rhyme with each other, but rhyme internally (i.e., the hemistich rhymes with the cadence of the line). The metrical source of Mickiewicz's ballad is generally agreed to be Sir Walter Scott's "Eve of Saint John," with the masculine rhymes changed to feminine to accommodate the Polish language (in which all polysyllabic words are stressed on the penultimate syllable).

Pushkin's rendering is, by his standards, remarkably faithful to the original both in terms of form and content. He retains the anapestic tetrameter alternating with anapestic trimeter as well as the exclusively feminine rhyme scheme.

Two lines reported to have been written by Pushkin suggest that he initially considered translating this poem in trochaic tetrameter (as in "Воевода"): "Там все жены, как иконы / В серебре и в жемчугах." The passage, which corresponds approximately to line 15 of the standard text, apparently renders an earlier version of Mickiewicz's own poem, which Pushkin would have known from his meetings with the Polish poet in the late 1820s. (See Gorlin, 235–36).

In Pushkin's edition of *Poezye Adama Mickiewicza*, Petersburg, 1829, the poem is found on pages 116–18 of volume 2.

TRZECH BUDRYSÓW
(Ballada Litewska.)

Stary Budrys trzech synów, tęgich jak sam Litwinów,
Na dziedziniec przyzywa i rzecze:
"Wyprowadźcie rumaki i narządźcie kulbaki,
A wyostrzcie i groty, i miecze.

Bo mówiono mi w Wilnie, że otrąbią niemylnie
Trzy wyprawy na świata trzy strony:
Olgierd ruskie posady, Skirgiełł Lachy sąsiady,
A ksiądz[1] Kiejstut napadnie Teutony.

Wyście krzepcy i zdrowi, jedzcie służyć krajowi,
Niech litewskie prowadzą was Bogi;
Tego roku nie jadę, lecz jadącym dam radę:
Trzej jesteście i macie trzy drogi.

Jeden z waszych biec musi za Olgierdem ku Rusi,
Ponad Ilmen, pod mur Nowogrodu;
Tam sobole ogony i srebrzyste zasłony,
I u kupców tam dziengi jak lodu.

Niech zaciągnie się drugi w księdza Kiejstuta cugi,
Niechaj tępi Krzyżaki psubraty,
Tam bursztynów jak piasku, sukna cudnego blasku
I kapłańskie w brylantach ornaty.

Za Skirgiełłem niech trzeci, poza Niemen przeleci;
Nędzne znajdzie tam sprzęty domowe,
Ale za to wybierze dobre szable, puklerze
I mnie stamtąd przywiezie synowę.

Bo nad wszystkich ziem branki milsze Laszki kochanki,
Wesolutkie jak młode koteczki,
Lice bielsze od mleka, s <sic> czarną rzęsą powieka,
Oczy błyszczą się jak dwie gwiazdeczki.

Stamtąd ja przed półwiekiem, gdym był młodym człowiekiem,
Laszkę sobie przywiozłem za żonę;
A choć ona już w grobie, jeszcze dotąd ją sobie
Przypominam, gdy spojrzę w tę stronę."

Taką dawszy przestrogę, błogosławił na drogę;
Oni wsiedli, broń wzięli, pobiegli.
Idzie jesień i zima, synów niéma <sic> i niéma <sic>,
Budrys myślał, że w boju polegli.

Po śnieżystej zamieci, do wsi zbrojny mąż leci,
A pod burką wielkiego coś chowa.
"Ej, to kubeł, w tym kuble nowogrodzkie są ruble?"
– "Nie, mój ojcze, to Laszka synowa."

Po śnieżystej zamieci, do wsi zbrojny mąż leci,
A pod burką wielkiego coś chowa.
"Pewnie z Niemiec, mój synu, wieziesz kubeł bursztynu?"
– "Nie, mój ojcze, to Laszka synowa."

Po śnieżystej zamieci, do wsi jedzie mąż trzeci,
Burka pełna, zdobyczy tam wiele,
Lecz nim zdobycz pokazał, stary Budrys już kazał
Prosić gości na trzecie wesele.

Note

1. Postermu zamiast: książe. (Mickiewicz's note.)

---

1 три литви́на – three Lithuanians. Ordinarily, Mickiewicz did not distinguish Lithuanians from Poles. However, this poem is purportedly derived from ancient Lithuanian folklore, in which the Lithuanians are indeed a separate people (see line 7).

2 с молодца́ми – with his (unmarried) sons

4 Даточи́те мечи́ с бердыша́ми – And sharpen your swords and pole-axes

6 Три замы́шлены в Вильне похо́да – In Vilnius three military campaigns are being planned. Vilnius was (and remains) the capital of Lithuania. The three campaigns are against Poland, Prussia, and Russia.

7 Паз – Pushkin chooses this name, presumably because it is more mellifluous than Skirgiełł. According to Venclova (52), it is an aristocratic Lithuanian family name.

на руса́ков – against the Prussians. In modern Russian, the stress would be "прусако́в."

8 А на русских Кесту́т воево́да – Kiejstut the commander <goes> against the Russians. The verb "идет" is implied here from the previous line.

13 Будет всем по награ́де – Each will get a reward

в Новегра́де – in Novgorod. ("Новоград" is an archaic form of "Новгород"; both parts of the name are declined.)

14 Поживи́тся от русских добы́чей – Profits from Russian prey

17 от проклятых крыжа́ков – from the cursed Teutonic knights. The word "крыжак" is a Polonism, borrowed from Mickiewicz's poem.

20 Янтаря́ – что песку́ там морско́го – Amber <which is as common> as the sand of the sea there. “Янтаря” and “песку” are in genitive case because of the verb “достать” in line 18.
26 что котёнок у печки – like a cat sitting in front of the stove
27 что смета́на – like sour cream
30 жонку (=жёнку) – a wife (diminutive form)
34 домови́тый – domestic (i.e., who stayed home)
37 доро́гою (=дорогой) – along the road
38 под буркою ноша больша́я – a heavy burden under a felt cloak
39 Ге! – Hey!

Воево́да – The Commander

A very free translation – in terms of both form and plot – of Mickiewicz’s “Ukrainian ballad” entitled “Czaty” (“The Watch”). Pushkin himself seemed to hint at his freedoms in his draft version, which he labeled an “Imitation of Mickiewicz” (“Подражание Мицкевичу”). One of the curious differences between the poems is that, in the Polish ballad, the unfaithful woman is the protagonist’s wife, whereas in Pushkin’s poem she is his mistress. It has been plausibly argued (Lednicki 1956, 44 and – on the basis of Pushkin’s own Polish-Russian dictionary – Levkovich 1974, 161–62) that this change is linked less to any profound rethinking of Mickiewicz’s work than to a basic linguistic error. Pushkin appears to have understood the Polish “niewiasta” (“woman”) as its Russian cognate (невеста = ”fiancée” or “woman of marriageable age”). He therefore refers to her throughout as “панна” (Polish “panna” or “young lady”).

Mickiewicz’s poem is in the identical form as “Будрыс и его сыновья” (see commentary to that poem), but Pushkin renders it differently. In a certain sense, Pushkin’s six-line stanzas remain true to the model of the Polish poem; he begins with a couplet rhyme (corresponding to the first line of a Mickiewicz stanza), then introduces another rhyme (Mickiewicz’s line 2), then another couplet rhyme (Mickiewicz’s line 3), then returns to the second rhyme (Mickiewicz’s line 4). However, Mickiewicz uses only feminine rhymes (typical of Polish verse), whereas Pushkin follows standard Russian practice by alternating feminine and masculine rhymes: A-A-b-C-C-b. Pushkin disregards the anapests altogether, writing his poem in trochaic tetrameter (a meter he often used for exotic and/or folkloric subjects).

In the edition Pushkin owned, “Czaty” comes directly before “Trzech Budrysów.” *Poezye Adama Mickiewicza* (Petersburg, 1829), 2:113–15.

Czaty
(Ballada Ukraińska)

Z ogrodowéj altany, wojewoda zdyszany,
Bieży w zamek z wściekłością i trwogą.
Odchyliwszy zasłony, spojrzał z łoże swej żony
Pojrzał, zadrżał, nie znalazł nikogo.

Wzrok opuścił ku ziemi i rękami drżącemi
Siwe wąsy pokręca i duma.
Wzrok od łoża odwrócił, w tył wyloty zarzucił,
I zawołał kozaka Nauma.

"Hej, kozaku, ty chamie, czemu w sadzie przy bramie,
Niema <sic> nocą ni psa, ni pachołka?
Weź mi torbę borsuczą i janczarkę hajduczą,
I mą strzelbę gwintówkę zdejm z kołka."

Wzięli bronie, wypadli, do ogrodu się wkradli,
Kędy szpaler altanę obrasta.
Na darniowém siedzeniu, coś bieleje się w cieniu,
To siedziała w bieliźnie niewiasta.

Jedną ręką swe oczy kryła w puklach warkoczy,
I pierś kryła pod rąbek bielizny;
Drugą ręką od łona, odpychała ramiona
Klęczącego u kolan mężczyzny.

Ten ściskając kolana,\ mówił do niej: "kochana!
Więc już wszystko, jam wszystko utracił!
Nawet twoje westchnienia, nawet ręki ściśnienia
Wojewoda już z góry zapłacił.

"Ja, choć z takim zapałem, tyle lat cię kochałem,
Będę kochał i jęczał daleki;
On nie kochał, nie jęczał, tylko trzosem zabrzęczał,
Tyś mu wszystko przedała na wieki.

Co wieczora on będzie, tonąc w puchy łabędzie
Stary łeb na twym łonie kołysał,
I z twych ustek różanych i z twych liców rumianych
Mnie wzbronione słodycze wysysał.

Ja na wiernym koniku, przy księżyca promyku,
Biegę tutaj przez chłody i słoty,
Bym cię witał westchnieniem, i pożegnał życzeniem
Dobrej nocy i długiej pieszczoty!"

Ona jeszcze nie słucha, on jej szepce do ucha
Nowe skargi czy nowe zaklęcia:
Aż wzruszona, zemdlona, opuściła ramiona,
I schyliła się w jego objęcia.

Wojewoda z kozakiem, przyklękneli za krzakiem,
I dobyli z za pasa naboje,
I odcięli zębami, i przybili sztęflami,
Prochu garść i grankulek we dwoje.

"Panie!" kozak powiada, jakiś bies mię napada,
"Ja niemogę <sic> zastrzelić tej dziewki.

Gdym półkurcze odwodził, zimny dreszcz mię przechodził,
I stoczyła się łza do panewki."

"Ciszej, plemię hajducze, ja cię płakać nauczę!
Masz tu s <sic> prochem leszczyńskim sakiewkę.
Podsyp zapał, a żywo szczyść paznogciem krzesiwo,
Potem palnij w twój łeb lub w tę dziewkę.

Wyżej..... w prawo..... pomału, czekaj mego wystrzału.
Pierwéj musi w łeb dostać Pan-młody."
Kozak odwiódł, wycelił, nie czekając wystrzelił,
I ugodził w sam łeb – wojewody.

Title: Воевода – Commander. Ordinarily, the term is historically limited to medieval times. Here it is chosen primarily because it is the word used in the Polish poem (albeit not in the title, though Mickiewiecz had considered using it as the title, see Lednicki 1956, 43).

4 к постéле – to the bed. This dative ending is based on the archaic noun "постеля" (rather than the "постель" of modern Russian).

5 Дёрнул полог – pulled <open> the bed curtain

8 потýпил грозны (=грозные) очи – cast down his fearsome eyes

9 свой сивый ус – his grey mustache

10 Рукавá назáд закúнул – threw back his sleeves

11 замóк задвúнул – closed the latch (behind him)

12 Гей, ты, кликнул, чортов кус! – Hey you, he called, you piece of the devil! (This curse is simply a fixed expression.)

14 ни затвóра – not a lock.

15 Я вас, хамы! – you louts, I <will show> you. The plural suggests that there are several servants, only one of whom plays a role in this poem. In a draft version, Pushkin had kept this in singular.

16 мешóк, верёвку – a bag, a rope. Presumably he is planning to mete out revenge.

18 Я ж её! – I <will show> her! The "ж" is simply emphatic here.

19 Пан и хлопец – The master and his servant. "Pan" is the standard word for "Mister" in Polish; it is used in the Mickiewicz poem. Strictly speaking "хлопец" means "guy" or "young man," but in the context of the poem he is obviously the servant. The fact that he is young is significant, for in the end he will take the side of the other young people against his (older) master.

21 сквозь ветвéй – through the branches. Ordinarily the preposition "сквозь" takes accusative case (as in line 45), but it can take genitive, as in this instance, which Pushkin takes advantage of for rhyming purposes.

22 у фонтáна – at the fountain. In the Polish poem, the meeting takes place in a gazebo, but Pushkin had a precedent for setting a nocturnal love encounter at a fountain: his own *Boris Godunov* (the Polish scene).

26–27 Чем лишь только я, бывáло, / Наслаждáлся – The <thing> that only I used to enjoy. The "чем" is governed by the verb "наслаждаться."

28 Белой груди воздыхáнье – the sigh of <your> fair breast

31 тобóй страдáл я – I was in love with you

33 От меня́ ты отперла́сь – you denied me
35 Серебро́м лишь побряца́л он – He only clanked silver <pieces>
36 И ему́ ты отдала́сь – And you gave yourself up to him
38 милой панны видеть очи – To see the eyes of <my> dear girl. According to Levkovich (1974, 162), the avoidance of the pronoun "you" in this phrase marks it as a Polonism. "Панна" is the standard Polish word for an unmarried woman.
47 По патро́ну откуси́ли – they each snapped off a cartridge
48 Вбили шомполом заря́д – they drove in the cartridge with a rod (i.e., they loaded their guns)
50 Пан мой, целить мне не можно – My lord, I can't aim. The phrase "мне не можно" is not accurate Russian and presumably is used to simulate Polish speech.
53 Дрожь берёт – I'm shaking
54 Порох в полку не попа́л – The gunpowder didn't go into the breech-block (i.e., the part where the gunpowder should be loaded)
55 гайду́чье племя – lackey race (a pejorative exclamation)
56 Будешь плакать, дай мне время! – Just give me time, you'll really have something to cry about!
57 Сыпь на полку … Наводи́ … – Pour it on the breech-block … Take aim
58 Цель ей в лоб – Aim for her forehead. Note that "цель" is here an imperative, not a noun.
59 С паном справлюсь сам – I'll take care of the guy myself
62 Хлопец пана не дожда́лся – The servant didn't wait for his master
65 Хлопец видно промахну́лся – The servant apparently missed
66 Прямо в лоб ему́ попа́л – He got (i.e., shot) him right in the forehead

„Когда б не смутное влече́нье" – "Were it not for the vague attraction"

Pushkin spent the month of September 1833 traveling, gathering materials for his *History of Pugachev*. Somewhere along the way he apparently spent the night at an estate where he encountered the woman who inspired these verses.

The text was never published in Pushkin's lifetime, and subsequent scholars (Tsiavlovskaia, then Lemin) have ingeniously and convincingly argued that it is probably the conclusion of a longer poem, the first part of which is traditionally printed as unconnected fragments. It is worth citing their reconstructed poem, as it gives the (indicative) context necessary to understanding the (subjunctive) eight-line piece that is otherwise unclear.

Она глядит на вас так нежно,
Она лепечет так небрежно,
Она так тонко весела,
Ее глаза так полны чувством,
Вечор она с таким искусством
Из-под накрытого стола
Свою мне ножку подала.

Зачем я ею очарован?
Зачем расстаться должен с ней?
Когда б я не был избалован
Цыганской жизнию моей,
Когда б не смутное влеченье
Чего-то жаждущей души,
Я здесь остался б – наслажденье
Вкушать в неведомой тиши:
Забыл бы всех желаний трепет,
Мечтою б целый мир назвал –
И все бы слушал этот лепет,
Все б эти ножки целовал.

In terms of form, this new work is somewhat unusual. The eight-line piece "Когда б не смутное влеченье" is written in iambic tetrameter with alternating rhymes, as are the four lines that precede them. However, the opening seven lines rhyme as A-A-b-C-C-b-b, making one wonder whether Pushkin might have altered them, had he ever prepared the poem for publication.

The commentary below follows the reconstructed poem, rather than the eight-line version of all Pushkin editions:

---

5 Вечо́р – yesterday evening

6 Из-под накры́того стола́ – from under the set table (i.e., under the tablecloth)

7 Свою́ мне ножку подала́ – gave me her foot. Pushkin's "passion for a pretty instep [...] would have been called 'foot-fetishism' by a modern student of the psychology of sex." Nabokov, 2:117.

11 Цыга́нской жизнию (=жизнью) – by my Gypsy life. The adjective here most directly connotes wandering, but it may also have a nuance of dissatisfaction with a settled existence.

13 Чего-то жаждущей души́ – of a soul yearning for something

14–15 наслажде́нье / Вкуша́ть в неве́домой тиши́ – to taste pleasure in unknown tranquility

19 ножки – feet. "The associative sense of the Russian "ножки" (conjuring up a pair of small, elegant, high-instepped, slender-ankled lady's feet) is a shade tenderer than the French *petits pieds*; it has not the stodginess of the English 'foot,' large or small, or the mawkishness of the German *Füsschen*." Nabokov, 2:115.

Literature: Lemin.

„Колоко́льчики звеня́т" – "Little bells ring"

Pushkin wrote this song at the request of his friend Mikhail Iur'evich Viel'gorskii (1788–1856), an amateur composer and major patron of the arts, for use in an opera called *Цыганы* (no relation to Pushkin's poem of that name). The resulting poem relies heavily on diminutives and sound repetitions, often in the same word (e.g., *колокольчики, барабанчики*).

Perhaps because it was intended as the text for an aria, Pushkin's poem is formally unusual. The two six-line stanzas have different rhyme schemes and even different meters. The first is a mixture of trochaic tetrameter (lines 1, 2, 4) and amphibrachic trimeter. The tetrameter lines rhyme with each other (masculine), while the amphibrachic lines rhyme with each other (feminine). Alternately, one may interpret these "amphibrachic" lines as trochees with one hypermetrical (incorrect) stress. Bondi (389) claims that this is a characteristic shift in Russian folklore, though his argument is by no means universally accepted. In any case, the second stanza is in standard trochaic tetrameter, with rhyme scheme A-b-A-b-C-C. Pushkin presumably chooses primarily trochees to convey the exotic theme. (Gypsies were, of course, hardly strangers to Russian poetry, thanks in part to Pushkin's own narrative poem about them. However, "Колокольчики звенят" derives its spirit less from that philosophical work than from Derzhavin's "Цыганская пляска," which emphasizes the strangeness of the wild Gypsy dance for the "civilized" Russian audience.)

---

1 Колоко́льчики – little bells. (These are not, as so often in Pushkin, carriage bells, but musical instruments.)

2 Бараба́нчики – little drums

4 Ой лю́шеньки-лю́ли – a meaningless refrain originating in lullabies (cf. "люлька," a cradle), but then found in songs of a more spirited and even raucous nature.

9 То шири́нкой алой машет – now waves a crimson kerchief. In the volume of "Editions and Corrections" to the Academy edition, this line is changed (based on the discovery of a new manuscript) to "Голубо́й шири́нкой машет" ("waves a light-blue kerchief").

10 Залива́ется-поёт – sings with abandon. The "поёт" is pleonastic (a common folkloric device).

11 плясу́нья – <female> dancer. The word is colloquial and would only be used in connection with folk dances.

12 Ворожи́ть я мастери́ца – I am an expert at sorcery

Осень (Отры́вок) – Autumn (A Fragment)

The title and subtitle are Pushkin's own. He is here referring to the Romantic usage of the term "fragment" as a work that is intentionally unfinished, because essentially unfinishable.

The poem is written in octaves, an eight-line stanza that features two rhymes used three times followed by a couplet: a-b-a-b-a-b-c-c. Given the alternating rhymes favored in the Russian tradition, poets had debated how best to domesticate the octave. After one attempt in 1821 ("Кто видел край"), Pushkin's solution was to start odd-numbered and even-numbered stanzas differently, that is, the first octave begins and ends with feminine rhymes, the second begins and ends with masculine rhymes. The source for the octave in European literature was Italian (Tasso's octaves, which Pushkin rhapsodizes about in *Eugene Onegin* 1:XLVIII; see also commentary to line 23 below), but that tradition had been revivified by English Romantics, often in comic works, for example, Byron's "Beppo" and several long poems of Barry Cornwall. As early as 1828, in the drafts to "Рифма, звучная подруга," Pushkin had connected the octave with Romanticism, apostrophizing rhyme as "Своенравная подруга романтических октав" ("Capricious friend of Romantic octaves"). It is probably not coincidental that the word "своенравный" also appears in "Осень" (line 40). In addition to "Осень," Pushkin turned to the octave in his long poem of 1830 "Домик в Коломне" ("The Little House in Kolomna"), the first half of which is a metapoetic discussion devoted to the octave. (In fact, the whole poem is devoted to this subject, though this is not immediately obvious; see Worthey.) Likewise, "Осень" itself is ultimately a poem about poetry, with the final stanzas being one of the rare descriptions of inspiration in all of Pushkin's works. While "Домик в Коломне" is written in iambic pentameter, "Осень" is in the more stylized iambic hexameter, which Pushkin takes pains to adapt to the "prosaic" subject of nature (see the explicit reference to "прозаизм" in line 64). Hence the extraordinary lexical range of "Осень" (Ginzburg, 211–12). The use of iambic hexameter in this poem surely draws on Prince Viazemskii's "Первый снег" ("First Snow"), a paean to winter from which Pushkin borrows liberally. Viazemskii begins his poem by noting that most poets delight in spring, whereas he (the Russian poet) prefers winter. He also dislikes autumn ("скучной осени," as he puts it), a view that Pushkin pointedly rejects.

Epigraph: Чегó в мой дремлющий тогдá не входит ум? – What then does not enter into my dreaming mind? This is a line from Derzhavin's great poem about domestic life in the countryside "Евгению. Жизнь званская" ("To Eugene. Life at Zvanka"). Derzhavin's poem is in quatrains of iambic hexameter (three lines) and iambic tetrameter (fourth line), but by quoting a single line of hexameter Pushkin creates an illusory sense of metrical continuity between Derzhavin's poem and his own.

6 В отъéзжие поля́ с охóтою (= охотой) своéй – To the fields far away from the manor house with his hunting companions. The noun "охота" can mean simply "hunt," or, in this case, "hunting retinue" (i.e., dogs and people who assist the hunter).

7 страждут озими – the winter crops suffer. A winter crop, common in Russian farming techniques, is a crop planted in the fall that matures beneath the earth during the winter. Here "озимь" can be understood more broadly (through metonymy) as the fields where the winter crop is planted. "Страждут" is archaic for "страдают."

10 вонь, грязь – stench, dirt. The striking spondee (particularly coming on these words) creates a distinctly "unpoetic" effect.

11 Кровь бродит – my blood ferments. This is an idiom for an agitated, uncomfortable state of mind.

15 под соболем – underneath the sable. The fur of the sable was (and still is) considered a luxury item, used for various winter garments. In "Первый снег," Viazemskii writes about his beloved: "И соболь на тебе чернеет и блестит"

("And the sable on you shows black and shines"). Pushkin clearly drew the final lines of this octave from a passage in that same poem: "Кто в тесноте саней с красавицей младой, / Ревнивых не боясь, сидел нога с ногой, / Жал руку." ("Whoever in the close quarters of a sleigh sat with leg next to leg, holding hands, not fearing jealous ones.") The phrase "нога с ногой" did not appear in the first publication of Viazemskii's poem because it was rejected by the censor.

17 обу́в желе́зом острым ноги – having shod feet with sharp steel, i.e., putting on ice-skates.

18 по зеркалу стоя́чих, ровных рек – along the mirror of still, even rivers. The description is of a frozen body of water.

20 Но надо знать и честь – (idiom) But enough is enough (i.e., winter goes on too long)

23 с Арми́дами млады́ми (=молодыми) – with young Armidas. Armida is the beautiful sorceress in Tasso's epic *Jerusalem Delivered.* Pushkin uses her name here not so much as an allusion as simply a synonym for beautiful young woman.

24 киснуть у пече́й за стёклами двойны́ми – spend one's day in boredom at the stoves behind doubled glass. These two panes of glass were a form of storm windows.

25 лето красное – beautiful summer. The epithet is distinctly folkloric, and its pleasant associations are undercut by the prosaicisms in the next line.

28 страждем (=страдаем) от засу́хи – we suffer from the drought. In modern Russian, the stress would be "за́сухи." Pushkin probably shifts the stress for the rhyme.

30 жаль зимы́ стару́хи – <we feel> sorry for old lady winter

31 проводи́в её блина́ми – having seen her off with pancakes. The antecedent is "old lady winter." The pancakes allude to Russian celebrations of "масленица" (Shrovetide), the holiday that marks the end of winter.

35 Красо́ю тихою (=Красой тихой), блиста́ющей смире́нно – In its quiet beauty, which shines modestly

36 нелюби́мое дитя́ – an unloved child

42 чахо́точная дева – a consumptive girl. Pushkin borrows an image from Sainte-Beuve's *Joseph Delorme*, where he described his muse as being consumptive (the passage had caused a furor in French criticism at the time, see Achinger 2000, 60–61). Pushkin had quoted these notorious verses in his 1831 review of Sainte-Beuve's poetry:

> … une toux déchirante
> La prend dans sa chanson, pousse en sifflant un cri,
> Et lance les graviers de son poumon meurtri.
>
> (A heart-wrenching cough racks her body in mid-song, she lets out a wheezing cry, and spits out grit from her sickened lungs.)

46 Моги́льной пропасти она́ не слышит зева – She does not sense the opening of the grave's abyss. The usual translation of "зев" is "maw," but the *Словарь языка Пушкина* renders it in this context as "зияние" (gaping

hole). Both meanings may be relevant. Additionally, there is probably a play on “зов” (“summons”), in which case “слышит” could be taken literally as “hears.”

52 в багре́ц и золото оде́тые – dressed in red and gold. The image calls to mind the dress of royalty, since “багрец” was traditionally associated with wealth.

53 ветра шум и свежее дыха́нье – the noise and fresh wafting of the wind. The words “шум” and “дыханье” are in accusative case (following “люблю” of line 51).

60 Чредо́й слета́ет сон, чредо́й нахо́дит голод – In turn sleep descends (i.e., I fall asleep), in turn hunger comes

69 в камельке́ – in the small fireplace

70 лиёт (= льёт) – spreads out

76 Душа́ стесня́ется лири́ческим волне́ньем – My soul is constricted by lyrical agitation

78 свобо́дным проявле́ньем – in a free manifestation

84 потеку́т – flow forth

88 грома́да – the colossus. The word is used by Pushkin to mean any large thing; here it refers to the ship.

Given the frequency of nautical imagery in poetry, it is not surprising that several potential sources have been mentioned for the metaphor beginning in line 85. Perhaps the most likely is Sainte-Beuve’s “Le Calme” (see Morozov, 86–87), given that Pushkin already alludes to his poetry in line 42.

Le Calme

> “Ma muse dort comme une marmotte de mon pays … comme il vous plaira, ma verve; ce qu’il y a de sûr, c’est que je ne ferai rien sans vous.”
>
> – Ducis.

Souvent un grand désir de choses inconnues,
D’enlever mon essor aussi haut que les nues,
De ressaisir dans l’air des sons évanouis,
D’entendre, de chanter mille chants inouïs,
Me prend à mon réveil; et voilà ma pensée
Qui, soudain rejetant l’étude commencée,
Et du grave travail, la veille interrompu,
Détournant le regard, comme un enfant repu,
Caresse avec transport sa belle fantaisie,
Et veut partir, voguer en pleine poésie.
A l’instant le navire appareille, et d’abord
Les câbles sont tirés, les ancres sont à bord,
La poulie a crié; la voile suspendue
Ne demande qu’un souffle à la brise attendue,
Et sur le pont tremblant tous mes jeunes nochers
S’interrogent déjà vers l’horizon penchés:
Adieu, rivage, adieu! – Mais la mer est dormante,
Plus dormante qu’un lac; mieux vaudrait la tourmente;
Mais d’en haut, ce jour-là, nul souffle ne répond;

La voile pend au mât et traîne sur le pont.
Debout, croisant les bras, le pilote, à la proue,
Contemple cette eau verte où pas un flot ne joue,
Et que rasent parfois de leur vol lourd et lent
Le cormoran plaintif et le gris goëland.
Tout le jour il regarde, inquiet du voyage,
S'il verra dans le ciel remuer un nuage,
Ou frissonner au vent son beau pavillon d'or;
Et quand tombe la nuit, morne, il regarde encor
La quille où s'épaissit une verdâtre écume,
Et la pointe du mât qui se perd dans la brume.

Pushkin would have known this poem from Sainte-Beuve's *Vie, poésies et pensées de Joseph Delorme* (Paris, 1829), 128–29. He also owned the 1830 edition of this work, in which the identical text of "Le Calme" is on pages 163–64. Another possibility (see Ivinskii, 1999) is the 1829 elegy "Отплытие" ("Departure") by the minor poet V. G. Tepliakov, a work that is largely derived from two sonnets by Adam Mickiewicz (which Pushkin may have known in the original; on this theory see Lednicki 1956, 57–59). However, neither Tepliakov nor Mickiewicz connect sailing to the motif of the imagination.

„Не дай мне бог сойти́ с ума́" – "God forbid I should go mad"

The theme of madness occurs in several of Pushkin's greatest works from the last years of his life (the story "Пиковая дама," the narrative poem "Медный всадник," the unfinished drama *Русалка*, in which the mad miller recites lines that clearly echo the present poem). It may be that the urgency and power of these works reflect Pushkin's own genuine fears of insanity. In all of these works, Pushkin rejects the clichés of Western literature (e.g., E. T. A. Hoffmann's conception of the madman as Romantic genius) as well as Russian cultural tradition (madness as holiness, the "юродивый" or "holy fool"), focusing instead on the misery and horrors of insanity.

This poem is written in iambs, with the rhyming third and sixth lines trimeter, the other lines tetrameter. The rhyme scheme is a-a-b-c-c-b. The exclusively masculine rhymes are rare in Russian poetry, but frequent in English tradition, and stanzas with this rhyme scheme and meter are not hard to find in English Romantic poetry (see Tomashevskii 1958, 83), but no precise source for Pushkin's poem has been adduced. The Academy edition suggests – on paleographical evidence – that the poem is unfinished, but this is hard to believe, since the conclusion works brilliantly as it stands.

---

2 посох и сума́ – the staff and the bag. An example of metonymy – these are the attributes of the wanderer (beggar).

3 глад (=голод) – hunger

4 Не то – It's not that

8 На воле – free

11 в чаду́ – in the intoxication
15 В пусты́е небеса́ – into the empty heavens
17 вихорь, роющий поля́ – a whirlwind that tears up the fields. In modern Russian, the form is "вихрь."
18 Лома́ющий леса́ – that breaks the forests. In the draft, Pushkin had the far less violent кача́ющий леса́ (that shakes the forests). Zakhar Ishov has pointed out to me that these violent images of madness are probably borrowed from Ariosto's *Orlando Furioso*, in the immediate continuation of the passage that Pushkin chose to translate in 1826.

> Quivi fe' ben de le sue prove eccelse,
> ch'un alto pino al primo crollo svelse:
> e svelse dopo il primo altri parecchi,
> come fosser finocchi, ebuli o aneti;
>
> (Here he gave a show of his excellent abilities / Destroying a tall pine with the first blow: / And after that one destroying several others / As if they were stalks of fennel, elderberry or anise.)

This passage was well known to Pushkin, who refers to it in "Ruslan and Liudmila" (Proskurin 2007, 130).
19 Да вот беда́: сойди́ с ума́ – But there's the misfortune (there's the rub): if you go insane. The second half of the line brilliantly echoes the opening line, shifting the emphasis from the first person to the second.
21 Как раз тебя́ запру́т – They'll just lock you up
22 Поса́дят на́ цепь дурака́ – They'll put the fool on a chain
23 как зверка́ – like a little beast
26 Не голос яркий соловья́ – Not the clear voice of the nightingale. The unusual Russian epithet is, according to Nabokov (3:74–75) a Gallicism, but more importantly, it recalls Konstantin Batiushkov's use of the word in "Последняя весна" ("The Last Spring"), a poem about a dying poet (a translation of the then enormously popular Charles Millevoye), which Pushkin also mined for his portrayal of Lensky in *Eugene Onegin*. In his translation Batiushkov describes the spring in terms of "яркий голос филомелы" ("the bright voice of Philomele" – according to Greek mythology the raped princess Philomele was turned into a nightingale). The Batiushkov reference is revealing. Batiushkov (1787–1855) had been one of Pushkin's early models for mellifluous poetry, but he spent the last decades of his life (beginning in 1822) in a permanent state of insanity and incoherence. In what was clearly a horrifying encounter, Pushkin had visited Batiushkov on 3 April 1830, but the mad poet did not recognize his former friend.

„Вам объясня́ть правле́ния нача́ла“ – "To explain to you the principles of government"

A translation of the opening of Shakespeare's *Measure for Measure*. Pushkin apparently abandoned the project (cutting off at the beginning of a lengthy speech) and decided instead to write his (final) narrative poem "Анджело" based on the same plot.

The opening is cited below according to the Shakespeare edition that Pushkin owned: *The Dramatic Works of Shakspeare* <sic> *Printed from the Text of Samuel Johnson, George Steevens and Isaac Reed, Complete in one Volume* (Leipzig, 1824), 74.

ACT I
Scene I – *An apartment in the Duke's palace. Enter Duke,* Escalus, *Lords, and Attendants.*

Duke. Escalus, –
Escal. My lord.
Duke. Of government the properties to unfold,
Would seem in me to affect speech and discourse;
Since I am put to know, that your own science
Exceeds, in that, the lists of all advice,
My strength can give you. Then no more remains,
But that to your sufficiency, as your worth is able,
And let them work. The nature of our people,
Our city's institutions, and the terms
For common justice, you are as pregnant in,
As art and practice hath enriched any,
That we remember. There is our commission,
From which we would not have you warp. – Call hither,
I say, bid come before us Angelo. –
Exit an Attendant
What figure of us, think you, he will bear?
For you must know, we have with special soul
Elected him our absence to supply,
Lent him our terror, drest him with our love,
And given his deputation all the organs
Of our own power. What think you of it?
Escal. If any in Vienna be of worth
To undergo such ample grace and honour,
It is lord Angelo.
Enter Angelo.
Duke. Look, where he comes.
Ang. Always obedient to your grace's will,
I come to know your pleasure.
Duke. Angelo,
There is a kind of character in thy life,
That, to the observer, doth thy history
Fully unfold.

Given the syntactic and lexical complexities of the English text (which are considerably lessened in the Russian translation), it is probable that Pushkin consulted a French prose translation as well as the original. In the edition Pushkin owned (*Oeu-*

vres complètes de Shakspeare <sic>, traduites de l'anglais par Letourneur [Paris, 1821]), the relevant passage is found in volume 8, pages 159–60.

> Le Duc. Escalus!
>
> Escalus. Seigneur.
>
> Le Duc. Vouloir vous expliquer les principes de l'administration paraîtrait en moi une affection vaine et discours inutiles, puisque je sais que vos propres connaissances dans l'art de gouverner surpassent tous les conseils et les instructions que pourrait vous donner mon expérience. Il ne me reste donc qu'un mot à vous dire: votre capacité égalant votre vertu, laissez-les agir ensemble et de concert. Le caractère de mes sujets, les lois de notre cité, le style et les formes de la justice sont des matières que vous possédez à fond, autant qu'homme instruit par l'art et la pratique. Voilà notre commission que nous voudrions voir ponctuellement suivie par vous. – (*A un domestique.*) Allez dire à Angelo de se rendre ici. – Quelle opinion avez-vous de sa capacité pour nous remplacer? Car vous savez que dans le secret de notre âme nous l'avons aussi choisi pour nous représenter dans notre absence, que nous l'avons armé de toute la terreur de notre autorité, revêtu de tout l'empire de notre amour, et que nous avons transmis à sa commission tous les organes de notre pouvoir. Que pensez-vous de notre choix?
>
> Escalus. S'il est dans Vienne un homme digne d'être revêtu d'un si grand honneur, et d'une si haute dignité, c'est le seigneur Angelo.
>
> (*Entre Angelo.*)
>
> Le Duc. Le voilà qui vient.
>
> Angelo. Toujours soumis aux volontés de votre altesse, je viens savoir vos ordres.
>
> Le Duc. Angelo, votre conduite passée présente un caractère où l'oeil observateur peut lire d'avance toute la suite de votre vie.

Pushkin's translation, like the English original, is in blank verse (unrhymed iambic pentameter).

---

7 Пости́гли вы верне́й (=вернее), чем кто б то ни́ был – You have understood more truly than anyone

8 нака́з – order

12 нами он назна́чен – he is appointed by us

14 И милостью <и> страхом облекли́ – clad in kindness and terror

15 Наме́стника всей нашей власти – the deputy of all our power

16 мните – think

21 Анджело, жизнь твоя́ явля́ет – Angelo, your life shows. The line is rhythmically extremely odd because, in order to scan correctly, the name "Анджело" would have to take a stress on the second syllable. In no other instance does Pushkin put the stress there (he uses the name in line 10 of this poem and numerous times in the narrative poem of that name). Either the line is unfinished or Pushkin was applying English rules of versification. (In Russian verse, one can stress the first syllable of an iambic line only in the case of monosyllabic words; in English, one can stress it also on polysyllabic words.) Pushkin was conceivably misled by the graphic layout of the English edition

he was using. In the corresponding English excerpt, the Duke's speech begins with the word "Angelo." Though this is actually the final foot of the previous line, Pushkin's English edition sets the word flush left. Thus, on first glance, it appears to be the beginning (rather than the end) of the line. The French prose translation would only have encouraged this misconception.

<Плетнёву> („Ты хочешь, мой напéрсник строгой") – To Pletnev ("You want, my stern confidant")

See commentary to "<Плетнёву>," "Вы за 'Онегина'" and especially "В мои осенние досуги" (all of 1835). Though the Academy edition dates the present poem as 1833, it is far more probable that, like these other poems, it was written in 1835 as a response to Pletnev's request that Pushkin continue his novel in verse.

Despite the absence of line 4 and the final word of line 9, this unfinished poem was clearly intended to take the form of an Onegin stanza: A-b-A-b-C-C-d-d-E-f-f-E-g-g.

---

1 напéрсник строгой (=строгий) – my strict confidant

2 Боёв парнáсских – of the wars of Parnassus. Parnassus, the mountain in Greece, is traditionally the symbol of all things poetic.

6 Давнó забы́того герóя – <My> long forgotten hero (i.e., Eugene Onegin)

14 Возьмýт обрóк его́ главы́ – His chapters take quit-rent (i.e., one can make money from them). In Pushkin's time, "оброк" was a fee that landowners took from their serfs. This same image occurs in "В мои осенние досуги" (also written in Onegin stanzas), which suggests that the two unfinished poems are connected and were composed at approximately the same time. In modern Russian, the stress would be "глáвы."

1834

„Я возмужáл средú печáльных бурь" – "I matured among sad storms"

An unfinished piece of what was probably intended to be a poem of many stanzas.

The verses are written in iambic pentameter, with caesura after the second foot (a somewhat old-fashioned touch in Pushkin's poetry of the 1830s). Apparently the poem was to take the form of quatrains with ring rhyme.

---

2 дней моúх потóк – the stream of my days. The entire stanza develops this not terribly original metaphor. Merlin (174) suggests a specific source in Lamartine's "Le vallon" ("The Vale"), a lengthy meditation in quatrains.

> La source de mes jours comme eux c'est écoulée;
> Elle a passé sans bruit, sans nom et sans retour:
> Mais leur onde est limpide, et mon âme troubleé
> N'aura pas réflêchi les clartés d'un beau jour.
>
> (The stream of my days has flowed away like them [i.e., the two hidden brooks of the previous stanza] / It has passed without noise, without name, and without return: / But their wave is clear, and my troubled soul / Will not reflect the splendors of a beautiful day.)

4 лазýрь – azure, the color of the sky

„Порá, мой друг, порá! Покóя сердце просит" – "It's time, my friend, it's time! <My> heart asks for peace"

One of Pushkin's most famous poems, first published after his death, and often admired for its brevity. However, on the manuscript page there is a prose "plan" for the poem's continuation.

> Юность не имеет нужды в at home, зрелый возраст ужасается своего уединения. Блажен кто находит подругу – тогда удались он домой.
>
> О скоро ли перенесу я мои пенаты в деревню – поля, сад, крестьяне, книги; труды поэтические – семья, любовь, etc. – религия, смерть.

In short, this frequently anthologized "poem" was intended as the beginning of a long work. The fact that only eight lines were completed gives them a stark and mysterious quality.

The presence of the English phrase "at home" (which, judging from the context, Pushkin understood in some non-existent idiomatic sense) has led scholars to search for an English source. However, no convincing model has been adduced. Pushkin's plan is hardly distinctive; the idea of retreating with one's beloved from the city to the countryside can be found frequently in Western literature, going back at least as far as Horace. Its potential literary pedigree aside, Pushkin's plan seems a fairly clear reflection of his own ideals of the 1830s.

The poem is in alexandrines (iambic hexameter couplets with caesura in the middle), a form that had a certain elevated and antiquated quality in the Russian poetry of Pushkin's day. The poem's lexicon mixes philosophical abstract nouns (счастье, покой, воля) with startling colloquialisms that one would not expect in a meditative poem of this type.

---

1 поко́я – peace. The word is in genitive case after the verb "просит."

3 Части́чку бытия́ – a little particle of existence

4 и глядь – как раз – умрём – and before you know it we'll up and die. The line is striking in its colloquial lexicon.

5 воля – freedom

6 мечта́ется мне доля – I dream of an <enviable> lot

8 В оби́тель дальную трудо́в и чистых нег – Into a distant abode of works and pure comforts. In modern Russian, the correct form would be "дальнюю."

„Он между нами жил" – "He lived among us"

In July 1833 Pushkin's friend S. A. Sobolevskii returned from Western Europe, bringing Pushkin a four-volume collection of Mickiewicz's poetry: *Poezye Adama Mickiewicza*, Paris, 1828–1832 (the first two volumes are dated 1828, the third 1829, and the final one 1832). Pushkin never cut the pages of the first three volumes, but the pages are all cut in the final volume, which also bears a dedication to Pushkin from Sobolevskii (cited in Modzalevskii 1910, 289). That final volume (pp. 283–85) closes with the poem "Do przyjaciół moskali" ("To My Russian Friends"). In that brief poem, Mickiewicz begins by recalling the Decembrists Ryleev and Bestuzhev, but then speaks of someone who "betrays his free soul to the tsar for hire" and "lauds the tyrant," lines that were transparently aimed at Pushkin and his jingoistic (yet sincere) poems on the taking of Warsaw in 1831. Pushkin's poem is in many ways a response to his erstwhile friend.

The poem – clearly unfinished – is written in blank verse (unrhymed iambic pentameter).

---

2 Средь племени ему чужо́го – Among a tribe foreign to him. Pushkin here raises the complicated subject of the relationship of Poland and Russia. In a draft, it is put more forcefully: Ему враждебным племенем – <among> a tribe hostile to him.

8 с высока́ – from a lofty perspective; from on high

10 распри – quarrels. It has been claimed (Levkovich 1974, 155–56) that the utopian vision described in these lines reflects the content of a poetic improvisation performed by Mickiewicz in Pushkin's own apartment.

13 Ушёл на запад – went to the West

15 ядом – with poison. Cf. Mickiewicz's poem: "Teraz na świat wylewam ten kielich trucizny" ("Now I am pouring over the world this goblet of poison").

19 знако́мый голос – familiar voice. Cf. Mickiewicz's poem: "Poznacie mię po głosie" ("You recognize me by my voice").

Literature: Lednicki 1956, 66–69; Frantsev, 133–34.

„Везу́вий зев откры́л – дым хлынул клубом – пламя“ – "Vesuvius opened its maw – smoke gushed in a cloud – a flame"

One of the main cultural events in Russia of 1834 was the public display of the picture *The Last Day of Pompeii* by Karl Pavlovich Briullov (1799–1852). This enormous canvas was immediately recognized as a masterpiece. Briullov spent the years from 1823 to 1835 working in Italy, and this picture was inspired by his visit to Pompeii. On the draft of his poetic response, Pushkin sketched the central figures of the painting. This brief (unfinished) poetic excerpt can be profitably compared with Pushkin's roughly contemporaneous depiction of another natural calamity – the flood in "Медный всадник."

Pushkin's poem is written in iambic hexameter with caesura after the third foot. The opening two lines form a couplet, leading one to expect a poem in alexandrines, but the rhyme scheme of the final four lines is a ring structure. The sound clusters (кр/хл/кл/пл) and enjambment of the first line help evoke the chaos it describes.

---

1 зев – maw. Aside from the striking personification, Pushkin chooses the word for its sound qualities: В*езувий зев*. The entire line stands out rhythmically, since it features six – and arguably seven – stresses; note also the insistent assonance in "откры́л – ды́м хлы́нул.")

2 как боево́е знамя – like a battle standard. Levitskii (7, note 14) argues that Pushkin's comparison of Vesuvius to a battle was inspired by Derzhavin's ode "На взятие Измаила" ("On the Taking of Izmail"), where a battle is compared to Vesuvius. Derzhavin's poem begins: "Везувий пламя изрыгает" ("Vesuvius spews flame").

5 Под каменным дождём, под воспалённым прахом – Under a rain of stones, under the inflamed earth. The description verges on the oxymoronic.

Literature: Lotman 1997, 293–99.

„Стою печа́лен на кладби́ще“ – "I stand sad at the graveyard"

"Graveyard poems" were a popular genre of Romanticism, beginning (in Russia) with Zhukovskii's 1802 translation of Gray's "Elegy in a Country Churchyard." It is interesting that Pushkin returns to this subject in his last years, reevaluating the possibilities of a genre that was now largely the province of epigones. It has been claimed that this turn also reflects the superstitious poet's presentiment of his own death.

The poem is written in iambic tetrameter. It begins with two quatrains rhymed alternately, but then shifts to a couplet rhyme. The last four lines also rhyme alternately, though some editions change their order, moving "Однообразны и унылы" to line 12, which creates a ring rhyme in the last four lines. The unfinished quality of the manuscript explains the editorial uncertainty about line order.

---

1 кладби́ще – graveyard. In modern Russian, the stress is on the first syllable: кла́дбище.
3 Свято́е смерти пепели́ще – the sacred hearth of death
4 степью – by the steppe. As usual, Pushkin uses steppe in a general sense to describe any flat area with sparse vegetation.
9 Одна́ равни́на справа, слева – A single plain to the right, to the left
10 Ни речки, ни холма́, ни древа – There is not a stream, not a hill, not a tree. Pushkin takes a poetic liberty and omits the word "нет," which is, strictly speaking, necessary. The combination of the diminutive "речка" with the Slavonicism "древо" is striking.
11 Кой-где (=Кое-где) – here and there

Песни западных славя́н – Songs of the Western Slavs

This curious cycle of poems reflects Pushkin's fascination with folklore. What Pushkin – following the usage of his day – calls the "Western" Slavs are what today would be designated as "South" Slavs (inhabitants of the former Yugoslavia). When Pushkin composed the songs, he was under the impression that he was translating genuine folkloric texts. Most of them came from *La Guzla, ou choix de Poésies Illyriques recueillies dans la Dalmatie, la Bosnie, la Croatie, et l'Herzegowine* (*The Guzla or Selected Illyrian Poetry Collected in Dalmatia, Bosnia, Croatia, and Herzegovina*), a collection that had been published anonymously in 1827. A "guzla" was a type of bowed instrument with a single string made of horsehair, used by folk singers to accompany their songs. These "strange songs" ("странных сих песен"), as Pushkin calls them in his introduction, were purportedly French translations of folksongs collected by the unnamed editor during his travels.

Shortly before publishing his cycle, Pushkin learned that the anonymous editor of *La Guzla* was none other than the celebrated French writer Prosper Mérimée and that the entire collection was in fact a mystification. (This information, which came in the form of a letter of Mérimée to Pushkin's friend S. A. Sobolevskii, did not deter Pushkin from publishing his work; he simply appended Mérimée's letter to his publication, and it can be found in all Pushkin editions.)

Pushkin was not the only one to be taken in by Mérimée's hoax: Mickiewicz had believed the poems to be genuine (see the first paragraph of Pushkin's own introduction to the cycle and his note 15), as had many Western readers. This is hardly surprising; despite Mérimée's claims that the work had been thrown together in a matter of days, scholars have shown that Mérimée consulted numerous collections of folklore (much of it Greek rather than Slavic), and his *Guzla* reads like typical ethnographic literature of the time, with its "poems" supplemented by copious explanatory footnotes and even a four-page biography of the supposed guzla virtuoso Hyacinthe Maglanovich (which Pushkin valued sufficiently to cite in its entirety in his note 18).

The French texts that Mérimée supplied were written in a rather colorless but supposedly "accurate" prose. In rendering them as Russian verse, Pushkin used all the poetic means at his disposal – versification, lexicon, and morphology (e.g., diminutives, truncated adjectives) – to evoke folkloric associations to a Russian ear. Whatever the sources of the originals, Pushkin's translations sound convincingly folkloric.

While Russian commentators invariably repeat the mantra that Pushkin treated his sources with great freedom, a comparison shows that in most ways he remained extremely faithful to them. Mérimée's texts are composed in numbered paragraphs; very often Pushkin organizes his translations in the same fashion, with stanzaic breaks marking the new paragraphs. Mérimée added notes in his *Guzla*, some of which Pushkin retained (only rarely crediting his source). In the *Guzla*, the texts Pushkin translated appear in the following order: "Notice sur Hyacinthe Maglanovich" (first – this "biography" is cited in the original French in Pushkin's note 18), "La vision de Thomas II, Roi de Bosnie" (fourth), "Le Morlaque à Venise" (fifth), "Chant de mort" (sixth), "Les braves Heyduques" (eighth), "La belle Hélène" (ninth), "La flamme de Perrussich" (thirteenth), "Le combat de Zenitza-Velika" (fifteenth), "Jeannot" (eighteenth), "Constantin Yacoubovich" (twentieth), "Les Monténégrins" (twenty-eighth), "Le cheval de Thomas II" (twenty-ninth).

Pushkin's poetic cycle comprises eleven translations from Mérimée, two translations of genuine Serbian folklore from the collection of the renowned philologist Vuk Karadžić (which, having first appeared in the original in 1814 and in German translation in 1825, inspired Mérimée's mystification [Solov'ev, 58]), and a few poems of uncertain provenance. Pushkin had been interested in Karadžić's work for at least a decade, and he owned the three-volume collection of Serbian folksongs that Karadžić published in 1823–1824.

The language of the "Songs" is a curious mixture of folkloric genres – songs, epic songs, fairy tale – and bookish forms (see Vinogradov 1949, 263–66).

The versification of the songs varies; in most cases Pushkin uses a type of accentual verse that he adapted from the talented scholar and poet Aleksandr Khristoforovich Vostokov (1781–1864); in a few of the poems he opts for trochees, a common means of folkloric stylization in Russian.

1. Виде́ние короля́ – The King's Vision

The poem is a translation of Mérimée's "La vision de Thomas II, Roi de Bosnie," (*La Guzla*, pp. 33–42, which is credited to the guzla player Hyacinthe Maglanovich). Mérimée's first footnote points the reader to a note to an earlier poem ("Le Mort de Thomas II"), which gives a detailed account of the historical context. Pushkin summarizes this in his own note: "Фома I был тайно умерщвлен своими двумя сыновьями Стефаном и Радивоем в 1460 году. Стефан ему наследовал. Радивой, негодуя на брата за похищение власти, разгласил ужасную тайну и бежал в Турцию к Магомету II. Стефан, по внушению папского легата, решился воевать с турками. Он был побежден и бежал в Ключ-город, где

Магомет осадил его. Захваченный в плен, он не согласился принять магометанскую веру, и с него содрали кожу." ("Thomas I was secretly killed by his two sons Stefan and Radivoi in 1460. Stefan took the throne. Radivoi, angry at his brother for stealing power, made known the horrible secret and escaped to Turkey to Mohammed II. Stefan, on the encouragement of the papal legate, decided to fight the Turks. He was defeated and escaped to Kliuch city, where Mohammed laid siege. Taken prisoner, he refused to convert to Islam and was flayed alive.")

Pushkin's poem is written in the accentual verse that he derived from Vostokov's 1820s translations of Serbian folklore from Karadžić's collection (see Gusev, 35). Vostokov had studied Russian folklore and done an impressive if not perfect imitation of its unusual rhythms (Gasparov 1976, 17–22). In Russian versification this is sometimes called a three-ictus "тактовик," a form in which each line has three metrical stresses (there may be a fourth stress – often either on the first syllable of the line or on a syllable adjacent to another stress – but it is minimized when the line is actually pronounced). The intervals between the metrical stresses range from one to three syllables. Individual lines may sometimes scan as syllabo-tonic (e.g., trochaic pentameter, amphibrachic trimeter), but at its most free, only the "тактовик" can explain the fluidity of the rhythm. See Gasparov (1984, 129) and Scherr (161–62), who prefers to call this "strict accentual verse." In keeping with Russian folkloric tradition, the poem is not rhymed, but the cadences are all feminine; most lines begin with two unstressed syllables followed by a stressed syllable.

The texts (and notes) from *La Guzla* cited below come from the 1827 edition that Pushkin used. Mérimée put the numbers above each paragraph; in the interests of saving space, they are placed before the paragraph here.

La vision de Thomas II, roi de Bosnie[1]

1. Le roi Thomas se promène dans sa chambre, il se promène à grands pas, tandis que ses soldats dorment couchés sur leurs armes; mais lui il ne peut dormir, car les infidèles assiégent <sic> sa ville, et Mahomet veut envoyer sa tête à la grande mosquée de Constantinople.

2. Et souvent il se penche en dehors de la fenêtre pour écouter s'il n'entend point quelque bruit; mais la chouette seule pleure au-dessus de son palais, parce qu'elle prévoit que bientôt elle sera obligée de chercher une autre demeure pour ses petits.

3. Ce n'est point la chouette qui cause ce bruit étrange; ce n'est point la lune qui éclaire ainsi les vitraux de l'église de Kloutch; mais dans l'église de Kloutch résonnent les tambours et les trompettes, et les torches allumées ont changé la nuit en un jour éclatant.

4. Et autour du grand roi Thomas dorment ses fidèles serviteurs, et nulle autre oreille que la sienne n'a entendu ce bruit effrayant; seul il sort de sa chambre son sabre à la main, car il a vu que le ciel lui envoyait un avertissement de l'avenir.

5. D'une main ferme il a ouvert la porte de l'église; mais, quand il vit ce qui était dans le choeur, son courage fut sur le point de l'abandonner: il a pris de sa main gauche une amulette d'une vertu éprouvée, et, plus tranquille alors, il entra dans la grande église de Kloutch.

6. Et la vision qu'il y vit est bien étrange: le pavé de l'église était jonché de

morts et le sang coulait comme les torren<t>s qui descendent, en automne, dans les vallées du Prologh; et, pour avancer dans l'église, il était obligé d'enjamber des cadavres et de s'enfoncer dans le sang jusqu'à la cheville.

7. Et ces cadavres étaient ceux de ses fidèles serviteurs, et ce sang était le sang des Chrétiens. Une sueur froide coulait le long de son dos et ses dents s'entrechoquaient d'horreur. Au milieu du choeur, il vit des Turcs et des Tartares armés avec les *Bogou-mili*,[2] ces renégats!

8. Et près de l'autel profané était Mahomet au mauvais oeil, et son sabre était rougi jusqu'à la garde; devant lui était Thomas Ier,[3] qui fléchissait le genouil et qui présentait sa couronne humblement à l'ennemi de la chrétienté.

9. A genoux aussi était le traître Radivoï,[4] un turban sur la tête; d'une main il tenait la corde dont il étrangla son père, et de l'autre il prenait la robe du vicaire de Satan,[5] et il l'approchait de ses lèvres pour la baiser, ainsi que fait un esclave qui vient d'être bâtonné.

10. Et Mahomet daigna sourire, et il prit la couronne, puis il la brisa sous ses pieds, et il dit: «Radivoï, je te donne ma Bosnie à gouverner, et je veux que ces chiens te nomment leur Beglierbey.»[6] Et Radivoï se prosterna, et il baisa la terre inondée de sang.

11. Et Mahomet appela son visir: «Visir, que l'on donne un caftan[7] à Radivoï. Le caftan qu'il portera sera plus précieux que le brocard de Venise; car c'est de la peau de Thomas écorché que son frère va se revêtir.» Et le visir répondit: «Entendre c'est obéir.»[8]

12. Et le bon Roi Thomas sentit les mains des mécréan<t>s déchirer ses habits, et leurs ataghans fendaient sa peau, et de leurs doigts et de leurs dents ils tiraient cette peau, et ainsi ils la lui ôtèrent jusqu'aux ongles des pieds,[9] et de cette peau Radivoï se revêtit avec joie.

13. Alors Thomas s'écria: «Tu es juste, mon Dieu! tu punis un fils parricide; de mon corps dispose à ton gré; mais daigne prendre pitié de mon ame <sic>, ô divin Jésus!» A ce nom, l'église a tremblé; les fantômes s'évanouirent et les flambeaux s'éteignirent tout d'un coup.

14. Avez-vous vu une étoile brillante parcourir le ciel d'un vol rapide et éclairer la terre au loin. Bientôt ce brillant météore disparaît dans la nuit, et les ténèbres reviennent plus sombres qu'auparavant: telle disparut la vision de Thomas.

15. A tâtons il regagna la porte de l'église; l'air était pur et la lune dorait les toits d'alentour. Tout était calme, et le roi aurait pu croire que la paix régnait encore à Kloutch, quand une bombe[10] lancée par le mécréant vint tomber devant lui et donna le signal de l'assaut.

Notes

1. Il faut se rappeler ici la note de la ballade précédente, qui contient un précis des événemen<t>s qui amenèrent la fin du royaume de Bosnie.
2. Les Paterniens. *Vid. ut suprà.*
3. Le père de Thomas II.
4. Son frère, qui l'avait aidé à commettre son parricide.
5. Mahomet II.
6. Ce mot signifie seigneur des seigneurs. C'est le titre du Pacha de Bosnie. Radivoï n'en fut jamais revêtu, et Mahomet se garda bien de laisser en Bosnie un seul des rejetons de la famille royale.

7. On sait que le grand-seigneur fait présent d'un riche *caftan* ou pelisse, aux grands dignitaires au moment où ils vont prendre possession de leurs gouvernemen<t>s.

8. Proverbe des esclaves turcs qui reçoivent un ordre.

9. Thomas II fut en effet écorché vif.

10. Maglanovich avait vu des bombes et des mortiers, mais il ignorait que l'invention de ces instrumens de destruction était bien postérieure à Mahomet II.

---

9 ночна́я птица – night bird. As we learn in line 13, this is a paraphrase for "сова" ("owl"), which in fact is present only in the protagonist's imagination.

10 беду́ немину́чу (=неминучую) – an unavoidable calamity

12 горемы́чных – unfortunate, long-suffering

13 Ключе-гра́де – the city of Kliuch. It is not clear that such a city ever existed. Mérimée's "Kloutch" may refer to Cluj, Romania, but Pushkin would probably not have recognized this, since in Russian that city is called "Клуж."

23 Ужасом в нем за́мерло се́рдце – His heart stopped beating in horror

30 по щи́колку – ankle. In a note, Pushkin points out that this is a Moscow pronunciation of щи́колодка (in modern Russian "щи́колотка").

33 *богуми́лы* – schismatics. The word (and explanatory footnote) come from Mérimée.

34 На амво́не – at the pulpit

35 на́-голо – at the ready (a phrase used with sabers, etc.)

37 С вострия́ (=С острия) – from the blade

38 неза́пный (=внезапный) – sudden

45 Басурма́нскою чалмо́ю – with an infidel turban

49 Как холо́п, нака́занный *фала́нгой* – Like a servant punished by having his heels whipped. Pushkin himself glosses the italicized word.

50 безбо́жный – godless (in this context this is synonymous with "not Christian")

54 Для гяу́р-христия́н беглербе́ем – <Be a> Begler Bey for the infidel-Christians. A Begler Bey was a title of certain governors-general in the Turkish provinces. Mérimée also uses (and glosses) the word.

62 Бусурма́не (=Басурмане) – infidels (Muslims)

64 Атага́ном (=Ятаганом) – yataghan. A double-curved Turkish saber. The word occurs repeatedly in the *Guzla*, where Mérimée glosses its first usage (in the opening poem "L'aubépine de Veliko," note 8).

69 взмоли́лся – began to pray

77 Коё-как – barely; with difficulty. This form, rather than the standard Russian "кое-как," is presumably used to give the text a Serbian flavor.

81 бомба – a bomb. Pushkin takes the word from Mérimée, noting (as Mérimée had) that it is anachronistic in the context of the fifteenth century.

2. Янко Марна́вич – Janco Marnavich

The source of the poem is Mérimée's *Guzla* ("La flamme de Perrussich," 117–23). Pushkin's stanzas of unequal length generally correspond to the breaks marked by numbers in Mérimée's text.

The versification is, as in the previous poem, a three-ictus "тактовик."

La flamme de Perrussich. Par Hyacinthe Maglanovich.

1. Pourquoi le bey Janco Marnavich n'est-il jamais dans son pays? Pourquoi voyage-t-il dans les âpres montagnes de Vergoraz, ne couchant jamais deux nuits sous le même toit? Ses ennemis le poursuivent-ils et ont-ils juré que le prix du sang ne serait jamais reçu?

2. Non. Le bey Janco est riche et puissant. Personne n'oserait se dire son ennemi, car à sa voix plus de deux cents sabres sortiraient du fourreau. Mais il cherche les lieux déserts et se plaît dans les cavernes qu'habitent les Heyduques; car son cœur est livré à la tristesse depuis que son pobratime[1] est mort.

3. Cyrille Pervan est mort au milieu d'une fête. L'eau-de-vie a coulé à grands flots et les hommes sont devenus fous. Une dispute s'est élevée entre deux beys de renom, et le bey Janco Marnavich a tiré son pistolet sur son ennemi; mais l'eau-de-vie a fait trembler sa main, et il a tué son pobratime Cyrille Pervan.

4. Dans l'église de Perrussich ils s'étaient juré de vivre et de mourir ensemble; mais deux mois après avoir prêté ce serment, l'un des pobratimi est mort par la main de son frère. Le bey Janco depuis ce jour ne boit plus de vin ni d'eau-de-vie; il ne mange que des racines, et il court çà et là, comme un bœuf effrayé du taon.

5. Enfin, il est revenu dans son pays, et il est entré dans l'église de Perrussich: là, pendant tout un jour, il a prié, étendu, les bras en croix sur le pavé, et versant des larmes amères. Mais quand la nuit est venue, il est retourné dans sa maison, et il semblait plus calme, et il a soupé, servi par sa femme et ses enfan<t>s.

6. Et quand il se fut couché, il appela sa femme et lui dit: «De la montagne de Pristeg, peux-tu voir l'église de Perrussich?» Et elle regarda à la fenêtre et dit: «La Morpolazza est couverte de brouillard, et je ne puis rien voir de l'autre côté». Et le bey Janco dit: «Bon, recouche-toi près de moi» et il pria dans son lit pour l'âme de Cyrille Pervan.

7. Et quand il eut prié, il dit à sa femme: «Ouvre la fenêtre et regarde du côté de Perrussich.» Aussitôt sa femme s'est levée et elle dit: «De l'autre côté de la Morpolazza, au milieu du brouillard, je vois une lumière pâle et tremblotante.» Alors le bey a souri, et il dit: «Bon, recouche-toi» et il prit son chapelet et se remit à prier.

8. Quand il eut dit son chapelet, il appela sa femme et lui dit: «Prascovie, ouvre encore la fenêtre et regarde.» Et elle se leva et dit: «Seigneur, je vois au milieu de la rivière une lumière brillante[2] qui chemine rapidement de ce côté.» Alors elle entendit un grand soupir et quelque chose qui tombait sur le plancher. Le bey Janco était mort.

Notes

1. L'amitié est en grand honneur parmi les Morlaques, et il est encore assez commun que deux hommes s'engagent l'un à l'autre par une espèce de fraternité nouvelle. Il y a dans les rituels illyriques des prières destinées à bénir cette union de deux amis qui jurent de s'aider et de se défendre l'un l'autre toute leur vie. Deux hommes unis par cette cérémonie religieuse s'appellent en illyrique *pobratimi*, et les femmes *posestrime*, c'est-à-dire, demi-frères, demi-sœurs. Souvent on voit les pobratimi sacrifier leur vie l'un pour l'autre; et, si quelque querelle

survenait entre eux, ce serait un scandale aussi grand que si, chez nous, un fils maltraitait son père. Cependant, comme les Morlaques aiment beaucoup les liqueurs fortes et qu'ils oublient quelquefois dans l'ivresse leurs sermen<t>s d'amitié, les assistans ont grand soin de s'entremettre entre les pobratimi, afin d'empêcher les querelles toujours funestes dans un pays où tous les hommes sont armés.

J'ai vu à Knin une jeune fille morlaque mourir de douleur d'avoir perdu son amie, qui avait péri malheureusement en tombant d'une fenêtre.

2. L'idée qu'une flamme bleuâtre voltige autour des tombeaux et annonce la présence de l'âme d'un mort, est commune à plusieurs peuples, et est généralement reçue en Illyrie.

Le style de cette ballade est touchant par sa simplicité, qualité assez rare dans les poésies illyriques de nos jours.

---

1 бей – bey. This is a Turkish term of respect along the lines of "lord" or "sir."
4 Под однóю кровлей – under the same roof
5 Али = Или
могýчи (= могучие) – powerful
6 Аль = Или
9 гайдýк – haiduk. A historical term among the South Slavs for patriotic outlaws fighting against Turkish dominion.
11 братовáлись – took vows of brotherhood. Pushkin's footnote to this line follows Mérimée's.
16 мéду и горелки – of mead and vodka
18 побранúлись – fought
19 из своегó пистóля – from his pistol. The more common Russian word would be "пистолет."
21 супротúвника (= противника) – enemy
24 Словно вол, ужáленный змиёю – Like an ox bitten by a snake. In modern Russian, the form would be "змеёй."
35 На дворé – outside
51 сия́нье – a radiance. Pushkin omits Mérimée's second note, which explains that a flame hovering next to tombs indicates the presence of the soul of a dead person.

3. Битва у Зенúцы-Велúкой – The Battle at Great Zenitza

A rendering of Mérimée's "Le combat de Zenitza-Velika" (129–33). Pushkin's note about the obscurity of the poem's origins follows Mérimée's more florid note to the same effect.

Pushkin uses the same three-ictus "тактовик" (unrhymed, feminine cadences) as in the previous poems. The poem is astrophic, which follows Mérimée's lead, as this is one of the few poems in the *Guzla* not broken down into numbered paragraphs.

Le combat de Zenitza-Velika[1]

Le grand bey Radivoï a mené les braves avec lui pour livrer bataille aux infidèles. Quand les Dalmates[2] ont vu nos étendards de soie jaune, ils ont relevé leurs moustaches et ils ont mis leurs bonnets sur l'oreille, et ils ont dit: «Nous aussi nous voulons tuer des mécréan<t>s, et nous rapporterons leurs têtes dans notre pays.» Le bey Radivoï répondit: «Dieu y ait part!» Aussitôt nous avons passé la Cettina et nous avons brûlé toutes les villes et tous les villages de ces chiens circoncis, et quand nous trouvions des juifs, nous les pendions aux arbres.[3] Le beglier-bey est parti de Banialouka[4] avec deux mille Bosniaques pour nous livrer bataille; mais aussitôt que leurs sabres courbés ont brillé au soleil, aussitôt que leurs chevaux ont henni sur la colline de Zenitza-Velika, les Dalmates, ces misérables poltrons, ont pris la fuite et nous ont abandonnés. Alors nous nous sommes serrés en rond et nous avons environné le brave bey Radivoï. «Seigneur, nous ne vous quitterons pas comme ces lâches; mais, Dieu aidant et la sainte Vierge, nous rentrerons dans notre pays, et nous raconterons cette grande bataille à nos enfants.» Puis nous avons brisé nos fourreaux.[5] Chaque homme de notre armée en valait dix, et nos sabres étaient rougis depuis la pointe jusqu'à la garde. Mais, comme nous espérions repasser la Cettina, le selichtar[6] Mehemet est venu fondre sur nous avec mille cavaliers. «Braves gens, a dit le bey Radivoï, ces chiens sont trop nombreux, nous ne pourrons leur échapper. Que ceux qui ne sont pas blessés tâchent de gagner les bois; ainsi ils échapperont aux cavaliers du selichtar.» Lorsqu'il eut fini de parler, il se trouva avec vingt hommes seulement, mais tous, ses cousins; et tant qu'ils ont vécu, ils ont défendu le bey leur chef. Quand dix-neuf eurent été tués, Thomas, le plus jeune, dit au bey: «Monte sur ce cheval blanc comme la neige; il passera la Cettina et te ramènera dans notre pays.» Mais le bey a refusé de fuir, et il s'est assis par terre les jambes croisées. Alors est venu le selichtar Mehemet qui lui a tranché la tête.

Notes

1. J'ignore à quelle époque eut lieu l'action qui a fourni le sujet de ce petit poëme, et le joueur de guzla qui me l'a récité, ne put me donner d'autres informations, si ce n'est qu'il le tenait de son père et que c'était une ballade fort ancienne.

2. Les Dalmates sont détestés par les Morlaques, et le leur rendent bien. On verra par la suite que l'auteur attribue à la trahison des Dalmates la perte de la bataille.

3. Les Juifs sont dans ce pays l'objet de la haine des Chrétiens et des Turcs, et dans toutes les guerres ils étaient traités avec la dernière rigueur. Ils étaient et sont encore aussi malheureux que le poisson volant, pour me servir de l'ingénieuse comparaison de sir Walter Scott.

4. Banialouka a été pendant long-temps <sic> la résidence du beglier-bey de Bosnie. Bosna Seraï est maintenant la capitale de ce pachalik.

5. Usage illyrien. C'est un serment de vaincre ou mourir.

6. Selichtar, mot turc qui veut dire *porte-épée*; c'est une des principales charges de la cour d'un Pacha.

---

1 жёлтое знамя – yellow banner

2 на бусурмáна (= басурмана) – against the infidel (a common usage of singular instead of the understood plural)

3 далмáты – Dalmatians (people from Dalmatia). As Pushkin's note 10 (itself a truncated version of a Mérimée note) indicates, the Dalmatians were disliked by the Montenegrins, who in this poem attribute their loss to Dalmatian cowardice (or treachery).

5 На бекре́нь (= набекрень) – aslant. Hats worn in this fashion traditionally indicate a daring attitude of the wearer.
7 воева́ть бусурма́нов (= басурманов) – to fight the infidels. The use of accusative with the verb "воевать" is substandard.
10 запове́дную речку – the forbidden river
12 жидо́в на дере́вьях вешать – to hang the Yids on trees. Pushkin again uses Mérimée's note. The Walter Scott reference is to chapter 6 of *Ivanhoe*: "His doubts might have been indeed pardoned; for, except perhaps the flying fish, there was no race existing on the earth, in the air, or the waters, who were the object of such an unintermitting, general, and relentless persecution as the Jews of this period."
13 Беглербе́й со свои́ми бошня́ками – The Begler Bey (see note to line 54 of "Видение короля") and his Bosnians
14 из Банялу́ки – from Banja Luka. Pushkin retains Mérimée's note.
24 Всяк из на́с троих во́инов сто́ил – Each of us was worth three warriors. The ordinary stress on "трои́х" is omitted for metrical reasons (because there are only three stresses in each line and because the subsequent syllable takes stress).
29 Селихта́р – Swordsman. Pushkin curtails Mérimée's note, which mentions that the word is Turkish in origin, a fact that would presumably be obvious to Pushkin's readers.
37 родны́е Родиво́ю – kin to Rodivoi
41 На коня́ моего́ вороно́го – On my black steed. In the French it is a "horse white as snow" ("ce cheval blanc comme la neige"). Pushkin changes it to a standard Russian epithet for a (noble) horse.
42 вплавь – swimming
43 вымчит – quickly take away

4. Феодор и Еле́на – Feodor and Helena

A translation of Mérimée's "La belle Hélène" (77–89). The meter is again the three-ictus "тактовик."

Pushkin begins with dots because he omits the opening passage of Mérimée's text. (The dots in the French text below are those of Mérimée.)

La belle Hélène

Première partie.

1. Asseyez-vous autour de Jean Bietko, vous tous qui voulez savoir l'histoire lamentable de la belle Hélène et de Théodore Khonopka, son mari. Jean Bietko est le meilleur joueur de guzla que vous ayez entendu et que vous entendrez jamais.

2. Théodore Khonopka était un hardi chasseur du temps de mon grand-père, de qui je tiens cette histoire. Il épousa la belle Hélène, qui le préféra à Piero Stamati,[1] parce que Théodore était beau et que Piero était laid et méchant.

3. Piero Stamati s'en est venu un jour à la maison de Théodore Khonopka: «Hélène, est-il vrai que votre mari est parti pour Venise et qu'il doit y rester un an?» – «Il est vrai, et j'en suis tout affligée, parce que je vais rester seule dans cette grande maison.» –

4. «Ne pleurez pas, Hélène, de rester seule à la maison. Il viendra quelqu'un pour vous tenir compagnie. Laissez-moi dormir avec vous, et je vous donnerai une grosse poignée de beaux sequins luisan<t>s, que vous attacherez à vos cheveux qui sont si noirs.» –

5. «Arrière de moi, méchant! .... ?» – «Mais, dit le méchant Stamati, laissez-moi dormir avec vous, et je vous donnerai une robe de velours avec autant de sequins qu'il en peut tenir dans le fond de mon bonnet.» –

6. «Arrière de moi, méchant! ou je dirai ta perfidie à mes frères, qui te feront mourir.»............................... Or, Stamati était un petit vieillard camus et rabougri, et Hélène était grande et forte.

7. Bien lui prit d'être grande et forte.................................... Stamati est tombé sur le dos, et il est rentré dans sa maison pleurant, les genoux à demi ployés, et chancelant..

8. Il est allé trouver un juif impie, et lui a demandé comment il se vengerait d'Hélène? Le juif lui a dit: «Cherche sous la pierre d'une tombe, jusqu'à ce que tu trouves un crapaud noir;[2] alors tu me l'apporteras dans un pot de terre.»

9. Il lui apporta un crapaud noir trouvé sous la pierre d'une tombe, et il lui a versé de l'eau sur la tête et a nommé cette bête Jean. C'était un bien grand crime de donner à un crapaud noir le nom d'un si grand apôtre!

10. Alors ils ont lardé le crapaud avec la pointe de leurs ataghans, jusqu'à ce qu'un venin subtil sortit de toutes les piqûres; et ils ont recueilli ce venin dans une phiole et l'ont fait boire au crapaud. Ensuite ils lui ont fait lécher un beau fruit.

11. Et Stamati a dit à un jeune garçon qui le suivait: «Porte ce beau fruit à la belle Hélène et dis-lui que ma femme le lui envoie.» Le jeune garçon a porté le beau fruit, comme on le lui avait dit, et la belle Hélène l'a mangé tout entier avec une grande avidité.

12. Quand elle eut mangé ce fruit, qui avait une si belle couleur, elle se sentit toute troublée, et il lui sembla qu'un serpent remuait dans son ventre.

Que ceux qui veulent connaître la fin de cette histoire, donnent quelque chose à Jean Bietko.

Deuxième partie

1. Quand la belle Hélène eut mangé ce fruit, elle fit le signe de la croix, mais elle n'en sentit pas moins quelque chose qui s'agitait dans son ventre. Elle appela sa sœur, qui lui dit de boire du lait; mais elle sentait toujours comme un serpent.

2. Voilà que son ventre a commencé à gonfler peu à peu, tous les jours davantage; si bien que les femmes disaient: «Hélène est grosse; mais comment cela se fait-il, car son mari est absent? Il est allé à Venise, il y a plus de dix mois.»

3. Et la belle Hélène était toute honteuse et n'osait lever la tête, encore

moins sortir dans la rue. Mais elle restait assise et pleurait tout le long du jour et toute la nuit encore. Et elle disait à sa sœur: «Que deviendrai-je quand mon mari reviendra?»

4. Quand son voyage eut duré un an, Théodore Khonopka pensa à revenir. Il monta sur une galère bien dorée et il est revenu heureusement dans son pays. Ses voisins et ses amis sont venus à sa rencontre, vêtus de leurs plus beaux habits.

5. Mais il eut beau regarder dans la foule, il ne vit pas la belle Hélène; et alors il demanda: «Qu'est devenue la belle Hélène, ma femme, pourquoi n'est-elle pas ici?» Ses voisins se prirent à sourire; ses amis rougirent; mais pas un ne répondit.[3]

6. Quand il est entré dans sa maison, il a trouvé sa femme assise sur un coussin. «Levez-vous, Hélène.» Elle s'est levée, et il a vu son ventre qui était si gros. «Qu'est-ce cela? il y a plus d'un an, Hélène, que je n'ai dormi avec vous?» –

7. «Mon Seigneur, je vous le jure par le nom de la bienheureuse vierge Marie, je vous suis restée fidèle; mais on m'a jeté un sort qui m'a fait enfler le ventre.» Mais il ne l'a point crue, il a tiré son sabre et lui a coupé la tête d'un seul coup.

8. Lorsqu'elle eut la tête coupée, il dit: «Cet enfant qui est dans son sein perfide n'est point coupable: je veux le tirer de son sein et l'élever. Je verrai à qui il ressemble, et ainsi je connaîtrai quel est le traître qui est son père, et je le tuerai.»

8 (*Variante*).[4] (Lorsqu'elle eut la tête coupée il dit: «Je veux le tirer de son sein perfide et l'exposer dans le pays, comme pour le faire mourir. Alors son père viendra le chercher, et par ce moyen je reconnaîtrai le traître qui est son père, et je le tuerai.»)

9. Il a ouvert son beau sein si blanc, et voilà qu'au lieu d'un enfant il n'a trouvé qu'un crapaud noir. «Hélas! hélas! qu'ai-je fait, dit-il; j'ai tué la belle Hélène, qui ne m'avait point trahi; mais on lui avait jeté un sort avec un crapaud!»

10. Il a ramassé la tête de sa chère femme et l'a baisée. Soudain cette tête froide a rouvert les yeux, ses lèvres ont tremblé, et elle a dit: «Je suis innocente, mais des enchanteurs m'ont ensorcelée par vengeance avec un crapaud noir.»

11. «Parce que je te suis restée fidèle, Piero Stamati m'a jeté un sort, aidé par un méchant juif, qui habite dans la vallée des tombeaux.» Alors la tête a fermé les yeux, sa langue s'est glacée, et jamais elle ne reparla.

12. Théodore Khonopka a cherché Piero Stamati et lui a coupé la tête. Il a tué aussi le méchant juif, et il a fait dire trente messes pour le repos de l'ame <sic> de sa femme. Que Dieu lui fasse miséricorde et à toute la compagnie.

Notes

1. Ce nom est italien. Les Morlaques aiment beaucoup à faire jouer aux Italiens un rôle odieux. *Pasa vjerro*, foi de chien, et *Lantzmantzka vjerro*, foi d'Italien, sont deux injures synonymes.

2. C'est une croyance populaire de tous les pays que le crapaud est un animal venimeux.

On voit dans l'histoire d'Angleterre qu'un roi fut empoisonné par un moine avec de l'ale dans laquelle il avait noyé un crapaud.

3. Ce passage est remarquable par sa simplicité et sa concision énergique.

4. J'ai entendu chanter cette ballade de ces deux manières.

---

1 Стама́ти – The name is stressed on the second syllable. In a note that Pushkin did not retain, Mérimée explains that the name is Italian and points out that Italians often play the role of the villain in Montenegrin folklore.

4 Охая да хрома́я – groaning and limping

5 По дело́м (=поделом) тебе, ста́рый бессты́дник – Serves you right, you shameless old man. (In this line the тебе́ is not stressed because it is adjacent to a major metrical stress (ста́рый).

6 Ай да баба! – Way to go, gal!

7 думать думу – to think a thought. (Such repetition is common in Russian folklore.)

9 к жиду́ лиходе́ю – to the evildoer, the Yid

15 жабу – a toad. Pushkin's note to the line repeats that of Mérimée.

19–20 христиа́нское имя / Нарещи́ тако́й пога́ной тва́ри – to give a Christian name to such a heathen creature. "Нарещи" is an archaic infinitive form of an archaic verb ("наречь"). Pushkin uses it to impart a foreign (Serbian) quality to the phrase.

31 бедной молоди́це – to the poor young woman

38 баить (=баять) – to say

39 Каково́-то будет е́й от му́жа – What will her husband do to her

40 Как – When. The use of "как" instead of "когда" is typically folkloric.

42 выдти = выйти

47 Вороти́лся на свою́ сторо́нку – returned to his homeland

76 понапра́сну (=напрасно) – for no reason

82 провеща́ла – spoke

89 И отпе́л по жене́ панихи́ду – And sang a requiem for his wife

5. Влах в Вене́ции – The Wallach in Venice

A translation of Mérimée's "Le Morlaque à Venise" (43–47). In the preface to the *Guzla* (viii), the anonymous author claims that his mother was a Morlaque and adds a note explaining that this is the term for the inhabitants of Dalmatia who speak either Slavic or Illyrian. Pushkin's translation "влах" ("Wallach") is, according to the *Словарь языка Пушкина*, a member of a Serbian tribe who lives in the mountains of Dalmatia.

The meter is the three-ictus "тактовик." Pushkin's six stanzas correspond to the six paragraphs of the French text.

Le Morlaque à Venise[1]

1. Quand Prascovie m'eut abandonné, quand j'étais triste et sans argent, un rusé Dalmate vint dans ma montagne et me dit: Vas <sic> à cette grande ville des eaux, les sequins y sont plus communs que les pierres dans ton pays.

2. Les soldats sont couverts d'or et de soie: et ils passent leur temps dans toutes sortes de plaisirs: quand tu auras gagné de l'argent à Venise, tu reviendras dans ton pays avec une veste galonnée d'or et des chaînes d'argent à ton hanzar.[2]

3. Et alors, ô Dmitri! quelle jeune fille ne s'empressera pas de t'appeler de sa fenêtre et de te jeter son bouquet quand tu auras accordé ta guzla? Monte sur mer, crois-moi, et viens à la grande ville, tu y deviendras riche assurément.

4. Je l'ai cru, insensé que j'étais, et je suis venu dans ce grand navire de pierres; mais l'air m'étouffe, et leur pain est un poison pour moi. Je ne puis aller où je veux; je ne puis faire ce que je veux: je suis comme un chien à l'attache.

5. Les femmes se rient de moi quand je parle la langue de mon pays, et ici les gens de nos montagnes ont oublié la leur, aussi bien que nos vieilles coutumes: je suis un arbre transplanté en été, je sèche et je meurs.

6. Dans ma montagne, lorsque je rencontrais un homme, il me saluait en souriant, et me disait: Dieu soit avec toi, fils d'Alexis; Mais ici je ne rencontre pas une figure amie, je suis comme une fourmi jetée par le vent au milieu d'un vaste étang.

Notes

1. La république de Venise entretenait à sa solde un corps de soldats nommés esclavons. Un ramassis de Morlaques, Dalmates, Albanais, composait cette troupe très- méprisée à Venise, ainsi que tout ce qui était militaire. Le sujet de cette ballade semble être un jeune Morlaque malheureux en amour et qui s'est laissé enrôler dans un moment de dépit.

Ce chant est fort ancien, à en juger par quelques expressions, maintenant hors d'usage et dont peu de vieillards peuvent encore donner le sens. Au reste, rien n'est plus commun que d'entendre chanter à un joueur de guzla des paroles dont il lui serait impossible de donner une explication quelconque. Ils apprennent par cœur fort jeunes ce qu'ils ont entendu chanter à leur père et le répètent comme un perroquet redit sa leçon. Il est malheureusement bien rare aujourd'hui de trouver des poètes illyriens qui ne copient personne et qui s'efforcent de conserver une belle langue, dont l'usage diminue tous les jours.

2. Grand couteau qui sert de poignard au besoin.

---

1 Как – When

2 промотáлся – went broke (i.e., spent all my money)

3 Вот далмáт – Then a Dalmatian. This is presumably a speaker of Dalmatian (a Romance language, now extinct) as against a Slav. As in "Битва у Зеницы-Великой," a Dalmatian is the villain.

4 Ступай, Дми́трий, в морскóй ты гóрод – Go, Dimitri, to the sea city (i.e., Venice). The inserted "ты" (unnecessary in ordinary Russian) is a folklorism, especially given its unusual syntactic placement. It also serves to avoid the problem of consecutive stresses, which folkloric verse does not tolerate. For this same reason, the beginning of the line would omit the usual stress on "Ступáй." (One could conceivably read that opening by including this stress, but omitting the subsequent stress on "Дмитрий." This is less probable, given the strong tendency in these verses to have the initial line stress fall on the third syllable.)

5 Там цехи́ны, что у нáс камéнья – There they have zecchini like we have

stones. Or, more idiomatically: the streets are paved with gold. A zecchino was an old Venetian coin. The use of "что" for "как" is markedly folkloric.

9 в ши́том долима́не – in an embroidered dolman. A dolman (sometimes written as "doliman") is a long robe with long sleeves, worn by Turks.

11 игра́й себе на гу́слях – just go and play on your guzla. The "себе" is not a reflexive pronoun, but a particle used in colloquial speech that emphasizes that the action is done freely. Pushkin uses "гусли" to translate the French "guzla," but the instruments are clearly different. The Russian "гусли" had many strings, was plucked, and was associated with ancient times, whereas the guzla that Mérimée describes has a single string, is bowed, and was still played in the nineteenth century.

14 отправля́йся морем – set off by sea

17 в этой мраморной лодке – in that marble ship (presumably a metaphor for Venice; in the French it is a "ship of stone," which Pushkin followed in his first publication of this poem, writing: "в этой каменной лодке")

25 Как у на́с быва́ло кого встре́чу – When I used to meet someone at home (in my country)

29 мура́шка – a tiny ant (i.e., completely insignificant)

6. Гайду́к Хризич – The Haiduk Khrizich

A translation of Mérimée's "Les Braves Heyduques" (67–71).

Pushkin uses the three-ictus "тактовик," though in a few lines (e.g., 36–37) with more than three unstressed syllables between the ictuses. The poem is astrophic, following Mérimée's text, which is not broken down into paragraphs (as in "Битва у Зеницы-Великой").

Les braves Heyduques[1]

Dans une caverne, couché sur des cailloux aigus, est un brave Heyduque, Christich Mladin. A côté de lui est sa femme, la belle Catherine; à ses pieds ses deux braves fils. Depuis trois jours ils sont dans cette caverne sans manger; car leurs ennemis gardent tous les passages de la montagne, et s'ils lèvent la tête, cent fusils se dirigent contre eux. Ils ont tellement soif, que leur langue est noire et gonflée; car ils n'ont pour boire qu'un peu d'eau croupie dans le creux d'un rocher. Cependant pas un n'a osé faire entendre une plainte,[2] car ils craignaient de déplaire à Christich Mladin. Quand trois jours furent écoulés, Catherine s'écria: «Que la sainte Vierge ait pitié de vous, et qu'elle vous venge de vos ennemis!» Alors elle a poussé un soupir et elle est morte. Christich Mladin a regardé le cadavre d'un œil sec; mais ses deux fils essuyaient leurs larmes quand leur père ne les regardait pas. Le quatrième jour est venu, et le soleil a tari l'eau croupie dans le creux du rocher. Alors Christich, l'aîné des fils de Mladin, est devenu fou: il a tiré son hanzar[3] et il regardait le cadavre de sa mère avec des yeux comme ceux d'un loup auprès d'un agneau. Alexandre, son frère cadet, eut horreur de lui; il a tiré son hanzar et s'est percé le bras: «Bois mon sang, Christich, et ne commets pas un crime:[4] quand nous serons tous morts de faim, nous reviendrons sucer le sang de nos ennemis.» Mladin s'est levé, il s'est écrié: «Enfants, debout! mieux vaut une belle balle que l'agonie de la faim.» Ils sont descendus tous les trois comme des loups enragés. Chacun a tué dix hommes, chacun a reçu dix balles dans la poitrine. Nos lâches ennemis leur ont coupé la tête, et quand ils la portaient en triomphe, ils osaient à peine la regarder, tant ils craignaient Christich Mladin et ses fils.[5]

Notes

1. On dit que Hyacinthe Maglanovich a fait cette belle ballade dans le temps où il menait lui-même la vie d'un heyduque, c'est-à-dire, à peu de chose près la vie d'un voleur de grand chemin.

2. Les Heyduques souffrent la douleur avec encore plus de courage que les Morlaques mêmes. J'ai vu mourir un jeune homme qui, s'étant laissé tomber du haut d'un rocher, avait eu les jambes et les cuisses fracturées en cinq ou six endroits. Pendant trois jours d'agonie il ne proféra pas une seule plainte; seulement lorsqu'une vieille femme qui avait, disait-on, des connaissances en chirurgie, voulut soulever ses membres brisés pour y appliquer je ne sais quelle drogue, je vis ses poings se contracter et ses sourcils épais se rapprocher d'une manière effrayante.

3. Grand couteau que les Morlaques ont toujours dans leur ceinture.

4. Ce mot rappelle celui de l'écuyer Breton au combat des trente: «Bois ton sang, Beaumanoir!»

5. Les soldats qui font la guerre aux Heyduques sont nommés Pandours. Leur réputation n'est guère meilleure que celle des brigands qu'ils poursuivent; car on les accuse de détrousser souvent les voyageurs qu'ils sont chargés de protéger. Ils sont fort méprisés dans le pays à cause de leur lâcheté. Souvent dix ou douze heyduques se sont fait jour au travers d'une centaine de Pandours. Il est vrai que la faim que ces malheureux endurent fréquemment est un aiguillon puissant pour exciter leur courage.

Lorsque les pandours ont fait un prisonnier, ils le conduisent d'une manière assez singulière. Après lui avoir ôté ses armes, ils se contentent de couper le cordon qui attache sa culotte, et la lui laissent pendre sur les jarrets. On sent que le pauvre heyduque est obligé de marcher très-lentement, de peur de tomber sur le nez.

---

2 гайдук Хри́зич – In Russian, the word "гайдук" is ordinarily stressed on the second syllable; in this line it is without stress because it is followed by an overdetermined invariant stress on the penultimate syllable of the line. Pushkin's note is mysterious; not all haiduks were leaders.

5 выдти = выйти

8 сорок ру́жей – forty guns

12 красно-солнце – the red sun (a standard folkloric epithet)

22 матерь = мать

30 Pushkin adds a note to this line about the belief in vampirism common among the South (he calls them "western") Slavs. Mérimée does not have such a note, mainly because he includes elsewhere in his book a lengthy excursus on the subject ("Sur le vampirisme," 135–56).

7. Похорóнная песня Иакúнфа Магланóвича – Hyacinthe Maglanovich's Funeral Song

A translation of Mérimée's "Chant de mort" (49–53), which was – according to Mérimée's note – an improvisation at a haiduk's burial by the great guzla player Hyacinthe Maglanovich (see Pushkin's note 18). Pushkin is unusually free in his treatment of the original. He omits the first refrain (section 4 of the French text), he shortens some passages and changes some of the proper names. In a note that Pushkin does not translate, Mérimée explains that it is customary to send messages to the dead using a recently deceased person as an intermediary.

Pushkin writes the poem in trochaic tetrameter (often used in Russian folkloric stylizations). The first and final stanzas are identical and use pair rhymes, the other stanzas all have alternating rhyme.

Chant de mort[1]

1. Adieu, adieu, bon voyage! Cette nuit la lune est dans son plein; on voit clair pour trouver son chemin, bon voyage!

2. Une balle vaut mieux que la fièvre: libre tu as vécu, libre tu es mort. Ton fils Jean t'a vengé; il en a tué cinq.

3. Nous les avons fait fuir depuis Tchaplissa jusqu'à la plaine; pas un n'a regardé derrière son épaule pour nous voir encore une fois.

4. Adieu, adieu, bon voyage! Cette nuit la lune est dans son plein; on voit clair à trouver son chemin, bon voyage!

5. Dis à mon père que je me porte bien,[2] que je ne me ressens plus de ma blessure, et que ma femme Hélène est accouchée d'un garçon.

6. Je l'ai appelé Wladin comme lui. Quand il sera grand, je lui apprendrai à tirer le fusil, à se comporter comme doit le faire un brave guerrier.

7. Chrusich a enlevé ma fille aînée, et elle est grosse de six mois. J'espère qu'elle accouchera aussi d'un garçon beau et fort.[3]

8. Twark a quitté le pays pour monter sur la mer; nous ne savons pas de ses nouvelles: peut-être le rencontreras-tu dans le pays où tu vas.

9. Tu as un sabre, une pipe et du tabac, avec un manteau de poil de chèvre:[4] en voilà bien assez pour faire un long voyage, où l'on n'a ni froid ni faim.

10. Adieu, adieu, bon voyage! Cette nuit la lune est dans son plein; on voit clair pour trouver son chemin. Bon voyage!

Notes

1. Ce chant a été improvisé par Maglanovich, à l'enterrement d'un heyduque son parent qui s'était brouillé avec la justice et fut tué par les Pandours.

2. Les parens et les amis du mort lui donnent toujours leurs commissions pour l'autre monde.

3. Jamais un père ne se fâche contre celui qui enlève sa fille, bien entendu lorsque tout se fait sans violence. (Voy. note 1, *L'Amante de Dannisich.*)

4. On enterre les heyduques avec leurs armes, leur pipe et les habits qu'ils portaient au moment de leur mort.

5 Пуля легче лихора́дки – a bullet is easier than a fever (i.e., a warrior's death is preferable to a death from illness)
16 хозя́йка – my wife (a folkloric use of the word)
19 Уж владе́ет атага́ном (= ятаганом) – He has already mastered the yataghan (see commentary to "Видение короля," line 64).
21 в Лизго́ре – in Lizgor. For mysterious reasons, Pushkin added this location to Mérimée's poem; such a place appears never to have existed (Yovanovitch, 504).

8. Марко Якубо́вич – Marko Iakubovich

A translation of Mérimée's "Constantin Yacoubovich" (177–85). Pushkin makes his source text far more obscure by omitting a central explanatory line of the French as well as the footnote to it: "A Greek who is buried in a Latin cemetery becomes a vampire, and vice versa." The change of the protagonist's name from "Constantin" to "Marko" is probably due to metrical necessity.

Constantin Yacoubovich

1. Constantin Yacoubovich était assis sur un banc devant sa porte: devant lui son enfant jouait avec un sabre; à ses pieds, sa femme Miliada était accroupie par terre.[1] Un étranger est sorti de la forêt et l'a salué, en lui prenant la main.

2. Sa figure est celle d'un jeune homme; mais ses cheveux sont blancs, ses yeux sont mornes, ses joues creuses, sa démarche chancelante. «Frère, a-t-il dit, j'ai bien soif et je voudrais boire." Aussitôt Miliada s'est levée et lui a vîte apporté de l'eau-de-vie et du lait.

3. – «Frère, quelle est cette éminence là-bas avec ces arbres verts?» – «N'es-tu donc jamais venu dans ce pays, dit Constantin Yacoubovich, que tu ne connaisses pas le cimetière de notre race?» – «Eh bien! c'est-là que je veux reposer, car je me sens mourir peu à peu.»

4. Alors il a détaché une large ceinture rouge, et il a montré une plaie sanglante. – «Depuis hier la balle d'un chien de mécréant me déchire la poitrine: je ne puis ni vivre ni mourir.» Alors Miliada l'a soutenu et Constantin Yacoubovich a sondé la blessure.

5. – «Triste, triste fut ma vie; triste sera ma mort. Mais sur le haut de ce tertre, dans cet endroit exposé au soleil, je veux que l'on m'enterre; car je fus un grand guerrier, quand ma main ne trouvait pas un sabre trop pesant pour elle.»

6. Et sa bouche a souri, et ses yeux sortaient de leur orbite: soudain il a penché la tête. Miliada s'écria: «Oh, Constantin, aide-moi! car cet étranger est trop pesant pour que je puisse le soutenir toute seule.» Et Constantin a reconnu qu'il était mort.

7. Puis il l'a chargé sur son cheval et l'a porté au cimetière, sans s'inquiéter si la terre latine souffrirait dans son sein le cadavre d'un Grec schisma-

tique.[2] Ils ont creusé sa fosse au soleil, et ils l'ont enterré avec son sabre et son hanzar, comme il convient à un guerrier.

8. Après une semaine, l'enfant de Constantin avait les lèvres pâles, et il pouvait à peine marcher. Il se couchait tout triste sur une natte, lui qui aimait tant à courir çà et là. Mais la Providence a conduit dans la maison de Constantin un saint hermite, son voisin.

9. «Ton enfant est malade d'une maladie étrange: vois sur son cou si blanc, cette tache rouge, c'est la dent d'un vampire.» Alors il a mis ses livres dans un sac, et il s'en est allé au cimetière, et il a fait ouvrir la fosse où l'on avait enterré l'étranger.

10. Or, son corps était frais et vermeil; sa barbe avait cru, et ses ongles étaient longs comme des serres d'oiseaux; sa bouche était sanglante, et sa fosse était inondée de sang. Alors Constantin a levé un pieu pour l'en percer; mais le mort a poussé un cri et s'est enfui dans les bois.

11. Et un cheval, quand les étriers lui coupent les flancs,[3] ne pourrait courir aussi vîte <sic> que ce monstre; et son impétuosité était telle, que les jeunes arbres se courbaient sous son corps, et que les grosses branches cassaient comme si elles eussent été gelées.

12. L'hermite a pris du sang et de la terre de la fosse, et en a frotté le corps de l'enfant; et Constantin et Miliada en ont fait autant; et le soir ils disaient: «C'est à cette heure que ce méchant étranger est mort.» Et comme ils parlaient, le chien a hurlé et s'est caché entre les jambes de son maître.

13. La porte s'est ouverte et un grand géant est entré en se baissant; il s'est assis les jambes croisées, et sa tête touchait les poutres de la maison; et il regardait Constantin en souriant, et celui-ci ne pouvait détourner les yeux, car il était fasciné par le vampire.

14. Mais l'hermite a ouvert son livre et il a jeté une branche de romarin dans le feu; puis, avec son souffle, il a dirigé la fumée contre le spectre, et l'a conjuré au nom de Jésus. Bientôt le vampire a tremblé et s'est élancé par la porte, comme un loup poursuivi par les chasseurs.

15. Le lendemain, à la même heure, le chien a hurlé et la porte s'est ouverte, et un homme est entré et s'est assis: sa taille était celle d'un soldat, et toujours ses yeux s'attachaient sur ceux de Constantin pour le fasciner; mais l'hermite l'a conjuré, et il s'est enfui.

16. Et le lendemain un petit nain est entré dans sa maison, et un rat aurait bien pu lui servir de monture. Toutefois ses yeux brillaient comme deux flambeaux, et son regard était funeste; mais l'hermite l'a conjuré pour la troisième fois, et il s'est enfui pour toujours.

Notes

1. Dans un ménage morlaque le mari couche sur un lit, s'il y en a un dans la maison, et la femme couche sur le plancher. C'est une des nombreuses preuves du mépris avec lequel sont traitées les femmes dans ce pays. Un mari ne cite jamais le nom de sa femme devant un étranger sans ajouter: *Da prostite, moya xena* (ma femme, sauf votre respect).

2. Un Grec enterré dans un cimetière latin devient vampire, et *vice versa*.

3. Les étriers turcs sont plats, assez semblables à des souliers, et tranchans sur les bords; ils servent ainsi d'éperons.

---

6 напи́ться – to quench his thirst
15 Отдыха́ть мне – I should rest
17 розви́л (=развил) – peeled away, twisted down
20 Бусурма́на (=басурмана) – of the infidel
21 Как=Когда
29 доле (=дольше) – any longer
32 коня́ вороно́го – black steed
40 на рого́же – on bast matting (a rough, inexpensive material used by peasants)
41 калуе́р – monk (in Serbian)
46 вурдала́ка – of a vampire. Pushkin glosses the word, which he introduces into the Russian language. (On the etymology and morphology, see Ivanov 1987, 31.) Mérimée gives the Illyrian word as "vudkodlak" on page 135.
55 коло́м замахну́лся – brandished a stake (in order to put it through the vampire)
63 моги́льною землёю (=могильной землей) – with earth from the grave. Pushkin's note is not found in Mérimée's poem, but it paraphrases a passage in the chapter "Sur le vampirisme" (137) in the *Guzla*: "Le remède le plus ordinaire contre une première attaque d'un vampire, est de se frotter tout le corps, et surtout la partie qu'il a sucée, avec le sang que contiennent ses veines, mêlé avec la terre de son tombeau." ("The most common remedy against the first attack of a vampire is to rub one's entire body and especially the part that was sucked, with the blood its veins contain, mixed with the earth from his grave.")
66 красного солнца – of the red sun (a common folkloric epithet)
79 запали́л – set fire to
87 це́сарский ре́крут – a recruit in the Austrian army. (In Russian, "цесарь" meant "Kaiser.")
89 про́гнал – chased away. As again in line 93, the stress falls on the first syllable for metrical reasons. (Ordinarily, the stress would fall on the second syllable.)

9. Бонапа́рт и черного́рцы – Bonaparte and the Montenegrins

A translation of Mérimée's "Les Monténégrins" (245–48), which Pushkin amplifies considerably. A note in Mérimée points out that this is simply local legend, made up by the proud Montenegrins. (Of course, it was in fact made up by Mérimée himself.) Pushkin omits the note, which has apparently made him a hero in Montenegro, where a Pushkin monument has been erected on the strength of this poem.

Pushkin renders the poem in trochaic tetrameter with alternating rhymes.

Les Monténégrins[1]

1. Napoléon a dit: «Quels sont ces hommes qui osent me résister? Je veux qu'ils viennent jeter à mes pieds leurs fusils et leurs ataghans ornés de nielles.»[2] Soudain il a envoyé à la montagne vingt mille soldats.

2. Il y a des dragons, des fantassins, des canons et des mortiers. «Venez à la montagne, vous y verrez cinq cents braves Monténégrins. Pour leurs canons, il y a des précipices; pour leurs dragons, des rochers, et pour leurs fantassins, cinq cents bons fusils.»

3. ....[3]

4. Ils sont partis: leurs armes luisaient au soleil: ils sont montés en ordre pour brûler nos villages; ils sont montés pour enlever dans leur pays nos femmes et nos enfan<t>s.[4] Quand ils sont arrivés au rocher gris, ils ont levé les yeux, et ils ont vu nos bonnets rouges.

5. Alors a dit leur capitaine: «Que chaque homme ajuste son fusil, que chaque homme tue un Monténégrin.» Aussitôt ils ont tiré et ils ont abattu nos bonnets rouges qui étaient plantés sur des piquets.[5] Mais nous, qui étions à plat ventre derrière eux, nous leur envoyâmes une vive fusillade.

6. «Ecoutez l'écho de nos fusils,» a dit le capitaine. Mais, avant qu'il se fût retourné, il est tombé mort et vingt-cinq hommes avec lui. Les autres ont pris la fuite, et jamais de leur vie ils n'osèrent regarder un bonnet rouge.

Celui qui a fait cette chanson était avec ses frères au rocher gris; il se nomme Guntzar Wossieratch.

Notes

1. Il n'est pas de petit peuple qui ne s'imagine que les regards de l'univers sont fixés sur lui. Du reste je crois que Napoléon ne s'est jamais beaucoup occupé des Monténégrins.

2. Ce sont des ornemens ciselés sur la poignée des armes précieuses, surtout sur les ataghans. On remplit les creux d'une composition d'un beau noir bleuâtre et dont le secret est, dit-on, perdu dans le Levant.

3. Ici manque une stance.

4. L'habitude de faire la guerre avec les Turcs faisait penser aux Monténégrins que toutes les nations exerçaient les mêmes atrocités dans leurs expéditions militaires.

5. Cette ruse fut fréquemment employée avec succès.

---

2 Бонапáрте – Napoleon Bonaparte. Note that it is spelled (and therefore pronounced) differently here than in the title. This is the Italian pronunciation, which was used along with the French in the early nineteenth century (Tolstoy uses both forms in *War and Peace*), perhaps to recall his Corsican origins and thus to signal disrespect.

3 Правда ль (=ли) – Is it true?

6 Объяви́ть их старшинáм – Announce to their leaders. The infinitive is used here as a brusque command.

9 шлёт – sends

11 своих мамлю́ков роту – a regiment of his mamelukes. "Mameluke" is a word of Turkish origin. Strictly speaking, they were young Christians (mainly Georgians) who were taken as slaves, converted to Islam, and raised to be warriors. After defeating them in his Egyptian campaign, Napoleon included units of Mamelukes in his own army.

12 космáтых кираси́р – hairy cuirassiers. Cuirassiers were armored cavalry. Napoleon's army had special cuirassier uniforms with a red tuft on the helmet, which probably explains the narrator's unusual epithet. (Ordinarily, "косматый" would describe either a person with long and disheveled hair or a furry animal.)

16 рвы – trenches

20–21 – The dots between these lines are also present in Mérimée's text with a note that a stanza is missing (another mystification).

25–26 Пусть каждый сбросит / Черногóрца одногó – Let each (of us) fell/take down one Montenegrin

30 с шестóв – from sticks. The hats were held on sticks to fool Napoleon's army.

33 Дружным залпом – with a coordinated volley (of shots)

42 наш вольный край – our free country

43 коль завидят – if they catch sight of

44 не взначáй (=невзначай) – by chance

10. Соловéй – The Nightingale

Pushkin translated this poem from the anthology of Vuk Karadžić's *Народне Српске пјесме, скупио их и на свијет издао Вук Стеф. Караџић* (Leipzig, 1824), 1:192–93.

Три највеће туге

Славіј птица мала свакомъ покој дала,
А мени јунаку три туге задала:[1]
Прва ми је туга на срдашцу моме,
Што ме није мајка оженила млада;
Друга ми је туга на срдашцу моме,
Што мој вранац коњиц пода мном не игра;
Трећа ми је туга, ах! на срцу моме,
Што се моја драга на ме расрдила.
Копајте ми раку у пољу широку,
Два копља широку, четири дугачку;
Више моје главе ружу усадите,
Сниже моји ногу воду изведите:
Које младо прође, нек се ружом кити,
Које л' старо прође, нека жеђу гаси.

Note

1. Мјесто ове прве двије врсте једни пјевају и овако:

Мрак на земљу паде, сваком покој даде,
А мени јунаку три туге зададе. (Vuk's note.)

Pushkin's translation is written in unrhymed trochaic tetrameter with feminine endings.

1 соловéйко – little nightingale

5 молóдца – young man. The stress is unusual (one would expect "мóлодца," as in line 8). However, different stresses on the same word (within a single poem) are common in Russian folklore.

7 Как уж – The phrase, a characteristic marker of the beginning of a clause in folk diction, is probably best left untranslated. (It is used again in line 12.)

8 Рано молодца жени́ли – They married the lad off early. The original reads: "Mother wouldn't allow the lad to marry." Pushkin either misunderstood the original or copied it incorrectly. See Speranskii, 97n2.
10 Ворон конь – Black steed. This is a variant of the common folkloric expression вороно́й конь (used elsewhere in this cycle, e.g., "Битва у Зеницы-Великой," line 41).
12 Красну-девицу – beautiful maiden (a common folkloric expression)
15 Во́ поле – in the field. The stress on the first syllable of this phrase is common in folklore.
17 Алы (= Алые) цветики-цвето́чки – crimson flowers (a truncated adjective cannot be used in this way in modern Russian, but it often occurs in folklore, cf. lines 19 and 22)
19 Чисту (= чистую) воду ключеву́ю – pure spring water
20 Пройдут мимо красны девки – When beautiful (unmarried) girls pass by. The perfective verb is not future tense, but rather repetitive present. "Пройдут" is here stressed on the first syllable (normally stress would fall on the second). The parallel verb in line 22 works the same way in terms of stress and meaning.
23 воды́ – some water (a partitive genitive)

11. Песня о Гео́ргие Чёрном – The Song of Black George

The precise sources of Pushkin's poem are not completely known; judging from Pushkin's own footnote 21, there must have been more than one. The essential difference between Pushkin's poem and many folkloric versions is that in the latter Black George kills his father-in-law rather than his father (see Medrish). Pushkin's most obvious source was the prose work of D. N. Bantysh-Kamenskii, *Путешествие в Молдавию, Валахию и Сербию* (*Journey to Moldavia, Wallachia and Serbia*) (Moscow, 1810).

The poem concerns a historical personage, Georgii Petrovich Karageorgii (1762–1817), nicknamed Black George ("Черный Георг," as Bantysh-Kamenskii calls him), a haiduk and hero in the Serbian war for independence against the Turks and, for a time, a ruler of Serbia. Pushkin's initial fascination with him can be traced to the politically rebellious days of his youth (see "Дочери Карагеоргия" ["To the Daughter of Karageorgii"] of 1820, the very first poem he wrote in his "southern exile"). This poem focuses on a famous and much disputed event in Georgii's biography, his killing of his father. Bantysh-Kamenskii explains the circumstances in the following way (121–22, italics in original):

> Со всех сторон стекаются Сербы к Черному Георгу; один только престарелый отец, живший с ним до того времени, хочет его оставить – упрекает его в чинимых им убийствах, в пролитии невинной крови, и в неминуемой гибели, угрожающей всем его соотечественникам. Он хочет идти к Туркам, предать им своего сына и всех его соумышленников. Тщетно Черный Георг умоляет его; он не внемлет его представлениям – отправляется в Белград. Черный Георг следует за ним – в последний раз

просит его воротиться; старик упорствует в отказе – и наконец сын находит себя принужденным застрелить отца своего!!! Здесь прерываю я на минуту повествование свое; не знаю, должно ли мне осуждать Черного Георга, или жалеть только о нем. Но не нам судить о делах подобных себе.

The poem is written in the three-ictus "тактовик" with unrhymed feminine cadences and (usually) the first stress falling on the third syllable of the line. There is one rhyme, at a particularly dramatic point (lines 38–39) and hence perhaps not coincidental. (According to Medrish [48], Serbian folklore uses rhyme rarely to emphasize key moments.)

---

1 Не два во́лка в овра́ге грызу́тся – It's not two wolves gnawing at each other in the ravine. A typical folkloric "negative" opening, in which one event is suggested, only to be replaced by another one. (Cf. the opening of "Сестра и братья," number fourteen in this cycle.)

6 Где тебе́ с султа́ном тяга́ться – What do you think you're doing, taking on the sultan? In this usage, "где" is a particle expressing doubt or disbelief in the possibility of the success of an undertaking.

7 с белгра́дским пашо́ю (= пашой) – with the Pasha of Belgrade (i.e., the Turkish ruler)

8 Аль (= Или) о двух голова́х ты роди́лся? – Are you daring to the point of foolhardiness? This is an idiom.

9 Пропада́й ты себе – Just go disappear. The "себе" is an emphatic particle, emphasizing that he should go away on his own, not getting anyone else involved.

18 Объяви́ть убе́жище сербов – to reveal the hideout of the Serbs

22 Отпусти́ мне нево́льное сло́во – Forgive me my freely spoken word(s)

24 "Вот ужо́, разбо́йник, тебе бу́дет!" – "Just you wait <and see what happens>, you bandit!" The stress on "тебе́" is omitted here, since the adjacent syllable must take stress (as the penultimate syllable in the line).

26 Старику́ кла́няется в но́ги – bows deeply to the old man. A rare case of consecutive stresses in the "тактовик."

29 за сивую косу – by his grey pigtail. This is a standard Serbian epithet (Medrish, 47).

32 Отпихну́л – pushed aside

44 пьян напи́лся – got drunk

49–50 There are several explanations for the epithet "black," the simplest of which is probably that "kara" means "black" in Turkish. The fact that Pushkin closes his poem in this apodictic way suggests that he was following the account given by Bantysh-Kamenskii, who concludes his nine-page retelling with the following passage (128–29): "Кончу тем, что настоящее имя его *Георгий Петрович*; зовут же его *Черным*, не по смугловатому лицу его, а потому, что в то время, как он убил отца своего, мать его дала ему сие название." ("I will conclude by saying that his real name is Georgii Petrovich; but he is called 'Black' not because of his rather swarthy complexion but because at the time he killed his father, his mother gave him this name.") Patronymics, while standard in Russian to this day, were no longer used in the Serbian of Pushkin's time, but they were present in Serbian folkloric texts (Medrish, 42).

12. Воевóда Милош – Milosh the Commander

The source of the poem is unknown, but the subject was a historical figure, alive and well at the time Pushkin was writing. Milosh Obrenovich (1780–1860) was made a commander by Georgii Karageorgii in 1807 and fought bravely against the Turks. He was the leader of the Second Serbian Uprising of 1815–1817. (He later turned against Karageorgii and treacherously caused his death; see "Менко Вуич грамоту пишет.")

The poem is written in the three-ictus "тактовик" with unrhymed feminine cadences (оплеухи/старухи is the sole exception, perhaps adding emphasis or perhaps to be understood as a coincidence) and an invariant third-syllable stress at the beginning of each line.

---

2 янычáры – Janissaries (Turkish soldiers)
6 Красных девок – beautiful maidens ("красная" in this meaning is a common folkloric epithet)
7 зазóрные – shameful
8 басурмáнские – infidel. (The Serbs are Eastern Orthodox Christians, while the Turks were Muslims.)
10 Унимáть нас – to keep us from getting upset; to pacify us. The possibility of generational disagreement recalls the father/son argument in the previous poem.
13 вам мирвóлить янычáрам – for you to be overindulgent toward the Janissaries
18 Велúйское ущéлье – the Veli Ravine. It is unclear if such a geographical location ever existed. Conceivably Pushkin based his adjective on the Slavic root for "large," in which case the phrase should be rendered as "Great Ravine.")
21 сербин – Serb (in Russian the more usual term is "серб")

13. Вурдалáк – The Vampire

A translation of Mérimée's "Jeannot" (169–71). Within Pushkin's cycle, it occupies a contrasting position to "Марко Якубович," in that it treats a "serious" theme in comic style, bringing a natural explanation to a potentially supernatural tale. Mérimée's text is also comic, but the conclusion is considerably bloodier than Pushkin's.

Pushkin translates Mérimée's text into trochaic tetrameter with alternating rhymes.

JEANNOT

1. Jeannot devait revenir à la ville, et il fallait passer, la nuit, par un cimetière Or, c'était un poltron plus lâche qu'une femme; il tremblait comme s'il avait eu la fièvre.

2. Quand il fut dans le cimetière, il regardait à droite et à gauche, et il entendit comme quelqu'un qui rongeait, et il pensa que c'était un brucolaque qui mangeait dans son tombeau.[1]

3. «Hélas! hélas! dit-il, je suis perdu. S'il me regarde, il voudra me manger, car je suis si gras: il faut que je mange de la terre de son tombeau;[2] autrement c'est fait de moi.»

4. Alors il s'est baissé pour prendre de la terre; mais un chien, qui rongeait un os de mouton a cru que Jeannot voulait le lui prendre. Il lui a sauté à la jambe et l'a mordu jusqu'au sang.

Notes

1. Espèce de vampire. (Voyez la notice sur les vampires.)
2. Ce préservatif est fort en usage et passe pour être très-efficace.

Title: Вурдала́к – Vampire. See note to line 46 of "Марко Якубович."
11 гложет – is gnawing. (The word appears again in line 20.)
14 упы́рь – vampire. This is the standard Russian word.
15 земли́ моги́льной – earth from the grave. The phrase is in genitive case because it is a negated direct object. Mérimée includes a note (already explained in Pushkin's note 20) to the effect that this is considered an effective way of thwarting a vampire.

14. Сестра́ и братья – The Sister and her Brothers

As Pushkin's note indicates, this was truly a work of folklore that Pushkin found in the collection of Vuk Karadžić (1:305–9), full reference in notes to "Соловей".

Бог ником дужан не остаје

Два су бора напоредо расла,
Међу њима танковрха јела;
То не била два бора зелена,
Ни међ' њима танковрха јела,
Већ то била два брата рођена:
Једно Павле, а друго Радуле,
Међу њима сестрица Јелица.
Браћа сеју врло миловала,
Сваку су јој милост доносила,
Најпослије ноже оковане,
Оковане сребром, позлаћене.
Кад то вид'ла млада Павловица,
Завидила својој заовици,
Па дозива љубу Радулову:
"Јетрвице, по Богу сестрице!
Не знаш кака биља од омразе?
Да омразим брата и сестрицу."

Ал говори љуба Радулова:
"Ој Бога ми, моја јетрвице!
Ја не знадем биља од омразе,
А и да знам, не би ти казала:
И мене су браћа миловала,
И милост ми сваку доносила."
Кад то зачу млада Павловица,
Она оде коњма на ливаду,
Те убоде вранца на ливади;
Па говори своме господару:
"На зло, Павле, сеју миловао,
На горе јој милост доносио!
Убола ти вранца на ливади."
Павле пита сестрицу Јелицу:
"Зашто, сејо? да од Бога нађеш!"
Сестрица се брату кунијаше:
"Нисам, брате, живота ми мога!
Живота ми и мога и твога!"
То је братац сеји вјеровао.
Кад то виђе млада Павловица,
Она оде ноћу у градину,
Те заклала сивога сокола,
Па говори своме господару:
"На зло, Павле, сеју миловао,
На горе јој милост доносио!
Заклала ти сивога сокола."
Павле пита сестрицу Јелицу:
"Зашто, сејо? да од Бога нађеш!"
Сестрица се брату кунијаше:
"Нисам, брате, живота ми мога!
Живота ми и мога и твога!"
И то братац сеји вјеровао.
Кад то виђе млада Павловица,
Она оде вече по вечери,
Те украде ноже заовине,
Њима закла чедо у колевци.
Кад у јутру јутро освануло,
Она трчи своме господару
Кукајући и лице грдећи:
"На зло, Павле, сеју миловао,
"На горе јој милост доносио!
Заклала ти чедо у колевци;
Ако ли се мене не вјерујеш,
Извади јој ноже од појаса."
Скочи Павле канда се помами,
Па он трчи на горње чардаке,
Ал још сестра у душеку спава,
Под главом јој злаћени ножеви;

Павле узе злаћене ножеве,
Па и вади из сребрни кора,
Али ножи у крви огрезли;
Кад то виђе Павле господару,
Трже сестру за бијелу руку:
"Сејо моја, да те Бог убије!
Буд ми закла коња на ливади
И сокола у зеленој башчи,
"Зашт' ми закла чедо у колевци?"
Сестрица се брату кунијаше:
"Нисам, брате, живота ми мога!
Живота ми и мога и твога!
Ако ли ми не вјерујеш клетви,
Изведи ме у поље широко,
Па ме свежи коњма за репове,
Растргни ме на четири стране."
Ал то братац сеји не вјерова,
Већ је узе за бијелу руку,
Изведе је у поље широко,
Привеза је коњма за репове,
Па и одби низ поље широко.
Ђе је од ње капља крви пала,
Онђе расте смиље и босиље;
Ђе је она сама собом пала,
Онђе се је црква саградила.
Мало време за тим постајало,
Разболље се млада Павловица,
Боловала девет годин' дана,
Кроз кости јој трава проницала,
У трави се љуте змије легу:
Очи пију, у траву се крију.
Љуто тужи млада Павловица,
Па говори своме господару:
"Ој чујеш ли, Павле господару!
Води мене заовиној цркви,
Не би ли ме црква опростила."
Кад то чуо Павле господару,
Поведе је заовиној цркви;
Кад су били близу б'јеле цркве,
Ал из цркве нешто проговара:
"Не ид' амо, млада Павловице:
Црква тебе опростити не ће."
Кад то зачу млада Павловица,
Она моли свога господара:
"Ој Бога ти, Павле господару!
Не води ме двору бијеломе,
Већ ме свежи коњма за репове,
Па ме одби низ поље широко,

Нек ме живу коњи растргају."
То је Павле љубу послушао:
Привеза је коњма за репове,
Па је одби низ поље широко.
Ђе је од ње капља крви пала,
Онђе расте трње и коприве;
Ђе је она сама собом пала,
Језеро се онђе провалило,
По језеру вранац коњиц плива,
А за њиме злаћена колевка,
На колевци соко тица сива,
У колевци оно мушко чедо,
Под грлом му рука материна,
А у руци теткини ножеви.

For his translation, Pushkin uses the three-ictus "тактовик" with unrhymed feminine cadences.

---

2 Между ими = Между ними (a similar instance where the "н" is omitted can be found in line 6)
9 Напосле́док – Then; in the end. (The word indicates the final step in a sequence of actions.)
10 Золочёный в серéбряной опрáве – gilt in a silver sheath
11 Павли́ха – this is the first time we hear of Pavlikha; the next line explains that she is Pavel's wife.
12 на золóвку – at her sister-in-law (husband's sister), that is, at Elitsa
13 Говори́т она Раду́ловой любе – She says to Radula's beloved
14 Невéстушка, по богу сестри́ца – O my sister-in-law, my dear little sister according to God
15–16 Не знáешь ли ты зéлия (= зелья) такóго, / Чтоб сестрá омерзéла брáтьям? – Do you know a potion that would make a sister despicable to her brothers?
23 к водопóю – to the watering hole (river)
24 коня́ воронóго – the black steed
25 своему́ господи́ну – to her husband (a folkloric use of the word "господин")
28 Извелá – destroyed
34 В ту пору – That time
36 Сивого сокола там заколóла – She slaughtered the grey falcon. According to Afanas'ev (1:230), the adjective "сивый" ("grey" in Russian) originally meant "white" or "bright," so that the fixed expression "сивый сокол" (in Ukrainian and, presumably, Serbian) corresponds to the Russian epic formula "свет-ясён сокол"). Pushkin was presumably unaware of these details; in any case, he took the Serbian phrase and translated it literally.
58 как = когда
61 В головáх – at the head of the bed
64 за белу (= белую) руку – by her fair hand (a truncated adjective)
73 в чистое поле – to the open field

84 соорудилась – was erected
91 страждет (=страдает) молода (=молодая) Павлиха – the young Pavlikha suffers
95 авось исцелюся – maybe I'll recover
101 Как=Когда
111 тернье да крапива – thorn and nettles
116 сокол-птица – a falcon-bird. (Such pleonasms are common in Russian folklore.)
119 тёткин – his aunt's (i.e., Elitsa's)

15. Яныш королевич – Ianysh the Prince

Though Pushkin's note suggests that he has translated only a part of the original, no source has ever been found, raising suspicions that it is a mystification on Pushkin's part. According to Tomashevskii (1961, 278), the poem borrows some details (e.g., the name of the Czech queen in line 4) from the "medieval" Czech work "Libušin soud" ("Libusha's Judgment") that the scholar Vaclav Hanka claimed to have discovered in 1818. (In the spirit of the time, Hanka wrote it himself and passed it off as folk poetry.) The poem's plot has obvious links to another folkloric work by Pushkin, the unfinished blank-verse drama *The Rusalka.*

The poem is written in the three-ictus "тактовик," with most lines beginning with two unstressed syllables followed by a stressed syllable and all lines ending with unrhymed feminine cadences.

---

7 с червонцами черес – a money belt with gold coins
8 Да гремучие серьги золотые – and loud gold earrings. Presumably the first epithet suggests their large size (capable of making a loud sound if struck together).
19 в Мораву – into the Morava River. The Morava River is located in Moravia, Slovakia (it meets the Danube near Bratislava), not to be confused with the river of that same name in Serbia.
23 её нарекла Водяницей – and called her Vodianitsa. The name is etymologically and logically connected to the water.
27 коня вороного – black steed
28 студёною водою (=студёной водой) – with ice-cold water
29 запененную – frothing. The word has an alternate (archaic) stress: запенённую. Both would fit the meter.
32 Хвать – It grabs. The word is a colloquial form that can substitute for various forms of the verb "хватать."
41 Осадив – Having reined in
46 Вила – A Slavic word for "rusalka"
62 Див-Рыба – the Magical Fish
73 по белые груди – up to her fair breasts
81 млада (=молодая) Елица – young Elitsa
82 Выдь (=Выйди) – Come out

96 Против ми́лой жена́ не уте́шит – Compared to the sweet one <my> wife does not give <me> pleasure

16. Конь – The Steed

A translation of Mérimée's "Le cheval de Thomas II" (249), the penultimate poem in Mérimée's collection. (On the final poem, see notes to "Что белеется.") Pushkin did not include this poem in the initial publication, but added it shortly thereafter. By making it the final poem in his cycle, he connects it to the first poem, since both conclude with the imminent flaying of King Thomas II. (For an echo of this motif in Pushkin's *Капитанская дочка* [*The Captain's Daughter*] see Bethea 2009, 293.)

The French text is written as a single paragraph, but Pushkin's poem, following the switch in speakers, is broken into two stanzas of uneven length. Pushkin's meter is trochaic tetrameter. The first stanza uses the rhyme scheme of an odic stanza, though the trochaic meter negates the association. The second stanza uses alternating rhymes throughout.

Le cheval de Thomas II

Pourquoi pleures-tu, mon beau cheval blanc? pourquoi hennis-tu douloureusement? N'es-tu pas harnaché assez richement à ton gré? n'as-tu pas des fers d'argent avec des clous d'or? n'as-tu pas des sonnettes d'argent à ton cou? et ne portes-tu pas le Roi de la fertile Bosnie? – Je pleure, mon maître, parce que l'infidèle m'ôtera mes fers d'argent et mes clous d'or et mes sonnettes d'argent. Et je hennis, mon maître, parce qu'avec la peau du Roi de Bosnie le mécréant doit me faire une selle.

---

1 конь рети́вый – fleet steed (a common folkloric expression)
5 Али (=Или) я тебя́ не холю – Or do I not care for you
6 вволю – to your heart's content
7 красна́ – beautiful
8 Аль = Или
10 злачёны (=золочёный) – gilt
22 сдерёт – will strip off. The verb is often used in the expression "сдирать/содрать кожу" ("to flay"), which is implicit in the poem's final image.
24 наме́сто чапрака́ (=вместо чепрака) – instead of a saddle-cloth

1835

(Из Анакре́она) Отры́вок – (From Anacreon) An Excerpt

Pushkin translated this and the following two poems from Anacreon on the same day, apparently intending to include them in a (never completed) prose piece that has come to be known as "Повесть из Римской жизни" ("A Tale from Roman Life").

Pushkin did not read ancient Greek and could only have known the Anacreontic poems in translation. Like many previous translators, he changes the final line of this particular poem, which in the original Greek is somewhat illogical (Cooper, 185–86). Given the wealth of translations available to Pushkin (in both French and Russian), it is difficult to say whom he consulted. His formal choices follow Russian tradition rather than French, since the latter opted to render these poems in prose. Pushkin's meter (trochaic tetrameter) fits in squarely with eighteenth-century Russian renditions of Anacreontic poetry. The presence of rhymes is unusual though not unprecedented in Russian Anacreontics. (Derzhavin and Lomonosov had used them.) Here Pushkin's rhyme scheme is that of an octave. However, two features make it unlikely that any comparison with traditional octaves was intended: the trochaic meter and the fact that the entire poem consists of only eight lines.

This particular poem is remembered largely because it is cited repeatedly (if inaccurately) by the vapid but charming Stepan Oblonsky in Tolstoy's *Anna Karenina.*

---

1 коне́й рети́вых – fleet steeds. The expression is common.
2 По их выжженным тавра́м – by the brands burned into them
3 парфя́н – Parthians. (The Parthians were an ancient civilization covering modern day Iran.)
4 По высо́ким клобука́м – by their high tiaras (i.e., high hats). The Russian word is Turkish in origin.

Ода LVI (Из Анакре́она) – Ode LVI (From Anacreon)

Like the preceding poem, this translation was to be included in the prose work about ancient Rome. The concluding lines of the poem (in both original and translation) are uncharacteristically dark.

Once again, Pushkin's poem is written in trochaic tetrameter, a standard Russian meter for Anacreontic poetry. The poem is astrophic, but breaks into two quatrains of alternating rhyme (with the even-numbered lines all rhyming on the same syllable), followed by a quatrain of ring rhyme. (In a variant, Pushkin altered the final four lines, giving them the same pattern of alternating rhyme as in the first eight lines.)

3 в дёснах – in <my> gums
5 Сладкой жизни – of sweet life
7 Парка счет ведёт им строго – The Parca strictly keeps an account for them. The Parca (or Moira) was one of the three goddesses also known as the Fates. The antecedent of "им" is the days of the previous line; the dative pronoun here is standard Russian usage.
8 Тартар тени ждёт моéй – Tartarus awaits my shade. Tartarus was the land of the dead in Greek mythology. (It also appears in Roman mythology, though there as a place for sinners, which is probably not implied in this poem.)
9 из-под спуда – from this hidden (closed-off) place
12 Нет исхóда уж оттýда – there is no exit from there. The "уж" is here emphatic.

Ода LVII – Ode LVII

Yet another translation from Anacreon, this one praising the virtues of moderation. As in the previous two poems, Pushkin follows convention by using trochaic tetrameter (here with alternating rhymes) to convey the Anacreontic meter.

1 Что же сухо в чаше дно – Why is the bottom in the cup dry
3–4 Только пьяное винó / Раствори́ водóю (=водой) трезвой – Only mix the intoxicating wine with sober water
5 скифы – Scythians. In the Greek context (this reference is found in the original Greek poem and presumably whatever translation served as Pushkin's source), the Scythians were barbarians. There is perhaps an irony here, in that the Scythians were a nomadic tribe who lived in a broad area that covered parts of southern Russia (as well as Ukraine and Central Asia). In other words, Russian readers might understand the Scythians as a synonym for Russians. (For an example of this, see "К вельможе," line 36.)
6 бесчи́нно – in an unseemly fashion
7 за чашей – while <drinking> a cup

„Юношу, горько рыдáя, ревни́вая дева брани́ла" – "Bitterly weeping, the jealous maiden scolded the youth"

The poem recalls both in form (elegiac distich) and genre "Царскосельская статуя." That poem was definitely an ekphrasis (a poetic depiction of a work of visual art), and this poem may also be one, though no specific statue has been adduced. Like that other poem, this one begins with a narrated action and finishes with the motif of permanent flow (here of tears, there of water).

3 сон его лёгкий лелéя – tenderly guarding his not <yet> deep sleep
4 лия́ – pouring. Note the echo on "лелея" and the numerous alliterative "л" sounds.

„Что белéется на горé зелёной" – "What shows white on the green mountain"

A partial translation of the "Hasanaginica," perhaps the most famous Serbian folk poem. The poem was not part of the Vuk Karadžić collection that Pushkin owned, but it was translated so many times (see Yovanovitch, 371–80) that it is difficult to determine which version(s) Pushkin knew. One can safely eliminate the German translations (including the one by Goethe that made the poem so widely known in Europe), since Pushkin did not know that language. Pushkin certainly had read Mérimée's version, which served as the concluding poem in his *Guzla* (see notes to "Песни западных славян") on pages 251–57. In a letter to Pushkin's friend Sobolevskii (intended for Pushkin and eventually published by him as part of his introduction to "Песни западных славян"), Mérimée had noted that this poem was the only genuine folkloric text in his entire book. As he explained, he used as a source Alberto Fortis's book *Viaggio in Dalmazia* (1774), where the poem appears in the original (written in Italianate transcription, see below) and in Italian verse. He claims to have supplemented the Italian by reading the Serbian poem aloud to a Russian friend, who helped him bring the translation closer to the original. (Mérimée seems not to have appreciated the differences between Russian and Serbian.)

Mérimée's letter to Sobolevskii is dated 15 January 1835. It is not known when Pushkin actually received it, nor when Pushkin began work on his own translation of the "Hasanaginica." If Pushkin's poem postdated his reception of the letter, then it is likely that Mérimée's discussion of his efforts in translating the "Hasanaginica" (at the end of the letter) inspired Pushkin to try his own hand at it. The title, "The sad ballad of the noble spouse of Hassan-Aga," comes from Fortis. Mérimée's version of the poem follows, cutting off where Pushkin did (though Mérimée included the entire poem).

Triste Ballade de la noble épouse d'Asan-Aga[1]

Qu'y a-t-il de blanc sur ces collines verdoyantes? Sont-ce des neiges, sont-ce des cygnes? Des neiges? elles seraient fondues. Des cygnes? ils se seraient envolés. Ce ne sont point des neiges, ce ne sont point des cygnes: ce sont les tentes de l'aga Asan-Aga. Il se lamente de ses blessures cruelles. Pour le soigner, sont venues et sa mère et sa sœur; sa femme, retenue par la timidité, n'est point auprès de lui.[2]

Quand la douleur s'est apaisée, il fait dire à sa fidèle épouse: «Ne me regarde pas dans ma maison blanche, ni dans ma maison, ni devant mes parens.» La dame, en entendant ces paroles, se renferme dans son appartement toute triste et accablée. Voilà que des pas de chevaux ont retenti près de sa maison, et la pauvre femme d'Asan-Aga, croyant que son mari s'approche, court à son balcon pour se précipiter. Mais ses deux filles ont suivi ses pas: «Arrête, notre mère chérie! ce n'est point notre père Asan-Aga, c'est notre oncle Pintorovich-Bey.»

L'infortunée s'arrête; elle serre dans ses bras son frère chéri. «Ah! mon frère! grande honte! Il me répudie, moi qui lui ai donné cinq enfan<t>s!»

Notes

1. On sait que le célèbre abbé Fortis a traduit en vers italiens cette belle ballade. Venant après lui, je n'ai pas la prétention d'avoir fait aussi bien; mais seulement j'ai fait autrement. Ma traduction est littérale, et c'est là son seul mérite.

La scène est en Bosnie et les personnages sont Musulmans, comme le prouvent les mots d'aga, de cadi, etc.

2. Il nous est difficle de comprendre comment la timidité empêche une bonne épouse de soigner un mari malade. La femme d'Asan-Aga est musulmane, et, suivant ses idées de décence, elle ne doit jamais se présenter devant son mari sans être appelée. Il paraît cependant que cette décence est outrée, car Asan-Aga s'en est irrité. Les deux vers illyriques sont remarquablement concis, et par cela même un peu obscurs:

Oblaziga mater i sestriza;
A glivbouza od stida ne mogla.

Pushkin was undoubtedly acquainted with the Russian translation of this poem by Aleksandr Vostokov (first published in 1827). Vostokov's translations of Serbian folklore had influenced his metrical choices in the "Песни западных славян" and in other folk stylizations. In this particular translation, Vostokov experimented with the form by using dactylic cadences (with one hyperdactylic exception) rather than feminine endings. If Pushkin was indeed following Vostokov (and there is no certainty of this), he disregarded the dactylic endings; otherwise, Vostokov's poem is metrically identical to the accentual verse in the "Песни западных славян."

Vostokov's translation follows, but only to the point where Pushkin's text stops.

Что белеется у рощи у зеленыя?
Снег ли то или белые лебеди?
Кабы снег, он скоро растаял бы,
Кабы лебеди были, улетели бы прочь.
Не снег то, не белые лебеди,
А белеется шатер Асан-Аги,
Где он лежит тяжко раненый.
Его мать и сестра посещали там,
Молода жена придти постыдилася.
Когда легче ему стало от тяжких ран,
Он послал сказать молодой жене:
"Не жди меня больше в дому моем,
Ни в дому, ни во всем роду-племени"!
Вняла жена таковы слова,
Стоит, цепенея от горести;
Вдруг конский топот заслышала:
Взметалась жена Асан-Аги,

Чтоб с башни из окна ей низринуться.
Бегут к ней две милые дочери:
"Постой, не мечися, матушка,
То едет не отец Асан-Ага,
Едет дядя Пинторович Бег."
Успокоилась тогда Агиница,
Обнимает брата с горькой жалобой:
"Ах, братец, какое посрамленье мне!
Выгоняют меня от пятерых детей!"

It is possible that Pushkin's main source was the Serbian text itself, which he had encountered in the French translation of Fortis's book: Abbé A. Fortis, *Voyage en Dalmatie* (Berne, 1778). This book was in his library. (Unlike Pushkin, Mérimée knew Fortis's book in the Italian original.) In the French book (1:142–49), the Serbian text appears side by side with a French translation. (While the Italian translation was in verse, the French – apparently translated from the Italian, not from the original Serbian – was in prose.) Once again, the citations below end at the point where Pushkin himself stopped translating.

Fortis's book gives the original Serbian in a transliteration (cited below) based largely on Italian phonetics that he himself seems to have devised.

Xalostna Pjesanza Plemenite Asan-Aghinize

Sto se bjeli u gorje Zelenoi?
Al-su snjezi, al-su Labutove?
Da-su snjezi vech-bi okopnuli;
Labutove vech-bi poletjeli.
Ni-su snjezi, nit-su Labutove;
Nego sciator Aghie Asan-Aghe
On bolu-je u ranami gliutimi.
Oblaziga mater, i Sestriza;
A Gliubovza od stida ne mogla.

Kad-li-mu-je ranam' boglie bilo,
Ter poruça vjernoi Gliubi svojoi:
Ne çekai-me u dworu bjelomu,
Ni u dworu, ni u rodu momu.
Kad Kaduna rjeci razumjela,
Josc-je jadna u toi misli stala.
Jeka stade kogna oko dwora:
J pobjexe Asan-Aghiniza
Da vrât lomi kule niz penxere.
Za gnom terçu dve chiere djevoike:
Vrati-nam-se, mila majko nascia:
Ni-je ovo babo Asan-Ago
Vech daixa Pintorovich Bexe.

J vratise Asan Aghiniza,
Ter se vjescia bratu oko vrâta.

Da! moi brate, welike sramote!
Gdi-me saglie od petero dize!

The following translation is found across from the Serbian text:

☞Chanson sur la mort de l'illustre épouse d'Asan-Aga

Quelle blancheur brille dans ces forêts vertes? Sont ce des neiges, ou des cygnes? Les neiges seroient fondues aujourd'hui, & les cygnes se seroient envolés. Ce ne sont ni des neiges ni des cygnes, mais les tentes du guerrier Asan-Aga. Il y demeure blessé & se plaignant amerement. Sa mère & sa soeur sont allées le visiter: son épouse seroit venue aussi, mais la pudeur la retient.

Quand la douleur de ses blessures s'appaisa, il manda à sa femme fidelle: «Ne m'attends pas ni dans ma maison blanche, ni dans ma cour, ni parmi mes parens». En recevant ces dures paroles cette malheureuse reste triste & affligée. Dans la maison de son époux, elle entend les pas des chevaux, & désespérée elle court sur une tour pour finir ses jours en se jettant par les fenêtres. Ses deux filles épouvantées, suivent ses pas incertains, en lui criant: Ah, chere mere, ah! ne suis pas: ces chevaux, ne sont pas ceux de notre père *Asan*; c'est ton frère, le Beg *Pintorovich* qui vient te voir.

A ces voix l'épouse d'*Asan* tourne ses pas, & courant les bras étendus vers son frère, elle lui dit: «Ah mon frère! vois ma honte extrême! Il me répudie, moi qui lui ai donné cinq enfans»!

---

1 на горé – on the mountain. In his letter to Sobolevskii, Mérimée pointed out that Fortis had mistranslated the word "gorje" as "bosco" ("forest"). What is remarkable is not that the French version of Fortis retains this error, but that Vostokov, a brilliant scholar, would repeat the mistake (he writes "роща"). This means that Pushkin had looked at the original, at Mérimée's translation, or at Mérimée's letter.

2 али (=или) лебеди белы (=белые) – or white swans

8 матерь = мать

9 люба – beloved. In Serbian, the word means "wife." (Maroevich, 127). It is not clear if Pushkin follows the Serbian or simply uses the Russian definition (as he does in the "Песни западных славян," number 15, line 81).

10 Как = Когда (see also line 14)

13 во всём моём роде – in my whole clan. The stress on "моём" would be omitted here, since the following syllable (the penultima) takes an obligatory stress.

14 мужнины речи – her husband's words

15 Каду́на – wife (Turkish). The fact that Pushkin capitalizes this word shows that he understands it (incorrectly) as a proper noun. This would suggest that he was consulting the original, since none of the translations (except his own) make this mistake.

17 Ас<ан>-агини́ца – the wife of Hassan-Aga

18 око́шко – window (diminutive)

Полково́дец – The Commander

The general referred to in the title is Mikhail Bogdanovich Barclay de Tolly (1761–1818). Barclay was vilified during the war with Napoleon as an incompetent leader, despite his bravery in battle and wisdom in retreating rather than facing the invading army directly. At this point in his life, Pushkin was clearly attracted to the figure of a misunderstood genius. (Note how the poem concludes with the emphatic distinction between the poet and the rabble.)

Pushkin's poem was inspired by his repeated visits (if we are to believe line 15) to the "Gallery of 1812" in the Winter Palace, which featured more than three hundred portraits of Russian war heroes. The paintings, commissioned by Alexander I in 1819, were created with incredible speed by the English artist George Dawe (see commentary to the 1828 poem "To Dawe, Esqr."), who worked with several Russian assistants.

Pushkin dated the poem in his notebook as 7 April 1835, Easter Sunday (Светл.<ое> вос.<кресение>), which has encouraged recent scholars to see Barclay as a Christ figure. In this way, Barclay as a suffering Christ is consciously opposed to the common poetic images of Kutuzov (and to an even greater extent Tsar Alexander) as Christ the savior. (On the topos of Alexander vs. Napoleon as Christ vs. Antichrist, see Gasparov 1992, 83–117.)

Shortly after publishing the poem, Pushkin was forced to defend himself against the accusation that he was slighting Kutuzov:

> Неужели должны мы быть неблагодарны к заслугам Барклая-де-Толли, потому что Кутузов велик? Ужели, после двадцатипятилетнего безмолвия, поэзии не позволено произнести его имени с участием и умилением? Вы упрекаете стихотворца в несправедливости его жалоб; вы говорите, что заслуги Барклая были признаны, оценены, награждены. Так, но кем и когда? Конечно, не народом и не в 1812 году. Минута, когда Барклай принужден был уступить начальство над войсками, была радостна для России, но тем не менее тяжела для его стоического сердца. Его отступление, которое ныне является ясным и необходимым действием, казалось вовсе не таковым: не только роптал народ ожесточенный и негодующий, но даже опытные воины горько упрекали его и почти в глаза называли изменником. Барклай, не внушающий доверенности войску, ему подвластному, окруженный враждою, язвимый злоречием, но убежденный в самого себя, молча идущий к сокровенной цели и уступающий власть, не успев оправдать себя перед глазами России, останется навсегда в истории высоко поэтическим лицом.
>
> (Should we really be ungrateful to the merits of Barclay de Tolly because Kutuzov is great? And after a twenty-five-year silence, should poetry really not be permitted to pronounce his name with sympathy and tender emotion? You reproach the poet for having complaints that are not fair; you say, that Barclay's merits have been recognized, valued, rewarded. Yes, but when and by whom? Of course, not by the people and not in 1812. The minute when Barclay was forced to give up leadership over the troops was joyous for Russia,

> but nonetheless difficult for his stoic heart. His retreat, which now seems a clear and necessary act, seemed nothing of the sort; not only did the cruel and angry people mutter, but even experienced soldiers bitterly reproached him and practically before his very eyes called him a traitor. Barclay, who did not inspire trust in the troops that were subservient to him, surrounded by enmity, injured by calumny, but convinced in himself, silently moving towards his cherished goal and giving up power without having had time to prove himself in Russia's eyes, will remain forever in history as a highly poetic figure.)

This paragraph appeared (with several others) under the title "Объяснение" ("Explanation") in Pushkin's own journal *Современник* (*The Contemporary*), in the fourth issue of 1836; the poem itself had been printed in the previous issue.

Unusually long for Pushkin's later lyrics, the poem is written in alexandrines, which – together with the high style of its lexicon – recall eighteenth-century poetics.

---

1 У русского царя́ в черто́гах есть пала́та – there is a chamber in the Russian tsar's splendid rooms

5 кистию (= кистью) – (with his) brush

6 разрисова́л – covered with drawings

21 Главо́ю (= Головой) лавровой – with their laurel head. From ancient times, the laurel wreath was worn by military heroes (and great poets). Note the sound repetition in this phrase. (For the standard image, see line 48.)

26 во весь рост – life-size. Most of the paintings in the gallery are not that large; hence Barclay's portrait stands out.

29 вое́нный стан – military camp

31 Свою́ ли точно мысль худо́жник обнажи́л – Did the artist reveal his own idea exactly

34 Доу – Pushkin's transliteration of "Dawe" (which may well reflect the actual British pronunciation)

39 в имени твоём звук чуждый не взлюбя́ – not loving the foreign sound in your name. (Pushkin forms a present verbal adverb from a perfective verb.) One of the reasons Barclay was mistrusted was that he was a foreigner (and not only in name). He was of Scottish descent, raised in the Baltics, with German as his native language. This was enough to convince many Russians that Barclay was colluding with Napoleon.

42 Руга́лся над твое́й свяще́нной седино́ю (= сединой) – Cursed your holy gray hair. The passage is polemically directed at Zhukovskii's poem in praise of Kutuzov "Вождю победителей" ("To the Leader of the Conquerors"): "И пред твоей священной сединою / Безумная гордыня пала в прах" ("And before your holy gray hair / Mad pride fell into the dust").

48 уступи́ть – to give up. In August of 1812, Barclay was forced to step down and allow Kutuzov to take over as the supreme commander of the Russian forces.

50 И в полковы́х ряда́х сокры́ться одино́ко – <You had to> hide alone in the regimental ranks. This is a bit of an exaggeration. Barclay was demoted, but he still remained a commander.

52 вперво́й (= впервые) – for the first time

53 Бросáлся ты в огóнь – You rushed into the fire. As commander of the right flank in the battle of Borodino, Barclay fought courageously.
54 вотщé – in vain
60 умилéнье – tender emotion. The same word is used by Pushkin in the prose passage cited above.

Literature: Proskurin 1999, 243–62.

Туча – The Storm Cloud

A nature lyric, addressed to the lone cloud lingering after the storm has passed. Khodasevich (1:162) notes that Pushkin usually uses the image of the storm cloud as a reference to dark events in his own life, but if this is the case here, the biographical circumstances are obscure.

The poem is written in the unusual form of amphibrachic tetrameter with pair rhymes (feminine, then masculine). No precise metrical model has been identified.

1 рассéянной бури – of the storm that has gone away (literally: that has been scattered)
2 Однá ты – You alone
5 облегáла – covered
6 тебя́ обвивáла – wound around you
9 Довóльно, сокрóйся! Порá миновáлась – Enough, disappear! That time has passed
11 древéс – of trees. This is the genitive plural of "древо" (archaic for "дерево").

Из А. Шеньé ("Покрóв, упи́танный язви́тельною кровью") – From A. Chénier ("The cover, soaked with caustic blood")

As Pushkin himself noted, this is a translation from André Chénier. The poem is based on a story from Greek mythology retold (among other places) in Ovid's *Metamorphoses* (Chénier's probable source). Hercules had slain the centaur Nessos, who had attempted to take advantage of Hercules' wife Deianeira. While dying, the centaur exacted his vengeance by telling Deianeira that she could use his blood as a love potion. When the jealous Deiancira later feared losing her husband's love, she soaked a cloak she had woven in the centaur's blood and sent it to her husband. As soon as Hercules put it on, he was wracked by tortuous pain, but could not remove it. He rushed to Mount Oite (in some versions of the myth he was already there), built a funeral pyre, and immolated himself on it. This led to his apotheosis; the gods, pitying his suffering, raised him up to Olympus.

Pushkin's interest in Chénier dates to the early 1820s. It is curious that the first seven lines of this translation were composed in 1825; a decade later Pushkin returned to the text and finished it.

The Russian translation, like the French poem, is written in alexandrines. Pushkin avoids the potential monotony of the form rhythmically (the spondee "Гнёт, ло́мит") and syntactically (e.g., the numerous pauses built into lines 9 and 12, the enjambments between lines 7 and 8 and 11 and 12). Ivanov (1997, 274) suggests that this poem sparked Pushkin's rediscovery of the alexandrine, which is used in so many of his major lyric poems of 1836.

In the edition Pushkin owned, the poem reads as follows:

Oeta, mont ennobli par cette nuit ardente,
Quand l'infidèle époux d'une épouse imprudente
Reçut de son amour un présent trop jaloux,
Victime du centaure immolé par ses coups.
Il brise tes forêts: ta cime épaisse et sombre
En un bûcher immense amoncèle sans nombre
Les sapins résineux que son bras a ployés.
Il y porte la flamme; il monte: sous ses piés
Etend du vieux lion la dépouille héroïque;
Et l'œil au ciel, la main sur la massue antique,
Attend sa récompense et l'heure d'être un dieu.
Le vent souffle et mugit. Le bûcher tout en feu
Brille autour du héros; et la flamme rapide
Porte aux palais divins l'âme du grand Alcide!

From *Oeuvres complètes d'André de Chénier* (Paris, 1819), 69.

---

3 Алкиду – to Hercules. In Russian the name Hercules is rendered either "Алкид" or "Геракл."
5 Се – behold
6 Эты – of Mount Oite
7 древеса́ – trees. This is the plural of "древо" (archaic for "дерево").
11 палица – club; cudgel
немéйский лев – the Nemean lion. The first of Hercules' twelve labors was to kill and flay the dread Nemean lion. Thereafter, he wore the lion's pelt as a type of armor. In this line, the reference is of course not to the lion, but to its pelt.

Literature: Sandomirskaja 1978.

„На Испа́нию родну́ю" – "To his native Spain"

The poem (see also commentary to "Родриг") represents a free retelling of the first two chapters of Robert Southey's lengthy narrative poem "Roderick, the Last of the Goths." Pushkin omits or changes numerous passages, transforming its meandering plot into a conversion narrative and thus aligning it with other poems of this period (e.g., "Странник"). Many of the plot changes (e.g., the temptations by the devil, the dream vision) are not in the poem proper, but rather in the extensive notes that Southey appended to the poem.

Pushkin owned an English edition of the work, but it is highly likely that he relied equally – if not more – on a French version, which translated the notes as well as the poem.

The minimal influence of the English original is reflected in the poem's form. In contrast to his standard practice in rendering English poetry (including his translation of "Madoc," another Southey poem), Pushkin changed the meter of the original. Southey's blank verse (unrhymed iambic pentameter) becomes Russian unrhymed trochaic tetrameter quatrains. This meter, sometimes called "Spanish trochees" or the "Romancero" meter, was used in translations from Spanish folklore and epic (e.g., Zhukovskii's translation of "El Cid," based on Herder's German model).

Southey himself included a preface in which he summarized the background to his rather obscure plot:

> The history of the Wisi-Goths for some years before their overthrow is very imperfectly known. It is however apparent, that the enmity between the royal families of Chindasuintho and Wamba was one main cause of the destruction of the kingdom, the latter party having assisted in betraying their country to the Moors for the gratification of their own revenge. Theodofred and Favila were younger sons of King Chindasuintho; King Witiza, who was of Wamba's family, put out the eyes of Theodofred, and murdered Favila, at the instigation of that Chieftain's wife, with whom he lived in adultery. Pelayo, the son of Favila, and afterwards the founder of the Spanish monarchy, was driven into exile. Roderick, the son of Theodofred, recovered the throne, and put out Witiza's eyes in vengeance for his father; but he spared Orpas, the brother of the tyrant, as being a Priest, and Ebba and Sisibert, the two sons of Witiza, by Pelayo's mother.

Southey even included a list of all of the characters of his poem as if it were a play. Those relevant to Pushkin's text are:

> Roderick … the last King of the Wisi-Goths: son of Theodofred.
> Count Julian … a powerful Lord among the Wisi-Goths, now a renegade.
> (*The Poetical Works of Robert Southey* [Paris, 1829], 384–85)

Title: На Испанию – The preposition "На" (rather than "В") is used in the context of a military attack.

11 готфов – of the Goths

16 Одолеет кто кого́ – who would conquer whom

23 почли́ – was considered

31 дротики – javelins

37 о́б земь – against the ground (the stress falls on the preposition here)

38 блестя́щую броню́ – his gleaming armor. (Presumably the armor was not quite so gleaming after eight days of battle.)

44 Весть о гибели его́ – news of his death. Cf. the English original: "the tidings of defeat."

56 Помоли́тесь за него́ – Pray for him. Roderick speaks of himself in the third person here.

62 заступ – spade
65 Тленье трупу не косну́лось – Decay had not touched the corpse. ("Трупу" is an archaic genitive after the verb "коснуться.")
78 лука́вый – the devil. Strictly speaking, the word means "crafty," but when used as a noun, it unambiguously connotes the devil.
83 Упое́ние собла́зна – the thrill of temptation
96 Заступи́лся – made a plea for. There is probably a play on заступ (line 62).
99 Белой ризою (=ризой) оде́ян – Clothed in a white garment

Literature: Dolinin 2007, 155–81.

„Менко Ву́ич гра́моту пи́шет" – "Menko Vuich writes a letter"

This fragment is clearly connected to the "Песни западных славян." The subject is the betrayal of Georgii Petrovich Karageorgii by his erstwhile comrade-in-arms Milosh Obrenovich (see commentary to "Песни западных славян," numbers 11 and 12).

The meter is the three-ictus "тактовик," so frequent in the earlier cycle.

---

1 Менко Вуич – There is no historical record of such a person. However, during his southern exile in Kishinev, Pushkin met numerous Serbian leaders who had fled the Turks and were taking advantage of Russia's hospitality, among them a mysterious "Вучич" (Trubetskoi 1983, 353). Pushkin may have misremembered the name or slightly altered it.
грамоту – letter. Strictly speaking, it is any sort of document, but the context makes "letter" a better translation here.
2 побрати́му – to his "blood-brother." This is not a familial relationship, but a symbolic one. The concept is at the center of "Янко Марнавич" ("Песни западных славян," number 2). See Pushkin's note 8 to the "Песни," a truncated version of Mérimée's lengthy first note to "La flamme de Perrussich" (cited as part of the commentary to "Янко Марнавич").
3 Чёрный Гео́ргий – Black George. The nickname of Karageorgii. Note also the repetition of "черные" in lines 10 and 11.
5 извести́ – to destroy
7 Хоти́н – a fortress town in Bessarabia (now in Ukraine), where Karageorgii lived in exile after the Turks routed him in 1813

<На Дондуко́ва-Корсако́ва> – On Dondukov-Korsakov

This nasty epigram was written at the expense of Prince Mikhail Aleksandrovich Dondukov-Korsakov (1794–1869), a man of limited intellect who was at the time the vice-president of the Academy of Sciences thanks to the good offices of S. S. Uvarov (see commentary to "На выздоровление Лукулла").

The poem is written in iambic tetrameter, with an opening couplet followed by alternating rhymes. As usual in an epigram, the key is the final line.

---

2 Дунду́к – blockhead. The word is unfortunately close to the first part of the prince's hyphenated name.
3 не подоба́ет – is not befitting
6 <- - -> – the missing word is "жопа" ("ass"). The line plays on the verb of the previous line. "Заседать" ("to meet, to be in session") is etymologically related to "сидеть," and the line could thus be understood as: "He sits, because he has an ass." However, a less literal and more obscene meaning would be apparent to those who knew that Dondukov achieved his high position because of his homosexual relationship with Uvarov.

„Кто из бого́в мне возврати́л" – "Who of the gods returned to me"

Like the Anacreontic poems of this same year, this poem was written for inclusion in the unfinished prose work traditionally called "Повесть из Римской жизни" ("A Tale from Roman Life"). It is a free translation of Horace's "To Pompeius Varus." Horace's poem recalls the battle of Philippi (42 BCE), in which the poet and his addressee fought on the side of Brutus. Brutus fought valiantly, but was ultimately defeated (he committed suicide when he recognized that his forces had lost), while Horace behaved less than heroically. Horace seems to describe his own cowardice, but Pushkin explains this differently in the context of his "Повесть": "Хитрый стихотворец хотел рассмешить Августа и Мецената своею трусостию, чтоб не напомнить им о сподвижнике Кассия и Брута." ("The clever poet wanted to amuse Augustus and Maecenas with his cowardice so as not to remind them about the comrade-in-arms of Cassius and Brutus.") In other words, Horace wanted to deflect their attention from the fact that he – and his guest Pompeius Varus – had fought with Augustus's enemies.

Pushkin's knowledge of Latin was limited, so he took advantage of translations. In addition to the bilingual Latin-French edition that he owned (facing-page, with the Latin original on the left), he used a Russian translation by Sergei Alekseevich Tuchkov (1767–1839), a professional military man and dilettante poet whom he had befriended in Kishinev in 1821.

In Pushkin's Horace edition (*Traduction des oeuvres d'Horace; par M. René Binet* [Paris, 1816], 1:92–95), this is the fifth ode of the second book:

V. AD POMPEIUM GROSPHUM.
Amicum sibi ac patriae restitutum gratulatur.

O, saepe mecum tempus in ultimum
Deducte, Bruto militiae duce,
Quis te redonavit Quiritem[1]
Dis patriis, Italoque caelo,
Pompei, meorum prime sodalium?

Cum quo morantem saepè diem mero
Fregi, coronatus nitentes
Malobathro[2] Syrio capillos?
Tecum Philippos, et celerem fugam
Sensi, relictâ non benè parmulâ;
Cum fracta virtus et minaces
Turpe solum tetigêre mento.
Sed me per hostis Mercurius[3] celer
Denso paventem sustulit aëre;
Te rursus in bellum resorbens
Unda fretis tulit aestuosis.[4]
Ergò obligatam redde Jovi dapem;
Longâque fessum militiâ latus
Depone sub lauru[5] meâ, nec
Parce cadis tibi destinatis.
Oblivioso laevia Massico
Ciboria exple. Funde capacibus
Unguenta de conchis. Quis udo
Deproperare apio coronas,
Curatve myrto? Quem Venus[6] arbitrum
Dicet bibendi? Non ego saniùs
Bacchabor Edonis: recepto
Dulce mihi furere est amico.

Notes

1. *Jam non militem, sed Quiritem, id est civem pacificum.*
2. Mot Syriaque latinisé.
3. Ce Dieu étoit regardé comme le protecteur des gens de lettres.
4. Il avoit sans doute été joindre Sextus Pompée, qui renouvela depuis la guerre en Sicile.
5. *Lauru* est pris ici dans un double sens.
6. On appeloit Vénus le coup de dés que nous nommons rafle de six. Celui qui l'amenoit étoit roi du festin.

V. A POMPEIUS GROSPHUS.

Horace témoigne à un ami la joie qu'il ressent de son retour inespéré.

Vous, près de qui je marchai plus d'une fois au trépas sous les étendards de Brutus; quel bienfait vous rend aux Dieux de vos pères, et renvoie à l'Italie le Romain qu'elle avoit perdu, cher Pompée, le premier de tous mes amis, avec qui j'ai souvent abrégé les longs jours, la coupe à la main, la couronne de fleurs sur la tête, et les cheveux embaumés des parfums les plus exquis de la Syrie? Avec vous je vis les champs de Philippes; et sans trop écouter l'honneur, je laissai mon bouclier pour mieux fuir, quand la valeur fut terrassée, et que nos braves eurent mordu la poussière. Pour moi, Mercure volant à mon secours, m'enleva tout tremblant dans un nuage à travers les ennemis. Et vous, le flot vous reporta encore au milieu des mers orageuses, et vous replongea dans nos funestes guerres. Acquittez-vous donc du festin que vous devez à Jupiter; venez à l'ombre de mon laurier reposer vos membres épuisés par tant de travaux et de combats. N'épargnez point les tonneaux qui vous sont destinés. Buvez à pleine coupe ce Massique divin qui fait oublier les maux. Versez de ces larges conques les essences qu'elles contiennent. A-t-on soin de nous faire à l'instant des couronnes d'ache ou de myrte? Vénus, qui nommeras-tu roi de la table? Je veux fêter Bacchus à la façon des Thraces. J'aime à perdre la raison, quand je retrouve un ami.

Tuchkov published his translation in: *Сочинения и переводы С. Тучкова* (Saint Peterburg, 1816), 1:120–21.

⇎Ода V. К Помпею Варусу
Проздравляет <sic> *его с возвращением в Рим*

О ты! С которым приближался
К последним жизни я часам,
Как, Марса славою пленялся
И Брут начальником был нам,
Какой блаженною судьбою,
Я зрю желанный твой ворзврат?
Возлюбленной Помпей! – С тобою
Делил я грусть и тьму отрад.
В день филиппинского[1] сраженья,
Воспомни, как я был с тобой,
И где исполнь геройска рвенья
Повергнул меч и щит я свой.[2]
О день ужасный! День жестокий!
В кой смерть, стремясь во всех полках,
Лила обильны крови токи,
Героев повергая в прах!
Меня трепещуща средь бою,
Меркурий щедрый сохранил;
Покрыв густою темнотою,
От лютой смерти удалил;
А ты, ревущими волнами,
Быв в бурно море увлечен,
Сражался паки со врагами,
Сколь ни был битвой утомлен. –
И так за жизни сохраненье,
За отвращенье многих бед;
Воздай Богам благодаренье,
Сверши Зевесу свой обет.
От службы трудной удалися,
Да усладится жизнь твоя;
Под лавры опочить склонися
Толь храбра воина как я.
Вкуси за бедствия отрады,
Наполни кубок сей вином,
Да воскурятся Ароматы,
Да свежей Гедеры венцом

Чело твое покрыто зрится,
Среди усердна торжества, –
Забота, грусть да удалится. –
Царем кто будет пиршества?
Тот знай, я пить расположился,
И как Фракиянин напьюсь.[3]
Мой дух к забавам устремился;
Я пеньем, пляской взвеселюсь.
Коль кто, чрез толь велико время
Мог друга в дом свой возвратить,
О нем забот отвергнув бремя,
Себя приятно позабыть!

Notes on page 329

1. *Филиппия*, деревня в Македонии, недалеко от Салоники, построенная на развалинах древней Филиппии. Знаменита победой одержанной Октавием и Антонием над Брутом и Касием.

2. Здесь Гораций смеется над своей трусостию смот. опыт жизни его. (This note, which also appears at the bottom of page 120, refers the reader to Tuchkov's introductory essay, where he writes (4–5): "В сем городе [in Athens] Гораций, участвуя в благополучии Брута, получил начальство над одним Легионом Римского войска. Слава не ожидала его под знаменами Марса; в день филипинского сражения бросил он недостойным образом свой щит и обесславил себя стремительным от неприятеля бегством.")

3. Фракияне почитались народом грубым, жестоким и большими пьяницами.

Pushkin's poem is written in iambic tetrameter in stanzas of varying length with unpredictable rhyming patterns. (Each stanza ends with an alternately rhymed quatrain, but until that point various rhyme schemes are used.)

---

2 похóды – (military) campaigns
3 браней ужас – the horror of battles
4 за призраком свобóды – <to achieve> the illusion of freedom
8 плющем увитые́ – entwined with ivy. In modern Russian, the form would be "плющóм."
9 Сирúйским мирром умащáл – anointed wih Syrian myrrh
11 квирúт – quirite. As footnote 1 to the Latin text makes clear, a "quirite" was a peaceful citizen of ancient Rome, as against a warrior.
15 Эрмий сам незáпной (=внезапной) тучей / Меня́ покры́л и вдаль умчáл – Hermes himself covered me in a sudden cloud and rushed me far away. Pushkin uses the Greek name rather than the Latin "Mercury."
17 от смерти неминýчей – from unavoidable death. "Неминучий" is a folk-poetic synonym for "неминуемый."
22 Садúсь под сень моúх пенáтов – Sit down under the cover of my household gods
25 Мальчик! лей – Servant! Pour <the wine>. The imperative is addressed to the servant boy. See the first French footnote to the Latin text cited in "Мальчику (Из Катулла)."
26 не кстати (=некстати) воздержáнье – it is not the time for abstaining

27 дикий скиф – a wild Scythian. See commentary to line 5 of “Ода LVII” (1835).

Literature: Al’brekht.

Странник – The Wanderer

The poem is Pushkin’s adaptation of the opening chapter of John Bunyan’s allegorical Christian novel *The Pilgrim’s Progress* (the first part was published in 1678), one of the most famous conversion narratives in world literature. *The Pilgrim’s Progress* was known primarily to pious readers of the middle and lower classes until a republication in 1830, which brought it to the attention of a broader educated public. This edition featured a lengthy introduction by Robert Southey, a poet whom Pushkin greatly admired.

Pushkin appears to follow the French translation rather than the English original (Dolinin 1987, 35). He renders the prose of the original in Russian alexandrines (couplets of iambic hexameter), the same form he would use for his profound religious poems of 1836. The style is markedly elevated with a distinct preference for archaisms, reflecting the religious theme. According to Dolinin (1987, 36), certain departures that Pushkin makes from the original indicate that he read Bunyan through the prism of Dante’s *Divine Comedy*.

The poem is apparently complete (it was listed by Pushkin under the title “Из Bunyan’a” for a collection of poems that he was preparing in the last months of his life), but it was not published in his lifetime.

---

2 Неза́пно (=Внезапно) был объя́т я скорбию (=скорбью) вели́кой – Suddenly I was seized by a great grief

4 Как тот, кто на суде́ в убийстве уличе́н – Like someone who is proved guilty of murder in court. In modern Russian, the form would be “уличён.”

5 в тоске́ ломáя руки – wringing my hands in anguish

13 Но скорбь час óт часу меня́ стесня́ла боле (=больше) – But from hour to hour grief weighed on me more and more

14 по невóле (=поневоле) – involuntarily

19 пламени и ветрам обрече́н – doomed to flame and winds. In contemporary Russian, the stress would be “обречён.”

20 Он в угли и золу́ вдруг будет обраще́н – It will be suddenly turned into coals and ash. In modern Russian, the form would be “обращён.”

21 коль не успе́ем вскоре – if we will not soon be able to

22 Обре́сть (=обрести) убе́жище – to find a refuge

23 Мои домáшние – My family members

28 оче́й тяжёлых не смыкáл – did not close <my> heavy eyes

29 Поу́тру я оди́н сиде́л, остáвя (=оставив) ложе – In the morning I sat alone, having left my bed

32 за должное почли́ – considered it necessary

34 и бранью и презре́ньем – both with cursing and with disdain

35 не внемля им – not paying heed to them

45 влачá свою́ вери́гу – dragging his chain
47 вопроси́л – asked (archaic)
49 жребий злобный – terrible fate
51 И вот о чём крушу́сь – And this is what I grieve about
54 отсéле – from here
55 Кудá ж бежáть – But where should I flee to
56 Не видишь ли, скажи́, чегó-нибу́дь – Tell <me>, do you not see something
57 даль указу́я перстом – pointing into the distance with his finger
59 Как от бельмá врачóм избáвленный слепéц – Like a blind man saved from a cataract by a doctor
60 некий свет – a certain light
61 держи́сь сегó ты света – follow that light
62 мета – goal
64 бежáть пусти́лся в тот же миг – set off in a run at that very moment
66 с порóгу – from the threshold. The ending on the noun is an archaic genitive form. Cf. a similar passage in Batiushkov's light-hearted poem "Странствователь и домосед," which contains the lines "Напрасно Клит с женой ему кричали вслед / С домашнего порога: – / 'Брат милый, воротись, мы просим, ради бога!'"
71 Кто поноси́л меня́, кто нá смех подымáл – Some people reviled me, some sought to make me a laughingstock
76 тесные вратá (=ворота) – narrow gates. Cf. Matthew 7:13–14: "Входите тесными вратами, потому что широки врата и пространен путь, ведущие в погибель, и многие идут ими; потому что тесны врата и узок путь, ведущие в жизнь, и немногие находят их." ("Enter ye in at the strait gate: for wide is the gate, and broad is the way, that leadeth to destruction, and many there be which go in thereat: Because strait is the gate, and narrow is the way, which leadeth unto life, and few there be that find it.")

„К кастрáту раз пришёл скрыпáч" – "Once a violinist visited a castrato"

The circumstances of composition of this brilliant and psychologically acute little poem are unknown. A castrato ("кастрáт") – as opposed to a eunuch ("éвнух" [sometimes stressed "евну́х"] or "скопéц") – was a male singer who was castrated before his voice changed. As a result, castratos could sing in high registers for their entire lives. Apparently, the tone quality differed considerably from the corresponding female voice range. Castrati were a fixture in eighteenth-century operas (for example, all of Händel's operas had a major castrato role), and the best of them were celebrated as stars; hence the rich castrato of Pushkin's poem. The vogue for castrato singers had already passed by Pushkin's day.

The poem is written in iambic tetrameter, in rhymed couplets until the final four lines, which are alternating.

---

1 скрыпáч (=скрипач) – violinist
2 Он – the antecedent is "скрыпач"

3 без<- - -> (=безму́дый) – without balls
5 Я их от скуки разбира́л – I was sorting them out from boredom
6 к стати=кстати
8 что твори́шь – what do you do?
10 я<- - -> себе́ чешу́ (=я <муде> себе чешу) – I scratch my balls. The form "муде" is a dual (a grammatical form no longer used in Russian); in modern Russian it would be "муди."

<Плетнёву> („Ты мне сове́туешь, Плетнёв любе́зный") – To Pletnev ("You advise me, dear Pletnev")

The minor poet Petr Aleksandrovich Pletnev (1791 [in Chereiskii 1792]–1865) was the publisher of many of Pushkin's works and a devoted friend. His close connection to *Eugene Onegin* earned him the dedication to chapters 4 and 5; in 1837, Pushkin made this the dedication to the entire work. As the opening lines indicate, the present poem (as well as the next two) was written in response to a letter from Pletnev (which has not survived) containing a request that Pushkin continue his "novel in verse."

This unfinished fragment is written in iambic pentameter octaves, a form Pushkin had used in his comic narrative poem "Домик в Коломне" ("The Little House in Kolomna").

---

2 Оста́вленный рома́н – the novel I have abandoned (i.e., *Eugene Onegin*)
6 Трево́гу славы – The frisson of fame. "Тревогу" is here used in a positive sense. In an early draft to this poem, Pushkin writes of his "труд приятный и полезный" – he retained "полезный" in line 5 and developed "приятный" in this phrase of line 6.
8 уме́ренную плату – a moderate fee
9 пока́ Оне́гин жив – while Onegin is <still> alive. Pushkin ends the novel suddenly, with the hero rejected but alive.
10 Дото́ль – until that time. "Дотоль" is syntactically linked to "пока" of the previous line: while Onegin still lives, the novel is not finished. Cf. the draft: "доколь Онегин жив, дотоль роман не кончен" as well as the corresponding lines (16–17) in "В мои осенние досуги."
11 план счастли́в – the plot is felicitous. Pushkin had used the word "план" in connection with *Eugene Onegin* (1:LX): "Я думал уж о форме плана" ("I've already thought of thc form of the plot")

„Вы за „Оне́гина" сове́туете, други" – "O, friends, you advise me to <take up> *Onegin*"

Another (incomplete) response to Pletnev's request, this time in the relatively lofty form of alexandrines.

1 други – friends. Note the high style. Presumably Pletnev made his request on behalf of several people.

2 осéнние досýги – autumnal leisure <hours>. Autumn was known to be a time of great productivity for Pushkin (see “Осень”), though 1835 proved an unfortunate exception (see Pushkin’s letter to Pletnev, written not later than 11 October 1835). He presumably received Pletnev’s request (now lost) at the season’s onset.

4 клад – a <potential> treasure (i.e., something with great possibilities)

5 Вставля́й в простóрную, вмести́тельную раму – Place into a wide, capacious frame. These are presumably the words that Pushkin’s friends address to him. (The direct speech of these friends begins midway in line 3 and ends after line 8.)

„В мои́ осéнние досýги“ – “In my autumnal leisure <hours>”

A final (also incomplete) response to Pletnev’s request, this time in Onegin stanzas, the form of Pushkin’s novel in verse. The tone of the piece reflects the mixed lexicon of the novel itself.

2 В те дни, как любо мне писáть – In those days when I love to write. This alludes to Pushkin’s preference for autumn over the other times of year as a period of inspiration (see “Осень”).

3 Вы мне совéтуете, други – You advise me, O friends. The line clearly recalls the first line of the previous poem.

7 Ромáн не конча перервáть – Having not finished, to stop working on the novel

10 Как бы то ни было жени́ть – To marry <him> no matter what. The line is rhythmically striking in that the only real stress falls on the final syllable (readers probably also place a stress “ни”; otherwise the line would be almost unpronounceable).

14 вывесть (= вывести) – to take away. The verb is in the infinitive because it is governed by “должно.”

20 Сбирáй обрóк хвалóй и бранью – Gather the quit-rent <in the form of> praise and cursing.

24 харéм (= гарем) – a harem. Pushkin obviously alludes to his narrative poem “Бахчисарайский фонтан” (“The Fountain of Bakhchisarai”), one of his bestsellers from the early 1820s.

28 ей-ей – really

„... Вновь я посети́л“ – “... Again I visited”

The poem is in many respects autobiographical. On 25 September 1835, Pushkin wrote a letter from Mikhailovskoe to his wife, which included numerous elements of the poem he would soon write:

> В Михайловском нашел я все по-старому, кроме того, что нет уж в нем няни моей, и что около знакомых старых сосен поднялась, во время моего отсутствия, молодая, сосновая семья, на которую досадно мне смотреть, как иногда досадно мне видеть молодых кавалергардов на балах, на которых уже не пляшу. Но делать нечего; всё кругом меня говорит, что я старею, иногда даже чистым, русским языком. Наприм.<ер> вчера мне встретилась знакомая баба, которой не мог я не сказать, что она переменилась. А она мне: да и ты, мой кормилец, состарелся да и подурнел. Хотя могу я сказать вместе с покойной няней моей: хорош никогда не был, а молод был.
>
> (In Mikhailovskoe I found everything as it was before, except that my nanny is no more and during my absence a young pine family has arisen next to the familiar old pine trees. I get annoyed looking at this, just as sometimes I'm annoyed to see the young horse guards at balls where I no longer dance. But there's nothing to be done; everything around me tells me that I am aging, sometimes even in plain Russian. For example, yesterday a familiar village woman met me; I couldn't but say that she had changed. And she <responded> to me: and you also, my benefactor, have become older and uglier. Though I could say to that together with my late nanny: I never was beautiful, but I was young.)

The letter reflects a rather depressed state of mind, which the poem does not. (The drafts contain several much darker passages that Pushkin ultimately chose to reject presumably because he wished the poem to have a philosophical rather than personal tone.)

The poem is probably finished, though it was not published in Pushkin's lifetime. Pushkin creates a fragmentary impression by truncating both the first and final lines as well as through the opening ellipsis.

The poem is written in blank verse without caesura, and Pushkin reflects the "prose" qualities of the form in his pared down poetic language, with few tropes and infrequent alliteration. This type of meditative poem is common in English Romanticism (e.g., Wordsworth's "Tintern Abbey," which conceivably influenced Pushkin's form and content), but in Russian poetry it was unprecedented, and it remains one of Pushkin's most famous works.

---

3 Изгна́нником два года незаме́тных – Two unnoticed years as an exile. Pushkin refers to his exile, two years of which (1824–1826) were spent at Mikhailovskoe, a family estate near Pskov. The adjective "незаметных" refers grammatically to "years," but logically to Pushkin himself, who was essentially under house arrest (Nabokov calls it "enforced rustication") far from Russia's cultural capitals.

6 поко́рный общему зако́ну – obedient to the general law (i.e., the law of nature)

8 Мину́вшее меня́ объе́млет живо – The past embraces me vividly

9 вечо́р – yesterday evening

10 Вот опа́льный домик – There's the disgraced house. A clear case of a transferred epithet: it was Pushkin himself who was "в опале" (in disfavor, in dis-

grace), not the house where he lived. The diminutive “домик” does not refer to size (the manor house in question was not so very small); rather it reflects a tender attitude on the part of the speaker.

12 Уже́ стару́шки нет – The old women is no more. Pushkin’s nanny Arina Rodionovna (see commentary to “Няне”) had died on 31 July 1828.

16 сиживал недви́жим – used to sit motionlessly

19 Меж нив златы́х (= золотых) и пажитей зелёных – Among golden fields of crops and green pastures

20 сине́я – showing blue

25 Скриви́лась мельница – the windmill has become crooked
наси́лу – with difficulty

27 Владе́ний дедовских – of <my> grandfather’s properties. Mikhailovskoe had initially been part of a larger parcel of land given to Pushkin’s illustrious great-grandfather Gannibal, who had in turn divided it among his sons. The adjective “дедовских” might simply mean “ancestral.”

31 им мимо = мимо них

40 разросла́сь – has grown up; has spread

42 Под сенью их – under their canopy

„Я думал, сердце позабы́ло“ – “I thought <that> my heart had forgotten”

This love poem, in its temporal shift from disenchantment to re-enchantment, recalls the 1825 К*** (“Я помню чудное мгновенье”), a resemblance that comes out still more clearly in the drafts (which include, for example, the line “Передо мной явилась ты”). In both poems, the speaker is transformed by the power of feminine beauty. In this case, however, the addressee is never even mentioned pronominally. Textological evidence, which shows that Pushkin began the poem in 1831 and returned to it in 1835, may suggest that the addressee changed over the course of time. (This would not be unprecedented in Pushkin’s lyric poetry.)

Though unpublished in Pushkin’s lifetime, the poem appears to be complete. It is written in iambic tetrameter with alternating rhymes. Though astrophic, it breaks logically and syntactically after the fourth line.

3–4 тому́, что было, / Уж не быва́ть – that which was cannot occur any more

7 Но вот опя́ть затрепета́ли – But now they again began to tremble. The antecedent is presumably the nouns of lines 5 and 6.

„О бедность! затверди́л я наконе́ц“ – “O poverty! I have learned at last”

An unfinished translation from Barry Cornwall’s “Dramatic Scene” entitled “The Falcon.” That Pushkin admired this genre of Cornwall’s work is clear from the fact that he initially used the term “драматические сцены” (“dramatic scenes”) to refer to the dramatic works now called his *Маленькие трагедии* (*Little Tragedies*). Pushkin repeatedly translated (or reworked) Cornwall’s lyric poems (especially in 1830), but this is the only instance where he translated from one of the dramas. Cornwall's entire work is only four pages long; Pushkin's translation comes from the opening monologue ("Scene I. Outside of a cottage. Sunset.").

The plot of the work comes from Boccaccio's *Decameron.* Cornwall himself offers the following introduction: "Frederigo, of the Alberighi family, loved a gentlewoman, and was not requited with like love again. But, by bountiful expences <sic> and over liberal invitations, he wasted all his lands and goods, having nothing left him but a Hawk or Falcon. His unkind mistress happeneth to come to visit him and he not having any other food for her dinner, made a dainty dish of his Falcon for her to feed on. Being conquered by this exceeding kind courtesie <sic> she changed her former hatred towards him, accepting him as her husband in marriage, and made him a man of wealthy possessions. Boccaccio. (*Old translation.*) Fifth day: novel 9."

The Russian translation, like the original, is written in blank verse (unrhymed iambic pentameter without caesura). The absence of rhymes allows Pushkin to remain quite close to Cornwall's text. His few departures from the original are probably due to his imperfect knowledge of English.

The text of the monologue reads:

Oh! poverty. And have I learnt <sic> at last
Thy bitter lesson? Thou forbidding thing,
That hath such sway upon this goodly earth,
Stern foe to comfort, sleep's disquieter,
What have I done that thou shouldst press me thus?
Let me not say how I did bear me in
Prosperity; much of the good we do
Lies in its secret – but away with this,
For here are skiey <sic> themes to dwell upon.
– Now do I feel my spirit hath not quite
Sunk with my fortunes. –

From *The Poetical Works of Milman, Bowles, Wilson, and Barry Cornwall* (Paris: A. and W. Galignani, 1829), 4:38.

---

7 В молча́нии добро́ должно́ твори́ться – Good <deeds> should be done in silence, in other words, one should not speak about the good things one has done. Pushkin seems to misunderstand the English here.

9 пищу я найду́ для дум мои́х – I will find food for my thoughts. Pushkin avoids the admittedly odd adjective "skiey" and freely paraphrases the line.

„Если ехать вам случи́тся" – "If you happen to travel"

The poem, unpublished in Pushkin's lifetime, gives an excellent example of the poet's "poetic economy." Begun and apparently abandoned as a rough sketch in 1833, Pushkin returned to it in 1835, applying it to a completely different geographical (and presumably personal) situation. The possibility of two mutually incompatible ways of filling in the asterisks marked by Pushkin has caused considerable confusion among scholars. Though the 1835 version is longer and more complete than the 1833 version, neither poem is finished.

The poem is in trochaic tetrameter with alternating rhymes.

---

2 От **** на * – Though other possibilities exist (see Arinshtein 1987, 91), the most probable way of filling in the blanks would be "От Тригóрского на Псков" ("From Trigorskoe to Pskov"). Trigorskoe was the location of the Osipova (Vul'f) estate adjacent to Pushkin's Mikhailovskoe. The use of the preposition "на" is standard in the context of traveling directions – even in contemporary Russian one says "поезд на Псков," even though the ordinary phrase would be "поехать в Псков." In the 1833 version the line reads: "От ** к Москве" (with a different fourth line that ends with the word "синеве").

3 Л. – Лýговка. The Lugovka River. Given that the last word of line 2 must be Pskov (the rhyme makes this unambiguous), Lugovka is the only river nearby that begins with an "L" and has three syllables. In Pushkin's day, the post chaise traveled along it.

4 Меж отлóгих берегóв – Between the sloping shores

6 холмóм – a hill. Some editions change this to "селóм" (a village), which the Academy edition treats as an earlier (rejected) version.

7 дубрáва – grove

8 барский дом – manor house. Assuming the point of departure (line 2) to be Trigorskoe, the manor house in question is probably Golubovo, the Vrevskii estate, where in 1835 Pushkin visited his longtime friend Evpraksiia Nikolaevna Vrevskaia (1809–1883), the daughter of P. A. Osipova (of Trigorskoe).

9 как – when

10 Утопáет солнца шар – the sun's sphere sinks

15 невидúмо – unremarked

Literature: Arinshtein 1987.

На выздоровлéние Лукýлла. Подражáние латúнскому – On Lucullus's Recovery. An Imitation of the Latin.

The subtitle ("подражание латинскому" – "An Imitation of the Latin") was a red herring, intended to confuse the censorship, which in fact it did. Pushkin's readers immediately recognized that the subject of the poem was not antiquity, but contemporaneity. Pushkin's "Lucullus" was the tremendously wealthy Count Dmitrii Nikolaevich Sheremetev (1803–1871), whose heir Sergei Semenovich Uvarov (1786–1855) had recently been appointed the head of the censorship committee and, in that capacity, had annoyed Pushkin considerably. (Up until that point, their relationship had been wholly unproblematic. Uvarov, by training a classicist, was an important figure in Russian education with considerable influence on official policy. It was he who coined the slogan "православие, самодержавие, народность" [usually translated as "orthodoxy, autocracy, nationality"] that served to guide education in Russia under Nicholas and well beyond.) When Sheremetev suddenly fell gravely ill, Uvarov had the property sealed to make certain that nothing would disappear from his future inheritance. Sheremetev's recovery put Uvarov in an embarrassing position, which Pushkin exploited in this poem. In a diary entry of February 1835, Pushkin had called Uvarov a "большой негодяй и шарлатан" ("big scoundrel and charlatan"). He also repeated several rumors that found their way into this poem, for example, that Uvarov, in order to ingratiate himself with the Minster of Finance, ran errands for his children (line 26), and that he stole government firewood (line 32).

The historical Lucullus (who lived in the first century BCE) was a great general who, in his later years, enjoyed fabulous wealth and a sybaritic lifestyle. His name was widely known because his biography was included in Plutarch's *Lives*. However, there is no anecdote in Plutarch similar to the incident related by Pushkin.

The poem is written in eight-line stanzas of iambs based on two different types of quatrains. This is often found in odes (e.g., Pushkin's own "Вольность"), but in the present case seven iambic tetrameter lines are followed by a line in iambic trimeter. This is unusual enough that Tomashevskii (1958, 91) suggests a specific source: Derzhavin's "Ко второму соседу" (1791), in which Derzhavin chides his wealthy neighbor about his arrogance. Stylistically, Pushkin's poem is extremely varied. Certain passages, particularly in the opening and closing stanzas, sound like stylized Derzhavin, but this is undercut numerous times, for example, by the absurd similes and by the colloquial speech of the heir.

---

1 Ты угаса́л – you were dying. The imperfective aspect is crucial here.

4 В дверя́х сене́й твои́х хруста́льных – At the doors of your crystal vestibule. In old Russian houses "сени" (not to be confused with the singular "сень") was the passageway between the entryway and the living quarters. In this case, the room in question probably had not merely windows, but also cut glass (a sign of wealth).

6 Заимода́вец – creditor

11 нахле́бников, цирце́й – hangers-on, kept women. The latter word is presumably also part of the "red herring" effect; see commentary to line 47.

16 судьбы́ – fates (in modern Russian, the stress is on the first syllable: су́дьбы)

20 Зноби́м стяжа́нья лихора́дкой – Becoming feverish with <the possibility of> gain

21 сургу́ч – sealing-wax

23 загре́сть – rake in

28 благо – luckily; thank goodness

29 Тепе́рь мне честность – трын-трава́! – Now honesty is easy for me! "Трын-трава" is extremely colloquial.

30 Жену́ обсчи́тывать – to cheat (in counting out money) my wife. Uvarov was married to Sheremetev's second cousin, hence the potential for inheritance.

38 взоры клонит – averts his gaze (the coffin being no longer needed)

40 в толчки́ – with a shove

43–44 Cf. the final stanza of Derzhavin's "На смерть князя Мещерского" (another poem about a wealthy nobleman's death): "Жизнь есть небес мгновенный дар; Устрой ее себе к покою." ("Life is a fleeting gift of the heavens; Use it for your peace.")

47 Жену́ краса́вицу – a beautiful wife. It was widely known that Sheremetev was

homosexual, but Pushkin suggests that this beautiful wife will produce an heir for him, thereby excluding Uvarov from future inheritance.

Literature: Binyon, 485–89.

„Когда́ влады́ка ассири́йский" – "When the Assyrian ruler"

This unfinished poem was presumably intended as a retelling of the legend of Judith and Holofernes (from the Book of Judith, a canonical book of the Roman Catholic and Eastern Orthodox Old Testament). However, Pushkin's text ends before the entrance of Judith (chapter 8). Pushkin focuses on the events that precipitate her heroism, which may be summarized as follows: the Assyrian King Nebuchadnezzar dispatched his general Holofernes to lay waste to all the peoples who refused to yield to him. Holofernes arrived before the Israelites of Judea, who chose to defy him.

Many of the details of Pushkin's text come directly from the fourth chapter of the Book of Judith, for example, the name of the city Bethulia (4:6), the motifs of draping the altar with sackcloth (4:12), and covering heads with ashes (4:15). Pushkin's poem cuts off at the beginning of chapter 5, when Achior, leader of the Ammonites, reports to Holofernes on the Jews.

The poem is in iambic tetrameter in stanzas of varying length with unpredictable rhyme scheme (a mix of quatrains and couplets, with occasional triple rhymes). The form recalls that of his southern poems, but the lexicon clearly draws on the biblical source, using frequent archaisms.

---

1 влады́ка ассири́йский – the Assyrian ruler (Nebuchadnezzar)

2 казнию казни́л – executed by execution. The pleonasm is meant to sound archaic (the use of "казнию" for "казнью" contributes to this effect).

3 весь край ази́йский – the entire Asian land. In biblical usage, Asia is not a continent, but rather the Persian empire (which stretched from Turkey to Iran). The word "азийский" is archaic for "азиатский," but it does not appear in the Book of Judith.

4 десни́це – (archaic) to his right hand

7 перед сатра́пом – before the satrap (a subordinate ruler, usually despotic, in this case Holofernes)

8 вы́и – (archaic) neck. The word is in genitive case because of negation. In sound it prepares the word "завыл" in line 12.

10 Иере́и – Priests

11 вре́тищем – with sackcloth. In the Bible, sackcloth is a sign of distress and lamentation.

13 золо́й – with ashes (in Russian this word is only used in the singular). Covering one's head with ashes was a ritual of mourning and repentance.

14 И внял ему́ всевы́шний царь – And the most-high Lord harkened to him. The antecedent is "народ."

15 Прите́к – <The satrap> came. (In older Russian течь = идти; this form would have sounded archaic even in Pushkin's day.)

17 Замко́м замкну́ты – closed with a lock. In structure similar to the construction in line 2 and to the "поясом/Препоясалась" in 18–19.
19 Препояса́лась высота́ – the high (place) was protected
26 сове́т разноплеме́нный – his council of many tribes. Assyria was an empire, so its army was composed of numerous different peoples.

Пир Петра́ Первого – The Feast of Peter I

The poem is both historical and political. In the most basic sense, it is dedicated to Peter the Great, a subject endlessly fascinating to Pushkin. In a more subtle way, it is directed at Nicholas, whom Pushkin had encouraged to "resemble his ancestor" in his "Стансы" of 1826 (see commentary to that poem). As we learn only in the penultimate stanza, the purpose of the celebration described is reconciliation; Peter is forgiving a subordinate. Such events were indeed part of the historical record, though Peter was not always so magnanimous. In the sketches to an introduction to his unfinished "History of Peter <The Great>," Pushkin noted: "Петр, простив многих знатных преступников, пригласил их к своему столу и пушечной пальбой праздновал с ними примирение (*Ломоносов*)." ("Peter, having forgiven many aristocratic transgressors, invited them to his table and celebrated his reconciliation with them by means of cannon shots. [*<From> Lomonosov*])." Given that Pushkin wrote this poem ten years after the Decembrist uprising (and published it on the first pages of the very first issue of his journal *Современник* [*The Contemporary*]), it seems likely that he was urging Nicholas – as in his earlier poem – to pardon the Decembrists. (See Gillel'son).

The poem is written in eight-line stanzas of trochaic tetrameter with alternating rhymes: A-b-A-b-C-d-C-d. The pattern is somewhat complicated in that the rhymes of one stanza are often picked up, repeated, or developed in other stanzas. Compare, for example, the final rhyme of each stanza: потрясена (1) /жена (4) /потрясена (6) and враг (2) /гром (3) /врагом (5). Moreover, the final (refrain) stanza takes its opening four lines from the second stanza and its final four lines from the first.

The poem is structured as a series of questions, eventually leading to an answer. The use of a refrain recalls the poems "Зимний вечер" and "Бесы," both written in this stanzaic form and meter.

---

4 дружные – harmonious
8 Далеко́ потрясена́ – is shaken up <near and> far. The *Словарь языка Пушкина* glosses this particular usage of "далеко" as "на большое расстояние вокруг" ("for a great distance all around").
10 В Питербу́рге-городке́ – in the town of Piterburg. This particular way of naming the city is peculiar. Probably Pushkin uses an older form that would place the reader in the context of the early eighteenth century (a draft version even reads "В Питербурхе"). The word "городок" probably reflects a closeness on the part of the speaker, though in one instance elsewhere Pushkin uses the word in connection with Petersburg to express disapproval or ironic distance. (See Pogosian, 169.)

12 эска́дра – squadron
13 Озарён ли честью новой – Is <the Russian bayonet or flag> illuminated by a new honor
14 русской = русский. Bayonet and flag are here metonyms for Russian military power.
15 швед суро́вый – the stern Swede. As in "Медный всадник" ("The Bronze Horseman") ("Отсель грозить мы будем шведу" – "From here we will threaten the Swede"), the singular "Swede" is either standing in for all Swedes or a paraphrastic naming of Karl, the Swedish king. (The Swedes were a great power at this time and Peter's main enemies.)
16 Мира ль просит грозный враг? – Does the fearsome enemy ask for peace? The line refers to the historical situation in 1721; before that Peter had sought peace with Karl.
17 в отъя́тый (= отнятый) край у шведа – In an area taken away from the Swede
18 Брантов утлый бот – Brandt's frail boat. In his youth, Peter discovered a rotting old sailboat and had a Dutch master named Karsten Brandt rebuild it and teach him to sail it. The boat is on display to this day in Petersburg's Military Maritime Museum. On 10 August 1723 Peter had organized a festival to honor it, as Pushkin himself noted in his "History of Peter": "триумф старого Ботика, дедушки русского флота" ("the triumph of the little old boat, the grandfather of the Russian fleet").
19 навстре́чу *деда* – To meet *the grandfather*. (In modern Russian, the dative "деду" would be used.) Italics ordinarily indicate a quote; Peter himself had called this boat "дедушка русского флота."
20 Всей семьёй – As a whole family
22 Стали в строй – Stood in formation
23 в честь Нау́ки – in honor of Science. Presumably military science is meant.
25 Полта́вы – of Poltava. Poltava (in Ukraine) was the site of Peter's triumph over the Swedish King Karl (cf. line 28 of this poem as well as Pushkin's narrative poem "Poltava").
29 Родила́ ль Екатери́на? – Did Catherine give birth? Catherine I, the wife of Peter the Great. They had seven children together. As Pushkin notes in the introduction to "Медный всадник" ("The Bronze Horseman"), it was a Petersburg tradition to fire cannons in celebration when the empress gave birth to an heir.
32 Чернобро́вая – dark-browed. This positive epithet is common in folk usage and chosen because the famously beautiful Catherine was of peasant (perhaps serf) origin.
33 с подданным – with a subject
34–35 Винова́тому вину́ / Отпуска́я – Forgiving a guilty man his guilt
36 Кружку пенит с ним одну́ – He fills a single frothy mug with him (i.e., they drink their beer together from a single glass)
37 цалу́ет = целу́ет
39 проще́нье торжеству́ет – <He> celebrates a pardon
43 музы́ки – of music. In modern Russian, the stress falls on the first syllable.

„На это скажут мне с улы́бкою неве́рной" – "To this they say to me with a false smile"

This brief poem is often assumed to be incomplete (and Pushkin made no effort to publish it), but it may well be finished. The poem fits in to a series of works Pushkin wrote on the relationship of the poet and his audience, dating back at least to "Разговор книгопродавца с поэтом" (1824), the final prosaic line of which recalls the truncated conclusion here. This list includes numerous poems on the poet (e.g., "Поэт и толпа") as well as the prose work "Египетские ночи" ("Egyptian Nights"), which was written at approximately the same time as "На это скажут мне."

The poem is written in alexandrines, with the final line truncated at the midpoint. Pushkin alters the usually stately flow of these long lines by including a striking enjambment after line 5 and by breaking the hemistichs of the final lines into smaller units. The contrast between the high-minded assumptions about poetry and the mercenary attitude of the poet himself are reflected in the lexicon, where, for example, the words "морочите" and "слава" occur in the same line.

1 На это – To this. A striking opening, as the reader has no idea what "это" refers to (though it can be inferred as the poem continues).
2 укло́нный – evasive
3 моро́чите – deceive; fool
4 она́ – the antecedent is "слава"
7 Почему́ ж – But why?

Подража́ние ара́бскому – Imitation of the Arabic

The source of the first six lines is unknown (and there may not be one), but the poem's final image seems to be borrowed from the thirteenth-century Persian poet and philosopher Saadi. Pushkin owned a French edition of his *Flower Garden* (widely considered his masterpiece): *Gulistan ou le parterre-de-fleurs du cheikh Moslih-Eddin Sadi de Chiraz traduit littéralement sur l'édition autographique du texte publiée en 1828 avec des notes historiques et grammaticales par N. Semelet* (Paris, 1834). However, beyond the translator's preface he did not cut the pages. The fifth chapter, called "Sur l'amour et la jeunesse" ("On Love and Youth"), contains a story that begins, "Je me souviens que dans l'ancien temps, moi et un ami, nous faisions société comme deux amandes dans unc (*même*) enveloppe." (274) – "I recall that long ago my friend and I kept company like two almonds in one (*the same*) shell." If Pushkin was aware of this version, he could only have read it in someone else's copy.

Pushkin's poem takes nothing else from this passage except what appears to be a homosexual orientation. This fact was clearly troubling to Soviet Pushkin scholars, and one is struck by the alacrity with which certain editors – who otherwise do not concern themselves with drafts – cite the draft to this one, since it shows unambiguously that the speaker is a woman: "Отрок милый, отрок нежный, / Я твоя, навек ты мой."

Pushkin's poem is in trochaic tetrameter with rhyme scheme A-b-A-b-C-b-C-b. Pushkin consistently uses this meter for "exotic" subjects (Gasparov 1990, 9).

---

4 Жизнью мы живём однóй – We live a single life

6 Мы сдвоúлись меж (= между) собóй – We have become completely intertwined with each other. The verb "сдвоить" means "to bring two things into one, to intertwine." As such, it serves as an excellent example of the conceit that operates throughout the poem.

7 точь в точь (= точь-в-точь) – exactly

„Не видáла ль, девица" – "Maiden, did you not see"

An unfinished free translation from the collection of Serbian folklore of Vuk Karadžić (in the 1824 edition that Pushkin owned, it is in volume 1, page 107).

Коњ се срди на господара

Ој девојко, душо моја!
Јеси л' вид'ла коња мога? –
Нит' сам глала, ни видела;
Синоћ сам му звеку чула:
Седлом бије о јаворје,
А копитом о мраморје;
Коњиц ти се расрдио,
Што ти љубиш две девојке:
Аливеру и Тодору;
Аливера сина роди,
А Тодора сузе рони.

As usual, Pushkin does not hesitate to remove the specifically Serbian elements from the poem. It has been proposed (Solov'ev, 67) that this piece is connected to the wedding song of Pushkin's unfinished drama "Rusalka."

Since the poem is a fragment, it is difficult to determine its form. If one assumes that the word "коня" takes stress on the first syllable here (as it often does in folk poetry, see Bailey, 44), most of the lines scan as unrhymed trochaic trimeter. In not, then half of the completed lines (1–8) are trochaic and half have stresses on syllables two and five (making them either "тактовик" or – less likely because less typical of folklore – amphibrachic dimeter). All lines have either dactylic or masculine cadences.

---

5 красна дéвица – beautiful maiden (a standard Russian folkloric expression). The folkloric stressing of the noun is "дéвица," whereas in modern Russian the stress falls on the second syllable ("деви́ца").

8 На Дунáй рекý – To the Danube River. The Danube, not in the Serbian original, frequently appears in the heroic tales ("былины") of Russian folklore.

~1836

Д. В. Давы́дову – To D. V. Davydov

This poem accompanied a copy of Pushkin's *История Пугачева* (*The History of the Pugachev Rebellion*) that the author gave to his old friend Denis Vasil'evich Davydov (1784–1839) during one of the latter's infrequent visits to Petersburg. Davydov was famed as a "hussar-poet," – Pushkin admired him in both capacities. As a hero of the War of 1812, Davydov's picture hung in the gallery of the Winter Palace that Pushkin so admired (see "Полководец," opening lines).

The poem is written in iambic tetrameter with an unpredictable rhyme scheme (couplets followed by a ring pattern followed by alternating rhymes).

---

1 Тебе́, певцу́, тебе́, геро́ю – For you, singer, for you, hero. Pushkin slightly alters the first line of a dedication to Davydov by the French poet Antoine-Vincent Arnault (1766–1834), changing the form of address from formal to informal. In an edition that Pushkin owned (*Oeuvres de A. V. Arnault*, Paris, 1825), Arnault himself (on page 373) explains his poem's origins in his commentary to the fable "La Feuille" ("The Leaf"):

> *La Feuille* a obtenu dans plus d'une langue les honneurs de la traduction. Celle qui en a été faite en russe, par le général Davouidoff, est, dit-on, remarquable par son élégance et sa fidelité. M. Davouidoff est un de ces hommes qui, nés avec le don de la poésie, ne s'y livrent que par caprice, et pour se délasser de la guerre et des plaisirs. Instruit de l'honneur qu'il en avait reçu, l'auteur de ces fables lui en adressa un exemplaire avec cet envoi:
>
> A vous, poëte, à vous, guerrier,
> Qui, sablant le Champagne au bord de l'Hippocrène,
> Avez d'une feuille de chêne
> Fait une feuille de laurier.
>
> (*La Feuille* received the honor of being translated in more than one language. That which was done in Russian, by general Davydov is, it is said, remarkable for its elegance and fidelity. Mr. Davydov is one of those men who, born with the gift of poetry, only reads it on a whim and to distract himself from war and pleasures. Having learned of the honor that it received, the author of these fables sent him a copy with this poetic send-off [*envoi*]: "To you, poet, to you, warrior, who celebrating with champagne at the edge of the Hippocrene, made a laurel leaf from an oak leaf.)

In a brief essay called "Французская академия" ("The Academie Française"), written at approximately the same time as his poem to Davydov (it was published in *Современник*, volume 2 of 1836), Pushkin wrote about the recently deceased Arnault.

Арно сочинил несколько трагедий, которые в свое время имели большой успех, а ныне совсем забыты. Такова участь поэтов, которые пишут для публики, угождая ее мнениям, применяясь к ее вкусу, а не для себя, не вследствие вдохновения независимого, не из бескорыстной любви к своему искусству! Две или три басни, остроумные или грациозные, дают покойнику Арно более права на титло поэта, нежели все его драматические творения. Всем известен его "Листок" [...] Участь этого маленького стихотворения замечательна. Костюшко перед своею смертью повторил его на берегу Женевского озера; Александр Ипсиланти перевел его на греческий язык; у нас его перевели Жуковский и Давыдов [...] Может быть, и сам Давыдов не знает стихов, которые написал ему Арно, услыша о его переводе. Он поместил их в примечаниях к своим сочинениям.

After reading Pushkin's essay, Davydov responded with a letter to Pushkin of 10 August 1836, expressing surprise at the existence of Arnault's poem to him and dismay at his own translation, which he considered "unworthy" of Arnault's attention.

Arnault's fable (which explains elements of his dedicatory poem to Davydov) is cited below (in the above-mentioned edition, page 168), followed by Davydov's translation:

⇴La Feuille

De ta tige détachée,
Pauvre feuille desséchée,
Où vas-tu? – Je n'en sais rien.
L'orage a frappé le chêne
Qui seul était mon soutien.
De son inconstante haleine,
Le zéphyr ou l'aquilon
Depuis ce jour me promène
De la forêt à la plaine,
De la montagne au vallon.
Je vais où le vent me mène,
Sans me plaindre ou m'effrayer,
Je vais où va toute chose,
Où va la feuille de rose
Et la feuille de laurier.

⇴Листок

Листок иссохший, одинокой,
Пролетный гость степи широкой,
Куда твой путь, голубчик мой?
– "Как знать мне! Налетели тучи,
И дуб родимый, дуб могучий
Сломили вихрем и грозой.
С тех пор, игралище Борея,
Не сетуя и не робея,

Ношусь я, странник кочевой,
Из края в край земли чужой;
Несусь, куда несет суровый,
Всему неизбежимый рок,
Куда летит и лист лавровый
И легкий розовый листок!"

As Arnault relates in his note (371–72), the poem was immediately understood to be an allegory about exile, though it was not written with that intention. This theme is not relevant to Pushkin's poem, though it may explain his initial interest in Arnault's fable (and the poem's subsequent fame).

Curiously enough, Pushkin's first line seems also to echo a passage from Baratynskii's narrative poem "Eda," where the poet, addressing Davydov, writes: "Венком певца, венком героя / Чело украшено твое" ("Your forehead is decorated with the wreath of a singer, with the wreath of a hero"). These lines come from the "Epilogue," which was not included in the published poem and only published posthumously. Pushkin, a great admirer of "Eda" (see commentary to "К Баратынскому"), might well have known the epilogue from a manuscript copy. Virolainen notes that this formulation (певец, герой) is semantically closer to Pushkin's text than the Arnault (poète, guerrier). However, "поэт" and "певец" were virtually synonymous in Russian poetry of this time, and the rendering of "guerrier" as "герой" could also be explained as a phonetic transposition (the two words are strikingly similar in terms of sound). Nonetheless, the coincidences are undeniable; Pushkin's line may have two sources.

3 в огне́ – in fire (i.e., in battle)

5 Нае́здник смирного Пега́са – A rider of submissive Pegasus. By stamping its foot on the ground the winged horse Pegasus created the Hippocrene (mentioned in the second line of Arnault's *envoi* to Davydov).

6 Парна́са – of Parnassus, the mountain associated with poetic inspiration. (See commentary to line 10.)

10 Ты мой отéц и командúр – In a letter to Pushkin of 4 April 1834, Davydov had written: "Совестно мне посылать тебе сердечные мои бредни, но, если прикажешь, исполню повеление парнасского отца и командира." ("I'm ashamed to send you my heartfelt ravings <i.e., my poetry>, but if you order <me to do so>, I will fulfill the command of the father and commander of Parnassus.")

11 Пуга́ч – a familiar name for the bandit and pretender Emilian Pugachev (1740 or 1742–1775), the subject of Pushkin's historical work *История Пугачева*

12 Он виден – плут, каза́к прямо́й! – He is clearly a rascal, a true Cossack

14 Уря́дник был бы он лихо́й – He would have made a dashing officer

Literature: Virolainen 2009b.

Худо́жнику – To an Artist

The artist in question is the sculptor Boris Ivanovich Orlovskii (1792 [according to Chereiskii – other sources give 1793 or 1796]–1837), whose studio Pushkin visited either on or slightly before 25 March 1836, the date Pushkin noted below the poem in the fair copy. Most (perhaps all) of the statues Pushkin describes were works that he saw on that day.

The frequent appeals to antiquity (and, in particular, to art works on mythological subjects), explain why the poem is written in elegiac distichs.

---

2 Гипсу – to plaster of Paris (gypsum). Sculptors would initially do a plaster version, which would serve as a basis for a more costly (marble or bronze) rendition.

3 Зевс Громове́ржец – Zeus the Thunder-Hurler (a standard epithet already in Homer)

4 в цевни́цу – into a reed pipe. Orlovskii's statue of this satyr was a student work, but its final version (in marble) remained unfinished at the time of his death.

5 Здесь зачина́тель Баркла́й, а здесь соверши́тель Куту́зов – Here is Barclay the starter and here Kutuzov the finisher. The line refers to bronze statues that Orlovskii had made of Russia's two leading generals in the Napoleonic wars. It has been suggested that the primary purpose of Pushkin's visit was to see the statue of Mikhail Bogdanovich Barclay de Tolly (1761–1818), to whom he had dedicated "Полководец" (see commentary to that poem). On Mikhail Illarionovich Kutuzov (1745–1813), see commentary to "Перед гробницею святой." It is noteworthy that Pushkin supplies one-word noun "epithets" to these contemporary heroes much as he does to the Greek gods mentioned.

6 Аполло́н … Ниобе́я – Apollo and Niobe continue the references to Greek mythology (line 3) and develop the series of oppositions that can be found throughout the poem, beginning with the first three words. Niobe represents sadness because she has all of her fourteen children slain (the seven sons are, in fact, killed by Apollo, though that is perhaps irrelevant here). A statue of Apollo was listed as part of Orlovskii's estate at the time of his death, but it has since been lost. There is no record of a Niobe statue, though there were two bas reliefs on unspecified subjects from antiquity (Koka 1972, 108).

7 В толпе́ молчали́вых куми́ров – in the crowd of silent statues

8 Дельвига нет – Anton Del'vig (1798–1831), Pushkin's school friend. There is no direct confirmation that Del'vig was a connoisseur of the visual arts, but there is considerable circumstantial evidence (see Vatsuro 1994, 172–202). Pushkin was obsessed with his friend's premature death (see "Чем чаще празднует лицей" and commentary to "Когда за городом").

Literature: Panofsky, 76–77.

Мирска́я власть – Secular Power

The poem is at once a powerful religious statement and a searing critique of contemporary society. It must have been precipitated by an event or a story, but there has been little agreement on what that might be. Prince Viazemskii suspected that it "probably" referred to the fact that on Holy Friday at the Kazan Cathedral (in Petersburg), soldiers stood watch before the "плащаница" (a life-sized image [either painted or embroidered] of Christ after he was removed from the cross). Other possible sources include a French engraving showing the crucifixion and two soldiers from Napoleon's Old Guard standing in front of it. (See Lerner, 186–187).

The poem is written in alexandrines (iambic hexameter couplets). The lexicon is elevated (e.g., "зрим" instead of "видим," "мните" instead of "думаете"), lending a solemnity to the work.

The text published in the Academy edition was based on inaccurate copies of the poem. Subsequently a manuscript was discovered (Izmailov 1954). Izmailov's corrections based on this manuscript are noted below.

---

3 животворя́ща древа – of the life-giving tree. The adjective and its (genitive) ending are archaic, as is the noun.
4 Мари́я-грешница и пресвята́я дева – Maria the sinner and the most holy virgin (i.e., Mary Magdalene and the Virgin Mary)
5 жены́ – women. Pushkin originally wrote "Стояли, бледные, две слабые жены," then crossed out the two adjectives. Hence the line should be printed "Стояли <…> две <…> жены" lest the reader mistakenly think that Pushkin intended the hemistich "Стояли две жены."
7 креста́ честна́го – of the revered cross. The form "честнаго" is archaic.
9–10 These lines should read: "Мы зрим поста́вленных на место жён святы́х / В ружье́ и кивере двух грозных часовы́х." – We see two dread sentries armed and in a shako stationed in place of the holy women. A shako is a peaked military cap.
12 казённая покла́жа – state goods
14 Иль мните важности прида́ть царю́ царе́й? – Or do you think that you are lending importance to the king of kings?
16 тернием венча́нного колю́чим – crowned with a prickly thorn
18 копию́ – to a spear. The standard Russian word is "копьё" (dative "копью"). Pushkin adds the syllable for metrical reasons, but the additional vowel gives it an archaic and therefore elevated quality.
19 чернь – the rabble
20 Того́, чья казнь весь род Ада́мов искупи́ла – him, whose execution redeemed all of Adam's race (i.e., humankind). Note the curious echo of "казенная" (line 12) in "казнь."
21 потесни́ть гуля́ющих госпо́д – to crowd the gentlemen on their promenades
22 Пуска́ть не велено́ сюда́ просто́й наро́д – The simple folk are not allowed to enter here

Подража́ние италия́нскому – Imitation of the Italian

The title is not a mystification, but nonetheless somewhat misleading. Pushkin was indeed imitating an Italian original, a sonnet about Judas by Francesco Gianni (1760–1822). However, his primary source was a French translation of that work done by Antoni Deschamps (1800–1869), published in *Dernières paroles. Poésies* (Paris, 1835), 49–50 (cited below). The book was published anonymously, but Pushkin surely knew the author's name, since the particular edition he owned (according to Modzalevskii 1910, 222) bore the dedication: "à M. le Prince Elim Mestschersky Antoni D." ("to Prince Elim Mestschersky <from> Antoni D."). Moreover, Pushkin was interested in Deschamps; his was the only Dante translation in Pushkin's library with all the pages cut (Vatsuro 2000, 244). Indeed, the *Dernières paroles* volume begins with a poem dedicated to Dante. The particular poem that Pushkin renders here recalls Pushkin's own Dante stylization "И дале мы пошли," with its laughing demons and their sadistic pleasures.

Rossi (2009) has pointed out that Pushkin had in his library a poetry anthology edited by A<ntonio> Buttura, *I quattro poeti Italiani con una scelta di poesie Italiene dal 1200 sino a nostri tempi* (Paris, 1833 [first edition], 1836 [second edition] – which version Pushkin owned is unclear, since the book was subsequently lost). This book contains not only the original Italian text by Gianni, but also two sonnets on the same theme (i.e., of Judas's descent into hell) by Vincenzo Monti (1754–1828), a poet in the Dantesque tradition. If, as Rossi contends, these other poems are likewise reflected in Pushkin's, it would mean that the title "Подражание италиянскому" should be taken at face value.

Sonnet de Gianni. Supplice de Judas dans l'enfer.

Lorsqu'ayant assouvi son atroce colère
Judas enfin tomba de l'arbre solitaire,
L'effroyable démon qui l'avait excité
Sur lui fondit alors avec rapidité.
Le prenant aux cheveux, sur ses ailes de flamme,
Dans l'air il emporta le corps de cet infâme
Et descendant au fond de l'éternel enfer
Le jeta tout tremblant à ses fourches de fer.
Les chairs d'Iscariote avec fracas brulèrent <sic>;
Sa moëlle rotit <sic> et tous ses os sifflèrent.
Satan de ses deux bras entoura le damné,
Puis en le regardant d'une face riante,
Serein, il lui rendit de sa bouche fumante
Le baiser que le traître au Christ avait donné.

The Italian text, as cited in Buttura's book (second edition, page 888), reads as follows:

SONETTO

Sopra Giuda.

Allor che Giuda di furor satollo
Piombò dal ramo, rapido si mosse
L'instigator suo demone, e scontrollo
Battendo l'ali come fiamma <sic> rosse;
Pel nodo che al fellon rattorse il collo
Giù nel bollor delle roventi fosse
Appena con le scabre ugne rotollo

Ch'arser le carni e sibilaron l'osse;
E in mezzo al vampo della gran bufera
Con diro ghigno Satana fu visto
Spianar le rughe della fronte altera:
Poi fra le braccia si recò quel tristo,
E con la bocca fumigante e nera
Gli rese il bacio che avea dato a Cristo.

It is characteristic of Pushkin's low regard for the sonnet that he chose to render the poem in ten alexandrine lines. Still, he did not entirely disregard the formal qualities of the French poem, which is written in twelve-syllable lines that – for the first ten lines – are rhymed in couplets. The French text then shifts to a ring pattern for the last four lines. If Pushkin did consult the Italian original, he ignored its meter (*endecasillabo*) and rhyme scheme.

Thematically, the poem offers a demonic counterpoint to the story of Judas's betrayal and Christ's resurrection. By describing this scene with a high lexicon, solemn intonations, and complicated syntax, Pushkin creates an appropriately grotesque effect.

Title: италиянскому – Italian. In modern Russian the word would be spelled "итальянскому."

1 Как с древа сорвался́ преда́тель учени́к – When the traitor-disciple fell down from the tree. "Древо" is archaic. In modern Russian, the stress would be "сорва́лся."

2 Дия́вол (=Дьявол) – the devil

3 Дхнул (=Дохнул) – blew
с свое́й добы́чей смрадной – with his stinking booty

4 труп живо́й – the living corpse. An oxymoron.
в горта́нь гее́нны гладной (=голодной) – into the gullet of hungry Hell. Note the emphatic alliteration.

5 радуясь и плеща – rejoicing and applauding. In modern Russian, the stress would be "плеща́." Rossi (2009, 114) notes the use of the same grammatical construction (two verbal adverbs) in one of the Judas sonnets by Monti (page 869 of the Buttura edition). In that poem, the demons who receive Judas's body are described as "ululando e bestemmiando" ("howling and blaspheming").

6 Прия́ли (=Приняли) – took

7 к прокля́тому влады́ке – to <their> accursed ruler

8 сатана́, привста́в, с весе́лием на лике – Satan, having risen, with joy on his countenance. "Лик" is often (though not exclusively) used about holy images; its presence in an explicitly demonic context is jarring.

9 насквозь прожёг уста́ – burned through the lips. In Russian, the word Satan is feminine in form, but nonetheless a masculine concept; hence the masculine verb ending.

10 лобза́вшие Христа́ – which had kissed Christ

Literature: Tomashevskii 1930.

„Напрáсно я бегý к сиóнским высотáм“ – “In vain I rush to the heights of Zion”

An incomplete poem, of which so little exists that it is difficult to make judgments about the direction it was to take. However, the alexandrines and the religious reference in the first line suggest that the poem would probably have fit into the broader context of elevated themes and high seriousness of the other alexandrine poems of 1836. (It might also connect to “Странник” of 1835, since the pilgrim’s goal in Bunyan’s novel is Mount Zion.)

---

2 за мною по пятáм – at my heels

3 ноздри пыльные уткнýв в песóк сыпýчий – having buried its dusty nostrils in the dry sand

4 пахýчий – strong-smelling. A transferred epithet; logically it refers to the deer, grammatically it refers to its rapid movement. Anna Akhmatova noted that this final image appears to be borrowed from a passage by André Chénier that was first published in 1839. Either Pushkin somehow had the opportunity to read Chénier’s poetry before its publication (see Luknitskaia, 223) or this is simply a coincidence (though this same Chénier work appears to have influenced other passages in Pushkin). The lines in question (cited here according to “Documents sur André Chénier,” in Saint-Beuve’s *Critiques et portraits littéraires* [Paris: Imprimerie de Madame Poussin, 1839], 5:441) read as follows:

> Ainsi, dans les sentiers d’une forêt naissante,
> A grands cris élancée, une meute pressante,
> Aux vestiges connus dans les zéphyrs errants,
> D’un agile chevreuil suit les pas odorants.
> L’animal, pour tromper leur course suspendue,
> Bondit, s’écarte, fuit, et la trace est perdue.
> Furieux, de ses pas cachés dans ces déserts,
> Leur narine inquiète interroge les airs,
> Par qui bientôt frappés de sa trace nouvelle,
> Ils volent à grands cris sur sa route fidèle.
>
> (Thus, in the paths of a young forest, rushing with loud cries, an eager pack <of beasts> follows the steps of an agile deer by the smells they recognize in the blowing winds. The animal, in order to deceive their suspended run, bounds, turns aside, flees, and the trace is lost. Furious because the footsteps are hidden in the desert, their agitated nostril interrogates the air, for whoever soon is struck by its new trace, they fly with loud cries along the faithful path.)

Из Пиндемóнти – From Pindemonte

Most commentaries state that the title is a mystification, that the work has nothing to do with the poetry of Ippolito Pindemonte (1753–1828), whose name Pushkin transliterates inaccurately. After all, in an earlier version the poem is entitled "Из Alfred <de> Musset," which would suggest that Pushkin was simply looking for someone to whom he could attribute his own (subversive) thoughts.

However, it may well be that the title should be taken seriously. Pushkin may have been paraphrasing – though not translating – passages he found in both Pindemonte and Musset (Vickery 1983, 140–42; Davydov 1999, 98–100). The opening passage of Pindemonte's "Le opinioni politiche" ("Political Opinions") reads:

> Sotto qualunque reggimento uom viva
> Benché regni il terror, benché la gente
> Frenin tiranne Leggi, o Re tiranni,
> Quanto de' mali, onde il cor nostro geme,
> Scarsa parte è ciò mai, che i Re, o le Leggi,
> O ponno in noi causare, o sanar ponno!
>
> (Under whatever regime man lives / Whether terror reigns, whether the people / Are curbed by tyrant Laws or tyrant Kings, / How much of the evils, from which our heart groans / How small a part it is that Kings or Laws / Can cause in us or remedy.)

The relevant Musset poem, "La Loi sur la Presse" ("The Law on the Press"), first published in September 1835, begins "Je ne fais pas grand cas des hommes politiques" ("I don't think much of politicians").

Other scholars have sought a source for this poem further afield: either in Alexis de Tocqueville's *Democracy in America* (Vol'pert, 475–78) – which Pushkin would have had to read at breakneck speed (Dolinin 2007, 228) – or in Robert Southey's short poem "Inscription for a Monument at Old Sarum" (Dolinin 2007, 226–36). Both of these arguments are highly speculative, since the textual echoes are far less obvious than in the case of Pindemonte and Musset.

Regardless of his sources, Pushkin was predisposed at this point in his life to take an interest in the rights of the individual, and this poem is surely his most moving and profound statement on the subject.

Like "Когда за городом," the poem is written in alexandrines and divided into two distinct parts, with an ironic and critical first section followed by a brief – and brilliantly sketched – positive ideal. Here, too, the second section (relying on verbal adverbs) is briefer; in both poems the final line is truncated and the poem – though complete – concludes with an ellipsis. Like the other major poems of 1836, it was not published in Pushkin's lifetime.

---

2 не однá кружи́тся головá – more than one head spins
4 оспóривать (=оспаривать) налóги – to argue about taxes
7 Морóчит олухов – deceives fools
8 В журнáльных замыслах стесня́ет балагýра – constrains the joker in his jour-

nalistic schemes. One hears in this line the bitterness that Pushkin experienced in the nasty and generally ignorant criticisms that had been leveled at him since at least 1828.

9 *слова́, слова́, слова́* – words, words, words. The italics indicate that it is a quote, and Pushkin's own footnote names *Hamlet* as the reference. The passage in question comes from Act 2, Scene 2, when Hamlet responds to Polonius's question as to what he is reading.

13 Бог с ними – The Hell with them. In Russian, this is a common idiom and does not invoke a deity. However, in the present instance the word recalls the "боги" of line 3 and adumbrates the adjective "божественным" in line 18. In terms of intonation, the passage is intriguing. According to the iambic meter, the phrase should be scanned as "Бог с ни́ми," but the natural sentence intonation – which presumably should be used – would read as "Бо́г с ними," a hypermetrical stress that draws added attention to the line and the logical break marked by this phrase.

14 Отчёта не дава́ть – not to give an accounting

15 для ливре́и – for a uniform. Ordinarily the word describes a servant's attire; here Pushkin uses it pejoratively as a high-ranking official's uniform.

16 Не гнуть ни совести, ни помыслов, ни шеи – Not to bend one's conscience, one's thoughts, one's neck. A magnificent example of a zeugma, perhaps derived (Grechanaia, 101) from the far less interesting lines of André Chénier's "O jours de mon printemps, jours couronnés de rose" ("O days of my spring, days crowned by a rose"). In Pushkin's edition (*Oeuvres complètes de Chénier*, Paris, 1819, pp. 112–113), the passage reads:

> Qui ne sait être pauvre est né pour l'esclavage.
> Qu'il serve donc les grands, les flatte, les ménage;
> Qu'il plie, en approchant de ses superbes fronts,
> Sa tête à la prière et son âme aux affronts.
>
> (Whoever does not know how to be poor is born for slavery. / Let him therefore serve the important people, flatter them, humor them, / Let him bend when approaching their haughty brows / His head for prayer and his soul for insults.)

17 скита́ться здесь и там – to wander here and there. This exact formula can be found in Batiushkov's "Элегия из Тибулла" ("Elegy from Tibullus"). See Proskurin 1999, 271.

20 Трепе́ща радостно в восто́ргах умиле́нья – Trembling joyously in raptures of tender emotion. In modern Russian, the stress would be "трепеща́."

„Отцы́ пусты́нники и жены непоро́чны" – "Hermit fathers and chaste women"

An extraordinary religious poem, written in the alexandrines Pushkin favored in 1836. The second half of the poem brilliantly renders in modern Russian the prayer of repentance attributed to Saint Ephrem the Syrian (fourth century), one of the fathers of the Eastern Orthodox Church. This well-known prayer, which Pushkin had once parodied in a letter of 23 March 1821 to Del'vig, is recited at services during Lent: "Господи и Владыко живота моего, дух праздности, уныния, любоначалия и празднословия не даждь ми. Дух же целомудрия, смиренномудрия, терпения и любве, даруй ми рабу Твоему. Ей, Господи Царю, даруй ми зрети моя прегрешения, и не осуждати брата моего, яко благословен еси во веки веков, аминь." ("O Lord and ruler of my life, do not give me the spirit of idleness, of despondency, of lust for power, and of idle speech. Rather grant me your slave the spirit of chastity, of humility, of patience, and of love. Grant me, Lord King, to see my transgressions and not judge my brother, for you are blessed for eternity, amen.")

The language of Pushkin's poem relies on archaisms to create a solemn, religious effect. He frequently avoids the standard form, opting for the more archaic variant, for example, "возлетать" (rather than "взлетать"), "во дни" (rather than "в дни"), "сокрытой" (rather than "скрытой").

---

1 непоро́чны (=непорочные) – chaste. The short adjective is used attributively, not possible in modern Russian. Pushkin often does this for purposes of stylization (here to create an archaic effect). The same technique is used in "заочны," the rhyme word in the next line.

2 Чтоб сердцем возлета́ть (=взлетать) во области зао́чны – in order to ascend with their heart into invisible (i.e., holy) realms

3 Чтоб укрепля́ть его́ средь дольних бурь и битв – in order to strengthen it (i.e., the heart) among earthly storms and battles

4 Сложи́ли множество боже́ственных моли́тв – Created many divine prayers

5 умиля́ет – moves to tender emotion. The word has a distinctly religious quality. ("Умиление" is one of the standard icons, portraying Mary holding the infant Jesus.)

7 Вели́кого поста́ – of the Great Fast, the forty-day period of repentance that precedes "Пасха" (Easter).

8 прихо́дит на уста́ – comes to <my> lips

9 падшего крепи́т – strengthens the fallen one (me)

10 Влады́ко дней мои́х! – Master of my days (i.e., of my life). "Владыко," the vocative case of "Владыка" (or conceivably simply an archaic nominative), is the form used in Ephrem's prayer.

11 Любонача́лия, змей сокры́той сей – of lust for power, that hidden snake. As Grechanaia (98–99) notes, this metaphor (absent from the prayer that Pushkin otherwise stays so close to) seems to be derived from a poem by André Chénier ("Jeu de paume"): "Tout mortel dans son coeur cache, même à ses yeux, / L'ambition, serpent insidieux" ("Every mortal hides in his heart, even from his own eyes / Ambition, that insidious serpent"). In the edition that Pushkin owned (*Oeuvres complètes de Chénier* [Paris, 1819]), these verses are on page 254.

„Когда́ за городом, заду́мчив, я брожу́“ – “Whenever I wander, pensive, outside of the city”

One of Pushkin’s great meditations on death, the poem borrows extensively from the hackneyed “graveyard” tradition of European Romanticism, yet makes it new and highly personal.

Part of the impetus for the poem may have been biographical. On 29 March 1836 Pushkin’s mother passed away; on 13 April he attended the funeral service for her in Sviatogorskii Monastery (near Mikhailovskoe) and selected a burial place for himself next to hers in that same cemetery. Pushkin wrote his poem contrasting the city and country graveyards four months later.

Levitskii (10) ingeniously argues that poem’s point of departure should be traced to a laconic and undated jotting (apparently the “plan” for an unwritten lyric poem) entitled “Prologue.”

> Я посетил твою могилу – но там тесно; les morts m’en distrai<en>t – теперь иду на поклонение в Ц.<арское> С.<ело> и в Баб<олово.>
>
> Ц.<арское> С.<ело>! … (Gray) les jeux du Lycée, nos leçons … Delvig et Kuchel<becker>, la poésie –
>
> Баб<олово>
>
> (I visited your grave – but it’s crowded there; the dead distract me – now I make my pilgrimage to Tsarskoe Selo and Babolovo [a park outside of Tsarskoe Selo].
>
> Tsarskoe Selo! … (Gray) the games of the Lyceum, our lessons … Del’vig and Kiukhel’beker. Poetry –
>
> Babolovo.)

The addressee of this clearly autobiographical text appears to be Pushkin’s deceased friend Del’vig, and the opening sentence reflects an aversion to the city graveyard where he was buried. The first sentence scans as an irreproachable iambic hexameter line (with caesura after the third foot).

“Когда за городом” is written in this very form (with pair rhymes), that is, in alexandrines. The obvious metrical association is with the eighteenth century, but Pushkin was reevaluating the expressive possibilities of the form (see also “Подражание италиянскому,” “Мирская власть,” “Из Пиндемонти” and “Отцы пустынники”). The poem’s lexicon is striking; numerous coarse words are interspersed with the expected high style, but they ultimately serve to heighten the pathos rather than annul it. Structurally, the poem is clearly divided into two parts by the ellipsis at the caesura of line 17. The final line is truncated at the hemistich, but the poem is finished. The concluding verbal adverbs convey a sense of timelessness.

---

1 заду́мчив – pensive. A short-form adjective. Rossi (2009, 116) notes a striking similarity between this line and the opening line of a famous Petrarch sonnet: “Solo et pensoso i più deserti campi” (“Alone and pensive <through> the most deserted fields”).

2 публи́чное кладби́ще – a public cemetery. In modern Russian the stress is on the first syllable: “кла́дбище.”

3 наря́дные гробни́цы – elegant tombs

4 Под коими (=которыми) гнию́т – Under which rot

5 коё-как стеснённые рядко́м – sloppily crowded together one next to the other. The archaic spelling “коё” is not an indication of stress, which falls on the first syllable.

6 за нищенским столо́м – at a destitute table. This is probably a transferred epithet (i.e., the table attracts beggars)

8 Дешёвого резца́ неле́пые зате́и – the ridiculous flourishes of a cheap chisel. Another transferred epithet: it is not the chisel, but the artisan who is cheap.

11 По старом рогаче́ вдови́цы плач аму́рный – the amorous lament of the widow for <her> old cuckold. The rare Latinate word “амурный” adds to the irony.

12 Вора́ми со столбо́в отви́нченные урны – the urns that are unscrewed from columns by thieves. “Урна” was a standard word in Russian elegies, where it was essentially a synonym for “grave” and thus a symbol of death. Here it is used in its literal sense, as a decoration on a mausoleum. (Ginzburg, 213)

13–14 Моги́лы склизкие, кото́ры (=которые) также тут / Зева́ючи жильцо́в к себе́ на утро ждут – Slimy graves that, yawning, also there await their tenants in the morning. The personification of the graves, combined with the metaphor of “tenants” for corpses, creates an eerie and uncomfortable image.

15 Таки́е смутные мне мысли всё наво́дит – All this brings troubling thoughts to me

16 нахо́дит – comes over

17 Хоть плюнуть да бежа́ть – <To the point that I want> to spit and run away

19 кладби́ще родово́е – ancestral cemetery

24 Прохо́дит селяни́н – A villager passes. This is the standard topos of graveyard elegies going back to Gray’s “Elegy in a Country Churchyard” (first translated by Zhukovskii into Russian in 1802). Pushkin used it in *Eugene Onegin* 7:VII (where a shepherd replaces the villager).

25 На место праздных урн – In place of (i.e., instead of) empty urns

26 Безно́сых гениев, растрёпанных хари́т – of noseless <funerary> statues, of dishevelled graces. The adjectives mock the pretensions of the nouns. “Безносых” refers primarily to the fact that noses are the first part of statues to disappear (whether worn away by weather or inadvertently smashed by thieves), but secondarily to the effects of syphilis (the most common cause of noselessness in Pushkin’s era).

27 над важными гроба́ми – above the solemn graves

„Я памятник себе́ воздви́г нерукотво́рный“ – “I erected a monument not built by hands”

Often referred to simply as “Памятник” (a title that Pushkin did not give it), this is one of Pushkin’s most famous and most puzzling poems. The epigraph indicates that the poem is Horatian in origin, but the most obvious debt is to Derzhavin's translation of Horace's poem.

Pushkin's poem is written in quatrains of which the first three lines are iambic hexameter and the final iambic tetrameter. Such a form is similar to the major poems in alexandrines of 1836 and, like them, was probably intended as part of the "Stone Island Cycle" (see Davydov 1999; Levitskii). However, the tetrameter lines – and alternating rhymes – set it apart from those poems and also from Derzhavin's translation of Horace (which has the same alternating masculine/feminine rhymes, but is written in straight iambic hexameter). This precise form is not found anywhere else in Pushkin's lyrics, though some partial precedents have been found in the Lyceum poetry: the final four lines of the eight-line stanzas of "Воспоминания в Царском Селе" (1814; the form is used again in the 1829 poem of that name) and the final eight lines of the lengthy "Napoleon on the Elba" of 1815, where these lines are not set off as quatrains, but part of a longer stanza. However, if the rhymes are reversed (i.e., masculine and feminine), it recalls two major poems written in quatrains: Pushkin's own "К Мордвинову" and Derzhavin's "Евгению. Жизнь званская" ("To Eugene. Life at Zvanka"), both of which raise questions about legacies and monuments (see especially the end of the Derzhavin). The origin of the truncated final line has been traced to French odes. (On the issues treated in this paragraph, see Tomashevskii 1958: 75–77; Vickery 1973.)

In Pushkin's bilingual Horace edition (*Traduction des oeuvres d'Horace; par M. René Binet* [Paris, 1816], 1:202–3), this is the final ode of the third book. The relevant passages read as follows:

Carminum suorum gloriam aeternam fore.

Exegi monumentum aere perennius,
Regalique situ pyramidum[1] altius;
Quod non imber edax, non aquilo impotens,
Possit diruere aut innumerabilis
Annorum series, et fuga temporum.
Non omnis moriar; multaque pars meî
Vitabit Libitinam; usque ego posterâ
Crescam laude recens. Dum Capitolium
Scandet cum tacitâ virgine Pontifex,
Dicar, quà violens obstrepit Aufidus,
Et quà pauper aquae Daunus[2] agrestium
Regnavit populorum,[3] ex humili potens,[4]
Princeps Aeolium carmen ad Italos
Deduxisse modos. Sume superbiam,
Quaesitam meritis, et mihi Delphicâ
Lauro cinge volens, Melpomene, comam.

Notes

1. Les pyramides d'Egypte sont un des monumens les plus étonnans de l'antiquité. La plus haute a cent dix toises quarrées à sa base, et soixante-dix sept toises trois quarts de hauteur perpendiculaire.

2. Il transporte au Prince la sécheresse du pays: Hypallage.

3. Hellénisme: comme on diroit en Grec λαῶν ἐκράτησεν.

4. Daunus vivoit exilé nomme bien à dessein, dans la Pouille; il en comme ayant aussi fait devint Roi. Horace le fortune par son mérite.

☞ *Le Poète s'applaudit de l'immortalité qu'il s'est assurée par ses vers.*

> J'ai achevé un monument plus durable que le bronze, plus élevé que les pyramides bâties par les rois; que ne sauroient détruire ni la pluie qui ronge les pierres, ni l'aquilon furieux, ni des années sans nombre, ni la fuite rapide du tem<p>s.
>
> Je ne mourrai pas tout entier: la meilleure portion de moi-même n'entrera point dans le tombeau: je vivrai; et ma gloire, toujours nouvelle, s'accroîtra par l'estime de la postérité. Tant que la Vestale en silence accompagnera le Pontife montant au Capitole; on dira sur les bords du bruyant Aufide, dans ces lieux arides où Daunus gouverna des peuples rustiques, et s'élevant du sein du malheur, devint un monarque puissant; on dira que le premier j'ai porté dans la poésie Latine l'harmonie de la lyre Eolienne. Muse, prends des sentimens de fierté dignes de ton ouvrage, et viens avec joie ceindre ma tête des lauriers de l'Hélicon.

Horace's poem had been translated several times into Russian, but for Pushkin the most influential was Derzhavin's adaptation, in which the geography is "Russianized" (stanza 3) and the poet's attributes personalized in keeping with Derzhavin's own accomplishments (stanza 4). This poem is so close to Pushkin's own that Nabokov (2:310) has argued that it is essentially a quotation, except that the final stanza strikes out in a new direction.

Я памятник себе воздвиг чудесный, вечный,
Металлов тверже он и выше пирамид;
Ни вихрь его, ни гром не сломит быстротечный,
И времени полет его не сокрушит.

Так! – весь я не умру, но часть меня большая,
От тлена убежав, по смерти станет жить,
И слава возрастет моя, не увядая,
Доколь славянов род вселенна будет чтить.

Слух прóйдет обо мне от Белых вод до Черных,
Где Волга, Дон, Нева, с Рифея льет Урал;
Всяк будет помнить то в народах неисчетных,
Как из безвестности я тем известен стал,

Что первый я дерзнул в забавном русском слоге
О добродетелях Фелицы возгласить,
В сердечной простоте беседовать о боге
И истину царям с улыбкой говорить.

О муза! возгордись заслугой справедливой.
И презрит кто тебя, сама тех презирай;
Непринужденною рукой, неторопливой,
Чело твое зарей бессмертия венчай.

Derzhavin translated another poem by Horace that has relevance to Pushkin's poem. In Horace, it is book 2, ode 20 (the last one in the book, just as "Exegi monumentum" is the last one in book 3), and it also concerns poetic immortality (for more on its relevance and on the way Del'vig may be implicated here as well, see Bethea 1998, 228–30). Derzhavin's Russianized translation is called "Лебедь":

Необычайным я пареньем
От тленна мира отделюсь,
С душой бессмертною и пеньем,
Как лебедь, в воздух поднимусь.

В двояком образе нетленный,
Не задержусь в вратах мытарств;
Над завистью превознесенный,
Оставлю под собой блеск царств.

Да, так! Хоть родом я не славен,
Но, будучи любимец муз,
Другим вельможам я не равен
И самой смертью предпочтусь.

Не заключит меня гробница,
Средь звезд не превращусь я в прах;
Но, будто некая цевница,
С небес раздамся в голосах.

И се уж кожа, зрю, перната
Вкруг стан обтягивает мой;
Пух на груди, спина крылата,
Лебяжьей лоснюсь белизной.

Лечу, парю – и под собою
Моря, леса, мир вижу весь;
Как холм, он высится главою,
Чтобы услышать богу песнь.

С Курильских островов до Буга,
От Белых до Каспийских вод,
Народы, света с полукруга,
Составившие россов род,

Со временем о мне узнают:
Славяне, гунны, скифы, чудь,
И все, что бранью днесь пылают,
Покажут перстом – и рекут:

"Вот тот летит, что, строя лиру,
Языком сердца говорил,
И, проповедуя мир миру,
Себя всех счастьем веселил."

Прочь с пышным, славным погребеньем,
Друзья мои! Хор муз, не пой!
Супруга! облекись терпеньем!
Над мнимым мертвецом не вой.

Epigraph: Exegi monumentum <aere perennius> – I have erected a monument more lasting than steel. The opening line of Horace's ode. (A Horatian "ode" is simply a lyric poem, not to be confused with Russian usage, where it denotes a solemn poem of praise and is associated with the poetics of the eighteenth century.)

1 нерукотво́рный – not made by <human> hands. In Russian the word is rarely found in poetry. (This is the only time in Pushkin's oeuvre that it appears.) It is ordinarily associated with the realm of the sacred. Cf. Mark 14:58: "мы слышали, как Он говорил: Я разрушу храм сей рукотворенный, и через три дня воздвигну другой, нерукотворенный." ("We heard him say, I will destroy this temple that is made with hands, and within three days I will build another made without hands.") Presumably coming from this biblical passage, it is often used in conjunction with icons (i.e., "Спас нерукотворный"). Feinberg (584) notes that the eighteenth-century poet Vasilii Ruban (1742–1795) had used the phrase "нерукотворная гора" in his poem "К памятнику Петра Великого" ("On the Monument of Peter the Great"). The poem is worth quoting in full, because it intersects in numerous ways with Pushkin's poem. Feinberg cites it to argue that the poem is a polemic with Tsar Alexander, since the creation of the Alexander Column was from its inception compared to the monument to Peter the Great. However, given that Ruban compares this famous pedestal to two wonders of the ancient world, the poem would also lend support for a reading of Pushkin's "александрийский" as referring to the lighthouse of Alexandria (see commentary to line 4).

Колосс Родосский, свой смири прегордый вид,
И, Нильских здания высоких пирамид,
Престаньте более считаться чудесами:
Вы смертных бренными соделаны руками.
Нерукотровная здесь росская гора,
Вняв гласу Божию из уст Екатерины,
Прешла во град Петров, чрез Невские пучины
И пала под стопы Великого Петра.

(Colossus of Rhodes, humble your proud glance. And you buildings of the Nile's high pyramids, Stop being considered as wonders; You are made by mortal perishable hands. Here a Russian mountain not made by human hands, Having heard God's voice from the mouth of Catherine, Passed through the depths of the Neva to Peter's city, And fell under the footsteps of Peter the Great.)

2 К нему́ не зарастёт (=зарастёт) наро́дная тропа́ – The people's path to it (the monument) will not be overgrown. The point of the line is *not* that people will

constantly walk over this path, but rather that this path is spiritual, not physical, and therefore cannot be overgrown.

4 Александри́йского столпа́ – <than> the Alexander column. This line has tormented commentators. In Russian (and in Pushkin's Russian) the word александри́йский means "of Alexandria." It is conceivable that this is simply a Gallicism formed from the name Alexander (Meilakh 2005, 350–52), but the normal way to say "Alexander Column" is "Александровская колонна." This twenty-five-meter-high column, a monument to Tsar Alexander, was begun in 1829 and completed in 1834. (Pushkin intentionally left the capital to avoid having to witness the official unveiling ceremonies; see Jakobson, 346.) It was the highest structure in Petersburg, making it a logical subject of comparison. Given that Pushkin was known to detest Tsar Alexander (who had, after all, exiled him), it would be logical that Pushkin was comparing himself, another Alexander (see the "непокорной главой" of line 3) to the tsar. If the word really connotes Alexandria, it would suggest the Diocletian Column in Alexandria (built in AD 297), measuring twenty-six meters. It has further been argued that Pushkin, by metonymy, means the lighthouse of Alexandria, one of the seven wonders of the ancient world, in which case it would develop logically from the "pyramids" (in Horace and Derzhavin), another of the ancient wonders. Be that as it may, there is no question that Zhukovskii (who had attended the official unveiling of the Alexander Column and written an enthusiastic endorsement thereof) assumed that the line would be read as a reference to the tsar. When he prepared the first publication of the poem after Pushkin's death, he changed it to "Наполеонова столпа" a reference to the Colonne Vendôme in Paris (erected by Napoleon in his own honor), which the Alexander Column was meant to "answer" (and dwarf). The word "столп" (as against "колонна") has an archaic coloration (Alekseev 1967, 69–71).

5 в заве́тной лире – in <my> cherished lyre

7 доко́ль (=доколе) в подлу́нном мире – as long as in the sublunar world. The word "подлунный" is probably a Gallicism: "le monde sublunaire" is found in French texts, both poetic and prosaic. In Russian it is distinctly high style, but it appears in poetry with some frequency. See, for example, Zhukovskii's poem that begins "Я Музу юную, бывало, / Встречал в подлунной стороне" ("I used to meet the Muse in the sublunar realm") or Gnedich's poem "К К. Н. Батюшкову": "Над всей подлунною страною / Мечты промчимся на крылах" ("Over the entire sublunar land / We will hurry on the wings of our dream").

8 пии́т (=поэт) – poet (archaic)

9 Слух обо мне – The word about me (i.e., my fame)

10 язы́к – ethnicity; people (*not* language). The various peoples are enumerated in the next lines. Compare Matthew 24:14: "And this gospel of the kingdom shall be preached in all the world for a witness unto all nations." In Russian: "И проповестся сие евангелие царствия по всей вселенней, во свидетельство всем языком."

11 финн – the Finn. Finland belonged to Russia after a brief war of 1808–1809, in which Tsar Alexander wrested it from Sweden.

12 Тунгу́з (=Тунгус) – The Tungus, a Siberian tribe. Though drafts indicate that Pushkin took a while to settle on this ethnicity (he had tried "черкес,"

which would recall his first "southern poem," "Кавказский пленник" ["The Prisoner of the Caucasus"]), his choice of this particular tribe and the modifier "ныне дикой (=дикий)" can probably be traced to a letter of 12 February 1836 (the first in twelve years) that he received from his old Lyceum friend, the poet Vil'gel'm Kiukhel'beker. Kiukhel'beker, who was living in a remote section of Siberia after years of imprisonment for his participation in the Decembrist uprising, wrote: "Тунгусов я встречал мало: но в них что-то есть; звериное начало (le principe animal) в них сильно развито и, как человек-зверь, тунгус в моих глазах гораздо привлекательнее расчетливого, благоразумного бурята." ("I met few Tungus people: but they possess something distinctive; an animal quality [le principe animal] is extremely developed in them and, as a combination of beast and man, the Tungus in my eyes are far more attractive than the calculating, prudent Buriat.")

калмы́к – the Kalmyk. Though Eastern in origin, for Pushkin they were a southern people (see notes to "Калмычке"). In choosing the specific nationalities he does, Pushkin emphasizes the geographical breadth of the Russian empire – east (Tungus), south (Kalmyk), north (Finn). This would lead one to conclude that the paraphrastic "гордый внук славян" ("proud grandson of Slavs") refers not simply to Slavic descendents generally, but to Poles specifically (the westernmost Slavs in the Russian empire). "Pride" is a negative term in Pushkin's Russian, and he constantly attributes it to the Poles, for example, in *Boris Godunov* and the 1831 poems on the Polish uprising. If this hypothesis is correct, then "внук" should be understood not as a reference to future generations, but rather to the fact that both the Russians and the Poles (and presumably all other Slavic peoples) are descended from the same "pan-Slavic" ancestor. This notion of kinship fits in neatly with Pushkin's famous claim (see commentary to "Клеветникам России") of the "fraternal" relationship between Russia and Poland. On the sources of this geographical topos, see commentary to "Клеветникам России," line 37.

14 чувства добрые – kind (good) feelings. Insofar as the entire poem appears to have as a subtext Pushkin's relationship to Tsar Alexander (cf. line 4), this may be a reference to an incident that occurred in 1819. When Tsar Alexander was trying to determine what sort of (unpublished, subversive) poems were making Pushkin so famous, he was shown the anti-serfdom poem "Деревня" ("The Village"). This actually corresponded to his liberal views at the time, and he responded: "Faites remercier Pouchkine des bons sentiments que ses vers inspirent" ("Have Pushkin thanked for the good feelings that his verses inspire"). Another memoir quotes the line as "Remerciez Pouchkine des nobles sentiments qui inspirent ses vers" ("Thank Pushkin for the kind (noble) feelings that inspire his verses"). See Tsiavlovskii (1958) on the veracity of these accounts.

15 Что в мой жесто́кой (=жестокий) век воссла́вил я Свобо́ду – that in my cruel age I sung the praises of Freedom. In a draft version Pushkin had written: Что в след Ради́щеву воссла́вил я свобо́ду ("that following Radishchev I sung the praises of freedom"). This version – conceivably rejected in an act of "self-censorship" to head off eventual problems with the official censorship – makes clear that Pushkin refers to his own poem "Вольность" (since

Radishchev had also written a poem by that name). The notion of including the name of one's own works in a "monument" poem can be traced to Derzhavin's "Лебедь" (the line "Чтобы услышать богу песнь" [To hear the song to God"] alludes to Derzhavin's own poem "Бог").

Pushkin had been rereading Radishchev a few weeks before writing his poem, and he surely recalled that author's "Слово о Ломоносове" ("<Laudatory> Speech on Lomonosov") – part of the final chapter of his masterwork *Путешествие из Петербурга в Москву* (*Journey from Petersburg to Moscow*; on Pushkin's acquaintance with this banned book, see Kunin, 51–54), which contains the following passage: "Не столп, воздвигнутый над тлением твоим, сохранит память твою в дальнейшее потомство […] Слово твое, живущее присно и вовеки во творениях твоих, слово российского племени, тобою в языке нашем обновленное, прелетит в устах народных за необозримый горизонт столетий. Пускай стихии, свирепствуя сложенно, разверзнут земную хлябь и поглотят великолепный сей град, откуда громкое твое пение раздавалося во все концы обширныя России; пускай яростный некий завоеватель истребит даже имя любезного твоего отечества: но доколе слово российское ударять будет слух, ты жив будешь и не умрешь."

To return to the specific line in question, even the version without Radishchev's name proved unacceptable: when Zhukovskii prepared the first publication, he changed the line to "Что прелестью живой стихов я был полезен," and, to create the new rhyme, shifted the word order of line 13 to read "… народу я любезен."

16 милость к падшим – mercy to those who have fallen. The line refers to the Decembrists. Kiukhel'beker's letter (see commentary to line 12), which begins with heartfelt thanks to Pushkin for not forgetting him through the years of his imprisonment, is surely in the background here.

19 Хвалу́ и клевету́ прие́мли равноду́шно – Accept praise and slander with equanimity. Rossi (2009, 107–8) suggests that this is a reference to Petrarch, though recognizes that the sentiment can be found in Baratynskii as well as in Pushkin's own work (the sonnet "Поэту").

20 оспо́ривай (= оспаривай) глупца́ – argue with a fool

Literature: Feinberg, 577–91; Lednicki 1954; Proskurin 1999, 275–300.

Родосло́вная моего́ геро́я. (Отры́вок из сатири́ческой поэ́мы) – The Genealogy of My Hero (Excerpt from a Satirical Long Poem)

Though published in 1836 (in Pushkin's own journal *Современник*), this excerpt was written earlier. The subtitle is not a mystification; this really was part of a larger work, but that larger work was never completed. A more extensive (though still unfinished) version of the poem is traditionally printed among Pushkin's narrative poems under the title "Езерский." Numerous obvious parallels to "Медный всадник" ("The Bronze Horseman") have encouraged scholars to read the two works as being contemporaneous (i.e., 1832–1833). However, there are no less obvious parallels to Pushkin's attacks on Bulgarin (see, in particular, "Моя родословная"), making it possible that the poem, at least in part, was written as early as 1830. (On the dating, see Solov'eva.) The description of Ezerskii's ancestry is, in broad outlines, parallel to Pushkin's own.

The work is in Onegin stanzas, the form that Pushkin devised for his novel in verse *Eugene Onegin*. Onegin stanzas are composed of fourteen lines, using three different types of quatrains (first alternating, then couplets, then ring) followed by a couplet. All stanzas begin with a feminine rhyme and end with a masculine rhyme.

---

1 ab ovo – (Latin) from the egg (i.e., from the beginning)

3–4 Чей в древни (=древние) веки парус дерзкий / Поработи́л брега́ море́й – whose daring sail in ancient times enslaved the shores of the seas. The passage is based on synecdoche: the sail denotes the sailors on the ships, the shores of the seas represent the people who lived along those shores.

5 Оду́льф – Odulf. As the name makes clear, this is not a Russian but a Varangian, one of the ancient Scandinavians who – according to the chronicles – came and ruled the ancient Slavs.

6 Вельми́ бе грозен воево́да – <Odulf> was a very fearsome commander. The first two words are old Russian, in imitation of the source (see line 7).

7 Софи́йский Хроногра́ф – the *Sophian Chronograph*. Often called the *Софийская летопись*, this was a historical record written in Novgorod some time in the fifteenth century. In modern Russian, the stress is "хроно́граф."

8 При Ольге – In Olga's time. This refers to the colorful figure of the crafty and intelligent Princess Olga in the *Повесть временных лет* (*Primary Chronicle*; tenth century AD).

9 Прия́л (=Принял) крещéнье в Царегра́де – Was baptized in Constantinople. According to the *Primary Chronicle*, Olga herself was baptized in Constantinople sometime between 948 and 955, making her the first Russian Christian.

10 С прида́ным – with a dowry

12 В заса́де – In an ambush

16 да – and

17 И в лавре схимился Печéрской – And took the vows in the Monastery of the Caves. This refers to the famous monastery in Kiev, founded in the eleventh century.

19 При Калке – On 31 May 1224 the Russians were soundly defeated by the Mongols (Tatars) at the Kalka River (today in Ukraine), losing most of their leaders.

23 Зато со славой, хоть с уро́ном – But on the other hand with glory, though with a loss. In the published version, for reasons of censorship, this line was replaced by "За то на Кулико́вом Поле." Since it does not rhyme, this clearly was not the original version. However, it does spell out what is otherwise only implicit: that the battle in question in these lines is the Russian victory at the Kulikovo Field in 1380, generally viewed as the turning point in Russia's wars with the Tatars. Kulikovo is located between the Napriadva and Don Rivers (see line 26).

27 табор – encampment

28 С дружи́ной суздальцев свои́х – with his detachment of Suzdal men. Suzdal was one of many cities that supplied soldiers for the battle with the Tatars.

31 Крамо́л и смут во дни крова́вы (=кровавые) – In the bloody days of treachery and darkness. In Russian “смутное время” refers to the Time of Troubles, the period encompassing the reign of Boris Godunov and the numerous False Dimitris.

32 Блестя́т Езе́рских имена́ – The names of Ezerskiis shine (i.e., the Ezerskiis were important)

34 в отве́те – in the embassy. Pushkin himself glosses this archaism.

39 выводи́м – removed; forced out. This is a present passive participle agreeing with “он.”

42 Сицких *пересе́в* – occupying a place in rank above the Sitskii family. Pushkin italicizes the word to indicate a quotation. In this case, as his own footnote explains, the expression is archaic. In 1408 Prince Semën Fedorovich (a descendant of Riurik) received land along the Sit’ River and became the first Prince Sitskii. The line died out in the seventeenth century.

44 Прия́л (=Принял) Рома́нов свой вене́ц – When Romanov accepted his crown. The Romanov dynasty began in 1613.

45 Как=Когда

47 во́роги – archaic for враги

51 статься может – perhaps

54 Вас спесь дворя́нская не гложет – aristocratic arrogance does not gnaw at you (i.e., questions of aristocracy do not concern you)

58 Мстисла́в, князь Курбский, иль (=или) Ерма́к – Mstislav Vladimirovich (son of Vladimir Monomakh) or Mstislav the Great (1076–1132), famed for his military prowess and wise rule. Prince Andrei Mikhailovich Kurbskii (1528–1583), a valiant warrior, the right-hand man and later sworn enemy of Ivan the Terrible. Ermak Timofeevich Alenin (sixteenth century), a Cossack bandit who then served the Stroganov family and conquered Siberia for the Russians.

59 Митю́шка целова́льник – Mitiushka the tax collector. Mitiushka is a diminutive from Dmitrii. A “целовальник” (or “цаловальник”) was someone who traveled around the empire making certain that all subjects kept their oath of obedience (“целование креста”); this went hand in hand with collecting taxes (often on alcohol). The *Словарь языка Пушкина* states, without explanation, that in this particular instance the word means wine-seller. In any case, the line refers not to a specific historical personage, but to an insignificant person, someone who – in contrast to those named in the previous line – could not lay claim to participating in the major events of Russian history.

61 Вы презира́ете отца́ми – You scorn your fathers. Pushkin here uses this verb with instrumental case (rather than the usual accusative), probably because he regards it as synonymous with “пренебрегать” (French “braver”). See Vinogradov 2000, 289.

63 Великоду́шно и умно́ – Magnanimously and wisely

65 Прямо́го просвеще́нья ради – for the sake of true enlightenment

67 Красо́ю (=Красой) *собственных заслу́г* – <Taking pride in> the beauty of *your own accomplishments*. The italics indicates that the phrase is a cliché. (The irony becomes clear in the next lines.)

68 Звездо́й двоюродного дяди – <Taking pride in> the medal of your cousin once removed

71–72 хоть в книжках и словéсно / Собрáтья надо мной труня́т – although in <their> books and in their speech / My comrades-in-arms mock me. This is an exceedingly rare instance of a typographical error in the Academy edition (3:427), which gives the verb "Собраться" instead of the noun "Собратья." The word "собрат" clearly recalls the first line of "Моя родословная," while the verb "трунить" calls to mind "Румяный критик мой." Both of these 1830 poems are aimed at Pushkin's critics, most probably Bulgarin.

73 Я мещани́н – I am a bourgeois (cf. "Моя родословная")

75 новый Ходако́вский – a new Khodakovskii. Pushkin's own footnote explains that this was a "lover of antiquity" who had recently died. Khodakovskii was the pen name of Adam Chernotskii (1784–1825).

78 О толстобрю́хой старинé – About the fat-bellied days of yore. The rhyme родне/старине appears in "Медный всадник" ("The Bronze Horseman") in a similar context (first stanza of part 1).

80 спростá – through our simplicity; without reflection

81 Из бар мы лезем в tiers-état – We try hard to turn ourselves from aristocrats into commoners. "Бар" is genitive plural of "барин" (landowning gentry), while "tiers-état" (the stress falls on the last syllable) is French for "third estate." Beginning in the Middle Ages, European society was often classified based on estates – the first two included the nobility and clergy, with everyone else (peasants and the bourgeois) occupying the third. The same sentiment is expressed in Pushkin's unfinished prose piece "Гости съезжались на дачу" ("Guests Gathered at the Dacha"): "древнее русское дворянство […] упало в неизвестность и составило род третьего состояния" ("The ancient Russian nobility […] fell into obscurity and formed a type of third estate"). See Driver, 21–51.

87 что нет князе́й Пожáрских – that there are no <more> Pozharskii princes. Prince Dmitrii Mikhailovich Pozharskii (1577–1642) is considered one of Russia's greatest heroes, liberating Moscow from the Poles in 1612 and soon after helping to usher in the Romanov dynasty. The Pozharskii line died out by the end of the seventeenth century.

89 Что их поно́сит и Фигля́рин – That even Figliarin berates them. Figliarin was a common nickname for Bulgarin (see commentary to "На Булгарина," line 6).

90 Что русский ветреный боя́рин – That an empty-headed Russian boyar

92 пыльный сбор календаре́й – a dusty collection of calendars. The type of "calendar" in question is probably the "Придворный календарь," an official court publication that gave information on promotions and awards. (This is what Grinev's father studies at the beginning of *Капитанская дочка* [*The Captain's Daughter*]).

95 геральди́ческого льва – the heraldic lion. In heraldry lions are common the world over (the lion statues in "Медный всадник" are part of this tradition). It seems to be chosen here less as a specific reference than for the colorful image of the "king of beasts" being kicked by the "democratic donkey." However, earlier versions of the text indicate that the "democratic donkey" was originally a reference to Nikolai Polevoi and his attacks on the "literary aristocracy," which included Pushkin and his friends (Izmailov 1975, 241–42).

99 архи́вы роя – rummaging in archives

106 Имел двена́дцать тысяч душ – Had twelve thousand serfs. Male serfs were commonly referred to as "souls," as in Gogol's novel *Мертвые души* (*Dead Souls*). Twelve thousand serfs was an enormous number. In the eighteenth century, most gentry families had less than twenty serfs, and only one percent of them had more than a thousand serfs.

108–109 Осьма́я (= Восьмая) часть, и та сполна́ / Была́ давно́ заложена́ – an eighth part, and that <part> was long ago completely mortgaged. Because Russia did not have a law of primogeniture (something Pushkin greatly regretted), estates inevitably became smaller with every generation, as parents chose to divide their wealth equitably among numerous children. Thus, the grandchildren of the wealthy could easily become destitute. In modern Russian, the stress would be "зало́жена."

110 И ежего́дно продава́лась – And was each year for sale

112 регистра́тором служи́л – worked as a registrar. In the table of ranks, registrar was at the bottom of the fourteen possible civil ranks (numbers thirteen and fourteen). In stanza 11 of his narrative poem "Езерский," Pushkin explicitly calls him a "коллежский регистратор," which places him unambiguously in the lowest rank.

„От западных море́й до самых врат восто́чных" – "From the Western seas to the very gates of the East"

Prince Kozlovskii (see commentary to "Кн. Козловскому") had urged Pushkin to translate his favorite satire by Juvenal. As these fragments indicate, the satire in question was the tenth. Since that work is more than three hundred lines long, it is hard to imagine that Pushkin intended to translate it in its entirety. These brief passages render two different parts of Juvenal's poem: the opening lines (1–5) and lines 188–195 (which Pushkin renders extremely freely).

Pushkin owned a facing-page bilingual Latin-French edition of Juvenal with extensive commentary: *Satires de Juvénal, traduites par J. Dusaulx, nouvelle edition revue et corrigée par Jules Pierrot* (Paris, 1826). The poem proper is on pages 118–47, the commentary on 148–85. It is worth noting that the second excerpt ("Da spatium vitae") is in Pushkin's edition clearly marked as the beginning of a new section, since it is preceded by several skipped lines in both the Latin and French (bottom of 132–33).

The relevant passages read as follows:

Vota.

Omnibus in terris, quae sunt a Gadibus usque
Auroram et Gangen, pauci dinoscere possunt
Vera bona, atque illis multum diversa, remota
Erroris nebula. Quid enim ratione timemus
Aut cupimus?
[…]
Da spatium vitae, multos da, Jupiter, annos!
Hoc recto vultu solum, hoc et pallidus optas.

Sed quam continuis et quantis longa senectus
Plena malis! Deformem et tetrum ante omnia vultum,
Dissimilemque sui, deformem pro cute pellem,
Pendentesque genas, et talis aspice rugas,
Quales, umbriferos ubi pandit Tabraca saltus,
In vetula scalpit jam mater simia bucca.
Plurima sunt juvenum discrimina: pulchrior ille
Hoc, atque ore alio; multum hic robustior illo.
Una senum facies; cum voce trementia labra,
Et jam leve caput, madidique infantia nasi.

Les vœux.[1]

Parcourez la terre depuis Cadix jusqu'au Gange, voisin des portes de l'Aurore, vous trouverez peu d'hommes capables de discerner les vrais biens des maux réels;[2] car enfin la raison règle-t-elle nos craintes?

[...]

Prolonge ma vie, ô Jupiter! accorde-moi de nombreuses années! Voilà le vœu que vous adressez au ciel et dans la prospérité et dans l'infortune (68). Cependant, à combien de maux une longue vieillesse n'est-elle pas condamnée? D'abord, le visage devient difforme et méconnaissable; la peau se flétrit; les joues sont pendantes et sillonnées de rides, comme celles d'une vieille guenon des forêts de Tabraca (69). Les jeunes gens diffèrent entre eux; l'un est plus beau, l'autre est plus fort. Tous les vieillards se ressemblent; tous ont la voix et les lèvres tremblantes, la tête chauve, le nez humide comme celui d'un enfant.

Notes

1. ARGUMENT. Juvénal fait sentir la folie de la plupart de nos vœux. Après avoir examiné ceux qui ont pour objet les richesses, les honneurs, le pouvoir, l'éloquence, la gloire, la vieillesse et la beauté, il finit par indiquer les vœux que nous pouvons raisonnablement adresser au ciel.

Cette satire a toujours été regardée comme le chef-d'œuvre de Juvénal. Cependant, qu'offre-t-elle au premier coup d'œil? une vérité sur laquelle les hommes, dans tous les temps, ont été d'accord; car on n'a jamais douté que les vœux des mortels ambitieux n'appelassent le plus souvent le malheur sur leurs têtes imprudentes: tant il est vrai que ce ne sont pas les sujets les plus recherchés qui l'emportent! En général, le sentiment et la manière de traiter décident du succès.

O le puissant levier que le sentiment! Heureux l'écrivain qui sait, comme Juvénal, s'en servir au gré de son âme enflammée par la vertu! Tous les sujets lui seront égaux, parce qu'il saura les rajeunir ou les féconder, parce qu'il les enrichira du fruit de ses veilles et de ses profondes méditations; qu'il leur donnera, selon les occurrences, de nouveaux aspects, des relations nouvelles; mais surtout parce qu'il y imprimera fortement le sceau durable de son caractère individuel.

Dans la fameuse satire du Turbot (satire 4), la plus grande partie du succès de notre poète vient de l'art: il n'appartient ici qu'à la nature des choses fidèlement représentées, qu'à la raison secondée de toutes les ressources de l'éloquence, de l'imagination, et d'un fonds immense de l'érudition la mieux choisie. Ce qu'il y a peut-être de plus remarquable dans l'exécution de cet ouvrage, consacré par l'estime publique, c'est d'en avoir soutenu l'intérêt jusqu'à la fin; et cela, en détruisant nos plus chères illusions, en nous montrant le néant de tout ce que les hommes, séduits par de vaines apparences, ont, de générations en générations, constamment préféré à la sorte de bonheur dont nous sommes susceptibles.

Comment se fait-il que le genre humain, qui aime tant qu'on le flatte, ne cesse de courir après ceux qui le gourmandent et le châtient, et pourquoi les principes les plus austères ne manquent-ils jamais d'approbateurs? c'est qu'il est de notre essence, sans désirer peut-être de devenir meilleurs, de chercher la vérité jusqu'au dernier soupir; et cet attrait irrésistible est le plus beau triomphe de l'auguste vérité.

2. *Parcourez la terre depuis Cadix jusqu'au Gange*, etc. v. I. Boileau a dit, sat. 8, v. I et suivans:

De tous les animaux qui s'élèvent dans l'air,
Qui marchent sur la terre, ou nagent dans la mer,
De Paris au Pérou, du Japon jusqu'à Rome,
Le plus sot animal, à mon avis, c'est l'homme …

(68) *et dans la prospérité et dans l'infortune*, v. 189. C'est, je pense, le sens de *recto vultu*, et de *pallidus*. "Lorsque la misère a imprimé la pâleur sur ton visage, non moins que dans la bonne fortune, lorsque tu portes la tête avec fierté." *Recto vultu* et *pallidus* expriment des idées opposés, et c'est mal à propos que des critiques, et particulièrement Dusaulx dans sa traduction, ont voulu les rattacher à la seule idée *d'optare*: ils n'ont pas songé d'ailleurs à la force de la conjonction ainsi placée, *hoc et pallidus*.

(69) *des forêts de Tabraca*, v. 194. Tabraca, ville de Numidie, située sur le fleuve Tusca, et qui, selon Pline (lib. V, sat. 3) appartenait aux Romains. Quant aux singes qui habitaient les forêts voisines, Juvénal paraît être le seul qui en fasse mention.

Pushkin's text is written in alexandrines, which recall less antiquity than French neoclassicism (e.g., the Boileau excerpt cited above in footnote 2) and Russian eighteenth-century imitations thereof.

---

2 от благ прямы́х и прочных – from true and real blessings

5 долгу (=долгую) жизнь и многие года́ – a long life and many years. A pleonasm. The line is not in quotation marks in Pushkin's Juvenal edition.

6 Зеве́са – Zeus. The name is in the accusative case. Pushkin opts for the Greek equivalent to Juvenal's "Jupiter."

8 рубца́ми – with scars

<Кн. Козло́вскому> – To Prince Kozlovskii

Prince Petr Borisovich Kozlovskii (1783–1840) was one of the most colorful figures of the age. He served in Russian embassies (among other places, in Cagliari [Sardinia], Rome, and Stuttgart), where he stood out by virtue of his erudition, wit, and girth. His liberal views and outspokenness probably led to his retirement in 1820. He continued to live abroad until 1835. In Europe he was completely at home, knowing the languages and the cultural and political elite of many countries. Upon returning to Petersburg in 1835 be became a contributor to Pushkin's journal *Современник* (*The Contemporary*), for which he wrote articles on scientific and mathematical subjects.

Pushkin's unfinished poem to him is written in alexandrines.

---

2 Друг бардов а́нглийских – Friend of the English bards. In modern Russian the stress falls on the second syllable of "английских." Among these English bards was Byron himself, who mentions Kozlovskii in "Don Juan" canto 7,

stanza 17: "Scherematoff and Chrematoff, Koklophti, Koclobski, Kourakin, and Mouskin Pouskin." The fourth name in this list is Byron's idiosyncratic transliteration of the name "Kozlovskii" (with English "b" for Russian "в").

6 боро́ться с Ювена́лом – to battle with Juvenal. The Latin poet Juvenal (first and early second century) was known primarily for his satires. Kozlovskii had urged Pushkin to translate his favorite Juvenal satire, a task Pushkin began shortly before his death. (See commentary to "От западных морей до самых врат восточных.")

8 Стиха́ми переве́сть (=перевести) я было дал обет – I was about to promise to translate in verse. The word "было" is here a particle (not a verb) that indicates that an action was about to take place, but then was either not done or not completely executed.

9 разверну́в – having opened up. The verb "развернуть" adds an archaic quality, since it is usually used in connection with a scroll.

10 Не мог я одоле́ть пугли́вого смуще́нья – I could not overcome my fearful embarrassment. This is presumably ironic; Pushkin was hardly prudish in his own verse.

11 Стихи́ бессты́дные прия́пами торча́т – The shameless verses stick up like Priapuses. Priapus was an ancient Greek god of fertility, traditionally portrayed with an enormous phallus. In modern Russian, the form is "Приап."

12 В них звуки странною (=странной) гармо́нией треща́т – In them (i.e., the verses) the sounds crackle in strange harmony

„Была́ пора́: наш праздник молодо́й" – "There was a time: our young holiday"

The "holiday" of the first line is the October 19 celebration of the founding of the Lyceum. These verses were written for the twenty-fifth anniversary; it was the last such event Pushkin was to attend. According to the memoirs of an eyewitness, Pushkin began to read his poem aloud, but became overcome with emotion and could not finish. This account may simply be a retrospective embellishment of the actual circumstances; namely, that the poem itself was unfinished, and Pushkin simply stopped because he had written no more (see Levkovich 1974, 94–95). Even in unfinished form, the poem is one of Pushkin's most brilliant and powerful.

It is written in iambic pentameter with caesura after the second foot. As Tomashevskii notes (1958, 61), Pushkin had ceased writing iambic pentameter with caesura in 1830. By using it here, he clearly is recalling his earlier Lyceum poem of 1825 ("Роняет лес багряный свой убор"), with which this poem also shares the stanzaic form otherwise unique to Pushkin's oeuvre (an eight-line stanza with two different types of rhyme with a ring rhyme followed by alternating rhymes: a-B-B-a-C-d-C-d). The combination of quatrains rhymed differently within an eight-line stanza is characteristic of the ode, and the elevated lexicon (e.g., "о други"), archaic forms (truncated adjectives such as "новы [rather than "новые"] тучи"), and historical allusions encourage such an association – notwithstanding the fact that odes were written in iambic tetrameter, not pentameter.

---

3 И с песнями бока́лов звон меша́лся – And the clinking of goblets mixed with the songs. Though grammatically ambiguous, the word "бокалов" belongs with "звон," not with "песнями."

4 И тесною (=тесной) сиде́ли мы толпо́й – And we sat in an intimate crowd. The word "тесно" had figured prominently in the 1831 Lyceum poem ("Чем чаще празднует лицей").

5 неве́жды – unknowing ones. The word is usually strongly pejorative, but here it expresses inexperience rather than stupidity.

6 смеле́й (=смелее) – more daringly

8 всех её зате́й – of all of its escapades. "Её" here refers to "юность."

9 Тепе́рь не то́ – now it is otherwise

10 перебеси́лся – ran its wild course

13 льётся – pours. This metaphoric use of the verb draws on the drinking imagery of the previous line.

18 день заве́тный – the cherished day

19 чредо́ю (=чередой) незаме́тной – in an imperceptible sequence

24 Уже́ль оди́н недви́жим будет он – Will he alone really be motionless

27 Чему́, чему́ свиде́тели мы были – To what, to what have we been witnesses

28 Игра́лища – playthings

29 Мета́лися (=Метались) смущённые наро́ды – Agitated peoples rushed about

34 черто́г цари́цын – the tsarina's palace. This was a part of the Lyceum (Jakobson, 336).

35 Куни́цын – Aleksandr Petrovich Kunitsyn (1783–1840), a progressive thinker and talented scholar, taught ethics and political science. He had just returned from three years of study abroad (in Göttingen, Heidelberg, and Paris) before he took up his post at the Lyceum. His speech at the opening ceremonies (19 October 1811) was considered to be the highpoint of the celebration not only by the students, but also by (then still liberal) Tsar Alexander, who rewarded him with a medal. Pushkin was particularly interested in Kunitsyn's courses and always remembered him fondly thereafter. (Liubavin, 25–32).

37 гроза́ двена́дцатого года – the storm of 1812. The word "гроза" should be understood figuratively here (as "woe" or "misfortune"); it refers to the war with Napoleon.

41 текла́ за ратью рать – division went after division. The use of "течь" for "идти" was archaic in Pushkin's day, but standard in Russian odic poetry of the eighteenth century.

47–48 И заревом моско́вским озари́лись / Его полка́м гото́вые снега́ – And the snows that were ready for his troops were illuminated by Moscow's glow. The "glow" refers to the burning of Moscow. (Pushkin subscribed to the general belief that Russian patriots set fire to the city soon after Napoleon had taken it to ensure that he would not benefit from his conquest. "Мы жгли Москву," he wrote in a draft version of his Lyceum poem of 1831 "Чем чаще празднует лицей.") The snows refer to the vicious winter that, according to most accounts, defeated Napoleon.

49 наш Агамемно́н – our Agamemnon. Tsar Alexander, whom Pushkin generally remembered with displeasure. His military successes here merit him compari-

son with the leader of the Greeks in the Trojan War. This same comparison can be found in Zhukovskii's "Императору Александру" ("To Emperor Alexander"), Pushkin's probable source (Al'tshuller, 109).

55 сии́ живы́е воды – those living (i.e., life-giving) waters. The "living waters" is a folkloric image.

57 и Русь оста́вил о́н – And he left Russia. A solemn paraphrase for "he died" (see Ivanova, 354). It is essentially a repetition (pleonasm) of the first part of the line, but with a particularly elevated style.

58 Взнесе́нну (=Вознесенную) им над миром изумле́нным – Raised up by him above the amazed world. The truncated adjective "Взнесенну" (likewise a marker of high style) refers to "Русь."

59 на скале́ – on a crag. Pushkin has in mind the island of Saint Helena, Napoleon's final place of exile. The crag can be explained either as an appealing Romantic image or a reflection of the island's volcanic terrain.

60 уга́с – became extinguished (i.e., died)

61 И новый царь, суро́вый и могу́чий – And the new tsar, stern and powerful. This is Nicholas, who had come to power in 1825 and reigned long after Pushkin's death.

64 урага́н – hurricane. The weather imagery recalls the "гроза" of line 37. The still more violent hurricane is probably an allusion to the Decembrist rebellion. The poem breaks off at the mention of this historical watershed.

На статую игра́ющего в свайку – On a Statue of a "Svaika" Player

A poem on a statue by Aleksandr Vasil'evich Loganovskii (1812–1855), whom Pushkin probably met at the exhibition of 1836 (see commentary to "На статую играющего в бабки"). "Svaika" (like "babki") was a traditional Russian game of obscure origins. The point of the game was to throw the "svaika" (an iron object the shape of an oversized nail with a very large head) deep into the ground inside of a metal ring. The statue depicts a youth naked above the waist with a muscled torso about to throw.

As in "На статую играющего в бабки," Pushkin views the Russian game through the prism of antiquity, using elegiac distichs as a formal marker to emphasize a timeless quality.

---

1 напряже́нья, уси́лия чуждый – free of tension <and> effort.

2 тешится быстрой игро́й – gets pleasure from the quick game

3 дискобо́л – discus thrower. The particular discus thrower alluded to by Pushkin is a statue of Myron of Eleutherae (fifth century BCE), an Athenian sculptor famed for his harmonious representations of athletes. None of Myron's works exist, but some (such as this one) are known because of ancient Roman copies. In the eighteenth century, Ivan Ivanovich Shuvalov (1727–1797), the first president of Saint Petersburg's Academy of the Arts, went to Italy and ordered plaster casts of numerous sculptures of antiquity. These were then brought to the Academy's Museum in Saint Petersburg for the edification of generations

of artists and artistically inclined Russians. Among these statues was the discus thrower of Myron. It is safe to assume that Pushkin knew the statue from this copy.

На статую игрáющего в бабки – On a Statue of a "Babki" Player

The poem was inspired by a statue by Nikolai Stepanovich Pimenov (1812–1864), which Pushkin viewed at an exhibition of works by students at the Academy of Arts in 1836. The exhibit took place in the "Античная галерея," a location that may have contributed to Pushkin's reception of the "classical" qualities of the statues he saw. According to memoirs, Pushkin was especially enthusiastic about this particular work; he rushed up to the sculptor and exclaimed "Слава Богу, наконец и скульптура на Руси явилась народною" – "Thank God, finally there is even national sculpture <i.e., sculpture that expresses the common man> in Russia" (Koka 1962, 183). The game of "babki" was akin to skittles except that it was played with the bones of domestic animals (usually from the ankle). Each player throws a bone and tries to knock as many other bones as possible out of a clearly delineated area. The statue in question pictures a youth (naked above the waist) in precisely the position Pushkin depicts (one hand on his knee, the other about to throw the bone).

The poem takes the form of two elegiac distichs, an obvious metrical allusion to antiquity.

---

1 рукóй о колéно – <one> hand against his knee
2 Бодро опéрся, другóй поднял меткую кость – Leaned full of strength, with his other <hand> he lifted the well-aimed bone.
3 раздáйся – move aside
4 русской удáлой игрé – the daring Russian game. In modern Russian the stress would be "удалóй."

„Альфóнс садúтся на конѧ́" – "Alphonse mounts <his> steed"

This unfinished work is a poetic (and somewhat free) rendering of parts of the first chapter of the novel *Dix journées de la vie d'Alphonse Van-Worden* or *Ten Days in the Life of Alphonse Van-Worden* (often called *Manuscrit trouvé à Saragosse – Manuscript Found in Saragossa*) by Jan Potocki (1761–1815). Pushkin greatly admired the book. Potocki was a wealthy and widely traveled Pole, educated in Switzerland, who wrote in French. The novel, which purports to be a French translation of a Spanish manuscript, is composed of numerous short tales, with a loose structure formally reminiscent of the *Thousand and One Nights* or the *Decameron*. The subject matter is macabre and at times supernatural, revolving around Alphonse Van-Worden, a Walloon officer serving in Spain in the first half of the eighteenth century.

Pushkin's poem is in the form of his southern narrative poems: iambic tetrameter with unpredictable rhyme scheme.

3 послу́шайтесь меня́ – listen to my advice
4 Пуска́ться в путь тепе́рь не время – it's not a good time to set off on your journey now
6 вента – inn (in Spain). The word is used repeatedly in Potocki's novel.
8 разложён ого́нь – the fire is set. In modern Russian, the form is "разло́жен."
9 Посте́ля – a bed. In modern Russian the standard form is посте́ль.
10 к стойлу тянется – is yearning for <his> stall (i.e., in the stable)
12 был бы путь – as long as there is a path
19 рысью – in a trot
21 Уще́льем тесным и глухи́м – Through a narrow and dense ravine
24 дичь и голь – wilderness and barrenness
25 торчи́т глаго́ль – a gallows sticks out. The word глаголь is an old word for the Russian letter "г." Because its shape resembles a gallows, it has this as a secondary definition.
29 Лишь только – as soon as
30 гита́нов – Gypsies. To add local color, Pushkin uses the Spanish word (which he and his readers would have recognized, since it is a cognate with the French "gitanes"). The word "citanas" (Spanish for "Gypsy women," apparently a typo for "gitanas") appears in Pushkin's edition of the first chapter of Potocki's novel, but Potocki's two hanged men are not Gypsies. The image of the gallows with corpses hanging recalls "Какая ночь! Мороз трескучий" (see commentary to that poem) and may be connected to Pushkin's obsession with the hanged Decembrists.
31 братьев-атама́нов – bandit-chief brothers
39 обрыва́ясь по ноча́м – coming down at night. The idea is presumably that the hanged men come down off the ropes.
41 мстя свои́м врага́м – taking vengeance on their enemies
42 Альфо́нсов конь – Alphonse's steed
43 их мимо = мимо них
44 Понёсся – rushed off

Literature: Chernobaev; Virolainen 2009a.

„Забы́в и рощу и свобо́ду" – "Having forgotten both <its> grove and <its> freedom"

The source or occasion for this poem is unknown. It is tempting to view the image of a caged bird enjoying its song as a statement about the poet, perhaps autobiographical. In this regard, Vasilii Kapnist's poem "Чижик" might have set a precedent.

The poem is written in iambic tetrameter with alternating rhymes: A-b-A-b.

2 чижик – siskin (diminutive of "чиж"), a type of finch
3 брызжет – splashes
4 тешится – amuses itself

<Из письмá к Яковлеву> – From a letter to Iakovlev

These lines appear in a short, undated letter to Mikhail Luk'ianovich Iakovlev (1798–1853). Iakovlev had been one of Pushkin's fellow students at the Lyceum (where his nickname was "паяц" ["the clown"]). He later became the archivist of Pushkin's Lyceum class (October 19 reunions were sometimes held at his house) and an official of high rank. In the 1830s he was director of a publishing house, and in that capacity he and Pushkin renewed their old acquaintance. The poem in question owes its existence to a debt. In its entirety, the letter in question begins with this quatrain, which is directly followed by two brief, rather prosaic sentences: Завтра получу деньги в 2 часа пополудни. А ввечеру тебе доставлю. ("Tomorrow at 2:00 I receive the money. And I'll get it to you in the evening.")

The context of this epigram suggests that Smirdin had been slow to pay Pushkin, hence Pushkin himself has been delayed in paying Iakovlev back.

The poem is written in iambs (line 2 is a hexameter; the others tetrameter) with rhyme scheme a-B-B-a. Semantically, it depends on two Russian idioms, both based on days of the week (lines 2 and 4).

---

1 Смирди́н – A. F. Smirdin (1795–1857), a well-known Petersburg bookseller, whose store (and adjacent library) was a meeting place for literati.

2 У торгашá сегó семь пятниц на недéле – For <this> salesman there are seven Fridays in a week. This idiom is used about someone who is always changing his mind.

4 после дождичка четвéрг – Thursday after a rain. This is an idiom that means "no one knows when."

От меня́ вечóр Лейла – Yesterday evening Leila <was leaving me>

The poem is a translation of an Arab poem that Pushkin read in French translation. The book in question was J. Agoub, *Mélanges de Littérature orientale et française* (Paris, 1835). The first section, called "Maouals arabes," begins with an introduction which, at some length, discusses Anacreon and the Anacreontic tradition in Western Europe.

> Si tout à coup, au milieu d'une assemblée littéraire, un heureux explorateur de l'antiquité venait annoncer la découverte inattendue d'un nouveau manuscrit d'Anacréon, il produirait sur tous les esprits une sensation vive et sympathique: l'attente du plaisir se peindrait dans tous les regards, et chaque parole de l'orateur serait recueillie avec une ardente curiosité.
>
> Il n'est pas une seule pensée du chantre de Téos qui n'ait été mille fois traduite, mille fois imitée, reproduite de mille manières, et tourmentée dans tous les sens; nous possédons si bien Anacréon, que nous devinerions sans effort, et comme par sentiment, les beautés de son nouveau recueil. Malheureusement cette jouissance nous est à jamais interdite: le poète le plus aimable de la Grèce n'offrit aux muses qu'un encens tardif. La vieillesse qui avait blanchi

ses cheveux, n'était pas descendue jusqu'à son coeur. Joyeux vieillard, le front caché sous des roses, tenant d'une main la coupe, et de l'autre la lyre, il chanta le plaisir sur les bords même de la tombe; et ces chants, qui ont retenti jusqu'à nous, furent les derniers et probablement les seuls de sa vie.

Mais pourquoi ne chercherions-nous pas ailleurs des consolations? La littérature moderne ferait à coup sûr d'utiles conquêtes, si, par un choix bien entendu, elle s'appropriait quelques-unes des richesses poétiques de l'Asie; elle y puiserait, comme à une source vierge encore, une série féconde de sentimens <sic> et de pensées, d'images et d'expressions; elle s'y empreindrait surtout de ce charme oriental qu'on ne saurait définir, mais qui semble rajeunir la physionomie de nos idées en les dépouillant un moment des formes d'une civilisation trop mûrie. Il existe, entre autres, chez les Arabes, un chant jusqu'ici peu connu de l'Europe, qui est à la fois érotique et élégiaque, qui tantôt se rapproche de la romance française, et tantôt revêt la couleur anacréontique. Ce chant, appelé *maoual*, et dont l'origine remonte au temps des Barmécides, est ordinairement écrit en langue vulgaire, et ne consiste qu'en une seule strophe. Quoique dans un espace aussi restreint, les développemens <sic> soient impossibles, les maouals arabes présentent en général un sens complet: ce sont autant de petits tableaux, esquissés sans art, souvent avec négligence, mais où respire toute la naïveté des poésies primitives. Un souvenir, une plainte, un message, un désir, quelquefois une simple pensée suffit au sujet d'un maoual. Chanté par les Arabes sur un air lent et expressif, il est propre à faire ressortir les charmes d'une belle voix, dont il emploie les accents les plus pathétiques et les plus tendres. En Egypte, le maoual fait encore les délices de tous les harems.

The reference to Anacreon's gray hair recalls a famous Anacreontic ode that was translated into Russian many times. In Lomonosov's version, from "Разговор с Анакреоном" ("Conversation with Anacreon") it begins:

Мне девушки сказали:
"Ты дожил старых лет,"
И зеркало мне дали:
"Смотри, ты лыс и сед."

This passage would surely have occurred to Pushkin when he read the sixth "maoual" and decided to translate it. (He had not read far – the poem is on pages 15–16 in the book, and the poetic texts only begin on the middle of page 13.) In its entirety, the French text reads:

Elle se levait: Assieds-toi, lui dis-je; elle répond: Les cheveux blancs ont paru. – Hélas! m'écriai-je, ce qui n'est aujourd'hui que du camphre était autrefois du musc. – Tu dis vrai, me répliqua-t-elle, mais ce que tu parais ignorer, c'est que le musc sert aux fêtes de l'hyménée, tandis que le camphre n'est bon que pour les sépultures.

(She was getting up: sit down, I said; she replied: White hairs have appeared. – Alas! I cried, only camphor remains of what once was musk. – You speak truly, she replies, but perhaps you do not know that musk is used for marriage celebrations whereas camphor is only good for burials.)

In short, the influence of the Anacreontic ode is clearly suggested both in the book's introduction and in the specific text Pushkin chose to translate. It is also reflected in his choice of rhymed trochaic tetrameter as the meter, which recalls Pushkin's own Anacreontics of 1835. (The French translation, in keeping with the tradition of the time, is in prose.) However, the complicated rhyme scheme (which, following the semantics, breaks down into units of five lines, four lines, and then five lines) sets it apart from the alternating rhymes of Pushkin's more traditional Anacreontics. The fact that it is astrophic reflects either the Anacreontic tradition or Agoub's introduction (or both).

---

1 Лейла – the name is chosen less for its Byronic connotations (though these may be relevant) than because it appears (as "Leïla") in the previous poem in Agoub's collection, which is found on the same page as the beginning of the one Pushkin chose to translate.
8 мускус – musk. Musk is black in color.
9 камфорá – camphor. Camphor is white.
13 The main use of musk is in perfumes.
14 The main use of camphor was as an embalming fluid.

Literature: Stroganov.

∾1830–1836 (year of composition uncertain)

Родри́г – Roderick

This mysterious dramatic monologue is presumably connected to Southey's "Roderick, Last of the Goths" (see commentary to "На Испанию родную"), but the precise nature of that connection is difficult to determine. The passage does not directly correspond to any scene in the poem; it does, of course, recall the dream in the third part of "На Испанию родную."

Even the title is uncertain, because in the manuscript it is written not at the top of the page, but at the bottom (and in parentheses, no less), suggesting either a general reference to the Roderick theme or perhaps even a stage direction ("Enter Roderick"), who would appear in response, as it were, to the closing words of the monologue ("Кто там идет?"). Given this ambiguity, there is no overwhelming reason to identify the speaker as Roderick; it may be the hermit whom Roderick meets.

The form is equally puzzling. Like "На Испанию родную," it is written in trochaic tetrameter. However, the earlier work was in unrhymed four-line stanzas (the standard form of "Spanish trochees"), whereas this one is in two stanzas of unequal length, with the first seven lines (and lines 10 and 12) rhyming, but all others unrhymed.

---

4 старец некой (=некий) – a certain old monk
17 На после́дней борозде́ – at the last furrow
18 вели́кой=вели́кий
23 испове́довать себя́ – to make a confession. The expression is somewhat archaic; modern Russian would be "исповедоваться."
24 разреше́нье – absolution
32 Казны вечныя старшу́ся – I fear eternal torment. The archaic genitive "вечныя" (rather than modern Russian "вечной") gives an ecclesiastical tone to the line.
33 Милосе́рдия наде́юсь – I hope for mercy. The use of "надеяться" with a genitive complement (i.e., without a preposition) is now archaic, but this is not the only instance in Pushkin's writing when it appears.
35 Но твоя́ да будет воля – But let it be your will

Literature: Dolinin 2007, 171–81.

Works Consulted

Achinger, Gerda. "Die Lyrik Sainte-Beuves als Faktor der lyrischen Textgenese bei Puškin." *Arcadia* 35 (2000): 45–65.

———. *Victor Hugo in der Literatur der Puškin-Zeit (1823–1840)*. Köln: Böhlau, 1991.

Afanas'ev, A. *Poeticheskie vozzreniia slavian na prirodu*. 3 vols. Moscow: Indrik, 1994.

Akhmatova, Anna. *Sobranie sochinenii v shesti tomakh*. Vol. 6. Moscow: Ellis Lak, 2002.

Al'brekht, M. G. "K stikhotvoreniiu Pushkina 'Kto iz bogov mne vozvratil . . .'" *Vremennik Pushkinskoi komissii* 1977 (1980): 58–68.

Alekseev, Mikhail Pavlovich. "Pushkin i nauka ego vremeni (Razyskaniia i etiudy)." *Pushkin: Issledovaniia i materialy* 1 (1956): 9–125.

———. "Spory o stikhotvorenii 'Roza'." In *Pushkin: Sravnitel'no-istoricheskie issledovaniia*, 326–77. Leningrad: Nauka, 1972.

———. *Stikhotvorenie Pushkina "Ia pamiatnik sebe vozdvig . . . ": Problemy ego izucheniia*. Leningrad: Nauka, 1967.

Al'tshuller, Mark. *Mezhdu dvukh tsarei: Pushkin 1824–1836*. Saint Petersburg: Akademicheskii proekt, 2003.

Arinshtein, L. M. "Esli ekhat' vam sluchitsia." *Vremennik Pushkinskoi komissii* 21 (1987): 85–96.

———. "Nezavershennye stikhotvoreniia Pushkina: Tekstologicheskie problemy." *Pushkin: Issledovaniia i materialy* 13 (1989): 279–305.

Averintsev, Sergei. "Tsvetiki milye brattsa Frantsiska: Ital'ianskii katolitsizm russkimi glazami." *Pravoslavnaia obshchina* 38 (1997): 97–105.

Azadovskii, M. K. "Istochniki skazok Pushkina." *Vremennik Pushkinskoi komissii* 1 (1936): 134–63.

Bailey, James. *Three Russian Lyric Folk Song Meters*. Columbus, OH: Slavica, 1992.

Beliaev, M. D. "Pol'skoe vosstanie po pis'mam Pushkina k E. M. Khitrovo." In *Pis'ma Pushkina k Elizavete Mikhailovne Khitrovo, 1827–1832*, edited by S. F. Platonov, 257–300. Leningrad: Izd-vo Akademii nauk SSSR, 1927.

Belousov, Aleksandr Fedorovich. "Stikhotvorenie A. S. Pushkina 'Zimnii vecher'." In *Russkaia klassicheskaia literatura: Analiz khudozhestvennogo teksta*, 14–33. Tallinn: Valgus, 1988.

Berezkina, S. V. "'Alina, zhal'tes' nado mnoiu . . .': (Iz kommentariia k 'Priznaniiu' A. S. Pushkina)." *Vremennik Pushkinskoi komissii* 24 (1991): 131–40.

———. "Iz kommentariev k 'tverskim' stikhotvoreniiam A. S. Pushkina, 1828–1829 gg." *Vremennik Pushkinskoi komissii* 25 (1993): 127–35.

———. "Iz kommentariia k stikhotvoreniiam Pushkina." *Russkaia literatura*, no. 2 (1995): 118–31.

Berkov, P. N. "Poeticheskoe tvorchestvo Lomonosova." In *Stikhotvoreniia*, by Mikhail Lomonosov, v–xxxvi. [Moscow]: Sovetskii pisatel', 1948.

Bethea, David. *Realizing Metaphors: Alexander Pushkin and the Life of the Poet*. Madison: University of Wisconsin Press, 1998.

———. *The Superstitious Muse: Thinking Russian Literature Mythopoetically*. Boston: Academic Studies Press, 2009.

Binyon, T. J. *Pushkin: A Biography*. London: HarperCollins, 2002.

Bitsilli, P. M. "Derzhavin – Pushkin – Tiutchev i russkaia gosudarstvennost'." In *Sbornik statei, posviashchennykh Pavlu Nikolaevichu Miliukovu, 1859–1929*, edited by B. A. Evreinov, 351–74. Prague: Izd. Redaktsionnogo kom-ta, 1929.

Blagoi, D. D. *Tvorcheskii put' Pushkina (1813–1826)*. Moscow: Izd-vo Akademii nauk SSSR, 1950.

———. *Tvorcheskii put' Pushkina (1826–1830)*. Moscow: Sov. pisatel', 1967.

Blank, Ksana. *Dostoevsky's Dialectics and the Problem of Sin*. Evanston: Northwestern University Press, 2010.

Bondi, S. M. *O Pushkine: Stat'i i issledovaniia*. Moscow: Khudozhestvennaia literatura, 1978.

Botvinnik, N. M. "O stikhotvorenii Pushkina 'Net, ia ne dorozhu miatezhnym naslazhden'em'." *Vremennik Pushkinskoi komissii* (1979): 147–56.

Briggs, A. D. *Alexander Pushkin: A Critical Study*. Totowa, NJ: Barnes & Noble Books, 1983.

Brown, James Edwin. "The Verse Epistles of A. S. Puskin." PhD diss., University of Wisconsin–Madison, 1983.

Bukalov, Aleksei. "Ital'ianskii Pushkin." *Novoe vremia*, no.32 (2004): 38–40.

Burgi, Richard, "Puškin and the *Deipnosophists*." *Harvard Slavic Studies* 2 (1954): 265–70.

Butakova, V. I. "Karamzin i Pushkin: (Neskol'ko sopostavlenii)." *Pushkin i ego sovremenniki* 37 (1928): 127–35.

Chereiskii, L. A. "K datirovke odnogo stikhotvoreniia Pushkina." *Vremennik Pushkinskoi komissii* (1973): 78–80.

———. *Pushkin i ego okruzhenie*. Leningrad: Nauka, 1988.

Chernobaev, V. G. "K istorii nabroska 'Al'fons saditsia na konia'." *Vremennik Pushkinskoi komissii* (1939): 405–16.

Cooper, Brian. "Pushkin and the Anacreontea." *The Slavonic and East European Review* 52, no. 127 (April 1974): 182–87.

Davydov, Sergei. "The Evolution of Pushkin's Political Thought." In *The Pushkin Handbook*, edited by David Bethea, 283–320. Madison: University of Wisconsin Press, 2005.

———. "Poslednii liricheskii tsikl Puskina." *Russkaia literatura*, no. 2 (1999): 86–108.

———. "Strange and Savage Joy: The Erotic as a Unifying Element in *The Little Tragedies*." In *Alexander Pushkin's Little Tragedies: The Poetics of Brevity*, edited by Svetlana Evdokimova, 89–106. Madison: University of Wisconsin Press, 2003.

———. "Zvukovoe khoziaistvo Pushkina (poeziia i proza)." In *Russian Literature and the West: A Tribute for David M. Bethea*, edited by Alexander Dolinin, Lazar Fleishman, and Leonid Livak, 1:157–76. Stanford: Stanford Slavic Studies, 2008.

Dolinin, Aleksandr. "K voprosu o 'Strannike' i ego istochnikakh." In *Pushkinskie chteniia v Tartu: Tezisy dokladov nauchnoi konferentsii 13–14 noiabria 1987 g.*, edited by A. E. Mal'ts, 34–37. Tallin: Tartuskii gos. universitet, 1987.

———. *Pushkin i Angliia: Tsikl statei*. Moscow: Novoe literaturnoe obozrenie, 2007.

Dovgii, O. L. and A. V. Kulagin. "Tomu [odno, odno] mgnoven'e." *Vremennik Pushkinskoi komissii* 21 (1987): 83–85.

Driver, Sam. *Puškin: Literature and Social Ideas*. New York: Columbia University Press, 1989.

Dunning, Chester. *The Uncensored Boris Godunov: The Case for Pushkin's Original Comedy*. Madison: University of Wisconsin Press, 2006.

Eidel'man, N. *Istoriia i sovremennost' v khudozhestvennom soznanii poeta*. Moscow: Sov. pisatel', 1984.

Esipov, Viktor. "Iz chego b'emsia?" *Moskovskii Pushkinist* 12 (2009): 269–79.

———. "Vokrug 'Proroka'. Okolo 'Teni Barkova'." *Moskovskii Pushkinist* 11 (2005): 8–61.

Evdokimova, Svetlana. *Pushkin's Historical Imagination*. New Haven: Yale University Press, 1999.

Faibisovich V. M. "K istochniku perevoda Pushkina 'Iz Katulla'." *Vremennik Pushkinskoi komissii* (1980), 69–75.

———. "Stikhotvorenie Pushkina 'Kto iz bogov mne vozvratil' (K pushkinskoi kontseptsii Goratsiia)." *Pushkin: Issledovaniia i materialy* 15 (1995): 184–95.

Feinberg, Il'ia. *Chitaia tetradi Pushkina*. Moscow: Sov. pisatel', 1985.

Fomichev, S. A. "K istolkovaniiu pushkinskogo nabroska 'Kriton, roskoshnyi grazhdanin." *Russkaia literatura*, no. 4 (2001): 114–18.

———. "'Pesni o Sten'ke Razine' Pushkina: Istoriia sozdaniia, kompozitsiia i problematika tsikla." *Pushkin: Issledovaniia i materialy* 13 (1989): 4–20.

Frantsev, V. A. "Pushkin i pol'skoe vosstanie 1830–1831 g.: Opyt istoricheskogo kommentariia k stikhotvoreniiam; 'Klevetnikam Rossii' i 'Borodinskaia godovshchina'." In *Pushkinskii sbornik*, 65–208. Prague: Politika, 1929.

Gardzonio, Stefano, "'I tvoi beznosyi Kasti': Nekotorye kommentarii k pushkinskomu poslaniiu 'K vel'mozhe'." In *Pushkinskie chteniia v Tartu: Materialy mezhdunarodnoi nauchnoi konferentsii 18–20 sentiabria 1998 g./2*, edited by A. A. Danilevskii, 134–45. Tartu: Tartuskii universitet, 2000.

Gasparov, B. M. *Poeticheskii iazyk Pushkina kak fakt istorii russkogo literaturnogo iazyka*. Vienna: Gesellschaft zur Förderung slawistischer Studien, 1992.

Gasparov, M. L. *Ocherk istorii russkogo stikha: Metrika, ritmika, rifma, strofika*. Moscow: Nauka, 1984.

———. "Perevod Pushkina 'Iz Ksenofana Kolofonskogo'." *Vremennik Pushkinskoi komissii* 20 (1986): 24–35.

———. *Russkii narodnyi stikh v literaturnykh imitatsiiakh*. Lisse: Peter de Ridder Press, 1976.

———. "Semanticheskii oreol pushkinskogo chetyrekhstopnogo khoreia." In *Pushkinskie chteniia: Sbornik statei*, edited by S. G. Isakov, 5–14. Tallinn: Eesti Raamat, 1990.

———. "Stikhotvorenie Pushkina i 'Stikhotvorenie' M. Shaginian." In M. L. Gasparov, *Izbrannye trudy*, 2:58–65. Moscow: Iazyki russkoi kul'tury, 1997.

Gershenzon, Mikhail. *Mudrost' Pushkina*. Moscow: Kn-vo pisatelei v Moskve, 1919.

———. *Stat'i o Pushkine*. Moscow: Akademiia, 1926.

Gillel'son, M. I. "Otzyv sovremennika o 'Pire Petra Pervogo' Pushkina." *Vremennik Pushkinskoi komissii* (1963): 49–51.

Ginzburg, Lidiia. *O lirike*. Moscow: Intrada, 1997.

Glebov, G. S. "Ob 'Arione'." *Vremennik Pushkinskoi komissii* 6 (1941): 296–304.

Gorlin, Michel. "Les ballades d'Adam Mickiewicz et Puškin." *Revue des études slaves* 19, no. 3 (1939): 227–41.

Grechanaia, E. P. "Pushkin i A. Shen'e: Dve zametki k teme." *Vremennik Pushkinskoi komissii* 22 (1988): 98–108.

Grekhnev, Vsevolod. *Mir pushkinskoi liriki*. Nizhnii Novgorod, 1994.

Grigor'eva, A. D. *Poeticheskaia frazeologiia Pushkina*. Moscow, 1969.

Grombakh, S. "K istorii stikhotvoreniia 'Poedem, ia gotov ...'" *Voprosy literatury*, no. 4 (1983): 204–10.

Gukovskii, G. A. *Pushkin i russkie romantiki*. Moscow: Khudozhestvennaia literatura, 1965.

Gusev, V. E. "Pushkin i Vuk Karadzhich." *Vremennik Pushkinskoi komissii* 24 (1991): 29–41.

Gustafson, Richard F. "The Upas Tree: Pushkin and Erasmus Darwin." *PMLA* 75, no. 1 (March 1960): 101–9.

Hokanson, Katya. "In Defense of Empire: 'The Bronze Horseman' and 'To the Slanderers of Russia'." In *Beyond the Empire: Images of Russia in the Eurasian Cultural Context*, edited by Tetsuo Mochizuki, 149–66. Sapporo: Hokkaido University, 2008.

Iakovlev, N. V. "K voprosu ob angliiskikh istochnikakh stikhotvoreniia Pushkina 'Tsygany' ('Nad lesistymi bregami')." *Pushkin i ego sovremenniki* 36 (1923): 63–70.

———. "'Poslednii literaturnyi sobesednik Pushkina': Barry Cornwall." *Pushkin i ego sovremenniki* 28 (1917): 5–28.

Iakubovich, D. P. "K pushkinskomu nabrosku 'Shumit kustarnik'." *Pushkin i ego sovremenniki* 38–39 (1930): 122–34.

Iezuitova, R. V. "Stikhotvorenie Pushkina 'Vsem krasny boiarskie koniushni' kak opyt sozdaniia 'prostonarodnoi ballady'." *Vremennik Pushkinskoi komissii* (1979): 31–42.

Il'in-Tomich, A. A. "Pushkin i stikhotvorenie Bairona 'Written in an Album'." *Pushkinskie chteniia v Tartu: Tezisy dokladov nauchnoi konferentsii 13–14 noiabria 1987 g.*, edited by A. E. Mal'ts, 37–41. Tallin: Tartuskii gos. universitet, 1987.

Ivanov, Viach. Vs. "Ob izomorfizme dvukh stikhotvorenii Pushkina." *Lotmanovskii sbornik* 2 (1997): 273–78.

———. "Zametki na poliakh tekstov Pushkina." *Pushkinskie chteniia v Tartu: Tezisy dokladov nauchnoi konferentsii 13–14 noiabria 1987 g.*, edited by A. E. Mal'ts, 30–32. Tallin: Tartuskii gos. universitet, 1987.

Ivanova, N. N. "Poeticheskaia glagol'naia perifraza u Pushkina." In *Poeticheskaia frazeologiia Pushkina*, edited by A. D. Grigor'eva, 293–372. Moscow, 1969.

Ivinskii, D. P. "K literaturnomu fonu pushkinskoi 'Oseni'." *Pushkin: Sbornik statei*, edited by M. L. Remneva, 189–97 Moscow: Izd-vo MGU, 1999.

———. *O Pushkine*. Moscow: Intrada, 2005.

Izmailov, N. V. *Ocherki tvorchestva Pushkina*. Leningrad: Nauka, 1975.

———. "Stikhotvorenie Pushkina 'Mirskaia vlast'." *Izvestiia akademii nauk SSSR: otdelenie literatury i iazyka* 13, no. 6 (1954): 548–56.

Jakobson, Roman. *Language in Literature*. Cambridge: Belknap Press, 1987.

Kahn, Andrew. *Pushkin's Lyric Intelligence*. Oxford: Oxford University Press, 2008.

Kalinowska, Izabela. *Between East and West: Polish and Russian Nineteenth-Century Travel to the Orient*. Rochester, NY: University of Rochester Press, 2004.

Khitrova, Dar'ia. "Stikhotvorenie Pushkina 'Rifma, zvuchnaia podruga': genealogiia i semantika liricheskogo narrativa." *Novoe literaturnoe obozrenie* 95, no. 1 (2009): 81–126.

Khodasevich, Vladislav. *Pushkin i poety ego vremeni*. Vol. 1. Oakland: Berkeley Slavic Specialties, 1999.

Kibal'nik, S. A. "Antologicheskie epigrammy Pushkina." *Pushkin: Issledovaniia i materialy* 12 (1986): 152–74.

Kiseleva, L. "Legenda o vechnom zhide v zamyslakh Pushkina i Zhukovskogo." In *Koran i Bibliia v tvorchestve A. S. Pushkina*, edited by D. Segal and S. Shvartsband, 93–100. Jerusalem: Hebrew University, 2000.

Kogan, Igor'. *Taina venetsianskogo stikhotvoreniia A. S. Pushkina*. Saint Petersburg: Kosta, 2008.

Koka, G. M. *Pushkin ob iskusstve*. Moscow: Izd-vo Akademii khudozhestv, 1962.

———. "Pushkin pered madonnoi Rafaelia." *Vremennik Pushkinskoi komissii* (1967): 38–43.

———. "Stikhotvorenie 'K biustu zavoevatelia'." *Pushkin: Issledovaniia i materialy* 2 (1958): 324–33.

———. "Stikhotvorenie Pushkina 'Khudozhniku'." *Vremennik Pushkinskoi komissii* (1972): 100–109.

Kolmogorov, A. N. and N. G. Rychkova. "Russian Poetry Rhythm Analysis and Probability Theory." *Theory of Probability and its Applications* 44, no. 2 (2000): 375–85.

Kulagin, A. V. "Shumit kustarnik." *Vremennik Pushkinskoi komissii* 27 (1996): 102–7.

Kunin, V. V. *Bibliofily pushkinskoi pory*. Moscow: Kniga, 1979.

Lednicki, Waclaw. *Adam Mickiewicz in World Literature*. Berkeley: University of California Press, 1956.

———. "Grammatici Certant: Puškin's 'Aleksandrijskij stolp'." *Harvard Slavic Studies* 2 (1954): 241–63.

———. *Pouchkine et la Pologne: A propos de la trilogie antipolonaise de Pouchkine*. Paris: E. Leroux, 1928.

Leibov R. and A. Ospovat. "Siuzhet i zhanr stikhotvoreniia Pushkina 'Olegov shchit'." *Pushkinskie chteniia v Tartu, 4: Pushkinskaia epokha; problema refleksii i kommentariia*, edited by L. Kiseleva, 71–88. Tartu: Tartuskii universitet, 2007.

Lemin, A. Iu. "Iz istorii odnogo stikhotvoreniia Pushkina." *Pushkin: Issledovaniia i materialy* 12 (1986): 341–50.

Lerner, N. O. "Pushkinologicheskie etiudy." In *Zven'ia: Sborniki materialov i dokumentov po istorii literatury, iskusstva i obshchestvennoi mysli XIX veka*, edited by Vladimir Bonch-Bruevich, 44–187. Moscow: Akademiia, 1935.

Levitskii, Aleksandr. "Derzhavin kak ispovednik Pushkina." *Russkaia literatura*, no. 1 (2011): 3–23.

Levkovich, Ia. L. "Kavkazskii dnevnik Pushkina." *Pushkin: Issledovaniia i materialy* 11 (1983a): 5–26.

———. "K datirovke perevoda Pushkina iz 'Konrada Vallenroda' Mitskevicha." *Vremennik Pushkinskoi komissii* (1983b): 118–22.

———. "Litseiskie 'godovshchiny.'" In *Stikhotvoreniia Pushkina 1820–1830-kh godov: Istoriia sozdaniia i ideino-khudozhestvennaia problematika*, edited by N. V. Izmailov, 71–106. Leningrad: Nauka, 1974.

———. "Perevody Pushkina iz Mitskevicha." *Pushkin: Issledovaniia i materialy* 7 (1974): 151–66.

———. "Rabochaia tetrad' Pushkina PD no. 841: (Istoriia zapolneniia)." *Pushkin: Issledovaniia i materialy* 12 (1986): 243–77.

Liapunov, Vadim. "Mnemosyne and Lethe: Puškin's 'Vospominanie'." In *Alexander Puškin: A Symposium on the 175th Anniversary of His Birth*, edited by Andrej Kodjak and Kiril Taranovsky, 27–41. New York: New York University Press, 1976.

———. "Not in Vain and Not by Chance: Pushkin and Philaret (Drozdov), Metropolitan of Moscow." In *Philaret, Metropolitan of Moscow, 1782–1867: Perspectives on the Man, his Work, and his Times*, edited by Vladimir Tsurikov, 36–51. Jordanville, NY: Variable Press, 2003.

Liprandi, A. P. "Iz dnevnika i vospominanii." In *Pushkin v vospominaniiakh sovremennikov*, edited by Vadim Vatsuro, 1:285–343. Saint Petersburg: Akademicheskii proekt, 1998.

Liubavin, M. A. *Litseiskie uchitelia Pushkina i ikh knigi*. Saint Petersburg: Izd-vo Sudarynia, 1997.

Lobanova, A. S. "'Voron k voronu letit': Russkii istochnik 'Shotlandskoi pesni' Pushkina." *Vremennik Pushkinskoi komissii* 26 (1995): 111–12.

Lo Gatto, Ettore. "L'Ariosto nella letteratura russa." *Nuove lettere emiliane* 9/11 (1965): 5–12.

Loseff, Lev. "The Toy Town Ruined." In *A Sense of Place: Tsarskoe Selo and its Poets*, edited by Lev Loseff and Barry Scherr, 35–50. Columbus, OH: Slavica, 1993.

Lotman, Iu. M. *O poetakh i poezii*. Saint Petersburg: Iskusstvo-SPB, 1996.

———. *Pushkin*. Saint Petersburg: Iskusstvo-SPB, 1995.

Luknitskaia, V. "Rannie pushkinskie shtudii Anny Akhmatovoi (po materialam arkhiva P. Luknitskogo)." *Voprosy literatury* 1 (1978): 185–228.

Maroevich, R. "Pervye russkie perevody Khasanaginitsy: (Poeticheskaia polemika Vostokova i Pushkina)." *Vremennik Pushkinskoi komissii* 26 (1995): 121–28.

McNally, Raymond T. "The Origins of Russophobia in France: 1812–1830." *American Slavic and East European Review* 17, no. 2 (April 1958): 173–89.

Medrish, D. N. "'Pesnia o Georgii Chernom' i fol'klornaia traditsiia." *Moskovskii Pushkinist* 5 (1998): 32–48.

Meilakh, B. *Khudozhestvennoe myshlenie Pushkina kak tvorcheskii protsess*. Moscow: Izd-vo Akademii nauk SSSR, 1962.

Meilakh, M. B. "Eshche raz ob 'Aleksandriiskom stolpe'." *Pushkin i ego sovremenniki* 4, no. 43 (2005): 340–63.

Merlin, V. V. "Ob odnom iz istochnikov stikhotvoreniia 'Ia vozmuzhal sredi pechal'nykh bur'." *Vremennik Pushkinskoi komissii* 20 (1986): 174–77.

Mikhailova, N. I. "Stikhotvorenie A. S. Pushkina 'Zaklinanie': (Iz nabliudenii nad tekstom)." *Vremennik Pushkinskoi komissii* 26 (1995): 95–100.

———. "'Svodnia grustno za stolom …': (K kommentariiu stikhotvoreniia A.S. Pushkina)." *Vremennik Pushkinskoi komissii* 29 (2004): 198–201.

Mirsky, D. S. *Pushkin*. New York: Dutton, 1963.

Modzalevskii, B. L. "Biblioteka A. S. Pushkina." *Pushkin i ego sovremenniki* 9–10 (1910): 1–442.

———. *Pushkin i ego sovremenniki: Izbrannye trudy (1898–1928).* Saint Petersburg: Iskusstvo-SPB, 1999.

Morozov, P. "Pushkin i St.-Beuve." *Russkii bibliofil* 7 (1915): 82–89.

Murav'eva, O. S. "Iz nabliudenii nad 'Pesniami zapadnykh slavian'."*Pushkin: Issledovaniia i materialy* 11 (1983): 149–63.

Nabokov, Vladimir. Translation and Commentary to *Eugene Onegin: A Novel in Verse*, by Aleksandr Pushkin. 4 vols. New York: Pantheon Books, 1964.

Nemirovskii, I. V. *Tvorchestvo Pushkina i problema publichnogo povedeniia poeta.* Saint Petersburg: Giperion, 2003.

Oksman, Iu. G. Commentary to *Polnoe sobranie stikhotvoreniii*, by Kondratii Ryleev. Leningrad, 1934.

———. "Siuzhety Pushkina (Otryvochnye zamechaniia)." In *Pushkinskii sbornik pamiati professora Semena Afanas'evicha Vengerova*, edited by N. V. Iakovlev, 24–39. Moscow: Gos. izd-vo, 1922.

Ospovat, Kirill. "Ob 'odicheskom diptikhe' Pushkina: 'Stansy' i 'Druz'iam'." In *Pushkinskaia konferentsiia v Stenforde 1999*, edited by David M. Bethea, A. L. Ospovat, N. G. Okhotin, and L. S. Fleishman, 133–42. Moscow: OGI, 2001.

Panofsky, Gerda S. "The Napoleonic Subtext of Andrei Belyi's 'Peterburg'." *Europa Orientalis* 24 (2005): 47–102.

Pogosian, Elena. "'Slovo pokhval'noe Petru Velikomu' Lomonosova v krugu istoricheskikh istochnikov 'Pira Petra Velikogo' A. S. Pushkina." *Pushkinskie chteniia v Tartu 2: Materialy mezhdunarodnoi nauchnoi konferentsii 18–20 sentiabria 1998 g.*, edited by A. A. Danilevskii, 166–82. Tartu: Tartuskii universitet, 2000.

Proskurin, O. A. Commentary to *Poemy i povesti*, by Aleksandr Pushkin. Vol. 1 of *Sochineniia: Kommentirovannoe izdanie*. Edited by David M. Bethea. Moscow: Novoe Izd-vo, 2007.

———. *Poeziia Pushkina, ili podvizhnyi palimpsest.* Moscow: Novoe literaturnoe obozrenie, 1999.

———. "Pushkin and Politics." In *The Cambridge Companion to Pushkin*, edited by Andrew Kahn, 105–17. Cambridge: Cambridge University Press, 2006.

Rak, V. D. *Pushkin, Dostoevskii i drugie: Voprosy tekstologii, materialy k kommentariiam.* Saint Petersburg: Akademicheskii proekt, 2003.

Ram, Harsha. *The Imperial Sublime: A Russian Poetics of Empire*. Madison: University of Wisconsin Press, 2003.

Rice, James L. "Six Short Poems by Pushkin Englished and Annotated." *Pushkin Review* 5 (2002): 1–45.

Rodnianskaia, Irina. "Stikhotvorenie 'Blazhen v zlatom krugu vel'mozh …' – propushchennoe zveno v razgovore o naznachenii poeta." *Moskovskii Pushkinist* 7 (2000): 28–37.

Ronen, Omry. "Emulation, Anti-Parody, Intertextuality, and Annotation." *Nabokov Studies* 5 (1998/1999): 63–70.

Rossi, Laura. "Ital'ianskii 'Pamiatnik', ili Pushkin, Petrarka i drugie v 1836 g." In *Memento Vivere: Sbornik pamiati L. N. Ivanovoi*, edited by K. A. Kumpan and E. P. Obatnina, 105–21. Saint Petersburg: Nauka, 2009.

———. "Kommentarii k pushkinskoi stroke, ili pochemu Onegin stoial, 'opershisia na granit'?" In *Pushkinskie chteniia v Tartu, 4: Pushkinskaia epokha; problema refleksii i kommentariia*, edited by L. Kiseleva, 32–46. Tartu: Tartuskii universitet, 2007.

Salupere, Malle. "Iz kommentariev k stikhotvoreniiam Pushkina Mikhailovskogo perioda ('Pesni o Sten'ke Razine' i 'Akvilon')." In *Pushkinskie chteniia v Tartu, 4: Pushkinskaia epokha; problema refleksii i kommentariia*, edited by L. Kiseleva, 54–70. Tartu: Tartuskii universitet, 2007.

Sandomirskaia, V. B. "O datirovke stikhotvoreniia Pushkina 'Kogda v ob''iatiia moi.' *Pushkin: Issledovaniia i materialy* 4 (1962): 354–61.

———. "Perevody i perelozheniia Pushkina iz A. Shen'e." *Pushkin: Issledovaniia i materialy* 8 (1978): 90–106.

Scherr, Barry P. *Russian Poetry: Meter, Rhythm, and Rhyme*. Berkeley: University of California Press, 1986.

Shapir, M. I. "O nerovnosti ravnogo: Poslanie Pushkina 'Kalmychke' na fone makroevoliutsii russkogo poeticheskogo iazyka." In *Tekst i kommentarii: Kruglyi stol k 75-letiiu Viacheslava Vsevolodovicha Ivanova*, edited by V. N. Toporov, 404–17. Moscow: Nauka, 2006.

———. "Otpoved' na zadannuiu temu. K sporam po povodu tekstologii 'Evgeniia Onegina'." *Novyi mir*, no. 4 (2003): 144–56.

Shebunin, A. N. "Pushkin i 'Obschestvo Elizavety'." *Vremennik Pushkinskoi komissii* 1 (1936): 53–90.

Shein, P. "Narodnaia pesnia i Pushkin." *Ezhemesiachnye sochineniia*, nos. 5–6 (1900): 1–21.

Shvartsband, Samuil. "Stikhotvornyi opyt A. S. Pushkina." *Toronto Slavic Quarterly* 33 (Summer 2010): 420–89.

Slovar' iazyka Pushkina, edited by V. V. Vinogradov, C. G. Barkhudarov, D. D. Blagoi, B. V. Tomashevskii. 4 vols. Moscow: Gosudarstvennoe izdatel'stvo inostrannykh i natsional'nykh slovarei, 1956–1961.

Smirnov, Igor' P. *Psikhodiakhronologika: Psikhoistoriia russkoi literatury ot romantizma do nashikh dnei*. Moscow: Novoe literaturnoe obozrenie, 1994.

Solov'ev, A. V. "Iugoslavskie temy v proizvedeniiakh Pushkina." In *Belgradskii Pushkinskii sbornik*, edited by E. V. Anichkov, 45–71. Belgrade: Izd. Russkogo Pushkinskogo komiteta, 1937.

Solov'eva, O. S. "'Ezerskii' i 'Mednyi vsadnik': Istoriia teksta." *Pushkin: Issledovaniia i materialy* 3 (1960): 268–344.

Speranskii, M. N. "K voprosu o pesniakh, zapisannykh A. S. Pushkinym." *Pushkin i ego sovremenniki* 38–39 (1930): 95–107.

Stennik, Iu. V. *Pushkin i russkaia literatura XVIII veka*. Saint Petersburg: Nauka, 1995.

Stroganov, M. V. "O stikhotvorenii Pushkina 'Ot menia vechor Leila'." *Pushkin: Issledovaniia i materialy* 15 (1995): 168–75.

Surat, I. Z. "Bibleiskoe i lichnoe v tekstakh Pushkina." *Moskovskii Pushkinist* 7 (2000): 85–95.

———. "Tri zametki." *Moskovskii Pushkinist* 5 (1998): 201–16.

Tomashevskii, B. V. "Belkin i Gibbon." *Vremennik Pushkinskoi komissii* 4/5 (1939): 483–85.

———. "Genezis 'Pesen zapadnykh slavian." *Atenei: Istoriko-literaturnyi vremennik* 3 (1926): 35–45.

———. "Istochnik stikhotvoreniia 'Kak s dreva sorvalsia predatel'-uchenik'." *Pushkin i ego sovremenniki* 38/39 (1930): 78–81.

———. "Istochniki stikhotvorenii 'Vse moe – skazalo zlato' i 'Glukhoi glukhogo zval'." *Pushkin i ego sovremenniki* 28 (1917), 56–64.

———. *Pushkin i Frantsiia*. Leningrad: Sovetskii pisatel', 1960.

———. "Pushkin i iuzhnye slaviane." In B.V. Tomashevskii, *Pushkin, kniga vtoraia: materialy k monografii*, 269–81. Moscow, 1961.

———. "Strofika Pushkina." *Pushkin: Issledovaniia i materialy* 2 (1958): 49–184.

Trubetskoi, B. A. *Pushkin v Moldavii*. Kishinev: Lit-ra artistike, 1983.

Tsiavlovskaia, T. G. "Dnevnik A. A. Oleninoi." *Pushkin: Issledovaniia i materialy* 2 (1958): 247–92.

Tsiavlovskii, M. A. "Kommentarii k ballade A. Pushkina 'Ten' Barkova'." *Philologica* 3 (1996): 159–265.

———. "Predstavlenie 'Derevni' Pushkina Aleksandru I." *Pushkin: Issledovaniia i materialy* 2 (1958): 382–85.

———. *Stat'i o Pushkine*. Moscow: Izd-vo Akademii nauk SSSR, 1962.

———. "'Zapretnaia roza' stikhotvoreniia Pushkina." *Pushkin i ego sovremenniki* 38/39 (1930): 218–22.

Tsiavlovskii, M. A., L. B. Modzalevskii, and T. G. Zenger, eds. *Rukoiu Pushkina: Nesobrannye i neopublikovannye teksty.* Moscow: Academia, 1935.

Tynianov, Iurii. *Pushkin i ego sovremenniki*. Moscow: Nauka, 1969.

Vatsuro, V. E. "Epigramma Pushkina na A. N. Murav'eva." *Pushkin: Issledovaniia i materialy* 13 (1989): 222–41.

———. "Iz istoriko-literaturnogo kommentariia k stikhotvoreniiam Pushkina." *Pushkin: Issledovaniia i materialy* 12 (1986): 305–23.

———. "Poeticheskii manifest Pushkina." *Pushkin: Issledovaniia i materialy* 14 (1991): 65–72.

———. *Pushkinskaia pora*. Saint Petersburg: Akademicheskii proekt, 2000.

———. *Zapiski kommentatora*. Saint Petersburg: Akademicheskii proekt, 1994.

Venclova, Tomas. *Neustoichivoe ravnovesie: Vosem' russkikh poeticheskikh tekstov*. New Haven: Yale Center for International and Area Studies, 1986.

Veresaev, V. *Sputniki Pushkina*. 2 vols. Moscow: Sov. sport, 1993.

Vickery, Walter. "'Arion': An Example of Post-Decembrist Semantics." In *Alexander Puškin: A Symposium on the 175th Anniversary of His Birth*, edited by Andrej Kodjak and Kiril Taranovsky, 71–84. New York: New York University Press, 1976.

———. "'Ia vas ljubil ...': A Literary Source." *International Journal of Slavic Linguistics and Poetics* 15 (1972): 160–67.

———. "Lexical Similarities and Thematic Affinities: Three Puškin Lyrics." *International Journal of Slavic Linguistics and Poetics* 28 (1983): 137–47.

———. "'Vospominaniia v Tsarskom Sele' (1814) i 'Pamiatnik': k voprosu o strofike." In *Slavic Poetics: Essays in Honor of Kiril Taranovsky*, edited by Roman Jakobson, C. H. van Schooneveld, and Dean S. Worth, 485–97. Hague: Mouton, 1973.

Vinogradov, V. V. *Iazyk Pushkina: Pushkin i istoriia russkogo literaturnogo iazyka*. Moscow: Nauka, 2000.

———. *Ocherki po istorii russkogo literaturnogo iazyka XVII–XIX vv.* Leyden: E. I. Brill, 1949.

———. *Stil' Pushkina*. Moscow: Gos. izd-vo khudozh. lit-ry, 1941.

Virolainen, Mariia, and Aleksandr Dolinin, eds. *Pushkin: Boris Godunov*. Vol. 2 of *Sochineniia: Kommentirovannoe izdanie.* Edited by David M. Bethea. Moscow: Novoe Izd-vo, 2008.

Virolainen, Mariia N. "Al'fons saditsia na konia." In *Pushkinskaia entsiklopediia: Proizvedeniia*, 1:29–32. Saint Petersburg: Nestor-Istoriia, 2009a.

———. "D. V. Davydovu." In *Pushkinskaia entsiklopediia: Proizvedeniia*, 1:408–10. Saint Petersburg: Nestor-Istoriia, 2009b.

Vol'pert, Larisa. *Pushkinskaia Frantsiia.* Saint Petersburg: Aleteiia, 2007.

Weintraub, Wiktor. *The Poetry of Adam Mickiewicz*. 's-Gravenhage, 1954.

Worthey, Glen. "Gender Poetics and the Structure of Pushkin's 'Little House in Kolomna'." *Elementa* 3 (1997): 271–90.

Yovanovitch, Voyslav M. *"La Guzla" de Prosper Mérimée: Étude d'histoire romantique*. Paris: Librairie Hachette, 1911.

Zinger, Elena, "Ia tvoi po-prezhnemu, tebia liubliu ia vnov'..." *Moskovskii Pushkinist* 11 (2005): 124–31.

Index of Poems by Title and First Line

NOTE: Poems addressed to individuals are alphabetized by the last name of the addressee. For example, the poem called „Кн. П. П. Вяземскому“ can be found under „Вяземскому, Кн. П. П.“ However, poems addressed to individuals that have a title beginning with the preposition “К” (“To”) are alphabetized under “К.” Hence „К Вяземскому” will be found under “К.”

Index of Names

NOTE: This index is limited to names of people who actually existed, not of fictional or mythological personages. For example, "André Chénier" and "Boris Godunov" are included when the references are to the poet and the tsar; they are not included when the references are to characters in Pushkin's works.

PUBLICATIONS OF THE WISCONSIN CENTER FOR PUSHKIN STUDIES

Realizing Metaphors: Alexander Pushkin and the Life of the Poet
David M. Bethea

The Pushkin Handbook
Edited by David M. Bethea

The Uncensored Boris Godunov: The Case for Pushkin's Original Comedy, with Annotated Text and Translation
Chester Dunning with Caryl Emerson, Sergei Fomichev, Lidiia Lotman, and Antony Wood

Alexander Pushkin's Little Tragedies: The Poetics of Brevity
Edited by Svetlana Evdokimova

Pushkin's Tatiana
Olga Hasty

Derzhavin: A Biography
Vladislav Khodasevich; Translated and with an introduction by Angela Brintlinger

The Imperial Sublime: A Russian Poetics of Empire
Harsha Ram

Pushkin and the Genres of Madness: The Masterpieces of 1833
Gary Rosenshield

Pushkin's Rhyming: A Comparative Study
J. Thomas Shaw

A Commentary to Pushkin's Lyric Poetry, 1826–1836
Michael Wachtel